MW01168431

ISBN: 9781313818353

Published by:
HardPress Publishing
8345 NW 66TH ST #2561
MIAMI FL 33166-2626

Email: info@hardpress.net
Web: http://www.hardpress.net

THE

ELDER PLINY'S CHAPTERS

ON THE

HISTORY OF ART

batissimam ipsorum astisi
cum quipraesenteserant
iudicio.cumapparuit eam es
se qua omnes secundam asua
quisq. iudicassent haecest
policlit proxima abeaphi
diae tertia clesilae quar
ta crdonis quintaphrae
monis phidias praeter io
uem olimpium quemnemo
aemulatur fecit exaebore
aeque mineruam athenis
quaeest inparthenone stans
exaere uero praeter amazo
nem supradictam mineruã
tam eximiae pulchritudi
nis utformae cognomen
acceperit fecit &cliducum
&aliam mineruam quam
romae paulus aemilius
adaedemfortunaehuiusce
diei dicauit item duo sig
na quaecatulus ineadem
aede palliata &alterum co
losssiconnudum primusq
astem fore uticen aperu

isse atquedemonstrasse
merito iudicatur poli
clitus sicronius hagela
dae discipulus diadume
num fecit molliter iuue
nem centumtalentis no
bilitatum idem &dori
phorum uiriliter puerũ
fecit &quem canona
artificesuocant linia
menta artis exeopeten
tes uel uti alege quadam
solusquehominum ar
temipsam fecisse artis
opere iudicatur fecit &
destringentem se &nu
dum talo incessentem
duosque pueros item
nudos talis ludentesqui
uocantur astragalizon
tes &sunt incitit in p
atrioduo.hocoperenul
lum apsolutius pleriq
iudicant itemmercuri
um quifuit lisimachaeae
herculem quiromae

THE

ELDER PLINY'S CHAPTERS

ON THE

HISTORY OF ART

PLINIUS SECUNDUS, C.

TRANSLATED BY

K. JEX-BLAKE

CLASSICAL LECTURER AT GIRTON COLLEGE, CAMBRIDGE

WITH COMMENTARY AND HISTORICAL INTRODUCTION

BY

E. SELLERS

FORMER STUDENT OF GIRTON COLLEGE, CAMBRIDGE,
AND OF THE BRITISH SCHOOL AT ATHENS

AND

ADDITIONAL NOTES CONTRIBUTED BY DR. HEINRICH LUDWIG URLICHS

London

MACMILLAN AND CO., Ltd.

NEW YORK: THE MACMILLAN CO.

1896

s

.

PREFACE

THE text printed in the following pages is based upon that of *Detlefsen*, but free use has been made of both earlier and later critical auxiliaries. We differ from Detlefsen mainly in adhering more closely to the *Codex Bambergensis*, whose superiority in respect of those parts of the *Historia* now reproduced must be regarded as incontestable. Our short critical apparatus is limited to notices of our deviations from Detlefsen, or of readings offering special interest or difficulty. For brevity's sake the name of Detlefsen stands in our apparatus not only for his own readings but also for those of the scholars whose views he adopts. In none but a few important cases do we print Detlefsen's sources. I have to thank *Mr. Fischer* of Bamberg for kindly verifying a number of readings in the Bambergensis, and *Dr. Leitschuh*, Chief Librarian at Bamberg, for permission to reproduce in facsimile a page of the famous codex. The present text has been prepared under the guidance of *Dr. Ludwig Traube*, who, moreover, has generously placed at our disposal a number of his own readings or conjectures.

Out of the many problems which even this short selection from the *Historia Naturalis* offers, the Introduction professes to deal only with the question of Pliny's Greek sources for the history of art ; it touches upon his Roman authorities only in so far as these were the channel through which the Greek authors reached him. The question is

one which, so far from being, as was supposed, either
exhausted or incapable of solution, is still in its infancy.
Where an earlier school was content to trace back Pliny's
debt to his Roman predecessors, a newer method of
inquiry enables the student to work backwards not only
from the Roman to the Greek authors, but from one Greek
author to another. So it is that, returning to the Introduction after an interval, it became clear to me (see footnotes
on p. xliii f.) that in matters of anecdote and biography
Antigonos of Karystos was seldom, if ever, to be regarded
as an ultimate source, and was to a far greater extent than
I had at first supposed the debtor of Duris. Nay, I believe that we may in time recover (to some extent) the
authorities which Duris himself had at his command. I am
profoundly indebted to *Dr. F. Münzer* for reading and
criticizing the proofs of the Introduction up to p. lxxiii,
and for allowing me to publish as footnotes and *Addenda*
the suggestive remarks made to me in the course of a
detailed correspondence.

I have endeavoured to make the notes printed below
the text a real commentary to the author's meaning, not
a bundle of bibliography.   Modern commentators might
still lay to heart the criticism passed by Scaliger on the
Pliny of his friend Dalecampius : *le bon homme est docte,
mais il farcit trop ses annotations de je ne sais quelle fatraille
d'auteurs* . . . But wherever further revision showed that
I had done but scant justice to important though dissentient
views I have tried to remedy the omission in the *Addenda*.
There too a few notes are printed the necessity for which
occurred to me later, and reference given to quite recent
literature.

One group of contributions has been made to this book
calling for special notice. When my work was already advancing towards completion, I learnt that *Dr. H. L. Urlichs*
was himself engaged upon an edition of the same parts of

Pliny. With ready generosity, however, Dr. Urlichs offered me at once for my own book a number of his notes, which we agreed should be printed in square brackets and marked with his initials H. L. U. Subsequently, however, Dr. Urlichs informed me, to my regret and surprise, that the present edition would block the way for his own ; accordingly, since he had given us notes, whose value is undeniable, we acceded to his request that his name should be placed as a third on our title-page. In fairness to Dr. Urlichs, I should add that his contributions and his responsibility begin and end with the notes that bear his initials.

Besides those scholars who have given me constant and special help, I have to thank *Mr. A. S. Murray*, *M. S. Reinach*, and *Professor Wilhelm Klein* for many friendly hints, *Mr. Bernhard Berenson* for helping me to a better understanding of passages concerned with the technique of art, and *Director G. von Laubmann* for the singular privileges accorded to me as a reader in the Royal Library at Munich. Above all am I beholden to my friend *Miss K. Jex-Blake*, not only for undertaking the translation, but for her liberality in allowing certain readings to be printed, of whose soundness she was not fully convinced. She has also found time, amid the arduous tasks imposed by College lecturing, to compile both Indices, and to assist in the revision of the book throughout.

EUGÉNIE SELLERS.

SCHWABING, MUNICH.
July, 1896.

CONTENTS

PLINY THE ELDER

and this too was why he rode in a litter in Rome. I can remember his blaming me for walking; I need not, he said, have lost those hours, for he thought all time lost that was not given to study.

INTRODUCTION

THE *Historia Naturalis* of Pliny was intended not only to embrace the whole of the Natural Sciences, but to consider them in their application to the Arts and Crafts of Civilized Life. Hence it is that in a work, whose title would least suggest it, a short yet complete History of Art finds a logical place within the scheme. To Pliny the arts of chasing in silver and of casting in bronze are simply the indispensable complement of the chapters on metals, while, in the same way, the arts of sculpture, of painting, and of gem-engraving come under the head of kinds of earth and precious stones. Pliny's larger and compacted purpose might thus, on the face of it, seem to condemn this present detachment of the History of Art for separate treatment. But that general commentary on Pliny in the light of modern research, to which the texts of *Sillig* and *L. von Jan* were but to serve as preliminaries [1], seems likely, owing to the multifarious contents of the *Historia*, to remain in the region of unachieved possibilities, if not further away still—in Utopia : *il faut plus d'un homme pour écrire sur le grand Pline* [2]. Meanwhile, from the nature of the subject, the Plinian account of Ancient Art and Artists forms an episode sufficiently complete in itself to be made, without further apology, the subject of a special inquiry.

In the Dedicatory Letter addressed with the *Historia* to the co-Emperor Titus, Pliny has himself announced that the 'twenty thousand matters worthy of attention' contained in the thirty-six volumes of his work were 'gathered from some two thousand books' [3]; we must therefore regard his work as nothing more than a compilation from other records, in which personal observation plays no part outside the range of contemporary events.

[1] The gigantic scheme had been conceived by Lorenz Okens (1779–1859) ; see Stark, *Archäologie der Kunst*, p. 264.

[2] *Scaligerana* (ed. 1657), p. 189.

[3] *Praef.* § 17.

An irreparable accident, however—the total loss of the art-literature which preceded Pliny—has given to the books with which we are here concerned an unique value. It so happens that from his pages only can we now obtain something like a connected impression of the art-literature of the Greeks, as it lay open, if no longer actually to him, at any rate to some of his immediate predecessors. For although Pliny in his Preface makes a great show of acknowledgement to his authorities, and announces his intention, which he duly carried out, of compiling *Indices* of their names [1], a very slight acquaintance with his work is sufficient to show that for no part of it did he ever read a Greek author systematically through [2], while for the history of the artists we are safe in asserting that not one of these authors was directly consulted. If the names of Apelles, of Melanthios, of the Sikyonian Xenokrates, of biographers such as Antigonos

---

[1] These lists are suffixed in the MSS. to the table of contents of each book, with which they together make up the first book of the *Historia*, and are also given singly before each book; they contain the names of 146 Roman and 327 foreign authors. For the convenience of the reader I print here the *Indices* to Bks. xxxiv–xxxvi, italicizing the names of the writers upon art:

Libro xxxiv continentur (here follow the contents) . . . *Ex auctoribus*: L. Pisone, Antiate, Verrio, *M. Varrone*, Cornelio Nepote, Messala Rufo, Marso poeta, Boccho, Iulio Basso qui de medicina Graece scripsit, Sextio Nigro qui item, Fabio Vestale. *Externis*: Democrito, Metrodoro Scepsio, *Menaechmo* qui de toreutice scripsit, *Xenocrate* qui item, *Antigono* qui item, *Duride* qui item, *Heliodoro* qui de Atheniensium anathematis scripsit, *Pasitele* qui de mirabilibus operibus scripsit, Timaeo qui de medicina metallica scripsit, Nymphodoro, Iolla, Apollodoro, Andrea, Heraclide, Diagora, Botrye, Archedemo, Dionysio, Aristogene, Democle, Mneside, Xenocrate Zenonis, Theomnesto.

Lib. xxxv continentur . . . *Ex auc-* *toribus*: Messala oratore, Messala sene, Fenestella, Attico, *M. Varrone*, Verrio, *Nepote Cornelio*, Deculone, *Muciano*, Melisso, Vitruvio, Cassio Severo, Longulano, *Fabio Vestale* qui de pictura scripsit. *Externis*: *Pasitele*, *Apelle*, *Melanthio*, *Asclepiodoro*, *Euphranore*, *Parrhasio*, *Heliodoro* qui de anathematis Atheniensium scripsit, Metrodoro qui de architectonice scripsit, Democrito, Theophrasto, Apione grammatico, Timaeo qui de metallica medicina scripsit, Nymphodoro, Iolla, Apollodoro, Andrea, Heraclide, Diagora, Botrye, Archedemo, Dionysio, Aristogene, Democle, Mneside, Xenocrate Zenonis, Theomnesto.

Lib. xxxvi continentur . . . *Ex auctoribus*: *M. Varrone*, C. Galba, Cincio, *Muciano*, Nepote Cornelio, L. Pisone, Q. Tuberone, Fabio Vestale, Annio Fetiale, Fabiano, Seneca, Catone censorio, Vitruvio. *Externis*: Theophrasto, *Pasitele*, Iuba rege, Nicandro, Sotaco, Sudine, Alexandro polyhistore, Apione Plistonico, *Duride*, Herodoto, Euhemero, Aristagora, Dionysio, Artemidoro, Butorida, Antisthene, Demetrio, Demotele, Lycea.

[2] See Teuffel, p. 761.

of Karystos, or Duris of Samos, figure in the *Indices*, rousing the curiosity and ambition of the modern scholar, they are there simply because Pliny had found them quoted by the Roman authors from whom he habitually drew—in this case by Varro, who, in turn, had presumably taken his own information on the subject from a single writer in whose pages the others were already cited. /Thus, although the Plinian *Indices* might mislead us into believing that his work was a mosaic, a piecing together of the several statements of all the authors, Greek or Roman, whose names he quotes, we shall find, on the contrary, that it resembles a stratification of which the superimposed layers can still be distinguished at many points, even though at a number of others they have so run together as to baffle analysis.

The result of such an analysis, if complete, would be nothing less than to isolate and restore to each writer his own contribution; nothing proves so well the difficulty of the task as the great amount of labour already expended in this direction. And this brings me to record the debt which every student of the Plinian art-books owes to the scholars by whose undaunted industry Pliny and his authors have gradually been brought into right relation : to *Otto Jahn*, who by detecting the homogeneous character of a number of scattered art-criticisms, and pointing out their immediate Varronian authorship and ultimate Greek origin, laid a solid basis for all future research in this field [1]; to *A. Brieger*, who made the first attempt to determine the names of the Greek writers whose views Varro had latinized [2]; to *Heinrich Brunn*, who first tried to restore Pliny's system of quotation from his authors [3]; to the scholars—among them *Theodor Schreiber* [4], *Adolf Furtwängler* [5], *Gustav Oehmichen* [6], *Karl Robert* [7],

---

[1] O. Jahn: *Ueber die Kunsturtheile des Plinius* in *Berichte der Sächs. Gesellschaft d. Wissenschaften*, 1850, pp. 105–142.

[2] A. Brieger: *De Fontibus Librorum*, xxxiii–xxxvi, *Nat. Hist. Plin. quatenus ad artem plasticam pertinent.* Dissert. Greifswald, 1856.

[3] H. Brunn: *De Auctorum Indicibus Plinianis.* Disp. Inaug. Bonn, 1856.

[4] Th. Schreiber: *Quaestionum de Artificum Aetatibus in Plin. Nat.*

Hist. Lib. relatis Specimen. Dissert. Leipzig, 1872.

[5] A. Furtwängler: *Plinius u. seine Quellen über die Bildenden Künste* in Supplebd. ix der Jahrbb. f. Klass. Phil. Leipzig, 1877.

[6] G. Oehmichen: *Plinianische Studien zur geographischen und kunsthistorischen Literatur.* Erlangen, 1880.

[7] C. Robert: *Archäologische Märchen aus alter u. neuer Zeit*, Berlin, 1886 (ch. i–iv and vi–viii).

L. von Urlichs [1], and his son *H. L. Urlichs* [2],—who, following
in the steps of these pioneers, developed or corrected their views;
and last, but not least, to *F. Münzer*, who only the other day [3],
when the question had begun to show signs of exhaustion, gave
it a new stimulus through his vigorous attempt to ascertain the
Greek element in Pliny by a minute comparison of those parts
suspected to be Greek with the extant fragments of certain
authors mentioned in the *Indices*. In what follows, I propose
to bring together, in a survey of the gradual growth of the Plinian
history of the artists, such results as have been attained, carrying
forward by the way the task of identifying and disengaging the
Greek writers upon art mentioned by Pliny.

§ 1. *Xenokrates of Sikyon (fl. about 280 B.C.).*

In the criticisms or verdicts upon celebrated artists, now dis-
jointedly scattered throughout the Plinian narrative, but recognized
by Otto Jahn (*op. cit.*) as vitally interdependent, we touch at
once upon the original groundwork. These criticisms have it in
common that they all culminate in a broad statement of the
special services rendered to art by the artist in question; they are
presented for the most part as the effect produced by the artist's
works upon the critic; and they are all consistently free from
anecdote or epigram, in contrast to the phraseological character
of so much of the ancient art-criticism. Their principle is most
readily grasped in the judgements passed upon the five most
famous statuaries—Pheidias, Myron, Polykleitos, Pythagoras,
and Lysippos—in xxxiv, 54–65. It is instructive minutely to
analyze these criticisms when freed so far as may be from the
additions made to them by later writers [4]. In the following
scheme I have indicated, within square brackets, the nature of
these additions.

[1] L. Urlichs: *Die Quellenregister zu Plinius letzten Büchern*. Progr. Würzburg, 1878.
[2] H. L. Urlichs: *Über Griechische Kunstschriftsteller*. Dissert. Würzburg, 1887.
Besides the works cited as of leading importance, mention may also be made of the two following dissertations: J. Dalstein, *Quibus Fontibus*

Plinius in Artificum Historia usus sit, Metz, 1885: and H. Voigt, *De Fontibus earum quae ad artes pertinent partium Nat. Hist. Plin. quaestiones*. Halle, 1887.
[3] F. Münzer: *Zur Kunstgeschichte des Plinius* in Hermes, vol. xxx, 1895.
[4] In doing this I have been guided almost entirely by the analysis of Münzer, *op. cit.* p. 502 ff.

I. Pheidias.

Phidias praeter Iovem Olympium ... fecit ex ebore ... Minervam Athenis, qnae est in Parthenone stans, ex aere vero (*follows allusion to 'Amazon' in* § 53) ... Minervam tam eximiae pulchritudinis ut formae cognomen acceperit. fecit et cliduchum [*follows mention of an Athena in Rome, of two draped figures and a nude colossos, all from Rom. Museogr.* p. xci] primusque artem toreuticen aperuisse atque demonstrasse merito iudicatur.

II. Polykleitos.

Polyclitus Sicyonius Hageladae discipulus diadumenum fecit [*follows epigrammatic qualification,* p. lxviii, *and price paid for the Diadumenos,* p. lxxxiv], idem et doryphorum [*follows epigrammatic qualification; second mention under the name 'canon' of the doryphoros,* p. xli] fecit et destringentem se et nudum telo incessentem [*follows mention of knucklebone players, at Rome, in Hall of Titus,* p. xcii; *of a Hermes at Lysimacheia, on authority of Mucianus,* p. xc; *of a Herakles at Rome*] hagetera arma sumentem [*follows from an anecdotic source, the mention of Artemon surnamed 'periphoretos'*—Add. p. 235] hic consummasse banc scientiam iudicatur et toreuticen sic erudisse ut Phidias aperuisse. proprium eius est uno crure ut insisterent signa excogitasse, quadrata tamen esse ea ait Varro et paene ad exemplum.

III. Myron.

Myronem Eleutheris natum Hageladae et ipsum discipulum bucula maxime nobilitavit [*follows allusion to epigrams upon the heifer*], fecit et canem et discobolon et Perseum et pristas et Satyrum admirantem tibias et Minervam, Delphicos pentathlos, pancratiastas [*follows mention* (a) *of a Herakles in Rome,* (b) *of the grave of a grasshopper and locust, see Comm.* p. 46, l. 4, (c) *of an Apollo restored to Ephesos by Augustus,* p. lxxxix]. primus hic multiplicasse veritatem videtur, numerosior in arte quam Polyclitus et in symmetria diligentior, et ipse tamen corporum tenus curiosus animi sensus non expressisse, capillum quoque et pubem non emendatius fecisse quam rudis antiquitas instituisset.

IV. Pythagoras.

Vicit eum Pythagoras Reginus ex Italia pancratiaste Delphis posito; eodem vicit et Leontiscum; fecit et stadiodromon Astylon qui Olympiae ostenditur et Libyn puerum tenentem tabellam eodem loco et mala ferentem nudum [*follows mention, from an epigram, of the Philoktetes at Syracuse,* p. lxix], item Apollinem serpentemque eius sagittis configi [*follows mention, from an anecdotic source, of the 'Citharoedus' at Thebes,* Münzer *op. cit.* p. 525], hic primus nervos et venas expressit capillumque diligentius. (πρῶτον δοκοῦντα Πυθαγόραν ῥυθμοῦ καὶ συμμετρίας ἐστοχάσθαι—Diogenes Laertios, viii, 46.)

V. Lysippos.

[*The account of Lysippos opens with an anecdote given on the authority of Duris,* p. xlvi.]

(Lysippus) fecit . . . destringentem se [*follows its dedication at Rome;*

b

anecdote of Tiberius's passion for the statue], nobilitatur Lysippus et temulenta tibicina et canibus ac venatione [*mention, on authority of Mucianus* (p. lxxxvii), *of the chariot of the Sun at Rhodes*]. fecit et Alexandrum Magnum multis operibus a pueritia eius orsus [*follows Nero's maltreatment of the statue*]. idem fecit Hephaestionem Alexandri Magni amicum [*its ascription by other authorities to Polykleitos; Pliny's own comment*, p. xciii], item Alexandri venationem quae Delphis sacrata est, Athenis Satyrum, turmam Alexandri in qua amicorum eius imagines summa omnium similitudine expressit [*mention of removal of the group to Rome*], fecit et quadrigas multorum generum. statuariae arti plurimum traditur contulisse capillum exprimendo, capita minora faciendo quam antiqui, corpora graciliora siccioraque, per quae proceritas signorum maior videretur. *non habet Latinum nomen symmetria* quam diligentissime custodit nova intactaque ratione quadratas veterum staturas permutando [*follows apothegm quoted from Duris*, p. lxii f]. propriae huius videntur esse argutiae operum custoditae in minimis quoque rebus.

To which may be added :

VI. Pupils of Lysippos, and Telephanes of Phokaia.

Filios et discipulos reliquit laudatos artifices Laippum, Boedan, sed ante omnes Euthrycraten, quamquam is constantiam potius imitatus patris quam elegantiam austero maluit genere quam iucundo placere. itaque optume expressit Herculem Delphis et Alexandrum Thespis venatorem et Thespiadas, proelium equestre, simulacrum ipsum Trophonii ad oraculum, quadrigas complures, equum cum fuscinis, canes venantium. huius porro discipulus fuit Tisicrates et ipse Sicyonius, sed Lysippi sectae propior, ut vix discernantur complura signa, ceu senex Thebanus et Demetrius rex, Peucestes Alexandri Magni servator, dignus tanta gloria. artifices qui compositis voluminibus condidere haec miris laudibus celebrant Telephanen Phocaeum ignotum alias, quoniam in Thessalia habitaverit, et ibi opera eius latuerint, alioqui suffragiis ipsorum aequatur Polyclito, Myroni, Pythagorae. laudant eius Larisam et Spintharum pentathlum et Apollinem [*follows, from a different source, a variant explanation of the obscurity of Telephanes*].

It is now a commonplace of archaeology that these closely connected criticisms were designed to establish a comparison of the five principal artists (*insignes*), based upon their gradual conquest of the problems of symmetry and proportion, and of certain minor technical details such as the rendering of the hair, of the sinews, or the veins : Pheidias discovers the possibilities of statuary ; Polykleitos perfects it and makes his statues rest their weight on one leg, yet he fails because his figures are too square and monotonous ; Myron surpasses him by attaining not only to symmetry but to variety, yet he fails in the rendering of the hair ; Pythagoras is more successful with hair and moreover learns how to express the sinews and the muscles ;—at this point we are brought up short by finding that, in Pliny, nothing is said of the relation of Pythagoras to symmetry. This is however an omission for which the Roman author, Pliny or Varro, is responsible ; for the record of that artist's contribution to symmetry is preserved in the passage quoted above from Diogenes Laertios[1] (cf. Comm. p. 48). There we learn that Pythagoras was considered the first artist to aim not only at symmetry but also at rhythm—in other words at the correct rendering of proportion, not only in figures at rest, but also in figures in motion. Lysippos, finally, achieves the perfect proportion, by modifying in a manner peculiar to himself the ancient canons, and solves by the way the minor technical difficulties in the rendering of the hair. The guiding thought is analogous to that which prompted Dionysios to classify the orators into inventors of their art— εὑρεταί, and its perfectors—τελειωταί[2].

The mention of Varro in § 56 certainly proves, as Jahn saw, that he was Pliny's immediate authority for the whole series of the criticisms ; but it is equally certain that they did not originate with him. So rigid a scheme of artistic development would be a most unlikely product of the varied and miscellaneous literary activity of that compiler. It is moreover strongly coloured by the partisanship of a school and obviously devised to the honour of the Sikyonian Lysippos, the greatest artists falling into place as his precursors. Besides, the words *non habet latinum nomen symmetria . . .* in § 65 show sufficiently that Varro had only been translating from the Greek. He appears here as the intermediary between Pliny and the Greeks precisely as, in the earlier books of the *Historia*, Trogus or Nigidius Figulus are named as authorities for facts or observations drawn by these writers from Aristotle[3].

The Greek author whose views on the gradual development of art passed, through Varro, into the pages of Pliny was not only a warm admirer of the Sikyonians, but, to judge from the exclusive

---

[1] Furtwängler, *Plinius u. seine Quellen*, p. 70.

[2] Dionysios Halik. *De Dinarcho iud.*: Περὶ Δεινάρχου τοῦ ῥήτορος οὐδὲν εἰρηκὼς ἐν τοῖς περὶ τῶν ἀρχαίων γραφεῖσιν, διὰ τὸ μήτε εὑρετὴν ἰδίου γεγονέναι χαρακτῆρος τὸν ἄνδρα, ὥσπερ τὸν Λυσίαν, καὶ τὸν Ἰσοκράτην, καὶ τὸν Ἰσαῖον· μήτε τῶν εὑρημένων ἑτέροις τελειωτήν, ὥσπερ τὸν Δημοσθένην, καὶ

τὸν Αἰσχίνην, καὶ Ὑπερείδην ἡμεῖς κρίνομεν.

[3] Nigidius is quoted for Aristotle in ix, 185, Trogus in xi, 275, 276 ; see F. Aly, *Zur Quellenkritik des älteren Plinius*, p. 10 f.; Montigny, *Quaestiones in Plin. Nat. Hist de Animalibus Libros.* Bonn,1844 ; Teuffel, p. 761.

stress which he lays upon certain sides of technical progress, an
artist judging from the standpoints which he had himself been
trained to esteem most highly. We have not far to go to fix upon
his name. He must be, as Robert first definitely pointed out[1],
that Xenokrates, himself a pupil of two distinguished Sikyonians,
Teisikrates and Euthykrates, who is cited in the Index to Bk.
xxxiv and in § 83 as having written on bronze statuary, and in xxxv,
68 upon painting[2]. In the latter passage he is named conjointly with Antigonos, another art-writer, who, as we shall
presently see, is in great measure responsible for the additions of
epigrammatic or anecdotic character made to the earlier history
by Xenokrates.

But the scheme of development propounded in the famous
five criticisms involves a curious anachronism : Myron is made
posterior to Polykleitos, Pythagoras posterior to both. That this
anachronism cannot be due to mere negligence appears from the
carefully thought-out nature of the context. I think it is clear
from the remark preserved in Diogenes, concerning the *rhythm*
contributed to statuary by Pythagoras, that, alongside considera-
tions of symmetry and proportion, the idea of an evolution from
figures at rest to figures in motion influenced the chronological
order adopted by the author of the criticisms. After the stately
seated or standing gods, goddesses, and temple-attendants of
Pheidias come first the quiet athletes of Polykleitos, just shifting
the weight of the body to one leg as in the act of walking, then

[1] *Archäologische Märchen aus alter und neuer Zeit*, pp. 28 ff. A. Brieger, *De Fontibus*, p. 46, had first pointed out that the verdicts on the bronze statuaries could be traced beyond Varro back to Antigonos and Xeno-krates ; cf. also Th. Schreiber, *Quaes-tionum de Artif. Aetat.*, p. 27 ff., and Furtwängler, *op. cit.* p. 68 ; but it was Robert who first disentangled the special contribution of Xenokrates.

[2] His identification with the Athe-nian Xenokrates, son of Ergophilos, of the inscriptions from Oropos and Elateia (Loewy, *Inschriften der Grie-chischen Bildhauer*, 135 *a, b, c*) ap-pears to me, on the other hand, doubtful (see Comm.). The strongest argument in its favour is that Loewy,

135 *a, b*, are from Oropos, a region for which both Teisikrates, the master of Xenokrates, and Thoinias, son of Teisikrates, were at one time active (*I. G. B.* 120–122 *a*). But it is strange that an Athenian, who in inscribing his name was careful in at least two cases (*I. G. B.* 135 *a*, and the new inscription—also from Oropos—'Εφημ. ἀρχ. 1892, 51, cf. Diels, *Anzeiger*, 1893, p. 138 f.) to record the country of his birth, should have come so completely to identify himself with the Sikyonians as did the Plinian writer, or have so often entirely passed over, or dismissed with only a passing allusion, the famous artists of his own country.

the works—athletes also for the greater part—of Myron and Pythagoras. Now, if we place the Myronian 'Diskobolos' with its audacious movement next to the Polykleitan 'Diadumenos' or 'Doryphoros,' and adopt the recent conjecture [1], which attributes to Pythagoras the fine boxer in the Louvre [2], and the athlete in violent motion of the Boboli gardens [3]—two statues which surpass even the Diskobolos in movement and animation—we shall at least understand how, at a time when art-criticism in our modern sense was scarcely existent, such statues would give rise to the perverse chronology of §§ 55–59.

The account of the pupils of Lysippos is obviously inseparable from the account of Lysippos himself. To Telephanes we shall return presently. Before we proceed to track out Xenokrates further, we should, however, note the significant fact that wherever, in the passages just discussed, the locality of a work of art is either given or can be recovered from other sources, it lies within a restricted geographical beat, comprised by Olympia (§§ 54, 59), Delphoi (§§ 57, 59, 64, 66), Lebadeia, Thespiai, and Thebes (§§ 66, 67), and finally Athens (§§ 54, 64) [4]. From this we may gather that Xenokrates (who probably had little opportunity for distant travel) confined himself to the mention of monuments of which he had personal knowledge.

A glance at the chronological tables of §§ 49–52 shows them to be by the author of the criticisms; in the one as in the other Pheidias opens the series—Lysippos with the brilliant attendance of sons and pupils closes it. If the Xenokratic authorship of the chronology needed confirmation, we should find it in the fact that Polykleitos, Myron, Pythagoras, are placed in the same curious order as in the verdicts. The activity of Xenokrates cannot have extended much beyond Ol. 121, the date he assigns to the pupils of Lysippos, and it is noteworthy that, although his treatise was extensively enlarged by later writers, yet the period with which it closed was adopted as representing the close of art in Greece. *Cessavit deinde* (after Ol. 121) *ars*, writes Pliny, *ac rursus Olympiade CLVI revixit*, the *revixit* not so much

[1] Furtwängler, *Masterpieces of Greek Sculpture*, p. 171 f; cf. E. Reisch, *Weihgeschenke*, p. 44.

[2] Phot. Giraudon, 1207.

[3] Phot. Arndt-Bruckmann (*Einzelverkauf*), 96.

[4] Cf. Münzer, *op. cit.* p. 505. Of the works whose locality is not indicated, the Athena *tam eximiae pulchritudinis* of Pheidias (see Comm. to xxxiv, 54, l. 2), the cow of Myron, and his Perseus were at Athens.

marking a real revival as affording a convenient formula to introduce the Greek artists who decorated at Rome the famous monuments erected by Q. Metellus Macedonicus [1].

It is evident that the chronological and narrative parts of the Xenokratic treatise had originally formed one consistent whole, which some later writer afterwards subdivided into a chronology and alphabetical lists (cf. p. lxxx). The five most famous artists, however, and the pupils of Lysippos were left, owing to their great reputation, in the original Greek order, though sundered from the chronology. Moreover, Telephanes of Phokaia (§ 68) and Praxiteles (§§ 69-71) were assigned places—in no sort of chronological order—between the pupils of Lysippos and the first alphabetical list. The reasons for the exception made in their favour are sufficiently instructive. The Xenokratic character of the account of Telephanes comes out in the comparison instituted to Polykleitos, Myron, and Pythagoras, whose names are given in the same order as in the verdicts; since, however, Xenokrates had not deemed Telephanes worthy of comparison with the two greatest names—with either Pheidias, the founder, or Lysippos the perfecter of the art—he had also not accredited him with any distinct contribution to the progress of statuary. Now the comparison of Telephanes to Polykleitos, Myron, and Pythagoras on the one hand, and the absence of any precise estimate of his merits on the other, were explained by some later Greek writer in a rationalizing anecdotic manner, alien to Xenokratic practice : Telephanes was excellent, the reasoning seems to be, or he could not be compared to great names, but he must have been obscure or we should hear more about him ; and as Xenokrates had given a list of works, some, or all, of which were in Thessaly [2], their remoteness was made the reason for the artist's want of fame : *quoniam in Thessalia habitaverit et ibi opera eius latuerint.* These additions are so nicely welded into the Xenokratic account that they must have been made at a quite early date, as we shall see by Antigonos (p. xxxvi). Puzzled by the mention of this excellent yet unknown artist, the Roman authors next introduced him under cover of their Greek authorities : *artifices qui haec condidere* (i.e. Xenokrates and Antigonos) *miris laudibus celebrant*

---

[1] The *cessavit* and *revixit* first explained by Brunn, *K. G.* i. p. 504 f. Cf H. L. Urlichs, *Griechische Kunstschriftsteller*, p. 31 f.

[2] A region to which Xenokrates might easily have extended his researches northwards from Phokis and Boeotia.

Telephanem Phocaeum, and placed him outside the *insignes*, but yet in a more distinguished place than the alphabetical lists. Practically the same happened in the case of Praxiteles (§§ 69–71). This artist appears to have been only summarily discussed by Xenokrates [1], who, like the rest of his school and Lysippos himself, was exclusively a worker in bronze, and therefore only wrote concerning works in bronze, entirely ignoring the marble sculpture wherein lay the chief strength of Praxiteles and the new Attic school. Yet Praxiteles was much too great a favourite of the Romans for a Roman writer to be content with assigning to him a place among the artists of the alphabetical lists, so he linked him on to Telephanes with a *quoque*, adducing as an apology for not placing Praxiteles among the *insignes* that he was *marmore felicior ideo et clarior*. The argument practically comes to : Praxiteles also, like Telephanes, has an excuse for the place assigned to him—in his case not want of fame, but the fact that he is better known as a worker in marble than as a worker in bronze [2].

An analysis of the first alphabetical list (§§ 74–83) will reveal further traces of Xenokrates. In the subjoined tables I have marked with an X those artists the account of whom seems Xenokratic, and placed within square brackets the names of artists or works manifestly introduced from other sources.

X. *Alcamenes : encrinomenos* [3].
X. *Aristides : quadrigae bigaeque.*
　　[*Amphicrates : Leaena*, periegetic, see Comm. and p. lxxxvi.]
X. *Bryaxis : Aesculapius, Seleucus.*
X. *Boedas : adorans.*
　　[*Baton : Apollo, Iuno*, Roman museography, cf. p. xci f.]
　　[*Cresilas : volneratus, Pericles*, both from epigrams, see Comm. and p.lxix.]
　　[*Cephisodotus : ara*, on authority of Heliodoros, p. lxxv.]
X. *Canachus* : [*Apollo*, anecdotic, see Comm. and p.lxxxviii] *celetizontes pueri.*
X. *Chaereas : Alexander, Philippus.*
X. *Ctesilaus : doryphorus, Amazon.*
　　[*Demetrius : Lysimache* (inscrip., p. lxxxvi), *Minerva mus.* (periegetic), Simon (literary source, p. lxv, note 1).]

[1] Münzer, *op. cit.* p. 507, considers the Xenokratic material to be somewhat as follows : *Praxiteles ... fecit ex aere. ... Proserpinae raptum item catagusam, et Liberum patrem et Ebrietatem nobilemque una Satyrum, quem Graeci periboeton cognominant ... item stephanusam, pseliumenen,* *Oporan* (where M. wrongly retains *canephoram*).

[2] I am indebted to Dr. H. L. Urlichs for giving me what I believe to be the correct explanation of the passage.

[3] The list is based on that of Oehmichen, *Plin. Studien*, p. 163 f.

X. *Daedalus: destringentes se.*
X. *Dinomenes: Protesilaus, Pythodemus.*
X. *Euphranor:* [*Alexander Paris* (epigr. p. lxix), *Minerva, Latona* (Roman
            museogr.)], *quadrigae bigaeque, cliduchus. Virtus et
            Graecia; mulier adm. et ador.; Alex. et Philippus.*
    [*Eutychides: Eurotas* (epigr. p. lxix f.).]
X. *Hegias: Minerva, Pyrrhus, celetizontes.*
    [*Hagesias: Hercules in Pario colonia* (Mucianus, p. xc).]
X. *Isidotus: buthytes.*
    [*Lycius: puer sufflans* (epigr. p. lxx)], *Argonautae.*
    [*Leochares: Ganymedes* (epigr. p. lxx), *Autolycus* (literary source, p.
            xlv, note 1), *Jupiter, Apollo* (Rom. museogr.), *Lyciscus*
            (epigr. p. lxxiii, note 2).]
X. *Lycius: puer suffitor.*
    [*Menaechmus: vitulus* (epigr. p. lxxiii, note 2).]
X. *Naucydes: Mercurius, discobolus, immolans arietem.*
X. *Naucerus: luctator anhelans.*
    [*Niceratus: Aesculapius et Hygia* (Roman museogr.).]
X. *Pyromachus: quadriga cum Alcibiade.*
X. *Polycles: Hermaphroditus.*
X. *Pyrrhus: Hygia et Minerva.*
X. *Phanis: epithyusa.*
    [*Styppax: splanchnoptes* (periegetic and epigr. p. lxx).]
    [*Silanion: Apollodorus, Achilles, epistates* (epigr. p. lxx).]
    [*Strongylion: Amazon* (Roman anecdote, cf. p. xcii).]
    [*Theodorus: se ipse fudit* (anecdotic).]
    [*Xenocrates: copia signorum* (Antigonos).]

Reference to the text of Pliny will show that the works of the
nineteen artists marked X are enumerated with a simple directness which contrasts as forcibly as possible with the literary
allusions, anecdotic tags, and epigrammatic descriptions attaching
to the notices of the names placed in brackets. This same
directness characterized the lists of works of the *insignes*, and
is a clear mark of Xenokratic authorship. Ten of these names,
moreover, still retain their place in the Xenokratic chronology
(*Alcamenes, Aristides, Canachus, Daedalus, Dinomenes, Euphranor,
Hegias, Naucydes, Pyromachus, Polycles*).

An attentive study shows how a second, a third, and perhaps
even a fourth hand worked over or added to the Xenokratic
material, sometimes to its suppression. *Cephisodotus, Eutychides,
Leochares*, all appear in the Xenokratic chronology, but, if any of
their works were mentioned, these have been omitted to make
way for others which brought the added interest of anecdote or
epigram; in the case of Euphranor (§ 77) the mention of the
' Paris,' derived from an epigram, was prefixed to the arid Xeno-

kratic lists. This method of introducing new material from other sources has led to the double mention of *Lycius* (§ 79) and of *Hegias* (§ 78), the latter of whom appears the second time, under the alternative form of his name, *Hagesias*. As to the mention of Xenokrates himself (§ 83), it is probable that if it had come from him its wording would be at once more modest and less vague. I therefore adopt Münzer's suggestion (*op. cit.* p. 509) that it is due to the reverence ('Pietät') of the later writer, who worked the Xenokratic treatise into his own, namely Antigonos. A number of other additions, made from evident Roman sources, or concerning works to be seen at Rome, in Varro's or Pliny's day, need no comment here. In the same way certain additions came to be made also to the chronology. The most obvious is the notice of Seilanion (see p. xlix, note 2, and Add. to Comm. on xxxiv, 51), who is tacked on to the artists of Ol. 113.

The Plinian account of the bronze-workers from § 49 to § 83 represents roughly, then, the original compass of that portion of the treatise of Xenokrates which treated of the period from the great revival after the Persian wars down to the sons and pupils of Lysippos, in Olympiads CXIII and CXXI. But it would be an error to suppose that this history of statuary took no notice of the earlier phases of the art. Through some accident which we are now no longer in a position to determine, the whole earlier part seems however to have been suppressed, with the exception of one unmistakable fragment, which oddly enough has found its way to the beginning of Pliny's account of the sculptors in marble (xxxvi, 9–10). The passage, as it now stands, is a little mosaic of most diverse materials, but the original Xenokratic conception is still evident from the stress laid upon the early fame of the Sikyonian workshops, from the fact that Dipoinos and Skyllis, the scene of whose labours lay chiefly in Sikyon and adjacent or dependent regions, are chosen among all archaic craftsmen to represent the beginnings of their art [1]. Their works had been of wood (note on xxxvi, 10) and could thus fall within the range of a writer upon bronze statuary, describing the gradual evolution from wood or wood gilt to metal. To the Xenokratic

---

[1] The Xenokratic kernel of the passage has been rightly detected by Münzer (*op. cit.* p. 523), whom it is therefore surprising to find support-ing the view that Xenokrates left the whole of the archaic period unnoticed (*ib.* p. 505).

contention that the art of sculpture in bronze was elaborated by Daidalid artists on the mainland of Greece, a later writer—presumably Antigonos (p. xliii f)—adjusted the account of the rise of sculpture in marble in the islands of the Aegean, under the auspices of Chian sculptors. Thus it was that the Xenokratic account of Dipoinos and Skyllis came in time to be placed at the opening of a history of sculpture in marble, where it has long proved a crux to archaeologists [1]. We have learnt, then, that Xenokrates, in treating of the bronze-workers, began with the earliest beginnings. The current notion that he took no account of archaic bronze statuary is as false as it is arbitrary [2]. It is not improbable that, if the Xenokratic account of the statuaries, as we have it in Pliny's thirty-fourth book, opens with Pheidias, this is somehow due to a very ancient misunderstanding of the statement that 'Pheidias first revealed the capabilities of sculpture and indicated its methods.' We shall immediately see how a similar expression, in the case of the painter Apollodoros, misled both ancient and modern critics into the erroneous supposition that the Greek writers—Xenokrates *in primis*—had ignored the early painters.

The Xenokratic history of the painters, preserved in Pliny's thirty-fifth book, can be recovered far more completely than that of the bronze-workers. Since in xxxv the alphabetical principle does not make its appearance till § 138, where it is employed to group together artists of comparatively minor importance, the original scheme is, in parts at least, still sufficiently clear.

Xenokrates is quoted by name, along with Antigonos, as the authority for the verdict upon Parrhasios (§ 68). The judgement in its essence is so indubitably his, as a comparison with the judgement passed upon Lysippos and his son Euthykrates (xxxiv, 66) proves, that if the later writer's name appears it can only

---

[1] Münzer, *loc. cit.*

[2] Cf. among others Robert, *Arch. Märchen*, pp. 36, 41, where the post-dating of Kritios and Nesiotes (§ 49) is explained by supposing that the fame of their 'Tyrant-Slayers' would attract the attention of the compiler of the chronology, who, since he ignored the archaic period, made them into contemporaries of Pheidias, the earliest bronze-worker

known to him. I take it rather that Xenokrates, having but very few dates at his command (see Comm. on xxxiv, 49), grouped about Pheidias, as their representative, a number of other artists who had been engaged upon the restoration of Athenian monuments after the Persian sack. The anachronism at any rate affords no proof that Xenokrates had neglected the archaic period.

be in his character of compiler, or 'editor,' of the Xenokratic history.

(Lysippus) statuariae arti plurimum traditur *contulisse* capillum exprimendo, capita minora faciendo quam antiqui, corpora graciliora siccioraque, per quae proceritas signorum maior videretur. non habet Latinum nomen *symmetria quam diligentissime custodit* nova intactaque ratione quadratas veterum staturas permutando, vulgoque dicebat ab illis factos quales essent homines, a se quales viderentur esse. propriae huius videntur esse *argutiae* operum custoditae in minimis quoque rebus. filios et discipulos reliquit laudatos artifices Laippum, Boedan, sed ante omnes Euthycraten, quamquam is constantiam potius imitatus patris quam *elegantiam* austero maluit genere quam iucundo placere.

Parrhasius Ephesi natus et ipse multa *contulit. primus symmetrian picturae dedit*, primus *argutias* voltus, *elegantiam* capilli, venustatem oris, confessione artificum in lineis extremis palmam adeptus. haec est picturae summa suptilitas. corpora enim pingere et media rerum est quidem magni operis sed in quo multi gloriam tulerint, extrema corporum facere et desinentis picturae modum includere rarum in successu artis invenitur. ambire enim se ipsa debet extremitas et sic desinere ut promittat alias pone se ostendatque etiam quae occultat. hanc ei gloriam concessere Antigonus et Xenocrates qui de pictura scripsere, praedicantes quoque, non solum confitentes [1].

But the criticism of Parrhasios is closely linked with a row of similar criticisms, not only interconnected, but dictated by the same spirit as the judgements passed upon the statuaries [2]. Robert has pointed out that identical standards were set up in each case, while the final appreciations were similarly formulated; as Pheidias (xxxiv, 54) discloses the possibilities of statuary, so Apollodoros (xxxv, 60) discloses those of painting. The initiative of either master was carried further in the one art by Polykleitos (xxxiv, 56), by Zeuxis (xxxv, 64) in the other. Both these artists, however, fail in the rendering of proportion, a point in which Myron (xxxiv, 57) and Parrhasios (xxxv, 68) surpass them. The former is *symmetria diligentior* than Polykleitos; of the other it is said that *primus symmetrian picturae dedit*. Pythagoras (xxxiv, 59) and Euphranor (xxxv, 128) each progress towards the attainment of symmetry; of the one the critics said πρῶτον . . . συμμετρίας δοκοῦντα ἐστοχάσθαι, of the other *primus videtur . . . usur-*

---

[1] I have chosen these two passages for comparison, because of the marked verbal similarities, but of course the real counterpart, among the painters, of Lysippos, among the statuaries, was Apelles.

[2] Robert, *Arch. Märch.* p. 67 ff., conveniently prints the passages side by side. After the detailed analysis of the verdicts upon the bronze-workers, it seems sufficient to refer to the text.

passe symmetrian. The highest mastery, finally, is embodied in Lysippos (xxxiv, 65) and in Apelles (xxxv, 79).

We may now proceed to recover traces of Xenokrates in the earlier sections of xxxv. It has been noted above that the contribution to symmetry, made respectively by Pythagoras and Euphranor, was couched in almost identical terms. But the statement that Pythagoras was the first to mark the sinews and the muscles, *primus nervos et venas expressit,* recalls the improvements attributed in an early part of the History of the Painters to Kimon of Kleonai : *articulis membra distinxit, venas protulit* (§ 56) [1]. That both are from the same hand is indubitable.

Again, the criticism of Kimon is inseparable from a whole series of similar passages, in which the earlier stages of painting were discussed. These began at § 16, and, after sundry excursus on paintings in Rome and on colours (§ 18 ff.), were resumed again at § 56. When exhibited together, the original coherence of the passages is self-evident [2].

§ 16. Inventam liniarem a Philocle Aegyptio vel Cleanthe Corinthio primi exercuere Aridices Corinthius et Telephanes Sicyonius, sine ullo etiamnum hi colore, iam tamen spargentes linias intus. ideo et quos pingerent adscribere institutum. primus invenit eas colore testae, ut ferunt, tritae, Ecphantus Corinthius.

§ 56. . . . eosque qui monochromatis pinxerint, quorum aetas non traditur, . . . fuisse, Hygiaenontem, Dinian, Charmadan et qui primus in pictura marem a femina discreverit Eumarum Atheniensem figuras omnis imitari ausum, quique inventa eius excoluerit Cimonem Cleonaeum. hic catagrapha invenit, hoc est obliquas imagines, et varie formare voltus, respicientes suspicientesve vel despicientes. articulis membra distinxit, venas protulit, praeterque in vestibus rugas et sinus invenit.

§ 57. Panaenus quidem frater Phidiae etiam proelium Atheniensium adversus Persas apud Marathona factum pinxit. adeo iam colorum usus increbruerat, adeoque ars perfecta erat ut in eo proelio iconicos duces pinxisse tradatur, Atheniensium Miltiaden, Callimachum, Cynaegirum, barbarorum Datim, Artaphernen.

§ 58. . . . Polygnotus Thasius qui primus mulieres tralucida veste pinxit, capita earum mitris versicoloribus operuit plurimumque picturae primus contulit, siquidem instituit os adaperire, dentes ostendere, voltum ab antiquo rigore variare. [*follows mention of a picture in Rome*] hic Delphis aedem pinxit, hic et Athenis porticum quae Poecile vocatur . . . cum partem eius Micon . . pingeret.

These primitives are represented as not yet sufficiently ad-

---

[1] The parallelism of the two passages is noted—but in a different context—by Hartwig, *Meisterschalen,* p. 165.

[2] I here follow Münzer entirely (*op. cit.* p. 514), who gives the passages freed, so far as possible, from later additions.

vanced to grapple with problems of harmony and symmetry; it is sufficient for them to attempt to conquer step by step, first a knowledge of their materials, then by slow degrees the correct presentment of objects. Philokles, Kleanthes, and the earliest painters, are scarcely painters at all; they practise mere outline. Then Ekphantos fills up this outline with red colour. Hygiainon and his fellows (§ 56) continue to use only one colour till it occurs to Eumaros to distinguish in painting between the sexes; this he doubtless does by introducing white for the flesh of the women[1] *and thus marks the first stage in the progress from monochrome to polychrome painting.* So far, however, figures have only been drawn in full face or in profile (though Pliny nowhere states this, it can be supplied from what follows); but now Kimon of Kleonai *invents* foreshortening, κατάγραφα[2]. He further correctly marks the articulations and the muscles, and 'discovers the wrinkles and the windings of drapery.' Artists, having now learnt to distinguish between the sexes, to articulate their figures, and to present them in various attitudes, are able to turn their attention to distinguishing between individuals. Panainos, accordingly, in his Battle of Marathon, introduces *portraiture*. But mere draughtsmanship—outline simply filled in with colour—was susceptible of still further improvements. Thus Polygnotos of Thasos first permits the draperies to reveal the bodies beneath them, and shows at the same time how to give movement not only to the body, as Kimon had done, but also to the face. Then, the capacities of this limited technique being exhausted, there appeared on the scenes the great painter Apollodoros (§ 90 above, p. xxvii), who by discovering 'the fusion and management of shade[3]'—we should rather say of light—first gave to objects their real semblance (*primus species instituit*): thus he contributed to painting its most important factor, and thereby, as an epigrammatist pointedly said, he 'opened the gates of art' to the great masters of Greek painting—to Zeuxis and Parrhasios and their illustrious contemporaries. The coherence of the whole history of the development and perfection of painting—the consistent logic which underlies it, of an evolution from the simpler to the more complex—is so patent that it is incomprehensible how so many

---

[1] Eumaros's innovation is generally so explained, but I am not aware that the significance of the introduction of this white colour has ever been accurately grasped.

[2] See note on xxxv, 56.

[3] ἐξευρὼν φθορὰν καὶ ἀπόχρωσιν σκιᾶς, Plutarch, *De Glor. Athen.* 2.

scholars—at least in the period between Jahn's Essay and Münzer's—entirely failed to apprehend it.

It remains, however, to ask how in face of this consecutive Treatise by a Greek writer there could ever arise the complaint in xxxv, 54 : *non constat sibi in hac parte* (sc. *historia pictorum*) *Graecorum diligentia multas post olympiadas celebrando pictores quam statuarios ac toreutas, primumque olympiade LXXXX.* The question involves a difficult problem. One can only imagine that the complaint, in its present form, is the result of a misunderstanding ; it is not impossible that some later writer, intermediate between the earlier Greek art-writers and the Roman, had found fault with the Greeks for failing to appreciate the naïve charm and simple methods of the painters who lived previous to the innovations of Apollodoros. Such a criticism, combined with the words used by Xenokrates of Apollodoros, *hic primus species instituit*, might lead in time to the supposition that the Greek art-writers had completely failed even to mention pre-Apollodorian painters. The Roman compilers, drawing from books (Pasiteles? p. lxxix) where the names of Xenokrates and Antigonos as authorities for the history of the early painters had long dropped out, piled up as proofs of the supposed inaccuracy of these writers [1] a number of facts [2] for which their Treatises were in reality the chief sources. Theophrastos, also, had been misrepresented in precisely the same manner. According to Pliny (vii, 205) he had attributed the invention of painting to Polygnotos, whereas Theophrastos can have intended nothing more than that Polygnotos was the first painter who could be properly so called ; writing doubtless under the influence of Aristotle's admiration for the ethical qualities of this artist (*Poet.* 1450a). Theophrastos had assigned to him the place which the Plinian authors, intent rather upon technical progress, gave to Apollodoros. In truth Pliny's statement as regards Theophrastos, and his or Varro's complaint of the Greek inaccuracy, are, I believe, but the distorted reflection of the old controversy whether draughtsmanship or colouring was the more powerful means of expression. The opinion of Aristotle may be

[1] It is universally acknowledged that the Greeks alluded to in the words *Graecorum diligentia* are the main authorities, i.e. Xenokrates and Antigonos (perhaps also Duris); cf. Robert, *Arch. Märchen*, p. 25.

[2] E.g. the activity of Pheidias and Panainos as painters (cf. p. li) ; the whole list of painters and their works from the early monochromatics down to Polygnotos. The account of Boularchos (§ 55) may have been derived by Varro (cf. p. lxxxiv and Comm. on xxxv, 55) from some independent source.

guessed from his predilection for the pre-Apollodorian Polygnotos[1]. The testimony of Dionysios to the value which a school of criticism, practically unrepresented in Pliny, attached to the pre-Apollodorian paintings is of importance:

'In ancient paintings the scheme of colouring was simple and presented no variety in the tones; but the line was rendered with exquisite perfection, thus lending to these early works a singular grace. This purity of draughtsmanship was gradually lost; its place was taken by a learned technique, by the differentiation of light and shade, by the full resources of the rich colouring to which the works of the later artists owe their strength[2].'

We learn from this passage that the methods of the later painters were practically looked upon as hostile to those of the earlier, and Xenokrates, a hot partisan of the post-Apollodorians, may well have expressed himself in language which would eventually lead to the erroneous supposition that he had ignored all earlier paintings, from Polygnotos and Panainos up to the early monochromatics.

As we have it in Pliny, the argument against the Greeks is presented with skill and vigour (Comm. on xxxv, 54); the theme was evidently congenial to the Roman authors, who doubtless felt for the archaic the enthusiasm—common to all decadent periods—which was to rouse the subtle satire of Quinctilian[3].

After § 70 it becomes more difficult to follow Xenokrates (cf. Münzer, *op. cit.* p. 516), and scarcely any sentence can be picked out as bearing the indubitable signs of his method. Later writers, as shown by the Plinian *indices*, had, when it came to the artists

---

[1] Bertrand, *Études sur la Peinture*, p. 17, singularly misapprehends Aristotle when he assumes that A. definitely stated his preference for drawing over painting, and translates *Poet.* 1450 b, 'en étalant les plus belles couleurs on ne fera pas le même plaisir que par le simple trait d'une figure.' What A. says is that colours laid on *confusedly* or *indiscriminately* will not produce as much pleasure as simple outline: εἰ γάρ τις ἐναλείψειε τοῖς καλλίστοις φαρμάκοις χύδην, οὐκ ἂν ὁμοίως εὐφράνειεν καὶ λευκογραφήσας εἰκόνα.

[2] Dionys. Halik. de Isaeo iudic. 4 εἰσὶ δή τινες ἀρχαῖαι γραφαί, χρώμασι μὲν εἰργασμέναι ἁπλῶς, καὶ οὐδεμίαν ἐν τοῖς μίγμασιν ἔχουσαι ποικιλίαν, ἀκριβεῖς δὲ ταῖς γραμμαῖς, καὶ πολὺ τὸ χαρίεν ἐν ταύταις ἔχουσαι· αἱ δὲ μετ' ἐκείνας, εὔγραμμοι μὲν ἧττον, ἐξειργασμέναι δὲ μᾶλλον, σκιᾷ τε καὶ φωτὶ ποικιλλόμεναι, καὶ ἐν τῷ πλήθει τῶν μιγμάτων τὴν ἰσχὺν ἔχουσαι.

[3] *Primi, quorum quidem opera non vetustatis modo gratia visenda sunt, clari pictores fuisse dicuntur Polygnotus atque Aglaophon, quorum simplex color tam sui studiosos adhuc habet, ut illa prope rudia ac velut futurae mox artis primordia maximis, qui post eos exstiterunt, auctoribus praeferant, proprio quodam intelligendi, ut mea opinio fert, ambitu.* Quinct. xii, 10.

of the fourth century, a large mass of literature to draw from. Moreover popular anecdotes concerning the painters now take in great measure the place of more serious criticism.

The next clear trace of Xenokrates is in the special emphasis laid (§ 76) upon the fame of the Sikyonian painters. Sikyon, the cradle of art-painting (§ 16), is now shown to be the home also of its splendid maturity; as she had produced Lysippos, the greatest master of statuary, so she produces Apelles, the greatest master of the rival art of painting, whose contributions to his art are appraised (§ 79) according to the canons applied to Lysippos in xxxiv, 65. Though Apelles was probably already an artist of established renown when he left his native Ephesos to study in the schools of Sikyon, the claims of his obscurer early masters must fade entirely before the glorious reputation of Eupompos and Pamphilos.

The Theban-Attic school, which branched off from the Sikyonian, with Aristeides I—brother-pupil of Eupompos—also claimed the attention of Xenokrates. We must recognize with Robert [1] that the account of Aristeides II in § 98 originates with him; we note the Xenokratic intent to connect the name of a great artist with some definite progress or contribution. In this case the progress accomplished is of ethical rather than of technical import; Aristeides discovers how to render not only character but transient emotions [2], and in this there is a vague reminiscence of the criticism passed upon Myron, that he had failed to express 'the sensations of the mind.'

Between the two Aristeides must naturally have intervened the account of Nikomachos, son of Aristeides I, and his pupils, which in Pliny appears in §§ 108–110, away from its original context.

After a long digression in §§ 112–121, due, as we shall see, in part to Varro (p. lxxxiv), in part to Pliny himself (cf. p. xcii), we again come upon clear traces of Xenokrates in the History of the Painters in Encaustic [3]. In § 122 we find it stated first that, according to certain authorities, Aristeides was the *inventor* of encaustic;

---

[1] *Archäologische Märchen*, p. 69; cf. Münzer, p. 516.

[2] i.e. *perturbationes*: Furtwängler, *Plinius u. s. Quellen*, p. 65 f., points out that this Ciceronian translation of the Greek πάθη (see Comm.) is presum-

ably due to Varro. It affords one of the many proofs of the passage of the Greek Treatises upon Art through Varro's hands.

[3] Münzer, *op. cit.* p. 517 ff.

immediately after it is asserted that there existed pictures in this technique older than the time of Aristeides, namely those by Polygnotos, by the Parians Nikanor and Mnasilaos, and by Elasippos. In a word, the claims of the island-schools to priority of invention are opposed to the claims of the artists of the mainland, precisely as in xxxvi, 9–12 the Xenokratic contention that statuary was invented by the Daidalids Dipoinos and Skyllis was confronted by Antigonos with the assertion that long before their time sculpture in marble had flourished in the islands of the Aegean (p. xxvi)[1]. Thus it seems safe to conclude that the tradition attaching the invention of Encaustic to the name of Aristeides goes back to Xenokrates, and that Antigonos, faithful to his programme of exhibiting the various sources at his command, appended to it the account now represented in Pliny by the words *aliquanto vetustiores encaustae picturae extitere . . . nisi encaustica inventa.*

The school partisanship of Xenokrates at once betrays itself in § 123 in the preeminence assigned to the Sikyonian Pausias, pupil of the Sikyonian Pamphilos (§ 75), and accordingly brother-pupil of Apelles. Pausias is not only praised as the *first* to achieve fame in the wax technique, but is also credited in true Xenokratic fashion with two distinct contributions : he is the *first* to paint the panels of ceilings, the *first* also to decorate the vaults of roofs. It may be noted at this point that the Plinian division into painters in the ordinary tempera and painters in encaustic was probably no part of the original Greek treatise. Pausias must have been discussed in connexion with Pamphilos and the artists of § 75, while the discussion of Euphranor must have followed upon that of his master Aristeides I. That the pupils of Pausias, Aristolaos (§ 137) and Nikophanes, had also originally been discussed by Xenokrates is almost certain[2]; but the criticism passed upon Euphranor in § 130 is to my mind the last passage in the Plinian narrative of the painters where Xenokratic authorship can be pointed to with certainty. Students, however, will read with interest Münzer's attempts (*op. cit.* p. 518) to disengage further Xenokratic threads.

---

[1] The parallelism has been kindly pointed out to me by Münzer in a private letter; see note 3 on p. xliv.

[2] The epithet *elegans* applied to Nikophanes in xxxv, 111, recalls the *elegantia* attributed to Lysippos, xxxiv, 66, the *elegantia* in rendering of hair attributed to Parrhasios, xxxv, 67.

Before dismissing the history of the painters we still have to note a few scattered passages which afford proof that Xenokrates had not only summed up but analyzed the problems which the great artists in turn had set themselves to solve. The appreciation of Parrhasios (xxxv, 67), with the appended analysis of his special artistic achievement, contained in the words *haec est picturae summa suptilitas . . . occultat*, is a striking instance. That highest and hardest aim of the painter to produce about his figures the illusion of ambient space, of enveloping light and air, could not be more vigorously or happily expressed than in the phrase: *corpora enim pingere et media rerum est quidem magni operis sed in quo multi gloriam tulerint, extrema corporum facere et desinentis picturae modum includere rarum in successu artis invenitur. Ambire enim se ipsa debet extremitas, et sic desinere ut promittat alia post se ostendatque etiam quae occultat* (see Comm.). Again we can, I think, trace the hand of Xenokrates in xxxv, 29, in the analysis of the various effects attempted by painting; with subtle understanding of artistic procedure it is told how painting after shaking off its early monotony discovered first light and shade, then the effects attainable by the juxtaposition of colours; finally, how it discovered glow and the passage from the more lit-up to the less lit-up parts of a picture, in a word what the moderns call 'values' (see Comm.) Such observations had doubtless formed part of the history of the development of painting from the early monochromatics to the successors of Apollodoros, and became detached from their original context, perhaps at the time when the Xenokratic Treatise was schematized as noted on p. xxii. Furthermore it is possible that the Treatise had originally included, besides statements of the personal contribution made to the progress of art by the principal artists, and aesthetic analysis of special problems, a discussion of the materials employed. Perhaps therefore we should follow Münzer (*op. cit.* p. 512; p. 499 ff.) in crediting Xenokrates with the chapters on colours (xxxv, 29 ff.)[1] and consequently also with the notice of the various kinds of bronze (xxxiv, 9 ff.) employed by the statuaries.

The short account of modelling[2] in clay in xxxv, 151–153, con-

[1] After considerable hesitation, we decided on omitting these chapters from the present edition, which is concerned only with those portions of the *Historia* that treat of artists and actual works of art.

[2] Münzer, *op. cit.* p. 509 f.; cf. Furtwängler, *Plinius u. s. Quellen,* p. 59 f.

tains the last marked traces of Xenokrates that we come across in Pliny. Boutades, a potter (*figulus*), and of course a Sikyonian, invents the fashioning of portraits in clay (*fingere ex argilla similitudines*). To this statement is now attached from another source an anecdote which represented this Sikyonian workman as active in Corinth (p. xxxvii). In § 152 a variant version of the discovery of modelling is given. Then with the words *Butadis inventum* we get back to our Sikyonian potter, who, having learnt to fashion a face in clay, is now the first (*primus*) to adapt faces to tile ends, whence arose in time the whole decoration of the eaves of temples. Further, he invents (*invenit*) how to take moulds off the clay models for statues (*de signis effigies exprimere*), and is thus the discoverer of the preliminary indispensable process of casting statues in bronze. Hundreds of years later another Sikyonian, Lysistratos, the brother of Xenokrates's special hero Lysippos, first discovers (*primus . . . instituit*) how to take a mould off the living face. Hence the last and crowning progress of art, the advent of realistic portraiture. Münzer is certainly right in his conjecture that the account of modelling was originally prefixed to the history of bronze-statuary, since bronze-casting presupposed the clay model (see Comm. on xxxiv, 35, and xxxv, 153), and therefore modelling passed as the older art : *etenim prior quam statuaria fuit* (xxxiv, 35). The place which Pliny assigns to modelling in his *History* is an obvious necessity of his scheme ; clay being the material of modelling, he is forced to bring the discussion of this art under ' kinds of earth.'

This closes the list of passages that can be traced back with any certainty to Xenokrates. It is a proof of the vigour of his conceptions that they could so impose themselves upon subsequent writers as never entirely to lose their original character, which still asserts itself throughout the whole of the Plinian account of the bronze statuaries and the painters. Nowhere do we grasp so readily what Pliny's history of art owed to Xenokrates as in the account of sculpture, given in Bk. xxxvi, where, failing the strong thread which bound together—at least in considerable parts— the narrative of the preceding books, we get little more than a loose patch-work of facts brought together without guiding thought or dominating interest. Meagre as are the fragments that we have disengaged, they point back to a critic of other calibre than the mere maker of anecdote and epigram—to a critic who, conscientiously endeavouring to judge of works of art on their own merits, fails, not from garrulous digression or the desire to make a witty point, but rather from preconceived theory and love of schematizing. Xenokrates allows nothing for the fantastic freaks of artistic growth; in his rigidly constructed system monochrome is made to precede colour, artists may not attack the problems of drapery till they have solved the rendering of muscle, and the gracious advent of perfect harmony and proportion is presented as the inevitable sum to which each of five artists had contributed his measured share. Besides, in common with most artists who have also been art-critics, he insists upon fixing the measure of artistic achievement in the successful solution of the problems which chiefly interested the school of which he showed himself the jealous partisan. Yet, crude as the scheme must appear to our modern world with its deeper sense of the complexity of things, it should win respect and sympathy as a first genuine attempt to tell the still unfinished tale of the rise and growth of art. And there is even to be traced, at a distance great enough from the modern method of comparison, that same purpose which distinguishes the modern critic—to let the actual monuments tell the tale.

§ 2. *Antigonos of Karystos* (*born about* 295 B. C.).

When a writer aims, like Xenokrates, at formulating his criticism of an artist as the unbiassed impression received from a series of that artist's works, he will be anxious not to impair the strength of this impression by digressive criticism of single works; above all, he will jealously guard the integrity of his judgement against anything that might look like borrowed appreciation. A writer who appraises an artist in the words applied by Xenokrates to Polykleitos will be the last to introduce material so foreign to the final judgement as that which describes how the boy binding a fillet about his head was 'a boy yet a man,' or his companion athlete 'a man yet a boy'—words written, moreover, with a view to rhetorical antithesis rather than to criticism of artistic qualities.

Yet little epigrammatic or anecdotic tags are plentiful even in those parts of the Plinian account which have been shown to be essentially Xenokratic. Such, for instance, are the legends interwoven in xxxv, 9 with the account of the early Sikyonian artists Dipoinos and Skyllis (see Comm.); the rationalizing statements in xxxv, 16 and 151, intended to reconcile the conflicting claims to greater antiquity of the art centres of Sikyon and Corinth; the additions made in xxxv, 59 to the Xenokratic account of Polygnotos and Mikon, to the effect that the former took no payment for his paintings in the *Stoa Poikile,* while the latter did; the anecdotic flavour given to the account of Telephanes of Phokaia (xxxiv, 68), the epigrammatic touch added in xxxv, 61 to express the connexion between Apollodoros and Zeuxis. These additions are generally so closely compacted with the original fabric that it is only recent criticism, the growing recognition of the whole tendency of the Xenokratic methods, which has detected them as extraneous. They differ totally, in this respect, from the loose and not unfrequently awkward additions to the Greek Treatises made at a later date by Varro or Pliny himself in order to introduce the mention of works in Rome or allusions to contemporary events.

It becomes evident that the Xenokratic treatise was minutely worked over by a writer, who used it not simply to quote from, but as a solid framework into which to fit new material of his own. This writer, who appears almost as close collaborator of Xenokrates, must be one of the writers included in xxxiv, 68 in the words *Artifices qui compositis voluminibus condidere haec,* where the *haec* refers (see p. xxii) to the previous account of the *insignes,* which, as we have seen, is Xenokratic in the main. Now in xxxv, 67, in the discussion of Parrhasios, writers upon art are referred to in similar manner: *confessione artificum in liniis extremis palmam adeptus (Parrhasius).* Immediately below, the names of these *artifices* are given; the one is, as we expected, *Xenocrates,* the other is *Antigonus.*

Antigonos is no longer a mere name. The brilliant essay in which Wilamowitz proved his identity with the Antigonos of Karystos [1], author of a book of Marvels or Ἱστοριῶν παραδόξων

[1] v. Wilamowitz-Moellendorff, *Antigonos von Karystos,* in *Philologische Untersuchungen,* iv, Berlin, 1881; see Susemihl, *Geschichte der Griechischen Literatur in der Alexandriner Zeit,* i. p. 519 ff. I consider it superfluous to discuss the question of identity. It was questioned by Diels in his review of Wilamowitz's book, *Deutsche Lit.-Zeitung,* 1882, p. 604 (cf. also Voigt, *De Fontibus Plinianis* p. 24), and disputed by H. L. Urlichs, *Griechische Kunstschriftsteller,* p. 34. Since then it has been accepted without reserve by Susemihl, and quite lately by Münzer, *op. cit.* p. 521 ff.

συναγωγή, and of certain Biographies of the Philosophers, from which Diogenes Laertios drew extensively[1], has made almost familiar the artist who was likewise pupil of the philosopher Menedemos of Eretria, who contributed to the revival of Attic sculpture under Attalos and Eumenes of Pergamon, and was at the same time a versatile *littérateur*, equally at home in the poems of Euripides or Philoxenos and in the technical treatises of the painters. Scarcely a strong individuality, perhaps, but a highly finished type of his age in its wide culture and many-sided curiosities. In addition to the passages already referred to (xxxiv, 68; xxxv, 66–68), Antigonos is quoted by Pliny in the *Indices* of Books xxxiii and xxxiv as a writer *de toreutice*, and in xxxiv, 84 as one of the sculptors in the service of the Court of Pergamon. Diogenes mentions the sculptors Anaxagoras (ii, 45) and Demokritos (ix, 49) on his authority, and recounts (vii, 7, 187) of a namesake of the philosopher Chrysippos, the physician Chrysippos of Knidos, that he had invented concerning Zeus and Hera certain intolerable obscenities not described by the writers upon painting: 'they are found neither in Polemon, nor in Xenokrates, nor yet in Antigonos[2].'

It further appears from the two following passages that, in his Lives of the Philosophers, Antigonos had allusions to the history and literature of art:

Diogenes ix, 11, 62: Antigonos of Karystos says in his account of Pyrrhon that he began life in obscurity and poverty, and was at first a painter, and that a picture by him—of very moderate execution—representing torch-bearers, is in the Gymnasium of Elis[3].

Diogenes iv, 3, 4: On the whole he (Polemon) was the sort of man described by Melanthios in his Book upon Painting, who says that a certain self-reliance and austerity should make itself felt in portraiture, precisely as in character[4].

[1] The fragments of Diogenes referable to Antigonos will be found conveniently put together by Wilamowitz, *op. cit.*

[2] Diog. vii, 7, 187: οὐδὲ παρὰ τοῖς περὶ πινάκων γράψασι κατακεχωρισμένην (sc. *historiam*)· μήτε γὰρ παρὰ Πολέμωνι μήτε παρὰ Ξενοκράτει (Wilam. *op. cit.* p. 8; Köpke, *De Antigono Carystio*, p. 25 note; the MSS. have παρ' Ὑψικράτει), ἀλλὰ μηδὲ παρ' Ἀντιγόνῳ εἶναι.

[3] Ἀντίγονος δέ φησιν ὁ Καρύστιος ἐν τῷ περὶ Πύρρωνος τάδε περὶ αὐτοῦ,

ὅτι τὴν ἀρχὴν ἄδοξός τ' ἦν καὶ πένης καὶ ζωγράφος· σώζεσθαί τ' αὐτοῦ ἐν Ἤλιδι ἐν τῷ γυμνασίῳ λαμπαδιστὰς μετρίως ἔχοντας.

[4] Καὶ ὅλως ἦν τοιοῦτος οἷόν φησι Μελάνθιος ὁ ζωγράφος ἐν τοῖς περὶ ζωγραφικῆς· φησὶ γὰρ δεῖν αὐθάδειάν τινα καὶ σκληρότητα τοῖς ἔργοις ἐπιτρέχειν, ὁμοίως δὲ καὶ (so Wilam. p. 64; the MSS. have δὲ κἂν) τοῖς ἤθεσιν. I am not able to apprehend the precise meaning which the words ὁμοίως . . . ἤθεσιν are intended to convey. The sense of the rest of the

Lastly, the learned traveller and antiquary, Polemon of Ilion (contemporary of Ptolemaios V. Epiphanes, 202–131 B.C.), who wrote against Antigonos a controversial work in at least six books [1], gives, in order to combat it, a verbatim quotation from Antigonos. The Polemonic fragment, which is of incomparable interest as affording an insight into the methods of these ancient controversialists, has found its way into the collection of Proverbs of the sophist Zenobios (age of Hadrian); it runs as follows :—

Zen. v. 82 : At Rhamnous is an image of Nemesis ten cubits high, made wholly of marble, the work of Pheidias, holding an apple branch in her hand. From this branch, *according to Antigonos of Karystos*, hangs a little tablet bearing the inscription ' Agorakritos the Parian made me.' But this is no proof (οὐ θαυμαστὸν δέ), for many also have inscribed another's name upon their own works, a complacency which Pheidias probably showed to Agorakritos, whom he loved . . .[2]

These accredited fragments prove the varied experience of Antigonos in the province of art-history : we find him appealing to the testimony of inscriptions as carefully as his rival Polemon, whose industry in this respect won for him the nickname of ὁ στηλοκόπας [3] ; he is ready to apply a phrase in a Treatise upon Portraiture to his characterization of a philosopher ; he had himself written a statistical book upon pictures, containing minute descriptions of their subjects [4] ; nor had he neglected to note the apocryphal tale which connected a certain mediocre picture at Elis with the name of the philosopher Pyrrhon.

The miscellaneous character of his information, and the passage is finely indicated by Wilamowitz, p. 147 ; cf. also H. L. Urlichs, *Griech. Kunstschrift.* p. 18 ff.

[1] The work bore the title πρὸς 'Αδαῖον καὶ 'Αντίγονον ; of Adaios of Mitylene, who appears to have written upon sculptors, περὶ ἀγαλματοποιῶν (Athenaios, xiii, 606 a), very little is known, cf. Susemihl, *op. cit.* i, p. 518 ; for Polemon, see Susemihl, i, p. 665 ff. ; for the fragments of his treatise against Antigonos, Preller, *Polemonis periegetae fragmenta*, Leipzig, 1838, p. 97 ff. ; Müller, *F. H. G.* iii, p. 132, fr. 56–69 ; for the nature of the controversy, see especially H. L. Urlichs, *op. cit.* p. 33 ff.

[2] 'Ραμνουσία Νέμεσις : ἐν 'Ραμνοῦντι Νεμέσεως ἵδρυται ἄγαλμα δεκάπηχυ, ὁλόλιθον, ἔργον Φειδίου, ἔχει δὲ ἐν τῇ χειρὶ μηλέας κλάδον. ἐξ οὗ φησιν 'Αντίγονος ὁ Καρύστιος πτύχιόν τι μικρὸν ἐξηρτῆσθαι τὴν ἐπιγραφὴν ἔχον "'Αγοράκριτος Πάριος ἐποίησεν." οὐ θαυμαστὸν δέ· καὶ ἄλλοι γὰρ πολλοὶ ἐπὶ τῶν οἰκείων ἔργων ἕτερον ἐπιγεγράφασιν ὄνομα· εἰκὸς οὖν καὶ τὸν Φειδίαν τῷ 'Αγορακρίτῳ συγκεχωρηκέναι, ἦν γὰρ αὐτοῦ ἐρώμενος, καὶ ἄλλως ἐπτόητο περὶ τὰ παιδικά. It was first conjectured by Wilamowitz, *op. cit.* p. 13 f., that the whole passage goes back to Polemon ; the view has been accepted without reserve by H. L. Urlichs *loc. cit.*

[3] Herodikos, *ap.* Athen. vi, 234 d.

[4] Cf. Wilamowitz, *op. cit.* p. 8.

varying trustworthiness of the quarters whence he obtained it, prove at once that Antigonos, unlike Xenokrates, belonged to the class of people who are curious of facts rather than critical of their significance.

Xenokrates had been guided in his selection of material by a strongly marked principle, whence the comparative ease in recovering and closing up the dissevered members of his treatise. The treatise of Antigonos on the other hand, with its looser method of synthesis, is more difficult to retrace. We cannot point to this or that fragment of the Plinian history as bearing his individual stamp. But we can distinguish certain elements in Pliny which go back to those general sources — art-historical, epigrammatic, anecdotic, &c.—whence we know Antigonos to have drawn, and, on examining these, we shall find the majority of cases to afford such strong proof of his handling that, failing contrary evidence, it will not be unfair to assume the remainder also to have come into Pliny through his medium.

From the fact that Antigonos incorporated the Treatise of Xenokrates into his own work, and from his allusion in his life of Polemon (above, p. xxxviii) to a Treatise upon Portraiture by the painter Melanthios, we may infer that it was he who introduced references to a number of artists as having also written upon their art. These are the bronze-worker Menaichmos (xxxiv, Index and § 80)[1], the painter Apelles (xxxv, Ind. and § 79, § 111), Melanthios, Asklepiodoros and Parrhasios (*ib.* Ind.), and Euphranor (*ib.* Ind. and § 128). Apelles as a writer upon art is fortunately more than a mere name. One trace of the work or works in which he expounded—presumably for the use of his pupils (cf. xxxv, § 111)—the theories of his art has survived, as Robert justly points out[2], in § 107 in the words *Asclepiodorus, quem in symmetria mirabatur Apelles*, which at the close of § 80 had been rendered by *Asclepiodoro de mensuris* (*cedebat Ap.*). If the conjecture be correct for Asklepiodoros it follows that Apelles's appreciation of Melanthios in the grouping of figures was also expressed in the same work. There, likewise, it must have been that he discussed the art of Protogenes (§ 80) and criticized his laborious finish. In fact, from the words *quorum opera cum admiraretur omnibus conlaudatis*, it is fair to assume that besides original theories the Apellian treatise contained criticisms—for the

---

[1] He is otherwise unknown either as artist or writer ; see Münzer, *op. cit.* p. 520, note 1 ; cf. Susemihl, i, p. 113, note 2.   [2] *Arch. Märchen*, p. 70.

most part favourable—of contemporary artists [1]. The statement as to his own *venustas*, like the *quod manum de tabula sciret tollere*, is the later concrete expression, practically thrown into proverbial formula, of the aims and theories expounded by Apelles as being those of himself and his school.

Antigonos, too, may be responsible for a few more Plinian passages which are faintly coloured by reminiscences of other technical treatises by artists, though these are not definitely alluded to. I have already indicated in the notes that in the words *solusque hominum artem ipsam fecisse artis opere (Polyclitus) iudicatur* in xxxiv, 55, there appears to lurk an allusion to the book, the Κάνων [2], in which, as we learn more fully from Galenos, Polykleitos had laid down his theories on the proportions of the human body [3]; we have accordingly translated the passage 'he is the only man who is held to have embodied his theory of art in a work of art,' the work being the famous Spear-Bearer, which is here introduced, quite irrespectively of its first mention in § 55, as a separate work under its alternative name of the *Canon* [4].

[1] Schubert, *Fleckeisen's Jahrbb.*, Supplementband ix, p. 716, detects a reference to the work of Apelles in Plut. *Dem.* 22 καὶ φησιν ὁ Ἀπέλλης αὕτως ἐκπλαγῆναι θεασάμενος τὸ ἔργον ὥστε καὶ φωνὴν ἐκλιπεῖν αὐτόν. ὀψὲ δὲ εἰπεῖν, μέγας ὁ πόνος καὶ θαυμαστὸν τὸ ἔργαν, οὐ μὴν ἔχειν χάριτας, δι' ἃς οὐρανοῦ ψαύειν τὰ ὑπ' αὐτοῦ γραφόμενα.

[2] The passage was first so explained by Otto Jahn, *Rhein. Mus.* ix, 1854, p. 315 f. ('Das Kunstwerk war ein Inbegriff der Regeln der Symmetrie, ein Compendium derselben'), who argued that here *ars* = the theories of art, a compendium of the rules of art, by extension of the meaning common in the rhetors and grammarians ; Cic. *Brut.* 12, 46 *Aristoteles ait ... artem et praecepta Siculos Coracem et Tisiam conscripsisse.* 12, 48, *similiter Isocratem ... orationes aliis destitisse scribere, totumque se ad artis componendas transtulisse.* Cf. Quinct. x. 1, 15 (where see Spalding's note); Servius on *Aen.* vii, 787, *legitur in arte.* The Greek τέχνη was commonly used in the same manner, *Life of Ten Orators, Isokrates*, ii, p. 838 (= Bernardakis, v, p. 164), εἰσὶ δ' αἱ καὶ τέχνας αὐτὸν (sc. *Isocr.*) λέγουσι συγγεγραφέναι.* At a later period Jahn abandoned his earlier opinion and saw a latent epigram in the words *solus hominum ... iudicatur (Kunsturtheile*, p. 120); he is followed by Münzer, *op. cit.* 530, note 1.

[3] The few extant fragments of this incomparably interesting work, in which Polykleitos reveals himself as an ancient Leonardo or Albrecht Dürer, have been carefully collected and commented on by H. L. Urlichs, *Griechische Kunstschriftsteller*, p. 1 ff. See also Diels, in *Arch. Anz.*, 1889, p. 10.

[4] It is quite possible that Antigonos, who had added to the Xenokratic mention of Doryphoros and Diadumenos the epigrammatic description which placed the two statues in pointed relation to one another (above, p. xxxvi), now introduced from his acquaintance with the literature of art a second account of the statue in its relation, not to the other works

If the proposed interpretation of the words *artem ipsam fecisse artis opere iudicatur* be correct, it follows that we have traces in xxxv, 74 of another such compendium of art by the painter Timanthes : *pinxit et heroa absolutissimi operis artem ipsam complexus viros pingendi* ; i. e., like the Doryphoros of Polykleitos, the ' hero ' of Timanthes was to serve as a ' Canon,' as the embodiment of theories which had been expounded in an *ars* or τέχνη.

Finally in § 76 it is said of Pamphilos that he was especially learned in arithmetic and geometry, without which sciences, he used to declare, art could make no progress. H. L. Urlichs [1] has pointed out that these words are distinguished from the ordinary floating apothegm by a precise character such as we should expect from an opinion recorded in a written Treatise ; and indeed an opinion emanating doubtless from the whole artistic personality of Pamphilos could nowhere have been preserved intact so well as in a technical treatise, written, like the work of Apelles, for the guidance of his pupils.

The Zenobian gloss showed that Antigonos had maintained the Agorakritan authorship of the Nemesis at Rhamnous on the ground of the inscription,—an argument against which Polemon, supporting the current attribution to Pheidias, retorts that Pheidias had doubtless permitted his own work to be inscribed with the name of the pupil he loved. Now, since Pliny ascribed the Nemesis quite simply to Agorakritos, without any reference to its attribution to Pheidias by other authorities, or to the Polemonic compromise, there can be little doubt that his ultimate source was Antigonos. Pliny gives the statement, however, in close connexion with the story of a competition between Agora-

---

of the master, bnt to his theories. This second mention, made with no precise reference to the first, was afterwards understood by the Roman authors to concern a distinct work. In the commentary I have given Furtwängler's explanation that the *Canon* appears in Pliny as a separate work to the *doryphorus*, owing to the introduction of a fresh authority at the words *facit et quem*. I would differ only in so far that, while F. supposes Pliny to have been the first to combine the two notices, my own opinion is that the combination was already

effected by the Greek authors. It is possible, of course, though scarcely probable, that a Greek writer had already heen guilty of assnming the *canon* and *doryphorus* to be separate works.

[1] *Op. cit.* p. 14 ff., where it is shown that the Pamphilos who wrote a work περὶ γραφικῆς καὶ ζωγράφων ἐνδόξων is a distinct person to the painter, and is presumably identical with the Alexandrian grammarian, first centnry B. C. ; see Urlichs, *Rhein. Mus.* xvi, 1861, pp. 247–258, and Susemihl, i, p. 903 f.

kritos and Alkamenes, and this again follows in natural sequence upon the mention of these artists in their common relation, as pupils, to Pheidias. The various episodes are so indissolubly linked[1] that the passage as a whole must be referred to Antigonos. Indeed, that he is Pliny's ultimate authority for the information concerning Agorakritos is confirmed by the closing attribution (§ 18, *s. f.*) to Agorakritos of the 'Mother of the Gods' at Athens : another vindication for that artist—doubtless, this time also, on the evidence of the inscription—of a work popularly ascribed to Pheidias (*Schriftqu.* 831–833), of which popular ascription Polemon, whose version is represented in Pausanias, would not be slow to avail himself. It is noteworthy that by retailing, though quite generally and in no relation to any one work, the scandal about Pheidias and Agorakritos (*eiusdem*—sc. *Phidiae—discipulus fuit Ag. Parius et aetate gratus, itaque e suis operibus pleraque nomini eius donasse fertur*) Antigonos may have supplied to Polemon, as Münzer acutely suggests (*op. cit.* p. 522), the weapon wherewith to combat the Agorakritan authorship of the Nemesis[2].

We have seen how the Xenokratic accounts of the beginning of painting in encaustic (xxxv, 121 ; see above, p. xxxii) and of the beginning of statuary (xxxvi, 9 ; above, p. xxv f.) were combined by a later writer, surmised to be Antigonos, with variant traditions that proclaimed the priority of invention of the island-schools over the schools of the mainland. The theory that these combinations or contrasts of traditions were effected at an early date by Antigonos is now confirmed by the fact that in both cases appeal is made to the testimony of inscriptions in xxxv, 121 ; the ἐνέκαεν in an artist's signature is quoted in proof of the antiquity of encaustic, while in xxxvi, 11–13, the genealogy of the Chian sculptors 'Melas,' Mikkiades, and Archermos, and the

[1] See on this point Furtwängler, *Plinius u. s. Quellen*, p. 72, who however does not trace the passage further back than Varro. That Varro was the intermediary source is obvious from the words *quod M. Varro omnibus signis praetulit* ; to the account of the Nemesis which he found in his handbook he appended, according to the wont of travellers, remarks of his own.

[2] The impression has grown upon me, since I wrote the above, that Antigonos drew from Duris the main part, if not the whole, of his account of Alkamenes and Agorakritos: the stress laid upon relations of pupilship, the supposed competition (p. lxiv), the hint thrown out of a scandalous story (see below, p. lx)—above all, the imaginative element in the tale of how the discomfited Agorakritos turned his Aphrodite into a Nemesis— are so many Duridian traits. Addenda.

mention of works by Boupalos and Athenis, sons of Archermos [1], at Delos, and of works by Archermos at both Delos and Lesbos, are all based upon inscriptional evidence [2] (Münzer, *op. cit.* p. 524 f.). Further, as Münzer indicates (*loc. cit.*), Antigonos went so far in the latter instance as to quarrel with his sources; he corrected the legend according to which Hipponax had driven Boupalos and Athenis to hang themselves in despair [3] by adducing proofs

[1] The genealogy of Boupalos and Athenis is mentioned only once again in literature—in the Scholia to Ar. *Birds,* 574 : Ἀρχερμον (MSS. Ἀρχενvον) γάρ φασι, τὸν Βουπάλου καὶ Ἀθήνιδος πατέρα, οἱ δὲ Ἀγλαοφῶντα τὸν Θάσιον ζωγράφον, πτηνὴν ἐργάσασθαι τὴν Νίκην, ὡς οἱ περὶ Καρύστιον τὸν Περγαμηνόν φασι. There is much to commend Münzer's suggestion (*loc. cit.*) that Karystios of Pergamon (end of second century, Müller, *Fragm. Hist. Graec.* iv, p. 356) appears here by confusion for our Karystian Antigonos, sometime resident in Pergamon. (The words οἱ δὲ ... ζωγράφον are in any case introduced from a source other than that cited for B. and A.) We should thus obtain important confirmation of Antigonos's authorship of the Plinian passage.

[2] The Zenobian gloss alone shows that Susemihl (i, p. 672) does Antigonos an injustice when he credits Polemon with the 'epoch-making' idea of basing researches in the province of art-history and periegesis upon a study of inscriptions. In this connexion we may recall as illustrative of the method employed by Antigonos, without on that account proposing to refer them definitely to him, the notices, derived from the inscriptions on their bases, of the group of Alkibiades and 'Demarate' of Nikeratos (xxxiv, 89), and of the trainer of athletes by Apollodoros (*ib.* 89); for the portrait statue of Lysimache by Demetrius (*ib.* 76), see below, p. lxxvi.

[3] Repeated study of the passage xxxvi, 11–13, convinces me that Anti-

gonos borrowed from Duris of Samos the genealogy of the Chian sculptors and the whole story of Hipponax; especially Duridian is the adjustment to a new set of personages of the story of Archilochos and Lycambes (see Comm.). I am glad to receive on this point confirmation from Münzer, who (in a private letter) explains Antigonos as having corrected Duris somewhat as follows : 'It is true that the Chians were already practising the art of sculpture (i. e. at the time when, according to the Xenokratic theory, the Daidalids were inventing statuary), but it is not true that the verses of Hipponax (as probably maintained by Duris) drove Boupalos and Athenis to death, for works by these artists exist which were created after the portrait of the poet, as, for example, the Delian statue bearing the inscription *non vitibus tantum,* &c.' Moreover, in another note, the gist of which he also allows me to publish, Münzer observes that Antigonos seems likewise to have borrowed from Duris that notice of the existence of paintings in encaustic older than Aristeides which he confronted with the Xenocratic account: 'The appeal to the signature of the otherwise totally unknown Elasippos would be characteristic of Duris (cf. below, p. liii). Equally unknown are Nikanor and Mnasilaos, and it is not clear whether the ethnic *Pariorum* applies also to Polygnotos, and whether this Polygnotos should accordingly be distinguished from the celebrated Thasian artist.' In the

to the contrary, again borrowed from inscriptions : *quod falsum est, complura enim in finitimis insulis simulacra postea fecere sicut in Delo quibus subiecerunt carmen non vitibus tantum censeri Chion sed et operibus Archermi filiorum.*

It is reasonable to suppose that Antigonos, who diligently studied the inscriptions carved on the actual monuments, did not neglect so fruitful a source as the literary epigram. He is almost certainly to be credited, as we have seen (p. xxxvi), with the epigrammatic qualification attached to the Xenokratic mention of the Diadumenos and the Doryphoros of Polykleitos, while the ascertained fragments of his writings display a wide-ranging familiarity, not only with the greater poets, but also with the poetasters and epigrammatists of his day [1]. Since, however, the actual extent of his responsibility for the epigrammatic element in Pliny cannot be precisely determined, it will be best to reserve for separate consideration (p. lxviii) material which plays a considerable part in the Plinian descriptions of works of art.

The Lives of the Philosophers reveal Antigonos as a lover of personal anecdote and characteristic *bons mots* [2]. Hence we are naturally disposed to credit him with the anecdotic material which forms so large a bulk of the Plinian narrative, and, as a fact, there are frequent proofs of its passage through his hands. The preservation, however, in the case of one highly distinctive anecdote, of the name of Duris of Samos (xxxiv, 61) enables us to penetrate further—to the very source whence Antigonos drew the larger part of his anecdotes [3].

text I have adopted the reading *Mnasilai* as beyond dispute, but Münzer provides me with a satisfactory proof that the *Arcesilai* of the inferior codices is impossible ; were this reading correct, we should expect to find that Antigonos in his biography of the Akademic Arkesilaos had mentioned this namesake of the philosopher (Antig. Kar. *ap.* Diog. Laert. iv, 45; cf. Wilamowitz, p. 70 ff.) ; but he only notes the sculptor Arkesilaos of Paros on the evidence of an epigram of Semonides.

[1] Münzer, *op. cit.* p. 529. Münzer, I may note here, lays considerable stress on the learning of Antigonos, in searching for traces of his art-treatise in Pliny; he accordingly inclines to trace back to him certain passages which evince literary interest: e. g. the allusions to the 'Banquet' of Xenophon (xxxiv, 79) and to his Treatise on Horsemanship (*ib.* 76).

[2] See on this point Wilamowitz, *Antigonos*, p. 33.

[3] That Antigonos drew from Duris for his Treatise upon art, and was thus the 'first intermediary' through which Duridian material found its way into Pliny, was first suggested by Susemihl, i, note 325, p. 588.

3. Duris of Samos (born about 340 B. C.); the anecdotic element in Pliny.

Duris, historian and tyrant of Samos, is one of the most striking figures among those older Greek writers whom German scholarship—the researches of Roesiger [1] and Schubert [2], the brilliant sketch by Wachsmuth [3], call for grateful mention—has succeeded in calling back to a new life. The facts we know about his career are few, but the scanty fragments [4] of his writings suffice to prove the strength of his literary personality. Together with his brother Lynkeus he had been a pupil of Theophrastos [5], and, like the later Peripatetics, he became a curious inquirer into personal anecdote, which he freely used for purposes of history. His imagination was stimulated by his studies of the tragedians [6] till he developed into an accomplished master of dramatic anecdote, where heroes and heroines, dressed in appropriate costume, play on a stage whose properties seem inexhaustible. It is to Duris that Plutarch owes some of his most picturesque descriptions—such as the gorgeous pageantry of the return of Alkibiades, and the picture of the admiral's galley entering the harbour with purple sails ' as if some maske had come into a man's house after some great banquet made [7].' Yet Plutarch more than once casts severe doubts on the historical trustworthiness of Duris [8], and the censure has been confirmed by Grote [9].

From Diogenes, who mentions a painter Thales on the authority of Duris (Diog. i, 1, 39 = Duris fragm. 78), we learn that he wrote Lives of the Painters (περὶ ζωγράφων), and, as we shall

---

[1] A. F. Roesiger: (1) *De Duride Samio Diodori Siculi et Plutarchi auctore Diss.*, Göttingen, 1874; (2) *Die Bedeutung der Tyche bei den späteren Griechischen Historikern*, Konstanz, 1880. For Duris, see especially p. 20 f.

[2] Rudolf Schubert: (1) *Die Quellen Plutarchs in d. Lebensbeschreibungen des Eumenes, Demetrios und Pyrrhos*, in Supplementband ix of the *Jahrbücher für Philologie*, pp. 648–833; (2) *Geschichte des Agathokles*, Breslau, 1887, p. 13 ff.; and (3) *Geschichte des Pyrrhus*, Königsberg, 1894, pp. 11–24, give a full and vivid account of Duris.

[3] Curt Wachsmuth, *Einleitung in das Studium der alten Geschichte*, Leipzig, 1895, pp. 543–546; see also Susemihl, i, p. 585 ff.

[4] To the collected fragments in Müller, *F. H. G.* ii, pp. 466–468, must be added the new fragments noted by Schubert, *Pyrrhus*, p. 12.

[5] Athen. iv, 128 a.

[6] Fr. 69, Fr. 70, and the remarks of Schubert, *Pyrrhus*, p. 15.

[7] *Alcib.* xxxii, tr. North, ed. Wyndham, ii, p. 133.

[8] Plnt. *loc. cit.*; *Perikl.* 28, &c.

[9] In reference to the story of Alkibiades' return, *Hist.* vi, p. 368.

presently see (cf. p. xlix), that he also wrote Lives of the Sculptors. Pliny mentions him in the Index to Book XXXIV as having written *de toreutice*. In the same book (§ 61) he appears as the authority for the statement that Lysippos of Sikyon had no master, but that he was originally a coppersmith and ventured upon a higher profession at a word of the painter Eupompos, who in presence of the young craftsman had enounced the dictum that 'nature and not any artist should be imitated.' The story will repay careful analysis. The meeting between the young Lysippos and Eupompos, though not chronologically impossible, belongs to a class of anecdote devised in order to bring the celebrity of one generation into pointed contact with the rising genius of the next. The story of Lysippos and Eupompos reminds one of nothing so much as of those legends invented by the Italian art-historians, on a hint afforded by two famous lines in Dante [1], in order to bring the young Giotto into connexion with Cimabue—legends which represent Giotto neglecting his clothmaker's trade to watch Cimabue at his work, or Cimabue opportunely passing along the road 'da Fiorenza a Vespignano [2]' precisely at the moment that the boy Giotto, while tending his flock, had drawn a sheep with such surprising fidelity that the delighted Cimabue begged Giotto's father to let him have the boy as pupil. But antiquity was rich in similar examples; the young Thukydides was said to have burst into tears of emotion on hearing Herodotos recite his History at Olympia, so that the elder historian was moved to congratulate the father of so gifted a son [3]. The undoubted pupilship of Xenophon to Sokrates was invested, by the later biographers of the philosophers, with the additional interest of that first meeting ' in a narrow lane' where Sokrates, barring the way with his stick, had refused to let the young man pass till he should have answered the question ' where men were made good and virtuous [4].' So, too, an exquisite legend had been spun to connect

[1] *Purgat.* xi, 94–96 :
'Credette Cimabue nella pittura
Tener lo campo, ed ora ha Giotto
il grido
Si che la fama di colui oscura.'
The entirely apocryphal character of the Cimabue-Giotto legend has been thoroughly exhibited by Franz Wickhoff, *Ueber die Zeit des Guido von Siena* (Mitth. des Inst. f. Oesterr. Geschichtsforschung, Bd. x, pp. 244 ff.).

[2] Vasari ed. Milanesi, p. 370.

[3] Souidas, s. v. *Thuc.*

[4] Diog. Laert. ii, 6, 2 ; the analogy to the Lysippos-Eupompos story is pointed out by H. L. Urlichs, *Griechische Kunstschriftsteller*, p. 27. For further instances of such relationships cf. Diels, *Rhein. Mus.* xxxi, p. 13 ff.

the greatest of the Sokratic disciples with the master already from the hour of birth : not only was Plato born the day after one of Sokrates' birthdays, but on the eve Sokrates had dreamed of a swan flying from the altar of Eros in the Academy, to take refuge in his bosom, and lo ! as the philosopher was recounting the vision Ariston brought in the new-born babe, in whom Sokrates at once divined the swan of his dream [1]. In the case of Eupompos and Lysippos there was no pupilship to emphasize, nor could pupilship be invented, since they practised different arts ; yet there remained the temptation to link the most brilliant of the Sikyonian statuaries, the chosen portraitist of Alexander, to the celebrity of the passing generation, that greatest of Sikyonian painters, whose fame had occasioned, in order to comprise him, a redivision of the schools (xxxv, 75).

The statement that Lysippos had no master arose in great measure, I take it, out of the good advice put into the mouth of Eupompos ' to imitate nature and not any artist '—advice which amounted to an aphorism expressing the naturalistic tendencies of the Lysippian school. But from saying that Lysippos followed nature and no special master it was but a step to concluding that he never had a master at all. Then, once the master's name suppressed or forgotten, legend and the art-historians might fill up the gap as they pleased, and the theory of self-taught genius was the readiest to hand. But here was an opportunity for further elaboration : the self-taught boy, the poor coppersmith, is destined to become the leading artist of Sikyon, at that time the acknowledged head of the Greek schools. Not only so, but he achieves great wealth, as we learn from another Duridian fragment preserved in Pliny (xxxiv, 37), but now separated from its original context [2]. So that the information as to the early career of Lysippos, which has been accepted with the utmost gravity by archaeologists and historians of art, is found to resolve itself into three apocryphal stories : (1) the *autodidaktia* assumed to account for the artist's master being unknown ; (2) the meeting with Eupompos, intended to bring into presence Sikyon's greatest painter and her greatest sculptor ; (3) the rise from obscurity to fame and riches. Armed with these observations, we shall have

---

[1] Apuleius, *de Platone* I.
[2] The authorship of Duris for this passage had been pointed out by Brieger, *De Fontibus*, p. 61 ; I cannot understand on what grounds it is doubted by Susemihl, i, p. 587, note 325. (See also Münzer, *op. cit.* p. 542.)

no difficulty in detecting the Duridian authorship of a number of other anecdotes preserved in Pliny. We can at once follow Münzer[1] in attributing to him the story which tells how Protogenes, whose master, like that of Lysippos, was unknown (*quis eum docuerit non putant constare*, § 101), began his career in abject poverty (*summa paupertas*) as a ship-painter, yet lived to decorate the most celebrated spot in the world, even the Gateway of the Athenian Akropolis; the story of Erigonos (xxxv, 145), the slave who rubbed in the colours for the painter Nealkes, who yet lived to be a great master himself, and to leave in Pasias a pupil of distinction; further, the kindred story of how the sculptor Seilanion (xxxiv, 51)[2] became famous *nullo doctore*, and yet, like Erigonos, formed a pupil of his own, Zeuxiades. The kinship of the whole group is self-evident, and even if the name of Duris in xxxiv, 61 were not there to reveal the author we should be led to fix upon him, because of the precise parallelism of these stories to that recounted by Plutarch, on the authority of Duris, of how, through the unexpected favour of Philip, Eumenes of Kardia rose from being the son of a poor carrier, who earned a scanty living in the Chersonese, to wealth and position[3]. Such anecdotes seem in measure prompted by the desire to illustrate the changes of Fortune, of that Τύχη whose caprices were so favourite a theme of the Peripatetics[4].

Duris was the author of yet one more anecdote of an artist's rise from obscurity to fame, which has been preserved in two scattered fragments in Pliny and in Diogenes. In Plin. xxxvi, 22 we read: *non postferuntur et Charites in propylo Atheniensium*

<hr>

[1] *Op. cit.* p. 534.
[2] The Duridian authorship is detected by H. L. Urlichs, *op. cit.* p. 28. The notice of Seilanion appears in the chronological table, awkwardly tacked on to the artists of the 113th Olympiad, where it is evidently out of place; Add. to Comm. on xxxiv, 51, 1.
[3] Plut. *Eum.* 1 Εὐμένη δὲ τὸν Καρδιανὸν ἱστορεῖ Δοῦρις πατρὸς μὲν ἀμαξεύοντος ἐν Χερρονήσῳ διὰ πενίαν γενέσθαι, τραφῆναι δὲ ἐλευθερίως ἐν γράμμασι καὶ περὶ παλαίστραν· ἔτι δὲ παιδὸς ὄντος αὐτοῦ Φίλιππον παρεπιδημοῦντα καὶ σχολὴν ἄγοντα τὰ τῶν Καρδιανῶν θεάσασθαι παγκράτια μειρα-

κίων καὶ παλαίσματα παίδων, ἐν οἷς εὐημερήσαντα τὸν Εὐμένη καὶ φανέντα συνετὸν καὶ ἀνδρεῖον ἀρέσαι τῷ Φιλίππῳ καὶ ἀναληφθῆναι. The analogy is pointed out by Münzer, *op. cit.* p. 534, who also refers to Duris all the stories discussed above of artists rising to fame from humble beginnings. The Duridian authorship had become evident to me since analysing the anecdotic material in Pliny in the light of the hints thrown out by H. L. Urlichs, *op. cit.* p. 21 ff. Addenda.
[4] See especially Roesiger, *Bedeutung der Tyche*, passim. Susemihl, i, p. 592.

quas Socrates fecit, alius ille quam pictor, idem ut aliqui putant. In his Life of Sokrates, Diogenes (ii, 5, 4) has the story on the authority of Duris that a Sokrates had begun life in slavery, and as a stone mason[1]. Now, although Diogenes applies this story to the philosopher, there is nothing in the fragment as it stands to show that Duris had this Sokrates in his mind. Indeed, since nothing is known of the slavery of the philosopher[2], there is every reason to suppose that Duris was speaking of the sculptor, and was recounting of him the same tale of modest beginnings as in the cases of Lysippos, of Protogenes, and of Erigonos. Like Erigonos he had been a slave, and in this capacity had practised an inferior branch of the art in which he was afterwards to excel. Like Protogenes, moreover, this man rose from the humblest circumstances to see his works—the famous Charites—*in propylo Atheniensium!* Further, the peculiar use in both passages of *propylon* for the gateway of the Akropolis, instead of the invariable *propylaion* or *propylaia*, affords satisfactory corroborative evidence of their common origin[3]. We get an interesting trace of the story's passage through the hands of Antigonos in the words *alius ille quam pictor, idem ut aliqui putant.* The identity of

---

[1] Diog. Laert. ii, 5, 4 Δοῦρις καὶ δουλεῦσαι αὐτὸν (Σωκράτη) καὶ ἐργάσασθαι λίθους. The statement which immediately follows, concerning the Charites on the Akropolis, which some said (ἔνιοί φασιν) to be by Sokrates, does not concern us; H. L. Urlichs (*Griechische Kunstschriftst.* p. 43) is certainly right in referring it to another source than Duris.

[2] Duris was quite capable of inventing the story had it suited him; but in the first place there is nothing to show that he wrote concerning the philosophic Sokrates or any philosophers; in the second, it is odd that so striking a circumstance as that of the philosopher's slavery, once invented, should not have found its way to any authors besides Diogenes.—As to the legend that the philosopher had been the sculptor of the Charites (Paus. i, 22, 8; ix, 35, 3; Schol. Aristoph. νεφελαί, 773; Souidas, s. v. *Sokrates*: Pliny, it should be noted, knows

nothing about it), it was inevitable that it should arise in face of the said Charites by a namesake, combined with the fact that the father of Sokrates, Sophroniskos, was a sculptor. That the *contaminatio* of philosopher and sculptor occurred at an early period is proved by some Attic coins of Hellenic date bearing the name of an official Sokrates who, in evident allusion to his famous namesake, had the group of the Charites from the Akropolis stamped on the Reverse. (See Furtwängler, *ap.* Roscher, i, p. 881.) The celebrity of the relief, owing to the supposed authorship of Sokrates, accounts for its numerous copies. See note on xxxvi, 32, and Furtwängler, *Statuenkopien im Alterthum*, p. 532 f. (where the writer modifies his earlier view as to the date of the extant Charites reliefs).

[3] Wachsmuth, *Stadt Athen*, i, p. 36, note 2; cf. also B. Keil in *Hermes*, xxx, 1895, p. 227.

Sokrates the sculptor with the painter of the same name was maintained against a previous writer who had disputed it. The nature of the controversy recalls at once Antigonos and his hostile critic Polemon[1]. (See Addenda.)

We have seen that one factor in these stories is the desire to account for the absence of any record concerning the masters of certain celebrated artists. We may therefore suspect that a second little group of Plinian anecdotes of sculptors who were *initio pictores* and who exchanged painting for sculpture may be traced back to the same workings[2]. The case of Pheidias (xxxv, 52) is specially deserving of analysis. The ambiguous character of the information concerning the painted shield, upon which his reputation as a painter rests, has been detected by H. L. Urlichs (see Commentary). We may now carry the argument further and recognize in the statement that Pheidias was *initio pictor* an attempt to solve a problem which greatly exercised the ancient art-historian, namely the problem who was the real master of Pheidias.

Three answers to this question may be distinguished in ancient criticism. According to one tradition, Pheidias had, like Myron and Polykleitos, been the pupil of Hagelaidas of Argos[3], a view which has long been shown—by Klein[4], Robert, and others—to be improbable, if not as impossible as it apparently is in the case of Polykleitos[5]. The tradition has all the apocryphal air of those stories, common to all times and countries, which group great names together without regard to temporal probabilities[6]. In certain circles, however, the real fact, as recent morphological study reveals it[7], that Pheidias was the pupil of Hegias, had

[1] So H. L. Urlichs, *Gr. Kunstschriftsteller*, p. 43.

[2] Cf. Münzer, *op. cit.* p. 533.

[3] Schol. to Aristoph., *Frogs*, 504, whence the information was copied by Tzetzes and Souidas.

[4] Klein, *Arch.-Ep. Mitth. aus Oesterreich*, vii, p. 64; cf. Robert, *Arch. Märchen*, p. 93 f.; Furtwängler, *Masterpieces*, p. 53.

[5] Robert, *l. c.*

[6] Lately Ernest Gardner, *Handbook of Greek Sculpt.* i, p. 193, has attempted, by straining the dates to the utmost, to defend the tradition for all three sculptors. Failing, however, sufficient evidence for its truth, a

sound criticism requires us rather to lay it aside, if not absolutely to reject it. The chronological difficulties have been hinted at above. Moreover, by exhibiting Hagelaidas as the master of the three most representative artists of the fifth century, the tradition betrays that tendency which is, to quote a modern writer, ' so easily explained pyschologically, but so fatal to criticism, of making one great name stand for a whole epoch or style.' (Bernhard Berenson, *Lorenzo Lotto, an Essay in Constructive Criticism*, p. 26.) Add.

[7] Furtwängler, *loc. cit.* The Hegias tradition is preserved by Dio Chrysostom, *Or.* lv, περὶ Ὁμ. καὶ Σωκρ. 1.

either remained unforgotten or, as is more probable, had been recovered from the monuments.   Neither tradition, however, can have been widely current, for had it been generally reported that Pheidias was the pupil of either artist some mention of the fact, or at least some argument disputing it, would surely have filtered into Pliny, who mentions Hegias twice (xxxiv, 49, 78) and Hagelaidas three times (*ib.* 49, 55, 57), noting, moreover, that the latter artist was the master of Myron and of Polykleitos.   The Plinian authors were on a totally different track, and their solution of the problem reveals the existence of a third class of critics, who, ignorant of the Hagelaidas and Hegias theories, filled up the gap in tradition by declaring that the early training of Pheidias was that of a painter.   To this theory some writer of the stamp of Duris would give more point by the opportune discovery of a shield reputed to be painted by Pheidias, though, strange to say, unable to fix the whereabouts of so weighty a piece of evidence more precisely than by saying it *had* been at Athens.

But if Duris of Samos is to be held responsible for the story that Pheidias had begun life as a painter it follows that we must likewise trace back to him the similar story concerning Pythagoras of Samos, and hence the whole ridiculous splitting into two of an artist who happened to sign sometimes Σάμιος from the home of his birth, sometimes Ῥηγῖνος from that of his adoption (see Comm.). Πυθάγορας Σάμιος would have a triple interest for Duris: as a native of Samos ; as a namesake of the philosopher Pythagoras, also a Samian celebrity, whom Duris had mentioned in his second Book of the History of Samos (fr. 56) ; and as a famous portraitist of athletes, for Duris, who had himself as a boy won a victory at Olympia (Paus. vi, 13, 5 [1]), appears in later life to have written a book on athletic games, περὶ ἀγώνων [2], the material for which he would doubtless derive in great measure from the inscriptions on the bases of the athlete statues.   It was perhaps thus that, coming upon the alternative ethnic of Pythagoras, he jumped at the conclusion that there were two artists of the name.   Then, having discovered a Πυθάγορας Σάμιος, it became necessary to find out his master.   Klearchos—himself a Rhegine—must be left for Pythagoras of Rhegion (Paus. vi, 4, 3), and so Duris, instead of involving

[1] See the reading proposed by Susemihl, i, p. 586, note 323. Schubart's emendation of the corrupt passage seems entirely erroneous.
[2] Susemihl, i, p. 587 f.

himself in false school genealogies, simply filled up the gap by declaring the Samian Pythagoras to have, like Pheidias, begun life as a painter. Finally, since a sentimental harping upon family relationships has been acutely detected by Münzer (*op. cit.* p. 533) as a characteristic of Duridian anecdotes, we may trace back to Duris the mention of Sostratos, the pupil and nephew— *filius sororis*—of Pythagoras of Rhegion. I have noted in the Commentary that there is nothing to lead us to identify this Sostratos with any of the other sculptors of the name, and Duris was nothing loth to provide his heroes with pupils, with children or other near relations, of whom history has otherwise no record. So the Arimnestos (Duris, fr. 56), son of the philosopher Pythagoras, and himself master of the philosopher Demokritos, appears a pure creation of Duris, as, for the rest, do the pupils of Seilanion and of Erigonos.

The whole group of stories we have been considering were precisely of the kind to attract Antigonos of Karystos, who in his Life of Pyrrhon (above, p. xxxviii) had especially noted the poverty and obscurity of the philosopher's early days, adding that he had begun as a painter [1]. In the case of Pythagoras there is a further interesting little proof that the story was handled by Antigonos. The words in § 61, *hic (Pyth. Samius) supra dicto (Pyth. Rhegino) facie quoque indiscreta similis fuisse traditur*, contain a sharp criticism, which has amusingly escaped Pliny and before him Varro, upon the statement that the Rhegine and Samian Pythagoras were different persons. The fact of the criticism turning upon a question of identity of artists, no less than the manner in which the criticism is passed, at once betray Polemon of Ilion, the indefatigable assailant of Antigonos, whose error, as regards Pythagoras, Polemon now corrects. 'Your second Pythagoras, my friend Antigonos,' wrote the amused Polemon, 'looks to me suspiciously like your first [2].' 'Polemon's whole book was merely the comprehensive criticism, the improvement and enlargement of that of Antigonos' (Münzer, *op. cit.* p. 526), and it was characteristic of its controversial parts, as H. L. Urlichs was

---

[1] The analogy between the anecdotes is pointed out by Münzer, *op. cit.* p. 533.

[2] Polemon's authorship of the criticism was rightly detected by H. L. Urlichs, *Griechische Kunstschrift-* *steller*, p. 39 ff., but I owe it to Prof. W. Klein to have explained to me, as I believe correctly, the whole satirical force of the words *hic supra dicto*, &c. . . .

the first correctly to apprehend, that, while Antigonos had inclined to multiply names and attributions, Polemon on the contrary wished to reduce them [1]. He was wrong in the case of the Agorakritan Nemesis ; in that of Pythagoras of Samos and Rhegion he was—as it happens—quite right.

Having thus detected in Pliny a number of anecdotes betraying the Peripatetic, and more especially Duridian, delight in dwelling upon unexpected turns of fortune or upon paradoxical changes of profession, we now turn to another class of story, intended primarily to give point to striking traits of character. In xxxiv, 71 it is recounted of the painter Parrhasios that he made an insolent use of his success, taking to himself the surname of the 'Lover of Luxury' (ἁβροδίαιτος), boasting moreover of his descent from Apollo, and that he had painted Herakles even as the hero had appeared to him in a dream. Finally the artist's intolerable pride finds its highest expression in the insult flung at his rival Timanthes. The story recurs in an amplified form, though with the Apolline descent omitted, in Athenaios, who has the first part of it on the authority of the Peripatetic Klearchos of Soloi.

Athen. xii, p. 543 c [2] : 'Among the ancients ostentation and extravagance were so great that the painter Parrhasios was clothed in purple and wore a golden wreath upon his head, as Klearchos says in his Lives. Parrhasios,

[1] Zenobios, v, 82 (above, p. xxxix); with Athenagoras, Πρεσβεία, 17 (= our App. XI), cf. Paus. ii. 27, 2 ; see also Paus. i, 24, 8 and the remarks of Furtwängler, *Masterpieces*, p. 412, on the artist of the *Apollo Parnopios*. With the statement preserved in Pliny xxxv, 54, to the effect that the gold-ivory Athena at Elis was the work of Kolotes, it is interesting to compare Paus. vi, 26, 3, where the words εἶναι μὲν δὴ Φειδίου φασὶν αὐτήν (i. e. the Eleian Athena) seem to imply, as Münzer kindly points out to me in an unpublished note, that the authorship of the statue was a controverted point—in other words, the phrase of Pausanias is the echo of a Polemonic criticism such as that surviving in the Zenobian gloss, and that which doubtless attached to the question of the authorship of

the 'Mother of the Gods.'

[2] The alternative account in Athenaios (xv, 687 b) should be compared (lack of space compels omission of the Greek):—

'Though Parrhasios the painter was vain beyond the measure of his art, and had, as the saying goes, drunk deep of the cup of liberty that his pencil gave, yet he had pretensions to virtue, writing on all his paintings at Lindos,

"One who lived in luxury... (ἁβροδίαιτος)."

But a wit, who was, I imagine, angry with him for defiling the delicacy and beauty of virtue by diverting to vulgar luxury the fortune given to him by chance, wrote at the side,

"One worthy of the stick... (ῥαβδο-δίαιτος)."

In spite of all, however, he must be

while arrogant beyond what his art warranted, yet laid claim to virtue, and would write on his paintings

One who lived in luxury (ἀβροδίαιτος) and honoured virtue painted this.

'And some person who was stung by the words wrote at the side :—

One worthy of the stick (ῥαβδοδίαιτος), &c.

'He further wrote these lines on many of his works :—

A man who lived in luxury and honoured virtue painted this, Parrhasios born in famous Ephesos. Nor have I forgotten my father Evenor, who begat me as his lawful son, first in my art among all Greeks [1].

'And he spoke a vaunt with no offence in the lines :—

Though they that hear believe not, I say this. For I aver that now have the clear limits of this art been discovered by my hand, and a bound is set that none may overpass. Yet is nothing faultless among mortals [2].

'Once at Samos, when competing with his Aias against an inferior picture, he was defeated ; and when his friends condoled with him he said that, for himself, he cared little, but he was grieved for Aias, who was worsted a second time.

'As signs of his luxurious living he wore a purple cloak and had a white fillet upon his head, and leaned upon a staff with golden coils about it, and fastened the strings of his shoes with golden latchets.

'Nor was the practice of his art toilsome to him, but light, so that he would sing at his work, as Theophrastos in his treatise on Happiness tells us. And he uttered marvels when he was painting the Herakles at Lindos, saying that the god appeared to him in a dream and posed himself (rd. αὐτόν) as was fitting for the picture. Hence he wrote upon the painting :—

As many a time in nightly visits he appeared unto Parrhasios, such is he here to look upon [3].'

Jahn has pointed out, in his discussion of the passage [4], that Klearchos had only the story of the artist's effeminacy. That Athenaios derived the rest of his information concerning Parrhasios from another source is manifest from the clumsy repetition of the

pardoned, because he said that he loved virtue. This is the story of Klearchos.

[1] ἀβροδίαιτος ἀνὴρ ἀρετήν τε σέβων
τόδ᾽ ἔγραψα
Παρράσιος, κλεινῆς πατρίδος ἐξ
᾽Εφέσαν.
οὐδὲ πατρὸς λαθόμην Εὐήνορος, ὅς
ῥά μ᾽ ἔφυσε
γνήσιον, Ἑλλήνων πρῶτα φέραν-
τα τέχνης.

[2] εἰ καὶ ἄπιστα κλύουσι, λέγω τάδε·
φημὶ γὰρ ἤδη

τέχνης εὐρῆσθαι τέρματα τῆσδε
σαφῆ
χειρὸς ὑφ᾽ ἡμετέρης· ἀνυπέρβλητος
δὲ πέπηγεν
οὖρος· ἀμώμητον δ᾽ οὐδὲν ἔγεντα
βροταῖς.

[3] Οἷος δ᾽ ἐννύχιος φαντάζετα παλλάκι
φαιτῶν
Παρρασίῳ δι᾽ ὕπνου, τοῖος ἅδ᾽
ἐστὶν ὁρᾶν.

[4] *Kleine Beiträge z. Geschichte d. alten Literatur* (in *Sächsische Berichte* for 1857), p. 285, note 1.

epigram ἀβροδίαιτος ἀνήρ, as also from the variant details respecting the artist's headgear—a gold crown in the first passage, a white fillet in the second. If we analyze the stories in Pliny and in Athenaios we obtain the following elements:

(1) The story of the artist's effeminacy and luxury, given in Athenaios, first on the authority of Klearchos, and repeated from an unnamed author; in Pliny it occurs combined with that of the artist's arrogance: *fecundus artifex, sed quo nemo insolentius usus sit gloria artis habrodiaetum se appellando.*

(2) The boast recorded both in Athenaios and Pliny that Herakles often appeared to the artist in dreams while he was engaged upon the hero's picture.

(3) The story, given also by both writers, of the competition at Samos, and the insult to Timanthes.

(4) The story, preserved *only in Pliny*, of the artist's boasted descent from Apollo.

It is evident that these *membra disiecta* must all have been found united in some older writer, from whom they found their way through different channels into Pliny and Athenaios respectively. Now Klearchos of Soloi was himself a pupil of Aristotle[1]; and, although Athenaios does not name his authority for the rest of the story, it is evident from its character, and from the mention moreover of Theophrastos for the parenthetical anecdote that Parrhasios was in the habit of singing at his work, that we are full among the Peripatetics. Therefore, as H. L. Urlichs has pointed out, the original authority must be a Peripatetic who had written upon the painters; in a word, it must be Duris of Samos[2]. This conjecture finds confirmation in the comments respectively made by Schubert[3] and Münzer[4] on the especial delight which Duris takes in describing details of dress (above, p. xlvi). It is significant that out of eighty-four fragments in Müller no less than ten[5] are concerned with elaborate descriptions of costume. Parrhasios the effeminate, with his purple robe and his golden crown, is reminiscent of the effeminate Demetrios, with his yellow hair and painted face, of frag. 27; of the regal Demetrios, with the gold-embroidered robes and the hair-band shot with gold (μίτρα χρυσόπαστος), of frag. 31.

[1] Athen. xv, p. 701 c.

[2] *Griechische Kunstschriftsteller,* p. 25.

[3] *Pyrrhus,* p. 15.

[4] *Op. cit.* p. 536.

[5] Fr. 14, 20, 22, 24, 27, 29, 31, 47, 50, and 64.

But Parrhasios was not the only painter who delighted in gorgeous apparel. According to Pliny (xxxv, 62), his rival Zeuxis carried the same taste so far as to make his appearance at Olympia displaying his own name woven in letters of gold into the embroideries of his garments—*aureis litteris in palliorum tesseris intextum nomen*—a detail which recalls the description of the chlamys of Demetrios, into which was inwoven the vault of heaven with its golden stars and twelve signs of the zodiac [1]. Robert [2] had already pointed out that the similarity of the stories narrated by Athenaios of the costume of Parrhasios, and by Pliny of that of Zeuxis, showed them to be derived from the same author. Since in the case of Parrhasios this author was Duris of Samos, it follows that it is to him also we must refer the Plinian anecdote of the luxury of Zeuxis [3].

A word remains to be said about the epigrams out of which the stories concerning Parrhasios are in great measure elaborated. It was the opinion of Jahn that all the epigrams purporting to have been written by Parrhasios upon himself, and inscribed upon his pictures—with the exception perhaps of the one celebrating the nocturnal apparitions of Herakles—were apocryphal [4]. Jahn included in the same category the self-laudatory epigrams placed in the mouth of the painter Apollodoros by one Nikomachos [5], and the epigram which, according to the orator Aristeides (Or. xlix, vol. ii, p. 521 Dindorf), had been elicited from Zeuxis in answer to the boasts of Parrhasios.

' Listen now,' writes Aristeides, ' to another swaggering painter,' and quotes the following epigram of Zeuxis :

' Herakleia my Fatherland, Zeuxis my name ; if any among men pretend to have attained the limits of my art, let him come forward and be proclaimed conqueror. . . . Yet methinks that mine is not the second place [6].'

[1] Duris *ap.* Athen. xii, 535 f (= fr. 31): αἱ δὲ χλαμύδες αὐτοῦ ἦσαν ὄρφνινον ἔχουσαι τὸ φέγγος τῆς χρόας, τὸ δὲ πᾶν [*verba suspecta*, Keil] ὁ πόλος ἐνύφαντο χρυσοῦς ἀστέρας ἔχων καὶ τὰ δώδεκα ζῴδια. Cf. Plut. *Demetrios*, 41.

[2] *Arch. Märchen*, p. 80.

[3] The remarks made above will show sufficiently why I have thought it unnecessary to refer either here or in the Comm. to the witty explanation of the *pallia* of Zeuxis as the curtains hung in front of pictures which he exhibited at Olympia (see *Arch. Ep. Mitth. aus Oesterreich*, xii, 1888, p. 106 f., and the article *Pictura* in Smith's *Dict. of Ant.* vol. ii, p. 410).

[4] *Kleine Beiträge*, p. 286 ff.

[5] *Apud* Hephaistion περὶ μέτρων καὶ ποιημ. iv, 7 :
Οὗτος δή σοι ὁ κλεινὸς ἀν' Ἑλλάδα πᾶσαν Ἀπολλό-
δωρος· γιγνώσκεις τοὔνομα τοῦτο κλύων.

[6] Ἡράκλεια πατρίς, Ζεῦξις δ' ὄνομ'·

These poetical criticisms, passed in similar vocabulary by three great contemporary painters upon their own or one another's achievements, seemed suspicious to Jahn. Bergk, however, saw no reason to dispute their authenticity [1], and in the case of Zeuxis at least it has lately been pointed out that his epigram has a parallel in the acrostic inscribed upon the grave of the rhetor and sophist Thrasymachos of Chalkedon, a younger contemporary of Sokrates : Τοὔνομα Θῆτα Ῥῶ Ἄλφα Σὰν Ὗ Μῦ Ἄλφα Χεῖ Οὗ Σάν, | πατρὶς Χαλκηδών· ἡ δὲ τέχνη σοφίη (Athen. x, 454 f = *Anth. App.* 359) [2]. We may gather from the observation that Zeuxis stood, as probably also Polykleitos, in close relation to the Sophists [3]. And the same is possibly true also of Parrhasios.

But to return to Duris. We have seen that those episodes of the Zeuxis-Parrhasios legends, designed to point the ethical qualities of the artists, might with certainty be referred to him. Now it has been finely discerned by Robert that the amiable Apelles and Protogenes are conceived as a pendant, so to speak, to the haughty and arrogant Zeuxis and Parrhasios, ' the faults of the older couple serving as a foil to the virtues of the younger. As a contrast to the productive and luxurious Parrhasios, we get Protogenes, struggling with the bitterest poverty, working with the most painstaking care, and accordingly producing but little : *summa paupertas initio artisque summa intentio et ideo minor fertilitas.* The portrait of Apelles is drawn with an even more loving hand ; his *simplicitas*, which manifests itself in his ungrudging recognition of the superiority of masters who surpassed him in special points ; his *comitas*, to which he owed the intimacy of Alexander ; his *benignitas* displayed towards Protogenes—are dwelt upon with admiration, and instances are adduced in their support [4].'

The intercoherence of the two sets of anecdotes is so patent

εἰ δέ τις ἀνδρῶν ἡμετέρης τέχνης
πείρατά φησιν ἔχειν δείξας νικάτω·
δοκῶ δέ, φησίν, ἡμᾶς οὐχὶ τὰ δεύτερ'
ἔχειν.

The resemblance to the second epigram of Parrhasios, quoted by Athenaios, is striking.

[1] *Lyrici Graeci*, ed. 4, vol. ii, p. 316 f.

[2] Imitated as late as the second half of the sixth cent. A.D. by Agathias (pp. 8, 18, ed. Niebuhr), who intro-

duces himself to the reader as : ἐμοὶ Ἀγαθίας μὲν ὄνομα, Μύρινα δὲ πατρὶς (Μεμνόνιος δὲ πατήρ), τέχνη δὲ τὰ Ῥωμαίων νόμιμα καὶ οἱ τῶν δικαστηρίων ἀγῶνες. See Reitzenstein, *Hermes*, xxiv, 1894, p. 238.

[3] Robert, *Votivgemälde eines Apobaten*, p. 20 ; Diels, *Deutsche Liter.-Ztg.* May 29, 1886, p. 784, and *Arch. Anz.* 1889, p. 10.

[4] *Arch. Märchen*, p. 81.

as of itself to justify us in assuming Duris, to whom we owe the one set, to be the author also of the other. This assumption is confirmed when we look more clearly into the details.

Most of the anecdotes recounted of Apelles and Protogenes are intended, as Robert has already remarked, to give concrete expression, above all, to the moral qualities of the artists, and at times also to their technical excellencies. The famous story of the 'splitting of the line' (xxxv, 80–82), like that of the circle traced by Giotto in presence of the Pope's envoy[1], is merely a comment on the delicate draughtsmanship of Apelles. Protogenes is made to split the line which Apelles divides once more, that the latter's superiority may be only the more triumphantly established by a great rival's acknowledged discomfiture. The setting of this particular anecdote moreover—the description of the studio with the solitary old woman (see Comm.) guarding in the master's absence the large easel with the panel ready to be worked upon—is specially Duridian in its picturesque detail.

The two proverbs attributed to Apelles, 'No day without a stroke' (§ 84), and 'Cobbler, stick to thy last' (§ 85), were intended to bring out his industry, and his respect for the opinion of others, though naturally only in so far as they speak of what they understand. The moralizing tone of the Peripatetic is heard in both the anecdotes elaborated out of the proverbs; nor is it superfluous to note that Duris seems to have had a strong leaning to proverbial sayings, possibly actually to have collected them[2].

The anecdote recounted in §§ 85, 86 of Alexander the Great's visit to Apelles illustrates another of the artist's qualities, his *comitas* or amiability. The kindly snub administered by Apelles to the king is evidently apocryphal, belonging to that class of anecdotes which, as Freeman would say, 'go about the world with blanks for the names[3],' for Ailianos (see Comm.) has it of Zeuxis and a *Megabyzos* or Priest of Kybele. The story of Pankaspe, which, on the other hand, is a comment on the monarch's generosity and self-control, is not only practically inseparable from the first, but Alexander's detection of his artist friend's trouble, and the magnanimous self-denial with which he gives up

---

[1] Vasari, ed. Milanesi, vol. i, p. 383.

[2] See fr. 49 = Zenob. v, 64; fr. 68 =

id. ii, 28; fr. 65 = Plut. *Lysander*, 18.

[3] Freeman, *Methods of Historical Study*, p. 134.

to him the most beloved of his mistresses, bear an extraordinary resemblance to the tale recounted by Plutarch (*Demetr.* xxxviii) of how King Seleukos gave up his wife Stratonike to his sick son Antiochos, whose love to his step-mother had been discovered by the physician Erasistratos as the cause of the young man's disease. The Plutarchian story has been traced back to Duris [1], whose partiality for erotic subjects, moreover, is abundantly proved by the extant fragments [2].

The story told in § 87 emphasizes the *benignitas* of Apelles towards all rivals, by singling out for our admiration his conduct in the case of Protogenes. The episode was evidently originally of a piece with the visit recounted in §§ 81, 82. To the story of the horses in § 95 we shall return later (p. lxiv); it may, however, be noted here that it shows the amiable and good-tempered artist losing patience, as in the case of the cobbler, with people pretending to know more about art than himself.

The Duridian character of the story of the rise of Protogenes from poverty to fame (§ 101) has already been noted in another connexion. His homely fare of soaked lupins gives point to his poverty and sobriety. The story in § 103, telling how the froth at the dog's mouth in the picture of 'Ialysos' was rendered by a lucky accident, when all the artist's efforts had failed, is eminently Peripatetic and Duridian in its delighted insistence upon the miracle of chance (*canis . . . quem pariter et casus pinxerit; fecitque in pictura fortuna naturam*) [3]. It is almost the anecdotic

---

[1] Schubert, *Pyrrhus*, p. 21.

[2] Cf. fragm. 2, 3, 19, 27, 35, 37, 42, 43, 58, 63. Thus he might possibly be responsible for the story of Pausias and Glykera (xxxv, 125), and for the anecdote recounted in xxxv, 140, of a Queen Stratonike, who may be identical with the Stratonike mentioned above. Perhaps too he had the stories of the lovers of the Knidian Aphrodite (xxxvi, 21) and of the Eros at Parion (*ib.* § 22) and of the Eros it true, were derived by Pliny from Mucianus (p. xc), but the latter may quite well have had access to Duris (cf. p. xci) or to art-literature based upon Duris; at any rate we find a similar anecdote recounted by Klearchos of Soloi (fragm. 46 *ap.* Athen.

xiii, p. 605 E), who not impossibly had himself got it from Duris, the statue in question having been at Samos. We learn, moreover, from Athenaios (xiii, p. 606 A), on the authority of Adaios of Mitylene, that it was the work of one Ktesikles (cf. Brunn, *K. G.* i, p. 424): he is otherwise unknown, and the name happens to be identical with that of the painter of 'Stratonike and the Fisherman.'

[3] The similar story recounted of Nealkes (xxxv, 104) is probably a mere *doublette* of that of Protogenes; but there is nothing in the date of Nealkes, as now established by Münzer (see Comm.), to prevent its having originated with Duris.

illustration of a line of Agathon quoted by Aristotle : τέχνη τύχην
ἔστερξε, καὶ τύχη τέχνην [1].' (Addenda.)

The story of the protection accorded by Demetrios (who by
the way is a favourite hero of Duris) to Protogenes [2], and of the
friendly intercourse between the warrior and the artist (§§ 104,
105), recalls the intercourse of Alexander and Apelles. Moreover,
the scenic setting, the description of the artist living *in hortulo
suo* (see Comm.), must be by the hand which had described the
anus una keeping watch in the empty studio. Of the Satyr
upon which Protogenes was at work when Demetrios besieged
Rhodes, Strabo (xiv, p. 652) tells an anecdote characteristic of
Duris. The Satyr was represented leaning against a column
upon which perched a partridge ; now so greatly was the painting
of the bird admired that it detracted from the attention due to
the central figure ; the painter, accordingly, vexed because his
main theme had become subsidiary (τὸ ἔργον πάρεργον γεγονός),
erased the bird. The story is identical in spirit and intention
with that of the boy and grapes painted by Zeuxis, and recounted
by Pliny (xxxv, 66) and Seneca Rhetor (see Comm.). I incline
to credit the Samian historian with the authorship of both. Lastly,
the story of Aristotle's advice to Protogenes to paint the feats of
Alexander is obviously more likely to proceed from the Peripatetic
Duris than from any other of the Plinian authors.

We have thus recovered considerable fragments of as many as
four of Duris's Lives of the Painters. There still remain scattered up and down the Plinian narrative a number of Duridian
passages, which I propose to examine in conclusion.

Closely connected with the anecdotes illustrative of character
comes another series, designed to give concrete form to certain
art-problems which had at different times exercised different
schools. A striking instance is the story told in xxxv, 64, of how
Zeuxis combined the beauty of his Helen painted for Kroton
(the Agrigentum of Pliny is a mistake, see Comm.) from the best
features of the five fairest maidens of that city. The anecdote
embodies the axiom that since 'there is no excellent *Beauty*, that
hath not some strangenesse in the proportions,' the artist, striving
for the ideal perfection, must needs 'take the best Parts out of
Divers Faces to make one Excellent [3].' Both the problem and

---

[1] *Ethics*, vi. 4. See *Addenda*.
[2] The story is also told with only
slight discrepancies by Plutarch in the
Demetrios, for which Duris is one of
the main sources.
[3] Bacon, *Essays*, xliii.

its solution had been discussed by Sokrates in the studio of Parrhasios [1]. Cicero, recounting the story of Zeuxis and the maidens as an illustration of the method he had himself followed in his study of rhetoric, had naturally combined it with the axiom it was originally intended to illustrate. The long passage (*de Invent. Rhet.* ii, 1, 1) is too well known to need full quotation, but the closing words are significant for our purpose, as showing how the anecdote had its rise in philosophic speculations :—

'. . . he (Zeuxis) did not believe that all the excellencies he needed for his beauteous image could be found in one body, for this reason, that nature never puts the perfect finishing touch to all the parts of any one object. Therefore, precisely as though by bestowing everything on the one she would have nothing left for the rest, she confers some benefit, now here now there, which is always inseparable from some defect [2].'

Dionysios (τῶν ἀρχ. κρίσις I), by using the anecdote to prove that we may, out of a varied erudition (πολυμάθεια), combine and inform the indestructible image of Art, shows his thorough appreciation of the philosophic lesson it was intended to convey. To a genial inventor like Duris, trained moreover in philosophic doctrine, may well be attributed the shaping of a story so much more apt to clothe an aesthetic problem than to convey an actual artistic practice. The fable of the five maidens of Kroton is of perennial interest ; it haunted the imagination of Raphael, who, writing of his Galatea to Baldassare Castiglione, says that 'per dipingere una bella, mi bisognerei veder più belle,' and at a later date we find it astutely criticized by Bernini [3] (see Add.).

Duris may also be credited, I think, with the expression of another problem of kindred nature, conveyed this time, however, not as an anecdote but as an apothegm. The judgement which Lysippos had passed upon his predecessors (xxxiv, 61), saying that, while *they* represented men as they are, *he* strove to represent them as they appeared to be, expresses, as I have pointed out in the notes, a dominant problem of art, the

---

[1] Xenophon, *Memorab.* iii, 10, 1 : . . . ἐπειδὴ οὐ ῥᾴδιον ἐνὶ ἀνθρώπῳ περιτυχεῖν ἄμεμπτα πάντα ἔχοντι, ἐκ πολλῶν συνάγοντες τὰ ἐξ ἑκάστου κάλλιστα·οὕτως ὅλα τὰ σώματα καλὰ ποιεῖτε φαίνεσθαι ; ποιοῦμεν γάρ, ἔφη, οὕτως.

[2] *Neque enim putavit omnia, quae quaereret ad venustatem, uno se in corpore reperire posse ideo, quod nihil simplici in genere omnibus ex partibus perfectum natura expolivit. Itaque, tanquam ceteris non sit habitura quod largiatur, si uni cuncta concesserit, aliud alii commodi, aliquo adiuncto incommodo muneratur.*

[3] See Baldinucci, *Notizie dei Professori del Disegno da Cimabue in qua* (Firenze, ed. 1847), p. 661.

problem of impressionism *versus* realism. Münzer[1] has lately referred the passage to Antigonos, who records a somewhat similar judgement passed by the philosopher Menedemos upon his predecessors[2]. This, however, only proves the later hand of Antigonos. So illuminating an aphorism could only have arisen in the brain of a far more powerful writer. The Lysippian judgement recalls, as has often been noticed[3], that which Aristotle makes Sophokles pass on himself and Euripides (Arist. *Poetics*, 1460 b[4])—is, in fact, but the application to a new problem of a phrase traditional in Aristotelian circles[5]. It is evident that Duris, who moreover is expressly named by Pliny as the authority for the early career of Lysippos, is far the likeliest of the Plinian authors to be responsible for the Lysippian apothegm[6]. The attribution is corroborated, moreover, by his partiality for such sayings, which he possibly collected systematically in emulation of the ἀποφθέγματα or ἀπομνημονεύματα of his brother Lynkeus[7].

He was an adept at deducing apothegms out of well-known lines of the poets and dramatists, even at the cost of occasional misapplication (Plutarch, *Demetr.* 14, 35, 45, 46; with Athen. vi, 249 c, cf. Odyss. xi, 122; Schubert, *Pyrrhus*, p. 20 f.); and I would therefore likewise refer to him the apothegm of Euphranor to the effect that ‘his Theseus was fed on meat, but that of Parrhasios on roses’ (xxxv, 128). Münzer has detected in the words the latent reminiscence of an Aristophanic line preserved in Diogenes on the authority of Antigonos[8] (see Comm.), but this

[1] *Op. cit.* p. 527.
[2] Antig. Kar. *ap* Diog. ii, 134 (= Wilam. p. 98): τῶν δὲ διδασκάλων τῶν περὶ Πλάτωνα καὶ Ξενοκράτην ἔτι δὲ Παραιβάτην τὸν Κυρηναῖον κατεφρόνει, Στίλπωνα δ᾽ ἐτεθαυμάκει· καί ποτε ἐρωτηθεὶς περὶ αὐτοῦ ἄλλο μὲν οὐδὲν εἶπε πλὴν ὅτι ἐλευθέριος. The resemblance to the Lysippian phrase is little more than formal and verbal.
[3] Among others by Vahlen in the notes to his ed. of the *Poetics* (Leipzig, 1885), p. 265.
[4] ‘Further, if it be objected that the description is not true to fact, the poet may perhaps reply,—“ But the objects are as they ought to be ”: just as Sophokles said that he drew men as they ought to be drawn ; Euripides as they are.’ Tr. S. H. Butcher,

p. 95 (for Greek, see Comm.).
[5] To say this, however, is far from admitting the theory of Ottfried Müller (*Kunst-Archäol. Werke*, II. p. 165 ff.), lately revived by Kékulé (*Arch. Jahrb.* viii, 1893, p. 39 ff.), that the original Greek of the Lysippian saying was a slavish imitation of the Sophoklean (Kékulé, p. 45)—and the *quales viderentur esse* of Pliny a clumsy misunderstanding of something like οἵους ἔοικεν εἶναι. On the contrary, the *viderentur* is the very pith of the apothegm, which conveys a problem totally different to the Sophoklean.
[6] Duridian authorship seems hinted at by Diels, *Arch. Anz.* 1893, p. 11.
[7] Ath. vi, 245 ; viii, 337.
[8] I trust I am not misapprehending

is no proof that Antigonos is also responsible for the new turn given to the phrase in the mouth of Euphranor.

There remains to note, with H. L. Urlichs [1] and Münzer [2], that Duris was presumably the source for sundry stories of art-competitions preserved in Pliny. Their authenticity is suspicious, as Jahn long ago maintained [3], because in all of them the competition itself offered no interest whatsoever to the writer, but was merely used—we may at once say invented—in order to bring great artists of the same or adjoining epochs into presence, and often to point some saying supposed to have been uttered on the occasion. The animating idea is the same as in the story which represented the young Lysippos venturing upon the higher paths of art at the bidding of Eupompos. Such is the contest between Parrhasios and Timanthes, already discussed in another connexion (above, p. liv), where we are not even told the subject of the picture by the latter artist ; the competition between Zeuxis and Parrhasios with the curtain and the grapes (*ib.* 65) ; and the kindred anecdote of Apelles' appeal from the verdict of human judges to that of beasts (*ib.* 95).

The story of the four statues of Amazons made in competition by four great artists for the Temple of Ephesos belongs to the same series. The garb it borrows from the legend of the award of the prize of valour after Salamis (see Comm.) sufficiently betrays its apocryphal character, even though it have a groundwork of truth. There is the undoubted existence of four distinct types of Amazons, similar in size and pose ; and Furtwängler has lately made the acute suggestion that the anecdote of the evaluation grew out of the order in which four statues of Amazons by the said four masters were exhibited in the Ephesian Artemision (see Comm.). Certainly such an order of exhibition [4], could it be proved, would

the *rapprochements* attempted on p. 527 f. of Münzer's article.

[1] *Griechische Kunstschriftsteller,* p. 28 f.

[2] *Op. cit.* p. 534.

[3] *Kleine Beiträge,* p. 289 f.

[4] It may be worth pointing out here that the story of the Four Amazons has a curious parallel, not, I believe, observed before, in Augustine's explanation of the origin of the number of the Muses ; it is quoted on the authority of Varro, who of course had

it from Greek art-writers : Aug., *De Doctrina Christiana,* ii, 8 : *Non enim audiendi sunt errores gentilium superstitionum qui novem Musas Iovis et Memoriae filias esse finxerunt. Refellit eos Varro, quo nescio utrum apud eos quisquam talium rerum doctior vel curiosior esse possit. Dicit enim civitatem nescio quam, non enim nomen recolo, locasse apud tres artifices terna simulachra musarum, quae in templo Apollinis dono poneret, et quisquis artificum pulchriora for-*

be a fine opportunity for imagining the rivalry of the four artists, precisely as a joint inscription of (the Elder) Praxiteles and Kalamis had given rise to some popular explanation, afterwards elaborated by Duris or a writer of his stamp into the anecdote recorded in xxxiv, 71, of the kind consideration of Praxiteles for the artistic reputation of Kalamis—an anecdote, by the way, that recalls the kindness of Apelles to Protogenes. Finally, the competition between Panainos and a totally unknown Timagoras (xxxv, 58), on the testimony of a *carmen vetustum*, of whose content, however, no hint is given, looks suspiciously like fiction.

There is still one passage in conclusion where Münzer (p. 535) detects, I believe rightly, the influence or authorship of Duris. This is the account of the women painters in xxxv, 147, ' woman' being one of the most favourite Duridian themes [1]. Münzer further remarks that the painter Olympias is a namesake of the mother of Alexander the Great, for whom Duris evinced a lively interest,[2] as for every one connected with Alexander ; that Aristarete is the daughter of Nearchos, who, as the namesake of one of Alexander's generals [3], would likewise interest Duris ; and that the three women Timarete (xxxv, 59), Irene, and Aristarete, at once daughters and pupils of their respective fathers, Mikon, Kratinos, and Nearchos, are conceived too manifestly on the same pattern to be above suspicion. Finally, the dancer Alkisthenes and the juggler Theodoros, painted by Kalypso, are evident Duridian personages ; they recall the θαυματοποιοί, Xenophon and Nymphodoros, of fragm. 44 (= Ath. i, p. 19, f.), where the clever tricks of Xenophon's pupil Kratisthenes of Phlious are described. The analogous formation of the names Alkisthenes—Kratisthenes, Theodoros—Nymphodoros, is certainly significant.

This closes the list of passages that may be attributed with any certainty to Duris. It is most improbable that either Varro or Pliny had direct access to his writings ; he seems so certainly the authority of Antigonos for the statement concerning Pythagoras of Samos (above, p. liii), and so many of the passages traced back to

---

masset ab illo potissimum electa emeret. Itaque contigisse ut opera sua quoque illi artifices aeque pulchra explicarent, et placuisse civitati omnes novem atque omnes emptas esse, ut in Apollinis templo dedicarentur. Quibus postea dicit Hesiodum poetam im-

posuisse vocabula. Non ergo Iupiter novem Musas genuit, sed tres fabri ternas creaverunt.

[1] Cf. fragm. 2, 3, 19, 24, 35, 42, 58, 63.

[2] Fr. 24.

[3] Plut. *Alex.* 66, 73 and often.

Duris were likely to interest Antigonos from their purely anecdotic character, that it is not unreasonable to assume that all the Duridian stories we meet with in Pliny were brought in by Antigonos, who had drawn largely from Duris for his Book of Marvels (Münzer, *op. cit.* p. 531). Antigonos presumably did not always give the name of his authority; like Pliny and most ancient writers, he would be willing enough to assume the credit of the greater part of his information, and would only mention his authorities by name in cases where the statements seemed to him to outpass belief. So, too, Varro quoted the *artifices qui condidere haec*, in xxxiv, 68, and again in xxxv, 68 (giving them here a second mention by name), in cases where he felt he needed an excuse for a weak explanation, or a warrant for an over-bold criticism. Thus it was that, after passing through many different hands, the name of Duris of Samos, preserved in xxxiv, 61 in testimony of the incredible story that the great Lysippos of Sikyon had been wholly a self-taught artist, has given us a clue leading us to assign, as I believe, to their right author no inconsiderable portion of the Plinian anecdotes.

At the same time the vindication of these tales for the Samian historian throws considerable light on the nature of his art-writings. They reveal him as above all a biographer in spirit and not only in form. He seeks to bring before his readers the individuality of the man rather than the technical or aesthetic quality of his work. For this purpose he employs popular traditions, giving to these *voces populi* the literary form which was to secure them from oblivion. In the attention he bestowed upon character-drawing, real and fictitious, he was a true product of his age in its newly awakened desire to ascertain the features of great men present or past. The words of Pliny were as true of the third century as of his own : *pariunt ... desideria non traditos vultus, sicut in Homero evenit:* sculptors were not content to portray contemporaries— a Menander or a Poseidippos—but must needs discover and fix for a late posterity the likeness of Aisop, Archilochos, Epimenides, nay of Homer himself[1]. In many cases the monuments are still there to show how nearly a deep intuition of the genius peculiar to each personage portrayed might help to restore the ‘image which no contemporary hand had traced. The same occurred in literature : the Peripatetics, Chamaileon of Herakleia,

---

[1] See the remarks of Wilamowitz, *Antigonos von Karystos*, p. 149 ff.

or Dikaiarchos of Messana—to quote two out of a host—had attempted to reconstruct the lives of Alkman, of Alkaios, or of Semonides. Duris himself had written a biography of Euripides[1], of which recent criticism has recovered at least one characteristic fragment, which tells how Sophokles on receiving the news of the death of Euripides clad himself in robes of mourning. When Duris wrote his biographies of the artists he determined they should be 'Lives' in the most realistic sense of the word, refusing to discuss the works divorced from the artists' personalities. It is little wonder if in essaying to breathe back life into the persons of Lysippos, of Apelles, or Protogenes, his vivid imagination and strong powers of presentment led him, when historic facts failed, to offer telling anecdote in their place.

We may feel impelled from the side of historical verity to echo the complaint of Plutarch that Duris shows, even where not misled by interest, an habitual disregard of truth[2], but we are none the less indebted to him for what is perhaps the most enduring charm in the history of the ancient artists. The stories we have been studying, like those countless others which enliven the pages of Greek history, have their rise in a profoundly popular instinct, in the desire to find expression, at once simple and striking, for distinguishing qualities of temperament or of workmanship. And in their graphic force, that 'power,' if we may borrow from the words which Dionysios applies to the oratory of Lysias, of 'driving home to the senses the subject of discourse[3],' they have entered into the very substance of our thought. While every schoolboy is familiar with the tale of Zeuxis and the grapes, a scholar such as August Boeckh could express his ideal of the learned life in the words *dies diem docet ut perdideris quam sine linea transmiseris*, or the orator Burke sum up the qualities of that masterly state-paper, 'whose every stroke had been justified by historic fact,' in the telling phrase *Thus painters sign their names at Co.*[4]

---

[1] Printed at the commencement of Kirchhoff's ed. Berlin, 1867, vol. i, p. viii. Cf. Schubert, *Pyrrhus*, p. 16.

[2] *Pericl.* xxviii: Δοῦρις μὲν οὖν οὐδ' ὅπου μηδὲν αὐτῷ πρόσεστιν ἴδιον πάθος εἰωθὼς κρατεῖν τὴν διήγησιν ἐπὶ τῆς ἀληθείας. . . . Cicero, however, in his

one allusion to Duris (*Att.* vi, i, 18) judges him more leniently.

[3] Dion. Hal. *de Lys.* vii δύναμίς τις ὑπὸ τὰς αἰσθήσεις ἄγουσα τὰ λεγόμενα.

[4] Burke, *Works* (ed. 1823), vol. viii, p. 129 (Letters on a Regicide Peace).

INTRODUCTION

IV. Literary Epigrams.

The literary epigram, at once descriptive of a work of art and embodying its criticism or eulogy, was among the most fruitful sources of information at the disposal of ancient writers upon art[1]. It plays accordingly, as Otto Jahn first perceived[2], a considerable part in Pliny's descriptions of pictures or statues, where it becomes of the highest importance to the critic to detect it : for, as it strongly coloured the Plinian narrative, so it has gone on to this day, colouring our appreciation of ancient works of art, nay, predisposing us in many cases to read into them intentions, which are within the expressive range of poetry rather than of the plastic arts.   Pliny's own phrase describing what the Apellian Aphrodite owed to the verses written in her praise remains true in greater or less degree of all works extolled in epigrams : *versibus Graecis tali opere, dum laudatur, victo sed illustrato.*

A first list of the Plinian passages based upon epigrams was drawn up by Otto Jahn (*loc. cit.*), and afterwards supplemented by Benndorf[3].   The subjoined list is compiled from theirs, but with some few additions indicated by an asterisk.

1.—xxxiii, 156 Antipater (sc. Diodoros, see note)—qui *Satyrum in phiala gravatum somno conlocavisse verius quam caelasse dictus est.*

    Cf. *Anth. Plan.* 248 :

        τὸν Σάτυρον Διόδωρος ἐκοίμισεν, οὐκ ἐτόρευσεν·
        ἢν νύξῃς, ἐγερεῖς· ἄργυρος ὕπνον ἔχει[4].

2.—xxxiv, 55 Polyclitus ... diadumenum fecit *molliter iuvenem* ... et doryphorum *viriliter puerum.*

(The epigrammatic qualification is so finely knitted to the mention of the works that it must have been brought in at a very early date[5].)

3.—xxxiv, 59 Pythagoras—fecit—*claudicantem, cuius ulceris dolorem sentire etiam spectantes* VIDENTUR.

---

[1] See in connexion with the epigrams of the *Anthology* which deal with works of art the admirable essay of J. W. Mackail, *Select Epigrams from the Greek Anthology*, p. 47 ff. ; cf. P. Vitry, *Étude sur les Épigr. de l'Anthol. Pal. qui contiennent la description d'une œuvre d'Art*, in *Rev. Arch.* xxiv. 1894, p. 315 ff.

[2] *Kunsturtheile des Plinius*, p. 118 ff.

[3] *De Anthologiae Graecae Epigrammatis quae ad artes spectant;* diss. Leipzig, 1862.

[4] 'This Satyr Diodorus engraved not, but laid to rest ; your touch will wake him ; the silver is asleep.'   Tr. J. W. Mackail, *op. cit.* p. 179.

[5] Münzer, *op. cit.* p. 529. Dilthey, *Rhein. Mus.* xxvi, 290, first pointed out the epigrammatic juxtaposition of the two works.

Cf. *Anth. Plan.* iv, 113; ll. 1–2 :

οἶδα Φιλοκτήτην ὁρόων, ὅτι πᾶσι φαείνει
ἄλγος ἐὸν καὶ τοῖς τηλόθι δερκομένοις [1].

*4.—xxxiv, 70 (Praxiteles) fecit et *puberem Apollinem subrepenti lacertae com-
minus sagitta insidiantem* quem sauroctonon vocant.

Cf. the same or perhaps identical epigram as adopted by
Martial, xiv, 172 :

> Ad te reptanti, puer insidiose, lacertae
> Parce ; cupit digitis illa perire tuis [2].

5.—xxxiv, 70 (Praxitelis) spectantur et *duo signa eius diversos adfectus exprimentia, flentis matronae et meretricis gaudentis.* hanc putant
Phrynen fuisse *deprehenduntque in ea amorem artificis et mercedem in voltu meretricis.*

The juxtaposition of the statues is purely epigrammatic ; in the
description of Phryne's portrait lurks perhaps a reminiscence of
Anth. Plan. iv, 204 (see Comm.).

*6.—xxxiv, 71 Ipse Calamis et alias *quadrigas bigasque fecit se impari, equis
sine aemulo expressis.*

The rhetorical point betrays the underlying epigram ; the
Propertian *Exactis Calamis se mihi iactat equis* (Prop. iii, 9, 10)
is doubtless from the same source, for where should Kalamis
boast of his horses so well as in some epigram purporting to be
written by the artist himself?

7.—xxxiv, 74 Cresilas *volneratum deficientem, in quo possit intellegi quantum
restet animae,*
et *Olympium Periclen dignum cognomine, mirumque in hac arte est
quod nobiles viros nobiliores fecit.*

8.—*ib.* 77 Euphranoris *Alexander Paris est, in quo laudatur quod omnia
simul intellegantur, iudex dearum, amator Helenae et tamen
Achillis interfector.*

9.—*ib.* 78 Eutychides *Eurotam, in quo artem ipso amne liquidiorem plurimi
dixere.*

---

[1] ' I behold Philoktetes. His agony
is made manifest, even to those who
look on from afar.' The analogy to the
Plinian description is pointed out by
Münzer, *l. c.* In the notes I have followed Brunn in quoting *Anth. Plan.*
112 (where the omission of the name
of Philoktetes is perhaps the cause of
its unusual omission in Pliny) : ' More
hateful than the Greeks was my maker,
a second Odysseus, who brought back
to me my woeful dire disease. The
rock, my rags and blood and wound
and grief, were not enough, but he has
even wrought my pain in bronze.'

[2] Pointed out by Münzer *op. cit.*
p. 527, note 1.

Cf. *Anth. Pal.* ix, 709 :

> Εὐρώταν ὡς ἄρτι διάβροχον, ἔν τε ῥεέθροις
> εἵλκυσ' ὁ τεχνίτης ἐν πυρὶ λουσάμενον·
> πᾶσι γὰρ ἐν κώλοις ὑδατούμενος ἀμφινένευκεν
> ἐκ κορυφῆς ἐς ἄκρους ὑγρορατῶν ὄνυχας
> ἁ δὲ τέχνα ποταμῷ συνεπήρικεν· ἆ τίς ὁ πείσας
> χαλκὸν κωμάζειν ὕδατος ὑγρότερον [1] ;

*10.—xxxiv, 79 Lycius . . . fecit *dignum praeceptore puerum sufflantem languidos ignes.*

The description of the 'dying fire,' which was of course not represented in bronze, betrays the epigram.

11.—xxxiv, 79 Leochares *aquilam sentientem quid rapiat in Ganymede et cui ferat parcentemque unguibus etiam per vestem puero.*

Cf. *Anth. Pal.* xii, 221 :

> Στεῖχε πρὸς αἰθέρα δῖον, ἀπέρχεο παῖδα κομίζων
> αἰετέ, τὰς διφυεῖς ἐκπετάσας πτέρυγας·
> στεῖχε τὸν ἀβρὸν ἔχων Γανυμήδεα, μηδὲ μεθείης
> τὸν Διὸς ἥδιστον οἰνοχόον κυλίκων·
> φείδεο δ' αἱμάξαι κοῦρον γαμψώνυχι ταρσῷ,
> μὴ Ζεὺς ἀλγήσῃ, τοῦτο βαρυνόμενος [2].

12.—xxxiv, 80 Naucerus (censetur) *luctatore anhelante.*

The analogy to xxxv, 71, makes it probable that the *anhelante* is from an epigram ; cf. Benndorf, *op. cit.*

xxxiv, 81 Styppax uno celebratur signo, splanchnopte—*Periclis Olympi vernula hic fuit exta torrens ignemque oris pleni spiritu accendens.*

The last words, the insistence on the swelling cheeks of the boy as he blows the fire, clearly point to an epigram. How far removed the real 'Entrail Roaster' would be from the Plinian description may be seen at a glance by studying the boy's statue from the Olympieion at Athens, which has lately been brought, with much probability, into relation with the statue by Styppax (see Comm. on passage).

13.—xxxiv, 81 Silanion Apollodorum fudit . . . *nec hominem ex aere fecit, sed iracundiam.*

(See Add. to the Comm. on the passage.)

---

[1] 'Dragged by the artist through a bath of fire, the Eurotas seems fresh from the water and amidst his streams. He bends to either side while water pours from all his limbs, and the drops fall from his head even to his feet. Art too hath joined in contest with the river; ah, who hath taught the bronze to burst into waves more flowing than the floods ? '

[2] 'Speed on to the heaven divine, go thy way, eagle, with the boy, spreading either pinion wide. Speed on with beauteous Ganymedes, nor suffer the boy to fall who poureth sweetest cups for Zeus. Yet spare to wound the boy with thy crooked talon, lest Zens sorrow in grief thereat.'

14.—xxxiv, 88 Epigonus ... praecessit in ... *matri interfectae infante miserabiliter blandiente.*

(From an epigram similar to the one on the 'dying mother' by Aristeides in xxxv, 98.)

15.—xxxiv, 141 *Ferreus Hercules,* quem fecit Alcon *laborum dei patientia inductus.*

16.—xxxv, 59 (Zeuxis) fecit et *Penelopen, in qua pinxisse mores videtur.*

17.—*ib.* 69 (Parrhasius) pinxit demon Atheniensium argumento quoque ingenioso. ostendebat namque *varium, iracundum iniustum inconstantem, eundem exorabilem clementem misericordem, gloriosum, excelsum humilem, ferocem fugacemque et omnia pariter.*

18.—*ib.* 70 (Parrhasius) *pueros duos, in quibus spectatur securitas et aetatis simplicitas.*

19.—*ib.* 71 (Parrhasi) duae picturae nobilissimae, *hoplites in certamine ita decurrens ut sudare videatur, alter arma deponens ut anhelare sentiatur.*

20.—*ib.* 94 (Apelles) pinxit et heroa nudum, *eaque pictura naturam ipsam provocavit.*

21.—*ib.* 98 (Aristidis) *oppido capto ad matris morientis ex volnere mammam adrepens infans, intellegiturque sentire mater et timere ne emortuo lacte sanguinem lambat.*

Cf. *Anth. Pal.* vii, 623 :

"Ελκε, τάλαν, παρὰ μητρὸς ὃν οὐκέτι μαστὸν ἀμέλξεις,
ἕλκυσον ὑστάτιον νᾶμα καταφθιμένης·
ἤδη γὰρ ξιφέεσσι λιπόπνοος· ἀλλὰ τὰ μητρὸς
φίλτρα καὶ εἰν Ἀΐδῃ παιδοκομεῖν ἔμαθεν [1].

22.—xxxv, 99 (Aristides pinxit) *supplicantem paene cum voce.*

*23.—*ib.* 99 (Aristides pinxit) *anapauomenen propter fratris amorem.*

(Cf. *Anth. Pal.* vii, 183, 184, and see H. L. Urlichs' note in the Comm. on the passage.)

24.—xxxv, 106 (Protogenis) Satyrus—est, quem anapauomenon vocant, *ne quid desit temporis eius securitati, tenentem tibias.*

(Cf. *Anth. Plan.* 244.)

*25.—xxxv, 138 Antiphilus *puero ignem conflante laudatur ac pulchra alias domo splendescente ipsiusque pueri ore.*

I suspect an epigram from the forced point made in the description of the room 'which is in itself beautiful.'

26.—xxxvi, 21 (Praxitelis Veneris) effigies *dea favente ipsa, ut creditur, facta.*

(Cf. *Anth. Plan.* 159–170.)

27.—xxxvi, 24 Cephisodotus ... *cuius laudatum est Pergami symplegma nobile digitis corpori verius quam marmori inpressis.*

---

[1] 'Drink, poor babe, from thy mother, whose breast thou shalt suck no more ; drink thy last draught from her in death. Now has the sword taken her life, yet a mother's love knows, even in Hades, how to care for her child.'

Cf. Herondas iv, 59 f. [1], quoted in the Comm. on the passage.

Besides the epigrams descriptive of works of art, we may note, for the sake of completeness, the allusion to the epigrams on Myron's cow (xxxiv, 57) and on the *Anadyomene* of Apelles (xxxv, 92); the epigram upon Zeuxis which lurks in the words *ab hoc (Apollodoro) artis fores apertas, Zeuxis . . . intravit* in xxxv, 61 (see Comm.); the epigram in which Apollodoros reproached Zeuxis with having not learnt—but stolen the art of his masters (*ib.* § 62); finally the reference to the laudatory verses composed by Parrhasios upon himself, discussed above (p. liv f.). In all these descriptive passages it is evident that the writer has been concerned to outstrip rather than to explain the artistic aim. We are confronted by a series of pointed sayings, inspired indeed, or they would miss their effect, by some quality actually existent in the work of art, but using this quality as a theme to be expanded freely into the fluidity of language, whereas the artist had been forced to compress his conceptions within the limits imposed by visible form. Whatever Euphranor's ethical conception of the separate or conflicting traits in the character of Paris, he must perforce combine and fuse them in the portrayal of one single personage. The versifier, on the other hand, remains within the limits of his art if he picks out the qualities suggested rather than definitely indicated by the Paris of Euphranor, and embodies these in a series of consecutive images: thus the Paris of the sculptor will be converted by the epigrammatist from a unit into a triad; the compacted whole is resolved into the judge of the goddesses, the lover of Helen, the murderer of Achilles—each trait calling up in the mind of the reader a distinct sensuous image, whereas the statue, however complex, called up only one. Or, again, the epigram may catch at a purely accidental detail — accidental so far as regards any ethical import—such as the drapery which Leochares gave as a background to his Ganymede, and interpret it to mean what it lay entirely outside the power of the formative arts to express,—the eagle's care to avoid wounding the boy. The achievement of artist and of epigrammatist is bound to be different, because of the dissimilarity of the material with which each clothes his thought. The question touches one of the

---

[1] 'Pray look at this naked child; if I pinch him can you not fancy I shall really hurt him Kynno? For the flesh palpitates in the picture like a warm spring'—(*ut fontes calidi*, v. Crusius, *ad loc.*).

most difficult of all the problems suggested by the study of art, the problem how far the language of form can be translated into that of words, and *vice versa*. It could only be adequately treated in context with the written Greek epigrams of the same class as those we have been considering, and with the various descriptions in ancient literature, outside Pliny, based upon such epigrams; and this, after all, would be only one chapter of a vast discussion that should embrace the literature, whether ancient or modern, that aims at the analysis of works of art. But I have touched upon it here only as a passing protest against the practice, still too common, of searching in what were often but plays of fancy for definite evidence concerning the intention to be conveyed by a work of art. The modern scholar shows himself scarcely less credulous in this respect than Pliny himself, who introduced most of his epigrammatic descriptions by the *intelligere*, which, as we learn from Cicero, was the special term used of the insight and criticism of the man who knows [1].

These descriptive epigrams were doubtless interwoven with the original Xenokratic fabric that underlies the Plinian account at different times. We have seen that some—perhaps even a large number—were certainly due to Antigonos of Karystos. Others may be due to the Greek artist and writer upon art, Pasiteles of Naples (p. lxxvii ff.); Varro or Mucianus may have brought in others; nor need we decide whether Varro, or Pliny, or another Roman, was first guilty of the comic blunder arising from the attribution in xxxiv, 57 to the sculptor Myron of the little monument, sung by two poets of the Anthology, which the girl Myro had raised to her pets, a cricket and a grasshopper [2].

[1] *Brutus*, 184 etenim necesse est, qui ita dicat, ut a multitudine probetur, eundem doctis probari; nam quid in dicendo rectum sit aut pravum, ego iudicabo, si modo is sum, qui id possim aut sciam iudicare: *qualis vero sit orator ex eo, quod is dicendo efficiet poterit intelligi.* See O. Jahn, *loc. cit.* p. 120.

[2] The list of works whose description is based upon literary epigrams should further include the notice in xxxiv, 79 of the group by Leochares of the slave-dealer Lykiskos and a boy 'on whose face may be read the wily craft of the servile character.' Possibly the notice in xxxiv, 88 of Nikeratos' group of Alkibiades and his mother 'Demarate sacrificing by torchlight' belongs to the same class (cf. note 2 on p. xliv). The description in xxxiv, 93 of the Hercules 'wearing the tunic,' considered by Benndorf (p. 55) as epigrammatic, seems inseparable from the notice of the three *tituli* on the statue, and is presumably an observation of Pliny's own, not borrowed from any special source.

V. Heliodoros of Athens (*fl.* 150 B.C.).

Heliodorus qui de Atheniensium anathematis scripsit is cited in the Indices of authors to Books xxxiv and xxxv ; the mention of his name in the Index to Book xxxiii, which contains no material that could be derived from him, must be looked upon as an interpolation. Till recently the literary personality of Heliodoros remained so shadowy [1] that all attempts to recover traces of him in Pliny had proved ineffectual [2]. Now, however, that Bruno Keil [3] has succeeded in proving Heliodoros to be the source for the periegetic portions in the Pseudo-Plutarchian *Lives of the Ten Orators*, it has become possible to ascertain also the extent of Pliny's debt—and it remains very small—to the Athenian periegete.

The interest of the results attained by Keil lies almost entirely outside Pliny ; it will suffice to indicate them briefly. The passage in the Life of Hypereides (849 c) concerning the burial-place of the orator πρὸ τῶν Ἱππάδων πυλῶν, ὥς φησιν Ἡλιόδωρος ἐν τῷ τρίτῳ περὶ Μνημάτων forms the basis of the inquiry. The reading of the MSS. Ἡλιόδωρος, which Ruhnken had unnecessarily altered to Διόδωρος, has been rightly retained in this place by both Keil (*l.c.*) and by Bernadakis in the new edition of the *Moralia* (vol. v, p. 193). For not only does the date of Heliodoros [4] accord precisely with the date required by certain other statements of periegetic nature contained in the *Lives* (cf. in particular Lyk. 842e = fr. 5[a] Keil [5]), but the information conveyed in these dateable fragments and in the remaining periegetic passages scattered through the *Lives* is of a strictly homogeneous character, which Keil defines as follows (*op. cit.* p. 237, cf. p. 201): 'The first interest of Heliodoros is for extant monuments; he gives details concerning the nature of the monument, its material, its locality and present condition ; then follow in natural sequence statements of an historical character, such as the original condition, change of locality, occasional details concerning cost,

---

[1] Seven fragments are collected by Müller, *F. H. G.* iv, p. 425. See also Susemihl, *Geschichte d. Al. Lit.* i, p. 692 f.

[2] E. g. the attempts of Wachsmuth, *Stadt Athen*, i, p. 36, note 2 ; on the difficulty of the Heliodoran question see Brieger, *De Fontibus*, p. 33.

[3] *Hermes*, xxx, 1895, pp. 199–240.

[4] After Antiochos Epiphanes (B.C. 175–164), cf. Athen. II, p. 45 c.

[5] Καὶ ἔστιν αὐτῶν (Lyknrg. and his children) τὰ μνήματα ἀντικρὺ τῆς Παιωνίας Ἀθηνᾶς ἐν τῷ Μελανθίου τοῦ φιλοσόφου κήπῳ (date of Melanthios circ. B.C. 150, Keil, *l. c.*).

artists, or donors. These statements are corroborated by the epigrams and inscriptions . . . relative to the monument described[1].'

Now if we turn to Pliny we shall find some four passages which bear this peculiar Heliodoran stamp. Three occur in Book xxxiv, in the first alphabetical list of the bronze-workers; one in Book xxxv, towards the close of the main account of the painters. In xxxiv, § 74, the passage *Cephisodorus Minervam mirabilem in portu Atheniensium et aram ad templum Iovis Servatoris in eodem portu, cui pauca comparantur* (sc. *fecit*) has long been admitted by a number of authorities[2], though on different grounds, to be from a source other than that of the main account. It will repay careful analysis. We know from Pausanias (i, 1, 3) that the 'Minerva' and the 'Jupiter' belonged to the same temple, namely to the Διισωτήριον, where Zeus and Athena were worshipped respectively as Σωτήρ and Σώτειρα[3]. Now, if we examine the Plinian passage we note at once a certain looseness of construction, a certain hesitancy in the wording; it is as if Pliny, or the author from whom he quotes, were not fully conscious—or at least fully persuaded—that the 'wondrous Athena' which was to be seen 'in the harbour of Athens' were really in the same place as the altar, which was in the same city, 'in the temple of Zeus the Saviour.' I accordingly believe that we have here the juxtaposition of two statements derived from separate sources. The words *Cephisodorus Minervam mirabilem in portu Atheniensium* would belong to the main account—the mention of the Athena, which was bronze (χαλκοῦ μὲν ἀμφότερα τὰ ἀγάλματα), being in place in a history of bronze-sculpture—while a later hand introduced from another source the mention of the *ara*, another work by Kephisodoros. Now this altar, which would naturally be marble and be decorated with reliefs, is obviously out of place in a history which was only concerned with works in the round and in bronze; this discrepancy, however, was unnoticed by the art-writer (Pasiteles (?), p. lxxx) who made the addition.

---

[1] Cf., in particular, Isokr. 838d (= Keil, fr. 4b), the inscription from the statue of Isokrates by Leochares, which Timotheos put up at Eleusis.

[2] Wachsmuth, *Stadt Athen*, i, p. 36, note 2; Furtwängler, *Master-pieces*, p. 145; Oehmichen, *Plin. Studien*, p. 151.

[3] See Comm. p. 60; cf. Liv. xxxi, 30, 9. The whole literature on the passage, both ancient and modern, given by Hitzig and Blümner, *Pausanias*, p. 120 f.

The connecting link was afforded by the name of Kephisodoros. Nor was any special attention bestowed upon the fact that the *ara* which was now mentioned stood not only *in eodem portu*, but actually in the same temple as the Athena. That the addition itself is Heliodoran seems probable from the precision with which the locality of the altar is noted (*ad templum Iovis Servatoris*), whereas the Minerva was simply cited as being *in portu Atheniensium*. The altar moreover—doubtless itself an ἀνάθημα—was a likely object to be included in a work *de anathematis*.

Close by the notice of Kephisodoros occurs the second passage detected as Heliodoran by Keil. The statement in xxxiv, 76 that 'Demetrios made a statue of Lysimache, who was priestess of Athena for sixty-four years,' has a precision of detail, due to the fact that the years of Lysimache's priesthood were taken from the inscription on her statue (see Comm.), unlike anything that meets us in the main account, where such detail is alien to the nature of the inquiry.

With these two passages recognized as Heliodoran by both Keil and Münzer[1] I incline to associate a third, claimed for Heliodoros by Wachsmuth[2], but rejected by Keil (*l. c.*). The passage (xxxiv, 72) concerning the 'Lioness' of Amphikrates, whose name was doubtless taken from the inscribed basis, belongs essentially to a book *de anathematis*, and accordingly to Heliodoros, one of whose works specially described the monuments of the Athenian Akropolis (περὶ τῆς Ἀθήνησιν ἀκροπόλεως, fr. 1— 3 Müller). At the same time, it must be admitted that the story related in connexion with the monument has, in its Plinian form, a more imaginative flavour than we find in any of the accredited Heliodoran fragments or in those more recently recovered by Keil. It is possible, therefore, that only the kernel of the passage is Heliodoran, and that the anecdote itself was expanded under the influence of other sources[3].

---

[1] *op. cit.* p. 541.

[2] *loc. cit.* The Heliodoran authorship seems admitted by Gurlitt, *Pausanias*, p. 96.

[3] It is noteworthy that the name of Amphikrates is preserved only in Pliny. As regards the mention of the statue and the anecdote attached thereto, Plut., *Garrul.* 8, and Polyainos, *Strategem.* viii, 45, appear to draw from the same source as Pliny, while the words of Pausanias (i, 23, 2), λέγω δὲ οὐκ ἐς συγγραφὴν πρότερον ἥκοντα, seem to indicate that Pausanias had the story merely from hearsay; moreover, he has no allusion to the animal's tonguelessness. The story, without mention of the statue, recurs once again in Pliny (vii, 87), and is told by Athen., xiii, 596 f.

We return to safer ground in the passage in Book xxxv, claimed for Heliodoros by Keil. He argues that the sentence (§ 134) *pinxit* (i. e. *Athenion*) *in templo Eleusine Phylarchum et Athenis frequentiam quam vocavere syngenicon* is marked off from the rest of the account of Athenion's pictures by the careful notice of locality, a special Heliodoran characteristic, while the rest of the enumeration, being resumed with *item*, points to the juxta-position of different sources. Both the 'Phylarchos' and the 'syngenicon,' moreover, being votive offerings, fall within the range of the *de anathematis*.

As already hinted, it seems probable that these additions from Heliodoros to the older text-books of Xenokrates and Antigonos were made by Pasiteles, the Plinian author whom we pass to consider next.

VI. *Pasiteles of Naples.*

This curiously many-sided man [1], at once worker in marble, in ivory, and in bronze, who was a careful student of animal life, who modelled and chiselled, who could raise a chryselephantine statue or make the design for a silver mirror, and who was the master of a considerable school, is known to us only from Pliny and from one mention in Cicero (*de Div.* i, 36, 79). His date is given by the former (xxxiii, 156) as *circa Pompei Magni* (b. 108 B.C., murd. 48 B.C.) *aetatem*. He received the right of Roman citizenship in 88 B.C. (xxxvi, 40, where see Comm.), at a time when he had presumably attained to manhood [2], if not yet to fame. Of his five volumes concerning famous works of art (*quinque volumina scripsit nobilium operum in toto orbe*, xxxvi, 40) we may expect to find traces in Pliny's work, where a distinguished place is assigned to him in the Indices of authors: in the Indices to xxxiii and xxxv he heads the list of Greek writers, in the Index to xxxiv he closes it; for xxxvi he appears as sole Greek authority. Brunn's researches have proved that a writer appearing in so prominent a position must be a main

---

See Jacobi, *Fleckeisen's Jahrb.* 1873, p. 367 f. ; Gurlitt, *loc. cit.* ; Kalk-mann, *Pausanias der Perieget*, p. 52, note 1 ; Reisch, *Weihgeschenke*, p. 13, note 1. Grote (*Hist.* iii, p. 332) inclined to accept the story of Leaina, but took no notice of the monument.

[1] The fullest account of Pasiteles is still that of Kékulé, *Die Gruppe des Künstlers Menelaos*, 1870, p. 11 ff.; see also Helbig, *Untersuchungen über die campanische Wandmalerei;* p. 10 f.; Wickhoff, *Wiener Genesis*, p. 26 f.

[2] Kékulé, *op. cit.*, p. 11 f.

authority—yet there is no writer so difficult to lay a definite hold on as Pasiteles, when we come to analyze the Plinian text. The only passage (xxxvi, 40) where he was thought to be cited by name for an expression of opinion has fallen away before Furtwängler's criticism : the reading *admirator et Pasitelis* must be restored in place of the unsatisfactory *admiratur et Pasiteles* of the editions [1]. The attempt of Brieger [2] to detect Pasitelean authorship in passages betraying periegetic interests or points of view, and that of Otto Jahn [3] to detect it wherever a work of art was qualified by the epithet *nobilis*, have likewise been disposed of by Furtwängler, whose own association of Pasiteles, however, with all the more properly artistic criticism in Pliny is inadequately based upon the fact that Pasiteles was an artist, since, as we have seen, he only shared that qualification with Xenokrates, Antigonos, and others. Nor are there any accredited fragments of his writings which could serve as clues. We are left, in order to account for his singular position in the Indices, with the sole alternative, already indicated by Brunn [4], of accrediting him with a final and wholesale working up of the old Greek Treatises upon art into his own five volumes. That Pasiteles should thus have elected to return to the Treatises of Xenokrates and Antigonos, rather than apply himself to formulate fresh theories and judgements, accords admirably with his artistic leanings : he created no style of his own, but turned back to Greek models—at times simply copying them, at others adapting or combining them for the presentment of a new subject [5]. Even as we doubtless owe to him and his school [6] not a few of those copies which have rescued Greek statues from complete oblivion, so we may owe it to his reverence for the art-literature of the Greeks that some part of it has filtered down to us through the subsequent medium of the Roman authors. Thus Varro, and Pliny after him, would quote, as their manner was, the names of Xenokrates,

---

[1] Furtwängler, *Plinius und seine Quellen*, p. 40 f.

[2] *De Fontibus*, p. 36.

[3] *Kunsturtheile*, p. 124.

[4] *Sitzungsberichte der Münchener Akademie* (phil.-hist. Classe), 1875, p. 313.

[5] On this point see especially Furtwängler, *Eine argivische Bronze* (50, Winckelmannsprogramm, Berlin, 1890), p. 134 f. ; Hauser, *Die neu-attischen Reliefs*, p. 182 ; cf. the interesting summary of Wolters, *Jahrb.* xi, 1896, p. 3 f, and now Furtwängler, *Statuenkopien im Alterthum*, p. 544 f.

[6] For Stephanos, pupil of Pasiteles, and Menelaos, pupil of Stephanos, see Commentary on xxxvi, 33.

of Antigonos, and other Greek writers, at second or third hand[1]. And that Pasiteles himself should chance not to be quoted in the actual text, for any of the additions which he made, is natural enough if we suppose that he gave merely an uncoloured enumeration of new material, unaccompanied by striking or disputable comment. For it is clear, if we inspect the cases in which authorities are cited in the Plinian text (xxxiv, 61, 68, &c.), that the mention is in no wise determined by the modern conscientiousness in such matters—not even by a sentiment of honour among thieves—but by the occasional wish to disclaim responsibility (cf. p. lxvi). Pliny, at any rate, thought it sufficient to acknowledge the debt which he owed indirectly to Pasiteles, whom he found cited as main Greek authority in Varro, by assigning him the leading place in the Indices, a place corresponding to that which he doubtless occupied in the Varronian lists of Greek authors[2]. Varro seems to have marked his debt to Pasiteles by a general complimentary allusion to his productiveness both as writer and artist (xxxvi, 40). The *quae fecisse nominatim non refertur* is an addition by Pliny, who, not seizing the precise intention of the passage, expected to find the works of Pasiteles enumerated singly in this particular connexion. He forgets that just above he has mentioned on Varro's authority the gold-ivory Jupiter in the temple of Metellus; Varro himself, who was a contemporary and possibly a friend of Pasiteles[3], must have known his works well.

To Pasiteles, moreover, may be traced almost certainly one important extension of the original Greek treatises. These terminated, as we have seen (p. xxi), with Ol. 121, a date which, though purely accidental, was accepted by subsequent writers

[1] That the name of Antigonos reached Pliny only through Pasiteles has been suggested by Wilamowitz, *Antigonos von Karystos*, p. 7.

[2] For Pliny's method of compiling long lists of authors from Varro see in especial the Index to Book viii; it contains the names of twenty-nine Greek authors, not one of which is cited in the text of the work; they appear to have been taken bodily over from Varro, *Re Rust.* i. 1, 8, Pliny even adopting for a long stretch the same order of enumeration; cp. *Amphilocho Athe-naeo—Menandris Prienaeo et Heracleote* with the Varronian *item Amphilochus Atheniensis ... Menandri duo unus Prienaeus alter Heracleotes*. Brunn (*de Indicibus*, p. 48) conjectures that the nine Greek writers περὶ μελιτουργικά, Index to Book xi, were taken straight over by Pliny from the lost work of Hyginus; cf. also Brunn, p. 50, and F. Aly, *Zur Quellenkritik des älteren Plinius*, 1885, p. 7 ff.

[3] Kékulé, p. 17.

as the close of a period of art. It was probably Pasiteles who, while preserving this date as the lower chronological limit for Greek art, brought in the mention of the revival in Ol. 156 (xxxiv, 52)[1]. This revival seems connected with the works of art and decorations executed for the buildings of Metellus, for which at a later date Pasiteles himself had made a Jupiter in ivory and gold. But if Pasiteles be the author of the additions to the chronology of the statuaries he must also be credited with the similar extension of the history of the painters, to include those who flourished from Ol. 156 onwards (xxxv, 135)[2].

To the actual contents of the five volumes *nobilium operum* we have no clue, but from their number a certain width of range may reasonably be argued. The design of Pasiteles was, we may conjecture, to give a general survey of all the arts of antiquity, rather than, like Xenokrates, to develop a definite scheme in relation to the department of art in which he was himself engaged, or which came within the sphere of his personal interest. We may therefore tentatively attribute to him—at any rate without violating any ascertained principle upon which he worked—the otherwise unallotted information in the early parts of xxxiv concerning bronze as used (*a*) for furniture, (*b*) for temple ornaments, (*c*) for statues of the gods, (*d*) for statues of mortals; each category is linked to the following by the purely artificial conception of progress from the less to the more noble. Under these headings the Roman authors afterwards fitted in, as best they could, fresh material concerning Roman art, committing themselves in the process to singular contradictions[3]. Statuary proper, moreover, was further divided into colossal images and lesser images (§ 49). These artificial categories seem likely enough to have been adopted by Pasiteles as a convenient mode of tabulating his vast material. Thus he would further break up the old Greek Treatises into a chronological table and an alphabetical list (above, p. xxii), into which new names or works of special merit were introduced from Heliodoros[4] or other sources, only the *insignes* being reserved for separate treatment. New lists were appended; of these it is significant that the first comprises almost solely the names of artists who were also distinguished for their silver-chasing, a branch of

---

[1] Münzer, *op. cit.*, p. 538; cf. Comm. on xxxiv, 52, l. 4.
[2] Münzer, *l. c.*; Robert, *Arch.*
Märch. p. 135, note 1.
[3] Cf. Münzer, p. 501.
[4] Cf. B. Keil, *Hermes* xxx, 1895, p. 226.

art in which Pasiteles himself specially excelled. Indeed, with regard to the account of the silver-chasers themselves in xxxiii, 154–157, failing information concerning the unknown writers Menaichmos[1] and Menander[2], who appear as authorities in the Index to Bk. xxxiii, or any clue to guide us here to Antigonos, Pasiteles must, for the present, be accepted as authority for the whole passage, with the sole exception of the subsequent interpolations and additions commented upon in the notes.

In Bk. xxxv, again, it may be Pasiteles who divided the painters into two classes, according as they painted in tempera (53–111) or in wax by the process called encaustic (122–149), and who elaborated the curiously artificial theories (§ 149) as to its development. The latter recall the conventional notions of artistic progress unfolded at the commencement of Bk. xxxiv; they are equally devoid of that apprehension of a living growth within a living organism which, in spite of all blunderings, never seems to have deserted Xenokrates. In his written works, as in many of the copies of Greek statuary attributed to him, Pasiteles had caught the sense but not the spirit of the masters he so zealously emulated. Lastly, he arranged the painters of second rank (§§ 138–145), those of third rank (§ 146), and the women painters (§ 148) in three closing alphabetical lists.

That the account of modelling (xxxv, § 151 f.) went through his hands is clear from the exceeding stress he laid upon the indispensable function of modelling in every branch of the plastic arts; his opinion on this subject, quoted by Varro, was probably the main addition Pasiteles made to the original Greek Treatise. That Pasiteles would leave the account of the modellers prefixed to that of the statuaries in bronze is evident from the connexion he established between the two, *plasticen matrem caelaturae et statuariae sculpturaeque dixit.* It has already been noted (p. xxxv) that the exigencies of his plan compelled Pliny to transfer the account to its present awkward position.

Pasiteles is the last writer upon art, properly so called, whose name meets us in the pages of Pliny. His comprehensive work proved not only a rich but a convenient store for the Roman encyclopaedists. Above all does he seem to have been excerpted

---

[1] Above, p. xl, note I.
[2] Only known through Pliny; cf. Susemihl, i, p. 524, note 47.

by Varro, whose extracts from Pasiteles, altered and re-adapted to his own purposes by Pliny, have thus survived down to our own day.

VII. *Varro* (116–28 B. C.)—*Cornelius Nepos* (*circ.* 99–24 B. C.)—
Fabius Vestalis.

The first step in Plinian criticism went from Pliny back to Varro as authority for the bulk of the history upon art.   In the light of a clearer analysis, Varro has fallen again into a subordinate place, overshadowed no longer indeed by his debtor Pliny, but by those earlier authorities to whom he was in his turn indebted.   By the emergence now into a certain definiteness of the Greek authorities : of Xenokrates and Duris, with their very distinctive histories, the one of art, the other of the artists ; of Antigonos in whom this uncongenial and even antagonistic material was worked up into a singular union ; and of Pasiteles, who yet further manipulated, rearranged, and amplified it, the Roman Varro is reduced from his position as authority to the humbler office of final intermediary.   Though he is undoubtedly the author whom Pliny quotes most frequently in his account of the Artists [1], as generally throughout the *Historia Naturalis*, yet any discussion of his literary or scientific personality would be foreign to the present enquiry [2].   It is perhaps fortunate for his great reputation that so few of his voluminous writings have survived : the criticism of their comparatively meagre fragments will, for the world at large, always be outmatched by that picture of his learning which we owe to the genius of Cicero (*Acad. Post.* i, 3, 9), who as a fact neither loved nor admired him, but who, in order to secure by a counter-compliment the gratification of his own vanity, was ready to flatter the πολυ-γραφώτατος *homo* [3]. Neither in the great list of his works preserved by Jerome, nor outside it, do we come upon traces of any work exclusively devoted to the history of art.   The probability is that in the case of Varro, as in that of Pliny, this history formed but

---

[1] xxxiv, 56 ; xxxv, 113, 136, 154, 155 ff. ; xxxvi, 14, 17, 39, 41 ; cf. Furtwängler, *Plinius*, p. 56 ff.

[2] For Varro, see especially Teuffel, *Geschichte der Römischen Literatur*, §§ 164–169, and the sketch in Momm-

sen, vol. III, p. 602 ff. On Varro's compilatory methods see the just estimate of G. Boissier, *Étude sur la vie et les ouvrages de Varron*, p. 27 ff.

[3] Cic. *Ep. ad Att.* xiii, 18.

an episode of a larger work, such for instance as the section on
'Human Affairs' in the 'Antiquities.' Further, we know from
extant fragments [1] that various notices of artists were scattered up
and down a number of Varro's lesser works.

It only remains to indicate the few and comparatively insigni-
ficant passages which we know, in most cases from Pliny's express
mention of him, to be in a more special sense Varronian, for
which Varro is, so far as we know, the final and sole authority.
Even these I shall be content to summarize very briefly,
apologizing for a brevity that may seem disproportioned by
reminding the reader that till lately the disproportion has been
all to the score of Varro, and that as a fact the value of the
Plinian sources increases in the order, not of their nearness to
Pliny, but of their approach to the distant fountain-head.

Varro seems occasionally, as in the passage (xxxiv, 69) on
Praxiteles, to have modified and doctored the Greek account
(above, p. xxii) so as to suit the Roman taste. Occasionally also
he brought in parenthetical scraps of interesting or curious information; for instance, to the statement in xxxvi, § 14, that the
archaic sculptors worked in marble he tacked on the truly
Varronian etymology of the word *lychnites* (see Comm.). For the
rest, his additions mostly express his personal opinion, or retail
his personal knowledge, in many cases, of contemporaries. Thus
from Pliny's paraphrase we learn that to the account he borrowed
from his Greek authors of the Nemesis at Rhamnous (xxxvi, 17)
he added a sentence expressive of his own admiration of the
statue, which he had doubtless seen during his stay at Athens.
Thus too his mention of the lady artist Iaia of Kyzikos, a friend
of his youth, is adjoined to the lists of women painters (xxxv, 147).
In like manner he praises the marvellously naturalistic modelling
of fruits by another acquaintance, Possis (*ib.* 155); this is followed
(*ib.* 155) by the laudatory notice of the friend of Lucullus, the
Athenian Arkesilaos—who may well have been known to Varro—
and of Pasiteles (above, p. lxxix). Further, it appears from § 154
that he had combined the Greek account of modelling, as he took
it from Pasiteles, with some account of the art in Rome, and in
this same connexion of modelling, though scarcely in its present
context, he had given yet another reminiscence of his Athenian

[1] When the whole of the Varronian fragments dealing with art-questions are collected and analyzed, con- siderable traces of lost Greek writings are certain to be revealed; see e.g. *Ling. Lat.* ix, 6, 12; *ib.* ix, 18.

visit in his explanation of the term *Ceramicus*. Two statements are still more closely personal: he mentioned that he had once possessed (*habuisse*) a bronze figure by the silver-chaser Mentor (xxxiii, 154), and a marble group of a Lioness and Cupids by Arkesilaos (xxxvi, 41). From his use of the past tense it has been justly surmised that Varro had lost these treasures at the time of the proscriptions of B. C. 43.

It is evident that Varro is the authority for both the genre pictures by Peiraikos and the huge pictures by Serapion, as well as for the portraits by Dionysios (xxxv, 113, 114). All three artists are placed antithetically to one another, and moreover, as we learn from § 148, they were evidently all three contemporaries of Varro. Upon these follows the mention of Kalates, a painter only once again mentioned in literature, namely in Varro's Life of the Roman People (fr. 1 Keil). Lastly, it is at least a significant coincidence that, while the pictures of Antiphilos mentioned by Pliny (*ib.* § 114) were either inside or in the neighbourhood of the Gallery of Pompeius, the same painter is mentioned in Varro's Treatise on Rustic Affairs (iii, 2, 5), in that part of the dialogue which is supposed to take place B. C. 54, a few months after the dedication of the theatre and the Gallery of Pompeius in the Field of Mars[1]. It shows, at any rate, that Varro, writing after his eightieth year, was still interested in the pictures of the Egyptian painter, whom he may have discussed in a previous work.

To Varro likewise Pliny owes, as appears from xxxv, 136, a number of notices of the high prices paid for works of art—mostly pictures. Varro had apparently collected together from his Greek authors a number of these instances, and had at the same time given, for the benefit of Roman readers, the Roman equivalent of the Greek talent: hence the *talentum Atticum $\overline{XVI}$ taxat M. Varro* (*loc. cit.*) of Pliny. Three of the works of art which obtained specially high prices are mentioned together in vii, 126 (where, however, there is no reference to Varro's evaluation of the talent), and again separately at different parts of the account of the painters: thus the price paid by Attalos for the 'Dionysos' of Aristeides of Thebes is given again twice in xxxv, 24 and 100; the price, 'its weight in gold,' of the picture by Boularchos, *ib.* 55; lastly, the price paid by Caesar for the 'Aias' and the 'Medeia' of Timomachos, *ib.* 136[2]. To these

---

[1] Münzer, p. 541.   [2] Münzer, *l. c.*

undoubted instances of Varronian authorship I incline to add as a fourth the notice of the price paid for the 'Diadumenos' of Polykleitos (xxxiv, 55).

Cornelius Nepos, who at one time (e. g. Furtwängler, *Plinius*, p. 25) was credited with the anecdotic portions in Pliny, which recent criticism has gradually but surely traced back to Duris, is mentioned in xxxv, 16 as Pliny's authority for the existence of an early Greek painter Ekphantos, who accompanied the Corinthian Damaratos in his flight to Italy. Presumably, therefore, Pliny also obtained from him the mention of the Corinthian potters, also companions of Damaratos (*ib.* 152). These extracts may be from the same work of Nepos, dealing apparently with Roman customs, from which Pliny has citations in other parts of the *Historia* (ix, 61, 136; x, 60, &c.) [1].

For Fabius Vestalis, *qui de pictura scripsit* (Index, xxxv), and who possibly had also written on statuary and sculpture, since he figures in the Indices to xxxiv and xxxvi, not even the acuteness of Münzer has been able to recover one single fragment out of the Plinian history. He is entirely unknown [2], save for the references in Pliny [3] (see Addenda).

VIII. *G. Licinius Mucianus* (date of birth unknown; died before B. C. 77, cf. Plin. xxxii, 62).

To the History of the Artists which he borrowed from Varro, Pliny made one notable group of additions from the work in which his contemporary G. Licinius Mucianus, *ter consul* [4], had published the more or less trustworthy observations compiled during a prolonged sojourn in the East. These additions concern the works of art of the coast cities of Asia-Minor and the adjacent islands, a region that had practically lain outside the ken of the Greek art-writers Xenokrates (cf. p. xxi) and Antigonos [5], and after them of Pasiteles [6].

[1] Münzer, p. 542 f.
[2] Teuffel, § 267, 11.
[3] Indices, vii, xxxiv–xxxvi; cf. vii, 213.
[4] Cited Indices to xxxi, xxxiii, xxxv, xxxvi, and repeatedly in the body of the *Historia* (see Detlefsen's Index).

[5] We must except, of course, the traditions derived by Antigonos from Duris concerning the island-schools of the Aegean.
[6] Pasiteles, so far as we can tell, seems not to have enlarged the geographical range of his predecessor, except for the notice of the Greek artists in

Mucianus, coming from the South [1], would first encounter the civilization of the Aegean in Rhodes (v, 132 ; xix, 12 ; xxxiv, 36) ; of the islands which he visited, Delos (iv, 66), Syros (*ib.* 67), and Andros (ii, 231) lay furthest to the West, Samothrake (xi, 167) to the North ; along the coast proper he came at least as far as Kyzikos (xxxi, 19). Pliny not unfrequently introduces the notices of works of art extant within this geographical district by such words as *hodie* or *nunc*, showing that he is quoting from a contemporary or recent authority. Finally, we have also to guide us, in our search for the information borrowed by Pliny from Mucianus, our knowledge of the man's superstitious credulousness, of his keen interest for everything marvellous or miraculous [2]. The greater number of the additions to be traced back to Mucianus have been detected by Leopold Brunn in an exhaustive dissertation [3], and accepted as Mucianian by the later commentators of Pliny [4]. The following list of the passages derived from Mucianus in the art-books follows a geographical order from south to north.

1. *Rhodes.*

LINDOS. That Mucianus visited its temple of Athena and noted its treasures and curiosities in detail, appears from xix, 12, where Pliny, specially using the word *nuperrime*, describes on the authority of Mucianus the cuirass of the Egyptian king Amasis, there preserved ; each thread in this cuirass was composed of three hundred and sixty-five strands ; Pliny adds that Mucianus, who had *verified* the fact, had remarked that 'almost nothing was left of the cuirass owing to these frequent verifications [5].' Hence the following descriptions of works of art in the same temple of Lindos have been justly referred to him [6].

1. xxxiii, 81 : a cup, with the strange story attached to it that

---

Rome employed on the buildings of Metellus.

[1] Münzer, *op. cit.*, p. 544.

[2] E. g. he was in the habit of wearing round his neck a fly tied up in a linen rag as a remedy against ophthalmia, Plin. xxviii, 5. I am not concerned here to reconcile such statements with the glowing tributes paid to Mucianus by Tacitus (*Hist.* i, 10 ; ii, 5, &c.). For an estimate of Mucianus see especially Teuffel, § 314.

[3] *De C. Licinio Muciano*, Diss., Leipzig, 1870.

[4] Cf. Furtwängler, *Plinius und seine Quellen*, pp. 52–56 ; Oehmichen, *Plinianische Studien*, pp. 141–149.

[5] . . . *Quod se expertum nuperrime prodidit Mucianus ter cos., parvasque iam reliquias eius superesse hac experientium iniuria.*

[6] First by Brieger, *de Fontibus*, p. 59 ff.

it was dedicated by Helena, who had moulded it on her breasts. (L. Brunn, 43.)

2. xxxiii, 155 : silver cups chased by Boëthos, the *hodie* showing that Pliny was quoting from a contemporary authority. (L. Brunn, 44.)

RHODES (city): 3. xxxiii, 155 : silver cups chased by Akragas and Mys. (L. Brunn, 44.)

4. xxxiv, 36 : *Rhodi etiamnum LXXIII signorum esse Mucianus ter cos. prodidit.* (L. Brunn, 12.)

5. *Ib.* 41, 42 : the description of the colossus of Rhodes (L. Brunn, 45); it evidently rests on the testimony of an eye-witness, and the delighted insistence on the marvellous appearance (*miraculo est*) of the fallen colossus, and its size and its cost, betrays the special bent of Mucianus [1].

6. *Ib.* § 42 : *Sunt alii centum numero in eadem urbe colossi minores* (L. Brunn, 45); the words are inseparable from the notices of the large colossus, and moreover recall xxxvi, 37.

7. xxxv, 69 : the picture by Parrhasios of Meleager, Herakles, and Perseus, thrice struck by lightning and yet not effaced— *hoc ipso miraculum auget*—(L. Brunn, 46), the insistence upon the miracle being thoroughly after the manner of Mucianus.

8. To the seven passages on Rhodian works of art, which critics agree in tracing back to Mucianus, should be added the mention in xxxiv, 63, of the chariot of the Sun by Lysippos, *in primis vero quadriga cum Sole Rhodiorum* [2].

II. *Knidos.*

9. xxxvi, 20, 21 : description of the Aphrodite of Knidos; it is that of an eye-witness, who is interested neither in the motive nor technique of the statue, but whose tourist's curiosity was roused by the story of King Nikomedes, by the tradition that the artist had made two rival statues, the one draped, the other not, and finally by the anecdote of the statue's lover [3].

10. *Ib.*: *Sunt in Cnido et alia signa marmorea inlustrium artificum*—inseparable from the preceding notice of the Aphrodite ; cf. above, 6 and 5 [4].

[1] Brieger, *l. c.*
[2] Münzer (p. 504) correctly omits it from the original Xenokratic list of Lysippian works, but makes no further suggestion as to its authorship.
[3] The passage first referred to Mucianus by Furtwängler, *op. cit.,* p. 53 f.; cf. Oehmichen, *op. cit.,* p. 148.
[4] Furtwängler, *l. c.*

III. *Halikarnassos.*

11. xxxvi, 30, 31 : description of the Mausoleion ; it resembles in character that of the Knidian Aphrodite ; the size, the beauty, and the labour expended upon the monument are described, but nothing is said of the subject presented ; the words *hodieque certant manus* point to a contemporary authority [1].

IV. *Miletos.*

12. xxxiv, 75 : Apollo of Kanachos, with the wonderful stag. That this is an addition to the original Greek account of the artist has already been pointed out (above, p. xxii) ; the periegetic character of the description, and the insistence upon trivial peculiarities which were perhaps only the result of accident [2], are characteristic of Mucianus [3].

V. *Samos.*

13. xxxv, 93 : portrait of Habron by Apelles [4].

VI. *Ephesos.*

14. xxxvi, 95 : description of Temple of Artemis ; it is evidently from the same hand as xvi, 213 (= App. IV), where Mucianus is quoted by name. Besides, the description bears the same character as that of the Mausoleion (No. 11): the interest of the describer centred in the wonder of the foundations, in the size and number of the columns, and in the apparition of the goddess to the tired artist.

15. *Ib.* 32 : the Hekate, against whose radiance the guardians of the temple advised visitors to shade their eyes. (L. Brunn, 51.)

16. xxxv, 92 : the portrait of Alexander by Apelles ; the description seems by Mucianus; the price of the work is dwelt upon, and the motive of the thunderbolt mentioned only because *digiti eminere videntur et fulmen extra tabulam esse.* (L. Brunn, 53.)

17. xxxv, 93 : picture of the procession of a Megabyzos by Apelles. (L. Brunn, 53.)

---

[1] First attributed to Mucianus by Furtwängler, *l. c.*

[2] See note on passage. Ernest Gardner, *Handbook of Greek Sculpture*, p. 194, note 1, hints at the same possibility. If my memory serves me right, it was Mr. A. S. Murray who, some years ago, in the course of conversation, first suggested to me that the puzzling Plinian description of the stag was a periegetic fable invented out of some trivial failure in the casting.

[3] Oehmichen, *Plin. Studien*, p. 142 f.

[4] Oehmichen, p. 146.

18. *Ib.* 129 : picture of the Madness of Odysseus by Euphranor ; Mucianus interpreted the action of Palamedes differently to other authorities [1] (see Comm.).

19. *Ib.* 131 : grave picture of a priest of Artemis by Nikias. (L. Brunn, 54.)

20. xxxiv, 58 : Apollo by Myron, taken away by Antonius and restored to the Ephesians by Augustus, in obedience to a dream. Münzer (p. 544) has astutely detected the apocryphal character of a story invented by a jealous priesthood in emulation of their Samian neighbours. (See Comm. on pass.)

VII. *Smyrna.*

21. xxxvi, 32 : the drunken old woman by Myron (for the epithet *ebria*, see Comm.) [2].

VIII. *Iasos.*

22. xxxvi, 12 : Artemis, by the sons of Archermos [3] ; evidently from the same writer as following fragment [4].

IX. *Chios.*

23. *Ib.* 13 : mask of Artemis by the same artists ; the Mucianian character patent in the description of the face, which appears sad to those who enter the temple, gay to those who leave it.

X. *Pergamon.*

From xxxvi, 131 we learn that Mucianus was in that region ; accordingly we should perhaps refer to him the notices concerning Pergamene art. These are foreign to the original treatises (above, p. xxi) : Xenokrates lived too early to take Pergamon into account ; Antigonos, although himself one of the artists employed by the Pergamene kings (xxxiv, 84), accepted the chronological limit of the Xenokratic Treatises. Pasiteles did the same, marking his only addition to the chronology as a 'Revival' (above, p. lxxix f.). It only remains to conjecture that Pliny took from Mucianus his descriptions of Pergamene works [5].

[1] Rightly attributed to Mucianus by Oehmichen, *l.c.*, as against Furtwängler (p. 44), who gave the passage to Pasiteles.

[2] Cf. Furtwängler, *op. cit.*, p. 54.

[3] Oehmichen, p. 147 ; cf. Münzer, *op. cit.*, p. 525, note 1.

[4] That Mucianus visited Iasos appears from ix, 33.

[5] Cf. Münzer, *op. cit.*, p. 544.

24. xxxiv, 84: *Plures artifices . . . Antigonus*; the words *qui volumina condidit de sua arte* may be an addition of Pliny's own.

25. xxxv, 60: *Aiax fulmine incensus* by Apollodoros, the *hodie* pointing clearly to a contemporary authority[1]. (Oehmichen, 71.)

26. xxxvi, 24: the 'symplegma' by Kephisodotos, with the epigram attached thereto. (Oehmichen, 81.)

XI. *Samothrake.*

From xi, 167 it appears that Mucianus visited this island; hence we may refer to him:

27. xxxvi, 25: an Aphrodite and Pothos by Skopas; the words *sanctissimis caerimoniis coluntur* are characteristic of the pious and superstitious Mucianus. (Oehmichen, 78.)

XII. *Parion.*

28. xxxiv, 78: Herakles by Hagesias (Oehmichen, 67). That this is an addition to the early Greek account was pointed out above, p. xxiv. Parion, moreover, only became a *colonia* under Augustus (see Comm.). It was not known as such to Varro, who only refers to it as Parion (cf. vii, 13, in *Hellesponto circa Parium*, on the authority of Varro); thus Mucianus remains the only one of the Plinian authors known to have visited this region at a time when it would be generally described as *P. colonia*.

29. xxxvi, 22: nude Eros by Praxiteles *in Pario colonia*, with the story of its lover Alketas of Rhodes, closely resembling the story of the lover of the Knidian Aphrodite. (Oehmichen, 68.)

XIII. *Lysimacheia.*

30. xxxiv, 56: a Hermes by Polykleitos, no longer extant when Mucianus visited the city[2].

This bald list serves to indicate the immediate indebtedness of Pliny to Mucianus, but there arises the further question whence Mucianus derived his own information. That he relied in great measure, perhaps mainly, on the tales of ciceroni, is evident from the nature of what he relates. Yet in some cases, e. g. in the description of the Mausoleion, or of the colossus of Rhodes, he

---

[1] Furtwängler, *Plinius*, p. 53.

[2] First attributed to Mucianus by Münzer, *op. cit.*, p. 525. In a private note Münzer further points out to me that the description of the temple of Erythreia (xi, 111, and xxxv, 161)—a city which lay in the route of Mucianus —must be referred to this author: ' it has all the characteristic signs: personal observation and interest in the miraculous.'

doubtless had handbooks which informed him of such details as price and size, or gave the names of the artists employed. To ascertain what these handbooks may have been, and whether fragments of Greek writings other than those of the Xenokrates-Antigonos-Pasiteles group reached Pliny through Mucianus, is a task which lies outside the compass of the present essay.

IX. *Pliny's own additions.—Roman Museography.*
Retrospect.

Besides the Varronian additions to the material derived from the Greek art-treatises, and besides the material which he derived independently from Varro, Pliny enriched his account of the artists by notices concerning the locality in Rome of a number of Greek works. It is well known that in the days of Pliny, and already long before his time, Rome displayed within her galleries, her temples, and her public places an unrivalled collection of works of art, gathered together from every part of the Hellenic world. From the day when Marcellus had first induced the Romans to admiration of Greek art by displaying the spoils of Syracuse[1], down to that crowning day of a triple triumph when Caesar Augustus celebrated his victory over the last of the Hellenic powers[2], statues and other works of art had come to be as much a part of the pageantry of triumphs as captives or military booty[3]. The solemn dedication of these objects in some public building was the natural sequel of the triumphal procession. The great generals of the Republic[4], and after them the Emperors[5], had shown themselves zealous for the preservation and arrangement of these collections. Only a short while before Pliny compiled

[1] Liv. xxv, 40; see Comm. on xxxv, 24, l. 16.

[2] In 23 B. C. ; for the works of art brought to Rome from Alexandria, see Wunderer, *Manibiae Alexandrinae.*

[3] So much so that works of art were even displayed in triumphs over barbaric and Western nations; the art booty acquired from Macedonia by Aemilius Paullus, for instance, seems to have formed an inexhaustible mine whence other conquerors could draw;

cf. Comm. on xxxiv, 54, the statues dedicated by Catulus in the temple of the Fortune of the Day, and on xxxiv, 77, the Minerva dedicated by Q. Lutatius Catulus below the Capitol.

[4] E. g. Gallery of Octavius, xxxiv, 13; Gallery of Pompeius, xxxv, 114, 126, 132.

[5] E. g. Gallery of Octavia, xxxiv, 31; xxxv, 139; xxxvi, 24, 35, &c.; and consult the Museographic Index (ii).

his history of the artists, his patron Vespasian had opened the great Temple of Peace, destined with its surrounding Forum [1] to receive, alongside the treasures of the Temple of Jerusalem, those Greek masterpieces which the greed of Nero had gathered within the Golden House [2]. The pages of Pliny are certainly the richest mine of information concerning the art treasures of Rome. Owing, moreover, to his preference for books over personal observation of actual fact, Pliny not unfrequently records the locality of works of art which had disappeared in his day [3]. Yet a discussion of the sources whence Pliny obtained his museographic information, though of matchless interest for the study of Roman history and topography, lies entirely outside an inquiry concerned with the Greek element in Pliny. It suffices to point out that Pliny doubtless had straight from Varro (p. lxxxiii f.) most of the Roman notices relating to events up to the close of the Republic; that for the Early Empire, up to the reign of Nero, he may have borrowed from authors such as Deculo [4] or Fenestella [5]; while his allusions to Nero [6], and his eulogies of the Flavian Emperors, and of the works of art in their possession [7], were probably part of the material he had himself compiled for his own *History of Rome*, a work embracing the period from the accession of Nero to the Judaic triumph of Vespasian and Titus [8].

It is little or nothing, then, of intrinsic importance from our point of view, that Pliny added to the Greek Treatises as he found them excerpted in Varro. At most does he bring the information thus derived from the Greeks into consonance with the taste of his day by occasional flashes of rhetoric, such as the repeated lament over the decay of art [9]; his outburst of admiration at the power of art, which 'could turn the eyes of the Senate of the Roman people for so many years upon Glaukion and his

[1] xxxiv, 84.

[2] *ib.*

[3] This remark applies to a great portion of the Roman statues mentioned in the earlier part of xxxiv. Cf. also xxxiv, 69 (statues by Praxiteles which had stood in front of the Temple of Felicity); xxxv, 99, the Dionysos and Ariadne of Aristeides.

[4] From whom he had the anecdote of Tiberius' passion for the *Apoxyomenos* of Lysippos, xxxiv, 62; it is

evidently from the same source as the mention of the 'Archigallus' loved by Tiberius, in xxxv, 70; see Oehmichen, *Plin. Studien*, p. 123.

[5] Cf. Oehmichen, *op. cit.* p. 125.

[6] xxxiv, 45, 48, 63, 84; xxxv, 51, 91, 120, &c.

[7] See especially xxxiv, 84; the appreciation of the *astragalizontes* belonging to Titus in xxxiv, 55, and of the *Laocoon* in xxxvi, 37.

[8] *Praef. Hist. Nat.* 20.

[9] Cf. xxxiv, 5 ff.; xxxv, 4, 29.

son Aristippos, persons otherwise quite obscure[1];' his simulated
indignation at the cruelty of Phalaris[2]; and his allusion to the
present merited dishonour of that Carthaginian Hercules to whom
human victims had once been offered up[3].

In estimating Pliny's account of the artists we must never
forget that it was inserted into the *Historia Naturalis* as a digression, which was artificially linked to the history of mineralogy on
the pretext of the materials employed. In doing this Pliny was
responding rather to the curiosity of his time in artistic matters[4]
than following any special inclination of his own. If Pliny cared
for art at all, it was only for its most realistic and imitative
aspects. He admires the brutal realism of the dog licking her
wounds[5], and in the workshop of Zenodoros his enthusiasm is
roused by the colossal model which, even when covered with its
wax tubings, betrayed an extraordinary likeness to Nero[6].
Occasionally too—and we may pay this tribute to our author as
we take our leave of him—we seem to detect that, if he appears
too often as an indiscriminating compiler, this is not so much
through total lack of the critical faculty as through lack of time.
At least he does not omit to rail at those critics who ascribed
to Polykleitos (the elder namesake being the only Polykleitos
known to him) the statue of Hephaistion, the friend of Alexander, although Hephaistion had lived nearly one hundred years
after the artist[7], while in xxxiv, 79 he expresses by a vigorous
turn of phrase his astonishment at finding Daidalos, whom in
his hurry he confuses with the old Homeric craftsman, figuring
among the artists of the historic age[8]. Yet the critical note
is rare, and, in the larger inquiry concerning the sources whence
Pliny drew, his own estimate of these sources appears but as
a trivial accident.

Thus the tendency of modern research is to lessen more
and more the importance of Pliny's personal contribution in his
account of the artists, as indeed in the whole of his great work.
Yet, by a singular irony, the fundamental faults of his work have
bestowed upon it a permanent value. He has given us what is
better than any original criticism which his century could have
produced—a short compilation which is, to borrow the word he

[1] xxxv, 28.
[2] xxxiv, 89.　[3] xxxvi, 39.
[4] Cf. Bertrand, *Études*, p. 329 ff.,
and his remarks, *ib.*, on the passages

in Plutarch treating of art.
[5] xxxiv, 38.　[6] *ib.* 45-46.
[7] *ib.* 64.
[8] *ib.* 76.

applies to the whole *Historia*, the ' storehouse ' or *thesaurus* wherein are consigned fragments from the lost text-books of Xenokrates, from the Biographies of Duris and Antigonos, nay, priceless sayings that had filtered through the ages from the very writings of Apelles and Pamphilos [1].

---

[1] A short but admirably just estimate of the precise value of Pliny's work is given by J. W. Mackail, *Latin Literature*, 1895, p. 197.

BIBLIOGRAPHY[1].

Editions. BARBARUS, Rome, 1492 ; DALECAMPIUS, Lyons, 1586 ; GRO-
NOVIUS, Leiden, 1669 ; HARDUINUS, Paris, 1685 ; SILLIG, Gotha, 1853–55 ;
LUDWIG VON JAN, Leipzig, 1854–65 ; DETLEFSEN, Berlin, 1866–1873 ;
URLICHS, *Chrestomathia Pliniana*, Berlin, 1857 ; LITTRÉ (Text and Trans-
lation), Paris, 1883.

AMELUNG, WALTHER : *Die Basis des Praxiteles aus Mantinea*
(Munich, 1895).

ARNDT–BRUCKMANN : *Photographische Einzelaufnahmen antiker
Sculpturen* (Munich, 1893, &c.).

BABELON : *Monnaies de la République Romaine* (Paris, 1885, 1886) ;
Cabinet des Antiques à la Bibliothèque Nationale (Paris, 1887).

BAUMEISTER : *Denkmäler des Klassischen Alterthums* (Munich
and Leipzig, 1885–1888).

BECKER, W. A.: *Römische Topographie* (being the first vol. of
Handbuch der röm. Alterthümer, Leipzig, 1843).

BERGER, ERNST : *Beiträge zur Entwickelungsgeschichte der Malertechnik* (I and II, Munich, 1893 and 1895).

BERGK : *Poetae Lyrici Graeci* (ed. 4, Leipzig, 1878–82).

BERNOULLI, J. J.: *Römische Ikonographie* (Stuttgart, 1882–1894).

BERTRAND, ÉDOUARD : *Études sur la Peinture et la Critique d'Art
dans l'Antiquité* (Paris, 1893).

BLÜMNER : *Technologie und Terminologie der Gewerbe und Künste
bei den Griechen und Römern* (Leipzig, 1875–1887).

BRUNN, HEINRICH : *Geschichte der Griechischen Künstler* (Brunswick,
1853 and 1859 ; the second edition, Stuttgart, 1889, is merely a
reprint of the first)=*K. G.*

---

[1] Only the most important works and those most constantly cited in the
notes are given. The bibliography of the Plinian sources will be found on
p. xv f. of the Introdnction.

BRUNN–BRUCKMANN : *Denkmäler Griechischer und Römischer Sculptur* (Munich, 1888–1895).

COLLIGNON, M. : *Histoire de la Sculpture Grecque* (vol. I, Paris, 1892) =*Sculpt. Grecque.*

CURTIUS, ERNST : *Stadtgeschichte von Athen* (Berlin, 1891).

DETLEFSEN : *De Arte Romanorum antiquissima* (I, II, III, Glückstadt, 1867, 1868, 1880).

DITTENBERGER AND PURGOLD : *Die Inschriften von Olympia* (Berlin, 1896).

FICK, A. : *Die Griechischen Personennamen* (second edition, Göttingen, 1894).

FÖRSTER, G. H. : *Die Sieger in den Olympischen Spielen* (I, II, Zwickau, 1891, 1892).

FRÄNKEL, MAX : *Die Inschriften von Pergamon* (Berlin, 1890).

FREEMAN, E. : *History of Sicily* (Oxford, 1891–1894).

FRIEDERICHS–WOLTERS : *Die Gipsabgüsse antiker Bildwerke* (Berlin, 1885).

FURTWÄNGLER, A. : *Der Dornauszieher und der Knabe mit der Gans* (Berlin, 1876).

—— *Die Sammlung Sabouroff* (Berlin, 1883, 1887).

—— *Meisterwerke der Griechischen Plastik* (Leipzig—Berlin, 1893).

—— *Masterpieces of Greek Sculpture*, ed. by E. Sellers London, 1895).

—— *Statuenkopien im Alterthum* (Munich, 1896).

GARDNER, E. A. : *A Handbook of Greek Sculpture* (London, 1896).

GARDNER, P. : *The Types of Greek Coins* (Cambridge, 1883).

GARDNER, P., and IMHOOF–BLUMER : *A Numismatic Commentary on Pausanias* (London, 1887, reprinted from *Journal of Hellenic Studies*).

GARDTHAUSEN, V. : *Augustus und seine Zeit* (Leipzig, 1891, 1896).

GILBERT, OTTO : *Geschichte und Topographie der Stadt Rom* (Leipzig, 1883–1890).

GURLITT, W. : *Ueber Pausanias* (Graz, 1890).

HARTWIG, PAUL : *Die Griechischen Meisterschalen* (Stuttgart and Berlin, 1893).

HEAD, B. V. : *Guide to the Coins of the Ancients* (second edition, London, 1881).

ḤELBIG : *Wandgemälde der vom Vesuv verschütteten Städte Campaniens* (Leipzig, 1868)=*Wandgem.*

—— *Untersuchungen über die Campanische Wandmalerei* (Leipzig, 1873)=*Untersuch.*

HELBIG : *Guide to the Public Collections of Classical Antiquities in Rome*, English ed. by James, F., and Findlay Muirhead (Leipzig, 1895) = *Class. Ant.*

HILLER VON GAERTRINGEN : *Inscriptiones Graecae Insularum Rhodi, Chalces, Carpathi cum Saro Casi* (Berlin, 1895).

HITZIG AND BLÜMNER : *Pausaniae Graeciae descriptio* (I, 1 Attica, Berlin, 1896).

HOLLAND, PHILEMON : *The Historie of the World, commonly called the Natural Historie of C. Plinius Secundus* (London, 1635).

JACOBI, FRANZ : *Grundzüge einer Museographie der Stadt Rom zur Zeit des Kaisers Augustus* (Part I, Spires, 1884).

JAHN, OTTO : *Kleine Beiträge zur Geschichte der Alten Literatur* (in Sächsische Berichte, Leipzig, 1857, p. 284).

JORDAN, H.: *Topographie der Stadt Rom im Alterthum* (1871–1885).

KIEPERT, H., ET HUELSEN, CH.: *Formae Urbis Romae Antiquae* (Berlin, 1896).

KROKER, E.: *Gleichnamige Griechische Künstler* (Leipzig, 1883).

KUHNERT, E.: *Statue und Ort in ihrem Verhältniss bei den Griechen* (in the Jahrbücher f. Classische Philologie, Supplementband xiv, Leipzig, 1884).

KÜLB, H.: *C. Plin. Secundus Naturgeschichte übersetzt und erläutert von . . .* (Stuttgart).

LANGE, JULIUS : *Fremstilling af Menneskeskikkelsen i dens aeldeste Periode indtil Højdepunktet af den graeske Kunst* (Kopenhagen, 1892).

LOEWY, E.: *Untersuchungen zur Griechischen Künstlergeschichte* (Vienna, 1883) = *Untersuch.*

—— *Inschriften Griechischer Bildhauer* (Leipzig, 1885) = *I. G. B.*

MARQUARDT : *Privatleben der Römer* (Leipzig, 1886).

—— *Römische Staatsverwaltung* (Leipzig, 1894).

MAYHOFF : *Lucubrationes Plinianae* (1865).

—— *Novae Lucubrationes Plinianae* (1874).

MOMMSEN, TH.: *Römische Geschichte* (7th edition, Berlin, 1882).

—— *Res Gestae divi Augusti* (Berlin, 1883).

—— *Römisches Staatsrecht* (Leipzig, 1887, 1888).

—— *Römische Forschungen* (Berlin, 1864).

—— *Geschichte des Römischen Münzwesens* (Berlin, 1860).

MÜLLER, J.: *Der Stil des älteren Plinius* (Innsbruck, 1883).

MÜLLER, OTTFRIED : *Handbuch der Archaeologie der Kunst* (third edition, by Welcker ; Stuttgart, 1878).

MURRAY, A. S.: *A Handbook of Greek Archaeology* (London, 1892).

OTTO : *Sprichwörter der Römer* (Leipzig, 1890).

OVERBECK : *Schriftquellen zur Geschichte der Bildenden Künste bei den Griechen* (Leipzig, 1868) = *S. Q.*

PAULY : *Real-Encyclopädie* (new edition, by G. Wissowa, Stuttgart, 1893–).

PREGER : *Inscriptiones Graecae Metricae ex scriptoribus praeter Anthologiam collectae* (Leipzig, 1891).

PRELLER : *Römische Mythologie* (third edition, by H. Jordan, Berlin, 1881).

—— *Griechische Mythologie* (fourth edition, by C. Robert, Berlin, 1894).

RAOUL-ROCHETTE : *Peintures antiques inédites* (Paris, 1836).

REINACH, S. : *Chroniques d'Orient* (1883–1895, reprinted from Revue Archéologique).

—— *Antiquités du Bosphore Cimmérien* (Paris, 1892).

—— *Bronzes figurés de la Gaule Romaine* (Paris, 1894).

REISCH, EMIL : *Griechische Weihgeschenke* (Leipzig, 1890).

ROBERT, C. : *Bild und Lied* (Berlin, 1881).

—— *Die Iliupersis des Polygnot*, Halle'sches Winckelmannsprogramm xvii (Halle, 1893).

—— *Die Marathonschlacht in der Poikile, und weiteres über Polygnot*, Halle'sches Winckelmannsprogramm xviii, 1895.

—— *Votivgemälde eines Apobaten nebst einem Excurs über den sog. Ares Borghese*, Halle'sches Winckelmannsprogramm xix, 1895.

ROSCHER, W. H. : *Lexikon der Griechischen und Römischen Mythologie* (Leipzig, 1884–).

v. SCHNEIDER, ROBERT : *Album auserlesener Gegenstände der antiken Sammlungen des allerh. Kaiserhauses* (Vienna, 1895).

SCHREIBER, THEODOR : *Die Alexandrinische Toreutik* (Leipzig, 1894).

—— *Hellenistische Reliefbilder* (Leipzig, 1894).

SILLIG, JULIUS : *Dictionary of the Artists of Antiquity* (trans. by H. W. Williams, London, 1837).

SUSEMIHL : *Geschichte der Griechischen Literatur in der Alexandrinerzeit* (I, II, Leipzig, 1891, 1892).

TEUFFEL : *Geschichte der Römischen Literatur* (fifth edition, by L. Schwabe, Leipzig, 1890).

TURNEBUS : *Adversariorum libri* xxx (Paris, 1580).

URLICHS, LUDWIG v. : *Anfänge der Griechischen Künstlergeschichte* (Würzburg, 1871, 1872).

—— *Die Malerei in Rom vor Caesar's Dictatur* (Würzburg, 1876).

URLICHS, LUDWIG V.: *Griechische Statuen im Republikanischen Rom* (Würzburg, 1880).

—— *Das hölzerne Pferd* (Würzburg, 1881).

—— *Pergamenische Inschriften* (Würzburg, 1883).

—— *Arkesilaos* (Würzburg, 1887).

WACHSMUTH, C.: *Die Stadt Athen im Alterthum* (I, II, Leipzig, 1874, 1890).

WEISSHÄUPL: *Grabgedichte der Griechischen Anthologie* (Vienna, 1889).

WICKHOFF, FRANZ: *Die Wiener Genesis* (Vienna, 1895).

WINCKELMANN: *Geschichte der Kunst des Alterthums* (first edition, 1763; I quote from the Vienna edition of 1776).

—— *History of Ancient Art*, tr. by G. Henry Lodge (London, 1881).

WUNDERER: *Manibiae Alexandrinae, eine Studie zur Geschichte des römischen Kunstraubes* (Würzburg, 1894).

Ann. Inst. = *Annali dell' Istituto di Corrispondenza Archeologica* (Rome, 1829–1885).

Ant. Denkm. = *Antike Denkmäler, herausgegeben vom K. Deutschen Archäologischen Institut* (Berlin, 1887).

Arch. Anz. = *Archäologischer Anzeiger* (a supplement printed at the end of the *Archäologisches Jahrbuch*).

Arch. Ep. Mitth. = *Archäologische Epigraphische Mittheilungen aus Oesterreich-Ungarn.*

A. Z. = *Archäologische Zeitung* (Berlin, 1843–1885).

Ath. Mitth. = *Mittheilungen des K. deutschen Archäologischen Instituts, Athenische Abtheil.* (Athens, 1876–).

Berl. Phil. Woch. = *Berliner Philologische Wochenschrift.*

B. C. H. = *Bulletin de Correspondance Hellénique* (Athens, 1877).

Bull. Inst. = *Bullettino dell' Istituto di Corrispondenza Archeologica* (Rome, 1829–1885).

Class. Rev. = *Classical Review* (London, 1887–).

Δελτ. = Δελτίον 'Αρχαιολογικόν (Athens, 1888–).

'Εφ. 'Αρχ. = 'Εφημερὶς 'Αρχαιολογική (Athens, 1883–).

Fleckeisen's Jahrb. = *Neue Jahrbücher für Philologie u. Pädagogik* (ed. Fleckeisen u. Masius).

Hermes = *Hermes, Zeitschrift für Classische Philologie* (Berlin, 1866–).

Jahrb. = *Jahrbuch des K. deutschen Archäologischen Instituts* (Berlin, 1886–).

J. H. S. = *Journal of Hellenic Studies* (London, 1880–).

c *BIBLIOGRAPHY*

Mon. Inst. = *Monumenti inediti dell' Istituto di Corrispondenza Archeologica* (Rome, 1829–1885).

Rev. Arch. = *Revue Archéologique* (Paris, 1844–   ).

Rhein. Mus. = *Rheinisches Museum für Philologie.*

Röm. Mitth. = *Mittheilungen des K. deutschen Archäologischen Instituts, Röm. Abtheil.* (Rome, 1886–   ).

T. J. B. = *Topographischer Jahresbericht* (contributed to the Römische Mittheilungen).

Woch. f. Klass. Phil. = *Wochenschrift für Klassische Philologie* (Berlin).

C. I. A. = *Corpus Inscriptionum Atticarum* (Berlin, 1873–   ).

C. I. G. = *Corpus Inscriptionum Graecarum* (Berlin, 1828–1870).

C. I. G. S. = *Corpus Inscriptionum Graeciae Septentrionalis* (vol. I, Berlin, 1892).

C. I. L. = *Corpus Inscriptionum Latinarum* (Berlin, 1863–   ).

C. I. Rhen. = *Corpus Inscriptionum Rhenarum* (Elberfeld, 1867–   ).

MANUSCRIPTS REFERRED TO.

Bamb. = the *Codex Bambergensis* M. V. 10, of the ninth to tenth century (see our plate); in the Royal Library at Bamberg (it contains only the last six books of the *Hist. Nat.*).

Ricc. = the *Codex Riccardianus* M. II. ii. 488, written abont the year 1100 according to Detlefsen, bnt probably older ; in the *Bibliotheca Riccardiana* at Florence.

Voss. = the *Codex Vossianus Latinus* 61 in folio, of the ninth century (cf. Chatelain, *Paléographie des Classiques Latins*, pl. cxli); in the University Library at Leiden.

Lips. = the *Codex Lipsii* 7 (see Geel, *Cat.* n. 465), copied from the *Vossianus* when this codex was more complete than it is now, and before it had been corrected (cf. Chatelain, pl. cxlii) ; in the University Library at Leiden.

e corr. = *e correctione* and refers to the corrections introduced into a MS. by a later hand.

reliqui = the remaining codices save the particnlar codex or codices anywhere quoted.

** = a corrupt reading which has not yet been satisfactorily restored.

† printed before an artist's name in the English translation signifies that the artist is so far known only from Pliny.

C. PLINII SECUNDI

NATURALIS HISTORIAE

LIBER XXXIII §§ 154-157
LIBER XXXIV §§ 5-93; 140-141

(CAELATURA ET STATUARIA)

I. CAELATURA.

154 MIRUM auro caelando neminem inclaruisse, argento multos. maxime tamen laudatus est Mentor de quo supra diximus. quattuor paria ab eo omnino facta sunt, ac iam nullum extare dicitur Ephesiae Dianae templi aut Capitolini incendiis. Varro se et aereum signum eius habuisse scribit. 5
155 proximi ab eo in admiratione Acragas et Boethus et Mys

§ 154. 2. maxime ... laudatus: the silver chasers are arranged in order of merit in four groups (a) *max. laudatus*, (b) *proximi ab eo*, (c) *post hos celebrati*, (d) *item laudantur*. Within each of these groups the names are arranged alphabetically, Benndorf, *de Anthol. Graec. Epigramm. quae ad artes spectant*, p. 52, note 1. The main account, derived, through a Roman source, from some Greek writer, is interrupted (1) by the mention of Varro's statue; (2) by a description (*extant ... habuit*) of chased works in Rhodes, drawn presumably from Mucianus (Brieger, *de Fontibus Plin.* p. 60), Introd. p. lxxxvi; (3) by the quotation of an epigram.

de quo supra diximus: the reference is to vii, 127, where the cups of Mentor are again alluded to as being in the Ephesian and Capitoline temples. The reader, however, would naturally think of (xxxiii, 147) *Lucius uero Crassus orator duos scyphos Mentoris artificis manu caelatos* HS. c̄ (sc. *emptos habuit*); but this statement being at variance with the present one, they must have been made indepen-

dently and at different times; the present passage seems a later addition, taken straight from vii, 127 (Furt-wängler, *Plinius u. s. Quellen*, p. 57, note 1).

3. quattuor paria: cups are mentioned in pairs, xxxiii, 147 (quoted above); xxxiv, 47 (*duo pocula Calamidis manu*); below § 156 (*in duobus scyphis*). It was apparently customary to decorate the pair with one continuous subject, as is expressly stated in the case of the cups by Zopyros (cf. Furtwängler, *Dornauszieher*, p. 96, note 63) and known from extant instances, e. g. the superb pairs of cups from Bernay, Schreiber, *Alex. Toreutik*, 54*, 55* (= Babelon, *Cab. des Antiques*, pl. 51 and 14, with Kentaurs and Kentauresses); *ib.* 67*, 68*; *ib.* 63*, 64* (at Naples) = *Mus. Borb.* xiii, pl. 49.

4. Ephesiae ... incendiis: vii, 127. The fire, which occurred in B.C. 356, gives us a lower limit for the date of Mentor. For the numerous passages in ancient authors referring to this, the most celebrated silver chaser of antiquity, see Overbeck's

I. SILVER CHASING.

CURIOUSLY enough, none have become famous as gold chasers, 154 many as chasers of silver. Of these the most esteemed is that *Mentor*, whom I have already mentioned. He made four pairs of cups in all, none of which, it is said, are extant; they perished when the temples of Artemis at Ephesos and of Jupiter on the Capitol were burnt down. Varro speaks of a bronze statue in his possession also from the hand of Mentor. Next to him †*Akragas*, 155 *Boethos*, and *Mys* were had in great admiration. Works by these

Schriftquellen, 2169–2181. The Capitoline fire occurred B. C. 83, during the Civil War, Appian, 'Εμφ. i, 83.

5. **Varro**: cf. xxxvi, 41, where Varro is likewise cited both as author and owner.—Like a number of other *caelatores* (so Kalamis, Ariston, Eunikos) Mentor was also a sculptor in bronze.

§ 155. 6. **Acragas**: the name, which is that of the eponymous river-god of Agrigentum (Ailian, Ποικ. Ἱστ. ii, 33), shows him to have been a native of that city, whose early connexion with Rhodes (cf. T. Reinach, *Rev. Arch.* xxiv, 1894, p. 178), would account for the artist seeking a field for his activity in the brilliant and art-loving city of Rhodes (cf. Museogr. Index) founded B.C. 408; at present, however, we have no nearer clue to his date. Against the theory of Th. Reinach, *op. cit.* pp. 170–180, that a chaser Akragas never existed, but was merely assumed owing to a misunderstanding of the legend ΑΚΡΑΓΑΣ on coins inserted as the *umbilici* of silver cups, Hans Dragendorff in *Terra*

Sigillata, p. 58, maintains that when a coin impression decorates the interior of a cup, it is always the only ornament and therefore inadmissible for cups decorated in relief, like those of Akragas. For names derived from river-gods cf. Αἴσηπος, as early as the sixth century (see Fick, *Gr. Personennamen*, p. 347, where a further list of such names is given). That the chaser Akragas appears only in Pliny need not astonish us: to mention only Epigonos (xxxiv, 88), this apparently very famous artist was up to the date of the Pergamene finds known from Pliny alone.

Boethus: xxxiv, 84. Cic. *Verr.* II, iv, 14, § 32 . . . *hydriam Boëthi manu factam*. A gem representing the wounded Philoktetes, signed ΒΟΗΘΟΥ is probably to be referred to him (Furtwängler, *Gemmen m. Künstlerinschriften*, Jahrb. iii, pl. VIII, 21 and p. 216).

Mys: he was a contemporary of Parrhasios (xxxv, 65, 68–73), from

fuere. exstant omnium opera hodie in insula Rhodiorum,
Boethi apud Lindiam Minervam, Acragantis in templo
Liberi patris in ipsa Rhodo Centauros Bacchasque caelati
scyphi, Myos in eadem aede Silenos et Cupidines. Acragantis et venatio in scyphis magnam famam habuit. post 5
156 hos celebratus est Calamis. et Antipater quoque Satyrum
in phiala gravatum somno conlocavisse verius quam caelasse
dictus est. Stratonicus mox Cyzicenus, Tauriscus, item
Ariston et Eunicus Mitylenaei laudantur et Hecataeus et
circa Pompei Magni aetatem Pasiteles, Posidonius Ephesius, 10
Hedys,Thrakides qui proelia armatosque caelavit, Zopyrus
qui Areopagitas et iudicium Orestis in duobus scyphis
HS [XII] aestimatis. fuit et Pytheas cuius duae unciae
✕ X̄ venierunt. Ulixes et Diomedes erant in phialae
157 emblemate Palladium subripientes. fecit idem et cocos 15
magiriscia appellatos parvolis potoriis, e quibus ne exem-

11. Hedys, Thrakides] *Furtwängler, Fleckeisen's Jahrb.* v, xxii, 1876,
p. 507 ; hedystrachides *Bamb.* ; iedis thracides *reliqui* ; Hedystrachides *Sillig,
Detlefsen*; Telesarchides *coni. Dilthey ap. Benndorf, de Epigr.* p. 53.

whose designs he executed the Ken-
tauromachia on the shield of the
Athena Promachos (Paus. i, 28, 2).
The epigram, from a cup at Herakleia
(Athen. xi, p. 782 B), beginning Γραμ-
μαὶ Παρρασίοιο, τέχνα Μυός . . . must
however, owing to the expression
τέχνα τινός, which does not occur in
pre-Imperial times, be a later forgery;
Preger, *Inscript. Graec. Metr.* p. 142,
note 185.

1. exstant . . . Cupidines: while
the introduction of the word *hodie*
points to a recent authority, the repetition of the artists' names in a different
order, marks the sentence as an interpolation (Introd. p. lxxxvii).

3. Centauros: for the subject cf.
the cups in the Biblioth. Nationale
and in Naples mentioned above.

⁕ 5. venatio: Dragendorff (*loc. cit.*)
suggests that the hunting scene on the
silvered terra-cotta cups, *Ann. d. Inst.*
1871 Pl. Q, and kindred compositions
may be derived from the *venatio* of

Akragas. in scyphis—the plural as
usual because two cups or perhaps a
set were decorated with one continuous
subject.

6. Calamis: xxxiv, 47, 71.

§ 156. 6. Antipater: the name of
the writer of an epigram has been
substituted for Diodoros, the real
name of the artist, and moreover that
required by the alphabetical arrangement; cf. *Anth. Plan.* 248

Τὸν Σάτυρον Διόδωρος ἐκοίμισεν, οὐκ
ἐτόρευσεν.

ἦν νύξης, ἐγερεῖς· ἄργυρος ὕπνον ἔχει·
an epigram similar to the one quoted
in the words *gravatum ... caelasse.*
Introd. p. lxviii.

8. Stratonicus: xxxiv, 85; he is
mentioned Athen. xi, p. 782 B, among
the ἔνδοξοι τορευταί.

Tauriscus: in xxxvi, 33 Pliny
expressly distinguishes him from the
sculptor of the same name.

9. Ariston, Eunicus . . . Hecataeus: xxxiv, 85.

three are still to be seen in the island of Rhodes : by Boethos in
the temple of Athena at Lindos, by Akragas cups with figures,
of Kentaurs and Bacchantes in the temple of Dionysos in the city
of Rhodes, and in the same temple cups by Mys, with figures of
Seilenoi and Erotes. Cups decorated round the interior with
hunting scenes by Akragas were also well known. Next in merit
to these chasers came *Kalamis*, +*Antipater*—whose sleeping Satyr 156
was said to have been not chased but laid to rest within the cup—,
Stratonikos of Kyzikos, and + *Tauriskos*. Other famous chasers
are +*Ariston* and +*Eunikos* of Mitylene, + *Hekataios*, *Pasiteles*, a
contemporary of the Great Pompeius, + *Poseidonios* of Ephesos,
Hedys, + *Thrakides*, whose favourite subjects were battles and
warriors, and + *Zopyros*, who represented the court of the Areiopagos
and the trial of Orestes on a pair of cups valued at 1,200,000
sesterces [£10,500 circ.]. + *Pytheas* too made a cup weighing two
ounces which sold for 10,000 denarii [£350 circ.]; the design on
the interior represented Odysseus and Diomedes stealing the
Palladion. He further made small drinking cups in the shape of 157
cooks, called μαγειρισκία, the delicate chasing of which was so liable

10. **Pasiteles**: xxxv, 156; xxxvi,
39 f. and above § 130. Cic. *de Div.*
i. 36, 79 mentions a toreutic work by
him representing the infant Roscius
wrapped in the coils of a serpent.
Possibly Pasiteles was influenced in
the presentation of the subject by the
'infant Herakles strangling the snakes'
of Zeuxis (xxxv, 63).

Posidonius: xxxiv, 91.

11. **Thrakides**: for the name cf.
Fick, *op. cit.* p. 141. The corrupt
Hedys conceals a name whose initial
letter lies between P—T.

12. **Areopagitas . . . Orestis**:
i. e. Orestes undergoing his trial
before the Areiopagos, the subject
being spread over both cups. Cf.
Winckelmann, *Mon. Ined.* pl. 151 for
a silver cup in the Corsini coll. representing this subject; better reproduced by Michaelis, *Das Corsinische
Silbergefäss*, Leipzig, 1859.

13. fuit et: like the *habuit et* below,
introduces a new artist who had no
place in the canonical lists quoted in

Pliny's main authority. Pytheas and
Teuker, therefore, lived presumably
in the period subsequent to Pasiteles.
The continuance of silver chasing at
least as late as the reign of Nero is
proved by the case of Zenodoros (xxxiv,
47). The decay of which Pliny com-
plains only applies to his own time;
nor need we attach too precise a meaning to this, or the similar complaint
on the decay of painting in xxxv, 4,
both being evidently rhetorical, cf.
Oehmichen, *Plinianische Studien*,
p. 161 f.; Furtwängler in *Berl. Phil.
Wochenschr.*, 1895, p. 814.

14. **Ulixes et Diomedes**: for the
subject cf. the celebrated Spada relief,
Schreiber, *Hell. Reliefbilder*, pl. VII,
the gem, signed Calpurnius Felix,
Jahrbuch iii, 1888, Pl. x, 7; cf.
Furtwängler, *ib.* p. 312 ; and the relief
on the neck of one of the Bernay oino-
choai, Babelon, *Cab. des Ant.* pl. 41.

§ 157. 15. cocos: [i.e. silver cups
in the shape of figurines.—H. L. U.]

16. **magiriscia**: from μάγειρος, a

plaria quidem liceret exprimere, tam opportuna iniuriae
subtilitas erat.   habuit et Teucer crustarius famam, subito-
que ars haec ita exolevit ut sola iam vetustate censeatur,
usuque attritis caelaturis, si nec figura discerni possit, auctoritas constet.   5

II. *STATUARIA.*

5 QUONDAM aes confusum auro argentoque miscebatur, et
tamen ars pretiosior erat, nunc incertum est peior haec sit
an materia, mirumque, cum ad infinitum operum pretia
creverint, auctoritas artis extincta est.   quaestus enim causa
ut omnia exerceri coepta est quae gloriae solebat—ideo 10
autem etiam deorum adscripta operi, cum proceres gentium
claritatem et hac via quaererent—adeoque exolevit fundendi
aeris pretiosi ratio ut iamdiu ne fortuna quidem in ea re ius
6 artis habeat.   ex illa autem antiqua gloria Corinthium
maxime laudatur.   hoc casus miscuit Corintho, cum cape- 15
retur, incensa, mireque circa id multorum adfectatio furit,
quippe cum tradatur non alia de causa Verrem quem
A.U.C. 711. M. Cicero damnaverat proscriptum cum eo ab Antonio,
quoniam Corinthiis cessurum se ei negavisset.   ac mihi
maior pars eorum simulare eam scientiam videtur ad segre- 20
gandos sese a ceteris magis quam intellegere aliquid ibi
7 suptilius, et hoc paucis docebo.   Corinthus capta est olym-

---

4. si nec] *Urlichs in Chrestom.* p. 301 ; sine *Bamb.*; ne *reliqui, Detlefsen.*
11. autem] *om. omnes praeter Bamb., Detlefsen.*

cook. [The subject influenced perhaps
by the Middle or New Comedy.—
H. L. U.]

 2. Teucer: possibly identical with
the gem engraver Τεῦκρος (cf. *Jahrb.*
iii, p. 323).

crustarius: this shows him to
have been especially a worker of
ἐμβλήματα or *crustae,* i.e. of figures
in relief, wrought separately and
attached to the object to be decorated;
cf. Cic. *Verr.* II, iv, 22, § 49 *duo
pocula non magna, verum tamen cum
emblemate*: also Juv. i, 76.   Add.

   § 5. 6. auro argentoque: up to

now the amount of precious metals
yielded by the analysis of ancient
bronzes is so small as scarcely to warrant Pliny's statement that gold and
silver were regularly employed in
the most ancient Greek alloys; cf.
Blümner, *Technol. u. Terminol.* vol.
iv, p. 178 ff.; O. Müller, *Handbuch*
306, Daremberg and Saglio, s. v. *aes.*

   § 6. 15. hoc casus miscuit: cf.
Florus, ii, 16 ; this and several other
anecdotes (see in especial Paus. ii, 3, 3,
and Plut. *De Pyth. Or.* 2, p. 395 B)
were invented to account for the origin
of Corinthian bronze when the secret

to injury that it was impossible to take a cast of them. *Teuker* also enjoyed some reputation for his embossed work. The whole art then suddenly disappeared so completely that nowadays we only value wrought silver for its age, and reckon its merit established when the chasing is so worn that the very design can no longer be made out.

II. BRONZE STATUARY.

BOOK XXXIV.

BRONZE was formerly alloyed with both gold and silver, and yet 5 the workmanship used to be more valuable than the metal; now *Decay of bronze* it is hard to say which is worse. It is extraordinary that when *work.* the price given for works of art has risen so enormously, art itself should have lost its claim to our respect. The truth is that the aim of the artist, as of every one else in our times, is to gain money, not fame as in the old days, when the noblest of their nation thought art one of the paths to glory, and ascribed it even to the gods. The process of founding valuable bronze is so completely lost that for generations even fortune has not been able to secure the results formerly ensured by skill.

Of the bronzes renowned in antiquity, the Corinthian is the 6 most esteemed. An accident first produced this alloy in the fire *Corinthian* which followed on the sack of Corinth and the rage for it is *bronze.* marvellously widespread. For instance, there is a story that when Antony proscribed Cicero he also proscribed Verres (whose 43 B. C. condemnation Cicero had once procured), simply because Verres had refused to give up to him his Corinthian bronzes. In my own opinion, however, most people affect a knowledge of the subject solely to exalt themselves above the common herd, without having any real insight into it; this I can prove in a few words. Corinth was taken in the third year of the hundred and 7

of its mixture had been lost. Pliny sees the impossibility of reconciling the story of the Corinthian alloy and the dates of famous statues, but instead of questioning the truth of the story, he proceeds to deny *in toto* the existence of Corinthian bronzes, though it is excellently and repeatedly attested: e.g. Martial, xiv, 172, 177, and often. The reader will feel reminded of the

witty satire in Petronius, *Sat.* 50, on Corinthian bronze and its wonderful alloy.

18. **proscriptum ab Antonio**: cf. Seneca Rhetor, *Suas.* vi, vii, *passim.* For the use to which Augustus put the proscriptions, in order to obtain Cor. bronzes, see Suet. *Aug.* 70; cf. Plin. xxxvii, 81, where Nonius is proscribed by Antonius for the sake of a fine opal.

piadis CLVIII anno tertio, nostrae urbis DCVIII, cum ante
saecula fictores nobiles esse desissent, quorum isti omnia
signa hodie Corinthia appellant.   quapropter ad coar-
guendos eos ponemus artificum aetates.   nam urbis nostrae
annos ex supra dicta comparatione olympiadum colligere 5
facile erit.   sunt ergo vasa tantum Corinthia quae isti
elegantiores modo ad esculenta transferunt, modo in lu-
8 cernas aut trulleos nullo munditiarum dispectu.   eius tria
genera : candidum argento nitore quam proxime accedens
in quo illa mixtura praevaluit, alterum in quo auri fulva 10
natura, tertium in quo aequalis omnium temperies fuit.
praeter haec est cuius ratio non potest reddi, quamquam
hominis manu sed ad fortunam temperatur in simulacris
signisque, illud suo colore pretiosum ad iocineris imaginem
vergens, quod ideo hepatizon appellant, procul a Corinthio, 15
longe tamen ante Aegineticum atque Deliacum, quae diu
optinuere principatum.

9   Antiquissima aeris gloria Deliaco fuit mercatus in Delo
celebrante toto orbe, et ideo cura officinis.   tricliniorum
pedibus fulcrisque ibi prima aeris nobilitas, pervenit deinde 20
et ad deum simulacra effigiemque hominum et aliorum
animalium.

10   Proxima laus Aeginetico fuit.   insula et ipsa est, nec
quod ibi gigneretur, sed officinarum temperatura nobilitata.
bos aereus inde captus in foro boario est Romae.   hoc erit 25
exemplar Aeginetici aeris, Deliaci autem Iuppiter in
Capitolio in Iovis Tonantis aede.   illo aere Myron usus

§ 7. 2. fictores : from meaning literally a modeller in clay, the word *fictor*
is extended to workers in bronze ; see
note on xxxv, 153.

4. ponemus . . . aetates : in §§
49–52.

nam : elliptical 'for of course, as
I shall draw from a Greek source,
I shall give them only in Olympiads,'
Furtwängler, *Plinius*, p. 19 ; for the
ellipse cf. xxxv, 137 (*nam Socrates*) ;
xxxvi, 32 (*nam Myronis illius*), where
see note.

7. lucernas : the familiar oval oil
lamp with flat top.

8. trulleos : apparently identical
with the *pelvis*, a basin to wash hands
or feet.   For a pelvis of bronze cf.
Juv. x, 64 ; for one of Corinthian
bronze, Orelli, 3838.

§ 8. 9. candidum argento : for
some bronze objects found at Suessula,
really containing small quantities of
gold and silver, see Blümner *op. cit.*
p. 184, note 5.

§ 9. 18. Deliaco : mentioned three
times, along with Corinthian bronze by
Cicero, *pro Sext. Rosc. Am.* 46, 133 ;
Verr. II, ii, 34, § 83 ; *ib.* 72, § 176.

mercatus in Delo : i.e. the fair

fifty-eighth Olympiad, that is, the year of Rome 608 [146 B.C.], centuries later than the celebrated workers, whose statues our amateurs still assume to be all of Corinthian bronze. I shall prove that they are wrong by giving the dates of the artists, for it will be easy to turn the Olympiads into years of Rome by referring to the two corresponding dates given above. It follows that the only vessels of Corinthian bronze are those which these connoisseurs use as dishes or lamps or basins, with no regard for their workmanship.

There were three varieties of Corinthian bronze—a white 8 bronze, that shone almost like silver, and contained a very large proportion of that metal; a second, in which a reddish tinge of gold prevailed; and a third, in which the three metals were blended in equal proportions. There is also a fourth alloy, of which no scientific account can be given; it is employed for images and statues, and though it is produced by the hand of man, yet fortune partly determines the result. It is known as ἡπάτιζον from the peculiar tint, verging on liver colour, which is its chief merit. It is inferior to the bronze of Corinth, but superior to those of Aigina and Delos, though these were long thought the best.

The bronze most celebrated in early times was that of Delos, 9 for as all nations resorted to the market of the island, great care *Delian bronze.* was bestowed on the manufacture of bronze. It was first employed there for the feet and framework (Add.) of couches, and afterwards its use was extended to images of the gods, and figures of men and animals.

Aiginetan bronze was the next to become celebrated. Aigina 10 also is an island; it had no mines, but owed its reputation to *Aiginetan bronze.* the admirable alloys produced in its foundries. A bronze bull, *Bull in* taken from Aigina, and now in the Cattle Market at Rome, may *Cattle Market.* stand for an example of Aiginetan bronze, and the Jupiter in the *Statue of* temple of Jupiter the Thunderer on the Capitol for an example of *Jupiter the Thunderer.*

held in connexion with the quinquen-
nial festival of Apollo and Artemis.

21. ad deum simulacra: cf. § 15
*transit deinde ars vulgo ubique ad
effigies deorum*: the imagined progress of art from furniture to images
of gods and hence to images of men
and animals is purely conventional;
see Münzer, *Hermes* xxx, 1895, p. 501.

§10. 23. Aeginetico: the alloy was
renowned because of the famous artists
who employed it. For a vivid picture
of the Aiginetan School, see Collignon,
Sculpt. Grecque, i, 280–307.

25. in foro boario: Tac. *Ann.*
xii, 24.

27. Iovis Tonantis aede. Cf.
xxxvi, 50. A small temple built (B.C.

est, hoc Polycletus, aequales atque condiscipuli, sed aemu-
latio et in materia fuit.

11   Privatim Aegina candelabrorum superficiem dumtaxat
elaboravit, sicut Tarentum scapos.   in his ergo iuncta com-
mendatio officinarum·est.   nec pudet tribunorum militarium 5
salariis emere, cum ipsum nomen a candelarum lumine
inpositum appareat.   accessio candelabri talis fuit Theonis
iussu praeconis Clesippus fullo gibber et praeterea et alio
12 foedus aspectu, emente id Gegania HS L̄.   eadem osten-
tante in convivio empta ludibrii causa nudatus atque 10
inpudentia libidinis receptus in torum, mox in testamentum,
praedives numinum vice illud candelabrum coluit et hanc
Corinthiis fabulam adiecit, vindicatis tamen moribus nobili
sepulchro per quod aeterna supra terras Geganiae dedecoris
memoria duraret.   sed cum esse nulla Corinthia candelabra 15
constet, nomen id praecipue in his celebratur, quoniam
Mummi victoria Corinthum quidem diruit, sed e compluri-
bus Achaiae oppidis simul aera dispersit.

13   Prisci limina etiam ac valvas in templis ex aere facti-
A.U.C. 587. tavere.   invenio et a Cn. Octavio qui de Perseo rege nava- 20
lem triumphum egit factam porticum duplicem ad circum
Flaminium quae Corinthia sit appellata a capitulis aereis
columnarum, Vestae quoque aedem ipsam Syracusana super-
ficie tegi placuisse.   Syracusana sunt in Pantheo capita

22) by Augustus near the great temple
of Jupiter Capitolinus to commemorate
his miraculous escape from death by
lightning (Suet. *Aug.* 29); *Mon. Ancyr.*
xix, 4, 5; Mommsen, *Res Gestae,*
p. 81.   The temple appears on coins
of Augustus, Cohen, *Aug.* 178-180;
184-186.   For the bronze statue by
Leochares, see below § 79.

   Myron . . . Polycletus, §§ 55-
58.

   § 11. 5. tribunorum . . . salariis:
cf. Juv. iii, 132.

   6. a candelarum lumine: the
etymology is Varronian; cf. Varro,
ap. Servius on *Aen.* ii, 225 . . . *ut in
quo figunt candelam candelabrum
appellant, sic in quo deum ponunt*

delubrum dicunt; and Macrob.
Satur. iii, 4, 2; cf. Martial, xiv, 43.

   8. Clesippus: the slave was of
course a Greek (Κλήσιππος).   The
story is attested by an inscription (close
of Republic) *C. I. L.* i, 805, *Clesippus-
Geganius mag. Capit[ol]-mag. luperc.
viat. tr.* apparently belonging to the
sepulchre mentioned in § 12.

   § 13. 19. limina etiam ac valvas:
either of massive bronze or plated,
Marquardt, *Privatleben der Römer,*
p. 223 ff.

   20. Cn. Octavio: the portico (built
B.C. 167) stood in the Campus
Martius near the Circus Flaminius
and the theatre of Pompeius.   It was
burnt down and rebuilt by Augustus

Delian bronze. Aiginetan bronze was employed by Myron, and *Bronzes* Delian by Polykleitos. These two artists were contemporaries *used by Myron and* and fellow-pupils, who carried their rivalry even into their choice *Polykleitos.* of a material.

At Aigina it was the trays, at Tarentum the stems of cande- 11 labra which were specially elaborated, so that the efforts of several *Cande-* workshops combine to recommend these utensils. They are *labra.* things without even a name except the one which they borrow from the light of their own candles, and yet we are not ashamed to give as much for them as the year's pay of a military tribune. Theon, the auctioneer, once included in the same lot as *Story of* one of these candelabra a slave, a fuller named Clesippus, who *Clesippus* was humpbacked and altogether hideous. The lot was bought for *Gegania.* 50,000 sesterces (£440 circ.) by Gegania, who displayed her 12 purchase at a banquet, and exposed Clesippus naked to the ridicule of the company, yet afterwards, through sheer wantonness, made him her lover, and at last her heir. Thus enriched, he worshipped the candelabrum as a deity, providing yet another story about Corinthian bronzes. Morality, however, was avenged in the magnificent tomb that he built only to keep the remembrance of Gegania's infamy alive upon the earth. Although none of these candelabra are really Corinthian, yet they are called so because Mummius destroyed Corinth; people forget that his victory also scattered the bronzes of various other Greek cities.

In early times the thresholds and folding-doors in temples 13 were commonly made of bronze. I find, too, that Gnaeus *Thresh-* Octavius, who was granted a triumph for his naval victory over 167 B.C. *olds.* King Perseus, built a gallery with double colonnade by the Circus of Flaminius, called the Corinthian Gallery, from the small bronze capitals of its columns. A decree was also passed that the temple of Vesta should be roofed with plates of Syracusan bronze.

(Festus, p. 178; *Mon. Anc.* xix, 4, 2–4. Mommsen, *Res Gestae*, p. 80), after the Dalmatian Triumph, B. C. 33. It must be distinguished from the *porticus Octaviae*, § 31. *Invenio* shows that Pliny is quoting from an ancient authority; either the building no longer existed in his day, or the outer colonnade had not been restored after the fire, so that the remarks as to the columns apply to the pre-Augustan building. (See O. Gilbert, *Gesch. u.*

Top. der Stadt Rom iii, p. 250, n. 2.) 23. **Vestae** . . . tegi: cf. xxxiii, 57. 24. placuisse: probably after the great fire of B.C. 241, cf. vii, 141. in Pantheo: built (B. C. 27) by Agrippa in his third consulate. This earlier building was altered to its present shape in the reign of Hadrian. For recent discoveries and literature, cf. C. Hülsen in *T.J.B.* iv, p. 305 (*Röm. Mitth.* viii, 1893) and Gardthausen *Augustus* ii, p. 430 f.

columnarum a M. Agrippa posita. quin etiam privata opu-
lentia eo modo usurpata est. Camillo inter crimina obiecit
A.U.C. 363. Spurius Carvilius quaestor ostia quod aerata haberet in
domo.

14   Nam triclinia aerata abacosque et monopodia Cn. 5
Manlium Asia devicta primum invexisse triumpho suo quem
duxit anno urbis DLXVII L. Piso auctor est, Antias quidem
heredes L. Crassi oratoris multa etiam triclinia aerata vendidisse. ex aere factitavere et cortinas tripodum nomine
Delphicas, quoniam donis maxime Apollini Delphico dica- 10
bantur. placuere et lychnuchi pensiles in delubris aut
arborum mala ferentium modo lucentes, quale est in templo
Apollinis Palatini quod Alexander Magnus Thebarum ex-
A.U.C. 419. pugnatione captum in Cyme dicaverat eidem deo.

15   Transiit deinde ars vulgo ubique ad effigies deorum. 15
Romae simulacrum ex aere factum Cereri primum reperio
A.U.C. 270. ex peculio Spuri Cassi quem regnum adfectantem pater
ipsius interemerit. transit et a diis ad hominum statuas

9. nomine] nomine ac *Bamb.*; nomine a *Voss.*

3. **Spurius Carvilius**: his part in
the trial is mentioned only by Pliny.

ostia quod aerata: καὶ δῆτα καὶ
θύραι τινὲς ἐλέγοντο χαλκαῖ παρ'
αὐτῷ φανῆναι τῶν αἰχμαλώτων. Plut.
Camill. xii.

§ 14. 5. abacosque: the use of
abaci as sideboards appears really to
date from the conquest of Asia, Marquardt, *Privatleben*, p. 319.

Cn. Manlium: Liv. xxxix, 6, 7
*ii primum lectos aeratos ... et quae
tum magnificae supellectilis habe-
bantur monopodia et abacos Romam
advexerunt.*

6. Asia devicta: cf. xxxiii, 148.

7. L. Piso: Lucius Calpurnius
Piso, surnamed Frugi; cos. B.C. 133;
frequently quoted by Pliny, Teuffel,
G.R.L. § 132, 4.

• Antias, Valerius, fl. ab. 45 B.C.;
frequently quoted by Pliny; Teuffel,
§ 155, 2.

9. nomine: cf. Diodoros, xvi, 26.
The corrupt *ac* of the MSS. must

arise from a copyist's misunderstanding
of *Delphicas* as a separate object.

11. lychnuchi: originally lamp-
stands (λυχνοῦχοι), whence the name
was transferred to the whole candelabrum, Marquardt, *op. cit.* p. 711;
Daremberg et Saglio, s.v. *candelabrum*.

pensiles: Verg.*Aen.*i, 726; Petron.
Sat. 30 *et lucerna bilychnis de camera
pendebat.*

12. quale: sc. *candelabrum*, to be
supplied from § 12.

templo Apollinis: dedicated by
Augustus B.C. 27, cf. xxxvi, 32.

§ 15. 15. Transiit ... ars: note
on § 9.

16. simulacrum: restricted as
usual to images of the gods, while
statua is more particularly used for
mortals. The notion that the Cassian
simulacrum was the first of its kind
at Rome is in flagrant contradiction to the mention in § 33 of a
Hercules, consecrated by Evander and
of Numa's Janus; moreover since in

Syracusan bronze was also employed by Marcus Agrippa for the capitals of the columns in his Pantheon. Wealthy individuals even adopted this fashion for their private houses. The quaestor Spurius Carvilius accused Camillus among other things of having had bronze plated doors to his house. 391 B.C. *Plated doors.*

The practice of using bronze for couches, side-boards and tables supported on a single foot, was first introduced, according to Lucius Piso, by Gnaeus Manlius, after the conquest of Asia, when he triumphed in the year of Rome 567 [187 B.C.]. Antias adds that the heirs of Lucius Crassus, the orator, sold a number of bronze couches. The cauldrons of tripods were also made of bronze; they were called *Delphicae*, because they were the gift most frequently dedicated to the Delphic Apollo. Hanging lamps in shrines were also made of bronze, and lamps with the lights fixed like apples on trees, as for instance, the lamp now in the temple of Apollo of the Palatine, which Alexander the Great carried off when he took Thebes, and dedicated, also to Apollo, at Kyme. 14 *Household furniture. Delphic tripods. Hanging lamps.* 335 B.C.

Later on bronze was universally employed for statues of the gods. I find that at Rome the first bronze image was made in honour of Ceres out of the confiscated property of Spurius Cassius, who was put to death by his father because he aimed at becoming king. From figures of the gods, bronze came to be used in various ways for statues and images of men. The 15 *Statues of gods and of mortals.* 484 B.C.

§§ 21, 29, a whole series of portraits from the period of the Kings and early Republic are mentioned, it is irreconcilable with the theory that art progressed from the statues of gods to those of men. Pliny is quoting from a variety of sources, without even attempting to harmonize them.

Cereri: in her temple near the Great Circus, vowed by Aulus Postumius the victor at Regillus, B.C. 493; for its paintings and plastic decorations see xxxv, 154.

17. pater ipsius: cf. Liv. ii, 41, 10 *sunt, qui patrem auctorem eius supplicii ferant: eum cognita domi causa verberasse ac necasse, peculiumque filii Cereri consecravisse: signum inde factum esse et inscriptum 'ex Cassia familia datum.'* Dionysios (viii, 79),

on the other hand, speaks of several statues. The story involves a complicated problem. There is much to commend the view of Gilbert, *Rom* ii, p. 243, note 2 *s. f.* that the consecration to Ceres, the special patroness of the plebeians, of the private property of Cassius was an extension—more accurately an ironic application (*Verhöhnung*) of the *lex sacrata* for the protection of the Trib. Pl. (cf. Liv. iii, 55) *ut qui trib. pl. nocuisset eius caput Ioui sacrum esset, familia ad aedem Cereris Liberi Liberaeque venum iret;* Dionys. x, 42 where the Patricians who offend against the assembly of the people convened under the Tribunes are punished by confiscation of their property to Ceres (τὰς οὐσίας αὐτῶν ἱερὰς εἶναι Δήμητρος).

atque imagines multis modis. bitumine antiqui tinguebant
eas, quo magis mirum est placuisse auro integere. hoc
nescio an Romanum fuerit inventum, certe etiam Romae
16 non habet vetustatem. effigies hominum non solebant ex-
primi nisi aliqua inlustri causa perpetuitatem merentium, 5
primo sacrorum certaminum victoria maximeque Olympiae,
ubi omnium qui vicissent statuas dicari mos erat, eorum
vero qui ter ibi superavissent ex membris ipsorum simili-
17 tudine expressa, quas iconicas vocant. Athenienses nescio
an primis omnium Harmodio et Aristogitoni tyrannicidis 10
publice posuerint statuas. hoc actum est eodem anno quo
A.U.C. 245. et Romae reges pulsi. excepta deinde res est a toto orbe
terrarum humanissima ambitione, et in omnium municipiorum
foris statuae ornamentum esse coepere prorogarique memoria
hominum et honores legendi aevo basibus inscribi, ne in 15
sepulcris tantum legerentur. mox forum et in domibus
privatis factum atque in atris honos clientium instituit sic
colere patronos.
18   Togatae effigies antiquitus ita dicabantur. placuere et
nudae tenentes hastam ab epheborum e gymnasiis exem- 20
plaribus, quas Achilleas vocant.   Graeca res nihil velare,

19. ita] ista *Riccard., Voss. (e corr.)* ; sta *Voss.*

1. **bitumine**: in order to give a
patina to the new bronze.

2. **auro**: xxxiii, 61, 82 ; xxxiv, 63.
The custom of gilding statues was
known in Greece, cf. the gilt statue
of Gorgias of Leontinoi, Paus. x, 18,
7 (Plin. xxxiii, 83, where, however,
it is stated that the Gorgias was of
solid gold), and the gilt Phryne by
Praxiteles, Paus. x, 15, 1 ; cf. Blümner,
Technol. iv, p. 308 ff.

4. **non habet vetustatem**: the
oldest recorded Roman instance of a
statua aurata is to M'. Acilius Glabrio
(B.C. 131), Liv. xl, 34, 5 *quae prima
omnium in Italia est statua aurata.*

§ 16. 6. **Olympiae**: the long
list of athlete statues began with the
ancient cypress wood statue of Praxi-
damas of Aigina, who won the prize

for boxing, Ol. 59 (= B.C. 544). Paus.
vi, 18, 7.

7. **ubi omnium . . . iconicas
vocant** : Lessing has made these
words the text for a famous passage
in the *Laokoon* (ii, § 13). Visconti
(*Iconographie Grecque*, Discours pré-
lim. p. viii, n. 4) arguing from Lucian,
ὑπὲρ τῶν εἰκόνων xi, takes *iconicas* to
mean 'grand comme nature'; Prof.
Klein, however, in a note which he
kindly allows me to publish, points
out that Pliny's statement bears an
apocryphal character, which has escaped every one save perhaps Blümner
in his Comm. on Lessing's *Laokoon*,
p. 503. It is evident that the discrepancies between ideal and iconic
statues were explained by Pliny,
or his author, as the result of an

ancients tinted the figures with bitumen, which makes the later practice of gilding them the more curious. This may very well be a Roman invention, and certainly even at Rome it is not of great antiquity. The ancients did not make any statues of individuals unless they deserved immortality by some distinction, originally by a victory at some sacred games, especially those of Olympia, where it was the custom to dedicate statues of all those who had conquered, and portrait statues if they had conquered three times. These are called *iconic*. (See Addenda.) **16** *Victors at Olympia.*

The Athenians were, I believe, introducing a new custom when they set up statues at the public expense in honour of Harmodios and Aristogeiton, who killed the tyrants. This occurred in the very year in which the kings were expelled from Rome. A refined ambition led to the universal adoption of the custom, and statues began to adorn the public places of every town ; the memories of men were immortalized, and their honours were no longer merely graven on their tombstones, but handed down for posterity to read on the pedestals of statues. Later on the rooms and halls of private houses became so many public places, and clients began to honour their patrons in this way. **17** *Public benefactors* **509 B.C.**

Formerly statues were dedicated wearing the toga. Nude statues holding a spear were also in favour, modelled after young men in the gymnasia ; these were called Achillean. The Greek **18** *Draped and nude statues.*

improbable rule, simply because the ancients had no habit of applying historical criticism to art, and consequently of discriminating between the works of a time when only the type was aimed at, from those of periods when art had advanced to individual portraiture. It is instructive to compare with Pliny's words a passage in Dio Chrysostom, *Or.* xxi, 1 περὶ κάλλους, where he attempts to explain the difference between the statues of an earlier and a later date by alleging physical degeneration. The difference observable in the Olympic statues generally, distinguished *pre-* from *post-* Lysippian portraiture; as it is very well said in xxxv, 153 *hic* (Lysistratos) *et simili-tudines reddere instituit, ante eum quam pulcherrimas facere studebatur.*

§ 17. 10. **Harmodio et Aristogi-**

toni: below § 70.

§ 18. 19. **togatae effigies :** such as the statues of the kings, § 23.

20. **tenentes hastam :** statues of athletes in the scheme of the Polykleitan Doryphoros, or leaning on their spear. *Achilleas* (from Achilles, the typical hero of the ephebes) a convenient generic term under which to group such portraits, Furtwängler, *Plinius*, p. 47, note 11. The custom of portraying mortals other than athletes in heroic nudity *during their lifetime*, seems to have been introduced by Alexander and his successors ; cf. the bronze portrait of a Hellenistic ruler in the Museo delle Terme (Helbig, *Class. Ant.* 1052).

21. **Graeca ... addere :** no precise historical information can be drawn from these words, which merely contain a broad comparison between

at contra Romana ac militaris thoraces addere. Caesar
quidem dictator loricatam sibi dicari in foro suo passus est.
nam Lupercorum habitu tam noviciae sunt quam quae
A.U.C. 617. nuper prodiere paenulis indutae. Mancinus eo habitu sibi
19 statuit quo deditus fuerat. notatum ab auctoribus et 5
L. Accium poetam in Camenarum aede maxima forma
statuam sibi posuisse, cum brevis admodum fuisset. equestres utique statuae Romanam celebrationem habent orto
sine dubio a Graecis exemplo, sed illi celetas tantum dica-
bant in sacris victores, postea vero et qui bigis vel quadrigis 10
vicissent. unde et nostri currus nati in iis qui triumpha-
vissent. serum hoc, et in his non nisi a divo Augusto
seiuges, aut elephanti.

20   Non vetus et bigarum celebratio in iis qui praetura
functi curru vecti essent per circum, antiquior columnarum, 15
sicuti C. Maenio qui devicerat priscos Latinos, quibus ex

13. aut] *E. Sellers*; sicut *codd.*, *Detlefsen*.

the typical Greek athlete statues and
the numerous Roman portraits of late
Republican and Imperial times.

 1. thoraces: the statue of Augustus
in the Vatican, Helbig, *Class. Ant.* 4,
well illustrates the combination of the
military element with the nude athletic
type. As a reminiscence of the athlete
statues the legs are left bare, but the
Emperor wears the cuirass, with the
mantle rolled round below the waist.

 2. loricatam, sc. effigiem: belonging to the class of statues just
mentioned, of which there are numerous examples, see Rohden in *Bonner
Studien*, pp. 1-80. Very little is known
about this particular statue of Caesar
or the spot in his Forum where it
stood. Pliny the Younger (*Ep.* viii,
6, 14) says that a decree of the Senate
in favour of Pallas, the freedman of
Claudius, was put up *ad statuam
loricatam divi Iulii*.

 • 3. Lupercorum, i.e. with only a
goatskin about the loins, like the priests
of Lupercus at the festival of the Lu-
percalia (Ov. *Fast. v*, 101).

 5. quo deditus fuerat: *nudus ac*

post tergum religatis manibus Vell.
Paterc. II, i, 5.

 not. ab auctoribus: probably
the statue was no longer extant when
Pliny wrote.

 § 19. 6. L.Accium: the tragic poet,
B.C. 170-103. There is no reliable
copy of the statue, Bernoulli, *Röm.
Iconographie*, i, p. 289.

 Camenarum = Musarum, in the
first region, *Porta Capena*.

 10. postea vero: the notion that
art progressed from the representations
of statues of horsemen to chariot-
groups, is in harmony with the for-
malizing theories of the growth of art,
hinted in § 9 and § 15, but it is the in-
verse of fact (cf. Münzer, *op. cit.* p. 502):
the race with four-horsed chariots was
introduced at Olympia, Ol. 25 (B.C.
680), the race on horseback (ἵππος
κέλης), Ol. 33 (B.C. 648), and the race
with two-horsed chariots, Ol. 93 (B.C.
408). The earliest monument of a
victor on his four-horsed chariot was
that of Kleosthenes of Epidamnos by
Hagelaidas, Ol. 66 (B.C. 516), Paus.
vi, 10, 2.

custom was to leave the body quite nude ; but the Roman and
military custom was to add a breastplate, while Caesar, when
Dictator, allowed a statue of himself wearing a cuirass to be set
up in his forum. Statues in the dress of the Lupercals are as *Lupercals.*
recent an innovation as those lately introduced wearing short *C. Hostil-*
cloaks. Mancinus set up a statue in his own honour, wearing *lius Man-*
the dress in which he had been given up to the enemy. I find 19 *cinus ;*
it mentioned by some authors that Lucius Accius the poet set up *137 B.C.*
in his own honour in the temple of the Camenae a statue, which *Lucius*
was of great size, although he was a very small man. *Accius.*

Equestrian statues, which are so common at Rome, were *Equestrian*
undoubtedly first borrowed from Greece. The Greeks, however, *statues.*
only dedicated equestrian statues of those who had been victors
on horseback at the sacred games ; later on we find statues of
the victors in the two and four-horse chariot races. From this
arose our custom of setting up chariots in honour of those who *Chariots.*
had triumphed. Until recent times this was unknown, and
chariots drawn by six horses or by elephants were only introduced
by the god Augustus.

The erection of two-horse chariots in honour of those who as 20
praetors have led the procession round the Circus is also of late
date. The custom of erecting statues on columns is more ancient, *Statues on*
witness the column in honour of Gaius Maenius, conqueror *columns.*
of the Ancient Latins, a people to whom the Romans were *G.Maenius.*

11. **currus**: Juv. viii, 3, mentions
the statue of a *triumphator* standing
erect in his triumphal car in the
vestibulum.

13. **seiuges**: a gilt chariot, drawn
by six horses, had already been dedicated to Jupiter Capitolinus in B. C.
169, by the Consul P. Cornelius (*seiuges
in Capitolio aurati* Liv. xxxviii, 35, 4).
Pliny's meaning must be that under
Augustus the team of six horses was
first used for other than religious
purposes. Mommsen, *Staatsrecht*, i,
3rd ed. p. 395, n. 1, points out that,
according to Dio Cassius, lix, 7,
Caligula was the first to drive in the
circus with six horses: τὸ ἅρμα τὸ
πομπικόν ... ἐξ ἵπποι εἵλκυσαν ὃ μη-
πώποτε ἐγεγόνει.

elephanti: from Pliny's words

it might be inferred that *triumphal*
chariots were drawn by elephants as
early as Augustus, whereas this occurred for the first time in the reign
of Alexander Severus, cf. Aelius Lam-
pridius, *Vita Al. Sev.* 57, 4. The
chariots drawn by elephants on early
imperial coins refer to the *Pompa
circensis*, Marquardt, *Staatsverw.* ii,
p. 586, note 7. Addenda.

§ 20. 15. **per circum**, sc. *Maximum*, on the occasion of the *Ludi
Apollinares*, instituted B.C. 212. For
the praetorial *biga*, cf. Mommsen,
Staatsrecht, i, 3rd ed., p. 394, note 4;
pp. 412, 447.

columnarum: from § 26 it is
evident that the *columnae* were statues
placed on high pedestals.

16. **C. Maenio**: cf. vii, 212. He

C

foedere tertias praedae populus R. praestabat, eodemque
in consulatu in suggestu rostra devictis Antiatibus fixerat
anno urbis CCCCXVI, item C. Duillio qui primus navalem
A.U.C. 494. triumphum egit de Poenis, quae est etiam nunc in foro,
21 item L. Minucio praefecto annonae extra portam Trige- 5
A.U.C. 315. minam unciaria stipe conlata—nescio an primo honore tali
a populo, antea enim a senatu erat—praeclara res, nisi
frivolis coepisset initiis. namque et Atti Navi statua fuit
A.U.C. 702. ante curiam—basis eius conflagravit curia incensa P. Clodii
A.U.C. 304. funere—fuit et Hermodori Ephesii in comitio, legum quas 10
22 decemviri scribebant interpretis, publice dicata. alia causa,
alia auctoritas M. Horati Coclitis statuae, quae durat hodie-
A.U.C. 246. que, cum hostes a ponte sublicio solus arcuisset. equidem
et Sibyllae iuxta rostra esse non miror, tres sint licet: una
quam Sextus Pacuius Taurus aed. pl. restituit, duae quas 15
M. Messalla. primas putarem has et Atti Navi, positas

had conquered the Latins with Furius
Camillus ; *additus triumpho honos,
ut statuae equestres eis, rara illa
aetate res, in foro ponerentur* Liv.
viii, 13, 9. The statue of Camillus had
stood on the old Rostra (§ 23), and
was apparently still extant in the days
of Pliny the Younger (see *Paneg.* 55,
6). The exact site of the statue of
Maenius is unknown, cf. Jacobi,
Museographie, p. 60.

1. ex foedere, i. e. the treaty concluded by Sp. Cassius in B.C. 493,
cf. *Röm. Forsch.* ii, p. 163, note 22.

2. Antiatibus: the orator's platform was from that time called the
rostra (Liv. viii, 14, 12). For its
statues, see Gilbert, *Rom*, p. 153, note 3.

3. C. Duillio: a portion of the inscribed basis, restored in antiquity,
belonging to the *columna Duilia*, was
found in 1565 (Helbig, *Class. Ant.* 543;
C. I. L. i, 195).

4. de Poenis. After the battle
of Mylae, B.C. 260.

§ 21. 5. L. Minucio : his column,
surmounted by the statue, is shown on
the reverse of a denarius of B.C. 129
of C. Minucius Augurinus (Babelon,

Monn. de la Rép. Rom., ii, p. 228;
Mommsen, *Röm. Münzw.* p. 550, no.
265). Livy, iv, 16, 2, mentions only
a gilt ox erected in honour of Minucius.

praefecto annonae : Liv. iv, 12, 8,
cf. Hirschfeld, *Verwaltungsgeschichte*,
p. 134.

6. unciaria stipe collata: according to Mommsen, *Staatsrecht*, iii,
p. 1185, note 3, this possibly means
that the expenses were met by volun-
tary contributions, whereas they otherwise fell to the *Aerarium*.

8. frivolis, because the statue was
set up in honour of the supposed
miracles of the whet-stone (Liv. i, 36)
and of the *Ficus ruminalis*. For
Pliny's scepticism in these matters see
xv, 77.

Atti Navi : he was represented
as under average height, and wearing
the priestly fillet (Dionysios iii, 71,
5). The statue stood on the left of
the steps leading up to the curia
(Livy, *loc. cit.*). The mention of
this statue, in confirmation of the
statement *antea enim a senatu*, brings
with it a long digression, thoroughly

bound by treaty to give one third of the spoils taken in war.
In the same consulship, in the year of Rome 416 [338 B.C.], he
defeated the people of Antium, and fixed the beaks of *The*
their ships upon the platform in the forum. Another column, *'Rostra.'*
in honour of Gaius Duillius, who enjoyed the first naval triumph *C. Duil-*
for his victory over the Carthaginians, is still standing in the forum. *lius ;*
Another was set up outside the Porta Trigemina, in honour of 21
Lucius Minucius, chief commissioner of the corn supply, and *Lucius*
for it a rate of one twelfth of an *as* was levied. This was, *Minucius.*
I believe, the first time this honour was conferred by the people, 439 B.C.
for previously it had been left in the hands of the Senate. Certainly the distinction were an honourable one save for the
slight grounds for which it was first conferred. For instance,
there was in front of the Senate House a statue of Attus *Statue of*
Navius, the base of which was destroyed when the Senate House *Attus*
was burnt down at the funeral of Publius Clodius, and in the 52 B.C.
comitium there was another, dedicated at the public expense, of *Hermo-*
Hermodoros, the Ephesian, who expounded the laws drawn up *doros ;*
by the Decemvirs. Very different were the reasons which 22
entitled Horatius Cocles to the statue which is still standing : *Horatius*
single-handed he had held the Sublician bridge against the foe. 508 B.C.
Nor am I astonished that a statue, or even three statues, of the *The three*
Sibyl should stand near the Rostra. One of these was replaced *Sibyls.*
by Sextus Pacuvius Taurus, when plebeian aedile, and the two
others by Marcus Messala. I should consider these statues and
that of Attus Navius, which date from the reign of Tarquin the
Ancient, to be the earliest we have, were it not that on the Capitol

in Pliny's manner, on ancient statues
in Rome; the subject of the statues
raised on columns is not resumed till
§ 27.

    fuit, i. e. the statue had disappeared
when Pliny wrote.

    10. **Hermodori** : cf. Strabo xiv,
p. 642 ; Cic. *Tusc. Disp.* v, 36, 105.
The statue presumably stood in front
of the old rostra, by the Twelve Tables
upon which the laws were inscribed.
It had been removed in Pliny's day,
cf. Jacobi, *Museographie*, p. 50.

    § 22. 12. **Horati Coclitis** : below
§ 29. The statue stood *in comitio*
Liv. ii, 10, 12 ; afterwards removed to

the *area Volcani* Aul. Gell. iv, 5, 1.
Cocles was represented full-armed,
with perhaps an indication of his
lameness, Dionysios v, 25 ; Plut. *Publ.*
xvi.

    14. **iuxta rostra**, i. e. the old ros-
tra. These new Sibyls are probably
identical with the τρία φᾶτα mentioned
by Procop. *De Bell. Goth.* i, 25, p. 122,
as standing between the curia and the
temple of Janus (O. Gilbert, *Rom*, iii,
p. 228, note 2).

    15. **Sextus Pacuius Taurus**,
probably identical with the trib. pl.,
B. C. 27.

aetate Tarquinii Prisci, ni regum antecedentium essent in
23 Capitolio. ex his Romuli et Tatii sine tunica, sicut et
Camilli in rostris. et ante aedem Castorum fuit Q. Marci
Tremuli equestris togata, qui Samnites bis devicerat capta-
A.U.C. 448. que Anagnia populum stipendio liberaverat. inter anti- 5
quissimas sunt et Tulli Cloeli, L. Rosci, Spuri Nauti,
A.U.C. 316. C. Fulcini in rostris, a Fidenatibus in legatione interfectorum.
24 hoc a re p. tribui solebat iniuria caesis, sicut aliis et P. Iunio,
A.U.C. 524. Ti. Coruncanio, qui ab Teuta Illyriorum regina interfecti
erant. non omittendum videtur quod annales adnotavere 10
tripedaneas iis statuas in foro statutas. haec videlicet mensura honorata tunc erat. non praeteribo et Cn. Octavium
ob unum SC. verbum. hic regem Antiochum daturum se
responsum dicentem virga quam tenebat forte circum-
scripsit priusque quam egrederetur circulo illo responsum 15
A.U.C. 592. dare coegit. in qua legatione interfecto senatus statuam
poni iussit quam oculatissimo loco, eaque est in rostris.
25 invenitur statua decreta et Taraciae Gaiae sive Fufetiae
virgini Vestali, ut poneretur ubi vellet, quod adiectum
non minus honoris habet quam feminae esse decretam. 20
meritum eius ipsis ponam annalium verbis : quod campum
Tiberinum gratificata esset ea populo.

---

1. **regum.** Cf. xxxiii, 9, 10, 24.

in Capitolio: cf. Appian, 'Εμφ.
i, 16, where Tib. Gracchus is killed
by the doors of the temple of Capitoline
Jupiter near the statues of the kings.

§ 23. 2. **sine tunica,** i. e. wrapped
in the toga alone, cf. Aul. Gell. vi,
12 ; Asconius (on Cic. *pro Scaur.* 30)
says that the younger Cato as praetor
used to lay aside the tunic *ex vetere
consuetudine, secundum quam et
Romuli et Tatii statuae in Capitolio
et in rostris Camilli fuerunt togatae
sine tunicis.* The difference of costume
shows that the statues of the kings were
put up at different dates. Pliny's information seems derived from Verrius,
cf. xxxiii, 63 *tunica aurea triumphasse
Tarquinium Priscum Verrius docet.*

et Camilli: see the passage from
Asconius quoted above.

3. **Q. Marci Tremuli:** Liv. ix, 43,
22 *statua equestris in foro decreta
est quae ante templum Castoris posita
est* ; cf. Cic. *Phil.* vi, 5, 13. For a possible echo of the statue see Mommsen,
Röm. Münzw. p. 549, n. 263.

qui . . . liberaverat : these words
appear to come from an inscription
in Saturnine verse, qui bís devícit
Sámni | -teís Anágniámque ‖ cepít
populúm stipéndi | ó líberavit (Urlichs
in *Chrestom.* p. 307).

5. **stipendio :** according to the
treaty concluded by Sp. Cassius in
B. C. 486, the Hernicans had been entitled to a third of the war booty ;
on this clause see Mommsen, *Röm.
Forsch.* ii, p. 163, n. 22.

inter antiquissimas sunt : the
use of the present shows that
Pliny is transcribing direct from his

we have the statues of Tarquin's predecessors. Among these the 23
figures of Romulus and Tatius are without the tunic, and so is *Ancient kings.*
that of Camillus on the Rostra. In front of the temple of Castor
there also stood an equestrian statue of Quintus Marcius Tremulus *Q. M.*
wearing the toga. He had conquered the Samnites in two battles, *Tremulus.*
and by taking Anagnia had freed Rome from payment of 306 B.C.
the war tax. The statues on the Rostra to Tullus Cloelius, *Roman*
Lucius Roscius, Spurius Nautius, and Gaius Fulcinus, ambassadors *ambassa-dors killed*
killed by the people of Fidenae, are also among the earliest. *by the*
This honour was usually paid by the state to those who had *Fidenates.*
been killed in violation of the law of nations; it was done in many 24
cases, notably that of Publius Junius and Tiberius Coruncanius, 230 B.C.
who were put to death by Teuta, queen of Illyricum. It is worth *Publius Junius and*
noticing that according to the annals the statues set up in the *Tiberius*
forum on these occasions were three feet high; apparently this was *Corun-canius.*
the height in vogue in those days. I shall mention the statue of
Gnaeus Octavius, on account of one clause in the decree of the *Cn.*
Senate. King Antiochos had wished to delay an answer, where- *Octavius.*
upon Octavius drew a circle round him with a rod which he
chanced to have in his hand, and compelled the king to give an
answer before he stepped outside the circle. Octavius was killed 162 B.C.
while on this embassy, and the Senate ordered a statue to be set
up in his honour 'in as visible a place as possible': the statue
accordingly stands on the Rostra. I find a decree giving a statue 25
to Taracia Gaia or Fufetia, a Vestal virgin, 'to be placed where *Taracia Gaia.*
she pleased,' a clause no less to her honour than the actual
dedication of a statue to a woman. According to the words of
the annals, which I will quote, she received these honours
'*because she had presented to the people the field by the Tiber.*'

anthor; the statues had already dis-
appeared in Cicero's time: *Lars Tolumnius rex Veientium quattuor legatos populi Romani Fidenis interemit, quorum statuae steterunt usque ad meam memoriam in rostris. Phil.* ix, 2, 4.

§ 24. 8. P. Iunio, Ti. Coruncanio. Polybios, ii, p. 131 (ed. Büttner-Wobst), calls them Γάϊος and Λεύκιος (Κοραγκάνιοι). They had been sent to put down piracy on the Illyrian coast.

11. tripedaneas refers not only to

the last-mentioned statues, but also to those of the ambassadors to the Fidenates.

12. Cn. Octavium, § 13, murdered at Laodicea in B.C. 162; cf. Cic. *Phil.* ix, 2, 4 *statuam videmus in rostris.* By a confusion Pliny attributes to Octavius an act performed by C. Popilius Laenas, on the occasion of his embassy to Antiochus IV Epiphanes in B.C. 168, Cic. *Phil.* viii, 8, 23; Liv. xlv, 12.

§ 25. 18. Taraciae Gaiae sive Fufetiae ... populo: this curious

26 Invenio et Pythagorae et Alcibiadi in cornibus comitii
A.U.C. 411. positas, cum bello Samniti Apollo Pythius iussisset
fortissimo Graiae gentis et alteri sapientissimo simulacra
A.U.C. 666. celebri loco dicari. eae stetere donec Sulla dictator ibi
curiam faceret. mirumque est illos patres Socrati cunctis 5
ab eodem deo sapientia praelato Pythagoran praetulisse
aut tot aliis virtute Alcibiaden et quemquam utroque
27 Themistocli. columnarum ratio erat attolli super ceteros
mortales, quod et arcus significant novicio invento. primus
tamen honos coepit a Graecis, nullique arbitror plures 10
statuas dicatas quam Phalereo Demetrio Athenis, siquidem
CCCLX statuere nondum anno hunc numerum dierum
A.U.C. 670. excedente, quas mox laceravere. statuerunt et Romae in

8. tolli *omnes praeter Bamb.*, Detlefsen.

statement is best examined in the light of a passage from Aulus Gellius, vii, 7, 1–4 *Accae Larentiae et Gaiae Taraciae, sive illa Fufetia est, nomina in* antiquis annalibus *celebria sunt. earum alterae post mortem, Taraciae autem vivae amplissimi honores a populo Romano habiti. et Taraciam quidem virginem Vestalem fuisse lex Horatia testis est, quae super ea ad populum lata. qua lege ei plurimi honores fiunt, inter quos ius quoque testimonii dicendi tribuitur* 'testabilis'*que una omnium feminarum ut sit datur. id verbum est legis ipsius* Horatiae; *contrarium est in* duodecim tabulis*scriptum:* improbus intestabilisque esto. *praeterea si quadraginta annos nata sacerdotio abire ac nubere voluisset, ius ei potestasque exaugurandi atque nubendi facta est munificentiae et beneficii gratia, quod campum Tiberinum sive Martium populo condonasset.* Though the personality of Taracia is clearly defined in this passage, it cannot be supposed that the region of the Çampus Martius had been so late as republican times in the possession of a single person, and that a Vestal virgin; close examination shows the aitiological nature of the whole story.

The privileges granted to Taracia are simply the common privileges of all the Vestals; in order to account for these the story of the gift of the land was adapted from the myth of Acca Larentia. Taracia is in fact a mere double of Larentia; her name betrays an evident connexion with Tarutius, the Tuscan husband of Acca Larentia, to whom he leaves the Ager Turax, i. e. the Campus Tiberinus (Plut. *Rom.* v.), which Larentia in turn bequeaths to the Roman people; a genuine myth which has for kernel the fact that the region of the Campus Martius had once been Etruscan (see Plut. *Publ.* viii, where the story of the gift and the privileges is substantially the same, but the name of the heroine is Ταρκυνία; cf. Liv. ii, 5, 2 *ager Tarquiniorum*). A statue was possibly put up to the mythical Vestal, benefactress of the Romans, but as no statue is mentioned either by Gellius or Plutarch (see Detlefsen, *De Art. Rom. Ant.* ii, p. 13), and as Pliny does not say he saw the statue, but merely that the annals stated that one was decreed, it is probable that the statue only existed in the anecdote, and that its mention represented what was

I find that statues of Pythagoras and Alkibiades were erected **26**
at the corners of the comitium, after an oracle of the Pythian *Pythagoras and Alki-*
Apollo, delivered in the course of the Samnite war, had ordered *biades.*
that a statue in honour of the bravest man of Hellenic birth, 343 B.C.
and another in honour of the wisest should be dedicated in
a much frequented place. These statues remained until the
dictator Sulla built the Council Chamber there. It is strange 88 B.C.
that the Senate of the day chose Pythagoras in preference to
Sokrates, whom Apollo had declared to be wiser than all men,
or that they chose Alkibiades before many other brave men, and
in fact that they selected any one for either quality in preference
to Themistokles.

The use of the columns was to raise the statues above **27**
ordinary men, and this is also the purpose of the arches which *Origin of statues*
have been recently introduced. The Greeks, however, were the *raised on*
first who conferred statues as a mark of honour, and I imagine *columns and on*
that no man has had so many statues dedicated to him as *arches.*
Demetrios of Phaleron at Athens, inasmuch as three hundred *Demetrios*
and sixty were set up at a time when the year only contained *of Pha-leron;*
that number of days. All these statues were afterwards broken *Gaius*
up. At Rome too the tribes put up statues in every street in *Marius Grati-dianus.*

84 B.C.

most likely another clause of the *lex Horatia*, namely, the right of the Vestals to have their portrait-statues erected. O. Gilbert, *Rom*, ii, p. 112, note 3.

The praenomen *Gaia* was given to *Taracia* in order to latinize her; cf. Tanaquil, who also bore the Latin names of *Gaia Cecilia*. The alternative name *Fufetia* is according to Gilbert *loc. cit.* probably Etruscan. For the masculine *Fufetius* cf. the famous Alban dictator Metius Fufetius, Liv. i, 23, 4 &c.

§ 26. 1. Pythagorae et Alcib. in cornibus, ἐπὶ τῆς ἀγορᾶς Plut. *Num.* viii.

5. curiam: altered and enlarged by Sulla (B. C. 88), who caused many of the statues in or in front of the curia to be removed. This new curia was burnt in B.C. 52, on the occasion of the riots at the funeral of Clodius

(§ 21), and rebuilt by Faustus Sulla, son of the dictator.

§ 27. 8. columnarum: resumes the subject of § 21.

9. arcus: on which stood statues and chariots. The oldest known instance is the arch or *fornix* of Q. Fabius Maximus Allobrogicus (B.C. 120) of which remains are to be seen close to the temple of Faustina. The simpler *fornix* developed into the elaborate triumphal arches of the Emperors.

12. nondum, i. e. before the reform of the calendar by Julius Caesar. Add.

13. laceravere: on the entrance of Demetrios Poliorketes into the city, Strabo ix, p. 398; Diogenes Laertios v, 5, 75 f. Pliny evidently has this statement as to the number of statues put up to Demetrios from Varro (see *Imagines, ap.* Nonius, p. 528 M.); cf. Wachsmuth, *Stadt Athen*, p. 611, note 1. Addenda.

omnibus vicis tribus Mario Gratidiano, ut diximus, easdem-

A.U.C. 671. que subvertere Sullae introitu.

28   Pedestres sine dubio Romae fuere in auctoritate longo tempore, et equestrium tamen origo perquam vetus est cum feminis etiam honore communicato Cloeliae statua 5 equestri, ceu parum esset toga eam cingi, cum Lucretiae ac Bruto, qui expulerant reges propter quos Cloelia inter

29 obsides fuerat, non decernerentur.   hanc primam cum

A.U.C. 246. Coclitis publice dicatam crediderim—Atto enim ac Sibyllae Tarquinium ac reges sibi ipsos posuisse verisimile est—nisi 10 Cloeliae quoque Piso traderet ab iis positam qui una opsides fuissent, redditis a Porsina in honorem eius, e diverso Annius Fetialis equestrem, quae fuerit contra Iovis Statoris aedem in vestibulo Superbi domus, Valeriae fuisse Publicolae consulis filiae, eamque solam refugisse Tiberimque transnata- 15 visse ceteris opsidibus qui Porsinae mittebantur interemptis Tarquinii insidiis.

30   L. Piso prodidit M. Aemilio C. Popilio iterum cos.

A.U.C. 596. a censoribus P. Cornelio Scipione M. Popilio statuas circa forum eorum qui magistratum gesserant sublatas omnis 20 praeter eas quae populi aut senatus sententia statutae essent, eam vero quam apud aedem Telluris statuisset sibi Sp. Cassius qui regnum adfectaverat etiam conflatam a censori-

---

1. **Mario Gratidiano, ut diximus**: xxxiii, 132; he introduced a method of testing the *denarii* issued by the mint (cf. Cic. *de Off.* iii, 20, 80). According to Mommsen (*Röm. Münzw.* p. 388) this would be insufficient to account for the almost divine honours paid to him; it seems more than probable that he also withdrew the plated coins from circulation.

§ 28. 6. **Lucretiae ac Bruto**: of the statue of Lucretia nothing more is known. The statue of Brutus stood near those of the kings (§ 23) on the Capitol; see Plut. *Brutus*, i, where the statue is described as holding a drawn sword.

§ 29. 11. **ab iis qui ... fuissent**: Livy (*loc. cit.*) says simply that the Romans awarded the statue; see Nitzch, *Röm. Annalistik*, p. 52.

12. **e diverso ... Valeriae**: cf. Plutarch, *Publ.* xix. The doubt as to the name shows that the statue bore no inscription. Neither Pliny nor Livy could probably have seen it, since Dionysios (v, 35) speaks of it as having disappeared in his day. From Seneca (*Consol. ad Marciam*, 16) and Plutarch *loc. cit.*, it appears that it was restored at a later date (cf. Urlichs, *Quellen-Register*, p. 5).

Annius Fetialis: only known from Pliny (*Indices* to xvi, xxxiii, xxxvi).

13. **Iovis Statoris**, ii, 140. The temple stood on the Sacred Way, at the commencement of the *Clivus*

honour of Gaius Marius Gratidianus, as I have said, and overthrew them again when Sulla entered the city.   83 B.C.

It is certain that standing statues were customary in Rome at 28
a very early date.   Still the first equestrian statues are extremely *Compara-tive*
old, and women shared the honour of them with men when *antiquity*
Cloelia, as if it were not enough that she should be re- *of standing and of*
presented wearing the toga, was granted such a statue, though *equestrian*
none were given to Lucretia and Brutus, and yet they had *statues.*
expelled that royal family for whose interests Cloelia was a *Cloelia.*
hostage.   I should readily believe this statue and that of Cocles 29
to be the first dedicated by the state (for it is probable that Tar- 508 B.C.
quinius set up those to Attus and the Sibyl, and that the kings
each set up their own), were it not for Piso's statement that the
statue to Cloelia was raised by her fellow-hostages, who were sent
back by Porsenna in honour of her.   Annius Fetialis on the other
hand says that the equestrian statue which stood opposite the
temple of Jupiter the Upholder in the vestibule of the house of
Tarquin the Proud was that of Valeria, the daughter of the consul *Valeria.*
Publicola.   She alone, he says, escaped and swam across the
Tiber, while the other hostages sent to Porsenna were treacherously
killed by Tarquinius.   Lucius Piso states that in the second con- 30
sulship of Marcus Aemilius and Gaius Popilius all the statues of *158 B.C. Removal of*
magistrates standing round the forum, except those which had been *statues of*
set up in accordance with a decree of the people or of the Senate, *magistrates not erected*
were removed by the censors Publius Cornelius Scipio and Marcus *by a decree*
Popilius.   The one near the temple of Earth, set up in his own *of the people or*
honour by Spurius Cassius, who aimed at the kingship, was further *the Senate.*
melted down by the censors; thus even in the matter of a statue

---

Palatinus, near the arch of Titus; the
house of Tarquin was close to it (Liv.
i, 41, 4), cf. Liv. ii, 13, 11 *in summa
sacra via fuit posita virgo insidens
equo*, without any closer definition of
the spot.

§ 30. 21. **praeter eas** : the measure
would be intended to prevent the
crowding of public places by statues
put up by private individuals (*loca
tueri*) ; Mommsen, *Staatsrecht*, ii,
p. 437, cf. Liv. xl, 51, 3.

23. **conflatam a censoribus** : not
of course by the censors mentioned
above, or the sentence would have

ended at *conflatam*.   For the duties
of censors as regards the removing of
statues, cf. Mommsen, *op. cit.*, p. 443.
As there were, however, no censors
in the days of Spurius Cassius
(office created B.C. 445), we must conclude that Pliny's account is incorrect.
According to Mommsen (*Röm. Forschungen*, ii, p. 167, note 28) Piso,
in recounting the events of A. U. C. 596,
may have stated that Sp. Cassius had
set up a statue in his own honour on
the spot where at a later date stood
the temple of Tellus (vowed B.C. 268
and ded. B.C. 252 by P. Sempronius

bus. nimirum in ea quoque re ambitionem providebant
31 illi viri. exstant Catonis in censura vociferationes mulieribus
A.U.C. 570. statuas Romanis in provinciis poni. nec tamen potuit in-
hibere quo minus Romae quoque ponerentur, sicuti Corneliae
Gracchorum matri, quae fuit Africani prioris filia. sedens 5
huic posita soleisque sine ammento insignis in Metelli publica
porticu, quae statua nunc est in Octaviae operibus.

32   Publice autem ab exteris posita est Romae C. Aelio
A.U.C. 469. tr. pl. lege perlata in Sthennium Stallium Lucanum qui
Thurinos bis infestaverat. ob id Aelium Thurini statua et 10
corona aurea donarunt. idem postea Fabricium donavere
A.U.C. 472. statua liberati obsidione, passimque gentes in clientelas ita
receptae, et adeo discrimen omne sublatum ut Hannibalis
etiam statuae tribus locis visantur in ea urbe cuius intra
A.U.C. 543. muros solus hostium emisit hastam.   15

33   Fuisse autem statuariam artem familiarem Italiae quoque et vetustam indicant Hercules ab Evandro sacratus,
ut produnt, in foro boario, qui triumphalis vocatur atque
per triumphos vestitur habitu triumphali, praeterea Ianus
geminus a Numa rege dicatus, qui pacis bellique argumento 20
colitur digitis ita figuratis ut CCCLXV dierum nota per

---

3. Romanis statuas *omnes praeter Bamb., Detlefsen.*

Sophus), and that this statue was
melted down when he was con-
demned—some such statement mis-
leading Pliny into the double error of
supposing (1) that the statue stood in
the temple of Tellus, (2) that the
second measure recounted above was,
like the first, carried out by censors,
whom he was naturally at a loss to
name.

2. illi viri ; used by Pliny to cover
his ignorance of the censor's names.

§ 31. mulieribus: cf. Cato's speech
on the *Lex Oppia*, as narrated by
Livy, xxxiv, 2-4 ; for his dislike of
statues in general cf. the anecdote
told by Plutarch, *Praec. Gerend. Reip.*
xxvii, B (Bernardakis, v, p. 115).

4. Corneliae : vii, 57 ; Plutarch
C. Gracchus, iv. The rectangular
basis of this statue was found in 1878

on the site of the porticus Octaviae ;
it is inscribed (a) *Opus Tisicratis,*
(b) *Cornelia Africani f*(ilia) *Gracchorum* (sc. *mater*). (b) is the earlier
inscription ; it is probable that the
statue of Cornelia was destroyed in
the great fire of A.D. 80, after which
the basis was used a second time for
some copy of a work of Teisikrates
(§ 67), Löwy, *I. G. B.* 493. Cf.
Bernoulli, *Röm. Iconogr.* i, p. 72 ff.
From the shape of the basis, Cornelia
appears to have been represented
seated, in the scheme familiar from
the so-called statues of Agrippina.

6. Metelli ... porticu : erected
by Q. Metellus Macedonicus after his
triumph B.C. 146. On its site Augustus
built in honour of his sister the famous
porticus Octaviae.

§ 32. 9. lege perlata : this measure

they provided against possible ambition. We know the protests
of Cato, in his censorship, against the statues set up to Roman
women in the provinces, and yet he could not prevent their being
set up in Rome itself, for example to Cornelia the mother of
the Gracchi and daughter of the elder Africanus. It is a seated
figure, remarkable as having shoes without thongs, which was
formerly in the public colonnade of Metellus and is now in
the galleries of Octavia.

31
184 B.C.
*Protests of
Cato the
Censor
against
statues of
women.*

The first statue set up at Rome at the cost of a foreign
nation was to Gaius Aelius, tribune of the people. He had
carried a law against Sthennius Stallius Lucanus, who had on two
occasions molested the people of Thurii. They in return presented Aelius with a statue and a golden crown, and later on
also gave a statue to Fabricius, who had delivered them from
a siege. This method of receiving a people into clientship
became very general, and all distinction was so completely lost
that statues of Hannibal can be seen in three places in a city
within whose walls he, alone among its enemies, has hurled his
spear.

32
*Statues
erected by
foreign
cities.*
285 B.C.

282 B.C.

*Statues of
Hannibal
in Rome.*
211 B.C.

That there was an ancient art of statuary, native to Italy,
is proved by the tradition which assigns to Evander the consecration of the Hercules in the Cattle Market, which is known
as the triumphal Hercules and draped at every triumph in
a triumphal robe. There is moreover the two-headed Janus
dedicated by King Numa, which is honoured as marking peace
or war; his fingers are bent to form 365, which is the number of

33
*Native
Italian
statuary.*
Hercules.
*Two-
headed
Janus.*

is mentioned only in this passage;
nothing further is known of this statue
or that of Fabricius.

13. **Hannibalis :** brought either
from Carthage or from Asia Minor.

§ 33. 16. **statuariam :** see on *toreuticen* in § 54.

17. **Hercules :** in the ancient shrine
(Tac. *Ann.* xv, 41 : *magna ara fanum-
que, quae praesenti Herculi Arcas
Evander sacraverat*) near to which,
at a later date, was built the round
temple of Hercules, which contained
the paintings of Pacuvius ; Peter *ap.*
Roscher, i, 2911 ff. ; cf. note on xxxv,
19), and below on § 33.

19. **Ianus geminus :** in his temple

near the curia at the N.E. end of the
Forum. The head of the statue appears
on the oldest Roman libral asses
(Roscher s. v. *Janus*, Mommsen, *Röm.
Münzw.* p. 175). One of the faces
looked towards the West and the
Great Forum, the other towards the
East and the Forum Julium (cf. Pro-
cop. *Bell. Goth.* i, 25).

20. **pacis bellique arg. :** *indicem
pacis bellique fecit* Liv. i, 19, 2.

21. **digitis ita figuratis :** this
curious statement is confirmed by
Macrobius, *Sat.* i, 9, 10, and John
Lydos, περὶ μηνῶν, i, 4. A number of
ingenious explanations are quoted in
Hardouin's note on the passage.

significationem anni temporis et aevi esse deum indicent.
34 signa quoque Tuscanica per terras dispersa quin in Etruria
factitata sint non est dubium.   deorum tantum putarem ea
fuisse, ni Metrodorus Scepsius cui cognomen a Romani
A.U.C. 489. nominis odio inditum est propter M M statuarum Volsinios 5
expugnatos obiceret.   mirumque mihi videtur, cum statuarum origo tam vetus Italiae sit, lignea potius aut fictilia
deorum simulacra in delubris dicata usque ad devictam
35 Asiam, unde luxuria.   similitudines exprimendi quae prima
fuerit origo, in ea quam plasticen Graeci vocant dici con- 10
venientius erit, etenim prior quam statuaria fuit.   sed haec
ad infinitum effloruit multorum voluminum operi, si quis
plura persequi velit, omnia enim quis possit ?

36   M. Scauri aedilitate signorum M M M in scaena tan-
A.U.C. 695. tum fuere temporario theatro.   Mummius Achaia devicta 15
A.U.C. 608. replevit urbem non relicturus filiae dotem.   cur enim non
cum excusatione ponatur?   multa et Luculli invexere.
Rhodi etiamnum $\overline{\text{LXXIII}}$ signorum esse Mucianus ter
cos. prodidit, nec pauciora Athenis, Olympiae, Delphis
37 superesse creduntur.   quis ista mortalium persequi possit 20
aut quis usus noscendi intellegatur?   insignia maxime et
aliqua de causa notata voluptarium sit attigisse artificesque
celebratos nominavisse, singulorum quoque inexplicabili
multitudine, cum Lysippus MD opera fecisse prodatur,
tantae omnia artis ut claritatem possent dare vel singula, 25
numerum apparuisse defuncto eo, cum thensaurum effre-
gisset heres, solitum enim ex manipretio cuiusque signi

12. operi *Bamb.* ; opere *reliqui, Detlefsen.*   18. $\overline{\text{LXXIII}}$} *Bamb. Ricc.* ;
LXXIII *Voss. (teste Detlefsen)* ; *numerus aperte corruptus.*

1. aevi esse deum : ὡσεὶ τοῦ αἰῶνος
πατέρα, John Lydos, *loc. cit.*

§ 34. 4. Metrodorus Scepsius :
born about B.C. 145 ; Müller, *F. H. G.*
iii, pp. 202-205 ; Susemihl, *Griech.*
Lit. in der Alexandr. Zeit, ii, p.
352 ff.

7. lignea : in Italy, as in Greece,
statuary began with the wooden idols
which not unfrequently remained
objects of worship even in the greatest
periods of art, e. g. the Athene Polias

of olive wood in the Erechtheion at
Athens, Paus. i, 26, 6 ; 27, 1 ; ii,
25, 1, &c.

fictilia : xxxv, 157.

§ 35. 11. prior quam statuaria :
since a bronze statue presupposed
a clay model, note on xxxv, 153.

§ 36. 14. M. Scauri aedilitate :
viii, 64, xxxv, 127.   For the theatre
see xxxvi, 5, 50, 113-115, 189; it
was erected in the Campus Martius,
but the exact spot is unknown.

days in the year, and by thus indicating the year they mark him as the god of time and the age. We also find, scattered in 34 different countries, statues in the Tuscan style, which must certainly have been made in Etruria. I should incline to think that these were only figures of the gods, did not Metrodoros of Skepsis, whose other name of μισορωμαῖος or Roman-Hater was given him from his hatred of Rome, accuse us of having taken Volsinii for the sake of its two thousand statues. To me it seems 265 B.C. strange that, though statuary in Italy has so ancient an origin, *Images of wood or* the images of the gods dedicated in the shrines were by preference *terra-cotta* made of wood or of terra-cotta until the conquest of Asia intro- *preferred in the* duced luxury. It will be better to speak of the origin of the model- *temples.* ling of portraits when we treat of the art which the Greeks call 35 πλαστική, as it is earlier than statuary. The latter art has been infinitely developed; a fuller discussion would require many volumes, an exhaustive treatise is scarcely possible.

Marcus Scaurus in his aedileship adorned the stage of a mere 36 temporary theatre with three thousand statues. Mummius filled *58 B.C. Statues in* all Rome with sculpture after his conquest of Achaia, and yet *Theatre of* I must add in his favour that he eventually died too poor to *Marcus* leave his daughter a dowry. The Luculli too brought over a *Scaurus.* number of statues; seventy-three thousand are still to be seen at 146 B.C. Rhodes, according to Mucianus, who was three times consul, A.D. 67, 70, and it is supposed that at least as many still remain at Athens, 72. Olympia and Delphoi. A detailed knowledge of all these is 37 unattainable and would moreover serve no purpose; still I should like to touch on the most famous, and those which any par- ticular circumstance has made noteworthy, and to name the illustrious artists. Even the works of individual sculptors are too numerous to be catalogued; Lysippos, for example, is said to 1500 have made fifteen hundred pieces of statuary, all of such merit *statues by Lysippos.* that any one alone would bring him fame. Their number was

15. Achaia devicta: xxxiii, 149.
16. dotem: cf. Frontinus, *Strateg.* iv, 3, 15.
17. et Luculli: i.e. L. Licinius, the conqueror of Mithridates, cos. B.C. 74 (xxxv, 125, 155), and his brother Marcus, below § 39; cos. B.C. 73; triumphed B.C. 71.
18. Rhodi etiamnum: Jerome (see Addenda) *Chron.* Ol. 184, 4,

ed. Schoene, p. 139: *templa Rho- diorum depopulatus est Cassius*, but from Pliny it appears that the plundering cannot have been so thorough as set forth either by Appian ἐμφυλ. iv, 81, Val. Max. i, 5, 8, or Orosius, vi, 18, 3.
Mucianus: see Introd. p. lxxxv.
§ 37. 24. Lysippus: the anecdote of the money-box may be traced

38 denarios seponere aureos singulos. evecta supra humanam
fidem ars est successu, mox et audacia. in argumentum
successus unum exemplum adferam, nec deorum hominumve
similitudinis expressae. aetas nostra vidit in Capitolio,
A.U.C. 822. priusquam id novissime conflagraret a Vitellianis incensum, 5
in cella Iunonis canem ex aere volnus suum lambentem,
cuius eximium miraculum et indiscreta veri similitudo non
eo solum intellegitur quod ibi dicata fuerat, verum et satisdatione, nam quoniam summa nulla par videbatur, capite
tutelarios cavere pro ea institutum publice fuit.   10

39   Audaciae innumera sunt exempla.   moles quippe
excogitatas videmus statuarum, quas colossaeas vocant,
turribus pares. talis est in Capitolio Apollo tralatus a
A.U.C. 681. M. Lucullo ex Apollonia Ponti urbe, XXX cubitorum,
40 D talentis factus, talis in campo Martio Iuppiter a Claudio 15
Caesare dicatus, qui devoratur Pompeiani theatri vicinitate,
talis et Tarenti factus a Lysippo XL cubitorum. mirum in
eo quod manu, ut ferunt, mobilis—ea ratio libramenti est—
nullis convellatur procellis. id quidem providisse et artifex
dicitur modico intervallo, unde maxime flatum opus erat 20
frangi, opposita columna. itaque magnitudinem propter
difficultatemque moliendi non attigit eum Fabius Verru-
A.U.C. 545. cosus, cum Herculem qui est in Capitolio inde transferret.
41 ante omnis autem in admiratione fuit Solis colossus Rhodi,

back to Duris, below § 51 ; Introd.
p. xlviii.

1. **denarios** : the Roman golden
denarius was worth about £1, but the
reference here must be to the στατήρ=
16*s.* nearly. Introd. p. lxxxiv.

§ 38. 4. **in Capitolio** : after the
temple had been burnt down in B.C. 83,
Sulla undertook its reconstruction,
which was eventually carried out by Q.
Lutatius Catulus, who dedicated the
new temple in B. C. 69. It was burnt
again *a Vitellianis*, Tac. *Hist.* iii, 71.

6. **in cella Iunonis** ; on the
right of the central cella of Jupiter ;
the cella on the left was dedicated to
Minerva.

9. **capite** : cf. xxxvi, 29 . . . *capitali satisdatione fama iudicet dignos*
(i. e. two statuary groups).

§ 39. 13. **Apollo**: Καλάμιδος ἔργον.
Strab. vii, p. 319.

§ 40. 15. **a Cl. Caesare**. Claudius
restored the theatre of Pompeius
after a fire, and probably dedicated
the Jupiter on the same occasion. Tac.
Ann. iii, 72.

16. **Pompeiani theatri** ; near the
Great Circus.

17. **factus a Lysippo** : it represented Zeus, and according to Strabo,
p. 278, was the tallest colossus after
that of Rhodes.

discovered when his heir broke open his money-box after his death, for it was his custom to lay by a piece of gold out of the price he received for each statue.

Art has made extraordinary progress, in technique first and afterwards in audacity. As an example of successful technique I shall mention a figure representing neither god nor man. Before the last fire on the Capitol, caused by the soldiers of Vitellius, our own generation could see in the temple of Juno a bronze dog licking its wound: the wonderful workmanship and absolutely life-like treatment are sufficiently proved not only by the sacred spot where the work was dedicated, but also by the unusual guarantee demanded for it. No sum of money was considered equivalent: it was a public ordinance that the curators should pledge their lives for its safety. *38 Technical progress. A.D. 69. Bronze dog.*

Of audacity countless instances can be given. For example artists have conceived the idea of gigantic statues called *colossi*, as tall as towers. Of this class is the Apollo in the Capitol, brought from Apollonia in Pontos by Marcus Lucullus; it is forty-five feet high, and cost five hundred talents [£120,000]. Another is the Jupiter dedicated in the Field of Mars by Claudius Caesar, which, however, is dwarfed by its proximity to the theatre of Pompeius. Yet another is the Zeus at Tarentum by Lysippos, which is 40 cubits [58 ft.] in height and is noteworthy because the weight is so nicely balanced that the colossus can, they say, be turned round by a touch of the hand, and yet cannot be overthrown by the wind. The artist is said to have provided against this by placing a column a little way off, on the side where it was most necessary to break the violence of the wind. The size of the statue and the difficulty of transporting it prevented Fabius Verrucosus from touching it, although he brought the Herakles in the Capitol from Tarentum. The most marvellous of all, however, is the statue *39 Colossi. (a) Apollo in the Capitol. B.C. 73. (b) Jupiter in the Field of Mars. 40 (c) Zeus by Lysippos, at Tarentum. B.C. 209. (d) Herakles in the Capitol. 41*

mirum . . . procellis: periegetic explanation.

22. non attigit Fabius: cf. Liv. xxvii, 16, 8.

23. Herculem: Λυσίππου ἔργον, Strabo, *loc. cit.* The hero was represented without weapons and seated, resting his head on his left hand; cf. Niketas Akominatos *de signis Constantinop.*, p. 859. Near the Hercules stood a bronze equestrian statue of

Fabius himself (Plut. *Fab. Max.* xxii), which he doubtless set up in imitation of Carvilius.

§ 41. 24. ante omnis . . . in admiratione: cf. Luc. *Jup. Trag.* 11. It was even reckoned among the Seven Wonders of the world. The notion that it stood with one foot on each of the moles which formed the entrance to the harbour while ships passed full sail between its legs was unknown to

A.U.C. 527. quem fecerat Chares Lindius, Lysippi supra dicti discipulus.
LXX cubitorum altitudinis fuit. hoc simulacrum post LVI
annum terrae motu prostratum, sed iacens quoque miraculo
est. pauci pollicem eius amplectuntur, maiores sunt digiti
quam pleraeque statuae. vasti specus hiant defractis mem- 5
bris, spectantur intus magnae molis saxa quorum pondere
stabiliverat eum constituens. duodecim annis tradunt effectum CCC talentis quae contigerant ex apparatu regis
42 Demetrii relicto morae taedio opsessa Rhodo. sunt alii
centum numero in eadem urbe colossi minores hoc, sed 10
ubicumque singuli fuissent, nobilitaturi locum, praeterque
43 hos deorum quinque quos fecit Bryaxis. factitavit colossos
et Italia. videmus certe Tuscanicum Apollinem in bibliotheca templi Augusti quinquaginta pedum a pollice, dubium
aere mirabiliorem an pulchritudine. fecit et Sp. Carvilius 15
A.U.C. 461. Iovem qui est in Capitolio victis Samnitibus sacrata lege
pugnantibus e pectoralibus eorum ocreisque et galeis. amplitudo tanta est ut conspiciatur a Latiari Iove. e reliquiis
limae suam statuam fecit quae est ante pedes simulacri eius.
44 habent in eodem Capitolio admirationem et capita duo quae 20
A.U.C. 697. P. Lentulus cos. dicavit, alterum a Charete supra dicto
factum, alterum fecit... dicus conparatione in tantum victus
45 ut artificum minime probabilis videatur. verum omnem
amplitudinem statuarum eius generis vicit aetate nostra
Zenodorus Mercurio facto in civitate Galliae Arvernis per 25

the ancients, and arose in the Middle
Ages. See Cecil Torr, *Rhodes in
Ancient Times*, p. 96 f.
  2. **LXX** cub. altitudinis: presumably from Varro, the measurement
being practically identical with that
given by Vibius Sequester (*Colossus
Rhodi altus pedes CV*), who is known
to have drawn from Varro, Urlichs,
Quellen-Reg. p. 11.
  hoc simulacrum . . . **Bryaxis**:
the picturesque description of the
prostrate colossus, and the mention of
the hundred other colossal statues in
Rhodes, have been rightly referred to
Mucianus by Brieger, *de Font. Plin.*

p. 60. Introd. p. lxxxvii.
  8. ex apparatu: Plut. *Demetr.* 20.
  9. opsessa **Rhodo**: vii, 126;
xxxv, 104, 105.
  § 42. 12. Bryaxis: below, § 73.
  § 43. 13. Tuscanicum Apollinem:
from what we know of Etruscan workmanship, Pliny's admiration must be
prompted by patriotism.
  in bibliotheca: belonging to
the temple of Augustus (xii, 94),
built by Tiberius and Livia in B.C.
14, Dio Cassius, lvi, 46; cf. Suet.
Tib. 74 *in bibliotheca templi novi*.
Gilbert, *Rom*, iii, p. 121, n. 3; it also
contained, besides the customary busts

of the Sun at Rhodes, made by Chares of Lindos, a pupil of the Lysippos already mentioned. It was seventy cubits [102 feet] in height, and after standing for fifty-six years was overthrown by an earthquake, but even as it lies on the ground it arouses wonder. Few men can clasp their arms about its thumb, its fingers are taller than most statues and wide caverns gape within its broken limbs, while inside can be seen huge fragments of rock, originally used as weights to steady it. According to tradition, its construction lasted twelve years, and cost 300 talents [£72,000], contributed by the Rhodians out of the siege-train left with them by King Demetrios when he wearied of the siege of Rhodes. There are a hundred smaller colossal statues in this city, any one of which would have made famous the place it adorned, besides five representing gods, made by Bryaxis. In Italy too colossal statues have been made; we have before our eyes the Tuscan Apollo, in the library of the temple of Augustus, which mea-sures 50 feet from its toe. It is not easy to say whether the beauty of the statue or of the bronze is the more worthy of wonder. After the victory over the Samnites, who fought bound by a solemn vow, Spurius Carvilius made from their breastplates, greaves, and helmets the Jupiter in the Capitol, a statue large enough to be visible from the temple of Jupiter Latiaris. From the filings he made a statue of himself, to stand at the feet of the other. Two heads, also placed on the Capitol, deserve to be admired. They were dedicated by Publius Lentulus: one is the work of the Chares mentioned above, the other is by . . . dikos, who however suffers by the comparison so as to seem a most unattractive artist. In our own times however Zenodoros exceeded the proportions of all other statues of this class. His Mercury was made in Gaul, in the state of the Arverni; he spent ten years upon

(e) Colossus of Rhodes by Chares of Lindos. B.C. 227.

42 Other colossal statues at Rhodes. Five by Bryaxis.

43 Tuscan Apollo. Colossal statues in Italy.

B.C. 293. Jupiter.

44 Colossal heads.

45 Zenodoros. His Mercury.

of illustrious men, a statue of Minerva, Plin. vii, 210.

16. victis Samnitibus: cf. Liv. x, 38-46. It is at least curious that Livy in his elaborate account of the triumph of B.C. 293 should only men-tion the temple of *Fors Fortuna* (x, 46, 14) as erected out of the booty. A. Schaeffer (*Comm. phil. in hon. Momms.* p. 7) accordingly supposes the statue to have been set up at a

later date, and that Pliny, or his author, confused the first and second consulship of Carvilius.

18. Latiari Iove: on the Mons Albanus (Monte Cavo).

§ 44. 21. Charete supra dicto: in § 41. Pliny is the only author who mentions any work of Chares besides the *Colossus*.

§ 45. 25. Zenodorus: perhaps an Alexandrian established in Gaul, see S.

annos decem, HS [CCCC] manipreti, postquam satis artem
ibi adprobaverat, Romam accitus a Nerone, ubi destinatum
illius principis simulacro colossum fecit CXIXS pedum
longitudine, qui dicatus Soli venerationi est damnatis sceleri-
46 bus illius principis. mirabamur in officina non modo ex 5
argilla similitudinem insignem, verum et de parvis admodum
surculis quod primum operis instaurati fuit. ea statua
indicavit interisse fundendi aeris scientiam, cum et Nero
largiri aurum argentumque paratus esset et Zenodorus
scientia fingendi caelandique nulli veterum postponeretur. 10
47 statuam Arvernorum cum faceret provinciae Dubio Avito
praesidente, duo pocula Calamidis manu caelata, quae Cassio
Salano avonculo eius praeceptori suo Germanicus Caesar
adamata donaverat, aemulatus est ut vix ulla differentia
esset artis. quanto maior Zenodoro praestantia fuit, tanto 15
magis deprehenditur aeris obliteratio.
48   Signis quae vocant Corinthia plerique in tantum capiuntur
ut secum circumferant, sicut Hortensius orator sphingem
Verri reo ablatam, propter quam Cicero illo iudicio in
altercatione neganti ei aenigmata se intellegere respondit 20
debere, quoniam sphingem domi haberet. circumtulit et
Nero princeps Amazonem, de qua dicemus, et paulo ante

3. CXIXS] *Urlichs in Chrestom. Plin.*; CVIS *Detlefsen*; qui nonaginta
        Bamb.

Reinach, *Bronzes Figurés de la Gaule
Romaine*, p. 12, who shows that the
name is met with principally in Syria
and Egypt.

Arvernis : where Mercury had a
celebrated ritual in his temple on the
Puy de Dôme ; see Addenda.

3. colossum : in the vestibule of
the Golden House, Suet. *Nero*, 31.

4. dicatus Soli venerationi : i. e.
by Vespasian, Suet. *Vesp.* 18, who set
up the colossus on the Sacred Way,
Dio Cassius, 66, 15 ; Martial, *Spect.* 2,
i, 71, 6. The basis may still be seen *in
situ* between the temple of Venus and
Rome and the Colosseum. Com-
modus replaced the head by a portrait
head of himself (Herodian, i, 5, 9),
and gave to the statue attributes of

Hercules, which were afterwards removed (Aelian Lamprid. *Commod.* 17,
10). The size of the Neronian colossus
became proverbial, *C. I. L.* viii, 1,
212, p. 36, l. 82. Cf. in xxxv, 51,
the colossal painted portrait of Nero.

§ 46. 5. mirabamur: practically
the only instance where Pliny speaks
from personal observation.

in officina : sc. *aeraria*, cf. below,
§ 134; xvi, 23 ; xviii, 89 ; *C. I. L.* vi,
8455, &c. Addenda.

6. argilla : i. e. the πρόπλασμα,
cf. xxxv, 155.

7. surculis : the *surculi* must, I
think, be the τρυπήματα or wax tubes
with which the wax model was
covered previous to its being cased
in loam ; these tubes were intended

it and received in payment forty million sesterces [£350,000 circ.]. After he had won his reputation in Gaul, Nero sum- *His colossal* moned him to Rome, where he made a colossal statue 119½ feet *Nero.* in height. It was originally intended to represent the Emperor, but after Nero's crimes had met with their punishment, it was dedicated to the worship of the Sun. In his workshop **46** our wonder was excited not only by the extraordinary likeness in the clay model, but by the slender tubing which was the first stage towards the completion of the work. This statue proved that the secret of the composition of bronze was lost, since Nero had been ready to provide the gold and silver, and in modelling and chasing Zenodoros was the equal of any ancient artist. When he made the statue for the Arverni, during **47** the governorship of Dubius Avitus, he imitated two cups, chased *He copies* by the hand of Kalamis, which Germanicus Caesar had prized *two cups* *by Kalamis.* very highly, and had given to Cassius Silanus his tutor, the uncle of Dubius, with such nicety that scarcely any difference can be detected between the original and the copy. Thus the artistic cunning of Zenodoros only strengthens the proof that the art of alloying bronze was forgotten.

The figures known as Corinthian are often so much prized that **48** the owners carry them about with them, as the orator Hortensius *Great* did the figure of a sphinx which he had taken from his client *value of* *Corinthian* Verres. The image was mentioned in the course of the trial, for *bronzes.* when Hortensius declared that he could not guess riddles, Cicero *Sphinx of* *Hortensius.* replied that he should be able to do so since he kept a sphinx in his house. Nero when Emperor also took about with him an Amazon *Nero's* *Amazon.*

to produce in the loam-coating holes for the pouring in of the bronze, and the letting out of the air. The colossal wax cast of a horse covered with tubings, Clarac, *Musée de Sc.* i, pl. v, figs. 5, 6, p. 101 ff., exactly illustrates what I imagine would be the appearance which the Neronian colossus presented when Pliny saw it. Oddly enough neither Clarac nor Blümner (cf. *Technol.* iv, p. 325) comment, so far as I am aware, on this interesting passage.

8. indicavit interisse: cf. § 5.

§ 47. 11. Dubio Avito. Tac. *Ann.* xiii, 54.

12. Calamidis: xxxiii, 156; xxxvi, 36.

13. praeceptori : in oratory. Ovid addressed the *Pontic Ep.* ii, 5, to Salanus.

§ 48. 18. Hortensius : the celebrated orator and art amateur, repeatedly mentioned by Pliny, viii, 211 ; ix, 170; xxxv, 130, &c.

21. sphingem : according to Plut. *Apophthegm. Rom. Cic.* ii. it was silver, but according to the same author, *Cic.* vii, 2, it was of ivory. See Addenda.

22. de qua dicemus: below, § 82.

C. Cestius consularis signum, quod secum etiam in proelio
habuit. Alexandri quoque Magni tabernaculum sustinere
traduntur solitae statuae, ex quibus duae ante Martis Ultoris
aedem dicatae sunt, totidem ante regiam.

49   Minoribus simulacris signisque innumera prope artificum 5
multitudo nobilitata est, ante omnis tamen Phidias Atheniensis Iove Olympio facto ex ebore quidem et auro, sed et
ex aere signa fecit. floruit autem olympiade LXXXIII, circiter CCC urbis nostrae annum, quo eodem tempore aemuli
eius fuere Alcamenes, Critias, Nesiotes, Hegias, et deinde 10
olympiade LXXXVII Hagelades, Callon, Gorgias Lacon,
rursus LXXXX Polyclitus, Phradmon, Myron, Pythagoras,
50 Scopas, Perellus. ex his Polyclitus discipulos habuit

7. Olympiae *omnes praeter Bamb., Detlefsen.*

1. C. Cestius. Tac. *Hist.* v, 10.

consularis signum : where Fröhner (*Rhein. Mus.*, 1892, p. 292)
proposes *consularis ⟨laris⟩ signum.*
But Pliny is concerned merely with
proving what store was laid by Corinthian bronzes, and not with their
subjects. If he specifies Nero's
Amazon, it is only because it had
become a familiar object.

2. tabernaculum: Pliny has here
misunderstood the Greek word σκηνή
= tent *or* canopy. The description
in the original can only have been of
the golden Nikai, which according to
Diodoros (xviii, 26) supported at
each of its corners the canopy of the
chariot upon which Alexander's corpse
was borne to Alexandria ; Urlichs,
Chrest. p. 314.

3. Martis Ultoris: in the forum
of Augustus, dedicated B.C. 2. *Mon.
Anc.* (iv) xxi, 21–22 ; Mommsen, *Res
Gestae*, p. 88.

4. regiam : close to the temple
of Vesta.

§ 49. 5. Minoribus, i. e. *colossis
supradictis.*

7. Iove Olympio, § 54; xxxvi,
18.

8. floruit = ἤκμαζε.

olymp. LXXXIII :   probably
date of commencement of Parthenon.
Then about Pheidias as representative
are grouped—failing more precise historical information—other artists connected with the restoration of Athens
after the Persian wars and its subsequent embellishment. The group of
the Tyrant-slayers, made by Kritios and
Nesiotes (archonship of Adeimantos
B. C. 477, *Marm. Par.*), replaced the
older group by Antenor, which had
been carried away by Xerxes (§ 70).
Hegias appears as contemporary of
K. and N. (cf. Lucian, *Rhet. Praec.* 9) ;
Alkamenes worked chiefly for Athens
(*Schriftquell.* 812–822). The following groups likewise, when they can be
determined at all, seem the result of
similar uncritical combinations. As
a rule the given Olympiad strictly
refers only to the first artist in each
group.

circiter : i. e. more accurately, 306.

9. aemuli : the epithet is applied
quite loosely, and means little more
than ' of rival merit ': so in xxxvi, 30,
the fellow-workers of Skopas on the
Mausoleion are called his *aemuli;* in

which will be mentioned later on, and a little earlier Gaius
Sestius, a consular, had a statue which he even took into
battle. It is said too that the tent of Alexander the Great was *Tent of*
always supported by statues, of which two have been dedicated *Alexander.*
in front of the temple of Mars the Avenger, and two in front of
the Regia.

The number of artists whose reputation rests on images and **49**
statues of smaller size can hardly be counted. *Pheidias* of *Chronology of the*
Athens, however, stands first of all with his Olympian Zeus. *principal*
This was of ivory and gold, but he also worked in bronze. He *artists.*
flourished in the eighty-third Olympiad [448-445 B.C.], about
three hundred years after the foundation of Rome. Of the same
date were his rivals, *Alkamenes, Kritios, Nesiotes,* and *Hegias.*
In the eighty-seventh Olympiad [432-429 B.C.] came *Hagelaidas,*
Kallon and the Laconian *Gorgias,* and in the ninetieth [420-417
B.C.] *Polykleitos, Phradmon, Myron, Pythagoras, Skopas,* †*Perellos.*

xxxv, 64, illustrious contemporaries
of Zeuxis figure as his *aequales et
aemuli;* cf. also xxxv, 124.

11. **Hagelades** : a contemporary
of the Elder Kanachos; flourished circ.
B. C. 515-485, Robert, *Arch. März·*
pp. 39, 93. He is placed in Ol. 87,
because his Herakles, 'Αλεξίκακος (in
Melite, Schol. Aristoph. Βάτραχοι,
504), like the Apollo Alexikakos of
Kalamis, Paus. i, 3, 4 (cf. Brunn,
K. G. i, p. 126), was connected in the
popular imagination with the staying
of the great Plague in the third year
of the Peloponnesian war—the association arising of course from the
epithet (Brunn, i, p. 68). The real
occasion for the dedication of the
Herakles remains obscure ; cf. Robert,
loc. cit.; Studniczka, *Röm. Mitth.* ii,
1887, p. 99, note 27 ; Wolters, *Ath.
Mitth.* xvi, 1891, p. 160. The mention
of Hagelaidas brings with it that
of his contemporaries, Gorgias and
Kallon. See Addenda.

Callon : it is uncertain whether the
Eleian Kallon (Paus. v, 25, 4; 27,
8 = *I. G. B.* 33), or his more celebrated Aiginetan namesake (*I. G. B.*
27; Paus. ii, 32, 5; iii, 18, 8).

Gorgias: *I. G. B.* 36 = *C. I. A.* iv,
373 (214).

12. **Polyclitus** : § 55, possibly dated
by the gold and ivory Hera, which
he made for the new Heraion at
Argos, after the fire of B.C. 424.
Together with Polykleitos are grouped,
besides Phradmon (probably a real
contemporary, Paus. vi, 8, 1, below,
§ 53), Myron and Pythagoras, for no
other reason, I imagine, than that,
all three masters being celebrated for
their statues of athletes, they fitted in
better with him than with any other
fifth-century artist for whom a date
could be found. As a fact the best
activity of Myron falls within the first
half of the century (Furtwängler,
Masterpieces, p. 182), while Pythagoras, as we know from his statues of
athletes whose victories ranged from
B.C. 488-480, was considerably the
older artist.

13. **Scopas** : he appears here by
a singular anachronism : in xxxvi, 30,
he is correctly dated from the Manso-
leion at Halikarnassos. The error is
however insufficient reason for assuming (with Klein and Robert cf. *Arch.
Märchen,* p. 46) an elder Skopas.

Argium, Asopodorum, Alexim, Aristidem, Phrynonem, Dinonem, Athenodorum, Demean Clitorium, Myron Lycium.
LXXXXV olympiade floruere Naucydes, Dinomenes,
Canachus, Patroclus, centesima secunda Polycles, Cephisodotus, Leuchares, Hypatodorus, CIIII Praxiteles, Eu- 5
51 phranor, centesima septima Aetion, Therimachus. CXIII
Lysippus fuit, cum et Alexander Magnus, item Lysistratus
frater eius, Sthenis, Euphron, Sofocles, Sostratus, Ion,

1. Argium Asopodorum *Detlefsen.* Phrynonem Dinonem *omnes praeter*
Bamb., [Dinonem] *Detlefsen.*   8. Sofocles] *coni. Loewy in Inschr. Gr.*
Bildh. 103ᵃ *p.* 384; fucles *Bamb.*; icles *Ricc., Voss.*; Eucles *Jan, Detlefsen.*

§ 50. 1. **Asopodorum**: a later
artist than the Asopodoros who worked
on the bathron of Praxiteles of Kama-
rina at Olympia (*I.G.B.* 30). See Add.

Alexim: if identical with the
father of Kantharos of Sikyon in § 85
(the pupil of Eutychides; Paus. vi,
3, 6), he must have been a pupil of
Polykleitos II. His insertion here
would be due to an error of Pliny.

2. **Athenodorum, Demean**: mentioned together, Paus. x, 9, 7, as employed on the Lakedaimonian votive
offering set up at Delphoi in comme-
moration of Aigospotamoi (B.C. 405).

Lycium: as his father appears in
the same Olympiad with Polykleitos,
he is placed in the Ol. of the sons of
Polykleitos; but he was already a
flourishing artist in B.C. 446, if Lolling
(Δελτίον, 1889, p. 181 ff.) is right in
referring the statues of horsemen (Paus.
i, 22, 4), on whose basis his signature
occurs, to the expedition of Perikles
to Euboia.

3. **Naucydes**: § 80, son of Patrokles (*I. G. B.* 86), and brother of
Daidalos of Sikyon, Paus. vi, 34;
I. G. B. 88–89. On his relation
to the older Polykleitos, next to
whose statue of Hera at Argos had
stood a Hebe by Naukydes, Paus.
ii. 17, 4 (the two statues on coins of
Argos, P. Gardner, *Num. Comm.* I, xv),
see Furtwängler, *Masterpieces*, p. 226,
and cf. Robert, *Arch. März.* p. 104 ff.

Dinomenes: below, § 76.

4. **Canachus**, i.e. the younger:
a Sikyonian and a pupil of Polykleitos
(Paus. vi, 13, 7). His chronology,
like that of Patrokles, is determined
by the fact that he worked on the
votive offering of Aigospotamoi (Paus.
x, 9, 7).

Polycles: § 80.

Cephisodotus: father of Praxiteles? (Brunn, *K. G.* i. p. 269) or elder
brother? (Furtwängler, *Masterpieces*,
p. 295). His chronology seems determined by his Eirene holding the
infant Ploutos, which should probably
be dated shortly after B.C. 375 'to
correspond with the institution of the
annual offering to Eirene consequent
on the victories of Timotheus' (Furtwängler, *loc. cit.*).

5. **Leuchares** = Leochares. Cf.
Leutychides = Leotychides in Herodotos. For his works, see below, 79
and xxxvi, 30. The extant dates for
his activity are comprised between
(*a*) a period previous to the banish-
ment of Timotheus in B.C. 355, for
whom he made a statue of Isokrates
(Heliodoros *ap.* Ps. Plut. *Vita X
Orat. Isocr.* 27), and (*b*) the year in the
reign of Alexander, when, in conjunc-
tion with Lysippos, he made Alexander's Lion Hunt (below on § 64).

Hypatodorus: he is possibly
identical with the H. who, in con-
junction with another artist Sostratos,

The following were pupils of Polykleitos, *Argeios, Asopodoros,* 50 *Alexis, Aristeides,* †*Phrynon,* †*Deinon, Athenodoros,* and *Demeas* of Kleitor. Myron was the master of *Lykios.* In the ninety-fifth Olympiad [400–397 B.C.] *Naukydes* flourished, with *Deinomenes, Kanachos,* and *Patroklos ;* in the hundred and second [372–369 B.C.], *Polykles, Kephisodotos, Leuchares, Hypatodoros ;* in the hundred and fourth [364–361 B.C.], *Praxiteles* and *Euphranor ;* in the hundred and seventh [352–349 B.C.], *Aetion* and †*Therimachos. Lysippos* lived in the hundred and thirteenth [328–325 B.C.], in 51 the days of Alexander the Great ; so also did his brother *Lysistratos,* as well as *Sthennis,* †*Euphron, Sophokles, Sostratos,* †*Ion,*

made for the Arkadian Aliphera (previous to B.C. 372, see Brunn, *K. G.* ii, p. 295) a bronze Athena, Paus. viii, 26, 5; Polyb. iv, 78. He must however be a distinct personality from the Hypatodoros who, with his colleague Aristogeiton, made for a certain Orchomenian the monument of which the inscribed basis is still extant (*I. G. B.* 101). The archaic style of the epigraphy (Kirchhoff, *Studien,* 4th ed., p. 142, note L) compels us to follow Robert (*Hermes,* xxv, 1890, p. 412 ff., and *Hall. Winckelmannspr.* xviii, 1895, p. 4 ff.) in referring the artists to the early part of the fifth century. To this date accordingly we must also refer their group set up at Delphoi by the Argives, whatever view we may take of the date of the Attico-Argive victory at Oinoë which the group commemorated, or was supposed to commemorate Paus. x, 10, 3 (see especially Robert, *ll. cc.,* and Furtwängler, *Masterpieces,* p. 41).

Praxiteles : dated with reference to his activity in Mantineia (Paus. viii, 9, 1), the third year of Ol. 104 (B. C. 462) being the date of the great battle (Furtwängler, *Plinius,* p. 21).

Euphranor : although he appears here as a sculptor (§ 77), the clue to his date is afforded by his painting, in the Stoa of Zeus Eleutherios at Athens (Paus. i. 3, 4), of the cavalry engagement that preceded the battle

of Mantineia (*equestre proelium,* xxxv, 129).

6. **Aetion, Ther.:** Aetion being only known as a painter (xxxv, 78), and Therimachos being unknown except for this passage and xxxv, 78, it is reasonable to suppose with Furtwängler (*loc. cit.*) that the whole passage, *centesima . . . Therimachus,* has been interpolated from xxxv, 78.

§ 51. 7. **Lysippus :** his ἀκμή is determined by the central Olympiad of the reign of Alexander. (Loewy, *Untersuch.* p. 64.)

Lysistratus, xxxv, 153.

8. **Sthenis of Olynthos,** *inf.* § 90. From *I. G. B.* 83 we learn that he was a fellow-worker of Leochares; and from *I. G. B.* 103ᵃ (cf. on *I.G.B.* 541, p. 370) that he was still active in the reign of Lysimachos (B. C. 306–281).

Sofocles : Loewy's reading is made practically certain by Bulle's observation (*Olympia,* Bd. ii, p. 156) that the bases from the statues of riders by Sophokles at Olympia (*I. G. B.* 123–125) closely resemble, in form and profile, the basis (*I. G. B.* 103ᵃ) of Sthennis from the Amphiareion at Oropos. This near connexion of the two artists explains the place assigned to them in the Plinian chronology.

Sostratus : probably identical with the Sostratos, son of Euphranor, *I. G. B.* 105.

Silanion—in hoc mirabile quod nullo doctore nobilis fuit,
ipse discipulum habuit Zeuxiaden—CXXI Eutychides,
Euthycrates, Laippus, Cephisodotus, Timarchus, Pyromachus.
52 cessavit deinde ars, ac rursus olympiade CLVI revixit, cum
fuere longe quidem infra praedictos, probati tamen, Antaeus, 5
Callistratus, Polycles Athenaeus, Callixenus, Pythocles,
53 Pythias, Timocles. ita distinctis celeberrimorum aetatibus
insignes raptim transcurram reliqua multitudine passim
dispersa. venere autem et in certamen laudatissimi, quamquam diversis aetatibus geniti, quoniam fecerant Amazonas, 10
quae cum in templo Dianae Ephesiae dicarentur, placuit
eligi probatissimam ipsorum artificum qui praesentes erant
iudicio, cum apparuit eam esse quam omnes secundam a sua
quisque iudicassent. haec est Polycliti, proxima ab ea Phidiae,
54 tertia Cresilae, quarta Cydonis, quinta Phradmonis. Phidias 15

1. **Silanion**: from Paus. vi, 4, 5
we learn that he made a statue of
Satyros of Elis, who appears as winner
of a double victory in a catalogue of
the Amphiaraia (*C. I. G. S.* 414).
According to a conjecture of J. Delamarre (*Rev. de Phil.* xviii, p. 162 *sqq.*)
this catalogue belongs to the same
period as *C. I. G. S.* 4253 (under archonship of Niketas B.C. 332–1), and
C. I. G. S. 4254 (archonship of Kephi-
sophon B.C. 329–8). It would thus
appear that the date assigned by Pliny
to Seilanion is correct. For his works,
cf. below, § 81. See Addenda.

nullo doctore, i. e. his school dia-
dochy had been lost ; cf. the similar
case of Lysippos. Introd. p. xlvii ff.

2. **Zeuxiaden**: known from one
of the Mattei inscriptions (*I. G. B.* 483–
485) as sculptor of a statue of Hypereides (d. B.C. 322). See Addenda.

Eutychides: below, § 78 ; xxxv,
141. The date assigned to him by
Pliny coincides approximately with
the restoration of Antiocheia by Seleukos, Ol. 119, 3 = B.C. 302. For the
new city E. made an allegorical figure
of Tyche supported on the river-god
Orontes—a work of which a copy has

survived in the exquisite statue in the
Vatican, Helbig, *Class. Ant.* 376.

3. **Euthycrates**: § 66. *Laippus*
(*ibid.*) = the Daippos of Paus. vi, 12,
6 ; 16, 5. The name is correctly
given below, § 87. Either Pliny in
transcribing from the Greek mistook
Δ for Λ, or he is quoting from a Latin
author who had already been guilty
of the blunder.

Cephisodotus, Timarchus : sons
of Praxiteles, *Vit. X Orat. Lykurg.*
38. The fact that they made a statue
of Menander (Paus. i, 21, 1, *I. G. B.*
108 = *C. I. A.* ii. 1370), who died
B.C. 291, shows that they were
older than the sons of Lysippos.
After the great masters, their pupils
are lumped together without any strict
chronological order (cf. Furtwängler,
Masterpieces, p. 309).

Pyromachus: there appear to
have been several artists of that name,
see below on § 80, § 84 ; xxxv, 146.

§ **52. 4. cessavit deinde ars** :
marks the end, not of a period of art,
but of Pliny's main Greek authority
(cf. the similar break in the account
of the Painters, xxxv, 135), Brunn,
K. G. i, p. 504 f. Between B.C. 296

and *Seilanion*. It is remarkable that *Seilanion* owed nothing to the instruction of any master; his own pupil was *Zeuxiades*. In the hundred and twenty-first Olympiad [B.C. 296–293] came *Eutychides, Euthykrates, Laippos, Kephisodotos, Timarchos*, and *Pyromachos*. A period of stagnation followed, and again a revival 52 in the hundred and fifty-sixth Olympiad [B.C. 156–153], the age of †*Antaios, Kallistratos, Polykles* of Athens, †*Kallixenos*, †*Pythokles*, †*Pythias* and *Timokles*, artists of merit, but still far below those already mentioned.

Having given the dates of the most celebrated artists, I shall 53 *The five most* touch briefly on the great names, and group the others under *most* various heads. The most famous artists, although born at some *famous make* distance of time from each other, still came into competition, since *Amazons* each had made a statue of an Amazon, to be dedicated in the *for a competition.* temple of Artemis at Ephesos, when it was decided that the prize should be awarded to the one which the artists themselves, who were on the spot, declared to be the best. This proved to be the statue which each artist placed second to his own, namely that of Polykleitos; the statue of Pheidias was second, that of Kresilas third, Kydon's fourth, and Phradmon's fifth.

Besides his Olympian Zeus, a work which has no rival, Pheidias 54

and the 'revival' in B.C. 156 came the great school of Pergamon, which Pliny omits in his chronological table, but which he mentions below, § 84. The *revixit* in B.C. 156 appears connected with the family of Polykles, father of Timokles and Timarchides (below, § 92; xxxvi, 35), and grandfather of Polykles II and of Dionysios, who made the statues for the temples of Juno and Jupiter erected by Q. Metellus Macedonicus, B.C. 149, cf. Gurlitt, *Pausanias*, p. 361 ff.; Loewy, *I. G. B.* p. 177.

6. Callistratus : perhaps identical with the artist mentioned, Tatian p. 36, 14, ed. Schwartz (Brunn, *K. G.* i, p. 535).

§ 53. 9. quamquam . . . geniti : by which Pliny attempts to reconcile his chronology (where Polykleitos is placed twenty-eight years after Pheidias) with the story of the competition.

10. Amazonas : since four Amazon

types, distinct in conception, but with external resemblances of type and dress have been identified (Furtwängler, *Masterpieces*, p. 128 ff.), the story of the competition contains a kernel of truth. Two of the extant statuary types can be traced back to Kresilas and Polykleitos respectively.

11. placuit . . . iudicassent : we have here in another garb the identical anecdote told by Herodotos, viii, 123, Plut. *Themist.* xvii, of the allotting of the prize of valour after Salamis.

15. Cresilae . . . Cydonis. In three out of the four extant inscriptions of his name, Kresilas calls himself Κυδωνιάτης (*I. G. B.* 45–47; for the inscription recently found at Delphoi cf. Furtwängler, *Masterpieces*, p. 116); it is evident that Pliny's Latin author in transcribing from the Greek forged out of a form Κύδων, the name of a fifth artist (cf. O. Jahn, *Sächs. Ber.* 1850, p. 37).

praeter Iovem Olympium quem nemo aemulatur fecit ex
ebore aeque Minervam Athenis, quae est in Parthenone stans,
ex aere vero praeter Amazonem supra dictam Minervam
tam eximiae pulchritudinis ut formae cognomen acceperit.
fecit et cliduchum et aliam Minervam quam Romae Paulus 5
Aemilius ad aedem Fortunae Huiusce Diei dicavit, item duo
signa quae Catulus in eadem aede palliata et alterum
colossicon nudum, primusque artem toreuticen aperuisse
55 atque demonstrasse merito iudicatur.   Polyclitus Sicyonius Hageladae discipulus diadumenum fecit molliter 10
iuvenem centum talentis nobilitatum, idem et doryphorum
viriliter puerum.   fecit et quem canona artifices vocant liniamenta artis ex eo petentes veluti a lege quadam, solusque
hominum artem ipsam fecisse artis opere iudicatur.   fecit

§ 54. 1. Iovem Olympium:
xxxvi, 18, where the gold-ivory
Minerva is also described.

3. Minervam . . . pulchr.: i. e.
the bronze Athena surnamed the
'Lemnia,' Paus. i, 28, 2; Lucian,
εἰκόνες 4; for extant copies of the
statue, Furtwängler, *Masterpieces*, pp.
4 ff. ; see Add.

5. cliduchum: votive portrait
statue of a priestess, same subject by
Euphranor, below § 78. See Add.
P. Aemilius: probably on the
occasion of his triumph after Pydna
(B. C. 168). For the magnificent
statues and works of art which he
brought from Makedonia see Liv.
xlv, 33; they filled 250 chariots
which graced his triumph. Plut. *Aem.
Paull.* 32; cf. Vell. Pater. i, 9.

6. Fortunae Huiusce Diei: on
the Palatine where was a *Vicus
huiusce diei* (Gilbert, iii, p. 422);
there was another temple of *Fortuna
H. D.* in *campo* (see R. Peter *ap.*
Roscher, i, 1514. *C. I. L.* i, p. 298 f.).

7. Catulus: i. e. the Elder, who
on the day of the battle against the
Cimbri εὔξατο . . . ἀνασχὼν τὰς χεῖρας
καθιερώσειν τὴν τύχην ἡμέρας ἐκείνης.
Plut. *Marius,* 26: Plin. xvii, 2. Whence
Catulus obtained these Pheidian works

remains uncertain. Cf. Urlichs, *Gr.
Statuen in Rep. Rom,* p. 9 f.

palliata: i. e. portraits (cf. the *palliati,* xxxv, 136), while the *colossus
nudus* presumably represented a hero
or local god; cf. H. L. Urlichs in
Woch. f. Klass. Philol. 1894, 488.

alterum: the *duo palliata* are
to be considered as one group, in
apposition to *alterum,* by an extension
of the construction of xix, 34; xxi,
128; xx, 9; xxxv, 71. H. L. Urlichs
loc. cit. See Addenda to p. 38, 5.

8. primusque aperuisse: this
criticism forms, together with the
similar criticisms attached to Myron,
Polykleitos, Pythagoras and Lysippos,
a consecutive *canon* or series of axioms
intended to link with definite great
names the successive steps in the
development of bronze-casting. After
Pheidias, the reputed discoverer of the
possibilites of the art, each artist is
appraised in his relation to symmetry,
the highest award falling to Lysippos,
Otto Jahn, *Kunsturtheile des Pl.* p.
128 ff.; C. Robert, *Arch. Märch.*
p. 28 ff. For the author of the verdicts
cf. below on § 56. Introd. p. xvi ff.

toreuticen; a term applied by
Pliny to the whole of statuary as
opposed to *pictura* (cf. xxxv, 77),

made in ivory the Athena at Athens, which stands erect in the *Artists of*
Parthenon. In bronze, besides the Amazon already mentioned, *first rank. Pheidias.*
he made an Athena of such passing beauty that she was sur-
named the Fair. He also made a Key-Bearer, or κλειδοῦχος,
another Athena which Aemilius Paullus dedicated at Rome in
front of the temple of the Fortune of the Day, two draped
statues dedicated by Catulus in the same temple, and a nude
colossal statue. He is rightly held to have first revealed the
capabilities of sculpture and indicated its methods.

Polykleitos of Sikyon was a pupil of Hagelaidas. He made **55**
an athlete binding the diadem about his head, which was famous *Polykleitos of Sikyon.*
for the sum of one hundred talents [£21,000 circ.] which it
realized. This διαδούμενος has been described as 'a man, yet
a boy': the δορυφόρος or spear-bearer as 'a boy, yet a man.'
He also made the statue which sculptors call the 'canon,'
referring to it as to a standard from which they can learn the
first rules of their art. He is the only man who is held to have
embodied the principles of his art in a single work. He also made

while *Statuaria ars* is, according to
Latin usage, reserved for bronze statuary; cf. § 35; § 65; xxxv, 156; xxxvi,
15, 37.

§ 55. 9. Sicyonius: by Plato
(*Protag.* p. 311 C) Pol. is called
Ἀργεῖος; cf. also *I. G. B.* 91; Furtwängler, *Masterpieces*, p. 255 ff. It
is natural that a confusion as to
the exact place of his birth should
have arisen, as his family appear to
have migrated from Argos to Sikyon
(*I. G. B.* 89).

10. Hag. discipulus: this is chronologically impossible—the activity
of Hagelaidas reaching back as far as
Ol. 65 = B.C. 520, that of Polykleitos
as low down as Ol. 90 = B.C. 420
(above, § 49), Robert, *Arch. Märchen*,
p. 92 ff. By a loose juxtaposition the
greatest Argive master in the fifth
century is made into the pupil of the
greatest Argive master in the sixth.

diadumenum . . . puerum:
the neat antithesis points to an epigram as the source of this statement;
Dilthey, *Rhein. Mus.* xxvi, p. 290.

The Doryphoros represented an
athlete carrying his palaistric javelin.
The most complete copy of the Diadou-
menos is the Vaison statue (*Br. Mus.
Cat.* i, 500); of the Doryphoros the
statue in Naples (Collignon, *Sculpture
Grecque*, i, pl. xii). See Addenda.

11. centum talentis; cf. vii, 126,
where the same price is paid by
Attalos for a picture by Aristeides of
Thebes. Introd. p. lxxxiv.

12. et quem canona: the 'canon'
was, however, identical with the
Doryphoros (see the passages *Schriftquell.* 953 ff.). It erroneously appears
here as a separate statue, the comment
on the Doryphoros *qua* canon being,
as Furtwängler, *Masterpieces*, p. 229,
note 4, detected, taken from a different
source to what precedes; cf. Münzer,
Hermes, xxx, 1895, p. 530, note 1.

14. artem ipsam fecisse: apparently an allusion to the treatise
on art by Polykleitos, called the
Canon. What Pliny states in
epigrammatic form is told more
plainly by Galenos περὶ τῶν Ἱπποκρ.

et destringentem se et nudum telo incessentem duosque
pueros item nudos talis ludentes qui vocantur astragalizontes et sunt in Titi imperatoris atrio—hoc opere nullum
56 absolutius plerique iudicant—item Mercurium qui fuit Lysimacheae, Herculem qui Romae, hagetera arma sumentem, 5
Artemona qui periphoretos appellatus est. hic consummasse
hanc scientiam iudicatur et toreuticen sic erudisse ut Phidias
aperuisse.   proprium eius est uno crure ut insisterent signa
excogitasse, quadrata tamen esse ea ait Varro et paene ad
57 unum exemplum.   Myronem Eleutheris natum Hageladae et 10
ipsum discipulum bucula maxime nobilitavit celebratis versibus laudata, quando alieno plerique ingenio magis quam
suo commendantur.   fecit et canem et discobolon et Perseum

1. telo] *Benndorf in Gesammelte Stud. zur Kunstgesch. Festschr. für A. Springer,* 1885, *pag.* 260 ; talo *codd. Detlefsen.*   3. *vide* Addenda.

καὶ Πλατ. δογμ. 5: ἔργῳ τὸν λόγον
ἐκβεβαίωσε, δημιουργήσας ἀνδριάντα
κατὰ τὰ τοῦ λόγου προστάγματα καὶ
καλέσας δὴ καὶ αὐτὸν τὸν ἀνδριάντα
καθάπερ καὶ τὸ σύγγραμμα, κανόνα ;
cf. xxxv, 74 (Timanthes) *pinxit et
heroa . . . artem ipsam complexus
viros pingendi.* Introd. p. xli.

1. destringentem se: i. e. an
ἀποξυόμενος.

telo incessentem : Furtwängler
(*Masterpieces,* p. 249) compares Ovid,
Metam. 14, 402 *saevisque parant
incessere telis.* See also Woelfflin,
in *Archiv für Lat. Lexicogr.* ix, 1894,
p. 119 ff. Addenda.

2. astragalizontes : [possibly for
a votive or grave monument, *Woch.
f. Klass. Phil.* 1895, 548. For a
kindred subject on a Roman sarkophagos, see Helbig, *Class. Ant.* 97.
—H. L. U.] See Add. to p. 42, 5.

3. et sunt . . . atrio : this addition
concerning the Roman locality of the
astragalizontes is loosely co-ordinated
to the main account ; cf. Oehmichen,
Plin. Studien, p. 119. Introd. p. xxxvii.

§ 56. 4. fuit : before the destruction of Lysimachea by the Thracians in
Ol. 145,4 = B.C. 197 (Liv. xxxiii, 38,11).

Lysimacheae : built B.C. 309 by

Lysimachos in the Thracian Cher-
sonnese.   Where the statue had previously stood is not known.

5. hagetera : the Doric form
points to a metrical epigram which
was doubtless inscribed on the basis
of the statue ; cf. H. L. Urlichs in
Woch. f. Klass. Phil. 1894, p. 1299 ff.

6. Artemona : according to
Ephoros (*ap.* Plut. *Per.* 27), A. was an
engineer who directed the blockading
works during the siege of Samos by
Perikles. Owing to his lameness, he
was carried about in a litter, whence
he received the surname Periphoretos.
Plutarch adds, however, that the story
was confuted by Herakleides of Pontos,
who showed from Anakreon (cf.
Bergk, *Poetae Lyr.* iii, p. 261, Fr.
21–46, where see note), that Art.
Periphoretos lived long before the
Samian war.   It is evident that there
was *contaminatio* between the two
namesakes, the engineer becoming
credited with the surname of the
notorious voluptuary, while the story
of the lameness was invented to account for it.   Addenda.

7. hanc scientiam : harks back
to § 54 *Phidias . . . primus artem
toreuticem aperuisse.*

an athlete scraping himself, a nude figure advancing with a weapon, and two boys, also nude, playing with knucklebones, who are known as the ἀστραγαλίζοντες [dice-players], and are now in the Hall of the Emperor Titus. Many people think that the faultless execution of this work has never been surpassed. Other works of his are 56 a Hermes, which was at Lysimacheia; a Herakles at Rome; a captain or ἀγητήρ putting on his armour; and finally a portrait of Artemon, known by the name of περιφόρητος or 'Man in the litter.' He is considered to have brought the scientific knowledge of statuary to perfection, and to have systematized the art of which Pheidias had revealed the possibilities. It was his peculiar characteristic to represent his figures resting their weight on one leg; Varro however says that they are square and almost exactly after the same type.

Myron was born at Eleutherai, and was also a pupil of 57
Hagelaidas. He is best known by his heifer, thanks to the well- *Myron of Eleutherai.*
known verses written upon it, for people very generally owe
their reputation to the talent of others, rather than their own.
He also made a dog, and a δισκοβόλος, or athlete hurling the
disk, a Perseus, sawyers, a Satyr gazing with wonder at the

8. **uno crure ut insisterent**: implies a shifting of the weight from one leg to the other in the act of walking, and therefore accurately describes the favourite Polykleitan attitude of 'arrested motion.' Had the figure been represented at rest with its whole weight on one leg, the expression used must have been *uni cruri insist.*, Michaelis, *Ann. d. Inst.* 1878, p. 29 (cf. J. Lange, *Fremstilling*, p. 466).

9. **quadrata . . . ait Varro**: the mention of Varro shows that the criticism of Polykleitos and consequently the kindred criticisms of the remaining four artists were derived from him, though Varro himself was of course drawing directly or indirectly from a Greek author, whom we now know to have been Xenokrates of Sikyon (§ 83), Introd. p. xvi ff.

quadrata = τετράγωνα, cf. Plato, *Protag.* 344 d.

§ 57. 10. **Myronem . . . Hage-**

ladae: the pupilship can neither be proved nor disproved; possibly, however, the tradition only arose from a general likeness between the early works of Myron and those of Hagelaidas. Furtwängler, *Masterpieces*, p. 196. Introd. p. li, note 6.

Eleutheris: on the frontier between Boeotia and Attica (cf. *I. G. B.* 417).

11. **bucula**: the heifer (doubtless a votive offering) had originally stood in Athens, Cic. *Verr.* II, iv, 60, § 135. Later it was transferred to Rome, where Prokopios (*Bell. Goth.* iv, 21) saw it in the *Forum Pacis.*—No less than thirty-eight of the epigrams alluded to are extant (collected in Overbeck, *Schriftquell.* 550–588).

13. **canem**: votive-offering, cf. *Anth. Pal.* vi, 175; 176. The list of works down to *Delph. pentathlon* is alphabetic (Petersen, *A. Z.* xxxviii, 1880, p. 25).

discobolon: the best copy is

et pristas et Satyrum admirantem tibias et Minervam, Delphicos pentathlos, pancratiastas, Herculem qui est apud circum maximum in aede Pompei Magni. fecisse et cicadae monumentum ac locustae carminibus suis Erinna significat. 58 fecit et Apollinem quem ab triumviro Antonio sublatum 5 restituit Ephesiis divus Augustus admonitus in quiete. primus hic multiplicasse veritatem videtur, numerosior in arte quam Polyclitus et in symmetria diligentior, et ipse tamen corporum tenus curiosus animi sensus non expressisse, capillum quoque et pubem non emendatius fecisse quam 10 59 rudis antiquitas instituisset. vicit eum Pythagoras Reginus ex Italia pancratiaste Delphis posito ; eodem vicit et Leontiscum ; fecit et stadiodromon Astylon qui Olympiae ostenditur et Libyn, puerum tenentem tabellam eodem loco et mala ferentem nudum, Syracusis autem claudicantem, 15

14. loco, et *Detlefsen.*

in Palazzo Lancellotti (Collignon, *Sculpture Grecque*, i, pl. xi).

Perseum: presumably identical with the Perseus by Myron on the Akropolis (Paus. i, 23, 7).

1. **pristas** : Dalecampius was the first to give the true meaning of the word ; Furtwängler, *Dornauszieher*, p. 89, note 30, correctly explained the curious subject as a votive offering; cf. H. L. Urlichs in *Woch. f. Klass. Phil.* 1893, p. 220 f. See Addenda.

Satyrum . . . et Minervam = Paus. i, 24, 1 ; Collignon, *Sculpture Grecque*, i, p. 465 f. Petersen, *loc. cit.*, showed that the two must be considered as one group owing to the alphabetical enumeration noted above.

3. **in aede Pompei Magni**: this new temple of H. was presumably near to the *ara maxima* in the *foro boario*, the chief centre of the hero's worship (Gilbert iii, p. 434 ; cf. H. Peter *ap.* Roscher i, 2918 ; cf. above on § 33 ; xxxv, 19). Pompeius had probably dedicated it on the occasion of his last triumph in B.C. 61, and brought the Herakles from Asia Minor (cf. Urlichs, *Chrest.* p. 139).

Vitr. 3, 2, 5: *aedes . . . Herculis Pompeiani.*

4. **Erinna**: Hardouin (1685) had already detected that this ridiculous statement arose from a confusion between Μυρών and the maiden Μυρώ, for whom the poetess Erinna must have written an elegy similar to the extant one by Anyte (*Anth.* vii, 190).

'Ακρίδι τᾷ κατ' ἄρουραν ἀηδόνι καὶ δρυοκοίτᾳ
τέττιγι ξυνὸν τύμβον ἔτευξα Μυρώ.

§ 58. 5. **sublatum restituit**: cf. *Mon. Anc.* (xxiv) iv, 49–51 : *In templis omnium civitatium provinciae Asiae victor ornamenta reposui, quae spoliatis templis is cum quo bellum gesseram privatim possederat.* Mommsen, *Res Gestae*, p. 95 f. Münzer, *op. cit.* p. 545, suspects the Ephesian story of being a *doublette* of Augustus' restoration of Myronian works to Samos, recounted Strabo xiv, 1, 14.

7. **multiplicasse veritatem**: explained by Brunn (*K. G.* i, p. 151) to mean that Myron ' widened the range of representation in art, inasmuch as he laid hold on moments disclosed by attentive observation of nature, but not

pipes and Athena, winners in the five contests at Delphoi,
pankratiasts, and the Herakles which is near the great Circus
in the temple of the great Pompeius. A poem by Erinna also tells
us that he made the monument of a cicada and a locust; he also 58
made the Apollo which was taken from the Ephesians by the
triumvir Antonius, and restored to them by the god Augustus, in
obedience to a dream. He was apparently the first to multiply
truth; he was more productive than Polykleitos, and a more
diligent observer of symmetry. Still he too only cared for the
physical form, and did not express the sensations of the mind,
and his treatment of the hair of the head and of the pubes continued to betray an archaic want of skill.

Pythagoras of Rhegion in Italy surpassed Myron with the 59
pankratiast placed at Delphoi; with the same statue he also sur- *Pythagoras*
passed Leontiskos. He further made the statues of the runner *of Rhegion.*
Astylos and of a Libyan, which are to be seen at Olympia; for the
same place he made the boy holding a tablet, and a nude male
figure bearing apples. At Syracuse is a statue by him of a man

utilized before.' A striking example
of course is the Diskobolos, represented
in the act of hurling the disk.

numerosior: cf. xxxv, 130, *diligentior quam numerosior*; ibid. § 138
numerosaque tabula [*numerosus* in
Pliny always of number; cf. vii, 101,
143; x, 176 *numerosiora in fetu*;
xv, 8, and often.—H. L. U.].

9. animi sensus: the translation
given above is from Pater, *Greek
Studies*, p. 301.

§ 59. 12. eodem...Leontiscum:
Leontiskos was a winner both in the
Pythian and Olympic games, whose
portrait was made by Pythagoras
(Paus. vi, 4, 3). He figures here
as an artist, doubtless through misunderstanding of some Greek sentence such as ἐνίκα καὶ τοῦτον ποιῶν καὶ
Λεοντίσκον, i. e. 'he conquered, both
when he made the pankratiast and
when he made the Leontiskos'
(Urlichs, *Rhein. Mus.* 1889, p. 261).

13. Astylon: Paus. vi, 13, 1.

qui Olympiae ostenditur:
belongs to *Libyn* as well as to

Astylon. In the following sentence,
likewise, *eodem loco* belongs to both
puerum and *mala ferentem nudum;*
cf. the analogous construction in xxxiii,
5 *murrina ex eadem tellure et cry-
stalina effodimus.* (H. L. Urlichs in
Görlitz. Verhandl. p. 330.)

14. Libyn, i. e. Mnaseas of Kyrene.
Paus. vi, 13, 7; 18, 1.

puerum . . . tabellam: probably an iconic πινάκιον, Reisch,
Weihgeschenke, p. 44. The statue
may be identical with that of the boy
victor Protolaos, Paus. vi, 6, 1; cf.
H. L. Urlichs, *loc. cit.* See Addenda.

15. mala ferentem: cf. the statue
of Theognetos, who carried πίτυος τῆς
γ' ἡμέρου καὶ ῥοιᾶς καρπόν, Paus. vi,
9, 1. Pythagoras's statue of Euthymos (*I. G. B.* 29, Paus. vi, 6, 4–6) is
mentioned in Bk. vii, 152.

claudicantem: the identification of this statue with a wounded
Philoktetes is due to Gronovius (Blümner, *Comm. to Lessing's Laokoon*,
p. 508 f.). The following words
cuius . . . videntur are evidently epi-

cuius ulceris dolorem sentire etiam spectantes videntur, item
Apollinem serpentemque eius sagittis configi, citharoedum,
qui Dicaeus appellatus est, quod, cum Thebae ab Alexandro
caperentur, aurum a fugiente conditum sinu eius celatum
esset. hic primus nervos et venas expressit capillumque 5
60 diligentius. fuit et alius Pythagoras Samius, initio pictor,
cuius signa ad aedem Fortunae Huiusce Diei septem
nuda et senis unum laudata sunt. hic supra dicto facie
quoque indiscreta similis fuisse traditur, Regini autem
61 discipulus et filius sororis fuisse Sostratus. Lysippum 10
Sicyonium Duris negat ullius fuisse discipulum, sed primo
aerarium fabrum audendi rationem cepisse pictoris Eupompi
responso. eum enim interrogatum, quem sequeretur antecedentium, dixisse monstrata hominum multitudine naturam
62 ipsam imitandam esse, non artificem. plurima ex omnibus 15
signa fecit, ut diximus, fecundissimae artis, inter quae destringentem se quem M. Agrippa ante Thermas suas dicavit
mire gratum Tiberio principi. non quivit temperare sibi in
eo, quamquam imperiosus sui inter initia principatus, trans-

grammatic; *Anth. Plan.* iv, 112, of
a bronze Philoktetes, seems to refer
to the work of Pythagoras, the unusual omission of the name of the
hero portrayed accounting for its
omission by Pliny (cf. Brunn, *K. G.* i,
p. 134).

2. configi: for the construction
cf. xxxv, 144 (*pinxit*) *ab Oreste matrem et Aegisthum interfici.*

citharoedum: a Theban poet
named Kleon. The inscription on his
statue is quoted by Athenaios, i,
p. 19 b, who adds the story of the
gold on the authority of Polemon; cf.
Preger, *Inscriptiones*, 140.

5. hic primus nervos: his relation to *symmetry* is not given by
Pliny. It is preserved however,
by Diogenes Laërtios viii, 46: οἱ δὲ
καὶ . . . ἀνδριαντοποιὸν 'Ρηγῖνον γεγονέναι φασὶ Πυθ. πρῶτον δοκοῦντα
ῥυθμοῦ καὶ συμμετρίας ἐστοχάσθαι.
καὶ ἄλλον ἀνδριαντοποιὸν Σάμιον
(Furtwängler, *Plinius*, p. 70).

§ 60. 6. fuit et alius: in Paus.
vi, 4, 3, Pythagoras is called 'Ρηγῖνος,
and immediately after (vi, 6, 4) he is
named as the artist of the statue of
Euthymos. Now on the basis of the
Euthymos (*I. G. B.* 23). Pythagoras
signs himself Σάμιος; it is clear
therefore that the *Samius* and the
Rheginus were one and the same person. He was probably among the
Samians who migrated to Italy in Ol.
71 (Herod. vi, 23) and became subjects
of Anaxilas of Rhegion (Loewy on
I. G. B. 23). He evidently signed
sometimes with the one sometimes
with the other ethnic, a fact which
misled some art historian into dividing
him into two persons. A critic corrected this blunder and stated his belief
that the two were identical, a remark
which would afford the clue to Pliny's
ridiculous statement about the likeness. It is noteworthy that Diogenes
(*loc. cit.*) is likewise guilty of dividing
the sculptor into two.

limping, the pain of whose ulcer even the spectators seem to feel.
He also made an Apollo piercing a serpent with his arrows, and
a man with a cithara, which bears the name of δίκαιος [the Just],
because when Thebes was taken by Alexander, a fugitive concealed B.C. 335.
some money in its bosom, where it remained safely hidden. He
was the first to make the sinews and veins duly prominent, and
to bestow greater pains on the hair. A second Pythagoras, 60
a Samian, was a painter in early life. Near the temple of the
Fortune of the Day are seven nude figures by him, and an
old man, which are praised. According to tradition his personal
resemblance to the other Pythagoras was so strong that the two
could be mistaken; it was the Rhegine Pythagoras, however, of
whom Sostratos was the pupil and nephew.

Duris declares that Lysippos of Sikyon was no man's pupil; **61** *Lysippos of Sikyon.*
that he was originally a coppersmith, and was encouraged to ven-
ture on a higher path by the words of Eupompos. That painter
when asked which of the earlier artists he followed, pointed to
a crowd of people, and replied that nature should be imitated
and not any artist. Lysippos produced more works than any 62
other artist, possessing, as I have said, a most prolific genius.
Among them is the man scraping himself, which Marcus Agrippa
dedicated in front of his baths. In this statue the Emperor
Tiberius took a marvellous delight, and though capable of self-

6. **initio pictor**: so of Pheidias xxxv, 54.

7. **ad aedem Fortunae H. D.**: above § 54; it seems to have contained a real Museum; the *septem signa* need not have formed a group, but were seven athlete statues, collected together into one place for the first time at Rome. To these was added the portrait of an old man by the same artist (cf. H. L. Urlichs in *Woch. f. Klass. Phil.* 1894, p. 488, and Sauer, *Anfänge d. Stat. Gruppe,* p. 20, note 73).

8. **facie quoque indiscreta**: cf. the similar expressions above § 38; vii, 53; xxxv, 88 *similitudinis indiscretae, &c.*

10. **Sostratus**: his identity with Sostratos, sixth in artistic descent from Aristokles of Sikyon (Paus. vi, 9, 3), is quite doubtful. On this

Sostratus see Münzer, *Hermes,* 1895, p. 533.

§ 61. 11. **negat ullius fuisse discipulum**: in other words the name of his master was lost, cf. Seilanion above § 51, Protogenes in xxxv, 101.

12. **pictoris Eupompi**: xxxv, 75, among the *aequales et aemuli* of Zeuxis. On chronological grounds there is nothing to prevent Eupompos as an old man from having known the young Lysippos. The anecdote, however, was probably concocted in order to bring into connexion the greatest painter and the greatest sculptor of Sikyon; cf. Introd. p. xlvii f.

14. **naturam...non artificem**: a hit at the schools which worked according to a fixed *canon.* Introd. p. xlviii.

§ 62. 16. **ut diximus**: above, § 37.

17. **thermas**: at the back of the Pantheon. See Addenda.

tulitque in cubiculum alio signo substituto, cum quidem tanta
populi Romani contumacia fuit ut theatri clamoribus reponi
apoxyomenon flagitaverit princepsque quamquam adamatum
63 reposuerit.   nobilitatur Lysippus et temulenta tibicina et
canibus ac venatione, in primis vero quadriga cum Sole 5
Rhodiorum.   fecit et Alexandrum Magnum multis operibus
a pueritia eius orsus.   quam statuam inaurari iussit Nero
princeps delectatus admodum illa, dein, cum pretio perisset
gratia artis, detractum est aurum, pretiosiorque talis existimabatur etiam cicatricibus operis atque concisuris in quibus 10
64 aurum haeserat remanentibus.   idem fecit Hephaestionem
Alexandri Magni amicum, quem quidam Polyclito ad-
scribunt, cum is centum prope annis ante fuerit, item
Alexandri venationem quae Delphis sacrata est, Athenis
Satyrum, turmam Alexandri in qua amicorum eius imagines 15
A.U.C. 608. summa omnium similitudine expressit—hanc Metellus Macedonia subacta transtulit Romam—fecit et quadrigas multo-
65 rum generum.   statuariae arti plurimum traditur contulisse

§ 63. 4. temulenta tibicina : a
votive or grave statue, cf. the *anus
ebria* of Myron, xxxvi, 32 ; the *psaltria* by the painter Leontiskos, xxxv,
141, &c.

5. canibus ac venatione : cf. the
Alexandri ven. below, § 64. Large
hunting groups came largely into
vogue from Alexander onwards ; cf.
Kuhnert, *Statue und Ort*, p. 331. Urlichs (*Skopas*, p. 196) believes that the
fine fragment of a rider from the
Mausoleion (Brit. Mus.) had formed
part of such a group.

Sole Rhodiorum : for a head of
Helios with Lysippian characteristics,
found in Rhodes, cf. Hartwig, 'Testa di
Helios,' *Röm. Mitth.* ii, pp. 159–166.

6. Alexandr. Magnum : the most
famous was the Alexander with the
spear (Plut. περὶ τῆς ᾽Αλ. τύχης ii,
2) ; the motive seems reproduced in
the nude bronze portrait in the Terme
Mus. (Helbig, *Class. Ant.* 1052 ;
Ant. Denkm. i, 5 ; Furtwängler,
Masterpieces, p. 364, n. 2). For

portraits of Alexander see Koepp,
Winckelmannsprogramm, 1892. The
story told in Bk. vii, 125 (cf. Plut.
Alex. iv), that Lysippos alone was
privileged to make bronze statues of
Alexander, must like the similar stories
of Apelles (xxxv, 85) and Pyrgoteles
(xxxvii, 8) be accepted *cum grano.*

§ 64. 13. cum is centum prope
annis : Pliny's difficulty arises from his
only knowing of the Elder and more
famous Polykleitos, whereas a younger
P. is known from Paus. vi, 6, 2 (also
I. G. B. 92). Since the greater artists
often become credited with the works
of their less illustrious *confrères*, it is
probable that, as Loeschcke (*A. Z.*
1878, p. 10 ff.) has already pointed
out, the Hephaistion really was by the
younger Polykleitos. So too a number
of the works by the pupils of Pheidias
came to be reckoned as by the master
himself. Introd. p. xciii.

14. venationem . . . Delphis :
dedicated by Krateros on the occasion
narrated by Plutarch (*Alex.* 40), who

control in the first years of his reign, he could not refrain from
having the statue removed into his private chamber, substituting
another in its place. The populace of Rome resented this so
deeply that they raised an outcry in the theatre, demanding the
restitution of the ἀποξυόμενος, to which the emperor was fain to
yield, in spite of the passion he had conceived for the statue.
Lysippos has also won fame by his drunken flute-player, his dogs 63
and huntsmen, and above all by the four-horse chariot and the
figure of the Sun made for the Rhodians. He also made a number
of portraits of Alexander the Great, beginning with one of him as
a boy, which the Emperor Nero, who was greatly charmed with the
statue, ordered to be gilded. Then, as this costly addition spoiled
the beauty of the work, the gold was removed, and the statue was
considered more valuable without it, in spite of the scars upon it
and the incisions for fixing the gold. Further he made a statue 64
of Hephaistion, the friend of Alexander the Great, which some
ascribe to Polykleitos, although that artist lived almost a hundred
years earlier. We have also from his hand an Alexander in
a hunting group, which is consecrated at Delphoi, a Satyr at
Athens and a troop of Alexander's bodyguard, in which all his
friends' portraits are rendered with great fidelity. This group
was transported to Rome by Metellus after the conquest of 146 B.C.
Makedonia. By Lysippos also are various four-horse chariots. His 65
chief contributions to the art of sculpture are said to consist

states that the work was executed
conjointly with Leochares. According
to Loeschcke (*Jahrb.* iii, 1888, p.
139 f.) an echo of this work has survived on a relief from Messene in the
Louvre (*loc. cit.* pl. vii), cf. also Hans
Dragendorff, *Terra Sigillata*, p. 57.

15. **turmam Alexandri**: i. e. the
twenty-five officers who had fallen in
the first attack at the Granikos. A
statue of Alexander formed the centre
of the group, Vell. Paterc. i, 11, 3.

amicorum . . . imagines: this
assertion has been supposed to clash
with the statement that the dead were
buried on the battle-field (Arrian i,
16, 5). But seeing how extensively
portraiture was encouraged in the
circle of Alexander, there doubtless
were extant portraits of the officers,

which would serve Lysippos as guide;
cf. the undoubted portraits on the
'Alexander' sarkophagos from Sidon,
where, however, we can hardly suppose
the persons represented to have given
the artist sittings.

16. **Macedonia subacta**: the group
had stood in Dion, probably in the
temenos of Zeus, where were the statues
of the Makedonian kings (Heuzey,
Mont Olympe, p. 118). Arrian, writing
A.D. 124, mentions it as still at
Dion, probably because he is quoting
from some life of Alexander written
previous to the Roman conquest.

17. **Romam**: first in the *porticus
Metelli*, which was afterwards ab-
sorbed into the *porticus Octaviae* (Vell.
Paterc. *loc. cit.*). The statues were on
the *area* (cf. Varro *ap.* Macrob. iii,

capillum exprimendo, capita minora faciendo quam antiqui,
corpora graciliora siccioraque, per quae proceritas signorum
maior videretur.   non habet Latinum nomen symmetria
quam diligentissime custodit nova intactaque ratione quadratas veterum staturas permutando, vulgoque dicebat ab 5
illis factos quales essent homines, a se quales viderentur esse.
propriae huius videntur esse argutiae operum custoditae in
66 minimis quoque rebus.   filios et discipulos reliquit laudatos
artifices Laippum, Boedan, sed ante omnes Euthycraten,
quamquam is constantiam potius imitatus patris quam 10
elegantiam austero maluit genere quam iucundo placere.
itaque optime expressit Herculem Delphis et Alexandrum
Thespis venatorem et Thespiadas, proelium equestre, simulacrum ipsum Trophonii ad oraculum, quadrigas complures,
67 equum cum fuscinis, canes venantium.   huius porro 15
discipulus fuit Tisicrates et ipse Sicyonius, sed Lysippi
sectae propior, ut vix discernantur complura signa, ceu
senex Thebanus et Demetrius rex, Peucestes Alexandri

13. Thespiadas] *om. Bamb., Detlefsen.*   15. fiscinis *Bamb., Detlefsen.*

4, 2) in front of the temples—Jupiter
and Juno (*frontem aedium spectant*
Velleius *loc. cit.*), cf. xxxvi, 35, 40.

§ 65. 3. symmetria: so in xxxv,
67, 128 Pliny retains the Greek word,
although, as Otto Jahn has pointed
out (*Kunsturtheile*, p. 131) *proportio*
or *commensus* afforded an adequate
Latin equivalent. For a like reluc-
tance to translate a Greek word which
had come to have a precise meaning
cf. xxxv, 98 *quae vocant Graeci ethe.*

6. quales viderentur esse: Pliny,
or his authority, is here finding a
formula for the conflict between the
desire to represent things *as they are
known to be*, and that of presenting
them *as they appear to be.* The *form*
of the aphorism seems influenced by the
words Aristotle puts into the mouth of
Sophokles, *Poet.* 1460 b: Σοφοκλῆς ἔφη
αὐτὸς μὲν οἵους δεῖ ποιεῖν, Εὐριπίδην δὲ
οἷοι εἰσίν (cf. also in *Poet.* 1448, ff. the
judgement passed on Polygnotos, Pau-
son and Dionysios), Introd. p. lxii f.

13. Thespiadas] *om. Bamb., Detlefsen.*

7. argutiae operum: cf. xxxv,
67 *Parrhasius . . . dedit primus argutias voltus ;* Cic. *Brutus,* 45, 167
and O. Jahn's note.

§ 66. 8. filios et discipulos: the
notice of the sons of Lysippos is from
the same author as the preceding five
appreciations. Introd. p. xxi.

9. Laippum: above § 51; cf.
§ 87. — Boedan: below § 73. —
Euthykraten: § 83.

10. quamquam.... maluit: points
to a reaction within the Lysippian
school to the older and severer Argive
manner.

constantiam: cf. Petron. 88 *Lysippum, statuae unius lineamentis
inhaerentem, inopia extinxit.*

12. itaque optime: explanatory,
not of the preceding *quamquam*, but
of the general excellence of E. (Blümner, *Rhein. Mus.* xxxii, p. 610).

13. Thespiadas : a Praxitelean
subject, xxxvi, 39 ; so his father made
for the same Thespiai an Eros, as

in his vivid rendering of the hair, in making the heads smaller than older artists had done, and the bodies slimmer and with less flesh, thus increasing the apparent height of his figures. There is no word in Latin for the canon of symmetry [συμμετρία] which he was so careful to preserve, bringing innovations which had never been thought of before into the square canon of the older artists, and he often said that the difference between himself and them was that they represented men as they were, and he as they appeared to be. His chief characteristic is extreme delicacy of execution even in the smallest details.

He left artists of high reputation in his sons and pupils, Laippos, **66** † Boedas, and above all Euthykrates; the latter however imitated *Pupils of Lysippos.* not so mKch the refinement as the perseverance of his father, choosing to win approval by an austere rather than a lighter style of execution. In this manner he made for Delphoi an admirable statue of Herakles, for Thespiai an Alexander hunting, a group of the Thespiades and a combat between horsemen, a statue of Trophonios within his oracular cave, several chariots with four horses, a horse carrying hunting prongs, and hunting dogs.

His pupil was Teisikrates, also a native of Sikyon, who **67** followed more closely the school of Lysippos, so that many of his *Teisikrates* works can hardly be distinguished from those of the master: *pupil of Euthy-* witness his portrait of an old man at Thebes, of king Demetrios *krates.* and of Peukestes, who saved Alexander's life and well deserves the honour of a statue.

Praxiteles before him. It may be that the Thespians owed to the bounty of Alexander (whose allies they had become in B.C. 335) these Lysippian bronzes, rivals of the celebrated Praxitelean marbles. (So Klein, *Jahrb.* ix, 1894, p. 166.)

proelium equestre: a votive offering like the *turmam Alexandri*, § 64, cf. Kuhnert, *Statue u. Ort*, p. 331. [From *simulacrum* to *canes* we have an inverted alphabetical list.—H.L.U.]

14. ad oraculum: the actual cave as distinct from the temple, which contained a statue of the god by Daidalos (Paus. ix, 39, 8), and another by Praxiteles (*ib.* § 4).

15. fuscinis: two-pronged spears, such as are used by Meleager and

Mopsos on the cylix by Glaukytes and Archikles in Munich (Klein, *Meistersign.* p. 77 = Gerhard, *Auserlesene Vasenbilder*, iv, 235). Further, on an archaic cylix from Kameiros (mentioned, *A. Z.* xxiv, 1866, p. 296), Bellerophon, riding Pegasos, is represented with a similar pronged fork; also in hands of one of the huntsman on two amphoras in Berlin (Furtwängler, *Cat.* 1705, 1706), otherwise the pronged fork is known only as a fishing implement. The horse, the *quadrigae* just mentioned, and the following *canes* (cf. note on *canem* in § 57) all belong to the usual class of votive offerings.

§ 67. 16. Tisicrates: § 83.

18. senex Thebanus: not Pindar

68 Magni servator, dignus tanta gloria. artifices qui compositis voluminibus condidere haec miris laudibus celebrant Telephanen Phocaeum ignotum alias, quoniam in Thessalia habitaverit, et ibi opera eius latuerint, alioqui suffragiis ipsorum aequatur Polyclito, Myroni, Pythagorae. 5 laudant eius Larisam et Spintharum pentathlum et Apollinem. alii non hanc ignobilitatis fuisse causam, sed quod se regum Xerxis atque Darei officinis dediderit, existimant.
69 Praxiteles quoque marmore felicior, ideo et clarior fuit. fecit tamen et ex aere pulcherrima opera: Proserpinae 10 raptum, item catagusam, et Liberum patrem, et Ebrietatem nobilemque una Satyrum quem Graeci periboeton cognominant, et signa quae ante Felicitatis aedem fuere, Veneremque quae ipsa aedis incendio cremata est Claudii principatu,
70 marmoreae illi suae per terras inclutae parem, item stepha- 15

as some have supposed—or the name would almost certainly have been preserved, but merely a portrait. Furtwängler, *Dornauszieher*, p. 92.

Demetrius: i. e. Poliorketes, became king B.C. 307, died B.C. 283.

Peucestes: *tribus iaculis confossus, non se tamen scuto, sed regem tuebatur* Q. Curtius ix, ch. 5, 21; the episode occurred during a siege in the territory of the Oxydrakai, or according to Arrian vi, 10, and Plutarch, *Alex.* lxiii, in that of the Malloi.

§ **68. 1. artifices qui**: i.e. Xenokrates and Antigonos, see Introd. p. xxii. **haec**, i. e. everything mentioned §§ 49–68.

3. **Phocaeum**: from the Ionian Phokaia, Φωκαῖος; cf. Furtwängler, *Masterpieces*, p. 57. It is unnecessary to look upon the word as a variant for *Phocensis*.

6. **Larisam**: it is worth noting in this connexion the beautiful head of the nymph Larissa on the coin, P. Gardner, *Types*, pl. vii, 17; *Rev.* horse and horseman treated in a style reminiscent of Parthenon frieze.

7. **alii non**: see Introd. *loc. cit.* The names of Xerxes (B.C. 485–465)

and of Dareios (the First B.C. 521–485, the Second B.C. 425–405) are apparently only introduced to attach the statement to well-known names. The dates are plainly irreconcilable.

§ **69. 10. Proserpinae raptum**: the extant representations of the Rape of Persephone have been carefully collected by Förster, *Raub u. Rückkehr d. Perseph.* in *Philologus*, Supplementband iv. A number are reproduced by Overbeck, *Atlas d. Kunst Myth.* Taf. 17, 18; none however can be referred with any certainty, or even probability, to the group by Praxiteles. Förster hesitatingly suggests that the coin of Kasa (Overb. *K. M. Münztafel*, ix, 12) reproduces the group of Praxiteles. The subject of the Rape was treated by the painter Nikomachos, xxxv, 108.

11. **item**: introduces a new subject, **catagusa**: the true meaning was given as early as by Dalecampius, τὴν κατάγουσαν *quae pensa nendo ducet unde et* κάταγμα; so independently Loeschcke, *A. Z.* 38 (1880), p. 102 f. The meaning of κατάγειν is further discussed by Förster, *loc. cit.* p. 719; H. L. Urlichs (*Woch. f. Klass. Phil.*

Those sculptors who have written treatises on the subject give 68 high praise to Telephanes of Phokaia, who is otherwise unknown, *Telephanes of Phokaia.* since, they say, he lived in Thessaly, where his works remained unnoticed. These writers however adjudge him a place beside Polykleitos, Myron and Pythagoras, praising his statues of Larissa, of Spintharos, a winner in the five contests, and of Apollo. Others give a different reason for his comparative obscurity, saying that he passed into the service of king Xerxes and of Dareios.

Praxiteles also, though more successful and consequently 69 better known as a worker in marble, created admirable works *Praxiteles.* in bronze: a rape of Persephone, the κατάγουσα or Girl Spinning, a Dionysos, a figure of Intoxication grouped with an admirable Satyr known among the Greeks as the περιβόητος or Renowned, and also the statues which stood in front of the temple of Felicity, and an Aphrodite which was also destroyed when the temple was burned down in the reign of Claudius, the worthy peer of his famous marble Aphrodite. Other works of his are 70 the στεφανοῦσα, or woman presenting a wreath, the ψελιουμένη, or

1894, p. 227 f.) compares for the motive the spinning maiden, Furtwängler, *Samml. Sabouroff*, Pl. xix; and the bronze statue, Munich, *Glypth.* 314. I take the κατάγουσα to have been a grave statue; for spinning and similar motives on graves, see Weisshänpl, *Grabgedichte der Gr. Anthol.* p. 77, note 3.

Liberum patrem: [it is usual to understand the Dionysos as forming a group with the two following statues, but the fact that up to *Veneremque* the enumeration of single works is given by *et*, shows that Pliny, at any rate, understood the Dionysos as a separate statue, and the figure of Intoxication and the Satyr only (their close connexion being indicated by the use of *-que*) as forming a group together; the second *et* is omitted in Cod. Bamb., but in cases of omission of syllables or even words, little faith can be put in this otherwise excellent MS.—H. L. U.]. This observation disposes of a recent conjecture *Liberum*

ebriolatum (*Mus. Ital. d. Antich. Class*, iii, p. 787); not only is it irreconcilable with the evidence of the MSS., but the use of the word *ebriolare*, only known from a fragment of the *Hetaera* of Laberius (*ap.*Nonius, 108, 6), is quite unproved for prose writers.

13. Felicitatis aedem: on the Triumphal Street (Dio Cassius 43, 21) built by L. Lucullus, B.C. 151; see note on xxxvi, 39. The *signa* being bronze are of course distinct from the marble *Thespiades* of xxxvi, 39; a number of Praxitelean works had been gathered together in the precinct of Felicitas, just as the temple of the Fortune of The Day contained works by Pheidias and Pythagoras (above, §§ 54, 60).

15. marmoreae illi: xxxvi, 20.

§ 70. stephanusam: probably in a group with an athlete, in which case the στεφανοῦσα would be the personification of the festal city where the athletic victory had been won;

nusam, pseliumenen, oporan, Harmodium et Aristogitonem
tyrannicidas, quos a Xerxe Persarum rege captos victa
Perside Atheniensibus remisit Magnus Alexander.   fecit
et puberem Apollinem subrepenti lacertae comminus sagitta
insidiantem quem sauroctonon vocant.   spectantur et duo 5
signa eius diversos adfectus exprimentia, flentis matronae
et meretricis gaudentis.   hanc putant Phrynen fuisse deprehenduntque in ea amorem artificis et mercedem in vultu
71 meretricis.   habet simulacrum et benignitas eius, Calamidis enim quadrigae aurigam suum inposuit, ne melior in 10
equorum effigie defecisse in homine crederetur.   ipse Calamis
et alias quadrigas bigasque fecit se impari, equis sine aemulo
expressis.   sed, ne videatur in hominum effigie inferior,

1. oporan] *Ricc.*; operan *Voss.*; ephoram *Bamb.*; canephoram *Urlichs in Chrest.*, *Detlefsen.*   12. sem pari equis *Bamb.*, *corr. Traube*; equis semper *reliqui, Detlefsen.*

cf. Athen. xii, 534 D : ὁ μὲν (sc. πίναξ) εἶχεν Ὀλυμπιάδα καὶ Πυθιάδα στεφανούσας αὐτόν (ʼΑλκιβιάδην). For the artistic motive cf. the relief in the Akrop. Mus., *A. Z.* 1869, 24 = Friederichs-Wolters, 1188. [From *Stephan.* to *Harmod. et Arist.* we have an inverted alphabetical list (cf. § 66); this confirms the MS. reading *oporan*. —H. L. U.]

1. pseliumenen : for an analogous motive see the little bronze, *Jahrb.* ix 1894, pl. xi; its connexion with Praxiteles cannot however be pressed further.

oporan : [for a personification of autumn cf. Ar. Εἰρήνη 523 ff., where ὀπώρα is brought in to wed Trygaios; thus the subject, which fits excellently into the Praxitelean series, is also proved to have been a conception familiar in the fifth and fourth centuries, H. L. U.].

2. quos a Xerxe . . . Alexander: since this statement is true only of the group by Antenor, Paus. i, 8, 5, it seems probable that the mention of Praxitelean Tyrant-Slayers is due to a confusion. Urlichs, *A. Z.* 1861,

p. 144, supposes the displacement of a heading *Antenor*, belonging probably to the alphabetical list which begins in § 72.

3. Magnus Alexander : so also Arrian, *Anab.* iii, 7, 8 ; Antiochos according to Paus. *loc. cit.*; Seleukos according to Val. Max. ii, 10, *ext.* 1.

4. subrepenti lacertae : from a descriptive epigram ; cf. Martial, xiv, 172.

5. sauroctonon : finest replica in Louvre, phot. Giraudon 1200.

6. flentis . . . gaudentis : epigrammatic antithesis, cf. the *molliter iuvenis* and *viriliter puer* of § 55. The statues were certainly only juxtaposed in the epigram.   The *flens matrona*, like the similar figures by Sthennis (below § 90) was a portrait statue for a grave ; Praxiteles is known to have made at least two grave monuments ; (*a*) the warrior and his horse, Paus. i, 2, 3 ; (*b*) the monument to which *C. I. G.* 1604 belonged; cf. Furtwängler, *Dornauszieher*, p. 91, note 43 ; above note on *catagusa*. For the artistic motive see the fine statue in the Louvre, phot. Giraudon 1174.

woman clasping a bracelet on her arm, ὀπώρα or Autumn, and statues of Harmodios and Aristogeiton, the Slayers of the Tyrant. These were carried off by Xerxes, king of the Persians, and restored to Athens by Alexander the Great after his conquest of Persia. He also made a young Apollo with an arrow watching a lizard as it creeps up with intent to slay it close at hand; this is known as the σαυροκτόνος or Lizard-slayer. There are two statues by him expressing contrary emotions, a mourning matron and a rejoicing courtesan. The latter is believed to be Phryne. The sculptor's love may be read in the whole statue, and Phryne's satisfaction is depicted on her face.

There is also a statue which testifies to the kindness of Praxiteles, for he made a charioteer for a four-horse chariot by Kalamis, not wishing it to be thought that Kalamis failed in the man after succeeding in the horses. Kalamis made other four and two-horse chariot-groups with varying success, though unrivalled in his horses. And yet, for it must not be thought that

71 *Kindness of Praxiteles towards Kalamis.*

7. **putant Phrynen**: doubtless correctly; it should be noted, however, that Pliny mentions neither of the celebrated statues of Phryne at Thespiai and at Delphoi, Furtwängler, *loc. cit.*

8. **mercedem**: the meaning is not altogether clear; the words may contain an allusion to the μισθός given by Praxiteles to Phryne, in the shape of the Eros which she dedicated at Thespiai, *Anth. Plan.* 204 (cf. Benndorf, *Epigr.* p. 53). Again the *merces* may refer to Phryne's reward in the artist's love; or—in the lower sense of payment—it may contain an allusion to her venality as *meretrix*.

§ 71. 10. **aurigam suum imposuit**: since Kalamis (above § 47; xxxiii, 156; xxxvi, 36) flourished in the early part of the fifth century, the *auriga* must have been by the Elder Praxiteles (Klein, *Arch. Ep. Mitth.* 1879, p. 8; Benndorf, *Cultusbild der Athena Nike*, p. 47; Furtwängler, *Masterpieces*, p. 102 ff., &c.). A division of labour in the case of important monuments was quite common, e. g. for Hieron,

Onatas makes the chariot, while Kalamis makes the κέλητες ἵπποι at either side, Paus. vi, 12, 1. [In the case of the Younger (?) Praxiteles it is expressly mentioned as noteworthy, that for a grave monument he made *both* the horse and the horseman: καὶ τὸν ἵππον καὶ τὸν στρατιώτην Paus. i, 2, 3.—H. L. U.] The inscription on the *bathron* of the chariot gave the names of both artists, and the juxtaposition was sufficient to give rise to the story of the *benignitas*. The chariot was of course a votive offering, a ὑπόμνημα τῆς νίκης (cf. in this book §§ 64, 86, 88; xxxv, 27, 99, 108, 141, &c.). Introd. p. lxv.

12. **se impari, equis sine aemulo expressis**: the reading, while derived straight from Cod. Bamb., further brings out an epigrammatic antithesis; the full meaning is as follows: 'This same K. failed through his inability to do the human figure, in other chariot-groups as a whole, albeit the horses taken alone were unrivalled'; cf. Prop. iii, 9, 10 *exactis Calamis se mihi iactat equis*. Introd. p. lxix.

72 Alcman poeta nullius est nobilior. Alcamenes Phidiae discipulus et marmorea fecit et aereum pentathlum qui vocatur encrinomenos, at Polycliti discipulus Aristides quadrigas bigasque. Amphicrates Leaena laudatur. scortum haec lyrae cantu familiaris Harmodio et Aristogitoni con- silia eorum de tyrannicidio usque in mortem excruciata a tyrannis non prodidit, quamobrem Athenienses, et honorem habere ei volentes nec tamen scortum celebrasse, animal nominis eius fecere atque, ut intellegeretur causa honoris,
73 in opere linguam addi ab artifice vetuerunt.   Bryaxis Aesculapium et Seleucum fecit, Boedas adorantem, Baton Apollinem et Iunonem qui sunt Romae in Concordiae
74 templo, Cresilas volneratum deficientem in quo possit

---

1. Alcman poeta] *E. Sellers*; alcamen et *Bamb.* (alcame et *e corr.*); alchimena *reliqui*; Alcmena *Detlefsen*.

1. **Alcman poeta:** it was pointed out by Benndorf (*op. cit.* p. 47) that the original reading had been corrupted by the neighbouring *Alcamenes*. The readings *Alcmena* or *Alcumena* are unsatisfactory, since the subject could hardly be reckoned among *hominum effigies*. The reading *Alcman poeta* now proposed meets this difficulty, while the subject falls within the range of Kalamis. He is known to have worked for Sparta from Paus. x, 16, 4 (cf. Klein, *Arch. Ep. Mitth.* 1881, p. 84), and might well be called upon to execute a statue of its greatest poet. For a statue of Alkman cf. *Anth. Pal.* vii, 709, an epigram which Weisshäupl (*Grabgedichte der Gr. Anth.* p. 45) suggests may have belonged to a statue of the poet at Sparta, cf. also *Anth. Pal.* vii, 18, 19. *Nobilior*—cf. *nobilis* applied below to the portrait of Perikles by Kresilas.

§ 72. **Alcamenes:** above § 49, xxxvi, 16.

3. **encrinomenos:** *encrinomenos vocatur, qui athletis adnumeratur, id est qui in eorum numero recipitur,* so Turnebus (*Advers.* p. 486, cf. the note of Dalecampius) explains the

term with reference to the ἔγκρισις ἀθλητῶν. Modern commentators, however, generally refer the epithet to the statue, and explain it as *approved, chosen, classical* or *canonical* ('classisch' 'mustergiltig,' Urlichs in *Chrest.* p. 325; cf. O. Jahn, *Kunsturtheile,* p. 125; H. L. Urlichs, *Blätter f. d. bayr. Gymnasialsch.* 1894, pp. 609–613). But the ἔγκρισις ἀθλ. (Lucian, ὑπὲρ τῶν εἰκόν. 11; cf. Xen. *Hell.* iv, 1, 10), lit. the 'examination' of the athletes (*probatio* Cic. *Off.* i, 144) was too well known as an athletic term for the epithet ἐγκρινόμενος as applied to the portrait of an athlete to be understood in any other sense than the one given to it above. The present participle, instead of the more usual ἐγκριθείς (cf. the inscr. Ross. *Griech. Königsreisen,* i, p. 96) shows that the athlete was represented in the act of submitting to the ἔγκρισις. The occurrence of the epithet *Encrinomenus* as a Roman proper name (*C. I. L.* v, 1, 4429), by proving its familiarity, suffices to discredit the old emendation of Barbarus *encriomenos,* which had lately come again into favour. The proposed identification of the *encrinomenos* with the statue of an athlete holding

he was inferior to others in representing the human figure, no artist has better portrayed the poet Alkman.

Alkamenes, a pupil of Pheidias, produced works in marble as 72 well as a winner in the five contests in bronze, called the ἐγκρινόμενος [undergoing the test]. A pupil of Polykleitos, *Aristeides*, made chariots with four horses and with two. †*Amphikrates* is famous for his λέαινα or Lioness : this Leaina was a courtesan, intimate through her playing on the lyre with Harmodios and Aristogeiton, whose plot of assassination she refused to betray, although tortured to death by the tyrants. The Athenians were anxious to pay her honour, and yet unwilling to commemorate a courtesan by a statue ; they accordingly made a figure of the animal whose name she bore, and to indicate their reason for honouring her, they forbade the artist to give it a tongue. *Bryaxis* made an Asklepios and a Seleukos ; †*Boedas* a praying 73 figure, *Baton* the Apollo and Hera which are in the temple of Concord at Rome, *Kresilas*, a wounded man at the point 74

Monument of Leaina.

the disc preparatory to the throw (Brit. Mus. and Vatican ; Helbig, *Class. Ant.* 331, where see literature) is, to say the least, open to doubt.

Aristides : possibly identical with the painter, master of Euphranor, xxxv, 75 ; Kroker, *Gleichnamige Künstler*, p. 25.

4. **Leaena** : vii, 87 ; the story, told also Plut. *de Garrul.* 8 ; Paus. i, 23, 1 ; Polyainos, Στρατηγήμ. viii, 45 ; cf. Cicero, *Glor.* ii, fr. 12 (all without mention of artist's name), is an obvious invention. Had the 'Lioness' been originally connected with the Tyrant-Slayers her monument must have stood by theirs ἐν Κεραμεικῷ (Arrian, *Anab.* iii, 16, 8), instead of at the entrance to the Akropolis (Paus. *loc. cit.*). Further, since the oldest authorities, Herodotos and Thukydides, in their account of the murder of the Tyrants, know nothing of this Leaina, it is probable that she was an ordinary votive-offering ; the fact that the artist had failed to give the animal a tongue, or that in the course of time the tongue had got broken away, having given rise to the anecdote

(cf. also Athen. xiii, 596 f.) Introd. p. lxxvi, note 3.

§ **73.** 10. **Bryaxis** : above § 42 ; xxxvi, 30.

11. **Aesculapium** : for Megara he made an Asklepios grouped with Hygieia, Paus. i, 40, 6.

Seleucum : i.e. Nikator, reigned B.C. 312–280 ; cf. below § 86 ; for his portraits see Wolters, *Röm. Mitth.* iv, 1889, pp. 32-40.

Boedas : above § 66.

adorantem : in the scheme doubtless of the 'Praying Boy' (Berlin, *Cat.* 2), cf. *Jahrb.* i, 1886, p. 1 ff. (Conze) ; for the type of the *adorans* on coins *Jahrb.* iii, 1886, p. 286 ff. (Imhoof-Blumer), on a gem *ib.* I. p. 217 (Furtwängler).

Baton : below § 91 ; known from *I. G. B.* 61, as a native of Herakleia.

12. **Concordiae templo** : at the base of the Capitol, vowed B.C. 367 by Camillus, and built after his death by the State ; restored by Tiberius (ded. A.D. 9). It was the most usual meeting place of the Senate.

§ **74.** 13. **Cresilas** : above § 53.
vulneratum : apparently identical

intellegi quantum restet animae et Olympium Periclen
dignum cognomine, mirumque in hac arte est quod nobiles
viros nobiliores fecit. Cephisodorus Minervam mirabilem
in portu Atheniensium et aram ad templum Iovis Servatoris
75 in eodem portu, cui pauca comparantur, Canachus Apollinem 5
nudum qui Philesius cognominatur in Didymaeo Aeginetica
aeris temperatura, cervumque una ita vestigiis suspendit ut
linum subter pedes trahatur alterno morsu calce digitisque
retinentibus solum, ita vertebrato dente utrisque in partibus
ut a repulsu per vices resiliat. idem et celetizontas pueros, 10
Chaereas Alexandrum Magnum et Philippum patrem eius

3. Cephisodorus] *Bamb.*; Cephissidorus *reliqui.*   8. inlitum *Bamb.*
                                            trahantur *Bamb.*

with the statue of Dieitrephes
pierced by arrows, Paus. i, 23, 3
(where the artist is not named); the
extant inscription ('Ερμόλυκος Διειτρέ-
φος ἄπαρχεν· Κρεσίλας ἐπόεσεν *I. G. B.*
46) should place this beyond a doubt,
were it not that the epigraphy is too
early for the date of Dieitrephes, who
according to Pausanias was identical
with the Athenian general mentioned
Thuc. vii, 29 (B. C. 414); cf. Kirchhoff
on *C. I. A.* i, 402. Furtwängler
(*Masterpieces*, p. 122) accordingly
proposes to identify the Dieitrephes
of the statue with an older namesake, father of the Nikostratos,'who
was a general at the commencement
of the Peloponnesian war (Thuc. iii,
75; iv, 119, 129). For possible re-
productions of the statue see Furtwängler, *op. cit.* figs. 48, 49, 50
(against his views cf. C. Robert, *Hall.
Winckelmannspr.* 1895, p. 21 f.).

1. Periclen : for the portrait
(without name of artist), cf. Paus. i,
25, 1. Its inscribed basis was discovered in 1888, see Δελτίον, 1889,
p. 36 ff. (Lolling). A terminal portrait of Perikles, extant in several
replicas (*Br. Mus. Cat.* i, 549; Helbig,
Class. Ant. 281, where see literature)
has been identified as a copy of the
Kresilaian portrait. Addenda.

3. Minervam mirabilem . . . et
aram : cf. Paus. i, 1, 3 : θέας δὲ ἄξιον
τῶν ἐν Πειραιεῖ μάλιστα 'Αθηνᾶς ἐστι
καὶ Διὸς τέμενος· χαλκοῦ μὲν ἀμφότερα
τὰ ἀγάλματα, ἔχει δὲ ὁ μὲν σκῆπτρον
καὶ νίκην, ἡ δὲ 'Αθηνᾶς δόρυ. The
τέμενος has been shown to be probably
contemporary with the restoration of
the Peiraios by the architect Hippo-
damos of Miletos (Arist. *Pol.* ii, 8, 1),
under Perikles (so Wachsmuth, *Stadt
Athen*, ii, p. 141 f.). Thus, if the
monuments mentioned by Pliny and
Pausanias are, as seems reasonable to
suppose, identical, Kephisodoros would
be an artist of the Periklean age.—
I see no reason for following Furtwängler (*Masterpieces*, p. 145 f.) in
assuming a displacement of Pliny's
notes, and giving the works mentioned
to Kresilas (cf. B. Keil in *Hermes*, xxxi,
1895, p. 225). Introd. p. lxxv; Add.

§ 75. 5. Apollinem : it was the
exact replica of the same artist's Apollo
at Thebes, except that the latter was
of wood, cf. Paus. ix, 10, 2; ii, 10, 4;
the type is reproduced both on the
autonomous and Imperial coinage of
Miletos, *A. Z.* 18, ix, pl. vii, and page
90 (= Collignon, *Sculpt. Grecque*,
fig. 153) and in the 'Payne-Knight
bronze' (Br. Mus.); cf. Furtwängler,
ap. Roscher i, 451 : the god, nude,

of death, whose face betrays how fast his life is ebbing, and also an Olympian Perikles, worthy of the epithet. The marvel *Perikles.* of his art is that it made famous men yet more famous. †*Kephisodoros* made a wondrous Athena in the harbour of Athens, and in the same city, in the temple of Zeus the Saviour, an altar to which few are comparable. *Kanachos* made the nude Apollo, 75 which is named the Lover and is in the temple at Didyma, of Aeginetan bronze, and with it a stag so poised upon its feet, *Apollo and* that a thread can be drawn beneath them while the heel and toe *Stag.* alternately catch the ground, both parts working with a jointed mechanism in such a way that the impact suffices to make them spring backwards and forwards. He also made boys on race-horses. †*Chaireas* made an Alexander the Great and his father

stands erect, holding a small stag on the palm of his R. hand, and the bow in his L. The work was executed previous to Ol. 71, 3 (= B.C. 494), in which year Dareios (Herod. vi, 19; Paus. viii, 46, 3, erroneously says Xerxes) sacked Miletos and took away the statue. The Apollo was restored by Seleukos Nikator, Paus. *loc. cit.* and i, 16, 3.

'6. Philesius : aitiology sought to explain the epithet by allusion to Apollo's love for Branchos (Strabo, xiv, p. 634), so Varro, *p.* schol. to Statius, *Thebais,* viii, 198 (ed. Lindenbrog, p. 282 f.) ; Macrobius (*Sat.* i, 17, 2) gives a symbolic explanation.

Aeginetica temp.: above § 8.

7. suspendit : for the meaning given above cf. xxxvi, 117 *theatra iuxta duo fecit amplissima ligno, cardinum singulorum versatili suspensa libramento.* From the word *solum* it is evident that Pliny conceived the stag to have its feet on the ground, an arrangement however which is in irreconcilable contradiction to the testimony of the coins, which show the stag resting on the god's hand. We must suppose, therefore, that the exact place of the stag was not described in the original account, and that Pliny, unacquainted with the statue, assumed, naturally enough,

either that the animal was on the ground, or, according to a scheme familiar from statues of Artemis (also for Apollo in the gem *Cades, Impronte,* iv, 19, 20) that its hind feet were on the ground while its front feet were held in the hand of the god. It is evident that in the *inlitum* of cod. *Bamb.* we have a corruption, while the *linum* of the later codices is a mere interpolation intended to get an ordinary Latin word out of the corrupt reading ; the original word must have given the instrument provided with the *dens vertebratus.* Whether the stag was in reality provided with some curious mechanism, or whether the fact that it had been cast separate and did not accurately fit on to the god's palm had given rise to an explanation which has a flavour of concoction, it is now impossible to tell (cf. however the ingenious article of Petersen, *A. Z.* xxxviii, 1880, pp. 22, 192).

10. repulsu: cf. xi, 164 *pare eodem praegnas veneno impresso dentium repulsu virus fundit in morsus* (Petersen).

celetizontas pueros : cf. on the Akropolis the bronze statue of Isokrates as παῖς κελητίζων. Lives of Ten Orators, *Isokr.* 42 ; at Olympia Aisypos, son of Timon, Paus. vi, z, 8 ; cf. *id.* vi, 12, 1. A κελητίζων on the

76 fecit, Ctesilaus doryphoron et Amazonem volneratam,
Demetrius Lysimachen quae sacerdos Minervae fuit LXIIII
annis, idem et Minervam quae *musica* appellatur, quoniam
dracones in Gorgone eius ad ictus citharae tinnitu resonant,
idem equitem Simonem qui primus de equitatu scripsit. 5
Daedalus et ipse inter fictores laudatus pueros duos destringentes se fecit, Dinomenes Protesilaum et Pythodemum
77 luctatorem.   Euphranoris Alexander Paris est, in quo
laudatur quod omnia simul intellegantur, iudex dearum,
amator Helenae et tamen Achillis interfector.   huius est 10
Minerva Romae quae dicitur Catuliana, infra Capitolium
A.U.C. 676. a Q. Lutatio dicata, et simulacrum Boni Eventus, dextra
pateram, sinistra spicam ac papavera tenens, item Latona

---

1. Ctesilaus] *Sillig, Detlefsen*; G. tesilaus *Bamb.*; desilaus *reliqui.*
3. myetica *Bamb.*

---

coin of Tarentum, Head, *Guide*, pl.
24, 7. Addenda.

§ 76. 1. **Ctesilaus**: the name,
though uncommon, is a good Greek
formation (cf. the formations ending
-λεως, -λαος in Fick, *Gr. Personennamen*, pp. 186 ff.), so that I see no
grounds for altering the reading to
Kresilas as proposed by Bergk
(*Zeitschr. d. Alterth. Wissensch.* 1845,
p. 962), who is followed by most
archaeologists. The argument derived
from the Amazon (§ 53), though
strong, is scarcely sufficient.

2. **Demetrius**: the famous ἀν-
θρωποποιός, Lucian, *The Liars*, 18.

Lysimachen = Paus. i, 27, 4: πρὸς
δὲ ναῷ τῷ τῆς Ἀθηνᾶς, the following information is derived from the
inscription on the basis of the statue,
Töpffer, *Att. Geneal.* 128; for a
similar inscr. from the Akropolis (but
belonging to a larger statue) of a
priestess who had served (?) [ἑξή]κοντα
δ᾽ ἔτη [κ]αὶ τέσσορ[α], see *I. G. B.* 64;
Hitzig and Blümner, *Paus.* p. 295.

3. **musica**: the reading is an
obvious interpolation, to make sense
out of the corrupt *myetica;* the epithet
is not found of Athena or any other

god. Fröhner in *Rhein. Mus.* 1892,
p. 292, proposes to read *mystica* for
myetica, adding that 'the mysterious
resonance of the aegis recalled the
music of the Elensinian mysteries
when the Hierophant struck the
ἠχεῖον.' Dr. Traube suggests that the
reading might possibly be *mycetica*, i. e.
'the Roarer'—μυκητικός as an epithet
of Poseidon occurs *ap.* Cornutos, *Nat.
Deor.* ch. 22, p. 42, Lang—it is quite
possible that an aitiological explanation, derived from the resonance of the
bronze aegis, had been found for an
epithet of which the original meaning
had been forgotten.

5. **de equitatu**: περὶ ἱππικῆς Xen.
de Re Eq. i, 3.

6. **Daedalus**: son of Patrokles
(*I. G. B.* 88, 89; Paus. vi, 3, 9, cf.
above § 50). D. signs Σικυώνιος
(*I. G. B.* 89) and seems to be the first
member of the family who migrated
to Sikyon; cf. Furtwängler, *Masterpieces*, p. 225.

et ipse: marks Pliny's astonishment at the appearance of Daidalos
among the bronze-workers (rightly explained by Oehmichen, *Plin. Studien*,
p. 192), perhaps because the only

Philip. † *Ktesilaos* made a δορυφόρος, or Spear-bearer, and 76 a wounded Amazon ; *Demetrios* a statue of Lysimache, who was priestess of Athena for sixty-four years. He also made the Athena called the Musical because the snakes of her Gorgon resound to the notes of the cithara, and an equestrian statue of Simon, the first writer on horsemanship. *Daidalos*, who appears here among the famous statuaries, made two boys scraping themselves, *Deinomenes* a Protesilaos and a portrait of Pythodemos the wrestler. A statue of Alexander Paris by *Euphranor* is 77 said to display every phase of the Trojan's character : he is *Statue of Paris in* at once the judge of the goddesses, the lover of Helen, and yet *his triple* the slayer of Achilles. The Athena at Rome known as the *aspect.* Minerva of Catulus, which was dedicated below the Capitol by Quintus Lutatius, is by Euphranor ; so is the statue of Good B.C. 78. Luck holding in the right hand a bowl, and in the left an ear of corn and a poppy. He also made a Leto with the new-

personage of the name with whom he is familiar is the mythical Daidalos (vii, 198, 209 ; xxxvi, 85, cf. vii, 205).

destringentes se : for the motive cf. §§ 55, 62.

7. **Dinomenes** . above § 50 ; distinct from the artist of the first century who made the statues of Io and Kallisto (Paus. i. 25, 1 ; *I. G. B.* 233), cf. Gurlitt, *Pausanias*, p. 267 ff.

§ 77. 8. **Euphranoris** : above § 50 ; xxxv, 128. His activity ranges from B. C. 375–330.

Alexander Paris: the second name is added to distinguish him from the king. The statue has not yet been identified among our copies, Furtwängler, *Masterpieces*, p. 357 ff. and Robert, *Hall. Winckelmannsprogr.* xix, 1895, p. 20 ff. arrive at surprisingly different results. Addenda.

11. infra **Capitolium** : Urlichs (*Griechische Statuen im Rep. Rom*, p. 11). suggests on the open space afterwards occupied by the temple of Vespasian.

12. Q. **Lutatio**, i. e. *Catulo* : after the fire of B. C. 85, the restoration of the Capitoline temple and adjacent buildings was entrusted to him ; cf.

Tacit. *Hist.* iii, 72 ; Plutarch, *Popl.* 15 ; above xxxiii, 57, &c. It is not known whence he obtained Greek works of art ; possibly from the inexhaustible booty of Aemilius Paulus ; cf. Urlichs, *loc. cit.*

Boni Eventus : from the description it is evident that the statue originally represented the Greek Triptolemos (Urlichs, *Chrestom.* p. 326), and was re-christened as a Roman agrarian divinity. Fröhner (*Méd. de l'Empire Romain*, p. 35) was the first to recognize the type on the obverse of a bronze medal of Hadrian : youth, holding in one hand two ears of corn and two poppies, and in the other a libation cup, is sacrificing at an altar. For a still better reproduction on a gem (*Br. Mus. Cat.* 929) cf. Furtwängler, *op. cit.* p. 350, where the gem is made the starting-point for a suggestive reconstruction of the works of Euphranor.

13. **Latona** . . . sustinens : the work is still unknown ; cf. E. Reisch, 'Ein vermeintliches Werk des Euphranor' in *Festgruss aus Innsbruck an die Phil. Versamml. in Wien*, 1893.

puerpera Apollinem et Dianam infantis sustinens in aede
78 Concordiae. fecit et quadrigas bigasque et cliduchon eximia
forma, et Virtutem et Graeciam, utrasque colossaeas, mulierem admirantem et adorantem, item Alexandrum et
Philippum in quadrigis, Eutychides Eurotam, in quo artem 5
ipso amne liquidiorem plurimi dixere. Hegiae Minerva
Pyrrhusque rex laudatur, et celetizontes pueri, et Castor ac
Pollux ante aedem Iovis tonantis, Hagesiae in Pario colonia
79 Hercules, Isodoti buthytes. Lycius Myronis discipulus fuit,
qui fecit dignum praeceptore puerum sufflantem languidos 10
ignes et Argonautas, Leochares aquilam sentientem quid
rapiat in Ganymede et cui ferat parcentemque unguibus
etiam per vestem puero, Autolycum pancrati victorem propter
quem Xenophon symposium scripsit, Iovemque illum tonantem in Capitolio ante cuncta laudabilem, item Apollinem 15
diadematum, Lyciscum mangonem, puerum subdolae ac

2. cliduchon] *Barbarus*; cliticon *Bamb., Detlefsen*; cliticum *reliqui.*
16. luciscus langonem *reliqui.*

1. aede Concordiae: above § 73.
§ 78. 2. cliduchon: a subject also
treated by Pheidias, § 54.
4. admirantem et adorantem =
ἀποβλέπουσαν 'looking up with awe
at the image of the divinity,' Furtwängler, *Plinius*, p. 46, cf. *Dornauszieher*, p. 87, note 19.
Alexandrum et Philippum: a
suitable occasion for these statues
would be the battle of Chaironeia,
where Al. had distinguished himself
by the side of Philip.
5. Eutychides: above § 51; distinct from his two later namesakes
(*a*) *I.G.B.* 143; (*b*) *I.G.B.* 244-249,
and recently Homolle in *Bull. Corr.
Hell.* 1894, p. 336 f. To the pupil
of Lysippos, Studniczka (*Jahrb.* ix,
1894, p. 211) inclines to attribute the
superb sarkophagos 'of Alexander'
from Sidon.
Eurotam: cf. the Orontes that
supports the city of Antioch by the
same artist; above note on § 51.
6. plurimi: i.e. the writers of
epigrams, Benndorf, *Epigr.* p. 54; cf.

Anth. Pal. ix, 709 (Introd. p. lxx).
Hegiae: for an older namesake,
master of Pheidias, see § 49; for a
Hegias in the reign of Claudius see
I. G. B. 332.
7. Pyrrhusque rex: for portraits
of this king (born B.C. 319, died
272), see Six, *Röm. Mitth.* vi, p. 279;
Helbig in *Mélanges d'Arch. et d'Hist.*
xiii, 1893, pl. i, ii, pp. 377 ff.
The addition of *rex* gives such precision to Pliny's statement that it is
unnecessary to suppose that we have
in the words *Hegiae ... laudatur* a
confused repetition of the *Pyrrhus
Hygiam et Minervam* of § 80 (cf.
Wolters, *Ath. Mitth.* xvi, 1891, p.
155, note 2).
8. Iovis tonantis: above § 10;
below § 79.
Hagesiae: Ἡγησίας instead of
the more familiar diminutive Ἡγίας,
so Ζεύξιππος for Ζεῦξις Plat. *Prot.*
318 B (cf. Fick, *Gr. Personennamen*,
p. 35).
Pario colonia: v, 141, founded
by the Parians, Milesians, and Ery-

born Apollo and Artemis in her arms, now in the temple of Concord, and chariots with four and two horses, a κλειδοῦχος or 78 Key-bearer, of great beauty, a statue of Valour, and one of Hellas, both of colossal size, a woman in wonder praying, and Alexander and Philip in four-horse chariots. *Eutychides* made an image of the Eurotas of which many have said that the artist's skill is clearer than the stream itself.

The Athena and the king Pyrrhos by *Hegias* are praised, so are his boys riding on racehorses, the Kastor and Polydeukes which stand in front of the temple of Jupiter the Thunderer, and also the Herakles of *Hegesias* in the colony of Parion, and the βουθύτης, or Slayer of the Ox, by *Isodotos*. *Lykios* was a pupil of Myron; in 79 the boy blowing a dying fire he created a work worthy of his master; he also made statues of the Argonauts. The eagle of *Leochares* appears to know how precious a burden it is ravishing in Ganymede and to what master it bears him, and its talons hold the boy tenderly though his dress protects him. He also made a statue of Autolykos, who was victorious in the pankration and in whose honour Xenophon wrote the Banquet; the celebrated Zeus with the thunderbolt in the Capitol, a work of supreme excellence; an Apollo wearing the diadem; the slave-dealer Lykiskos and a boy, on whose face may be read the wily

Eagle ravishing Ganymede

thraians, Strabo, xiii, p. 588, 14; it was made into a Roman colony by Augustus (*Colonia Pariana Julia Augusta*).

§ 79. 9. **Lycius Myronis**: § 50.

10. **puerum sufflantem**: same subject treated by the painter Antiphilos xxxv, 138. The work is of course distinct from the *puer suffitor* below, and from the boy, also by Lykios, holding the holy water basin on the Akropolis, Paus. i, 23, 7, but the kinship of the subjects shows where the artistic strength of Lykios lay (cf. Wolters, *Ath. Mitth.* xvi, 1891, p. 153 ff. and Mayer, *Arch. Jahrb.* viii, 1893, p. 218 f.).

11. **Leochares**: § 50. [His works are enumerated in two alphabetical groups: from *aquilam* to *Iovem*, and after *item* from *Apollinem* to *puerum*. —H. L. U.]

aquilam . . . Ganymede: a copy

of this work has been recognized in the statuette, Helbig, *Class. Ant.* 400.

13. **Autolycum**: winner in the Pankration at the greater Panathenaia Ol. 89, 3 = B.C. 422 (the fictitious date of the 'Banquet,' Athen. v, p. 216 d), murdered B.C. 404 by the Thirty Tyrants. Since Leochares lived into the reign of Alexander, there can be no question of his having made a portrait of Autolykos, but the latter was sufficiently celebrated to have—like Miltiades and other heroes of Athenian history—statues raised to him after death (cf. Klein, *Arch. Ep. Mittheil.* vii, 1883. p. 72).

14. **Iovemque illum tonantem**: the motive of the statue may be recovered from coins; Cohen, *Médailles Impériales*, 2nd ed. i, p. 88; Roscher, ii, 748. Above § 10.

16. **Lyciscum mangonem**: Ur-

80 fucatae vernilitatis, Lycius et ipse puerum suffitorem. Me-
naechmi vitulus genu premitur replicata cervice. ipse
Menaechmus scripsit de sua arte. Naucydes Mercurio et
discobolo et immolante arietem censetur, Naucerus luctatore anhelante, Niceratus Aesculapium et Hygiam . . . qui 5
sunt in Concordiae templo Romae. Pyromachi quadriga
ab Alcibiade regitur. Polycles Hermaphroditum nobilem
fecit, Pyrrhus Hygiam et Minervam, Phanis Lysippi
81 discipulus epithyusan. Styppax Cyprius uno celebratur
signo, splanchnopte—Periclis Olympii vernula hic fuit exta 10
torrens ignemque oris pleni spiritu accendens—Silanion
Apollodorum fudit, fictorem et ipsum, sed inter cunctos
diligentissimum artis et iniquom sui iudicem, crebro perfecta

5. Hygiam] Hygiam fecit *Detlefsen*.

lichs (*Chrestom.* p. 328) refers the
subject to the influence of the Middle
Comedy. Λυκίσκος, as title of a play
by Alexis, is preserved by Athen. xiii,
p. 595 d; the *puer* must have formed
a group with the *mango;* but Pliny,
who is here giving an asyndetic
enumeration of single works, seems
to have understood them to be separate statues, cf. Furtwängler, *Dornauszieher*, p. 91, note 44 (against
the reading *Lyciscus langonem*, which
has lately again come into favour, see
Friedländer's note to Martial, ix, 50).

1. suffitorem: presumably holding
a censer suspended by chains; cf.
Mayer, *op. cit.* p. 222.

§ 80. 2. replicata cervice: i.e.
in the scheme known from the Nike
sacrificing an ox on the balustrade of
the Temple of Athena Nike, cf. Cecil
Smith in *J. H. S.* vii, 1886, pp. 275 ff.

3. scripsit de sua arte : Introd.
p. xl.

Naucydes: above § 50. His *immolans arietem* has been identified,
but on purely fanciful reasons, with
the Phrixos burning the thigh of a ram
on the Akropolis, Paus. i, 24, 2 (cf.
Furtwängler, *Masterpieces*, p. 231).

4. luctatore anhelante: epigram-

matic, cf. xxxv, 71, *ut anhelare sentiatur ;* Reisch, *Weihgeschenke*, p. 45.

5. Niceratus : Νικήρατος Εὐκτή-
μονος 'Αθηναῖος, Fränkel, *Inschr. aus
Perg.* 132; also *I. G. B.* 147, 496;
works conjointly with Phyromachos,
ib. 118 (from Delos).

Aesculapium et H.: Fränkel (*loc.
cit.*) suggests that the group was originally made for the *Asklepieion* at
Pergamon, in which case it was presumably transferred to Rome when
the Romans inherited the Pergamene
treasures by the will of Attalos II, 133
B. C.

6. Pyromachi: note on *Niceratus*
above ; for an older namesake cf.
§ 51.

quadriga: possibly as a pendant to
the group by Nikeratos of Alkibiades
and his mother sacrificing, § 88
(Fränkel, *loc. cit.*).

7. Polycles : not identical with
the artist of § 50, while his identity
with the Polykles of § 52 (=xxxvi, 35)
is uncertain. Nothing is known of his
Hermaphrodite ; it cannot of course
have been the marble recumbent figure,
extant in so many replicas : it should
perhaps be sought for among the
standing types of the Hermaphrodite

craft of the servile character. *Lykios* too made a boy burning perfumes.

By *Menaichmos* we have a calf on which a man is setting 80 his knee as he bends its neck back; Menaichmos also wrote a book on his art. The fame of *Naukydes* rests on his Hermes, his διϲκοβόλοϲ or Disk-thrower, and his man sacrificing a ram; that of †*Naukeros* on his panting wrestler. *Nikeratos* ⟨made⟩ the Asklepios and Hygieia now in the temple of Concord at Rome. By *Pyromachos* we have a four-horse chariot driven by Alkibiades. *Polykles* made a famous Hermaphrodite, *Pyrrhos* a Hygieia and an Athena, †*Phanis*, the pupil of Lysippos, an ἐπιθύουϲα, or woman sacrificing.

†*Styppax* of Cyprus is known by one statue only, the ϲπλαγχνόπ- 81 τηϲ, or Roaster of Entrails. This was a slave of Perikles the *The 'Roaster of* Olympian; he is roasting entrails and blowing hard on the fire to *Entrails.'* kindle it till his cheeks swell. *Seilanion* cast a portrait of Apollo- doros, who was also a statuary, and among the most painstaking, a severe critic of his own work, who often broke up a finished

(e. g. *Berlin Cat.* 193; see Herrmann *ap.* Roscher, i, pp. 2324 ff.). Addenda.

8. **Hygiam et Minervam**: from the extant inscription ('Αθηναῖοι τῇ 'Αθηναίᾳ τῇ 'Υγιείᾳ || Πύρροϲ ἐποίηϲεν 'Αθηναῖοϲ *I. G. B.* 53) it appears that Pliny made one work into two. The statue is mentioned Paus. i, 23, 4 (without name of artist), Plutarch, *Per.* 13, who says it was dedicated by Perikles to commemorate the miraculous cure of a favourite work- man employed on the Propylaia (see note on *vernula* below). Wolters, however, has shown on technical evidence (*Ath. Mitth.* xvi, 1891, p. 153 ff.) that the statue must have been dedicated at a period subsequent to the commencement of the Peloponnesian war, and that Plutarch's narrative must consequently be a mere invention.

§ 81. 9. **Styppax Cyprius**: I see no reason for the doubts with regard to this name expressed by Loewy *Untersuch.* p. 30, against which see also Wolters, *Ath. Mitth.* xvi, 1891, p. 156, note 1.

10. **splanchnopte**: the motive of the statue and a probable copy are fully discussed by M. Mayer, *Jahrb.* viii, 1893, p. 224 and pl. iv.

Periclis Ol. vernula: the story is told fully, xxii, 44; in spite of dis- crepancies it is apparently identical with the one narrated by Plutarch of the Athena Hygieia. The cause for the dedication of a statue by so im- portant a personage as Perikles would naturally be eagerly sought for; the vicinity of the *splanchnoptes* to that of Athena in her character of 'Healer' suggested a connexion between the two, and accounts for the legends told by Pliny and Plutarch. Cf. Wol- ters, *loc. cit.*; Kuhnerdt, *Stat. u. Ort,* p. 274.

12. **Apollodorum**: the date proved for Seilanion (§ 51) makes it impossible to identify the Apollodoros either with the Sokratic philosopher (fl. b. c. 430– 360) or with the artist of *I. G. B.* 55 (in Pre-Eukleidan characters). *I. G. B.* 218 records a third of the name. For the painter A. see xxxv, 60.

signa frangentem, dum satiari cupiditate artis non quit,
82 ideoque insanum cognominatum ; hoc in eo expressit, nec
hominem ex aere fecit, sed iracundiam, et Achillem nobilem,
item epistaten exercentem athletas, Strongylion Amazonem
quam ab excellentia crurum eucnemon appellant, ob id in 5
comitatu Neronis principis circumlatam. idem fecit puerum
quem amando Brutus Philippensis cognomine suo inlustravit.
83 Theodorus, qui labyrinthum fecit Sami, ipse se ex aere
fudit, praeter similitudinis mirabilem famam magna sup-
tilitate celebratus.   dextra limam tenet, laeva tribus digitis 10
quadrigulam tenuit translatam Praeneste, tantae parvitatis
ut—mirum dictu—eam currumque et aurigam integeret alis
simul facta musca.   Xenocrates Tisicratis discipulus, ut alii
Euthycratis, vicit utrosque copia signorum.   et de sua

8. fecit Sami, ipse] *editores ante Sillig* ; fecit, Sami ipse *Detlefsen.*   12.
mirum dictu] *coni. Traube* ; miraculo pictam *Bamb.* ; totam *reliqui, Detlefsen.*

§ 82. 2. nec hominem . . . sed
irac.: O. Jahn (*Kunsturtheile,* p.
112) detected in these words a latent
epigram; the phraseology, however,
which was originally confined to col-
loquial language and used as a rule
in a disparaging sense, had become
universal in Pliny's day; cf. Quinct.
x, 1, 112 *non iam hominis nomen sed
eloquentiae habeatur;* H. S. Jones,
Class. Rev. 1893, p. 224, cf. Baehrens,
Catullus, p. 608.   See Addenda.
    4. epistaten . . . athletas: votive
statue, put up presumably by the
athletes of a gymnasium ; thus the
gymnasiarchs Menas and Metodoros
at Sestos and Pergamon receive statues
for honourable discharge of their
duties, likewise the Κοσμητής Nym-
phodotos at Athens receives a statue
in the palaistra *C. I. A.* iii, 1104, see
Kuhnerdt, *Statue u. Ort,* p. 308 [the
words *exercentem athletas* were probably taken from the descriptive
epigram on the statue.—H. L. U.]
    Strongylion: *I. G. B.* 52 gives the
inscr. belonging to his δούριος ἵππος
(Paus. i, 23, 8), which from the allusion in Aristoph. Ὄρνιθες, 1128, must

have been erected shortly before that
play was produced in B. C. 414.
    Amazonem : we possibly have its
copy in the charming equestrian statuette in Naples (Friederichs-Wolters,
1781 ; the opinion first expressed by
Hoffman in Overbeck's *Plastik,* ed. 4,
i, p. 506, note 14).   By representing
the Amazon on horseback, S. could
not only display her legs, but likewise
find scope for his talent as a sculptor
of animals (Paus. ix, 30, 1).
    6. circumlatam : above § 48; we
may conclude from this fact that the
Amazon was a statuette.
    7. cognomine suo: *Bruti puer,*
Martial, ii, 77 : ix, 50 ; xiv, 171.
    § 83. 8. Theodorus : his date
may be approximately determined by
the fact that he worked for Kroisos
(B. C. 560–546), Herod. i, 51, and
for Polykrates, Herod. iii, 41 (B. C.
532 ?–521), cf. xxxvii, 3.   That there
was only one artist of the name has
now been admitted even by Overbeck
(*Plastik,* 4th ed. 1893, p. 78).
    labyrinthum . . . Sami : i. e. the
Heraion, of which his father Rhoikos
(Herod. iii, 60) was the first archi-

statue, being unable to reach the ideal he aimed at; from this he was called 'the madman.' This characteristic Seilanion ren- 82 dered, and made his bronze not a portrait of an individual, but a figure of Vexation itself. He also made a famous Achilles, and a trainer exercising his athletes. *Strongylion* made the Amazon surnamed the εὔκνημος from the beauty of her legs; it was because of this special feature that the Emperor Nero carried the statue about in his train. He also made the boy which Brutus of Philippi loved, and made illustrious by his name. *Theodoros*, the maker of the labyrinth at Samos, also cast a portrait 83 of himself in bronze, famed as a wondrous likeness, and also celebrated for the extreme delicacy of the workmanship. The right hand holds a file, while three fingers of the left hand support a tiny team of four horses, which is now at Praeneste, *Tiny* so small that the team, marvellous to relate, with chariot and *chariot and* charioteer could be covered by the wings of a fly which the artist *Theodoros.* made to accompany it. *Xenokrates* was a pupil of Teisikrates, or, according to some authorities, of Euthykrates; he outdid both in

tect; cf. xxxvi, 90, where the purely mythical *labyrinthus Lemnius* is a mistake of Pliny for *lab. Samius* (Urlichs, *Anfänge*, 1871, p. 3, cf. Klein in *Arch. Ep. Mitth.* ix, 1885, p. 184); of Rhoikos and Theodoros at least we know that they were *indigenae* not of Lemnos but of Samos (Σάμιοι, Paus. viii, 14, 8; Ῥοῖκος ἐπιχώριος, sc. of Samos, Herod. *loc. cit.*

ipse se : cf. the portrait of the Kretan Cheirisophos, presumably by himself, next to his gilt statue of Apollo at Tegea, Paus. viii, 53, 7.

10. laeva ... quadrigulam : it is generally supposed that the little chariot was engraved on the base of a scarab (see e.g. the scarab, *Brit. Mus. Cat. of Gems*, pl. D, 254); Benndorf, *Zts. für Oesterr.Gymnasien*, 1873, p. 406. Theodoros was a famous gem-graver; yet the extant marvels of μικροτεχνία accomplished in the goldsmith's art show that the execution in the round of a microscopic chariot was no technical impossibility; see note on *Mymercides*, xxxvi, 43.

11. **Praeneste** : where the celebrated temple of *Fortuna Primigenia*, like so many of the temples in Rome (cf. Friedländer, *Darstellungen*, ii, pp. 154 ff.), must have contained all sorts of curiosities (see R. Peter *ap.* Roscher, i, 1545).

12. mirum dictu: xviii, 160, so *facile dictu*, xxviii, 20 ; *rarum dictu*, xiv, 132 ; *incredibile dictu*, xxxv, 88.

eam: i. e. the team proper as distinct from the *currus* and the *auriga*, likewise in xxxvi, 36 *quadriga currusque*.

13. **Xenocrates**: his identity with the Xenokrates of Athens, son of Ergophilos of *I. G. B.* 135 a and b (from Oropos), of *I. G. B.* 135 c (from Elateia), and of Ἐφημ. ἀρχαιολ. 1892, 52 (from Oropos), though usually accepted, is nothing less than proven. See Introd. p. xx, note 2.

Tisicratis : *I. G. B.* 120, from Oropos.

14. **Euthycratis** : above § 67 [from the fact that this and the two

84 arte composuit volumina. plures artifices fecere Attali et
Eumenis adversus Gallos proelia, Isigonus, Pyromachus,
Stratonicus, Antigonus qui volumina condidit de sua arte.
Boethi, quamquam argento melioris, infans amplexando
anserem strangulat. atque ex omnibus quae rettuli clarissima 5
quaeque iam sunt dicata a Vespasiano principe in templo
Pacis aliisque eius operibus, violentia Neronis in urbem con-
85 vecta et in sellariis domus aureae disposita. praeterea sunt
aequalitate celebrati artifices, sed nullis operum suorum
praecipui, Ariston qui et argentum caelare solitus est, Cal- 10
lides, Ctesias, Cantharus Sicyonius, Dionysodorus Critiae
discipulus, Deliades, Euphorion, Eunicus et Hecataeus
argenti caelatores, Lesbocles, Prodorus, Pythodicus, Polygnotus idem pictor e nobilissimis, item e caelatoribus
86 Stratonicus, Scymnus Critiae discipulus. nunc percensebo 15

4. amplexando] *Traube*; sex anno *Bamb.* (sex annis *e corr.*) ; eximiae *Voss.* ;
eximie *Ricc.*, *Detlefsen* ; annosum *coni. Buecheler in Herondas*, p. 25 ;
vi annosum *coni. R. Meister in Mimiamben des Herondas*, p. 708. 11. Dionysius, Diodorus *Detlefsen* ; Diodorus *Bamb.*; dionysiodorus *Ricc.*, *Voss.*

preceding names contain the common
element -κρατης it would appear that
the bearers all belonged to the same
family, cf. Fick, *Griech. Personennamen*, p. xi.—H. L. U.].
   1. volumina : Introd. p. xvi.
   § 84. Attali : i. e. Attalos I, B.C.
241–197.
   2. Eumenis : i. e. II, B.C. 197–159.
   Gallos : *Attalus eos rex saepe fudit
fugavitque*, Liv. xxxviii, 17, 15, the
dates however are obscure (see Loewy
on *I. G. B.* 154, pp. 117 f.); the
other victories commemorated in the
Pergamene inscriptions are those of
Attalos I over Antiochos Hierax in
228 B.C.
   Isigonus : neither his name nor
those of Stratonikos (below § 90) or
Antigonos, have turned up among
the Pergamene inscriptions; Michaelis
(*Jahrb.* viii, 1893, p. 131) accordingly
proposes to alter the *Isigonus* of Pliny
to *Epigonus*, but on grounds which
are insufficient.

Pyromachus : above § 80.
   3. volumina : Introd. p. xxxvi.
   4. Boethi : of Chalkedon (Paus.
v, 17, 4, where Schubart, however,
reads Καρχηδόνιος) ; identical with the
silver-chaser of xxxiii, 155. In the
Heraion of Olympia Pausanias saw
the gilt statue of a boy by him.
quamquam elliptical, i. e. 'although
more renowned as a silver chaser, yet
I may mention . . .' The artist of
the portrait of Antiochos Epiphanes
(*I. G. B.* 210) belongs to a later
period, while a third Boëthos, belonging to the first quarter of the first
century B.C., is known from *Bull. d.
Corr. Hell.* xi, p. 263.
   infans : preserved in a number of
replicas, Munich, *Glypt.* 140 ; Capitol, Helbig, *Class. Ant.* 518. The
same subject (without the artist's
name) is mentioned Herond. iv, 31
τὴν χηναλώπεκα ὡς τὸ παιδίον πνίγει |
πρὸ τῶν ποδῶν γοῦν εἴ τι μὴ λίθος
τοὔργον | ἐρεῖς λαλήσει· (ed. O. Cru-

the number of statues that he produced, and he also wrote books on his art.

The battles of Attalos and Eumenes against the Gauls were represented by several artists, †*Isigonos, Pyromachos, Stratonikos* and *Antigonos* who also wrote books on his art.

Boëthos, though greater as a worker in silver, made a child hugging a goose till he throttles it.

The best of all the works I have mentioned have now been dedicated at Rome by the emperor Vespasian in the temple of Peace and in his other galleries, Nero having first brought them by the strong hand to Rome, and placed them in the apartments of the Golden House.

I add a list of artists whose works are of equal excellence, though no single one is of supreme merit. Such are *Ariston*, who also worked in silver, †*Kallides*, †*Ktesias, Kantharos* of Sikyon. *Dionysodoros* the pupil of Kritios, †*Deliades*, †*Euphorion, Eunikos* and *Hekataios*, the silver chasers; †*Lesbokles*, †*Prodoros*, †*Pythodikos*, and *Polygnotos*, who was also among the most famous painters. Others who were also silver chasers were *Stratonikos* and †*Skymnos* the pupil of Kritios.

84 *Works commemorating the victories of Attalos and Eumenes. Boëthos.*

85 *Artists of second rank.*

sins, who suggests the basis alone to have been of marble—cf. *Anth. Pal.* ix, 719—and accordingly assumes identity with the Plinian group, cf. *Untersuchungen zur Mimiamben des Herondas* 1892, p. 82). Identity likewise assumed by Buecheler and Meister (above text notes). The action of the child, who is really squeezing the goose in his embrace, is exactly described by the word *amplexando*, as now restored from the reading of Cod. Bamb. Addenda.

5. **ex omnibus . . . clarissima**: rhetorical flattery intended to please Pliny's patron Vespasian, cf. xxxvi, 102; so too Josephus, *Bell. Jud.* vii, 5, 7 (Niese, vol. vi, p. 591) says: πάντα . . . εἰς ἐκεῖνον τὸν νεὼ (sc. *Templ. Pac.*) συνήχθη καὶ κατετέθη, δι' ὧν τὴν θέαν ἄνθρωποι πρότερον περὶ πᾶσαν ἐπλανῶντο τὴν οἰκουμένην. The *templum Pacis* was ded. A. D. 75, after the conquest of Judaea ; full literature Gilbert, *Rom* iii, p. 135, note 3.

7. **violentia Neronis**: for hatred of Nero, cf. above § 45, xxxv, 51, 120. Introd. p. xcii.

§ 85. 9. **aequalitate**: i.e. of merit, Furtwängler, *Plinius*, p. 11.

10. **Ariston**: xxxiii, 156; a painter of the name, xxxv, 110–111; cf. on *I. G. B.* 275 a.

Callides: a painter of the name in Lucian, *Dial. Meretr.* viii, 3, cf. Brunn, *K. G.* ii, p. 311.

11. **Cantharus**: son of Alexis, pupil of Eutychides (above § 78), Paus. vi, 3, 6; 17, 7.

Dionysodoros: an artist of the name, *I. G. B.* 243 (from Delos, B. C. 110); a painter, xxxv, 146.

Critiae: perhaps identical with the Kritios in § 49.

12. **Eunicus et Hec.**: xxxiii, 156.

13. **Polygnotus**: xxxv, 58; known as a sculptor only from Pliny.

15. **Stratonicus**: presumably identical with the Str. of § 84 and of § 90.

eos qui eiusdem generis opera fecerunt, ut Apollodorus,
Androbulus, Asclepiodorus, Aleuas philosophos, Apellas
et adornantes se feminas, Antignotus et luctatores, perixyo-
menum tyrannicidasque supra dictos, Antimachus, Athenodorus feminas nobiles, Aristodemus et luctatores bigasque 5
cum auriga, philosophos, anus, Seleucum regem.   habet
87 gratiam suam huius quoque doryphorus.   Cephisodoti
duo fuere: prioris est Mercurius Liberum patrem in infantia
nutriens, fecit et contionantem manu elata, persona in
incerto est.   sequens philosophos fecit.   Colotes qui cum 10
Phidia Iovem Olympium fecerat philosophos, item Cleon et
Cenchramis et Callicles et Cepis, Chalcosthenes et comoedos
et athletas, Daippus perixyomenon, Daiphron et Damo-

§ 86. 1. qui eiusdem generis:
for the practice of classifying works
of art according to the artistic motive cf. Furtwängler, *Dornauszieher*,
pp. 20 f.

Apollodorus: above § 81.

2. Asclepiodorus: a painter of the
name, xxxv, 107.

philosophos: Furtwängler,*Dornauszieher*, pp. 24 f., has pointed out
that under this rubric must be understood not only philosophers in a restricted sense, but in general portraits
of distinguished personages.

Apellas: son of Kallikles, makes
for Olympia the chariot of Kyniska
(*I. G. B.* 99 = Paus. vi, 1, 6), sister of
Agesilaos (died B.C. 360) of Sparta.
Cf. note on Callicles in § 87.   Add.

3. adornantes se: cf. the *pseli-
umene* in § 70.

Antignotus: an artist of the name,
I. G. B. 314–316 (Augustan).

4. supra dictos: descriptive of
the actual personages portrayed; unnecessary difficulty has been caused
(cf. Loewy on *I. G. B.* 314) by assuming that they referred to the group
mentioned in § 70.

Athenodorus: xxxvi, 37.

5. Aristodemus: according to Tatian, p. 36, 9 (ed. Schwartz), makes a
statue of Aisop, i.e. a work which

would fall under the heading of
philosophi.

6. anus: votive portraits of priest-
esses, such as that of Lysimache, above
§ 76. Furtwängler,*Dornauszieher*, p.26.

Seleucum regem: above § 73.

7. quoque: [i.e. as well as the
more celebrated Doryphoros of Polykleitos in § 55.—H. L. U.].

§ 87. Cephisodoti duo: (*a*) the
artist of the Eirene, Paus. ix, 16,
1, possibly father or brother of the
great Praxiteles (cf. note on § 50); (*b*)
a son of Praxiteles, xxxvi, 24.

8. Mercurius . . . nutriens: the
motive is identical with that of the
Praxitelean Hermes.   Addenda.

9. manu elata: the raised hand
not being an action of Greek oratory
(where even to allow the hand to
protrude much from the cloak was
thought unseemly, Aischines *c. Tim.*
25), it is probable that the statue belonged to the class *adorantes*, and
that its gesture was misinterpreted by
a Roman writer as being the familiar
manus elata of the Roman orators
(Milchhöffer, *Arch. Studien H. Brunn
dargeb.* 1892, p. 39).   A recent conjecture *manu velata* as the equivalent
of the ἐντὸς τὴν χεῖρα ἔχων of Aisch.
loc. cit. has met with little favour, cf.
S. Reinach in *Chron. d'Orient*, 1893,

I will now enumerate those who made statues of the same class, as *Apollodoros*, †*Androboulos*, *Asklepiodoros* and †*Aleuas*, who made philosophers; *Apellas*, who also made women adorning themselves, *Antignotos*, who also made wrestlers, a περιξυόμενος or athlete scraping himself, and statues of the tyrant-slayers whom I have mentioned, and †*Antimachos* and *Athenodoros*, who made statues of renowned women. *Aristodemos* also made wrestlers, two-horse chariots with charioteer, and figures of philosophers, of old women, and of king Seleukos; his Spear-bearer too has a charm of its own. There were two artists of the name of *Kephisodotos ;* by the first we have a Hermes nursing the infant Dionysos. He also made a statue of a man haranguing with uplifted hand; the person represented is not known. The younger *Kephisodotos* made statues of philosophers, and so did *Kolotes*, who had worked with Pheidias on his Olympian Zeus, *Kleon*, *Kenchramos*, *Kallikles*, and †*Kepis ; Chalkosthenes* also made statues of comic actors and athletes. *Daippos* made a περιξυόμενος or athlete scraping himself, † *Daiphron*, *Damokritos*, and †*Daimon* philosophers

86
Artists who made statues of the same class.

87

p. 9; W. Gurlitt in *Berl. Phil. Woch.* 1895, p. 1230.

    persona in incerto: [i. e. the inscription was effaced, or no longer extant.—H. L. U.] So Pausanias, vi, 15, 7, speaks of the statue of an unknown individual as ἀνὴρ ὅστις δή.

    10. **Colotes**: xxxv, 54.

    11. **Cleon**: of Sikyon, pupil of Antiphanes, himself pupil of Polykleitos, Paus. v, 17, 4, where a bronze Aphrodite by him is mentioned; *ib.* 21, 3 (two bronze Zanes, *I. G. B.* 95, 96); the remaining four statues by him (vi, 1, 5; 3, 10; 8, 5; 9, 2; 10, 9) all belong to the class *athletae*. For his school cf. Furtwängler, *Masterpieces*, p. 278.

    12. **Cenchramis**: *I. G. B.* 70, 71 (both from Athens), where he is named with Polymnestos (*I. G. B.* 72). Add. **Callicles**: son of Theokosmos of Megara, Paus. vi, 7, 1 (where his statue of the illustrious περιοδονίκης Diagoras of Rhodes is mentioned); father of Apellas (above § 86). F. Hauser (*Röm. Mittheil.* x, 1895, pp. 97–119) would see in him the artist

of the lovely bronze head of the boy-pugilist, Munich, *Glypt.* 302, and of the original of the basalt statue of another pugilist in the Terme Mus. (*ib.* pl. I).

    Chalcosthenes: apparently an error for *Chaecosthenes* (Καἴκοσθένης), brother of Dies and son of Apollonides, *I. G. B.* 113–117, 220, see note on xxxv, 155. In connexion with the votive-statues of *comoedi* mentioned here, it is interesting to note that *I. G. B.* 220 is from the theatre of Dionysos at Athens; cf. Δελτίον, 1891, p. 84, 1. Like Epigonos (§ 88) he is known only from Pliny and the inscriptions.

    13. **Daippus**: above § 51; for athlete statues by him cf. Paus. vi, 12, 6; 16, 5.

    Damocritus: From Paus. vi, 3, 5 we learn that he was a Sikyonian, a pupil of Pison of Kalaureia (Paus. x, 9, 8), and fifth in school descent from the Attic artist Kritios. His identity with the Δημόκριτος of *I. G. B.* 484 and Diogenes Laertios, ix, 49 is doubtful.

88 critus et Daemon philosophos.   Epigonus omnia fere prae-
dicta imitatus praecessit in tubicine et matri interfectae
infante miserabiliter blandiente.   Eubuli mulier admirans
laudatur, Eubulidis digitis computans.   Micon athletis spectatur, Menogenes quadrigis.   nec minus Niceratus omnia quae 5
ceteri adgressus repraesentavit Alcibiaden lampadumque
89 accensu matrem eius Demaraten sacrificantem.   Tisicratis
bigae Piston mulierem inposuit, idem fecit Martem et Mercurium qui sunt in Concordiae templo Romae.   Perillum
nemo laudet saeviorem Phalaride tyranno, cui taurum fecit 10
mugitus hominis pollicitus igni subdito, et primus expertus
cruciatum eum iustiore saevitia.   huc a simulacris deorum

11. et] *Bamb.*; ex *reliqui*; exprimere *Detlefsen.*

§ 88. 1. **Epigonus**: known from
a series of Pergamene inscriptions.
Fränkel, *Inschriften aus Pergamon,*
12; 21–28; 29; 31 (= *I. G. B.* 157);
32 (= *I. G. B.* 157 a).   The great
bathron to which 21–28 belongs com-
memorates the close of the war in B. C.
228, against Antiochos and the Galatai.
    omnia fere: rhetorical; cf. *cla-
rissima quaeque* in § 84; *omnibus fere
quae fecit,* xxxvi, 13.
    2. **tubicine**: since Epigonos
worked for the Pergamene kings, it
has been suggested that his *tubicen*
represented a Gaul with his war
trumpet such as the famous 'dying
Gaul' of the Capitol (Helbig, *Class.
Ant.* p. 398, where see literature).
[The statue, however, may, as Winckelmann suggested, have been simply the
votive-portrait of the winner in the
contest of heralds, such as that of
Archias of Hybla at Delphoi, cf. Pollux, iv, 92, Preger, *Inscr.* 143, or that
of Phorystas at Olympia, *I. G. B.*
119.   For a *tubicen* by the painter
Antidotos see xxxv, 130.—H. L. U.]
Add.
    mätri interfectae: for the mo-
tive cf. xxxv, 98; S. Reinach (*Rev.
des Études Grecques,* 1894, p. 41 ff.)
suggests that the group was of a

Gaulish mother and her child, and
belonged to the same series as the
'Dying Gaul' and the so-called
'Arrius and Paeta' of the Villa Ludovisi, Helbig, *Class. Ant.* 884.   Add.
    3. **Eubuli**: his name has been
suggested in *I. G. B.* 235.   For his
mulier admirans cf. above § 78.
    4. **Eubulidis**: his name alter-
nates with that of Eucheiros (below
§ 91) on a series of inscriptions
(*I. G. B.* 223–229, 544) belonging
apparently to one family of artists;
dates uncertain.
    digitis computans: [the gesture
which is expressive of pondering or
meditation might be given to any
number of portraits of *philosophi;* cf.
Lucian, *Timon,* 122, συνεσπακὼς τοὺς
δακτύλους πρὸς τὸ ἔθος τῶν λογισμῶν;
Plin. *Ep.* ii, 20, 3: *composuit vultum,
intendit oculos, movet labra, agitat
digitos, computat.*   This observation,
coupled with the fact that, had the
digitis computans been the portrait of
a celebrated man, the name would
not have been forgotten, disposes of
Milchhöffer's theory (*Arch. Studien
H. Brunn dargebr.* pp. 37 ff.) that
the personage represented was Chrysippos.—H. L. U.]
    Micon: identical with the painter,

Epigonos produced examples of almost all the subjects I have 88
mentioned, and surpassed them in his trumpeter and his infant *Dead mother and*
piteously caressing its dead mother. †*Euboulos* is praised for *child by*
his woman in amazement, and *Euboulides* for his man reckoning *Epigonos.*
on his fingers. *Mikon's* athletes are admired, and the four-horse
chariots of *Menogenes*. *Nikeratos* too attempted the same subjects as these artists, and also made statues of Alkibiades and
his mother Demarate sacrificing by torchlight. *Piston* made a 89
woman, to be placed in a two-horse chariot by *Teisikrates*, also
the statues of Ares and of Hermes which stand in the temple of
Concord at Rome. *Perillos* it is impossible to praise : he showed *Bull of*
a cruelty greater than that of the tyrant Phalaris, for whom he *Phalaris.*
made a bull, promising that if a fire were lighted under it the
cries of the man inside would sound like the animal's bellowing,
a torture which cruelty for once righteous made him the first to
suffer. From representations of gods' and men he had dragged

xxxv, 59. The fact that he made statues of athletes has been confirmed by *I. G. B.* 41, from the statue of the περιοδονίκης Kallias (Ol. 77 = B. C. 472); and *I. G. B.* 42.

5. **Niceratus**: above § 80, where see note on his Alkibiades.

6. **lampadum accensu**: i. e. she held a torch, possibly in each hand; the word *accensu*, however, makes me suspect a latent epigram, Introd. p. xliv, note 2.

7. **Demaraten** . her name was however Δεινομάχη, Plat. *Alc.* 105, d, &c. [The name Demarate may have crept into Pliny's authority through an error in transcribing the inscription on the group.—H. L. U.]

§ 89. **Tisicratis**: above § 83; *mulierem inposuit*, cf. § 71 on Kalamis and the Elder Praxiteles; the *mulier* was possibly a Nike.

9. **Perillum**: the Latin form. He also appears as Perilaos in Lucian, according to whom (*Phal.* i, 11) he was a native of Akragas; for the late notion that he was an Athenian, see Freeman, *Hist. of Sicily*, ii, p. 75, note 2.

10. **Phalaride**: vii, 200; B.C. 570-

564 is now generally accepted as the date of his τύραννις, Bentley, *Diss. on the Epistles of Phalaris* (ed. 1699), pp. 27 ff.; Freeman, *Sicily*, ii, pp. 458 f.

taurum fecit: the earliest men-tion of the brazen bull is by Pindar, *Pyth.* i, 184; its mechanism is fully described by Polybios, xii, 25. The bull was reputed to have been taken to Carthage on the sack of Akra-gas by the Carthaginians, B. C. 403; it was brought back and restored to the Carthaginians by the Younger Scipio, Cic. *Verr.* II, iv, 34, § 73. See Freeman, *op. cit.* Appendix, vii, where the story of the bull is fully discussed. It early became a *locus communis* of rhetoric (cf. Kalkmann in *Rhein. Mus.* xlii, 1887, pp. 513 ff.), which accounts for the high colouring of Pliny's language. Introd. p. xciii.

11. **mugitus hominis**: *Mugiet, et veri vox erit illa bovis*, Ovid, *Trist.* iii, 11, 48.

primus expertus: cf. Diodoros, ix, 19; Ovid, *loc. cit.*; and *Ars Amat.* i, 653; Lucian, *Phalaris*, i, 12.

hominumque devocaverat humanissimam artem.   ideo tot
conditores eius laboraverant ut ex ea tormenta fierent!
itaque una de causa servantur opera eius, ut quisquis illa
90 videat oderit manus.   Sthennis Cererem, Iovem, Minervam
fecit, qui sunt Romae in Concordiae templo, idem flentes 5
matronas et adorantes sacrificantesque.   Simon canem et
sagittarium fecit, Stratonicus caelator ille philosophos,
91 Scopas *uterque*, athletas autem et armatos et venatores
sacrificantesque Baton, Euchir, Glaucides, Heliodorus,
Hicanus, *Iophon*, Lyson, Leon, Menodorus, Myagrus, Poly- 10
crates, Polyidus, Pythocritus, Protogenes idem pictor e
clarissimis, ut dicemus, Patrocles, Pollis, Posidonius qui
et argentum caelavit nobiliter, natione Ephesius, Periclymenus, Philon, Symenus, Timotheus, Theomnestus, Timarchides, Timon, Tisias, Thrason.   ex omnibus autem 15

8. scopas] *codd.* ; copas *Gerhard, Detlefsen.*   10. Iophon] *Urlichs in*
Chrest. p. 91 ; olophon *Bamb.* ; lophon *reliqui.*

§ 90. 4. **Sthennis**: above § 51.

5. **flentes matronas**: grave portrait statues, cf. above on § 70.

6. **adorantes sacrificantesque** :
cf. §§ 73, 78.   On these rubrics see
the remarks of Furtwängler, *Dorn-*
auszieher, pp. 22 ff.

Simon: his identity with the Aiginetan artist of the name (Paus. v,
27, 2), employed with Dionysios of
Argos on the Olympic votive-offer-
ings of Phormis of Mainalos, is
uncertain.

canem et sagittarium : i. e. a
votive-portrait of a Kretan or Scythian
bowman with his dog ; cf. Furtwängler,
op. cit., p. 93.

7. **Stratonicus**: xxxiii, 156; above
§§ 84, 85.

8. **Scopas uterque**: although the
MSS. are unanimous, no satisfactory
sense can be got out of the reading.
Skopas, as the name of the artist, is
quite in place in the alphabetical
enumeration, but we cannot follow
Klein (*Arch. Ep. Mitth.* iv, p. 22 ff.)
in assuming a lacuna after *uterque*, or
in seeing in the *uterque* a confirma-

tion of his double Skopas (above note
on § 49, l. 13).   My own view is that the
uterque is a very ancient corruption,
and conceals the name of the work of
art made by Skopas.   It has also been
suggested that *scopas* is the acc. pl.
either of σκώψ (Satyric dancers, see
Urlichs's note in *Chrest.* p. 331) or
σκόπας (Satyr on the look-out), in
which case the *uterque* would refer
back to Simon and Stratonikos.
ΣΚΟΓΑ< is inscribed above a Satyr
on a vase with the Apotheosis of
Herakles (Munich, Jahn *Cat.* 384 =
Mon. d. Inst. iv, pl. 41, *Ann.* xi, *Tav.*
d'Agg. O) ; but the fact that the
next Satyr is inscribed ΥΒΡΙΣ shows
that we have here no generic term,
but merely an epithet applied to one
particular Satyr (cf. the ἀποσκοπεύων
of Antiphilos in xxxv, 138).   Finally
besides the *copas* (= castanet dancers),
of Gerhard, Urlichs in *Pergamen.*
Inschriften, p. 23, has suggested
scyphos.   See Addenda.

§ 91. **athletas**: for this and the
following rubrics cf. *adorantes sacri-*
ficantesque above.

down the most humanizing of arts to this level, and the early masters had only laboured to the end that instruments of torture should be created by its means. The works of Perillos, in consequence, are preserved only that whoever sees them may loathe the hand that made them. *Sthennis* made statues of Demeter, 90 Zeus and Athena, which are at Rome in the temple of Concord; also matrons weeping, praying, or sacrificing. *Simon* made a dog and an archer, *Stratonikos*, known also as a silver chaser, made statues of philosophers, and Skopas . . .

We have statues of athletes, armed men, hunters, and men 91 sacrificing, by *Baton*, *Eucheir*, †*Glaukides*, *Heliodoros*, †*Hikanos*, †*Iophon*, *Lyson*, *Leon*, *Menodoros*, *Myagros*, *Polykrates*, †*Polyeidos*, *Pythokritos*, *Protogenes*, who was also, as will be said later on, a painter of the highest renown, *Patrokles*, †*Pollis*, *Poseidonios*, an Ephesian by nationality, who is also famous for his silver chasing, *Periklymenos*, *Philon*, *Symenos*, *Timotheos*, *Theomnestos*, *Timarchides*, *Timon*, †*Teisias*, and *Thrason*.

Artists who made statues of athletes.

Baton : above § 73.

Euchir: note on *Eubulidis* above § 88.

Heliodorus : xxxvi, 35.

10. Iophon: the *olophon* of *Bamb.* points to a longer name. Loewy, *Untersuch.* p. 39, note 31 suggests Herophon (*I. G. B.* 280, from a basis found at Olympia).

Lyson: he made a statue of *Demos* which stood in the Bouleuterion at Athens, Paus. i, 3, 5.

Leon: perhaps = *I. G. B.* 148.

Menodoros : an artist of the name made a copy of the Eros of Praxiteles at Thespiai, Paus. ix, 27, 4.

Myagrus : of Phokaia, Vitruv. iii, *Praef.* 2.

Polycrates : for a doubtful inscription with this name cf. *I. G. B.* 482.

11. Pythocritus : son of Timocharis of Rhodes, *I. G. B.* 174–176, *Ath. Mitth.* xvi, 1891, pp. 120 f. = *Jahrb.* ix, 1894, p. 41. It is interesting to note that *I. G. B.* 174 belonged to the statue of a priest, i. e. to the class *sacrificantes* (Brunn, *K. G.* i, p. 461);

while *I. G. B.* 176, from the statue of an Olympic winner, belongs to the class *athletae*.

12. Patrocles : above § 50.

Posidonius : xxxiii, 156.

13. Periclymenus : Tatian, p. 35, 28 (ed. Schwartz), τί μοι διὰ τὸν Περικλύμενον γύναιον (Eutychis Plin. vii, 34), ὅπερ ἐκύησε τριάκοντα παῖδας, ὡς θαυμαστὸν ἡγεῖσθε τὸ κατανοεῖν ποίημα; Brunn, *K. G.* i, p. 473.

14. Philon : Tatian, p. 36, 17 (ed. Schwartz), mentions a statue of Hephaistion (cf. above § 64) by him; he would thus belong to the age of Alexander.

Symenus : *I. G. B.* 84 (latter half of sixth century).

Timotheus : xxxvi, 35.

Theomnestus : a painter of the name, xxxv, 107.

Timarchides : xxxvi, 35.

15. Timon : probably = *I. G. B.* 234 (from Athens).

Thrason : a figure of Hekate and a fountain, a Penelope and Eurykleia (in a group?) are mentioned, Strabo, xiv, p. 641; cf. Brunn, *K. G.* i, p. 421.

92 maxime cognomine insignis est Callimachus semper calumniator sui, nec finem habentis diligentiae, ob id catatexitechnus
appellatus, memorabili exemplo adhibendi et curae modum.
huius sunt saltantes Lacaenae, emendatum opus sed in quo
gratiam omnem diligentia abstulerit.   hunc quidem et 5
pictorem fuisse tradunt.   non aere captus, nec arte, unam
A.U.C. 698. tantum Zenonis statuam Cypria expeditione non vendidit
Cato, sed quia philosophi erat, ut obiter hoc quoque noscatur
93 tam inane exemplum.   in mentione statuarum est et
una non praetereunda, quamquam auctoris incerti, iuxta 10
rostra, Herculis tunicati, sola eo habitu Romae, torva facie,
sentiensque suprema tunicae.   in hac tres sunt tituli: L.
A.U.C. 691. Luculli imperatoris de manubiis, alter: pupillum Luculli
filium ex S. C. dedicasse, tertius: T. Septimium Sabinum
aed. cur. ex privato in publicum restituisse.   tot certaminum 15
tantaeque dignationis simulacrum id fuit.

12. sentientique *reliqui.*   tunica *reliqui.*

§ 92. 1. Callimachus: his date
can be approximately fixed at the
close of the fifth century, from the fact
that he is credited (Vitr. iv, 1, 10)
with the 'invention,' i. e. introduction
into Greece, of the Corinthian capital,
which Skopas (Paus. viii, 45, 5) employed in the temple at Tegea (Ol.
96 = B. C. 396). Addenda.

calumniator sui: cf. Quinct. x,
1, 115: *inveni qui Calvum prae-*
ferrent omnibus, inveni qui Ciceroni
crederent, eum nimia contra se ca-
lumnia verum sanguinem perdidisse.

2. catatexitechnus: Paus. i, 26,
7; Vitruv. *loc. cit.: Call. qui propter*
elegantiam ac subtilitatem artis
marmoreae ab Atheniensibus catatexi-
technus fuerat nominatus; Brunn,
K. G. i, p. 254 aptly compares the
use of κατατήκειν in Dionys. *H. de vi*
Dem. 51: Οὐ γὰρ δή τοι, πλάσται μὲν
καὶ γραφεῖς ἐν ὕλῃ φθαρτῇ χειρῶν εὐ-
στοχίας ἐνδεικνύμενοι τοσούτους εἰσ-
φέρονται πόνους, ὥστε καὶ φλέβια καὶ
πτίλα καὶ χνοῦς καὶ τὰ τούτοις ὅμοια
εἰς ἄκρον ἐξεργάζεσθαι καὶ κοτατήκειν
εἰς ταῦτα τὰς τέχνας.

4. saltantes Lacaenae: Furt-
wängler (*Masterpieces*, p. 438; *ib.* fig.
179) inclines to recognize the type in
the dancing girls wearing the Kala-
thiskos so common on later reliefs
and gems.

5. gratiam . . . abstulerit: this
judgement flatly contradicts the words
of Vitruvius quoted above (cf. also Paus.
loc. cit.); an interesting evidence of diver-
gence of opinion among ancient critics.

et pictorem fuisse: cf. of Pythagoras, § 60; of Pheidias, xxxv, 54.

7. Zenonis: he was born at Kition.
His features are known from the bust
at Naples, Schuster, *Ueber die erhal-*
tenen Porträts der Gr. Philosophen,
pl. iv, 1, 1 a.

Cypria expeditione: vii, 113,
when Cato went to Cyprus as *Quaestor*
cum iure praetorio to confiscate the
property of Ptolemy, which was put
up to auction.

§ 93. 10. auctoris incerti: this
suffices to discredit the proposed
identification of this statue with the
Herakles of Polykles, mentioned Cic.
ad Att. vi, 1, 17.

Of all artists, however, *Kallimachos* has received the most dis- 92 tinctive name. He was always too severe a critic of himself, and *Kallima-chos, ' the* incessantly laborious; from this he received the surname of *Niggler.'* κατατηξίτεχνος, or the Niggler—a noteworthy warning that even diligence has its limits. By him we have a group of Spartan girls dancing, a work of faultless technique, which has, however, lost all charm through over elaboration. Some authorities say that Kallimachos was also a painter.

The statue of Zeno was the only one which Cato did not sell 56 B.C. when commissioner in Cyprus; this, however, was not because he valued the bronze or the workmanship, but because the statue was that of a philosopher, a trivial incident, yet not unworthy of passing notice.

In speaking of statues there is one which ought not to be 93 omitted, although the artist is unknown. It stands close to the *Herakles wearing* Rostra, and represents Herakles wearing the tunic; it is the only *the tunic.* one of him in Rome in that dress: the wild expression of the face shows that he is feeling the last agonies of the tunic. There are three inscriptions upon it: one states that it is part of the plunder taken by Lucius Lucullus, the second that the son of 63 B.C. Lucullus, while still a minor, dedicated it in pursuance of a de-cree of the Senate, the third that Titus Septimius Sabinus when curule aedile made it once more a public monument. These inscriptions show the rivalry occasioned by the statue, and the value set on it.

11. **torva facie**: the description shows clearly to what school the Herakles belonged; the hero trying to extricate himself from the burning robe irresistibly recalls the Laokoon tearing away the snakes. That the *tunica* was the fatal robe sent by Deianeira is a suggestion first made by Turnebus, *Advers.* lib. xvi, 487. Though the reading *sentiensque suprema tunicae* is not absolutely beyond suspicion, I see no reason for following Peter (*ap.* Roscher, i, 2941) in denying (cf. Urlichs in *Chrest.* p. 333) the allusion to the poisoned tunic. The subject seems to have been represented in painting by Aristeides (Polybios, *ap.* Strabo, viii, p. 381).

12. **tres sunt tituli**: showing that the statue had changed place three times; where it stood on its first dedication is unknown. The son of Lucullus re-dedicated it near the (old) Rostra. Then, owing to the numerous changes which took place in the Forum it was removed and fell into private hands; the restoration by T. Sep-timius Sab. was in virtue of his office as aedile, by which he had charge of public buildings and statues.

13. **de manubiis**: on the occasion of his triumph B.C. 63.

pupillum: he was the ward of Cato (Cic. *de Fin.* iii, 2) and Cicero (*Att.* xiii, 6).

140   Aristonidas artifex cum exprimere vellet Athamantis
furorem Learcho filio praecipitato residentem paenitentia,
aes ferrumque miscuit ut robigine eius per nitorem aeris
relucente exprimeretur verecundiae rubor.   hoc signum
141 exstat hodie Rhodi.   est in eadem urbe et ferreus Hercules, 5
quem fecit Alcon laborum dei patientia inductus.   videmus et Romae scyphos e ferro dicatos in templo Martis
Ultoris.

1. **Aristonidas** : xxxv, 146, where
his son Mnasitimos is mentioned
among the painters *non ignobiles ;* cf.
I. G. B. 197 (inscr. more completely
given by Hiller von Gaertringen,
I. G. Ins. i, 855),which shows that M.
was also a sculptor like his father.

Athamantis furorem : recalls such
subjects as Herakles grieving for his
madness, xxxv, 141.   The Athamas
was perhaps inspired by the *Ino* of
Euripides, where the murder of Lear-
chos occurred.

4. **verecundiae rubor** : cf. Plu-

The artist *Aristonidas* in a statue representing Athamas after **140**
the murder of his son sought to depict fury giving place to *Use of iron in*
repentance, and mixed copper and iron, that the rust might show *statues.*
through the metallic lustre of the copper and express the blush of
shame ; this statue exists to this day at Rhodes, where also is **141**
a Herakles which *Alkon* bethought himself to cast in iron, in
allusion to the fortitude of the god under his labours. We can
also see cups of iron at Rome, dedicated in the temple of Mars
the Avenger.

tarch's description of the Iokasta of
Seilanion, Συμπ. v, 1, 2, cf. πῶς δεῖ τὸν
νέονποιημ. ἀκ. iii, 30 .

   6. Alcon : according to Brunn,
K. G. ii, p. 402 (cf. i, p. 466) he is

perhaps identical with the chaser
Alkon, Athen. xi, p. 469 A, the
Pseudo - Virgil, *Culex,* 66 ; Ovid,
Metam. xiii, 683 ff.

   7. Martis ultoris : above § 48.

C. PLINII SECUNDI

NATURALIS HISTORIAE

LIBER XXXV, §§ 15–29; 50–149; 151–158

(PICTURA ET PLASTICE)

I. PICTURA.

LIB.
XXXV.

15 DE picturae initiis incerta nec instituti operis quaestio est.
Aegyptii sex milibus annorum apud ipsos inventam priusquam in Graeciam transiret adfirmant vana praedicatione,
ut palam est, Graeci autem alii Sicyone alii apud Corinthios
repertam, omnes umbra hominis lineis circumducta, itaque 5
primam talem, secundam singulis coloribus et monochro-
maton dictam postquam operosior inventa erat, duratque
16 talis etiam nunc.   inventam liniarem a Philocle Aegyptio
vel Cleanthe Corinthio primi exercuere Aridices Corinthius
et Telephanes Sicyonius, sine ullo etiamnum hi colore, iam 10
tamen spargentes linias intus.   ideo et quos pingerent ad-

§ 15. 1. incerta: in vii, 205 Pliny had already given two different versions.

2. Aegyptii: their contention was obviously a true one; the *vana prae-dicatione* is drawn from a Greek writer anxious to claim the invention of painting for Greece.

4. Sicyone: for its claims to artistic preeminence cf. below, § 75, xxxvi, 9, and note on xxxiv, 55; it is probable that Corinth was the earlier artistic centre, and that priority was claimed for Sikyon, when, in the latter half of the fifth century, it began to assume the leadership of the Peloponnesian schools. The allusion to Sikyon, and the theoretical character of the following genesis of painting

(Introd. p. xxviii f.) point to Xenokrates as authority.

5. umbra ... circumducta: this theory is purely arbitrary; it rests on the conventional supposition that the simpler method necessarily precedes the more complex—that pictures in outline precede pictures where the contours are filled in, and monochrome painting polychrome. The historical study of the monuments, i. e. of early painted fictile wares, has shown, however, that the operation was reversed in both cases; cf. Robert, *Arch. Märchen*, p. 121 ff. Studniczka (*Jahrb.* ii, 1887, p. 148 ff.) has made a vigorous attempt to reconcile fact with the Plinian tra-

I. PAINTING.

THE origin of painting is obscure, and hardly falls within the 15
scope of this work. The claim of the Egyptians to have dis- *Obscurity of its ori-*
covered the art six thousand years before it reached Greece is *gin.*
obviously an idle boast, while among the Greeks some say that it
was first discovered at Sikyon, others at Corinth. All, however,
agree that painting began with the outlining of a man's shadow;
this was the first stage, in the second a single colour was employed,
and after the discovery of more elaborate methods this style, which
is still in vogue, received the name of monochrome.

The invention of linear drawing is attributed to † *Philokles* of 16
Egypt, or to *Kleanthes* of Corinth. The first to practise it were *Philokles of Egypt.*
† *Arideikes* of Corinth, and † *Telephanes* of Sikyon, who still used *Kleanthes of Corinth.*
no colour, though they had begun to give the inner markings, and *Arideikes*
from this went on to add the names of the personages they *of Corinth. Telephanes of Sikyon.*

dition; see also Hollwerda in *Jahrb.*
v, 1890, p. 256 f. and C. Smith, art.
PICTURA in Smith's *Dict. Ant.* p. 400 f.,
who gives a lucid analysis of the
question.

§ 16. 8. **inventam liniarem**: the
use of *invenio* like that of *primus* (cf.
note on xxxiv, 54) must not be
pressed; it arises from the determina-
tion, already noted in the case of the
bronze statuaries, to connect each
stage of a progress with one definite
name.

Philocle Aegyptio: harks back
to the Egyptian tradition; Münzer,
Hermes, xxx, 1895, p. 512, note 1.

9. **Cleanthe**: known from Strabo,
viii, p. 343, as the painter of (*a*)
an Ilioupersis, (*b*) a Birth of Athena
(cf. Athen. viii, 346 C); for the
probable style of these paintings cf.
Studniczka, *op. cit.* p. 153.

11. **adscribere institutum**: the
names of the personages portrayed
were used ornamentally to fill up
space, as often on black-figured vases.

scribere institutum. primus invenit eas colore testae, ut
ferunt, tritae, Ecphantus Corinthius. hunc eodem nomine
alium fuisse quam quem tradit Cornelius Nepos secutum
in Italiam Damaratum Tarquinii Prisci regis Romani patrem
fugientem a Corintho tyranni iniurias Cypseli mox docebi- 5
mus.

17   Iam enim absoluta erat pictura etiam in Italia. exstant
certe hodieque antiquiores urbe picturae Ardeae in aedibus
sacris, quibus ego quidem nullas aeque miror, tam longo
aevo durantis in orbitate tecti veluti recentis. similiter 10
Lanivi, ubi Atalante et Helena comminus pictae sunt nudae
ab eodem artifice, utraque excellentissima forma, sed altera
18 ut virgo, ne ruinis quidem templi concussae. Gaius princeps
tollere eas conatus est libidine accensus, si tectori natura
permisisset. durant et Caere antiquiores et ipsae. fate- 15
biturque quisquis eas diligenter aestimaverit nullam artium
celerius consummatam, cum Iliacis temporibus non fuisse
eam appareat.

1. invenit] *codd.*; inlevit *Haupt, Detlefsen.*

1. **invenit**: the manuscript reading is defended by Holwerda (*op. cit.*
p. 259, note 54) who points out that
invenire eam colore testae tritae corresponds to *picturam invenire singulis
coloribus* above. For *primus invenit*
cf. below, §§ 151, 152.

testae tritae: the process, which
is known only from this passage,
probably died out early, Blümner,
Technol. iv, p. 478 f.

2. **Ecphantus**: the name is that
of a painter inscribed on the *columna
Naniana* (*I. G. B.* 5); the identity
suggested by Studniczka (*op. cit.* p.
151) is quite uncertain.

3. **alium fuisse quam**: attempts
to reconcile two variant traditions—
namely the attribution of the invention
of painting proper to Ekphantos, and
the Italian tradition that painting was
perfect in Italy long before the arrival
of the Greeks. Cf. § 152, where the
fictores who followed Damaratos into
Italy are mentioned.

4. **Damaratus**: below § 152; Tac.
Ann. xi, 14; Dionysios H. iii, 46 ff.,
Strabo v, p. 219, viii, p. 378, &c.

5. **mox docebimus**: Furtwängler
(*Plinius*, p. 25 f.; cf. Robert, *Arch.
Märchen*, p. 123) has shown that the
proof follows immediately: *iam
enim . . .*

§ 17. 8. **Ardeae**: iii, 56; for the
paintings by M. Plautius in its temple
of Juno, below, § 115; for paintings
in temple of Castor and Pollux see
Servius on *Aen.* i, 44 (Thilo i, p. 31):
*nam Ardeae in templo Castoris et
Pollucis in laeva intrantibus* (cf.
below, § 154) *post forem Capaneos
pictus est fulmen per utraque tempora
traiectus.*

11. **Lanivi**: iii, 64; viii, 221.

12. **altera ut virgo**: for the
ellipse of the first *altera* cf. below,
§ 71 *hoplites in certamine ita
decurrens ut sudare videatur*, alter
arma deponens ut . . . and see note on
xxxiv, 54, l. 7.

painted. The invention of painting with colour made, it is said, from powdered potsherds, is due to †*Ekphantos* of Corinth. *Ekphantos of Corinth.* I shall show presently that this Ekphantos is distinct from that namesake of his who, according to Cornelius Nepos, followed Damaratos, the father of Tarquin the Ancient, in his flight to Italy from Corinth to escape the insults of the tyrant Kypselos, for by that time painting in Italy also had already reached high **17** perfection. To this day we may see in the temples of Ardea *Antiquity of painting in Italy.* paintings older than the city of Rome, which I admire beyond any others, for though unprotected by a roof they remain fresh *Paintings at Ardea.* after all these years. At Lanuvium again are two nude figures by *Atalanta* the same artist, of Atalanta and Helen, painted side by side. *and Helen* Both are of great beauty, and the one is painted as a virgin; they *at Lanuvium.* have sustained no injury though the temple is in ruins. The **18** Emperor Caligula, who was fired by a passion for these figures, would undoubtedly have removed them if the composition of the stucco had allowed of it. Caere possesses some still more ancient *Paintings* paintings. No one can examine these carefully without confess- *at Caere.* ing that painting reached its full development more rapidly than *Rapid de-* any other art, since it seems clear that it was not yet in existence *velopment of the art.* in Trojan times.

13. ne ruinis quidem concussae : one may conjecture that the Atalanta and Helena had once formed part of a larger composition which was partially destroyed in Pliny's time. Engelmann (*ap.* Roscher, i, p. 1964) conjectures that the painting had originally represented a mortal counterpart of the 'Judgement of Paris'— on the analogy of a bronze Etruscan cista at Berlin (Friederichs, *Bronzen*, 542, cf. *Arch. Anz.* 1889, p. 42),where Paris appears in conversation with three nude women Fclena (Helen), Ateleta (Atalanta) and Alsir (?). Helen was a favourite subject of the Etruscan artists; cf. Gerhard, *Etr. Spiegel*, iv, 373–382.

§ 18. 14. libidine accensus : for similar stories cf. below, § 70; xxxiv, 62.

tectori natura : below, § 173. For the elliptical construction of *si permisisset* cf. Tac. *Ann.* ii, 46 ; spera-baturque *rursum pugna*, ni *Mara-boduus castra* subduxisset.

15. Caere, iii, 51 ; an interesting series of paintings from Caere (Cervetri) now in the Brit. Mus. has been published by A. S. Murray, *J. H. S.* x, 1889, pl. vii, pp. 243–252, who justly points out their dependence on Greek models. In asserting the independent development of painting in Italy, Pliny has evidently been misled by his patriotism. A similar, but somewhat later, series of paintings from Caere in the Louvre, *Mon. Inst.* vi, vii, pl. 30.

17. Iliacis temporibus : the statement is based on the Homeric poems, where, with the exception of the νῆες μιλτοπάρῃοι, and the ἵππου παρήιον (*Il.* iv, 141) which 'a woman of Paionia or Maionia dyes with purple,' there are no allusions to painting; see O. Müller, *Handbuch*, p. 51.

19   Apud Romanos quoque honos mature huic arti contigit, siquidem cognomina ex ea Pictorum traxerunt Fabii clarissimae gentis, princepsque eius cognominis ipse aedem Salutis pinxit anno urbis conditae CCCCL, quae pictura duravit ad nostram memoriam aede ea Claudi principatu exusta. 5 proxime celebrata est in foro boario aede Herculis Pacuvi poetae pictura. Enni sorore genitus hic fuit, clarioremque
20 artem eam Romae fecit gloria scaenae. postea non est spectata honestis manibus, nisi forte quis Turpilium equitem Romanum e Venetia nostrae aetatis velit referre pulchris 10 eius operibus hodieque Veronae exstantibus. laeva is manu pinxit, quod de nullo ante memoratur. parvis gloriabatur tabellis extinctus nuper in longa senecta Titedius Labeo praetorius, etiam proconsulatu provinciae Narbonensis functus,
21 sed ea re in risu etiam contumeliae erat. fuit et principum 15 virorum non omittendum de pictura celebre consilium.
A.U.C. 709. cum Q. Pedius nepos Q. Pedii consularis triumphalisque et a Caesare dictatore coheredis Augusto dati natura mutus esset, in eo Messala orator, ex cuius familia pueri avia fuerat, picturam docendum censuit, idque etiam divus 20 Augustus comprobavit, puer magni profectus in ea arte
22 obiit. dignatio autem praecipua Romae increvit, ut existimo,

§ 19. 2. Fabii clariss. gentis : *An censemus, si Fabio, nobilissimo homini, laudi datum esset quod pingeret, non multos apud nos futuros Polyclitos et Parrhasios fuisse ?* Cic. *Tusc. Disput.* i, 2, 4. The first *Pictor* is of course distinct from the historian (h. about B.C. 254; Teuffel, 116).

3. aedem Salutis : since the temple was dedicated by C. Junius Bubulcus, a hero of the second Samnite war, B.C. 311, and consecrated by him as Dictator, B.C. 302 (Liv. ix, 43, 25), the pictures probably related to his exploits in Apulia (Urlichs, *Malerei in Rom*, p. 7). From Valerius Max. viii, 14, 6 it appears that they were extensive compositions, covering perhaps the two long walls of the cella. Dionysios, xvi, 6, praises the fine drawing, and sharp clean contours

of these wall-paintings. (Against the proposed identification of a wall-painting from the Esquiline, *Bull. Comm.* 1889, pl. xi, xii, as ' riproduzione in piccolò ' of the pictures in the temple of Salus, see Hülsen, *Röm. Mitth.* 1891, p. 111.)

6. foro boario aede Herculis : this temple, which was called *aedes Aemiliana* (according to Scaliger's emendation of Festus, p. 242) was either founded or restored with great splendour by Aemilius Paullus the conqueror of Pydna ; cf. H. Peter, *ap.* Roscher, i, p. 2909 f. It was natural, as Urlichs (*Malerei*, p. 17) points out, that he should employ to decorate it Pacuvius, who had written in his honour the *Praetexta Paulus* (Ribbeck, *Röm. Trag.* 326), and whose intimacy with Laelius, the bosom friend

Among the Romans too this art was early had in honour, see- **19**
ing indeed that so distinguished a family as the Fabii drew from *Painting in Rome.*
it the name of Pictor [Painter] ; and the first of the name actually *Fabius Pictor.*
painted the temple of Safety, in the year of Rome 450 [304 B.C.].
These paintings lasted until my day, when the temple was burned
down in the reign of Claudius. Soon afterwards the poet *Pacu-* *Pacuvius.*
vius won great renown through his paintings in the temple of
Hercules in the Cattle Market. The mother of Pacuvius was
a sister of Ennius, whence it came about that the drama lent
a new lustre to the art of painting at Rome. Since that time. **20**
however, the profession of painter has received no honour at the
hands of men of good birth, unless we except in our own time
Turpilius, a Roman knight from Venetia, whose excellent pictures *Turpilius.*
are still to be seen at Verona. He painted with his left hand,
a peculiarity noted of no artist before him. *Titedius Labeo*, who *Titedius Labeo.*
died not long ago in extreme old age, was proud of the little
pictures that he painted : he was of praetorian rank and had even
been governor of Narbonensis, yet his art only brought upon him
ridicule and even scorn. Nor must I omit the famous decision **21**
with regard to painting arrived at by eminent statesmen. *Quintus* *Quintus Pedius.*
Pedius (grandson of that Quintus Pedius who had been consul,
had enjoyed a triumph and was named by the dictator Caesar as **45 B.C.**
co-heir with Augustus) having been dumb from his birth, it so
befell that Messala, the orator, to whose family the boy's grand-
mother belonged, advised that he should be taught to paint. The
god Augustus approved of the idea, and the boy had made great
progress in the art when he died. The esteem which the Romans **22**

of Aemilius' son Scipio, is known to
us from Cicero (*Laelius*, 7, 24).

§ 20. 9. honestis manibus : cf.
Cic. *Tusc. Disp. loc. cit.*, and the
ironical words applied to Fabius
Pictor by Val. Max. viii, 14, 6.

Turpilium : possibly a descen-
dant of the Turpilius who wrote comedies, and was a contemporary of
Terence (Rihbeck, *Com.* 2nd ed. 85).

11. Veronae : probably Pliny's
birthplace, since in Praef. 1 he speaks
of Catullus as his *conterraneus*.

13. Titedius Labeo : Tac. *Ann.*
ii, 85.

§ 21. 17. Q. Pedii consularis : be

was the grandson of Caesar's elder
sister ; he triumphed Dec. 13, B.C. 45,
after his Spanish campaign (Appian,
Bell. Civ. iii, 22, 23, 94–96), was
consul with Augustus in B.C. 43, in
which year he died.

18. coheredis dati : Snet. *Julius*,
83.

19. Messala orator : B.C. 64–A.D.
8 (Teuffel, 222), quoted in the indices
to Bks. ix, xxxiii, xxxv ; restores the
ancient Sibyls, xxxiv, 22. Cf. also
vii, 90, and above, § 8.

avia : i. e. the wife of Q. Pedius,
the legatee of Caesar.

§ 22. 22. dignatio ... increvit :

a M'. Valerio Maximo Messala, qui princeps tabulam pictam
proelii quo Carthaginienses et Hieronem in Sicilia vicerat,
proposuit in latere curiae Hostiliae anno ab urbe condita
CCCCLXXXX. fecit hoc idem et L. Scipio, tabulamque

A.U.C. 565. victoriae suae Asiaticae in Capitolio posuit, idque aegre 5
tulisse fratrem Africanum tradunt haut inmerito, quando
23 filius eius illo proelio captus fuerat.   non dissimilem
offensionem et Aemiliani subiit L. Hostilius Mancinus qui
primus Carthaginem inruperat situm eius oppugnationesque
depictas proponendo in foro et ipse adsistens populo spectanti 10
singula enarrando, qua comitate proximis comitiis con-

A.U.C. 609.
A.U.C. 655. sulatum adeptus est.   habuit et scaena ludis Claudii Pulchri
magnam admirationem picturae, cum ad tegularum similitudinem corvi decepti imaginem advolarent.

24   Tabulis autem externis auctoritatem Romae publice fecit 15
primus omnium L. Mummius cui cognomen Achaici victoria

A.U.C. 608. dedit.   namque cum in praeda vendenda rex Attalus
$X\lceil\overline{VI}\rceil$ emisset tabulam Aristidis, Liberum patrem, pretium
miratus suspicatusque aliquid in ea virtutis quod ipse

on Roman triumphal pictures generally
see the excellent remarks of Raonl-
Rochette, *Peint. Ant.* p. 303 f., and
recently Wickhoff, *Wiener Genesis*,
p. 30 f.

1. M'. **Valerio Maximo Messala**:
cos. B.C. 263; cf. vii, 214.

3. **in latere curiae Host.**: seeing the numerous changes undergone
by the Curia between the date of
Messala and that of Cicero, the identity of the picture with the *tabula
Valeria* (Cicero *in Vat.* 9, 21; *ad Fam.*
xiv, 2, 2) is improbable (it seems accepted by Becker, *Röm. Top.* p. 326,
note 99, and recently by Gilbert, *Geschichte u. Top.* iii, p. 165, note 2;
Urlichs, *Malerei*, p. 9, suggests that
the exhibition was only temporary).
The date usually assigned to Messala's
victory is A. U. C. 491 = B.C. 263.

4. **L. Scipio**: he triumphed on
the last day of the intercalary month
of B.C. 188, but his splendid games
were not celebrated till B.C. 186 (cf.
xxxiii, 138).   It is not known on

which of the two occasions he exhibited the picture of his exploits (cf.
Urlichs, *op. cit.* p. 14).

5. **aegre tulisse**: the injury felt
was far-fetched; from Val. Max. ii, 10
2, we learn that Antiochos treated
the son with marked courtesy, and
sent him back *celeriter*.

§ 23. 8. **Aemiliani**: the offence
presumably consisted in the omission
from the picture of any allusion to
the timely help of Scipio, Appian,
Λιβ. 113 ff.; cf. *ibid.* 134, where a
graphic account is given of the enthusiasm with which the Romans
received the news of the fall of
Carthage.

12. **scaena**: i. e. the *scaenae frons*
or wall of the stage-buildings, upon
which the scenic decorations were
hung, cf. § 65.

Claudii Pulchri: aedile B.C. 99;
on his games see viii, 19; Val.
Max. ii, 4, 6 *C. Pulcher scenam va-
rietate colorum adumbravit vacuis ante
pictura tabulis extentam.*

gave to painting was greatly increased (so it seems to me) by the
action of Manius Valerius Maximus Messala. He first caused
his victory over the Carthaginians and Hiero in Sicily to be
painted on wood, and exhibited the picture at the side of the
Curia Hostilia in the year of Rome 490 [264 B.C.]. Following
his example Lucius Scipio exhibited in the Capitol a picture representing his Asiatic victory, a step which not unnaturally displeased
his brother 'the African,' whose son had been taken prisoner in
the battle. In the same way Lucius Hostilius Mancinus, who
had been the first to enter Carthage, incurred the anger of Scipio
Aemilianus by exhibiting in the forum pictures of the site of
Carthage and the various attempts to storm it, while he himself
stood by, telling the whole story to the crowd of spectators with
a geniality which at the next elections won him the consulship.
At the games given by Claudius Pulcher, the painting of the
scenery excited great wonder, the very crows being deceived by
the painted tiles and flying down to settle on them.

    Foreign pictures, however, were first publicly brought into
vogue at Rome by Lucius Mummius, surnamed the Achaean from
his victories. At the auction of the spoils, King Attalos had bid
for a picture of Dionysos by Aristeides the sum of 600,000 denarii
[£21,000 circ.], whereupon Mummius, surprised at the price
offered, and suspecting some merit in the picture which escaped

*M'. Val.
Max. Mes-
sala com-
memorates
his victory
by a pic-
ture.
L. Scipio
Asiaticus.
189 B.C.*

23
*L. Hosti-
lius Man-
cinus.*

145 B.C.
99 B.C.

24
*'Mummius
introduces
foreign
pictures.*
146 B.C.

14. **corvi decepti**: cf. below, §§ 65, 66, and 155.

§ 24. 16. **L. Mummius**: in xxxiii, 149, however, the introduction of foreign pictures into Rome is attributed to Scipio's Asiatic victories; while Liv. xxv, 40, states that the first enthusiasm for Greek pictures at Rome was a result of the capture of Syracuse by Marcellus: *ceterum inde primum initium mirandi Graecarum artium;* cf. also Cato's speech as given Liv. xxxiv, 4 (below note on § 157), and Plut. *Marcell.* xxi.

17. **in praeda vendenda** : the notion of an auction is inaccurate : according to Paus. vii, 16, 8, Mummius had taken to Rome the most valuable works of art, and handed over to Philopoimen (see next note) the less important objects.

rex Attalus : see vii, 126. As a fact Attalos himself was not present at Corinth (Paus. vii, 16, 1); he had only sent an auxiliary force to the Romans, under the command of Philopoimen. There is a further inaccuracy in the account of the purchase : according to Polybios (*apud* Strabo, viii, p. 381), who was an eye-witness, the Roman soldiers were already using the pictures as dice-boards, when Philopoimen offered a hundred talents to Mummius in case he should feel disposed to assign the picture to Attalos' share of the booty. For the paintings collected by Attalos, see Fränkel, *Jahrb.* vi (1891), pp. 49-60, 'Gemälde-Sammlungen u. Gemälde-Forschung in Pergamon.'

18. **Aristidis** : below, §§ 98-100.
Liberum patrem: below, § 99.

nesciret, revocavit tabulam Attalo multum querente et in
Cereris delubro posuit, quam primam arbitror picturam
25 externam Romae publicatam. deinde video et in foro
positas volgo. hinc enim ille Crassi oratoris lepos agentis
sub Veteribus, cum testis compellatus instaret : dic ergo, 5
Crasse, qualem me noris? talem, inquit, ostendens in tabula
pictum inficetissime Gallum exerentem linguam. in foro
fuit et illa pastoris senis cum baculo, de qua Teutonorum
legatus respondit interrogatus, quantine eum aestimaret,
donari sibi nolle talem vivom verumque.   10
26   Sed praecipuam auctoritatem publice tabulis fecit Caesar
dictator Aiace et Media ante Veneris Genetricis aedem
dicatis, post eum M. Agrippa vir rusticitati propior quam
deliciis. exstat certe eius oratio magnifica et maximo
civium digna de tabulis omnibus signisque publicandis, 15
quod fieri satius fuisset quam in villarum exilia pelli. verum
eadem illa torvitas tabulas duas Aiacis et Veneris mercata
·est a Cyzicenis HS. [$\overline{XII}$]. in thermarum quoque calidissima parte marmoribus incluserat parvas tabellas paulo
ante, cum reficerentur, sublatas.   20

1. in Cereris delubro : xxxiv,
15; below, §§ 99, 154. Strabo, *loc.
cit.* τὸν δὲ Διόνυσον [sc. 'Αριστείδου]
ἀνακείμενον ἐν τῷ Δημητρείῳ τῷ ἐν
'Ρώμῃ κάλλιστον ἔργον ἑωρῶμεν· ἐμ-
πρησθέντος δὲ τοῦ νεὼ συνηφανίσθη καὶ
ἡ γραφὴ νεωστί.

§ 25. 4. Crassi oratoris : Cicero
(*de Orat.* ii, 66, 266 ; cf. Quinct. vi, 3,
38, where see Spalding's note) attributes the witticism to the orator, C.
Julius Caesar Strabo (Teuffel, 153, 3).

5. sub veteribus : sc. *tabernis,*
cf. § 113; these shops, with a colonnade in front of them, stood facing the
Sacra Via, on the site afterwards occupied by the *Basilica Julia.* The
tribunal, where the scene is imagined,
may, have stood close to the *Regia* ;
cf. Jordan, *Top.* i, 2, p. 382, note 92.
Cicero, *loc. cit.*, has *sub novis,* i. e. on
N. side of the Forum.

6. in tabula : Cic. *loc. cit. in*

Mariano scuto Cimbrico. The pro-
truding tongue was probably apotro-
paic (cf. Urlichs in *Chrestom.,* p. 343) ;
being misunderstood it gave occasion
to the witticisms recorded by Pliny,
Cicero and others with Quinctilian,
perhaps also to the remark in Liv.
vii, 10, 5 : (*Gallum*) *linguam etiam
ab irrisu exserentem.*

§ 26. 12. Aiace et Media : vii,
126 = App. I; below, §§ 136, 145.

ante V. G. aedem : whereas
in § 136 the same pictures are said to
be *in V. G. aede ;* the latter seems
the likeliest ; the first variant is probably due to Pliny's carelessness ; cf.
Münzer, *op. cit.* p. 542. The temple
was vowed by Caesar at Pharsalos
(B.C. 48), ded. with the Forum, Sept.
24 or 25, B.C. 46 (but see *Mon. Ancyr.*
iv, 12 ; Mommsen, *Res Gestae,* p. 84 f.).

13. M. Agrippa : B.C. 63–A.D. 12 ;
Teuffel, 220, 10–14.

his own eyes, withdrew it, in spite of the protests of Attalos, and afterwards dedicated it in the temple of Ceres. This was, I believe, the first foreign picture publicly dedicated at Rome. Later on I see that they were constantly put up even in the 25 Forum, a custom which gave the orator Crassus an opening for a witticism. He was pleading a case close to the Old Shops, when a witness under examination said to him, 'Pray what do you take me for, Crassus ?' 'Just such a man as that,' answered Crassus, pointing to a coarse picture of a Gaul with his tongue out. In the Forum too was the picture of an old shepherd with his staff, of which the envoy of the Teutons said, when asked what he thought it was worth, that he would not take such a man at a gift, even if he were alive and real.

But the highest public tribute to painting was paid by the 26 dictator Caesar when he dedicated the Aias and the Medeia in *Caesar's patronage* front of the temple of Venus the Mother, and after him by Marcus *Aias and Medeia.* Agrippa, whose natural tastes inclined to rustic simplicity rather *Agrippa.* than to the refinements of luxury ; a magnificent speech of his at least is extant, fully worthy of the first citizen in the state, urging that all pictures and statues should be made public pro-perty—certainly a wiser plan than to consign them to exile in our country houses. Yet the rude Agrippa bought two pictures—an *Aias and Aphrodite* Aias and an Aphrodite—from the people of Kyzikos for 1,200,000 *from Ky-* sesterces [£10,500 circ.], and further, in the hottest chamber of *zikos.* his baths were some small pictures, let into the marble, which were removed not long ago in the course of a restoration.

17. **Aiacis et Veneris**: nothing further is known of either picture ; the grounds for identifying either or both with the Ajax and Medea purchased by Caesar (Welcker, Helbig, Urlichs, &c.) are purely fanciful. From the *post eum* we may assume that Agrip-pa's purchases were later than Caesar's, and the price paid for the pictures was not the same (cf. § 136 where the price paid by Caesar is given). The question is fully discussed by F. Brandstätter, *Timomachos*, p. 16 ff. The occasion for Agrippa's pur-chases, and the spot where he exhi-bited them, are unknown. He may have bought the pictures as aedile in B.C. 33, or to adorn the buildings which several years later were carried out under his direction (the *Septa Julia* in B.C. 26; the *Thermae* and the *Porticus Neptunia* in the follow-ing year ; cf. Brandstätter, *loc. cit.*).

18. **thermarum**: immediately be-hind the Pantheon : the *calidissima pars* must be identical with the *cal-darium*.

19. **incluserat**: according to a custom general in Roman times ; cf. below the pictures in the Curia Julia (§ 27). The six celebrated mono-chrome pictures in red on white marble slabs (Naples) had been let into the wall in a similar manner; cf.

27   Super omnis divus Augustus in foro suo celeberrima in
parte posuit tabulas duas quae Belli faciem pictam habent
et Triumphum, item Castores ac Victoriam. posuit et quas
dicemus sub artificum mentione in templo Caesaris patris.
A.U.C. 725. idem in curia quoque quam in comitio consecrabat duas 5
tabulas inpressit parieti. Nemean sedentem supra leonem
palmigeram ipsam adstante cum baculo sene cuius supra
caput tabella bigae dependet, Nicias scripsit se inussisse,
28 tali enim usus est verbo. alterius tabulae admiratio est
puberem filium seni patri similem esse aetatis salva differentia 10
supervolante aquila draconem complexa. Philochares hoc
suum opus esse testatus est. inmensam, vel unam si tantum
hanc tabulam aliquis aestimet, potentiam artis, cum propter
Philocharen ignobilissimos alioqui Glaucionem filiumque
eius Aristippum senatus populi Romani tot saeculis spectet. 15
posuit et Tiberius Caesar minime comis imperator in templo
ipsius Augusti quas mox indicabimus.

29   Hactenus dictum sit de dignitate artis morientis. quibus
coloribus singulis primi pinxissent diximus, cum de his pig-
mentis traderemus in metallis: monochromata ea genera 20
picturae vocantur. qui deinde et quae invenerint et quibus
temporibus, dicemus in mentione artificum, quoniam indicare
naturas colorum prior causa operis instituti est. tandem

---

6. impressit parieti, Nemean *usque ad* bigae (bige *Voss.*, bigere *Bamb.*,
palmigere *Bamb.* e corr.) dependet. Nicias *Detlefsen; interpunctionem corr.*
Traube.   20. metallis: monochromata . . . vocantur] *Littré*; metallis. qui
monochromata—ea genera picturae vocantur—*Detlefsen, vid. errata, vol.* v
pag. 250.

Robert, *Hall. Winckelm. progr.* xix,
1895, p. 5 f.; Raoul-Rochette, *Pein-*
tures, p. 162; Wickhoff, *Wiener Gene-*
sis, p. 70.
    § 27. 1. in foro . . . parte: below,
§ 93, in *fori sui celeberrimis partibus.*
    2. Belli faciem . . . et Triumphum
=below, § 93 *Belli imaginem re-*
strictis ad terga manibus, Alexandro
in curru triumphante; ib. *Castorem*
et Pollucem cum Victoria.
    3. quas dicemus: i. e. the Anadyo-
mene of Apelles in § 91.
    5. in curia: sc. *Julia*, ded. by

Augustus B.C. 29: it had been begun by Caesar to replace the *Curia*
of Sulla.
    6. inpressit parieti: cf. note on
incluserat in § 26.
    Nemean . . . Nicias: §§ 130,
131. The *Nemea* was the personification of the festal city; the *senex*
with the staff one of the judges in the
games; the tablet with the chariot
indicated the particular contest of
which the picture was the memorial
(Brunn, *K. G.* ii, p. 194); cf. in Paus.
i, 22, 7 the picture commemorating

Above all the god Augustus placed in the most frequented part 27
of the Forum which bears his name, two pictures, the one containing *Augustus.* *Pictures in*
figures of War and of Triumph, the other Kastor and his twin, *his forum.*
with Victory. He also dedicated in the temple of his father Caesar *In temple*
certain pictures which I shall mention when I enumerate the artists. *of Caesar.*
Furthermore he let into the wall of the Council Chamber which *In Curia.*
he consecrated in the Comitium two pictures. On the one, which 29 B.C.
1. *Nemea*
represents the nymph Nemea holding a palm and seated on a *by Nikias.*
lion, while an old man with a staff stands by, above whose head
is suspended a tablet with a two-horse chariot, Nikias has written
that he burned in the painting, using that very word [ἐνέκαεν]. In 28
the other picture we admire the marked resemblance between 2. *Picture*
by Philo-
a young man and his aged father, although the difference of age *chares of*
is not lost; an eagle with a snake in its talons is flying over their *Glaukion*
and Aris-
heads. Philochares lays claim to the painting as his work. *tippos.*
Marvellous is the power of art, judged by this work alone, since
Philochares could turn the eyes of the Senate of the Roman
people for so many years upon Glaukion and his son Aristippos,
persons otherwise quite obscure. Tiberius Caesar too, rude *Tiberius.*
prince though he was, dedicated in the temple of Augustus
pictures which I shall name later on.

I have said enough concerning the dignity of a decaying art. 29
When treating of pigments in my account of metals I named the
colours used singly by the early painters; paintings in that style
are called monochromes. Subsequent innovators, together with
the character and date of their inventions, I shall treat of in my
account of the artists, since the scheme of my work obliges me
first to describe the composition of the pigments employed.

the victory of Alkibiades in the Nemean games: ἵππων δέ οἱ νίκης τῆς ἐν
Νεμέᾳ ἐστὶ σημεῖα ἐν τῇ γραφῇ; also
the *pinax* wtih *biga* on the 'Ikaorios'
relief (Br. Mus. = Friederichs-Wolters,
1844).

8. inussisse i. e. ἐνέκαεν: cf. 122.

§ 28. 9. alterius tabulae: since
placed in the open air, presumably
likewise in encaustic. The eagle and
snake, like the *tabella bigae*, must
have referred to the event commemorated by the picture. How the
work of Nikias came into the hands
of Augustus is unknown (§ 131); as

to the picture of Philochares, Wunderer (*Manubiae Alexandrinae*, p. 23)
suggests that it belonged to Augustus's Egyptian spoils.

11. Philochares: perhaps identical with the vase-painter, brother of
the orator Aischines, mentioned
derisively (ἀλαβαστοθήκας γράφων) by
Demosthenes, *Fals. Leg.* p. 415, 237
(Ol. 109, 2 = B. C. 343).

17. mox indicabimus: in § 131.

§ 29. 19. diximus: in xxxiii,
117.

20. monochromata: *ibid.*; cf.
above, § 15; below, § 56.

se ars ipsa distinxit et invenit lumen atque umbras, differentia colorum alterna vice sese excitante. postea deinde adiectus est splendor, alius hic quam lumen. quod inter haec et umbras esset appellarunt tonon, commissuras vero colorum et transitus harmogen.   5

50   Quattuor coloribus solis immortalia illa opera fecere—ex albis Melino, e silaciis Attico, ex rubris Sinopide Pontica, ex nigris atramento—Apelles, Aetion, Melanthius, Nicomachus, clarissimi pictores, cum tabulae eorum singulae oppidorum venirent opibus. nunc et purpuris in parietes 10 migrantibus et India conferente fluminum suorum limum, draconum elephantorumque saniem nulla nobilis pictura est. omnia ergo meliora tunc fuere, cum minor copia. ita est, quoniam, ut supra diximus, rerum, non animi pretiis excubatur.   15

51   Et nostrae aetatis insaniam in pictura non omittam. Nero princeps iusserat colosseum se pingi CXX pedum linteo, incognitum ad hoc tempus. ea pictura cum peracta esset

1. **lumen atque umbras**: cf. xxxiii, 160; below, § 131.

2. **alterna vice sese excitante**: this passage should be studied in connexion with Aristotle's doctrine, in the third book of the *Meteorologica*, of the juxtaposition of colours; cf. with relation to the Plinian words: μέλαν παρὰ μέλαν ποιεῖ τὸ ἠρέμα λευκὸν παντελῶς φαίνεσθαι λευκόν *Meteor*. p. 375 a, 20. See on the whole subject, Bertrand, *Études*, pp. 150–160.

3. **splendor**: the meaning suggested for this word by Blümner, *Technol.* iv, p. 428 is '*reflexion*' (for reflected lights cf. § 138). But reflexion comes simply under the same heading as treatment of light, whereas the words of Pliny, *alius hic quam lumen*, expressly show that *splendor* was a totally different factor to light. In truth it was neither more nor less than the 'glow' which—as distinct from any treatment of light and shade

—is so marked a quality of certain Renascence and modern artists (e. g. Titian, Turner). Külb rightly translates 'Glanz.' Introd. p. xxxiv.

4. **tonon**: what the modern French would call ' values,' i. e. the passages from the more lit up parts in a picture to the less, the 'value' being the quantity of light in a given colour.

commissuras . . . colorum: the arrangement of colours, resulting in ἁρμογή, or what the moderns would call the general 'tone' of a picture.

§ 50. 6. **Quattuor coloribus**: cf. Cic. *Brutus* 18, 70 *similis in pictura ratio est, in qua Zeuxin et Polygnotum et Timanthem et eorum qui non sunt usi plus quam quattuor coloribus, formas et lineamenta laudamus ; at in Aetione, Nicomacho, Protogene, Apelle iam perfecta sunt omnia.* These words do not necessarily contradict the statement of Pliny or prove that the later painters used more

Art at last differentiated itself and discovered light and shade, the several hues being so employed as to enhance one another by contrast. Later on glow—a different thing to light—was introduced. The transition between light and shade they called τόνος, but the arrangement of hues and the transition from one colour to another harmonization or ἁρμογή.

Four colours only—white from Melos, Attic yellow, red from **50** Sinope on the Black Sea, and the black called 'atramentum'— *Four colours* were used by Apelles, Aetion, Melanthios and Nikomachos in *used by* their immortal works; illustrious artists, a single one of whose *early* pictures the wealth of a city could hardly suffice to buy, while *artists.* now that even purple clothes our walls, and India contributes the ooze of her rivers and the blood of dragons and of elephants, no famous picture is painted. We must believe that when the painter's equipment was less complete, the results were in every respect better, for as I have already said, we are alive only to the worth of the material and not to the genius of the artist.

In our own days too painting has known an extravagance which **51** must not be forgotten : the Emperor Nero ordered a colossal por- *Colossal portrait* trait of himself, 120 feet in length, to be painted on canvas, a thing *of Nero on canvas.*

than four colours. The *perfecta omnia* need mean no more than that they had learnt endless combinations of the four colours, whereas the older painters used them pure or knew but of few combinations. The colour effects produced by Apelles and his contemporaries being far more elaborate than anything attempted in the period of Polygnotos, it is natural that the employment of only four colours should, in their case, be dwelt upon with special admiration. As an example of what can be accomplished with only four colours, the student will remember the 'Christ crowned with thorns' by Titian in the Munich Pinakothek (1114); cf. Morelli, *Galleries of Munich and Dresden*, p. 58 (Transl. C. J. Ffoulkes). The 'four colours' are elaborately discussed by Bertrand, *Études*, pp. 132–144. [The names Apelles — Nicomachus are in alphabetical order. H. L. U.]

8. **Apelles**: below, § 92 *legentes meminerint omnia ea* (sc. *opera*) *quattuor coloribus facta.*

11. **India . . . limum**: i. e. *indigo*, cf. xxxiii, 163; above, §§ 46, 49.

12. **draconum elephantorumque saniem**: also called *cinnabaris*, 'dragon's blood'; in viii, 34, Pliny gives a wonderful account of its production; cf. xxxiii, 116.

14. **ut supra diximus**: xxxv, 4: *honorem non nisi in pretio ducentes;* cf. the similar rhetorical complaint in xxxiv, 5.

§ 51. 17. **colosseum**: a counterpart to the colossal statue by Zenodoros in xxxiv, 45.

18. **incognitum**: if still unknown in Pliny's day, the practice of painting on canvas soon became general, as is witnessed by the portraits from the Fayoum; cf. Cecil Smith, *Pictura*, p. 329; Berger, *Beiträge*, ii, p. 52 f.

H

in Maianis hortis, accensa fulmine cum optima hortorum
52 parte conflagravit. libertus eius cum daret Anti munus
gladiatorum, publicas porticus occupavit pictura, ut constat,
gladiatorum ministrorumque omnium veris imaginibus redditis. hic multis iam saeculis summus animus in pictura, 5
pingi autem gladiatoria munera atque in publico exponi
coepta a C. Terentio Lucano. is avo suo a quo adoptatus
fuerat triginta paria in foro per triduum dedit tabulamque
pictam in nemore Dianae posuit.
53   Nunc celebres in ea arte quam maxima brevitate per- 10
curram, neque enim instituti operis est talis executio, itaque
quosdam vel in transcursu et in aliorum mentione obiter
nominasse satis erit, exceptis operum claritatibus quae et
54 ipsa conveniet attingi sive exstant sive intercidere. non
constat sibi in hac parte Graecorum diligentia multas post 15
olympiadas celebrando pictores quam statuarios ac toreutas,
primumque olympiade LXXXX, cum et Phidian ipsum
initio pictorem fuisse tradatur clipeumque Athenis ab eo
pictum, praeterea in confesso sit LXXX tertia fuisse fratrem
eius Panaenum, qui clipeum intus pinxit Elide Minervae 20

1. **Maianis hortis**: *C. I. L.* vi,
6152, 8668, where they are mentioned
along with the *horti Lamiani*,
which as we learn from Phil. Jud.
περὶ ἀρετ. καὶ πρεσβ. 2, p. 597, ed.
Mangey (cf. Becker, *Röm. Top.* p. 542,
note 1142), were close to the gardens
of Maecenas on the Esquiline.

§ **52.** 2. **Anti**: iii, 57 ; it was the
birthplace of Nero (Suet. *Nero* 6).

4. **gladiatorum . . . imaginibus**:
numberless representations of gladiators have come down to us in
mosaics ; such as the mosaic from
Trêves (Baumeister, *Denkm.* pl. xci);
cf. the great mosaic with portraits of
athletes in the Lateran (Helbig,
Class. Ant. 704).

7. **C. Terentio Lucano**: possibly
identical, according to Mommsen,
with the *Terentius Lucanus* on the
coin *Röm. Münzw.* p. 554, 164 (and
note 278).

9. **in nemore Dianae**: i. e. the

grove of Nemi; cf. xvi, 242 and
Strabo, v, p. 239.

§ **53.** 10. **Nunc celebres . . . per-
curram** : cf. xxxiv, 53.

13. **claritatibus**: ⌐xxviii, 87 *in
ceteris claritates animalium aut
operum sequemur* = for the rest, I
shall note remarkable animals . . .
H. L. U.⌐

§ **54.** 14. **non constat sibi . . .
adiutor**: the supposed proofs of
Greek inaccuracy are skilfully cumu-
lated, (*a*) *non constat sibi* . . . (*b*) § 56
quid quod in confesso . . . (*b*) § 57
quod si recipi necesse est . . . , the
argument culminating in § 58 in the
words *chronicorum errore non dubio*,
after which the case of Polygnotos is
thrown in as a kind of postscript.
The complaint was, however, unjust
and originally based on a misunderstanding, see Introd. p. xxx.

17. **olympiade LXXXX**: below,
§ 60.

previously unheard of. When the picture was finished, it was struck by lightning in the gardens of Maius, and burned together with the greater part of the gardens. A freedman of this emperor **52** gave a gladiatorial show at Antium, at which the public colonnades were adorned by a picture of all the gladiators and attendants, *Portraits of* portrayed from the life. Realistic portraiture indeed has for *gladiators.* many generations been the highest ambition of art; Gaius Teren-tius Lucanus, however, was the first to have a picture of a gladia-torial show painted and to exhibit it in public. He showed thirty pairs of gladiators in the Forum for three days, in honour of his grandfather, who had adopted him: moreover he dedicated a picture of them in the grove of Diana.

I now propose to mention the most famous painters as briefly **53** as may be, for a detailed account would be inconsistent with the *History of* scheme of my work. It will therefore be enough if I give some *painters.* artists only a passing notice, or name them in connexion with others; though I must still make a separate mention of the most renowned paintings, whether they be still in existence or whether they have perished. On this point the Greeks have **54** made a mistake in placing the painters many years later than the *Erroneous chronology* bronze workers and metal chasers, and in giving the ninetieth *of the* Olympiad [420-417 B.C.] as the date of the earliest painter, over- *Greeks.* looking the tradition that *Pheidias* himself was originally a painter, *Pheidias.* and painted a shield at Athens. It is further acknowledged that *Panainos* brother of Pheidias, who lived in the eighty-third *Panainos.*

18. initio pictorem : cf. xxxiv, 60 *Pythagoras Samius initio pictor* and Introd. p. li.

clipeum: the shield introduced without any further definition has an apocryphal air (cf. Münzer, *op. cit.* p. 553, and Introd. *loc. cit.*). It cannot of course be that of the Athena Parthenos as Urlichs (*Chrest.* p. 346), Robert (*Arch. März.* p. 24), and Furt-wängler (*Masterpieces*, p. 45), would have it, for so important a fact would have been noted; besides, we have the express statement in xxxvi, 18 that the inner side of the shield of the Parthenos was carved in relief, H. L. Urlichs, *Woch. f. klass. Phil.* 1895, p. 548.

tradatur: H. L. Urlichs (*loc. cit.*) points out that the expression is

opposed to *in confesso sit,* i. e. hearsay to ascertained fact.

19. **LXXX** tertia : the date is loosely assumed for Panainos, as being that of his brother Pheidias, xxxiv, 49; Robert, *op. cit.* p. 25; Furtwängler, *op. cit.* p. 40 f.

20. Panaenum : Panainos is again mentioned below, in his proper order in the history of the development of painting, without any reference to this first notice, which is from a different source, cf. Introd. p. xxviii f. and p. li f. *Fratrem,* so also Paus. v, 11, 6: ἀδελφιδοῦς Strabo viii, p. 354.

intus pinxit: with the device of a cock (Paus. vi, 26, 3, where the Athena is simply attributed to Pheidias). Introd. p. liv, note 1.

Elide: from xxxvi, 177 (=App.

quam fecerat Colotes discipulus Phidiae et ei in faciendo
55 Iove Olympio adiutor. quid quod in confesso perinde est
Bularchi pictoris tabulam, in qua erat Magnetum proelium,
a Candaule rege Lydiae Heraclidarum novissimo, qui et
Myrsilus vocitatus est, repensam auro? tanta iam dignatio 5
picturae erat. circa Romuli id aetatem acciderit necesse
est, etenim duodevicensima olympiade interiit Candaules
A.U.C. 37. aut, ut quidam tradunt, eodem anno quo Romulus, nisi
fallor, manifesta iam tunc claritate artis, adeo absolutione.
56 quod si recipi necesse est, simul apparet multo vetustiora 10
principia eosque qui monochromatis pinxerint, quorum
aetas non traditur, aliquanto ante fuisse, Hygiaenontem,
Dinian, Charmadan et qui primus in pictura marem
a femina discreverit Eumarum Atheniensem figuras omnis
imitari ausum, quique inventa eius excoluerit Cimonem 15
Cleonaeum. hic catagrapha invenit, hoc est obliquas
imagines, et varie formare voltus, respicientes suspicientesve
vel despicientes. articulis membra distinxit, venas protulit,

VIII) it appears that Panainos also decorated with paintings the walls of the temple of Athena.

1. Colotes: xxxiv, 87. *Iove Olympio*: xxxiv, 54; xxxvi, 18.

§ 55. 3. **Magnetum proelium**: according to vii, 126, a defeat (*excidium*), but the precise event is unknown. S. Reinach (*Rev. des Ét. Grecques*, 1895, p. 175 ff.), justly comments on the strangeness of the tradition that a Greek painter immortalized a Greek defeat, and tries to prove the *excidium* to have crept into Pliny's account by confusion with the celebrated defeat—or rather extermination—of the Magnetes by the Treres in B. C. 651 (Strabo xiv, p. 647), which gave rise to the proverbial τὰ Μαγνητῶν κακά. R. wishes to refer the picture to some one of the Magnete victories alluded to by Strabo (*loc. cit.*) on the testimony of Kallinos (cf. also Wilamowitz in *Hermes*, xxx (1895), p. 177 ff.). But where so much is uncertain, we shall

hesitate before throwing overboard our only piece of positive information—the *excidium* of vii, 126 (= App. I).

6. **circa Romuli aetatem**: the synchronism is based on Herod. i, 12, who gives the death year of Kandaules = accession of Gyges = *floruit* of Archilochos, and must be connected with Cicero (*Tusc. Disp.* i, 13), who places Archilochos *regnante Romulo*; cf. Münzer, *op. cit.* p. 542; cf. Introd. p. lxxxiv.

§ 56. 11. **monochromatis**: above, §§ 15, 29.

14. **discreverit**: as in black-figured vases, by painting the flesh parts of the women white (Introd. p. xxix). Indeed a conventional difference between the colouring of the sexes seems to have been observed down to the latest time. Thus albeit Alexander was remarkable for his fair skin, Apelles in his portrait of the king οὐκ ἐμιμήσατο τὴν χρόαν, ἀλλὰ φαιότερον καὶ πεπινωμένον ἐποίησεν Plut. *Al.* iv, 120.

Eumarum: the name is still known

Olympiad [448–445 B.C.], painted at Elis the inner surface of the shield belonging to an Athena by Kolotes, a pupil of Pheidias and his assistant in executing the Olympian Zeus. Again, is it not an undisputed fact that a picture of the defeat of the Magnetes by the painter *Boularchos* was bought by Kandaules, also called *Boular-* Myrsilos, the last Lydian king of the line of the Heraklids, for its *chos.* weight in gold, a proof of the honour already paid to painting? This must have taken place in the days of Romulus, for Kandaules died in the eighteenth Olympiad [708–705 B.C.], or, according to some authorities, in the same year as Romulus, and already then, B.C. 717. unless I am mistaken, the art had attained to greatness, even to perfection. And if we must accept this, it follows that its first origin 56 is much older, and that the early painters in monochrome, whose *Painters* dates have not been handed down to us, lived some time before. *in mono-* *chrome.* Such, for example, were †*Hygiainon*, †*Deinias*, †*Charmadas*, †*Eumaros* of Athens, who was the first to mark the difference *Eumaros* between man and woman in painting, and who ventured to *of Athens.* imitate every sort of figure, and *Kimon* of Kleonai, who developed *Kimon of* the inventions of Eumaros. He devised κατάγραφα, or profile *Kleonai.* drawings, and represented the features in different postures, looking backwards or upwards or downwards. He marked the attachments of the limbs, gave prominence to the veins, and also

only from Pliny, for the reading Εὔμαρος on the basis from the Akropolis, bearing the signature of Antenor (*Jahrb.* ii, 1887, p. 135 f.) is quite uncertain (cf. Hartwig, *Meisterschalen*, p. 154). Further, the conjecture of Urlichs,*Eumari* (*Hölz. Pferd*, p. 14 n. 12), for the corrupt *Arimnae* in Varro, *Ling. Lat.* ix, 6, 12, is impossible; see Spengel's critical apparatus, p. 198.

figuras = 'position' by a slight extension of one meaning given to the word by Cicero, *Verres* II, i, 21, 57, *non solum numerum signorum, sed etiam uniuscuiusque magnitudinem, figuram, statum litteris definiri vides*, upon which see Pseudo-Asconius, p. 174, 7 (ed. Orelli) *figura est circa gestum situmque membrorum* (Blümner, *Rhein. Mus.* 26, p. 353).

15. Cimon: cf. the improvements attributed to him by Ailian, ποικ. ἱστ. viii, 8.

16. catagrapha: the word is susceptible of meaning 'foreshortening' (Holwerda, *Jahrb.* v, 1890, p. 258; Hartwig, *Meisterschalen*, p. 156 f., Lange, *Fremstilling*, pp. 429, 464), and this was possibly the meaning intended by the Greek author, for profile figures, which had existed from the earliest times, could on no theory, however conventional, be interpreted as audacious inventions. It is clear however that Pliny or his Latin author understood *catagrapha* as simply = profile, since this is the meaning he gives to the Greek equivalent *obliqua imago* in § 90, where see note.

17. [respicientes suspicientesve vel despicientes: sudden change from asyndeton to disjunctive particle, cf. xxviii, 63 *contra renum aut lumborum, vesicae cruciatus*, J. Müller, *Stil*, p. 69. H. L. U.]

18. membra . . . protulit: cf. on

57 praeterque in vestibus rugas et sinus invenit. Panaenus
quidem frater Phidiae etiam proelium Atheniensium ad-
A.U.C. 264. versus Persas apud Marathona factum pinxit. adeo iam
colorum usus increbruerat, adeoque ars perfecta erat ut in
eo proelio iconicos duces pinxisse tradatur, Atheniensium 5
Miltiaden, Callimachum, Cynaegirum, barbarorum Datim,
Artaphernen.

58   Quin immo certamen etiam picturae florente eo in-
A.U.C. 306. stitutum est Corinthi ac Delphis, primusque omnium certavit
cum Timagora Chalcidense, superatus ab eo Pythiis, quod 10
et ipsius Timagorae carmine vetusto apparet chronicorum
errore non dubio. alii quoque post hos clari fuere ante
LXXXX olympiadem, sicut Polygnotus Thasius qui primus
mulieres tralucida veste pinxit, capita earum mitris versicoloribus operuit plurimumque picturae primus contulit, 15
siquidem instituit os adaperire, dentes ostendere, voltum
59 ab antiquo rigore variare. huius est tabula in porticu
Pompei, quae ante curiam eius fuerat, in qua dubitatur an
ascendentem cum clupeo pinxerit an descendentem. hic

---

1. vestibus rugas] *Traube*; veste brugas *Bamb.*; verrugas *reliqui*; veste
rugas *Detlefsen*.

xxxiv, 59, the improvements attributed
to Pythagoras of Rhegion. Introd.
p. xxvii.

57. 3. apud Marathona: on a wall
of the στοὰ ποικίλη (§ 59). The picture
was ascribed by other writers to Mikon
(Arrian, *Anab.* vii, 13, 5; Ailian, περὶ
ζόων vii, 38; Sopatros, διαιρ. ζητημ. i,
8), and may have been the work of both
painters, Wachsmuth, *Stadt Athen* ii,
p. 503. Others again (see Ailian, *loc.
cit.*) gave it to Polygnotos. Pausanias
in his description of the paintings of
the Poikile, i, 15, names no artists.
For the latest reconstruction of the
picture see Robert, *Hall. Winckelmannspr.* xviii, 1895. Addenda.

5. iconicos duces: the year of
the battle being B.C. 490, and the
Stoa dating presumably from Kimon's
recall in B.C. 457 (Furtwängler,
Masterpieces, p. 41), there can be no
question of real portraiture; but the

tradition of the names attaching to
each figure would be carefully preserved; perhaps too there was an
attempt at characterization, so that
in a history of the development of
painting Panainos might pass as the
first to have essayed portraiture (Introd. p. xxviii f.).

6. Miltiaden: his name was not
inscribed, but he was characterized
by his gesture of exhortation, Aischines *c. Ktesiph.* 186, &c., see Wachsmuth's fine criticism of the passage,
op. cit. p. 506, note 2. For the
motive see the warrior on the gold
sheath in the Hermitage, Benndorf,
Gjölbaschi p. 157 fig. 143 = *Compte
Rendu* 1864, pl. v, 1.

Callimachum, Cynaegirum: Ail.
loc. cit. τοὺς ἀμφὶ τὸν Κυνέγειρον
καὶ 'Επίζηλόν τε καὶ Καλλίμαχον,
cf. Wachsmuth, *op. cit.* p. 510 f. The
omission of Epizelos in Pliny is

discovered the wrinkles and the windings of drapery. Further- 57
more *Panainos* the brother of Pheidias painted the battle between *Panainos. Picture of*
the Athenians and Persians at Marathon. So extensively were *battle of*
colours now used, so perfect had technique now become, that he *Marathon.*
is actually said to have given the real portraits of the commander
on both sides, of Miltiades, Kallimachos and Kynaigeiros among
the Athenians, of Datis and Artaphernes among the barbarians.

Nay more, competitions for painters were instituted at Corinth 58
and Delphoi in the time of Panainos, when in the first contest he *Painting competi-*
tried for the prize against *Timagoras* of Chalkis, who conquered *tions.*
him, as we know from an old epigram by Timagoras himself, at 448 B.C. *Timagoras*
the Pythian games; an evident proof that the chroniclers are *of Chalkis.*
wrong in their dates. Yet other painters became famous before
the ninetieth Olympiad [420–417 B.C.], as for example *Polygnotos* *Polygnotos*
of Thasos, who first painted women with transparent garments *of Thasos.*
and gave them headdresses of various colours. This artist made
a first serious contribution to the development of painting by
opening the mouth, showing the teeth, and varying the stiff
archaic set of the features. He painted the picture now in the 59
gallery of Pompeius and formerly in front of his Council Chamber, *His 'warrior.'*
representing a warrior armed with a shield, about whom people
argue as to whether he is ascending or descending. He also

curious. The heroes are mentioned
as an indivisible triad by Plutarch,
Glor. Ath. 3, Diogenes Laert. i, 56.

§ 58. 9. Corinthi ac Delphis: i.e.
at the Isthmian and Pythian festivals
(*Pythiis* below); for contests between painters cf. §§ 65, 72 and
Introd. p. lxiv.

13. Polygnotus: son of the first
Aglaophon, and brother of Aristophon
(§§ 60, 138).

qui primus: introduces as usual,
the artist's special contribution to the
progress of his art, Introd. p. xxviii f.

14. tralucida veste: Ailian, ποικ.
ἱστ. iv, 3 ἱματίων λεπτότητας; Lucian,
εἰκόνες 7 ἐς τὸ λεπτότατον ἐξειργασ-
μένην (of the drapery of Kassandra in
the Nekuia).

§ 59. 17. porticu Pompei: in
the immediate vicinity of Pompeius's
theatre.

18. curiam: Gilbert, *Rom.* iii,
p. 325; numerous works of art
were collected by Pompeius in the
complex of buildings about his
Theatre.

in qua dubitatur: the warrior
(perhaps Kapaneus, cf. Benndorf, *op.
cit.* p. 190; pl. xxiv, A. 4: *Anth. Plan.*
iv, 106) was presumably on a ladder,
and it was difficult to tell whether he
was climbing up or coming down again.
Robert, *Hall. Winckelmannsprogr.*
xviii, 1895, p. 67, suggests that
the *tabula* was the votive picture of
an *apobates*, of whom it was uncertain
whether he was stepping up to, or
down from, his chariot; for the subject
see the beautiful monochrome picture
on white marble slab (Naples, Helbig,
Wandgemälde 1405[b]), published by
Robert, *Hall. Winckelmannsprogr.*
xix, 1895.

Delphis aedem pinxit, hic et Athenis porticum quae Poecile
vocatur gratuito, cum partem eius Micon mercede pingeret.
vel maior huic auctoritas, siquidem Amphictyones, quod
est publicum Graeciae concilium, hospitia ei gratuita de-
crevere. fuit et alius Micon qui minoris cognomine distin- 5
guitur, cuius filia Timarete et ipsa pinxit.

60   LXXXX autem olympiade fuere Aglaophon, Cephisodorus, Erillus, Evenor pater Parrhasi et praeceptor maximi
pictoris de quo suis annis dicemus, omnes iam inlustres, non
tamen in quibus haerere expositio debeat festinans ad lumina 10
artis in quibus primus refulsit Apollodorus Atheniensis
LXXXXIII olympiade. hic primus species exprimere
instituit primusque gloriam penicillo iure contulit. eius est
sacerdos adorans et Aiax fulmine incensus, quae Pergami

---

1. **Delphis aedem :** i.e. the
Λέσχη or covered portico where
people met to converse. The pictures,
which included an Ilionpersis and a
Neknia are described in Paus. x, 25–
31. For modern reconstructions see
Robert, *Hall. Winckelmannspr.* xvi,
1892 and xvii, 1893.

Poecile : where next to Mikon's
Amazonomachia (below) Polygnotos
painted an *Ilioupersis.* Next to
this again came the *Marathon* by
Mikon and Panainos (above). For
the distribution of the pictures see
Benndorf, *op. cit.* p. 156, and the new
arrangement proposed by Robert in
Hall. Winckelmannspr. xviii, 1895,
p. 44. The pictures, as appears
from Synnesios, *Ep.* 135 (= Overb.
Schriftquell. 1057), were not mural
paintings in the ordinary sense, but
were painted on wooden boards or
panels ; cf. Wachsmuth, *Stadt Athen,*
ii, p. 504.

2. **gratuito :** cf. Melanthios (cf.
Wilamowitz, *Arist. u. Athen.* p. 287,
n. 37) *ap.* Plutarch, *Kimon,* iv, p. 431 :
αὐτοῦ γὰρ δαπάναισι θεῶν ναοὺς
    ἀγοράν τε
Κεκροπίαν κόσμησ' ἡμιθέων
    ἀρεταῖς.

(The ναοί here referred to are those of
Thesens and the *Anakes,* Harpokration *s. v.* Πολύγνωτος.)

partem eius Micon : he painted
the battle of Theseus and the Amazons, Paus. i, 15, 2 ; Arrian vii, 13, 5,
where few will agree with Graef (*ap.*
Pauly *s. v.* AMAZONEN p. 1778) in
defending the old reading Κίμων ; cf.
Robert, *loc. cit.* p. 47, note 2. Mikon
was also a sculptor, xxxiv, 88, where
see note.

3. **Amphictyones :** the reward
they gave was more probably for the
decoration of the Λέσχη ; while for
his work at Athens he received the
Attic citizenship, Harpokration, *l. c.*

6. Timarete : below, § 147.

§ 60. 7. **LXXXX autem Olymp. :**
as in the case of the sculptors (xxxiv,
49), the first painter in each Olympiad is dated from a work brought
into connexion with an important
historical event ; about this central
date his contemporaries, whether
older or younger, are roughly grouped,
cf. Robert, *Arch. März.* p. 66 f.

Aglaophon : son of Aristophon
(below, § 138), and accordingly nephew
of Polygnotos (Plato, *Gorg.* p. 448 B)
and grandson of the first Aglaophon.

decorated the temple at Delphoi and at Athens the Painted Portico *He paints* [στοὰ ποικίλη], as it is called.   For this he took no money, while *the Lesche at Delphoi,* *Mikon,* to whom part of the work was entrusted, accepted pay- *and at* ment.   The position he thus won for himself was all the greater, *Athens the Stoa* so much so that the Amphyktionic council, or national assembly *Poikile.* of Hellas, decreed that he should be a public guest.   There was *Mikon.* another *Mikon,* distinguished as ' the younger,' whose daughter *Younger.* *Timarete* was also an artist.

In the ninetieth Olympiad [420–417 B.C.] lived *Aglaophon,* 60 † *Kephisodoros,* † *Erillos* and *Evenor,* the father and master of *Great masters* the great artist Parrhasios, whom I shall mention in due time. *of the* They were all painters of note, yet they need not prevent my *ninetieth Olympiad.* hastening on to the true luminaries of art, among whom the first to shine was *Apollodoros* of Athens in the ninety-third *Apollo-* Olympiad [408–405 B.C.].   He was the first to give his figures *doros of Athens.* the appearance of reality, and he first bestowed true glory on the brush.   He painted a priest in prayer, and an Aias struck *His works* by lightning, which is still to be seen at Pergamon.   No picture *1. Priest,* *2. Aias.*

His date (Robert, *loc. cit.*) seems determined by his picture of Olympias and Pythias crowning Alkibiades (Satyros *ap.* Athen. xii, p. 534 D), painted to commemorate the chariot victories of Ol. 90 (Grote, *Greece,* v, p. 456 f.) or Ol. 91 (Rutgers) ; see G. H. Förster, *Die Olympischen Sieger,* i, p. 20 f.   The companion picture of Alkibiades in the lap of Nemea was by Aristophon, Plut. *Alkib.* xvi, Paus. i, 22, 6 (artist unnamed).   Satyros, *loc. cit.*, attributes it however to the son.

8. Evenor, pater Parrhasi : Paus. i, 28, 2.   *suis annis* below, § 67.

11. Apollodorus : Overb. *Schriftquell.* 1641-1646.

12. primus species ... primusque gloriam : belongs to the series of Xenokratic art judgements begun in §§ 15–16 ; 56–58 : cf. Introd. p. xxix.

species : evidently the vague translation of some Greek technical term ; cf. Jahn, *Kunsturtheile,* p. 138. The discovery attributed to Apollodoros by Plutarch (*Glor. Ath.* ii) was

the φθορὰ καὶ ἀπόχρωσις σκιᾶς—(an advance also attributed to Zeuxis, Quinct. xii, 10, 4 *prior luminum umbrarumque invenit rationem*) i. e. he showed how to render—not the shadow cast, but the graduated passage from light to shadow on curved surfaces (Lange, *Fremstilling,* p. 465 ; cf. above, *tonon* and *harmogen* in § 29).   In this connexion may be noted the attempt at expressing by shadow the curving of surfaces, on two interesting polychrome lekythoi of the Berlin Museum (*Cat.* 2684, 2685—the latter published in facsimile by Winter, *Winckelmannsprogr.* 1895, cf. *id.* p. 9).

14. sacerdos adorans : votive portrait ; cf. the *sacerdos adstante puero* of Parrhasios (§ 70) the *supplicans paene cum voce* of Aristeides (§ 99).

Aiax fulmine incensus : Verg. *Aen.* i, 43 ff. *ipsa* (sc. *Minerva*) *Iovis rapidum iaculata e nubibus ignem* | *disiecitque rates, evertitque aequora ventis* | *illum expirantem*

spectatur hodie. neque ante eum tabula ullius ostenditur
61 quae teneat oculos. ab hoc artis fores apertas Zeuxis
Heracleotes intravit olympiadis LXXXXV anno quarto,
audentemque iam aliquid penicillum—de hoc enim adhuc
loquamur—ad magnam gloriam perduxit, a quibusdam falso
in LXXXVIIII olympiade positus. confuisse necesse est
Demophilum Himeraeum et Nesea Thasium, quoniam
62 utrius eorum discipulus fuerit ambigitur. in eum Apollodorus supra scriptus versum fecit, artem ipsis ablatam
Zeuxim ferre secum. opes quoque tantas adquisivit ut in
ostentationem earum Olympiae aureis litteris in palliorum
tesseris intextum nomen suum ostentaret. postea donare

6. positus. confuisse] *Traube*; positus cum fuisse (fuisset *omnes praeter
Bamb.*) *codd.*; positus, cum quo fuisse *Ritschl, Detlefsen.*

*transfixo pectore flammas | turbine
corripuit scopuloque infixit acuto;* cf.
Odyss. iv, 499 ff. [The *fulmine incensus* of the subject not (as Furtwängler, *Plinius*, p. 53 suggests) of
the picture, in which case Pliny would
use *tabula*, cf. below, § 69.—H. L. U.]
    Pergami : Introd. p. xc.
    § 61. 2. fores apertas : [ii, 31
*rerum fores aperuisse Anaximander
. . . traditur*; the metaphor is common
to Silver Latin, cf. Pliu. *Epist.* i, 18, 4
*illa (actio) ianuam famae (mihi)
patefecit*. Because a similar expression
occurs, Babrios, Proem. 1. 29, there is
no need to follow Schneidewin, *Rhein.
Mus.* vii (1850), p. 479, in thinking
that Pliny's words go back to a Greek
metrical epigram, cf. also Müller,
Stil, p. 126 ff. H. L. U.] At the
same time, the words exactly express
the position which the Greek writers
(Introd. p. xxix) assigned to Apollodoros at the opening of a series of
painters who, masters of their art,
each brought towards the final perfection to be attained by Apelles (§ 79)
a definite contribution : Apollodoros
among the painters is the counterpart
of Pheidias among the statuaries,
Robert, *Arch. März.* p. 67 f. (Introd.

p. xxvii). Therefore the words must
represent some closely similar Greek
expression ; for an analogous paraphrase cf. Add. to note on xxxiv, 81.
    3. Heracleotes : Plato, *Protag.*
318 B ὁ νεανίσκος ὁ νῦν νεωστὶ ἐπιδημῶν
Ζεύξιππος ὁ Ἡρακλεώτης (on the identity
of Zeuxis and Zeuxippos see Fick,
Griech. Personennamen, pp. 35, 132).
The dialogue being imagined as taking
place in B. C. 424, it is impossible to
reconcile this mention of Zeuxis with
the tradition that he was born at
Herakleia (founded B.C. 432), except
by either holding Plato guilty of an
anachronism (and likewise Xenophon,
who alludes to Z. in the 'Banquet,'
of which the scene is laid in B. C. 422),
or supposing with Robert (*Hall.
Winckelmannsprogr.* xix, 1895, p. 18),
that the parents of Zeuxis removed as
colonists to Herakleia when he was
already a boy of nine or ten. The artist
was evidently at home in Lower Italy
(he paints for Agrigentum, Kroton,
&c.) ; it is out of the question to
assume that he was born at the older
Pontic Herakleia. Addenda.
    Ol. 95, anno quarto : the occa-
sion for the date assigned to him here
is unknown. Since the 'Alkmena,'

by any of his predecessors really rivets the gaze. It was he who 61
opened the gates of art through which *Zeuxis* of Herakleia *Zeuxis of*
passed in the fourth year of the ninety-fifth Olympiad [397 B.C.], *Herakleia,*
giving to the painter's brush (for of the brush alone I speak as
yet) the full glory to which it already aspired. Zeuxis is erroneously placed by some in the eighty-ninth Olympiad [424–
421 B.C.]; it is evident that † *Demophilos* of Himera and † *Neseus* *taught by*
of Thasos were among his contemporaries, seeing that there is a *Demophilos or Neseus.*
controversy as to which of the two was his master. In an epigram 62
written against him by the Apollodoros whom I mentioned above,
it is said that 'Zeuxis bore away with him the art he had stolen
from his masters.' He amassed great wealth, and in order to *His wealth,*
make a parade of it at Olympia he showed his name woven in *luxury, and pride.*
golden letters into the embroideries of his garments. Later on

which belongs to his later period (see below Urlichs' note on *postea*), was yet painted previous to B.C. 406, in which year Agrigentum was destroyed by the Carthaginians, Zeuxis must have been an artist of note long before B.C. 398; cf. also the passage from Plato quoted above. On the other hand the ascription to Z. of the Ἔρως ... ὁ γεγραμμένος ἔχων στέφανον ἀνθέμων, Ar. *Acharn.* 991 (play produced B.C. 425), rests only on the doubtful authority of the scholia.

4. adhuc: i. e. in opposition to encaustic painting in § 149.

5. falso: Quinct. xii, 10, 4, dates Zeuxis, and Parrhasios *circa Peloponnesia ambo tempora*, from the fact that Xenophon (*Memorab.* iii, 10, 1) records a conversation between Parrhasios and Sokrates. The earlier date was the correct one.

7. Demophilum: distinct from the Damophilos (below, § 154, where see note) who decorated the temple of Ceres.

Himeraeum: Ἱμέρα on the N. coast of Sicily.

Thasium: the ethnic suggests that Neseus belonged to the circle of Polygnotos (§ 58) of Thasos. Robert, *loc. cit.*, points out that the young

Zeuxis very possibly placed himself under this master, on his arrival in Athens.

§ 62. 9. ipsis: sc. *Demophilo et Nesea* (Traube). Benndorf, *Epigr.* p. 30, and Jahn, *Kleine Beiträge*, p. 284, explain it as *sibi sociisque*, which is impossible.

10. in ostentationem: the story of the gorgeous robes worn by Zeuxis has its counterpart in the gorgeous robes of his rival Parrhasios (Athen. xii, 543 C—D), Introd. p. lvii.

12. tesseris intextum: the best explanation seems that of Urlichs, *Chrest.* p. 345; he takes the *tesserae* to have been small squares (of stuff) upon which the name was embroidered, and quotes Vopiscus, *Carinus* 20 *inscriptum est adhuc in choraulae pallio Tyrianthino Messalae nomen uxoris* (ed. H. Peter); see in Casaubon's edition, vol. ii, p. 851 ᵃ, Saumaise's note, who in reference to the Plinian passage explains *tesserae* = κύβοι, and quotes Hesychius (*s. v.* κύβος) οἱ Σαλαμίνιοι λέγουσι κύβον τὸ τοῦ ἱματίου σημεῖον.

postea: [i. e. in his latter period; the Alkmena and the Pan must therefore be reckoned among the artist's later works.—H. L. U.]

opera sua instituit, quod nullo pretio satis digno permutari
posse diceret, sicuti Alcmenam Agragentinis, Pana Archelao.
63 fecit et Penelopen in qua pinxisse mores videtur, et athletam,
adeoque in illo sibi placuit ut versum subscriberet celebrem
ex eo, invisurum aliquem facilius quam imitaturum. magni- 5
ficus est et Iuppiter eius in throno adstantibus diis et
Hercules infans dracones strangulans Alcmena matre coram
64 pavente et Amphitryone. reprehenditur tamen ceu grandior
in capitibus articulisque, alioqui tantus diligentia ut Agragentinis facturus tabulam quam in templo Iunonis Laciniae 10
publice dicarent inspexerit virgines eorum nudas et quinque
elegerit, ut quod in quaque laudatissimum esset pictura
redderet. pinxit et monochromata ex albo. aequales eius
et aemuli fuere Timanthes, Androcydes, Eupompus, Parrha-
65 sius. descendisse hic in certamen cum Zeuxide traditur, et 15
cum ille detulisset uvas pictas tanto successu ut in scaenam

2. **Alcmenam**: probably identical with the picture in § 63.

Archelao: for whom Zeuxis decorated the palace at Pella, Ailian
ποικ. ἱστ. xiv, 17.

3. **mores**: in the sense given to it
by Horace, *Ep.* i, 1, 57 *est animus
tibi, sunt mores.* Some commentators
however (chief among them Winckelmann), have understood *mores* to be
a translation of the Greek ἦθος, whereby endless difficulties have arisen,
seeing that ἦθος was precisely the
quality in which, according to Aristotle,
Poet. 6, 11, Zeuxis was deficient. But
ἦθος in its strictly philosophical sense
had no precise Latin equivalent, as
we learn from Quinct. vi, 2, 8, and
from Pliny himself (below, § 98,
where see note) ; cf. Brunn, *K. G.*
ii, p. 86 f.; Jahn, *Kunsturtheile*,
p. 105 f.

5. **invisurum**: μωμήσεταί τις
μᾶλλον ἢ μιμήσεται ; the proverb is
attributed by Plutarch (*Glor. Ath.* 2),
and Hesychios to Apollodoros. The
saying recurs from early times in a
variety of forms ; Bergk, *Lyr. Graec.*
ii, p. 318, Benndorf, *Epigr.* p. 27, n. 3 ;

cf. Preger, *Inscript. Gr. Metr.* 193.
Introd. p. lvii.

6. **Iuppiter . . . Amphitryone** :
the whole subject is preserved on a
vase-painting in the Brit. Mus.; A. S.
Murray, *Class. Rev.* 1888, p. 327 ; id.
Handb. of Greek Arch. p. 376. Add.

§ 64. 8. **reprehenditur tamen**: the
tamen presupposes a sentence of praise,
which has fallen out. Quinctilian (xii,
10, 5) says of Zeuxis *plus membris
corporis dedit . . .* but praises him on
the same grounds that Pliny blames
him, another instance of conflicting
criticisms in antiquity ; cf. note on
Kallimachos in xxxiv, 92.

9. **articulisque**: literally the
joints (knuckles, wrists, ankles, &c.)
and so by extension the extremities ;
see Robert, *Arch. März.* p. 76, *Hall.
Winckelmannsprogr.* xix, 1895, p. 25.
An almost identical criticism is passed
upon Euphranor in § 128. Zeuxis is
represented in the same relation to
Apollodoros as Polykleitos xxxiv, 56
to Pheidias (*ib.* 54). On the Xenokratic authorship see Introd. p. xxvii.

Agragentinis: from Cic. (*Invent.*
ii, 1, 1) it appears that this picture

he began to make presents of his pictures, saying that they were beyond all price. In this way he gave his Alkmena to the city of *His gifts* Agrigentum and his Pan to Archelaos. He also painted a Pene- *of the 'Alkmena,'* lope, in whom he embodied virtue's self, and an athlete with whom *and the* he was so well pleased that he wrote beneath it the line thence- *'Pan.'* forward famous : 'Another may carp more easily than he may copy.' **63** He also painted a superb Zeus enthroned amid the assembled gods, with the infant Herakles strangling the snakes in presence of his trembling mother Alkmena and of Amphitryon. Zeuxis is criti- **64** cized however as having exaggerated the heads and extremities of *For the temple* his figures ; for the rest he bestowed such minute pains upon his *of Hera* work that before painting for the people of Agrigentum a picture *Lakinia he paints* to be dedicated in the temple of Hera on the Lakinian pro- *a picture* montory, he inspected the maidens of the city naked, and chose *taken from the five* out five, whose peculiar beauties he proposed to reproduce in his *most* picture. He also painted monochromes in white. *Timanthes,* *beauteous maidens* *Androkydes,* †*Eupompos* and *Parrhasios* were contemporaries *of the city.* and rivals of Zeuxis. The story runs that Parrhasios and Zeuxis **65**

His con-

is identical with the famous Helena (below, § 66).

   10. Iunonis Laciniae : Cicero, *loc. cit.*, says the Helena was painted for the Krotoniates ; so too Dionysios H. (*de veter. script. cens.* 1), and this is doubtless correct, for as Freeman remarks (*Sicily*, vol. ii, p. 402, note 3) 'the Lakinian Hera, at home at Kroton, would have no place at Akragas ' (cf. Roscher, i, p. 2086).

   11. inspexerit virgines : Lange (*Fremstilling*, p. 354 n.) points out that the anecdote gives concrete expression to the saying that the best parts must be taken ' out of divers Faces, to make one Excellent,' cf. Xenoph. *Mem.* iii, 10, 2 ; Cicero and Dionysios (*ll. cc.*) incorporate the axiom with the anecdote which illustrates it. See Introd. p. lxi f.

   13. ex albo : i. e. on a dark ground, perhaps in imitation of marble reliefs (cf. Blümner, *Technol.* iv, p. 420, note 4), whereas monochrome paintings were usually carried out in red (*cinnabar, minium, rubrica, sinopis*, Plin. xxxiii, 117), presumably on a white ground. Of the latter technique we *tempora-* have imitations in the pictures painted *ries.* in red colour on the white marble slabs in Naples. Semper's theory (*Stil*, i, p. 470, ed. 1) that these had once been polychrome pictures in encaustic, whose colours were destroyed by the heat of the lava, has been disproved by Helbig, *Wandgemälde,* 170ᵇ; cf. Robert, *Hall. Winckelmannsprogr.* xix, 1895, p. 9 ; on the contrary, the slabs admirably prove the practice of painting in monochrome.

   14. Timanthes : below, § 73.

   Androcydes : of Kyzikos ; according to Plutarch (*Pel.* xxv) he painted at the time of the liberation of the Kadmeia (B.C. 379) the picture of a battle in which both Epameinondas and Pelopidas had been engaged ; i. e. probably the battle mentioned *Pel.* iv (Brunn, *K. G.* ii, p. 124). From Athen. viii, p. 341 A, we learn that he was celebrated for his accurate painting of fish.

   Eupompus : below, § 75.

   § 65. 16. uvas pictas : cf. below, §§ 66, 155 ; above, § 23.

   ut in scaenam : i. e. the pictures

aves advolarent, ipse detulisse linteum pictum ita veritate
repraesentata ut Zeuxis alitum iudicio tumens flagitaret
tandem remoto linteo ostendi picturam atque intellecto
errore concederet palmam ingenuo pudore, quoniam ipse
66 volucres fefellisset, Parrhasius autem se artificem.   fertur et 5
postea Zeuxis pinxisse puerum uvas ferentem, ad quas cum
advolassent aves, eadem ingenuitate processit iratus operi
et dixit : uvas melius pinxi quam puerum, nam si et hoc
consummassem, aves timere debuerant.   fecit et figlina opera,
quae sola in Ambracia relicta sunt, cum inde Musas Fulvius 10
Nobilior Romam transferret.   Zeuxidis manu Romae Helena
est in Philippi porticibus, et in Concordiae delubro Marsyas
67 religatus.   Parrhasius Ephesi natus et ipse multa contulit.
primus symmetrian picturae dedit, primus argutias voltus,
elegantiam capilli, venustatem oris, confessione artificum in 15
lineis extremis palmam adeptus.   haec est picturae summa

were exhibited in the theatre, and
hung on the *scaenae frons*, or front
wall of the stage-buildings.

§ 66. 7. pinxissé puerum: a
mere *doublette* of the preceding anecdote; the story is also told Senec.
Rhet. *Controv.* x, 5 (34), 27.

9. figlina opera: Pyrrhus had
probably inherited these works as king
of Macedonia. Zeuxis, it will be remembered, had worked for King
Archelaos, above, § 62.

10. sola . . . relicta sunt: donbt-
less because these painted terra-cottas
were architectural decorations, and
could not be removed without injury
to the buildings; Liv. xxxviii, 9, 13
*signa aenea marmoreaque et tabulae
pictae, quibus ornatior Ambracia quia
regia ibi Pyrrhi fuerat . . . sublata
omnia avectaque ; nihil praeterea tactum violatumve*, cf. Raoul-Rochette,
Peintures, p. 51.

Ambracia: the capital of King
Pyrrhus: for its art treasures cf.
Polyb. xxii, 13, 9; Liv. *loc. cit.*

Musas : these statues, which probably dated from the reign of Pyrrhus,

were dedicated by Fulvius in the
Temple of *Hercules Musarum*, with
a statne of Herakles as Μουσα-
γέτης (see in this connexion Eumenius
of Autun *pro restaurandis scholis*,
vii, in *Paneg. Lat.* ed. Baehrens,
p. 121; cf. also Ovid, *Fasti*, vi,
804). The Muses are figured on
the reverse of the coins of Q. Pom-
ponius Musa (reproduced and fully
discussed by O. Bie, *Die Musen in d.
antiken Kunst*, pp. 24–44). The
tragic Muse is preserved in a statuette
of the Vatican (Clarac, 507, 1013),
while a head from Frascati in the Brit.
Mus.(Friederichs-Wolters,1445)seems
to reproduce the head of another;
cf. Amelung, *Basis des Praxiteles*,
p. 44. For the one extant basis,
see *Bull. d. Inst.* 1869, p. 3 ff.—The
temple was surrounded by the *porticus
Philippi*, and was close to the *porticus Octaviae* on the W. side of the
Circus Flaminius.

11. Helena : the mention of the
Muses which Fulvius brought to
Rome, suggests to Pliny two more
works by Zeuxis, noted by him as

entered into competition, Zeuxis exhibiting a picture of some *Competi-* grapes, so true to nature that the birds flew up to the wall of the *tion be-tween* stage. Parrhasios then displayed a picture of a linen curtain, *Zeuxis and* realistic to such a degree that Zeuxis, elated by the verdict of the *Parrha-sios.* birds, cried out that now at last his rival must draw the curtain *The cur-* and show his picture. On discovering his mistake he surrendered *tain and the grapes.* the prize to Parrhasios, admitting candidly that he had deceived the birds, while Parrhasios had deluded himself, a painter. After 66 this we learn that Zeuxis painted a boy carrying grapes, and when *Boy with* the birds flew down to settle on them, he was vexed with his own *grapes.* work, and came forward saying, with like frankness, 'I have painted the grapes better than the boy, for had I been perfectly successful with the latter, the birds must have been afraid.' He also modelled certain terra-cottas which were the only works of art left in Ambrakia when Fulvius Nobilior brought the statues of the Muses to Rome. The paintings in Rome by the hand of Zeuxis *Helen.* are: the Helen in the gallery of Philip and the bound Marsyas *Marsyas bound.* in the temple of Concord. *Parrhasios*, a native of Ephesos, also 67 made great contributions to the progress of art. He first gave *Parrha-sios.* painting symmetry, and added vivacity to the features, daintiness to the hair and comeliness to the mouth, while by the verdict of artists he is unrivalled in the rendering of outline. This is the

being also in Rome. In making this addition he forgets that he had already mentioned the Helena, when quoting from his main authority. His oversight is, however, the easier to explain as in the previous passage the name of the picture had not been given.

12. **Philippi porticibus**: built by L. Marcius Philippus, the step-father of Augustus, round the *T. Hercules Musarum* (above); Suet. *Aug.* 29; Ovid, *Fasti*, vi, 801 ; cf. Gilbert, *Rom.* iii, p. 248.

Concordiae delubro: note on xxxvi, 73.

Marsyas religatus: the representations of Marsyas bound are all cited by Jessen *ap.* Roscher, ii, 2450 ff. None, however, can be traced back with any certainty to Zeuxis's picture. A reminiscence of the whole composition perchance survives in the

relief of a marble vase at Naples, *A. Z.* 1869, taf. 18.

§ 67. 13. **Ephesi natus**: Strabo xiv, p. 642 ; *Anth. App.* lix, 2.

14. **primus symmetrian pict. dedit**: his achievement as a painter marks a similar advance upon that of Zeuxis (§ 64) to Myron's (xxxiv, 57) upon that of Polykleitos among the statuaries, Introd. p. xxvii.

argutias: note on xxxiv, 65.

15. **confessione artificum**: refers to the artists and art-historians Antigonos and Xenokrates (below, § 68); cf. *artifices qui condidere haec* in xxxiv, 68, where the same two writers are meant, Introd. p. xxxvii.

in lineis: cf. Quinct. xii, 10, 4 *examinasse (Parrh.) subtilius lineas traditur.*

16. **haec est picturae ... occultat**: the passage is of unique aesthetic interest (Introd. p. xxxiv), it expresses

suptilitas. corpora enim pingere et media rerum est quidem
magni operis sed in quo multi gloriam tulerint, extrema corporum facere et desinentis picturae modum includere rarum
68 in successu artis invenitur. ambire enim se ipsa debet extremitas et sic desinere ut promittat alia post se ostendatque 5
etiam quae occultat. hanc ei gloriam concessere Antigonus
et Xenocrates qui de pictura scripsere, praedicantes quoque,
non solum confitentes. et alia multa graphidis vestigia
exstant in tabulis ac membranis eius, ex quibus proficere
dicuntur artifices. minor tamen videtur sibi comparatus in 10
69 mediis corporibus exprimendis. pinxit demon Atheniensium
argumento quoque ingenioso. ostendebat namque varium,
iracundum iniustum inconstantem, eundem exorabilem
clementem misericordem, gloriosum, excelsum humilem,
ferocem fugacemque et omnia pariter. idem pinxit et 15
Thesea, quae Romae in Capitolio fuit, et navarchum thoracatum, et in una tabula, quae est Rhodi, Meleagrum, Herculem, Persea, haec ibi ter fulmine ambusta neque obliterata
70 hoc ipso miraculum auget. pinxit et archigallum, quam

5. alia sponse (sponte *e correctione*) *Bamb.* (*scriptum erat* alias pos se; *an*
alias post se? *Traube*).

the dominant effort of painting to
represent objects not only as relieved
from the flat, but *as occupying space.*
It is suggestively discussed by Bertrand, *Études*, p. 65 ff.

1. media rerum : i. e. the modelling of the particular face chosen for
presentation, as it lies between its
bounding lines, without any necessary
suggestion of the parts which are
concealed from view.

2. extrema . . . modum includere : the subtle meaning conveyed
by these words is more easily felt
than translated. The idea is that the
supreme difficulty and consequently
the supreme achievement of painting
consists in bringing the painted outline (*modus desinentis picturae*) into
agreement with the contour of the
figure.

4. ambire . . . extremitas : Ber-

trand (*loc. cit.*) translates ' il faut en
effet que les *contours s'enveloppent
eux-mêmes.*' In other words, the contours must be so drawn *as to appear
to clasp what is behind them.*

§ 68. 5. ut promittat alia post
se : the meaning is so clear, the
aesthetic lesson so true, that I have
decided on keeping Detlefsen's reading, but not without hesitation, for the
MSS. are in favour of *alias* (sc. *extremitates*) *post se*—a reading recommended
by Dr. Traube. The meaning of
this alternative reading would be: in
any object, the face which the artist
chooses for presentation forms, where
it leaves off, a line against the background. But another view of the
same object would have afforded a
different system of bounding lines, of
extremitates, and as any object may
be viewed from an endless number

highest subtlety attainable in painting. Merely to paint a figure in relief is no doubt a great achievement, yet many have succeeded thus far. But where an artist is rarely successful is in finding an outline which shall express the contours of the figure. For the 68 contour should appear to fold back, and so enclose the object as to give assurance of the parts behind, thus clearly suggesting even what it conceals. Preeminence in this respect is conceded to Parrhasios by Antigonos and Xenokrates, writers on *Judgement* painting, who indeed not only concede but insist upon it. Many *of Antigonos and* other traces of his draughtmanship remain, both in pictures and *Xeno-* on parchments, which are said to be instructive to artists. Still, *krates.* if tried by his own standard, he fails in modelling. He painted 69 an ingenious personification of the Athenian 'Demos,' discovering *His works.* it as fickle, passionate, unjust, changeable, yet exorable, compassionate and pitiful, boastful, proud and humble, bold and cowardly, in a word, everything at once. He also painted the Theseus formerly in the Capitol at Rome, an admiral in armour, and Meleager, Herakles and Perseus in a picture at Rhodes, where it has thrice been set on fire by lightning without being destroyed, a miracle which increases our wonder.

of points, there is no limit to its bounding lines. It therefore becomes the business of the great artist, to give assurance, although working on the flat, of these hidden lines. This notion of fugitive, pursuant outlines, though somewhat rhetorical and over-subtilized, would also convey its peculiar truth.

9. tabulis : either small tablets, containing the artist's sketches for his large pictures, or, if in the usual sense of easel pictures, we must understand these *tabulae* to have been left unfinished, with the design merely sketched in.

§ 69. 11. demon Atheniensium : cf. the same subject by Euphranor, Paus. i, 3, 3 ; below note on § 129.

16. Thesea : the picture was originally in Athens (Plut. *Thes.* iv), whence it may have been brought by Sulla.

fuit : i.e. it was destroyed by the fire of B.C. 70 ; cf. xxxiii, 154; xxxiv, 38.

17. quae est Rhodi : Mucianus is therefore presumably the authority here followed by Pliny, Introd. p. lxxxvi f.

Meleagrum, Herculem, Persea ; grouped in a 'Santa conversazione,' such as were becoming popular in the period of Parrhasios ; they had little mythological significance, save as presenting, pleasantly grouped together, two or more of the popular national gods or heroes; cf. the 'Aineias, Kastor and Polydeukes' in § 71. (Robert, *Bild u. Lied,* p. 45.)

18. ter fulmine ambusta : the stress laid on the miraculous circumstance confirms the authorship of Mucianus, Introd. *loc. cit.*

§ 70. 19. archigallum : literally the word would apply to the chief of the priests of Kybele. But the following anecdote shows that the picture more probably represented the figure of a nude boy, surnamed the *archi-*

I

picturam amavit Tiberius princeps atque, ut auctor est
Deculo, HS. [LX] aestimatam cubiculo suo inclusit. pinxit
et Thressam nutricem infantemque in manibus eius et Philiscum et Liberum patrem adstante Virtute, et pueros duos in
quibus spectatur securitas et aetatis simplicitas, item sacer- 5
71 dotem adstante puero cum acerra et corona. sunt et duae
picturae eius nobilissimae, hoplites in certamine ita decurrens
ut sudare videatur, alter arma deponens ut anhelare sentiatur. laudantur et Aeneas Castorque ac Pollux in eadem
tabula, item Telephus, Achilles, Agamemnon, Ulixes. fecun- 10
dus artifex, sed quo nemo insolentius usus sit gloria artis,
namque et cognomina usurpavit habrodiaetum se appellando
aliisque versibus principem artis et eam ab se consummatam,
super omnia Apollinis se radice ortum et Herculem, qui est
Lindi, talem a se pictum qualem saepe in quiete vidisset. 15
72 ergo magnis suffragiis superatus a Timanthe Sami in Aiace
armorumque iudicio herois nomine se moleste ferre dicebat
quod iterum ab indigno victus esset. pinxit et minoribus
tabellis libidines, eo genere petulantis ioci se reficiens.

gallus, owing to some physical peculiarity (cf. Klein, *Arch. Ep. Mitth.*
xii, 1888, p. 123); perhaps therefore
the picture should be reckoned among
the *libidines* mentioned below in § 72.
1. amavit Tiberius: cf. the
similar story told of the *Apoxyomenos*
of Lysippos, xxxiv, § 62.
3. Thressam nutricem : a votive
portrait put up in gratitude for the
services of a favourite nurse ; cf. Furtwängler, *Dornauszieher*, p. 95, or a
grave picture; cf. *Anth. Pal.* vii,
663 :

'Ο μικκὸς τόδ' ἔτευξε τᾷ Θρείσσᾳ
Μήδειος τὸ μνᾶμ' ἐπὶ τᾷ ὀδῷ, κήπέ-
γραψε Κλείτας.
ἐξεῖ τὰν χάριν ἁ γυνὰ ἀντ' ἐκείνων
ὧν τὸν κῶρον ἔθρεψ'. ἔτυμ' ὧν ἔτι
ΧΡΗΣΙΜΑ τελευτᾷ.

From *pinxit et Thr. nutr.* down to *et
corona* we seem to have part of the
old account of Parrhasios by Xenokrates ; Münzer, *op. cit.* p. 515; cf.
Introd. p. xxvii.

Philiscum : a poet of the Middle
Comedy ; Kock, *Fragm. Com. Graec.*
vol. ii, p. 443.
5. sacerdotem adstante puero:
cf. above, note on § 60.
§ 71. 6. duae picturae: apparently
composed as pendants; the description is epigrammatic, Benndorf, *Epigramm.* p. 55, Introd. p. lxxi.
9. Aeneas Castorque ac Pollux:
for this group of heroes, who have
no mythological connexion with one
another, cf. above, note on § 69.
10. Telephus, Achilles, Agamemnon, Ulixes : i. e. a picture representing the healing of Telephos by
the rust from the sword of Achilles
(xxxiv, 152), in presence of Agamemnon and of Odysseus. Robert (*Bild.
u. Lied.* p. 35) conjectures the picture
to have been inspired by the lost play
of Euripides ; but Vogel (*Scenen
Euripid. Trag. in gr. Vasengemälden,*
p. 18) rightly points out that Euripides had assigned too marked a part

He also painted a priest of Kybele : a picture of which the 70
Emperor Tiberius was enamoured, and which, according to
Deculo, although valued at 6,000,000 sesterces (£52,500 circ.), he
placed in his private apartments. Furthermore he painted a
Thrakian nurse with an infant in her arms ; a portrait of Philiskos,
Dionysos by the side of Virtue, two boys whose features express
the confidence and the simplicity of their age, and a priest with
a boy at his side holding a censer and a wreath. Two other 71
pictures by him are most famous, a hoplite in a race who seems to
sweat as he runs, and a hoplite laying aside his arms, whose
labouring breath we seem to hear. His picture of Aineias, Kastor
and Polydeukes is praised, so is his Telephos with Achilles, Agamemnon and Odysseus. He was a prolific artist, but carried his *His luxury*
success with an arrogance that none have equalled ; he called *and arrog-*
ance.
himself ἁβροδίαιτος [the luxurious] and said in another epigram
that he was the prince of painting, that he had brought it to the
highest point of perfection, and more than all that he was of the
seed of Apollo, and had painted the Herakles at Lindos precisely *Herakles at*
Lindos.
as he had often seen him in sleep. Hence it was that when he 72
was defeated by a large majority of votes in a competition with *Competi-*
Timanthes at Samos, the subject of his picture being Aias and *tion with*
Timanthes.
the award of the arms, he said in the name of the hero that he .
was grieved at being worsted a second time by an unworthy rival.
He also painted small pictures of licentious subjects, seeking

in the action to Klytaimnestra, for
her to have been left out in a picture
taken straight from his drama. Vogel
therefore points to the Telephos of
Aischylos as the source of Parrhasios'
inspiration.

12. habrodiaetum : from the epigram preserved Ath. xii, p. 543 D,
= *Anthol. App.* 59 = Bergk. *L. G.* ii,
pp. 320, 635, 1 ; cf. O. Jahn, *Kleine
Beiträge*, p. 286 ff. ; Introd. p. lv.

13. consummatam : from the epigram Athen. xii, p. 543 E = *Anthol.
App.* 60 = Bergk, ii, p. 321, 636, 2 ; cf.
the epigram composed by Zeuxis upon
himself, Aristeides, *Or.* 49, ii, p. 521
= Bergk, ii, pp. 318, 634.

14. super omnia . . . ortum : according to Jahn (*loc. cit.*) these words
are from a lost epigram of similar
character to those preserved in Athe-

naios.

15. talem . . . pictum : Athen. xii,
543 F = *Anth. App.* 61 = Bergk, p. 321,
636, 3 ; these verses were probably inscribed on the picture ; cf. the epigram
which Parrhasios composed for his
picture of Hermes, Themistios *Orat.*
ii, p. 34 (Dindorf).

§ 72. 16. a Timanthe : the name of
Parrhasios' rival is given only by Pliny ;
the story of the competition also
Athen. xii, 543 E, Ailian, ποικίλη ἱστ.
ix, 11. Introd. p. liv f.

in Aiace armorumque iudicio :
it is unnecessary to suppose from
these words that 'The award of the
Arms' was also the subject of the
picture by Timanthes.

19. libidines : one instance on record is his 'Meleager and Atalanta,'
Suet. *Tib.* 44 ; Polemon (*ap.* Athen.

73 nam Timanthi vel plurimum adfuit ingenii. eius enim est
Iphigenia oratorum laudibus celebrata, qua stante ad aras
peritura cum maestos pinxisset omnes praecipueque patru-
um, et tristitiae omnem imaginem consumpsisset, patris
ipsius voltum velavit quem digne non poterat ostendere. 5
74 sunt et alia ingenii eius exempla, veluti Cyclops dormiens
in parvola tabella, cuius et sic magnitudinem exprimere
cupiens pinxit iuxta Satyros thyrso pollicem eius metientes.
atque in unius huius operibus intellegitur plus semper quam
pingitur et, cum sit ars summa, ingenium tamen ultra artem 10
est. pinxit et heroa absolutissimi operis artem ipsam complexus viros pingendi, quod opus nunc Romae in templo
75 Pacis est. Euxinidas hac aetate docuit Aristiden praeclarum artificem, Eupompus Pamphilum Apellis praeceptorem.
est Eupompi victor certamine gymnico palmam tenens. 15

xiii, p. 567 B) makes the same charge
of πορνογραφία against Aristeides,
Pausias and Nikophanes; cf. also
Euripides, *Hippol.* 1005.

§ 73. 1. **Nam**: resumes the subject
from *victus esset.*

Timanthi: a native of Kythnos,
Quinct. ii, 13, 13. Eustathios (on
Il. p. 1343, 60), whose authorities
are rarely trustworthy, calls him
Σικυώνιος. It must be by confusion
with a later Timanthes, who painted
the battle of Aratos against the
Aitolians at Pellene in Arkadia, in
B. C. 240 (Plut. *Arat.* 32), and who
was therefore presumably a Sikyonian.

2. **oratorum**: cf. Cic. *Orator,* 22,
74 *pictor* (name not mentioned) *ille
vidit, cum immolanda Iphigenia tristis
Calchas esset, tristior Ulixes, mae-
reret Menelaus, obvolvendum caput
Agamemnonis esse, quoniam sum-
mum illum luctum penicillo non posset
imitari.* That the Iphigeneia was a
stock rhetorical subject is proved by
Quinct. (*loc. cit.*) and Val. Max. viii,
11, ext. 6. A famous Pompeian wall-
painting, representing the sacrifice
(Helbig, *Wandgemälde,* 1304 = phot.
Alinari 12027), shows Agamemnon

with head completely veiled, but since
Iph. is being carried, and not standing, we must see in it only a later
adaptation of the picture by Timanthes (cf. also Helbig, *op. cit.* 1305, and
the mosaic in *A. Z.* 1869, taf. xiv).
The ancients entertained two distinct
views as to the veiling of Agamemnon; Pliny and Quinctilian arguing
that the painter did not show the
features of the father, in order to save
dignitas, while Cicero and Valerius
Maximus argued that he had recourse
to this means because the highest
pain cannot be expressed in art.
Both ancient and modern criticisms
are discussed by Blümner, *Comm.* to
Lessing's *Laokoon,* p. 506 f. As
Blümner points out, the veiling motive
in sorrow is common both in painting
and poetry; *e. g.* Euripides veils the
head of Agamemnon in the description
of the identical scene, *Iph. Aul.* 1550;
cf. also Brunn, *K. G.* ii, p. 124.
According to Quinctilian, this picture
gained for Timanthes the prize over
Kolotes of Teos.

4. **consumpsisset**: cf. the similar story of Euphranor, Val. Max.
viii, 11, ext. 5. According to Eusta-

relaxation in this wanton humour. To return—*Timanthes* was a 73
painter above all curious in invention, for by him is that Iphigeneia *Iphigeneia*
praised by the orators,whom he depicted standing by the altar ready *of Timan-*
for death. Having represented all the onlookers and especially *thes.*
her father's brother as plunged in sorrow and having thus exhausted
every presentment of grief, he has veiled the face of her father for
which he had reserved no adequate expression. There are other 74
examples of his inventiveness; for instance, being· desirous to
emphasize, even in a small picture, the huge size of a sleeping *Sleeping*
Cyclops, he painted some Satyrs at his side, measuring his thumb *Cyclops.*
with a thyrsos. He is the only artist whose works always suggest
more than is in the picture, and great as is his dexterity, his
power of invention yet exceeds it. He also painted a hero, a pic- *Hero in*
ture in which he touched perfection, having comprehended in it *temple of*
the whole art of painting the male figure. The picture is now at *Peace at*
Rome in the temple of Peace. *Rome.*

In this period †*Euxeinidas* was the master of *Aristeides*, 75
a famous artist, and †*Eupompos* of *Pamphilos*, who in turn was the *New di-*
master of Apelles. We have by Eupompos a victor in an athletic *vision of*
contest holding a palm. So great was this artist's reputation that *the schools*
into the
Attic, Ionic
and Si-
kyonian.

thios (*l. c.*),whose statement,however, 12. in templo Pacis: note on
savours of concoction, Timanthes was xxxiv, 84.
inspired to veil the head of Agamem- § 75. 13. Aristiden: identical
non, by the similar device employed with the Aristeides of § 111, the master
by Homer in describing the grief of of Euphranor, where Pliny however
Priam, *Il.* xxiv, 162. confuses him with his grandson
§ 74. 6. Cyclops dormiens: the Aristeides the Theban. According to
presentation of this subject in paint- Kroker (*Gleichnamige Gr. Künstler,*
ing was doubtless influenced by the p. 33) and Furtwängler (*Masterpieces,*
Kyklops of Euripides, in which the p. 349) he is further probably identical
Satyrs were brought on the stage with with the sculptor of xxxiv, 72, pupil of
Polyphemos; Robert, *Bild u. Lied,* Polykleitos; the dates favour the
p. 35; Winter,*Jahrb.* vi, 1891, p. 272, supposition.
who rightly refuses to refer the pic- 14. Eupompus: xxxiv, § 61;
ture (with Klein) to the younger above, § 64.
Timanthes. 15. palmam tenens: a number of
11. artem ipsam complexus: examples of a youth with palm in
the similarity of expression with the left hand, and raising the crown
xxxiv, 55, *solusque hominum autem* to his head with the right, are collected
ipsam fecisse artis opere iudicatur, by Milchhöfer, *Arch. Stud. Brunn*
suggests that the *heros* of Timanthes, *dargebracht,* 1892, p. 62, ff.; they
like the Doryphoros of Polykleitos, probably go back to the type created
was a canonical figure intended to by Eupompos, Furtwängler, *Master-*
illustrate the artist's theories of pro- *pieces,* p. 256; cf. also Reisch, *Griech.*
portion; cf. Kalkmann, *Jahrb.* x, *Weihgeschenke,* p. 41.
1895, p. 84, note 147; Introd. p. xli.

ipsius auctoritas tanta fuit ut diviserit picturam in genera.
quae ante eum duo fuere—Helladicum et Asiaticum appella-
bant—propter hunc, qui erat Sicyonius, diviso Helladico
76 tria facta sunt, Ionicum, Sicyonium, Atticum.   Pamphili
cognatio et proelium ad Phliuntem ac victoria Atheniensium, 5
item Ulixes in rate.   ipse Macedo natione, sed primus in
pictura omnibus litteris eruditus, praecipue arithmetica et
geometria, sine quibus negabat artem perfici posse, docuit
neminem talento minoris—annuis ✗ D—quam mercedem et
77 Apelles et Melanthius dedere ei.   huius auctoritate effectum 10
est Sicyone primum, deinde et in tota Graecia, ut pueri ingenui omnia ante graphicen, hoc est picturam in buxo,
docerentur recipereturque ars ea in primum gradum libera-
lium.   semper quidem honos ei fuit ut ingenui eam exerce-
rent, mox ut honesti, perpetuo interdicto ne servitia doce- 15
rentur.   ideo neque in hac neque in toreutice ullius qui
78 servierit opera celebrantur.   clari et centesima septima
olympiade exstitere Aetion   ac Therimachus.   Aetionis

4. **tria facta sunt** : above note on
§ 72. ' It is difficult to say wherein
this great local superiority consisted,
which tempted, moreover, wealthy
amateurs, like Ptolemy II and Attalos, to purchase at enormous prices
galleries of old Sikyonian masters.
Plutarch uses a special term for it,
χρηστογραφία, which is usually explained as indicating the reaction in
art against the methods of Zeuxis
and his contemporaries.' (C. Smith,
art. PICTURA, Smith's *Dict. Ant.* p.
413.)
    § 76. 5. **cognatio** : it may have
been a grave picture placed upon a
family grave, cf. in sculpture a similar
family gathering on the Eastern pediment of the tomb known as the
' Nereid monument ' (Brit. Mus.),
Michaelis, *A. Z.* 1845, pl. xxxiv, p.
145. Or it may have been merely a
votive commemorative picture. For
similar subjects cf. the *cognatio
nobilium* of Timomachos (136), the
frequentia of Athenion (134), the

syngenicon of Oinias (143), finally
the *stemmata* of Koinos (139).
    **proelium ad Phliuntem ac vic-
toria** : = victoria Atheniensium in
proelio ad Phliuntem : hendiadys,
cf. Müller, *Stil*, pp. 109, 15. The
picture is generally supposed to have
represented the episode narrated by
Xenophon, *Hellenika*, vii, 2, 18–23,
when the Phliasians and Athenians
under the command of Chares surprised and put to flight the Sikyonian
troops (B. C. 367); Brunn, *K. G.* ii, p.
132 f.; Schaefer, *Demosthenes*, i, p.
103 ff.; cf. Grote, *Greece*, viii, p. 258.
    6. **Macedo** : from Amphipolis
(Sonidas). His birthplace is of importance as giving the probable clue
to the subsequent connexion of his
pupil Apelles—and possibly to that
of Lysippos—with the Makedonian
court. (Against his identification, on
the insufficient testimony of the scholia,
with the Pamphilos of Aristoph. *Plut.*
385, see Judeich, *Fleckeisen's Jahrb.*
1890, p. 758.)

A. THE THEBANO-ATTIC SCHOOL.

Euxeinidas, *fl. circ.* 400 B.C.; § 75.

Aristeides I (§§ 75; 108, 111; xxxiv, 72 ?)

Nikomachos, son §§ 108–109.

Aristeides II, *Thebanus*, son §§ 98–100; 110.

Nikeros, son § 111.

Ariston, son §§ 110; 111.

Philoxenos of Eretria, § 110.

Antorides, § 111.

Euphranor, §§ 111; 128.

Antidotos, § 130.

Nikias (II), §§ 130–132.

B. THE SIKYONIAN SCHOOL.

Eupompos, *fl. circ.* 400 B.C.; § 75.

Pamphilos, §§ 75–76; 123.

Apelles, §§ 79–97.

Perseus, § 111.

Melanthios, §§ 76; 80.

Pausias, §§ 123–127.

Aristolaos, son § 137.

Nikophanes, § 137.

Sokrates, § 137.

[*To face page* 118.]

it occasioned a new division of the schools of painting. Before his time there had been two schools, known as the Helladic proper and the Asiatic; but now the Helladic was subdivided in his honour, and thus the schools became three, the Ionic, the Sikyonian and the Attic, Eupompos himself being a Sikyonian.

By Pamphilos we have a family group, the victorious engage- 76 ment of the Athenians at Phlious, and a picture of Odysseus on *Pamphi-los, master* his raft. A Makedonian by birth, Pamphilos was the first painter *of Apelles.* who was thoroughly trained in every branch of learning, more 367 B.C. particularly in arithmetic and geometry; without which, so he held, art could not be perfect. He taught no one for less than a talent [£210 circ.]—that is, five hundred denarii [£17 10s. circ.] a year—the fee paid him both by Apelles and by Melanthios. It was owing to his influence that first at Sikyon, and after- 77 wards throughout Greece drawing, or rather painting, on tablets *Drawing taught to* of boxwood, was the earliest subject taught to freeborn boys, and *freeborn* that this art was accepted as the preliminary step towards a liberal *boys.* education. It was at any rate had in such honour that at all times the freeborn, and later on persons of distinction practised it, while by a standing prohibition no slaves might ever acquire it, and this is why neither in painting nor in statuary are there any celebrated works by artists who had been slaves.

In the hundred and seventh Olympiad [352–349 B.C.] lived 78 Aetion and †Therimachos, both painters of note. By Aetion are *Aetion and Therima-chos.*

7. praecipue arithmetica . . . posse: these words are probably derived from a Treatise on Painting by Pamphilos; see Introd. p. xliii.

9. quam mercedem . . . Apelles: 'Ήνθει γὰρ ἔτι δόξα τῆς Σικυωνίας μούσης καὶ χρηστογραφίας, ὡς μόνης ἀδιάφθορον ἐχούσης τὸ καλόν, ὥστε καὶ 'Απελλῆν ἐκεῖνον ἤδη θαυμαζό-μενον ἀφικέσθαι καὶ συγγενέσθαι τοῖς ἀνδράσιν ἐπὶ ταλάντῳ, τῆς δόξης μᾶλ-λον ἢ τῆς τέχνης δεόμενον μεταλαβεῖν. Plut. *Arat.* xiii.

10. Melanthius: §§ 50, 80; and *Index* to this book. From Antigonos of Karystos, *ap.* Diogenes L. iv, 3, 18 (Introd. p. xxxviii), we learn that he wrote περὶ ζωγραφικῆς; Melanthios was also a master of Apelles (perhaps after the death of Pamphilos), who,

with other pupils, assisted him in the votive picture for Aristratos of Sikyon (Plut. *loc. cit.*).

§ 77. 11. pueri ingenui = ἐλεύ-θέριοι: cf. Aristotle, *Polit.* v (viii), 3, p. 1338 δοκεῖ δὲ καὶ γραφικὴ χρήσι-μος εἶναι πρὸς τὸ κρίνειν τὰ τῶν τεχ-νιτῶν ἔργα κάλλιον· οὐδ' αὖ καθάπερ ἡ γυμναστικὴ πρὸς ὑγίειαν καὶ ἀλκήν· οὐδέτερον γὰρ τούτων ὁρῶμεν γινό-μενον ἐκ τῆς μουσικῆς. λείπεται τοίνυν πρὸς τὴν ἐν τῇ σχολῇ διαγωγήν, ἐς ὅπερ καὶ φαίνονται παράγοντες αὐτήν· ἣν γὰρ οἴονται διαγωγὴν εἶναι τῶν ἐλευθέρων, ἐν ταύτῃ τάττουσιν.

§ 78. 18. Aetion et Therimachus: cf. note on xxxiv, 50. Therimachos is otherwise unknown, Aetion is a favourite artist of Lucian, who has given a famous description of his Alexander

sunt nobiles picturae Liber pater, item Tragoedia et
Comoedia, Semiramis ex ancilla regnum apiscens, anus
lampadas praeferens et nova nupta verecundia notabilis.
79 verum et omnes prius genitos futurosque postea superavit
Apelles Cous olympiade centesima duodecima. picturae 5
plura solus prope quam ceteri omnes contulit, voluminibus
etiam editis quae doctrinam eam continent. praecipua eius
in arte venustas fuit, cum eadem aetate maximi pictores
essent. quorum opera cum admiraretur omnibus conlaudatis,
deesse illam suam Venerem dicebat, quam Graeci Charita 10
vocant, cetera omnia contigisse, sed hac sola sibi neminem
80 parem. et aliam gloriam usurpavit, cum Protogenis opus
inmensi laboris ac curae supra modum anxiae miraretur,
dixit enim omnia sibi cum illo paria esse aut illi meliora,
sed uno se praestare, quod manum de tabula sciret tollere, 15
memorabili praecepto nocere saepe nimiam diligentiam. fuit
autem non minoris simplicitatis quam artis. Melanthio
dispositione cedebat, Asclepiodoro de mensuris, hoc est
81 quanto quid a quoque distare deberet. scitum est inter
Protogenen et eum quod accidit. ille Rhodi vivebat, quo 20
cum Apelles adnavigasset avidus cognoscendi opera eius

and Roxana ('Ηρόδ. ἢ 'Αετίων, 4);
cf. εἰκόνες, 7, περὶ τῶν ἐπὶ μισθ. συν.
42 ; cf. Cicero, *Brutus*, xviii, 70
(quoted above, note on § 50).

  2. **Semiramis:** Brunn (*K. G.* ii,
p. 245) points out that the nuptials
of S. and Ninos may have been conceived as a sort of mythical counterpart to those of Alexander and Roxana.

  anus . . . nova nupta : of course
in one picture. The *anus* is doubtless
the mother of the bride, to whom the
δᾳδουχεῖν, the carrying of the δᾳδες
νυμφικαί, usually fell (Hermann-Blüm-
ner, *Lehrbuch*, p. 275; Furtwängler,
S. Sabouroff, i. 58, 59; cf. the attendant (?) holding torches on the
marriage vases or λουτροφόροι). The
torch was doubtless made the occasion for effects of light; cf. the
marriage of Alexander and Roxana,

where Hephaistion holds a torch, the
marriage feast of Peirithoos by Hippys
(Athen. xi, p. 474), which was lit up
by a hanging candelabrum. The
enumeration from *Tragoedia* to *anus*
is asyndetical—*et* being reserved to
link *Comoedia* to *Trag.* (both in one
picture) and *nova nupta* to *anus*
—so that I cannot follow Brunn
(*K. G.* ii, p. 245) and Furtwängler
(*Dornauszieher*, p. 96, n. 57), in
understanding the words *anus . . .
notabilis* to be descriptive of the
picture of the Nuptials of Semiramis.

  § 79. 5. **Apelles Cous:** Ovid,
Ars Amat. iii, 401, *Pont. Epist.* iv, 1,
29 ; but Strabo (xiv, p. 642), Lucian,
διαβολ. 2, and after him Tzetzes (*Chil.*
viii, 392) call him an Ephesian ; that
this is correct is proved by Herondas,
iv, 72 ('Εφεσίου 'Απελλέω) who certainly would not have made Apelles

the well-known pictures of Dionysos, of Tragedy and Comedy, of Semiramis rising from slavery to royal power, and of an old woman carrying lamps and a bride, whose shamefacedness is very apparent.

Apelles of Kos, however, in the hundred and twelfth Olympiad **79** [332–329 B.C.] excelled all painters who came before or after him. *Apelles of Kos.* He of himself perhaps contributed more to painting than all the *His written Treatises.* others together; he also wrote treatises on his theory of art. The grace of his genius remained quite unrivalled, although the very greatest painters were living at the time. He would admire their *His esti-* works, praising every beauty and yet observing that they failed *mate of the works of his* in the grace, called χάρις in Greek, which was distinctively his *contempor-* own; everything else they had attained, but in this alone none *aries and of his own.* equalled him. He laid claim to another merit: when admiring **80** a work of Protogenes that betrayed immense industry and the most anxious elaboration, he said that, though Protogenes was his equal or even his superior in everything, he yet surpassed that painter in one point—namely in knowing when to take his hand from a picture; a memorable saying, showing that too much care may often be hurtful. His candour was equal to his genius: he acknowledged the superiority of Melanthios in the distribution of figures, and that of Asklepiodoros in perspective arrangement, that is in giving the accurate distances between different objects.

A neat story is told of him in connexion with Protogenes, who **81** was living in Rhodes. Thither Apelles sailed, eager to see the *His visit to Protogenes.*

into an Ephesian, if he could have claimed him for his native Kos. The tradition that the artist was a Koan arose because at Kos were some of his most celebrated works, among them the *Anadyomene.*

6. **voluminibus editis**: cf. § 111; it must be from these writings of Apelles that the judgements he passed upon his contemporaries were originally derived (Introd. p. xl).

7. **praecipua venustas**: Quinct. xii, 10, 6 *ingenio et gratia, quam in se ipso maxime iactat, Ap. est praestantissimus.* According to Plutarch (*Demetr.* xxii), and Ailian (ποικ. ιστ. xii, 41) this judgement on himself was passed when he saw the Ialysos of Protogenes (§ 102).

9. **quorum opera cum adm.**: i. e. in his writings.

§ **80**. 12. **Protogenis**: below, §§ 81, 101–106.

opus miraretur: presumably the Ialysos.

15. **manum de tabula**: = χείρ' ἀπὸ τραπέζης; Petron. 76 *postquam coepi plus habere, quam tota mea patria habet, manum de tabula;* also used of school-boys trifling in their master's absence, cf. Cic. *ad Fam.* vii, 25 *sed heus tu, manu de tabula!* (Otto, *Sprichwörter,* p. 210).

17. **Melanthio**: above, § 76.

18. **Asclepiodoro**: below, § 107.

§ **81**. 19. **scitum est**: the following anecdote appears to be elaborated out of the admiration which Apelles

fama tantum sibi cogniti, continuo officinam petiit.   aberat
ipse, sed tabulam amplae magnitudinis in machina aptatam
una custodiebat anus.   haec foris esse Protogenen respondit
interrogavitque a quo quaesitum diceret.   ab hoc, inquit
Apelles, adreptoque penicillo lineam ex colore duxit sum- 5
82 mae tenuitatis per tabulam, et reverso Protogeni quae gesta
erant anus indicavit.   ferunt artificem protinus contempla-
tum subtilitatem dixisse Apellen venisse, non cadere in
alium tam absolutum opus, ipsumque alio colore tenuiorem
lineam in ipsa illa duxisse abeuntemque praecepisse, si 10
redisset ille, ostenderet adiceretque hunc esse quem quaereret, atque ita evenit.   revertit enim Apelles et vinci
erubescens tertio colore lineas secuit nullum relinquens
83 amplius subtilitati locum.   at Protogenes victum se confessus
in portum devolavit hospitem quaerens, placuitque sic eam 15
tabulam posteris tradi omnium quidem, sed artificum prae-
A.U.C. 757. cipuo miraculo.   consumptam eam priore incendio Caesaris
domus in Palatio audio, spectatam nobis ante spatiose nihil
aliud continentem quam lineas visum effugientes inter egregia
multorum opera inani similem et eo ipso allicientem omnique 20
84 opere nobiliorem.   Apelli fuit alioqui perpetua consuetudo
numquam tam occupatum diem agendi ut non lineam du-
cendo exerceret artem, quod ab eo in proverbium venit.
idem perfecta opera proponebat in pergula transeuntibus,
atque ipse post tabulam latens vitia quae notarentur aus- 25
cultabat vulgum diligentiorem iudicem quam se praeferens,
85 feruntque reprehensum a sutore, quod in crepidis una pauci-
ores intus fecisset ansas, eodem postero die superbo emenda-

---

2. aptatam una] *Bamb.*; aptatam picturae una *reliqui, Detlefsen.*

had professed for Protogenes in his
writings, see Introd. p. xl.

3. una . . . anus: Leo, *Plautinische
Forschungen* (1895), p. 65, calls attention to the part played in classical
literature by the single *ancilla* or the
anus.   Like the *pistrinum* she is, so
to speak, one of the requisites of the
contented life.   We get the *ancilla*
in the amusing anecdote, Cic. *de Orat.*
ii, 276, while Chrysippos ἠρκεῖτο
γραιδίῳ, μόνῳ, Demetrios *ap.* Diog.

Laert. vii, 7, 185.   The motive is
Homeric ὥσπερ ὁ Λαέρτης . . . γρηὶ σὺν
ἀμφιπόλῳ, Teles, p. 25 (ed. Hense).

5. lineam . . . duxit: the anecdote
belongs to the same category as
Giotto's O, Vasaried. Milanesi I, p.383.

§ 83. 17. consumptam . . . audio:
oral tradition.

§ 84. 23. in proverbium: i. e.
nullus dies sine linea; cf. Otto, *Sprichwörter,* p. 194.

24. pergula: cf. Ulpian, *Digest.*

works of a man only known to him by reputation, and on his arrival immediately repaired to the studio. Protogenes was not at home, but a solitary old woman was keeping watch over a large panel placed on the easel. In answer to the questions of Apelles, she said that Protogenes was out, and asked the name of the visitor: 'Here it is,' said Apelles, and snatching up a brush he drew a line of extreme delicacy across the board. On the return **82** of Protogenes the old woman told him what had happened. *They split a line, in* When he had considered the delicate precision of the line he at *friendly* once declared that his visitor had been Apelles, for no one else *emulation.* could have drawn anything so perfect. Then in another colour he drew a second still finer line upon the first, and went away, bidding her show it to Apelles if he came again, and add that this was the man he was seeking. It fell out as he expected; Apelles did return, and, ashamed to be beaten, drew a third line of another colour cutting the two first down their length and leaving no room for any further refinement. Protogenes owned himself **83** beaten and hurried down to the harbour to find his visitor; they agreed to hand down the painting just as it was to posterity, a marvel to all, but especially to artists. It perished, I am told, A.D. 4. in the first fire of the house of the Caesars on the Palatine. Formerly we might look upon it; its wide surface disclosed nothing save lines which eluded the sight, and among the numerous works by excellent painters it was like a blank, and it was precisely this that lent it surpassing attraction and renown.

Apelles further made it an unvarying rule never to spend a day, **84** however busy, without drawing a line by way of practice; hence *His in-* the proverb. It was also his habit to exhibit his finished works *dustry.* to the passers-by in a balcony, and he would lie concealed behind the picture and listen to the faults that were found with it, regarding the public as more accurate critics than himself. There is **85** a story that when found fault with by a cobbler for putting one *The critical* loop too few on the inner side of a sandal, he corrected the *cobbler.* mistake. Elated by this the cobbler next day proceeded to find fault with the leg, whereupon Apelles thrust out his head in

ix, 3, 5, § 12 *cum pictor in pergula clipeum vel tabulam expositam habuisset eaque excidisset, et transeunti damni quid dedisset.* (It has been shown by F. Marx in *Studia Lucili-ana*, 1882, p. 16 f. that in Lucilius xv,
6, the old reading *pergula pictorum* should be altered to *pergula ficto-rum*, which is adopted by Buecheler.) For *pergulae* at Pompei, see Mau, *Röm. Mitth.* ii, 1887, p. 214 ff.

tione pristinae admonitionis cavillante circa crus, indignatum
prospexisse denuntiantem ne supra crepidam sutor iudicaret,
quod et ipsum in proverbium abiit.   fuit enim et comitas
illi, propter quam gratior Alexandro Magno frequenter in
officinam ventitanti—nam, ut diximus, ab alio se pingi 5
vetuerat edicto—sed in officina imperite multa disserenti
silentium comiter suadebat rideri eum dicens a pueris qui
86 colores tererent.   tantum erat auctoritati iuris in regem
alioqui iracundum.   quamquam Alexander honorem ei
clarissimo perhibuit exemplo, namque cum dilectam sibi 10
ex pallacis suis praecipue, nomine Pancaspen, nudam pingi
ob admirationem formae ab Apelle iussisset eumque, dum
paret, captum amore sensisset, dono dedit ei magnus animo,
maior imperio sui, nec minor hoc facto quam victoria aliqua.
87 quippe se vicit, nec torum tantum suum sed etiam adfectum 15
donavit artifici, ne dilectae quidem respectu motus, cum
modo regis ea fuisset, modo pictoris esset.   sunt qui Venerem
anadyomenen ab illo pictam exemplari putent.   Apelles et
in aemulis benignus Protogeni dignationem primus Rhodi
88 constituit.   sordebat suis ut plerumque domestica, percon- 20
tantique quanti liceret opera effecta parvum nescio quid
dixerat, at ille quinquagenis talentis poposcit famamque
dispersit se emere ut pro suis venderet.   ea res concitavit
Rhodios ad intellegendum artificem, nec nisi augentibus
pretium cessit.   imagines adeo similitudinis indiscretae 25
pinxit ut—incredibile dictu—Apio grammaticus scriptum
reliquerit quendam ex facie hominum divinantem, quos
metoposcopos vocant, ex iis dixisse aut futurae mortis annos

---

§ 85. 2. ne supra crepidam sutor:
cf. Valer. Max. viii, 12, ext. 3; Otto,
Sprichwörter, p. 97.   Introd. p. lix.

3. enim : corroborates *idem praeferens*, ignoring the intervening anecdote.

5. ut diximus: in vii, 125 = App. I;
cf. note on xxxiv, 63.

6. in officina : the following anecdote is told by Plutarch (*de Tranquill.
Anim.* 12), concerning the megabyzos
(§ 93), while Ailian, Ποικ. Ἱστ. ii, 2,
tells it of Zeuxis and a megabyzos.

7. qui colores tererent : τὰ παι-
δόρια τὰ τοῦ Ζεύξιδος τὴν μηλίδα τρί-
βοντα κατεγέλα, Ailian, *loc. cit.*

§ 86. 11. Pancaspen : ὄνομα ἦν
Παγκάστη, τὸ δὲ γένος Λαρισσαία,
Ailian, Ποικ. Ἱστ. xii, 34.   Lucian
(εἰκόνες, 7) calls her Πακάτη.

§ 87. 18. anadyomenen : = *exeuntem e mari*, below, § 91.

exemplari: according to Athen.
xiii, p. 590 F, the model was Phryne,
while according to *Anth. Plan.* 179
Apelles, like Praxiteles (xxxvi, 21),

a passion and bade the cobbler 'stick to his last,' a saying which
has also passed into a proverb.

The charm of his manner had won him the regard of Alexander *Friendship*
the Great, who was a frequent visitor to the studio, for, as we have *of Alexan-*
der and
said, he had issued an edict forbidding any one else to paint his *Apelles.*
portrait. But when the king happened to discourse at length in *Story of*
Pankaspe.
the studio upon things he knew nothing about, Apelles would
pleasantly advise him to be silent, hinting that the assistants who
ground the colours were laughing at him; such power did his 86
personality give him over a king habitually so passionate. Yet
Alexander gave him a signal mark of his regard : he commissioned
Apelles to paint a nude figure of his favourite mistress Pankaspe,
so much did he admire her wondrous form, but perceiving that
Apelles had fallen in love with her, with great magnanimity and
still greater self-control he gave her to him as a present, winning
by the action as great a glory as by any of his victories. He 87
conquered himself and sacrificed to the artist not only his mistress
but his love, and was not even restrained by consideration for the
woman he loved, who, once a king's mistress, was now a painter's.
Some believe that she was the model for the Aphrodite rising
from the sea.

Friendly even to his rivals, Apelles was the first to establish in 88
Rhodes the reputation of Protogenes, who, as so many in their *Kindness*
of Apelles
own homes, was neglected by his countrymen. When asked by *to Proto-*
Apelles the prices of his finished works, he mentioned some *genes.*
trifling sum, upon which Apelles offered fifty talents [£10,500
circ.] for each, and spread a report that he was buying the pictures
to sell as his own. This stirred up the Rhodians to a better
appreciation of the artist, but not until they offered a still higher
price would Apelles give up the pictures.

His portraits were such perfect likenesses that, incredible as it *His aston-*
may sound, Apio the grammarian has left it on record that *ishing*
merits as
a physiognomist, or μετωποσκόπος as they are called, was able to *portrait*
painter.

was privileged to see the goddess
herself: αὐτὰν ἐκ πόντοιο τιθηνητῆρος
'Απελλῆς | τὰν Κύπριν γυμνὰν εἶδε
λοχευομέναν.

§ 88. 25. similit. indiscretae :
xxxiv, 60 *facie quoque indiscreta*
similis, and note.

26. incredibile dictu: hence Pliny

waives the responsibility and immediately names his authority.

Apio grammaticus: *Praef.* 25,
xxx, 18, and often in Pliny; flor.
reign of Caligula. Müller, *F. H. G.*
iii, 506–516.

28. metoposcopos: cf. Suet. *Ti-*
tus 2.

89 aut praeteritae vitae. non fuerat ei gratia in comitatu
Alexandri cum Ptolemaeo, quo regnante Alexandriam vi
tempestatis expulsus subornato fraude aemulorum plano
regio invitatus ad cenam venit, indignantique Ptolemaeo et
vocatores suos ostendenti, ut diceret a quo eorum invitatus 5
esset, arrepto carbone extincto e foculo imaginem in pariete
deliniavit, adgnoscente voltum plani rege inchoatum proti-
90 nus. pinxit et Antigoni regis imaginem altero lumine
orbam primus excogitata ratione vitia condendi, obliquam
namque fecit, ut quod deerat corpori picturae deesse potius 10
videretur, tantumque eam partem e facie ostendit quam
totam poterat ostendere. sunt inter opera eius et exspirantium imagines. quae autem nobilissima sint non est
91 facile dictu. Venerem exeuntem e mari divus Augustus
dicavit in delubro patris Caesaris, quae anadyomene vocatur, 15
versibus Graecis tali opere, dum laudatur, victo sed inlus-

§ 89. 1. non fuerat ei gratia:
the following is a mutilated and somewhat different account of the events
narrated at length by Lucian (διαβολ.
4), for which, according to Lucian,
Apelles took vengeance by painting
his famous 'Calumny.' Both the
versions have an aitiological flavour, and probably arose in great
measure out of the picture itself (for
the historical inaccuracies in Lucian's
story see Brunn, *K. G.* ii, p. 208). For
the latest discussion of the Calumny,
and especially of the influence of
Lucian's description on artists of the
Renascence, see R. Förster in *Jahrb.
d. Preuss. Samml.* 1887, p. 29 ff.

3. aemulorum: from Lucian, *loc.
cit.*, we learn that the Egyptian painter
Antiphilos (§§ 114, 138) was among
them.

5. vocatores: i. e. the slaves in
charge of the invitations or *vocationes*,
Seneca, *Ira* iii, 37, 4; Suet. *Calig.*
39, &c.

§ 90. 8. altero lumine orbam:
Ant. was accordingly surnamed μονό-
φθαλμος and Κύκλωψ, Polyb. v, 67, 6 ;
Ailian, Ποικ. Ἰστ. xii, 43.

9. obliquam: Brunn, *K. G.* ii,
p. 10; Quinct. ii, 13, 12 *habet in pictura speciem tota facies; Apelles tamen
imaginem Antigoni latere tantum
altero ostendit, ut amissi oculi deformi-
tas lateret.* These words prove beyond
the possibility of doubt that the *obliqua imago* of Antigonos was a simple
portrait in profile. Hartwig, however,
(*Meisterschalen*, p. 157) argues that
to disguise a defect a simple profile
would be unworthy of the inventiveness
of so great an artist as Apelles, and,
starting from the meaning which he
claims for *catagrapha* (above, § 56,
where see note), tries to show that the
portrait was in ¾ and foreshortened.
The portrait of the squinting Tommaso
Inghirami by Raphael (original in
Pal. Inghirami at Volterra; the picture
in the Pitti is only a copy), which
Hartwig quotes in support of his
theory, seems as a fact to emphasize
rather than conceal the physical defect.

12. exspirantium imagines:
acutely explained by Brückner (*Sitz-
ungsber. d. Wiener Akademie*, vol.
116, p. 519, note 4) as grave pictures

tell from the portraits alone how long the sitter had to live or had ⅄
already lived.   When in Alexander's train he had been on un- 89
friendly terms with Ptolemy, during whose reign he was once
driven into Alexandria by a violent storm.   On Apelles appearing
at a banquet, to which his rivals had maliciously induced the
king's fool to invite him, Ptolemy flew into a passion, and pointing
to his chamberlains bade him say from which of them he had
received the invitation, whereupon the painter snatching up
a charred stick from the hearth traced on the wall a likeness, in
whose first strokes the king at once recognized the face of the
fool.

He also painted a portrait of king Antigonos, who was blind of 90
one eye, being the first to devise a means of concealing the *He paints king*
infirmity by presenting his profile, so that the absence of the eye *Antigonos.*
would be attributed merely to the position of the sitter, not to
a natural defect, for he gave only the part of the face which could
be shown uninjured.   There are among his works some pictures
of dying people, though it were difficult to say which are the best.
His Aphrodite rising from the sea was dedicated by the god 91
Augustus in the temple of his father Caesar: she is known as the *'Aphrodite rising from*
ἀναδυομένη, being, like other works of the kind, at once eclipsed *the sea.'*
yet rendered famous by the Greek epigrams written in her praise.

representing death-scenes; cf. the
γραπτὸς τύπος, described *Anth.* vii,
730; cf. also *ib.* vii,170; Weisshäupl,
Die Grabgedichte der Gr. Anthologie,
97 ff.; further, Paus. ii, 7, 3 praises the
excellent painting of a grave picture
at Sikyon, of Xenodyke, who died in
childbirth; cf. in sculpture the grave
relief of Malthake from the Peiraieus,
see Friederichs-Wolters, 1042. Praxiteles (xxxiv, 70), Nikias (below, § 132),
Nikomachos (mon. of Telestes, § 109),
likewise decorate graves; cf. the
iuvenis requiescens of Simos, § 143.

13. quae autem nobilissima
sint: [refers not to *opera* but to
imagines; rapid changes of gender or
number are common in Pliny, Mayhoff, *Lucubr. Plin.* (1865) p. 83; cf.
J. Müller, *Stil,* p. 56.—H. L. U.].

§ 91. 14. exeuntem e mari =
anadyomenen, above, § 87.   From
numerous descriptions (Overb.*Schrift-*

quellen, 1847–1866) we learn that
the goddess was represented wring-
ing her hair, in a type which
was likewise adapted to statuary
(Helbig, *Class. Ant.* 254). For the
picture itself see Benndorf, *Athen.
Mitth.* 1876, p. 50.

15. in delubro patris Caesaris:
the picture was previously in the
Koan Asklepieion, whence Augustus
obtained it by remitting 100 talents
of the Koan tribute; Strabo xiv,
p. 657. Since Ovid (exiled A. D. 8)
mentions the Anadyomene in *Trist.*
ii, 527 f., the picture must have been in
Rome previous to the year of his exile.
For further discussion of the dates see
Wunderer, *Manibiae Alexandrinae,*
p. 8.

16. victo sed inlustrato : 'surpassed' inasmuch as the poet can give
expression to more things than the
painter who is limited to one moment;

trato, cuius inferiorem partem corruptam qui reficeret non potuit reperiri, verum ipsa iniuria cessit in gloriam artificis. consenuit haec tabula carie, aliamque pro ea substituit Nero 92 principatu suo Dorothei manu.   Apelles inchoaverat et aliam Venerem Coi superaturus famam illam suam priorem. 5 invidit mors peracta parte, nec qui succederet operi ad praescripta liniamenta inventus est.   pinxit et Alexandrum Magnum fulmen tenentem in templo Ephesiae Dianae viginti talentis auri.   digiti eminere videntur et fulmen extra tabulam esse—legentes meminerint omnia ea quattuor colo- 10 ribus facta—manipretium eius tabulae in nummo aureo 93 mensura accepit, non numero.   pinxit et megabyzi sacerdotis Dianae Ephesiae pompam, Clitum cum equo ad bellum festinantem, galeam poscenti armigerum porrigentem. Alexandrum et Philippum quotiens pinxerit enumerare 15 supervacuum est.   mirantur eius Habronem Sami, Menan-

5. famam] etiam *omnes praeter Bamb.*, *Detlefsen.*

for the idea conveyed by *inlustrato* cf. xxxiv, 57, of the heifer of Myron, *celebratis versibus laudata, quando alieno plerique ingenio magis quam suo commendantur.*

3. substituit : this may be an exaggeration, as the picture of Apelles seems still to have been in existence under Vespasian, when Suetonius (*Vesp.* 18) speaks of its being again restored : *Coae Veneris . . . refectorem insigni congiario magnaque mercede donavit.*

§ 92. 4. inchoaverat : Cic. *Fam.* i, 9, 15, and *Off.* iii, 2, 10.

8. fulmen tenentem = κεραυνοφόρον, i. e. deified. Plutarch (περὶ τῆς Ἀλ. τύχης, ii, 2) relates that it was said of this picture that there were two Alexanders, the son of Philip who was invincible, and the Alexander of Apelles who was inimitable. It is a fascinating conjecture of King (*Anc. Gems* i, p. xii), followed by Furtwängler, *Jahrb.* iv (1889), p. 69, that an ancient copy of this famous picture is extant in the carnelian in St. Petersburg (*Jahrb.* iii, pl. xi, 26).

The position of the right arm holding the thunderbolt in the gem is specially significant.

9. eminere videntur: cf. in § 127 *quae volunt eminentia videri ;* § 131 *ut eminerent e tabulis picturae.*

10. legentes meminerint : harks back to § 50.

§ 93. 12. megabyzi : Strabo xiv, p. 641 ἱερέας δ' εὐνούχους εἶχον οὓς ἐκάλουν Μεγοβύζους.

13. pompam : from Herondas iv, 66 ff. we learn that the picture was at Kos, in the παστός (Sanctuary) of the Asklepieion, and that it represented a sacrifice of oxen. It is amusingly described by the gossips Kokkale and Kynno (ed. Crusius).

ΚΟΚ. ὁ βοῦς δὲ χὠ ἄγων αὐτόν, ἤ θ' ὁμαρτεῦσα

χὠ γρυπὸς οὗτος χὠ ἀνάσιμος ἄνθρωπος,

οὐχὶ ζόην βλέπουσιν ἡμέρην πάντες ;

εἰ μὴ ἐδόκευν τι μέζον ἢ γυνὴ πρήσσειν,

ἀνηλάλαξ' ἄν, μή μ' ὁ βοῦς τι πημήνῃ,

When the lower portion was damaged no one could be found to restore it, and thus the very injury redounded to the glory of the artist. In course of time the panel of the picture fell into decay, *Its restora-* and Nero when Emperor substituted for it another picture by the *tion by* hand of Dorotheos. Apelles had begun another Aphrodite at **92** Kos, intending to surpass even the fame of his earlier achievement, but when only a part was finished envious death interposed, and no one was found to finish the outlines already traced. He *'Alexander* also painted in the temple of Artemis at Ephesos a portrait of *holding the* Alexander holding a thunderbolt for twenty talents [£4,200 *bolt.'* circ.]: the fingers seem to stand out and the thunderbolt to project from the picture;—the reader should remember that all this was done with four colours. For this picture he was paid in gold coins, reckoned not by number but by measure. He painted **93** too the train of a μεγάβυζος, or priest of Artemis of Ephesos, Kleitos on horseback going out to battle, and the picture of a squire handing a helmet to one who asks for it. It were vain to enumerate the number of times he painted Alexander and Philip. At Samos we admire his Habron, at Rhodes his Menander, king of Karia, and his Antaios, at Alexandria Gorgo-

οὕτω ἐπιλοξοῖ, Κυννί, τῇ ἑτέρῃ
κούρῃ.
ΚΥΝ. ἀληθιναί, φίλη, γὰρ αἱ Ἐφεσίου
χεῖρες
ἐς πάντ᾽ Ἀπελλέω γράμματ᾽,
οὐδ᾽ ἐρεῖς "κεῖνος
ὤνθρωπος ἐν μὲν εἶδεν, ἐν δ᾽
ἀπηρνήθη."
ἀλλ᾽ ᾧ ἐπὶ νοῦν γένοιτο, καὶ
θεῶν ψαύειν
ἠπείγεθ᾽ . . .

The use of the past tense ἠπείγετο shows that Apelles was no longer alive at the time Herondas wrote the Mimiamboi (circ. B. C. 280–273). For similar subjects cf. on § 126 (Pausias) and § 137 (Aristolaos). A curious but arbitrary explanation of the Koan picture, as representing the Egyptian bull Apis, is given by R. Meister in his ed. of Herondas, p. 222.

Clitum: surnamed ὁ μέλας (Plutarch, *Alex.* 16), the bosom friend of Alexander, whose life he saved at the Granikos, and by whom he was

afterwards slain: Arrian. iv, 8, &c.

14. galeam poscenti: [generally taken as descriptive of the portrait of Kleitos. But the change from the accusative to the dative would be barbarous, while the asyndetic enumeration shows that we have here a fresh subject. It was perhaps a grave picture (*expir. imago*); very similar subjects appear on grave reliefs (1) in Syracuse, rider with horn of plenty, standing by his horse, to *r.* attendant leaning on spear, to l. boy bringing helmet, snake between boy and horse, unpublished; (2) the relief from Thyrea in Athens, Friederichs-Wolters, 1812, cf. Deneken, *ap.* Roscher ii, art. 'Heros,' col. 2563. Also on vases, Naples, Heydemann 2192, from Canosa.—H.L.U.]

15. quotiens pinxerit: cf. xxxiv, 63, of Alexander's portraits by Lysippos.

16. Habronem: probably the painter mentioned below, § 141.

Sami: where the Heraion con-

drum regem Cariae Rhodi, item Antaeum, Alexandreae
Gorgosthenen tragoedum, Romae Castorem et Pollucem
cum Victoria et Alexandro Magno, item Belli imaginem
restrictis ad terga manibus, Alexandro in curru triumphante,
94 quas utrasque tabulas divus Augustus in fori sui celeberrimis 5
partibus dicaverat simplicitate moderata, divus Claudius
pluris existimavit utrique excisa Alexandri facie divi
Augusti imagines addere. eiusdem arbitrantur manu esse
et in Dianae templo Herculem aversum, ut, quod est difficillimum, faciem eius ostendat verius pictura quam promittat. 10
pinxit et heroa nudum, eaque pictura naturam ipsam provo-
95 cavit. est et equus eius sive fuit pictus in certamine, quo
iudicium ad mutas quadripedes provocavit ab hominibus.
namque ambitu praevalere aemulos sentiens singulorum
picturas inductis equis ostendit, Apellis tantum equo adhin- 15
nivere, idque et postea semper evenit, ut experimentum
96 artis illud ostentaretur. fecit et Neoptolemum ex equo
adversus Persas, Archelaum cum uxore et filia, Antigonum
thoracatum cum equo incedentem. peritiores artis praefe-
runt omnibus eius operibus eundem regem sedentem in equo 20
et Dianam sacrificantium virginum choro mixtam, quibus

tained a collection of pictures (Strabo xiv, p. 637 τὸ Ἡραῖον . . . νεὼς μέγας, ὃς νῦν πινακοθήκη ἐστί).

Menandrum: one τῶν ἑταίρων, Arrian, *Anabasis* iii, 6, 8 ; iv, 13, 7 ; vii, 24, 1, Diodoros xviii, 59; he was satrap of Lydia, and as no king of Karia of the name of Menander is known, it may be that we have here a confusion on Pliny's part, cf. Brunn, *K. G.* ii, p. 212.

1. **Antaeum:** unknown.

Alexandreae: above, § 89.

2. **tragoedum:** cf. the *temulenta tibicina* of Lysippos, xxxiv, 63, the *saltator Alcisthenes* in § 147, &c.

Castorem ... Magno: above, § 27. The type of Alexander between the Dioskouroi was at a later date adapted to triumphal pictures of the Emperors, cf. *Mon. d. Inst.* iii, 10.

4. **restrictis ad terga manibus':**

in § 27 the subject of the picture is described as Triumph and War. Servius on *Aen.* i, 294 (ed. Thilo i, p. 109) *in foro Augusti introeuntibus ad sinistram fuit bellum pictum et furor sedens super arma devinctus eo habitu quo poeta dixit;* it is of course possible that Pliny forgot to mention the *Furor*, but, as Jacobi (*Museogr.* p. 73) has pointed out, it is more likely that Servius, in order to give a more striking explanation of the Virgilian lines (*Claudentur Belli portae ; Furor impius intus | saeva sedens super arma et centum vinctus aenis | post tergum nodis fremet horridus ore cruento*), split the personification of War into two. We may assume from Servius, *loc. cit.*, that the first picture was on the R. of the spectator entering the Forum.

§ 94. 8. **arbitrantur:** i.e. a judge-

sthenes the tragic actor, at Rome Kastor and Polydeukes with *Allegorical* Victory and Alexander the Great, and also a figure of War with *pictures of Alexander* his hands bound behind his back, and Alexander riding in triumph *the Great.* in a chariot. These two pictures had been placed in the most 94 crowded parts of his forum with the restraint of good taste by the god Augustus, but the god Claudius thought fit to cut out in both the face of Alexander and substitute that of Augustus. The Herakles with averted face, in the temple of Diana, is also attributed to Apelles; by a triumph of art the picture seems not only to suggest, but actually to give the face. He also painted a nude hero, a picture which challenges comparison with Nature herself. A horse also exists, or did exist, painted for a com- 95 petition, in which he appealed from the judgement of men to that *An unfair verdict.* of dumb beasts. When he saw that his rivals were likely to be *The horses* placed above him through intrigue, he caused some horses to be *approve the picture of* brought in and showed them each picture in turn; they neighed *Apelles.* only at the horse of Apelles, and this was invariably the case ever afterwards, so that the test was applied purposely to afford a display of his skill. He also painted Neoptolemos on horse- 96 back fighting against the Persians, Archelaos in a group with his wife and daughter, and a portrait of Antigonos in armour advancing with his horse. Skilled judges of painting prefer among all his works his equestrian portrait of Antigonos and his Artemis amid a band of maidens offering sacrifice, a painting

ment of connoisseurs not certified by the artist's signature.

9. **Dianae**: in the campus *Flaminius* dedicated by Lepidus B.C. 179; Liv. xl, 52. The reading *Annae* (sc. *Perennae*) is defended by Jordan (*ap.* Preller, *Röm. Mythol.* 2nd ed. i, p. 344, note 1), but against his view see Wissowa *ap.* Pauly, *s. v.* Anna Perenna.

§ 95. 12. **est et equus**: according to Ailian, Ποικ. Ἱστ. ii, 3, the story was told of Alexander and the horse in his equestrian portrait. The *est ... sive fuit* show how little importance Pliny himself attaches to such anecdotes.

§ 96. 17. **Neoptolemum**: *not* the son of Achilles, as Welcker and others have supposed, but the ἑταῖρος of

Alexander, son of Arrhabaios, Arrian i, 20, 10; ii, 27, 6, Diodoros xviii, 29.

ex equo: sc. *pugnantem.*

18. **Archelaum**: two Archelaoi are known among the soldiers of Alexander, (1) the son of Androkles, one τῶν ἑταίρων; he was placed in command of the garrison left at Aornos (Arr. iii, 29, 1); (2) the son of Theodoros, who was placed in command at Susa (Arr. iii, 16, 9).

21. **sacrificantium**: since the words are at variance with the Homeric description, endless emendations of the passage have been suggested (see Overbeck, *Schriftquell.* 1870). The best explanation seems that of Dilthey (*Rhein. Mus.* xxv, p. 327), who supposes that in translating

vicisse Homeri versus videtur id ipsum describentis. pinxit
et quae pingi non possunt, tonitrua, fulgetra, fulgura, quae
97 Bronten, Astrapen, Ceraunobolian appellant. inventa eius
et ceteris profuere in arte, unum imitari nemo potuit, quod
absoluta opera atramento inlinebat ita tenui ut id ipsum 5
repercussu claritatis colorem album excitaret custodiretque
a pulvere et sordibus, ad manum intuenti demum appareret,
sed etiam ratione magna, ne claritas colorum aciem offende-
ret veluti per lapidem specularem intuentibus et e longin-
quo eadem res nimis floridis coloribus austeritatem occulte 10
daret.

98 Aequalis eius fuit Aristides Thebanus. is omnium primus
animum pinxit et sensus hominis expressit, quae vocant
Graeci ethe, item perturbationes, durior paulo in coloribus.
huius opera : oppido capto ad matris morientis ex volnere 15

6. alhum] *Traube* ; alvum *Bamb.* ; alium *Bamb. e corr.*, *Detlefsen* ; *om.
reliqui.* 8. etiam] *Bamb. e corr.* ; etium *Bamb.* ; et cum *Voss.*, *Detlefsen.*
15. opera] *Bamb.* ; pictura *reliqui*, *Detlefsen.*

some Greek epigram beginning for
instance :
·θυούσαις δὲ κόραισιν ὁμορρόθος ἰοχέαιρα
ἐξάρχουσα χορόν, σεύεται ἀγροτέρη.
Pliny or his author mistook θυούσαις
from θυέω for the partic. of θύω.

1. Homeri versus : Od. vi, 102—
οἵη δ' 'Αρτεμις εἶσι κατ' οὔρεα ἰοχέαιρα
  *   *   *   *   *
τῇ δέ θ' ἅμα Νύμφαι, κοῦραι Διὸς
αἰγιόχοιο,
ἀγρονόμοι παίζουσι.

3. Bronten . . . Ceraunobolian :
personifications [κεραυνοβολία was
the personification of κεραυνός (Diels,
Doxographi Graeci, p. 367 foll. and
Aetios Mac. ii, 2, 3, p. 368); for Bronte
cf. Philostr. the Elder *Imag.* i, 14
Βροντὴ ἐν εἴδει σκληρῷ καὶ 'Αστραπὴ
σέλας ἐκ τῶν ὀφθαλμῶν ἰεῖσα πῦρ . . .
Possibly the three figures were united
in an allegory of a storm and formed
a votive offering to Zeus κεραυνο-
βόλος ; cf. *C. I. G.* 1513 ; βροντῶν and
κεραύνιος, *C. I. G.* 2641, 3446, 3810,
and often.—H. L. U.].

§ 97. 5. atramento : the exact

composition of Apelles's *atramentum*
still remains obscure ; we can only
gather that although some black substance formed its basis, this was so
diluted and spread out as to become
transparent and practically colourless.

6. colorem album excitaret :
this passage offers grave difficulties.
(1) If we follow the remaining codices
in omitting the word *album* we get
pure nonsense, since it is absurd to
talk of a glazing that raised the
picture's colour as a whole, and yet
toned it down. (2) If we follow
Detlefsen and adopt the *alium* which
a later hand wrote for the *alvum* of
cod. Bamb. we get worse nonsense,
for what is this *color alius?* (3) I
cannot help suspecting that *albus* (used
of a dead, opaque white) is a mistranslation of the Greek λευκός in its
sense of 'brilliant' ; the object of the
glazing, then, was to give a brilliant
surface to the whole picture ; this
brought the colours into unison, and
at the same time served the practical
purpose of protecting the painting
from dust.

thought to have excelled the lines of Homer that describe the same scene. He also painted the unpaintable, thunder, for example, lightning and thunderbolts, βροντή, ἀστραπή and κεραυνοβολία as they are called.

All have profited by his innovations, though one of these could 97 never be imitated; he used to give his pictures when finished a black glazing so thin that by sending back the light it could call forth a whitish colour, while at the same time it afforded protection from dust and dirt, only becoming visible itself on the closest inspection. In using this glazing, one main purpose of his was to prevent the brilliance of the colours from offending the eyes,—the effect was as when they are looked at through talc, —and also that when seen at a distance those which were vivid to excess might be imperceptibly toned down.

Aristeides of Thebes was his contemporary: he was the first 98 among all painters to paint the soul, and gave expression to the *Aristeides of Thebes.* affections of man—I mean to what the Greeks call ἤθη—and also the emotions. His colouring is rather harsh. His works are:

9. **lapidem specularem**: xxxvi, 160; it was a transparent highly laminated substance, used also for windows (*specularia*), cf. Plin. *Ep.* ii, 17, 4; Juv. iv, 21, &c.

§ 98. 12. **Aristides Thebanus**: below, § 111; he was the second of the name, son of Nikomachos, § 108, and grandson of the first Aristeides, *ib.*, above, § 75.

omnium primus: note on § 16.

13. **sensus . . . perturbationes**: as O. Jahn points out (*Kunsturtheile*, p. 115), Pliny is here giving a closer definition of *animus* by dividing it into ἤθη and πάθη, for the first of which, according to Quinct. vi, 2, 8, no precise Latin equivalent existed: *horum* (sc. *affectuum*) *autem, sicut antiquitus traditum accepimus, duae sunt species: alteram Graeci* πάθος *vocant, quod nos vertentes recte ac proprie affectum dicimus, alteram* ἤθος, *cuius nomine, ut ego equidem sentio, caret sermo Romanus: mores appellantur, atque inde pars quoque illa philosophiae* ἠθική *moralis est dicta* (cf. above, note on *mores* in § 63).

Pliny, therefore, to avoid misunderstanding, gives the Greek word also for ἤθη, while for πάθη he felt himself on safe ground in using *perturbationes*, the translation introduced by Cicero (*Tusc. Disp.* iii, 4, 7). Not a few commentators have considered ἤθος, πάθος to be incompatible qualities in one artist, yet Quinct. (vi, 2, 12) shows that in a sense πάθος is complementary to ἤθος, while Ailian (Ποικ. Ἱστ. iv, 3) especially attributes both qualities to Polygnotos—the ἀγαθὸς ἠθογράφος. (For a thorough and subtle discussion of the question cf. O. Jahn, *op. cit.* pp. 105–117.)

15. **matris morientis**: the motive was employed in sculpture by Epigonos (xxxiv, 88). The picture is described *Anth. Pal.* vii, 623. The Plinian passage doubtless inspired the group of a dead mother with a young child seeking her breast, on the left of the celebrated 'Morbetto' or 'Phrygian Plague' engraved by Marc. Antonio (reproduced Delaborde, *M. Antoine Raimondi*, to face p. 214) according to general supposition from

mammam adrepens infans, intellegiturque sentire mater et timere ne emortuo lacte sanguinem lambat, quam tabulam Alexander Magnus transtulerat Pellam in patriam suam.
99 idem pinxit proelium cum Persis, centum homines tabula ea conplexus pactusque in singulos minas denas a tyranno 5 Elatensium Mnasone.   pinxit et currentes quadrigas et supplicantem paene cum voce et venatores cum captura et Leontion Epicuri et anapauomenen propter fratris amorem, item Liberum et Ariadnen spectatos Romae in aede Cereris,
100 tragoedum et puerum in Apollinis, cuius tabulae gratia 10 interiit pictoris inscitia cui tergendam eam mandaverat M. Iunius praetor sub die ludorum Apollinarium.   spectata est

a drawing of Raphael. But the drawing in sepia wash and white in the Uffizi (cornice 265, no. 525) is only, Mr. B. Berenson informs me, a copy after an original, now lost, that may have been by Perino del Vaga.

3. transtulerat Pellam: after the sack of Thebes in B.C. 335.

§ 99. 4. proelium cum Persis: since Aristeides is a contemporary of Apelles and Alexander, the picture must have represented one of the battles of this king.   It is tempting to identify the *proelium* with the battle of Issos and to recognize its copy in the famous mosaic from Pompei in Naples: the powerfully characterized Alexander, the Dareios with his gesture of despairing command are conceptions worthy of the great master of *ἦθος* and *πάθος*, while motives such as the fallen Persian in the foreground recall the *mater moriens*.   It is possible, however, that the Pompeian mosaic should be rather traced back to Aristeides's fellow-pupil Philoxenos (§ 109) (Michaelis, *Jahrb.* vii, 1893, p. 134), whose battle-piece is more closely defined as *proelium cum Dario*. It is, at any rate, time to claim the picture for powerful artists such as Aristeides or Philoxenos, and to discard the opinion which attributes it to a lady-painter Helena, reputed indeed to have painted a battle of Issos, but only on

the authority of so notorious a liar as Ptolemaios Chennos. Addenda.

6. Mnasone: a pupil and friend of Aristotle, circ. B.C. 349 (Timaios *apud* Athenaios, vi, p. 264 D, Ailian, Ποικ. Ἱστ. iii, 19). He was made tyrant of Elateia after the battle of Chaironeia in B.C. 338.

currentes quadrigas: votive offerings for victories in the chariot course, cf. note on xxxiv, 71.

7. supplicantem: making a gesture of entreaty, probably the picture was that of an *adorans;* cf. xxxiv, 73, 90, &c.   *Cum voce* epigr. cf. Introd. p. lxxi.

venatores cum captura: note on xxxiv, 66; cf. the hunt of Ptolemaios Soter by Antiphilos in § 138.

8. Leontion Epicuri: friend and pupil of Epikouros (B.C. 341–270), and mistress of his favourite pupil Metrodoros; she was a rival of Glykera (Athen. xiii, p. 585 D), who came to Athens with Harpalos, B.C. 326. Aristeides probably painted her not much later than B.C. 320.   Although Epikouros did not reside in Athens before B.C. 306, it is natural that her portrait, whenever painted, should be described as that of the famous '*Leontion Epicuri*,' Kroker, *Gleichnamige Gr. Künstler*, p. 28; Urlichs, *Rhein. Mus.* xxv, p. 511 f.   Another portrait of her by Theoros below, § 144.

a picture of a mother lying wounded to death in the sack of *Wounded*
a city; she appears conscious that her babe is creeping towards *mother and her child.*
her breast, and afraid lest, now that her milk is dried up, he
should suck blood. This picture Alexander the Great carried off
to his native Pella. He also painted a battle with the Persians; 99
the picture contains a hundred figures, for each of which Mnason
the tyrant of Elateia had agreed to pay him ten minae [£35];
and furthermore a chariot race, and a suppliant whose very accents
we seem to hear, huntsmen with their game, Leontion the pupil
of Epikouros, a girl dying for love of her brother, the Dionysos
and Ariadne now to be seen at Rome in the temple of Ceres, and
a tragic actor and a boy in the temple of Apollo. This picture 100
was ruined through the ignorance of the painter to whom Marcus
Junius as praetor entrusted it to be cleaned before the games of
Apollo. In the temple of Faith on the Capitol was to be seen

anapauomenen . . . amorem:
[the subject, which has given rise to
much controversy (see especially Dilthey and L. Urlichs in *Rhein. Mus.*
xxv and xxvi) is sufficiently easy to
explain by reference to *Anth. Pal.* vii,
517—

Ἠῷοι Μελάνιππον ἐθάπτομεν, ἠελίου δὲ
δυομένου Βασιλὼ κάτθανε παρθενεκὴ
αὐτοχερί· ζώειν γὰρ ἀδελφεὸν ἐν πυρὶ
θεῖσα,
οὐκ ἔτλη. δίδυμον δ'οῖκος ἐσεῖδε κακὸν
πατρὸς 'Αριστίπποιο· κατήφησεν δὲ Κυ-
ρήνη
πᾶσα, τὸν εὔτεκνον χῆρον ἰδοῦσα
δόμον.

Evidently the *anapauomene* was a girl
who had died in grief at her brother's
death. The picture was a grave picture, an *expirantis imago* (§ 90), and
the name anapauomene was doubtless
derived from the epigram inscribed
upon it: ἀναπαύεσθαι, here of rest in
death.—H. L. U.] Introd. p. lxxi.

9. spectatos: before the fire which
took place in the reign of Augustus,
Strabo, viii, p. 381; see note above on
§ 24, where the Dionysos alone is
mentioned.

aede Cereris: note on xxxiv, 15.

10. tragoedum et puerum: has

sometimes been explained of a tragic
actor playing his part with a boy (e.g.
Maas, *Ann. d. Inst,* 1881, p. 142,
155, suggests Priam and Troilos), but
it more probably simply represented
an older actor teaching a boy his part;
for the subject cf. Schreiber, *Hell. Rel.*
pl. 47, 48; Helbig, *Wandgemälde,*
1455 (actor with poet), and the cylix by
Douris in Berlin (Furtwängler, *Vasen,*
ii, 2285), also a similar subject below;
an old man with a lyre teaching a
boy.

Apollinis: in the temple on the
Campus Flaminius, near the *porticus Octaviae,* xxxvi, 34; dedicated
B.C. 430, for the removal of a plague
(Liv. iv, 25), it remained down to the
age of Augustus the only temple to
the god in Rome (Asconius on Cic.
In toga candida, p. 91). In B.C. 32,
C. Sosius dedicated in it a cedar-wood
statue of the god which he brought
from Seleukia (xiii, 53); hence the
temple is sometimes called *templum
Apollinis Sosiani.*

§ 100. 11. M. Junius: probably
Silanus, cos. B.C. 25.

12. ludorum Apollinarium: held
on July 13; instituted B.C. 212.

et in aede Fidei in Capitolio senis cum lyra puerum docentis. pinxit et aegrum sine fine laudatum, tantumque arte valuit ut Attalus rex unam tabulam eius centum talentis emisse
101 tradatur. simul, ut dictum est, et Protogenes floruit. patria ei Caunus, gentis Rhodiis subiectae. summa paupertas 5 initio artisque summa intentio et ideo minor fertilitas. quis eum docuerit non putant constare, quidam et naves pinxisse usque ad quinquagensimum annum, argumentum esse, quod cum Athenis celeberrimo loco Minervae delubri propylon pingeret, ubi fecit nobilem Paralum et Hammoni- 10 ada, quam quidam Nausicaan vocant, adiecerit parvolas naves longas in iis quae pictores parergia appellant, ut appareret a quibus initiis ad arcem ostentationis opera sua
102 pervenissent. palmam habet tabularum eius Ialysus, qui est Romae dicatus in templo Pacis. cum pingeret eum, 15

1. **aede Fidei**: Livy (i, 21), attributes its foundation to Numa; restored B. C. 115 by M. Aemilius Scaurus; it was on the Capitol, see Gilbert, *Rom*, iii, p. 399, note 2.

2. **aegrum**: votive picture for a recovery ; for the subject Furtwängler (*Jahrb.* iii, p. 218) compares an excellent bronze statuette of a sick man (in the Cook coll. at Richmond).

3. **Attalus rex**: vii, 126. = App. I. § 101. 4. **ut dictum est** : in § 81.
patria Caunus: so also Paus. i, 3, 5, Plut. *Demetr.* 22, while Souidas names Xanthos in Lykia as his birthplace.

7. **quis eum docuerit** : cf. Seilanion xxxiv, 51 ; Lysippos, *ibid.* 61 ; see Introd. p. xlvi ff.
naves pinxisse: i.e. he would paint the παράσημα and ἐπίσημα of ships.

9. **Athenis**: he was probably twice at Athens ; Curtius conjectures that his picture of the 'Thesmothetai' (Paus. i, 3, 5), in the *Bouleuterion*, was connected with the re-organization of the νομοφύλακες by Demetrios of Phaleron, but that in the days of Pausanias, the origin of the picture

being forgotten, it was called after the old republican θεσμοθέται (*Stadt-Geschichte von Athen*, p. 229). Add.— The second visit was under his special patron Demetrios Poliorketes, on the occasion alluded to here.

10. **propylon**: cf. xxxvi, 32 *Charites in propylo Atheniensium quas Socrates fecit ;* the unusual form *propylon* for the more familiar *propylaeum* or *propylaea* justifies us in attributing both passages to the same authority ; Wachsmuth, *Stadt Athen*, i, 36, 2 ; Introd. p. l.
Paralum et Hammoniada : i.e. the patron-heroes of the two holy triremes. The Ammonias—ἡ τοῦ Ἄμμωνος ἱερὰ τριήρης—(see Kenyon's note on Aristotle, 'Aθην. Πολ. p. 152) replaced the old Salaminia. The choice of the name is characteristic of the Antigonids and their strenuous efforts to keep alive the memory of the deified Alexander (Curtius, *op. cit.* p. 233); for the holy triremes cf. Boeckh-Fränkel, *Staatsalterthümer*, p. 305 ff. ; Boeckh, *Seeurkunden*, p. 76 ff.

11. **Nausicaan** : both figures were, it seems, united in one picture which

a picture of an old man with a lyre teaching a boy. Aristeides also painted a sick man, a picture never sufficiently praised, and so great was his name that king Attalos, we are told, paid a hundred talents [£21,000 circ.] for a single picture by his hand.

Protogenes, as I have already said, was a painter of the same date. He was a native of Kaunos, a city subject to Rhodes. The great poverty of his early days and his scrupulous devotion to his art were the causes that he produced but few pictures. The name of his master is supposed to be unknown, while some say that he painted ships until his fiftieth year, and adduce in proof thereof that when he was at Athens decorating, in the most celebrated of spots, the gateway to the temple of Athene, for which he painted his famous Paralos and Hammonias,—a figure sometimes called Nausikaa,—he introduced some tiny warships in the part of the picture called the παρέργια, purposing to show the humble origin of the painter whose works had risen to such a height of glory. Among his pictures the Ialysos, dedicated in the Temple of Peace at Rome, bears off the palm. The story

101
Protogenes of Kaunos. Obscurity of his early life.

102
The 'Ialysos.'

lent itself to interpretation as Odysseus and Nausikaa ; but see C. Torr, *Class. Rev.* iv, 1890, p. 231.

parvolas naves: perhaps along the edge of the picture; they were merely ornamental, or, at the most, served to indicate that the hero and heroine depicted were connected with ships. C. Torr (*loc. cit.*) suggests that the little warships were represented in the background out at sea, the figures themselves being in the foreground upon the shore. In this case the 'smallness' was due simply to the necessities of perspective. The explanation given by Pliny is evidently aitiological, nor is it necessary to follow Curtius (*loc. cit.*) in bracketing the *et*, and taking these small triremes to indicate ' to what a height of glory — from what small beginnings—ship-building had attained.'

12. **parergia**: diminutive of πάρεργον. No specific part of the picture is intended, but only a subordinate or incidental detail. The word is best

explained by reference to Strabo xiv, p. 652, where it is related that Protogenes was vexed because in his picture of the Satyr (below, § 105) the admiration roused by the partridge had caused the work itself—τὸ ἔργον—to become a πάρεργον.

§ 102. 14. **Ialysus**: a Rhodian hero, after whom the city of Ἰάλυσος was named ; son of Kerkaphos and Kydippe, whose other sons were the eponymous heroes Lindos and Kameiros (Pindar, *Ol.* vii, 74). The dog shows that Ialysos was represented as a huntsman. Possibly the picture was one of a cycle of Rhodian heroes, likewise including the *Kydippe* and *Tlepolemos* (below, § 106). When Strabo wrote (*loc. cit.*), the picture was still at Rhodes; it was probably brought away by Vespasian and placed at once in his Temple of Peace. Plutarch (*Dem.* 22) says it was already burnt in his day.

15. **templo Pacis**: note on xxxiv, 84.

traditur madidis lupinis vixisse, quo simul et famem susti-
neret et sitim nec sensus nimia dulcedine obstrueret.   huic
picturae quater colorem induxit contra obsidia iniuriae et
vetustatis, ut decedente superiore inferior succederet.   est
in ea canis mire factus ut quem pariter et casus pinxerit. 5
non iudicabat se in eo exprimere spumam anhelantis, cum
in reliqua parte omni, quod difficillimum erat, sibi ipse
103 satisfecisset.   displicebat autem ars ipsa nec minui poterat,
et videbatur nimia ac longius a veritate discedere, spumaque
illa pingi, non ex ore nasci ; anxio animi cruciatu, cum in 10
pictura verum esse, non verisimile vellet, absterserat saepius
mutaveratque penicillum, nullo modo sibi adprobans.   postremo iratus arti, quod intellegeretur, spongeam inpegit
inviso loco tabulae, et illa reposuit ablatos colores qualiter
104 cura optaverat, fecitque in pictura fortuna naturam.   hoc 15
exemplo eius similis et Nealcen successus spumae equi
similiter spongea inpacta secutus dum celetem pingit ac
poppyzonta retinentem eum.   ita Protogenes monstravit et
fortunam.   propter hunc Ialysum, ne cremaret tabulam,
Demetrius rex, cum ab ea parte sola posset Rhodum capere, 20
non incendit, parcentemque picturae fugit occasio victoriae.
105 erat tunc Protogenes in suburbano suo hortulo, hoc est
Demetrii castris, neque interpellatus proeliis inchoata opera

1. quo] *Traube* ; quoniam, *codd.*, *Detlefsen.*   sustineret] *codd.* ; sustinerent
Detlefsen.   2. obstrueret] *Bamb.* ; obstruerent *reliqui, Detlefsen.*   17. dum
celetem pingit ac] *Traube* ; disceret cum pingitur *Bamb.* ; dicitur, cum
pingeret, *Detlefsen.*

3. obsidia iniuriae ac vetustatis : hendiadys, to avoid the
awkward co-ordination of genitives ;
cf. Petron. 84 *nondum vetustatis iniuria victus.* In spite of the ingenious
remarks of Berger (*Beiträge*, ii, p. 19),
I think the story of the four coats
of colour may still be considered
apocryphal.

§ 103. 15. fortuna: the whole anecdote is an amusing illustration of the
saying of Agathon (*ap.* Arist. *Nic.
Ethics*, vi, 4), τέχνη τύχην ἔστερξε
καὶ τύχη τέχνην. Introd. p. xli f.

§ 104. 16. Nealcen : below,
§§ 142, 145.   The following anecdote

is told also by Plut. περὶ Τύχης, p.
99 B. (= Bernardakis I, p. 240) and
by Val. Max. viii, 11, ext. 7 (without
naming the artist).   Dio Chrysostom
and Sextus Empiricus (see *S. Q.* 1889)
tell the story of Apelles.

17. celetem . . . poppyzonta :
for the subject in sculpture cf. (*a*)
Winter *Jahrb.* viii, 1893, p. 142 ; (*b*)
Parthenon W. frieze, viii, 15, 22 (*Cat.*
p. 180) &c. ; (*c*) a gem in the Coll.
Tyskiewiez (Furtwängler *Ant. Gemmen*, pl. ix, 14).

20. ab ea parte sola : cf. vii, 126.
The picture was in the temple of
Dionysos just outside the city (Strabo,

runs that while he was painting it he lived on lupins steeped in
water, that he might thus satisfy at once his hunger and his
thirst without blunting his faculties by over-indulgence. He gave
this picture four coats of colour to preserve it from the approach
of injury and age, so that if the first coat peeled off the one below
might take its place. The dog in this picture is the outcome as *The foam*
it were of miracle, since chance, and not art alone, went to the *of the dog is painted*
painting of it. The artist felt that he had not perfectly rendered *by miracle.*
the foam of the panting animal, although he had satisfied himself
—a difficult task—in the rest of the painting. It was the very 103
skill which displeased him and which could not be concealed, but
obtruded itself too much, thus making the effect unnatural; it
was foam painted with the brush, not frothing from the mouth.
Chafing with anxiety, for he aimed at absolute truth in his painting and not at a makeshift, he had wiped it out again and again,
and changed his brush without finding any satisfaction. At last,
enraged with the art which was too evident, he threw his sponge
at the hateful spot, and the sponge left on the picture the colours
it had wiped off, giving the exact effect he had intended, and
chance thus became the mirror of nature. Nealkes likewise 104
once succeeded in rendering the foam of a horse in the same *The same happens to*
way, by throwing his sponge at the picture he was painting of *a horse in*
a groom coaxing a race-horse. Thus Protogenes even taught the *a picture by Nealkes.*
uses of fortune. It was to preserve this Ialysos that king Demetrios
refrained from setting fire to the city, which was open to attack
on that side only, and by sparing the picture he forfeited his
chance of victory. At the time of the siege Protogenes was living 105
in his little garden beyond the walls, within the lines of Demetrios.
He did not allow the war to interrupt his work, but went on with *Generosity*
the pictures he was painting, except when summoned to the *of Deme-trios*
presence of the king, and when asked what gave him courage to *towards Protogenes.*

loc. cit.); for a fuller account of
the episode see in especial Plutarch,
Dem. 22; the story has little historical
credibility, but, as Helbig (*Unters.*
p. 181) points out, serves to emphasize
the love of art which characterized
'the most genial of the Diadochoi.'

Rhodum: i.e. the new city
founded in B.C. 408; for the siege cf.
xxxiv, 41.

§ 105. 22. erat tunc Protogenes:

the story, which recurs in a variety of
forms, is suspicious: thus Archimedes
was found quietly drawing geometric
figures when the Romans stormed
Syracuse (Liv. xxv, 31, 9); in modern
times the painter Parmegianino was
found calmly painting a Madonna
when the Spanish and Dutch troops,
under Constable of Bourbon, stormed
Rome in 1527, &c.

intermisit omnino nisi accitus a rege, interrogatusque qua
fiducia extra muros ageret respondit scire se cum Rhodiis
illi bellum esse, non cum artibus. disposuit rex in tutelam
eius stationes, gaudens quod posset manus servare quibus
pepercerat, et ne saepius avocaret, ultro ad eum venit hostis 5
relictisque victoriae suae votis inter arma et murorum ictus
spectavit artificem, sequiturque tabulam illius temporis haec
106 fama, quod eam Protogenes sub gladio pinxerit. Satyrus
hic est quem anapauomenon vocant, ne quid desit temporis
eius securitati, tenentem tibias. fecit et Cydippen, Tlepo- 10
lemum, Philiscum tragoediarum scriptorem meditantem et
athletam et Antigonum regem, matrem Aristotelis philosophi, qui ei suadebat ut Alexandri Magni opera pingeret
propter aeternitatem rerum. impetus animi et quaedam
artis libido in haec potius eum tulere. novissime pinxit 15
Alexandrum ac Pana. fecit et signa ex aere, ut diximus.
107 eadem aetate fuit Asclepiodorus, quem in symmetria mirabatur Apelles. huic Mnaso tyrannus pro duodecim diis
dedit in singulos mnas tricenas, idemque Theomnesto in
108 singulos heroas vicenas. his adnumerari debet et Nico- 20
machus Aristidi filius ac discipulus. pinxit raptum
Proserpinae, quae tabula fuit in Capitolio in Minervae
delubro supra aediculam Iuventatis, et in eodem Capitolio,

21. Aristidi] *Urlichs in Chrestom.*; aristiaci *Bamb. Detlefsen*; aristicheimi
Riccard; ariste //// *Voss.*; aristecheimi *Lips.*

§ 106. 9. ne . . . securitati :
Strabo describes the Satyr as leaning
on a column, apparently somewhat in
the scheme of the celebrated 'Resting
Satyr' by Praxiteles, Helbig, *Class. Ant.*
525. Furtwängler, *Masterpieces*, p. 329.
10. Cydippen, Tlepolemum :
above, note on *Ialysus* in § 102.
Tlepolemos led the Rhodian contin-
gent to Troy (*Il.* ii, 653).
11. Philiscum trag. script.: he
was a native of Kerkyra. According
to Athen. v, 198 c he took part in the
great πομπή of Ptolemy Philadelphos,
B.C. 284, in virtue of his office of
priest of Dionysos. The theory that
the beautiful relief in the Lateran

(Benndorf-Schöne,245 = Helbig,*Class.
Ant.* 663) is a copy of Protogenes'
picture is quite uncertain.
12. Antigonum regem : painted
by Apelles, above, §§ 90, 96.
matrem Aristotelis : her name
was Phaestis. Cf. Introd. p. lxi.
16. Alexandrum ac Pana : probably Alexander was represented as
Dionysos, to whom, according to the
legend, Pan acted as shieldbearer
during his progress through India,
Lucian, *Dionys.* 2 ; Helbig, *Untersuchungen*, p. 50.
ut diximus : xxxiv, § 91.
§ 107. 17. Asclepiodorus : above,
§ 80 ; he may be identical with the

remain outside the walls, he replied that he knew the king was making war against Rhodes, not against art. Demetrios placed sentinels to guard him, and took a pride in protecting the artist he had spared. Unwilling to call him from his work, Demetrios, enemy though he was, visited him in person, and in the midst of arms and of assaults neglected his hopes of victory to watch the painter. Hence comes the saying about the picture which Protogenes was engaged on at the time, that he had painted it under the sword. This is the Satyr called the ἀναπαυόμενος [resting], 106 and he is holding the pipes, to emphasize the painter's sense of security at the moment. He also painted a Kydippe, and a Tlepolemos, Philiskos the tragedian in meditation, an athlete, a portrait of king Antigonos, and the mother of Aristotle the philosopher, who had tried to persuade him to paint the exploits of Alexander the Great, on the ground that they deserved immortality, but the natural turn of his genius, and his artist's caprice drew the painter rather to these other themes. Alexander and Pan were the last subjects he ever painted; as already noted, he also made bronze statues.

The *Asklepiodoros* whose knowledge of symmetry was praised 107 by Apelles, belonged to the same epoch; the tyrant Mnason *Asklepiodoros.* gave him thirty minae [100 guineas circ.] for each of his twelve gods, and to †*Theomnestos* twenty minae [£70 circ.] for each of his heroes.

We must rank with these artists *Nikomachos*, the son and pupil 108 of Aristeides. He painted the rape of Persephone, which was in *Nikomachos, son o[f] Aristeides.* the temple of Minerva on the Capitol, above the little chapel of

---

sculptor xxxiv, 86. He must have held a high position since Plutarch, *Glor. Athen.* 2, mentions him along with Apollodoros (above, § 60), Euphranor (below, § 128); Nikias (§ 132), and Panainos (§ 59), as one of the masters who made Athens glorious through their paintings.

18. **Mnaso** : above, note on § 99.

§ **108.** 20. **Nicomachus** : the mention in Cic. *Brutus*, 18, 70, is alone sufficient to prove his high reputation, yet his works are known from Pliny only; to the list given here must be added the unfinished Tyndaridai, in § 145.

21. **Aristidi** : i. e. the Elder, cf. above, § 75; Urlichs' reading is confirmed by the fact that whereas in § 110 Ariston appears as brother and pupil of Nikomachos, he appears in § 111 as a son and pupil of Aristeides, hence Nikomachos too must have been the son of an Aristeides, Kroker, *Gleichnamige Gr. Künstler*, p. 26.

raptum Proserpinae : for the subject cf. note on xxxiv, 69.

22. **fuit** : before the fire of 69 A. D.; above, note on xxxiv, 38.

23. **aediculam Iuventatis** : in the actual cella of Minerva, near the statue of the goddess; the cult of *Iuventas*,

quam Plancus imperator posuerat, Victoria quadrigam in
sublime rapicns. Ulixi primus addidit pilleum. pinxit et
109 Apollinem ac Dianam, deumque matrem in leone sedentem,
item nobiles Bacchas obreptantibus Satyris, Scyllamque
quae nunc est Romae in templo Pacis. nec fuit alius in ea 5
arte velocior. tradunt namque conduxisse pingendum ab
Aristrato Sicyoniorum tyranno quod is faciebat Telesti
poetae monimentum praefinito die intra quem perageretur,
nec multo ante venisse tyranno in poenam accenso paucisque
110 diebus absolvisse et celeritate et arte mira. discipulos 10
habuit Aristonem fratrem et Aristiden filium et Philo-
xenum Eretrium, cuius tabula nullis postferenda Cassandro
regi picta continuit Alexandri proelium cum Dario. idem
pinxit et lasciviam, in qua tres Sileni comissantur. hic
celeritatem praeceptoris secutus breviores etiamnum quas- 15
111 dam picturae conpendiarias invenit. adnumeratur his et
Nicophanes elegans ac concinnus ita ut venustate ei pauci
conparentur. cothurnus ei et gravitas artis multum a

like that of *Terminus* (in the same
temple) was one of the oldest in
Rome; Liv. i, 55, 4; v, 54, 7; for
full literature cf. Wissowa, *ap.* Roscher,
ii, pp. 666, 708, *s. v.* Jupiter; *ib.*
p. 764, *s. v.* Juventas.

1. **Plancus imperator** : sc. L.
Munatius, triumphed B. C. 43 (for his
assumption of the title of *imperator* cf.
Cic. *Phil.* iii, 38, and the letters of
Plancus, *ap.* Cic. *ad Fam.* x, 8; 24).
His brother L. Plautius Plancus
(adopted by L. Plautius) struck in B.C.
45 a coinage with a type of Nike and
horses, which is apparently a copy of
the picture by Nikomachos (see next
note and cf. Helbig, *Untersuchungen*,
p. 154). Furtwängler (*Jahrb.* iv,
1889, p. 62) hence suspects an error on
the part of Pliny in naming the more
famous *Plancus Imp.* as dedicator of
the statue.

**Victoria quadrigam in sub-
lime rapiens**: Furtwängler (*loc. cit.*)
emphasizes the opinion already expressed by Panofka (13th *Winckelmannsprogramm*) and Schuchardt

(*Nikomachos*, p. 20 ff.) that the composition survives on a beautiful gem
signed Ροῦφος (*Jahrb.* iii, 1888, pl. xi,
10), in St. Petersburg, representing
Nike with outspread wings, bearing
away a team of four horses. This
theory is confirmed by the fact that
the composition is repeated on the
coins of the *gens Plautia* (Babelon,
Monnaies de la Rép. Rom. ii, p. 325).
The painting of Nikomachos was of
course a votive offering for a victory
in the chariot race. ' Instead of the
usual traditional type, in which the
winner appears in his chariot crowned
by victory, or else Nike standing in
the chariot guides the horses, Nikomachos ventured on a daring invention ; ignoring the chariot and the
earthly chariot course, he painted the
triumphant horses as they are borne
aloft to victory by Nike herself.'
(F.)

2. **Ulixi primus** : Servius on
Aeneid ii, 44 (Thilo i, p. 222) *huic
Ulixi primus Nicomachus pictor pilleo
caput texisse fertur*, but the Schol.

Youth, and a Victory snatching up to Heaven a team of horses; this was also to be seen in the Capitol, where Plancus had dedicated it when general. He was the first to give a cap to Ulysses. He also painted an Apollo and Artemis, a Mother of the Gods 109 seated on her lion, a celebrated picture of Mainades with Satyrs stealing upon them, and a Scylla now at Rome in the temple of Peace. No artist surpassed him in rapidity of execution. It *His* is said, for instance, that Aristratos, tyrant of Sikyon, com- *rapidity.* missioned him to paint before a fixed day the monument which he was raising to the poet Telestes; Nikomachos arrived only a little before the appointed time, and the tyrant in his annoyance wished to punish him, but the painter finished the work in a few days with a promptitude as marvellous as his success. His pupils 110 were his brother †*Ariston*, his son *Aristeides* and †*Philoxenos* of Eretria, who painted for king Kassander the battle between Alexander and Dareios, a picture second to none; he also painted a scene of revelry in which three Seilenoi are making merry. He imitated the swiftness of his master, and himself invented some shortened methods of technique. We must include in this list 111 *Nikophanes*, a painter at once graceful and precise, whose delicacy *Niko-* few can equal, though he lacks the grandeur and dignity found in *phanes.*

on *Iliad* x, 265 attributes the innovation to Apollodoros.

3. Apollinem ac Dianam: a group. deumque matrem: i. e. Kybele sitting on her lion, as for instance on the Pergamene frieze, and on the frieze from the temple at Priene (fragment in Br. Mus.).

§ 109. 4. nobiles Bacchas obrept. Sat.: for the subject, cf. *Wandgemälde*, 542–556 ; Schreiber, *Hell. Reliefs*, xxiv. None of these compositions can, however, be referred with certainty to Nikomachos.

Scyllamque: Schuchardt (*Nikomachos*, p. 40 ff.) proposes to recognize a copy of the picture of Nikomachos in the *Scylla, Mon. d. Inst.* iii, pl. liii, 3 = Helbig, *Wandgemälde*, 1063; the same composition recurs on coins struck by S. Pompeius.

7. Aristrato: tyrant of Sikyon, Ol. 105 = B.C. 360–357.
Telesti: a dithyrambic poet, native

of Selinos, who had apparently migrated to Sikyon (Athen. xiv, p. 616, 625). In B.C. 401 he won the first prize at Athens.

§ 110. 11. Aristidem filium: i. e. *Aristides Thebanus*, above, § 98, cf. below, § 111.

12. Cassandro regi: B.C. 306–296.

13. proelium cum Dario: at Issos in B.C. 433, or Gaugamela in B.C. 431. See note above on *proelium cum Persis*, in § 99.

16. compendiarias: what this 'shortened method' may have been it is impossible to tell; cf. Petron. 2 *pictura quoque non alium exitum fecit, postquam Aegyptiorum audacia tam magnae artis compendiariam invenit*. See Addenda.

§ 111. 17. Nicophanes: below, § 137 ; *adnumeratur his*, because he belongs to approximately the same date.

Zeuxide et Apelle abest. Apellis discipulus Perseus, ad
quem de hac arte scripsit, huius fuerat aetatis. Aristidis
Thebani discipuli fuerunt et filii Niceros et Ariston, cuius
est Satyrus cum scypho coronatus, discipuli Antorides et
Euphranor, de quo mox dicemus.   5
112 Namque subtexi par est minoris picturae celebres in
penicillo, e quibus fuit Piraeicus. arte paucis postferendus
proposito nescio an destruxerit se, quoniam humilia quidem
secutus humilitatis tamen summam adeptus est gloriam.
tonstrinas sutrinasque pinxit et asellos et obsonia ac similia, 10
ob haec cognominatus rhyparographos, in iis consummatae
voluptatis, quippe eae pluris veniere quam maximae multo-
113 rum. e diverso Maeniana, inquit Varro, omnia operiebat
Serapionis tabula sub Veteribus. hic scaenas optime pinxit,
sed hominem pingere non potuit. contra Dionysius nihil 15
aliud quam homines pinxit, ob id anthropographos cogno-
114 minatus. parva et Callicles fecit, item Calates comicis
tabellis, utraque Antiphilus. namque et Hesionam nobilem
pinxit et Alexandrum ac Philippum cum Minerva, qui sunt
in schola in Octaviae porticibus, et in Philippi Liberum 20

2. de . . . arte scripsit: above,
§ 79, Introd. p. xl.
  Aristidis Thebani: above, §§ 98–
100, 110; he appears here as master
of Nikeros-Euphranor, by confusion
with his grandfather Aristeides I,
above, note on § 108.
  5. Euphranor: he is erroneously
made into a pupil of Aristeides of
Thebes, whereas he was the pupil of
the older Aristeides, above, § 75. *mox
dicemus*, in § 128.
  § 112. 7. Piraeicus = Πειραϊκός fr.
Πειραιεύς, Helbig, *Untersuch.* 366 ff.
This artist is still known only from
Pliny, the *Pireicus* of Propert. iii, 9,
12, which rested on mere interpolation, having been abandoned for *Parrhasius* by recent editors: *Parrhasius
parva vindicat arte locum.*
  10. tonstrinas sutrinasque: cf.
the *lanificium* by Antiphilos in § 138,
the workshops by Philiskos and Simos
in § 143.

§ 113. 13. e diverso: in contradiction to the small pictures by Peiraikos.
  Maeniana: *maeniana appellata
sunt a Maenio censore qui primus in
foro ultra columnas tigna proiecit, quo
ampliarentur superiora spectacula,*
Festus, 134. This derivation is probably correct, though the word soon
became a common appellative, cf.
Vitruvius, v, 1, 1. Jordan (*Top. der
Stadt Rom*, vol. i, part 2, p. 383,
note 94) believes that Pliny alludes to
a temporary exhibition of a picture by
Serapion, and not to painted decorations of the *maeniana*. The date of
Serapion is unknown, except that it
must have been previous to Varro,
from whom the information as to his
pictures is derived.
  inquit Varro: from whom §§ 112–
114 appear to be almost wholly derived, Münzer, *op. cit.* p. 540 f.
  14. sub Veteribus: note on § 25.

Zeuxis and Apelles. *Perseus*, the pupil to whom Apelles dedicated his book on art, also belongs to this period. The pupils of Aristeides of Thebes were his sons †*Nikeros* and †*Ariston* (by the second of whom we have a crowned Satyr holding a cup) and also †*Antorides* and *Euphranor*, of whom I shall speak presently. *Pupils of Aristeides.*

It is well to add an account of the artists who won fame with the brush in painting smaller pictures. Amongst them was †*Peiraïkos*. In mastery of his art but few take rank above him, yet by his choice of a path he has perhaps marred his own success, for he followed a humble line, winning however the highest glory that it had to bring. He painted barbers' shops, cobblers' stalls, asses, eatables and similar subjects, earning for himself the name of ῥυπαρογράφος [painter of odds and ends]. In these subjects he could give consummate pleasure, selling them for more than other artists received for their large pictures. As a contrast, Varro mentions a picture by †*Serapion* which covered the whole of the balconies by the Old Shops. This Serapion was an excellent scene-painter, but could not paint the figure. *Dionysios* on the contrary painted figures only, and was called ἀνθρωπογράφος [painter of men]. *112 Genre painters. Peiraïkos. 113 Serapion. Dionysios, the 'painter of men.'*

Kallikles also painted small pictures, and so did †*Kalates*, who chose comic subjects; while *Antiphilos* painted in both styles, his being a famous Hesione, and the picture of Alexander and Philip with Athene now to be seen in the 'schools' of the gallery of Octavia. In the gallery of Philip are his Dionysos, his young *114 Kallikles. Kalates. Antiphilos.*

15. **Dionysius**: probably identical with the portrait painter named § 148, but not to be confused with the painter Dionysios of Kolophon, a contemporary of Polygnotos (Arist. *Poet.* 2).

§ **114.** 17. **parva et Callicles**: known besides only from the following passage of Varro, *neque ille Callicles quaternum digitum tabellis nobilis cum esset factus, tamen in pingendo adscendere potuit ad Euphranoris altitudinem*, Varro, *de Vita P. R.* 1, ap. Charisius, p. 126, 25.

comicis: i.e. in subjects borrowed from comedy, cf. § 140.

18. **utraque**: i.e. both small and large pictures; Urlichs, *Chrest.* p. 367.

Antiphilus: appears again in § 138 as a painter in encaustic. He was an Alexandrian and a rival of Apelles (above, note on § 89). Quinctilian (xii, 10, 6) praises him for his facility (*facilitate Antiphilus*); he is probably one of those who introduced that *ars compendiaria* (above, § 110, cf. on Pansias, in § 124), with the invention of which Petronius charged the Egyptians.

Hesionam: probably her deliverance by Herakles. For the subject cf. the large picture, Helbig, *Wandgemälde*, 1129.

19. **Alex. ac Phil. cum Minerva**: probably on a chariot, with Athena acting as charioteer, Furtwängler, *Jahrb.* iv, 1889, p. 86, note 42.

patrem, Alexandrum puerum, Hippolytum tauro emisso
expavescentem, in Pompeia vero Cadmum et Europen.
idem iocosis nomine Gryllum deridiculi habitus pinxit, unde
id genus picturae grylli vocantur. ipse in Aegypto natus
115 didicit a Ctesidemo. decet non sileri et Ardeatis templi 5
pictorem, praesertim civitate donatum ibi et carmine quod
est in ipsa pictura his versibus:

> Dignis digna. Loco picturis condecoravit
> reginae Iunonis supremi coniugis templum
> Plautius Marcus, cluet Asia lata esse oriundus,   10
> quem nunc et post semper ob artem hanc Ardea laudat,

116 eaque sunt scripta antiquis litteris Latinis; non fraudando et
Studio divi Augusti aetate qui primus instituit amoenissi-
mam parietum picturam, villas et portus ac topiaria opera,
lucos, nemora, colles, piscinas, euripos, amnes, litora, qualia 15
quis optaret, varias ibi obambulantium species aut navigan-
tium terraque villas adeuntium asellis aut vehiculis, iam
piscantes aucupantesque aut venantes aut etiam vindemi-
117 antes. sunt in eius exemplaribus nobiles palustri accessu
villae, succollatis sponsione mulieribus labantes trepidis quae 20
feruntur, plurimae praeterea tales argutiae facetissimi salis.

12. Latinis, non *Detlefsen*.

1. **Hippolytum tauro emisso**:
under the influence of the Euripidean
play, Kalkmann, *A. Z.* 1883 (41),
p. 43 ff.

2. in **Pompeia**: note on § 59.
Cf. again Varro, *de Re Rust.* iii, 2, 5,
and Münzer, *loc. cit.*; Introd. p. lxxxiv.
Cadmum et Europen: its great
reputation is apparent from Martial
ii, 14, 3, who uses the name of the
picture as synonymous for the porticus Pompeia (*currit ad Europen*).
The picture, which was doubtless originally in Alexandria, may, as Helbig
(*Untersuch.* p. 224 f.) points out, have
inspired Moschos during his stay in
that city to write the famous description in *Idyll* i, 125 ff. A number of
extant later representations of the
myth—the most celebrated of which
is the mosaic from Palestrina, Roscher,

i, p. 1414, are probably influenced
more or less remotely by the composition of Antiphilos.

3. **Gryllum**: the name, which was
that of the father and of one of the
sons of Xenophon, was common enough.
The *deridiculus habitus* must have
been in allusion to γρύλλος = a dancer
of the γρυλισμός, in which the per-
formers were originally masked as
pigs, though in time the term seems
to have come to include every kind of
wanton dancing (see Phrynichos, ed.
Lobeck, p. 101). Such performances
were especially in favour at Alexandria, so that it is natural to find
such a subject influencing an Alexandrian artist (cf. Urlichs, *Das hölzerne
Pferd*, p. 20 f.).

§ 115. 5. **Ctesidemo**: below,
§ 140.

Alexander, and Hippolytos terrified at the bull sent up from the sea, and in the gallery of Pompeius his Kadmos and Europa. Among his comic pictures is one of a man called Gryllos in a ridiculous costume, from which all such pictures are called γρύλλοι. Antiphilos was born in Egypt, and studied under †*Ktesidemos*. *His master Ktesidemos.*

I ought not to pass over in silence the painter of the temple at 115 Ardea, especially as he was honoured by receiving the citizenship of the town and the following verses written on the picture: 'To the deserving be due honour paid. The temple of queenly Juno, wife of the almighty, did Lykon adorn with paintings, even Plautius *Plautius* Marcus, born in wide Asia, whom for this his art Ardea praises *Marcus* now and for ever more.' The lines are in old-fashioned Latin *Lykon.* characters.

Nor must I neglect †*Studius*, a painter of the days of Augustus, 116 who introduced a delightful style of decorating walls with repre- *Studius.* sentations of villas, harbours, landscape gardens, sacred groves, woods, hills, fishponds, straits, streams and shores, any scene in short that took the fancy. In these he introduced figures of people on foot, or in boats, and on land of people coming up to the country-houses either on donkeys or in carriages, besides figures of fishers and fowlers, or of hunters or even of vintagers. Among 117 his works we know well the men approaching a villa through a swamp, and staggering beneath the weight upon their shoulders of the terrified women whom they have bargained to carry over, with many other scenes of like vivacity and infinite humour. He

Ardeatis templi: Verg. *Aen.* vii, 411 ff.; cf. above, § 17.

8. **Loco** = Λύκων; in addition to his Greek name he would, on receiving the citizenship of Ardea, assume the name of Plautius Marcus. M. Hertz, in *Index Lect.Vratislav.*(1867), suggests that he may have been both painter and poet, as was Pacuvius (above, § 19), and that he is identical with *Plautius*, a writer whose comedies passed under the name of Plautus, Varro, *ap.* A. Gellius, iii, 3, 3. The inscription on his picture being in hexameter, he cannot be dated earlier than Ennius (B.C. 239–169); cf. Mommsen, *Röm. Gesch* ed. 7, i, p. 941 note.

§ 116. 13. **qui primus**: note on § 16: as a fact from Vitruvius vii, 5, (cf. *Rhein. Mus.* xxv, 1870, p. 394

ff.) it appears that the painting of *topiaria opera* was older than the age of Augustus. Studius gave it a new impulse or perhaps made it for the first time really fashionable at Rome.

15. **topiaria opera**: in Livia's Villa at Prima Porta the walls of one room were decorated with the plan of a garden (see *Antike Denkmäler*, i, pl. 11,24), and afford an excellent example of the style of Studius (Brunn, *Bull.* 1863, p. 81 ff.); cf. also, Helbig, *Untersuchungen*, p. 62. Pliny the younger (*Ep.* v, 6, 22) describes a bedroom in his villa as follows: *nec cedit gratiae marmoris ramos incidentesque ramis aves imitata pictura.*

§ 117. 19. **exemplaribus**: sc. *ingenii*; cf. § 74 *ingenii . . . exempla.*

21. **argutiae**: § 67; xxxiv, 65.

idem subdialibus maritimas urbes pingere instituit, blandis-
118 simo aspectu minimoque inpendio.   sed nulla gloria artificum est nisi qui tabulas pinxere, eo venerabilior antiquitatis
prudentia apparet.   non enim parietes excolebant dominis
tantum, nec domos uno in loco mansuras quae ex incendiis 5
rapi non possent.   casa Protogenes contentus erat in hortulo
suo, nulla in Apellis tectoriis pictura erat.   nondum libebat
parietes totos tinguere, omnium eorum ars urbibus excuba-
119 bat pictorque res communis terrarum erat.   fuit et Arellius
Romae celeber paulo ante divum Augustum, ni flagitio 10
insigni corrupisset artem, semper ei lenocinans cuius feminae
amore flagraret, ob id deas pingens, sed dilectarum imagine.
120 itaque in pictura eius scorta numerabantur.   fuit et nuper
gravis ac severus idemque floridus et vividus pictor Famulus.   huius erat Minerva spectantem spectans quacumque 15
aspiceretur.   paucis diei horis pingebat, id quoque cum
gravitate, quod semper togatus, quamquam in machinis.
carcer eius artis domus aurea fuit, et ideo non extant
exempla alia magnopere.   post eum fuere in auctoritate
Cornelius Pinus et Attius Priscus, qui Honoris et Virtutis 20
aedes Imp. Vespasiano Aug. restituenti pinxerunt, Priscus
antiquis similior.

121   Non est omittenda in picturae mentione celebris circa
A.U.C. 711- Lepidum fabula, siquidem in triumviratu quodam loco
718. deductus a magistratibus in nemorosum hospitium minaciter 25
cum iis postero die expostulavit somnum ademptum sibi
volucrum concentu, at illi draconem in longissima membrana

---

14. floridis (floridus e corr.) umidus Bamb., corr. Traube ; floridissimus
Urlichs in Chrest., Detlefsen.

1. subdialibus : cf. xxxvi, 186.
§ 118. 4. excolebant dominis :
private patrons, cf. in § 30 (colores)
quos dominus pingenti praestat ; in
§ 44 e reliquis coloribus quos a dominis dari diximus . . .
'6. casa in hortulo : above, § 105.
The 'cottage' doubtless belonged to
the same class of loci communes as the
anus (note on § 81).
§ 120. 14. gravis ac severus : i.e.

in his person (cf. below, cum gravitate,
togatus), whereas his painting was
floridus and vividus ; the adjectives
are transferred from the colour to the
painter, cf. § 134 austerior colore,
though austerus like floridus was
a technical qualification of certain
colours, sunt autem colores austeri
aut floridi, § 30.
17. quod semper togatus : so
Vandyck painted in full dress.

also brought in the fashion of painting seaside towns on the walls
of open galleries, producing a delightful effect at a very small cost.
No artists, however, enjoy a real glory unless they have painted **118**
easel pictures, and herein the wisdom of past generations claims
our greater respect. They did not decorate walls to be seen only
by their owners, nor houses that must always remain in one place
and could not be carried away in case of fire. Protogenes was
content with a cottage in his little garden, and no fresco was to be
seen in the house of Apelles. It was not yet men's pleasure to
dye whole surfaces of wall; all the masters laboured for the cities,
and the artist was the possession of the whole world.

Not long before the time of the god Augustus, *Arellius* had **119**
earned distinction at Rome, save for the sacrilege by which he *Arellius.*
notoriously degraded his art. Always desirous of flattering some
woman or other with whom he chanced to be in love, he painted
goddesses in the person of his mistresses, of whom his paintings
are a mere catalogue. The painter †*Famulus* also lived not **120**
long ago; he was grave and severe in his person, while his *Famulus.*
painting was rich and vivid. He painted an Athena whose eyes
are turned to the spectator from whatever side he may be looking.
Famulus painted for a few hours only in the day, and treated his
art seriously, always wearing the toga, even when mounted on
scaffolding. The Golden House was the prison of his art, and
hence not many examples of it are known. After him †*Cornelius* *Cornelius*
Pinus and †*Attius Priscus* were painters of repute, who painted *Pinus.* *Attius*
the twin temples of Honour and Virtue when they were restored *Priscus.*
by the emperor Vespasian Augustus. Priscus approached more
nearly to the old masters.

While on the subject of painting I must not omit the well- **121**
known story of Lepidus. Once during his triumvirate he had 43–36 B.C
been escorted by the magistrates of a certain town to a lodging in *'Scare-crow,'*
the middle of a wood, and on the next morning complained with *painted fo:*
threats that the singing of the birds prevented him from sleeping. *Lepidus.*
They painted a snake on an immense strip of parchment and
stretched it all round the grove. We are told that by this means

machinis: here of scaffolding,
Blümner, *Technol.* iv, 430: for
machina=easel, above, § 81.

18. **carcer eius artis**: for Pliny's
hatred of Nero cf. above, § 51; xxxiv,
45, 84.

20. **Honoris et Virtutis aedes**:
built or rather restored by Marcellus,
in B. C. 212, to contain part of the art
treasures brought from Syracuse, Liv.
xxv, 40, cf. xxvii, 25; Cic. *Verr.* II, iv,
54, 120; Gilbert, *Rom,* iii. p. 97 f.

depictum circumdedere luco eoque terrore aves tunc siluisse
narratur et postea potuisse compesci.

122   Ceris pingere ac picturam inurere quis primus excogita-
verit non constat. quidam Aristidis inventum putant postea
consummatum a Praxitele, sed aliquanto vetustiores encau- 5
stae picturae exstitere, ut Polygnoti et Nicanoris ac Mnasilai
Pariorum.   Elasippus quoque Aeginae picturae suae in-
scripsit ἐνέκαεν, quod profecto non fecisset nisi encaustica
inventa.

123   Pamphilus quoque Apellis praeceptor non pinxisse solum 10
encausta sed etiam docuisse traditur Pausian Sicyonium
primum in hoc genere nobilem.   Bryetis filius hic fuit eius-
demque primo discipulus.   pinxit et ipse penicillo parietes
Thespis, cum reficerentur quondam a Polygnoto picti,
multumque conparatione superatus existimabatur, quoniam 15
124 non suo genere certasset. idem et lacunaria primus pingere
instituit, nec camaras ante eum taliter adornari mos fuit.
parvas pingebat tabellas maximeque pueros.   hoc aemuli
interpretabantur facere eum, quoniam tarda picturae ratio
esset illa.   quamobrem daturus et celeritatis famam absolvit 20
uno die tabellam quae vocata est hemeresios puero picto.
125 amavit in iuventa Glyceram municipem suam, inventricem
coronarum, certandoque imitatione eius ad numerosissimam
florum varietatem perduxit artem illam.   postremo pinxit

§ 122. 3. ceris pingere . .
inurere: i. e. encaustic; note on
§ 149.
   4. quidam ... inventum : for this
variant tradition, Introd. p. xxxiii.
   Aristidis : presumably the first of
the name, above, § 75.
   5. consumm. a Praxitele : who
would use encaustic for the *circumlitio*
of his statues (below, § 133).
   6. Polygnoti : above, §§ 58–59.
   8. ἐνέκαεν : cf. above, § 27.
   § 123. 10. Pamphilus : §§ 75–76.
We now come again upon distinct
traces of Xenokrates. Stress is laid
upon the pre-eminence of Sikyon, and
the painters are connected with definite stages of progress. Pamphilos

is awkwardly dragged in a second
time, in order to introduce his pupil
Pausias, who in the original Greek
account, where no arbitrary division
seems to have been drawn between
the painters in encaustic and others,
would certainly be discussed in connexion with his master and his contemporaries of §§ 75–76, Introd.
p. xxxiv.
   13. pinxit ... certasset: this
mention of wall-paintings shows that
encaustic was not treated separately
by the Greek authors.
   14. Thespis : the wall paintings
by Polygnotos had probably been
injured at the destruction of Thespiai
by the Thebans in B. C. 374. The

they terrified the birds into silence and that this has ever since
been a recognized device for quieting them.

We do not know with certainty who first invented the art of 122
painting with wax colours and burning in the painting. Some *Encaustic painting.*
believe that it was invented by Aristeides and afterwards brought
to perfection by Praxiteles, but encaustic paintings of a somewhat
earlier date exist, for example, by Polygnotos, and by †Nikanor
and †Mnasilaos of Paros. †Elasippos of Aigina also wrote on one
of his paintings ἐνέκαεν [burnt it in], which he certainly would not
have done before the invention of encaustic painting.

Tradition further says that Pamphilos the master of Apelles 123
not only painted in encaustic but also taught *Pausias* of Sikyon, *Practised by Pamphilos, and by Pausias of Sikyon.*
the first well-known master in this style. Pausias was the son of
†*Bryetes*, under whom he first studied. He also painted with the
brush certain walls at Thespiai, which had originally been painted
by Polygnotos and needed restoration. His work was held to
suffer very greatly by the comparison, as he had competed in
a style that was not his own. He was the first to paint panelled 124
ceilings, nor was it the practice to decorate vaulted roofs in this
way before his day. He habitually painted small pictures, boys
being his favourite subject. His rivals declared that this was
because his method of encaustic painting was slow, whereupon he
determined to acquire a reputation for rapid execution, and
painted in a single day a picture of a boy called the ἡμερήσιος
[day's work]. As a youth he loved his townswoman Glykera, 125
who first invented flower wreaths. By copying and rivalling her *Glykera, the flower-girl, beloved of Pausias.*
he enabled encaustic painting to represent a great variety of
flowers. Finally he painted a portrait of Glykera herself seated

---

restoration of the paintings would
take place on the restoration of the
city, after the capture of Thebes by
Alexander in 335 B.C.

§ 124. 16. idem et lacunaria
primus: Furtwängler (*Fleck. Jahrb.*
xxii, 1876, p. 507) has pointed out
that these words correspond to *qui
primus lacunaria pinxit* in the table
of contents, while the following *nec
camaras ante eum* corresponds to
quando primum camarae pictae (*ib.*).
The statements accordingly are quite
distinct.

20. absolvit uno die: cf. the

praise for swiftness bestowed upon
Nikomachos, § 109, and his pupil
Philoxenos, § 110; upon Iaia, in § 148,
and Quinctilian's estimate of Antiphilos (note on § 114).

§ 125. 22. Glyceram: xxi, 4,
whence we obtain *post Olympiada C*
(= B.C. 380) as a further guide to the
artist's date. Append. V.

inventricem: the passage in xxi
shows that she was really thought of
as the inventor of the art of plaiting
garlands; thus the old conjecture
venditricem (Gesner) becomes impossible.

et ipsam sedentem cum corona, quae e nobilissimis tabula
est appellata stephaneplocos, ab aliis stephanopolis, quoniam
Glycera venditando coronas sustentaverat paupertatem.
huius tabulae exemplar, quod apographon vocant, L. Lucul-
126 lus duobus talentis emit Dionysiis Athenis.   Pausias autem 5
fecit et grandis tabulas, sicut spectatam in Pompei porticu
boum immolationem.   eam primus invenit picturam, quam
postea imitati sunt multi, aequavit nemo.   ante omnia, cum
longitudinem bovis ostendi vellet, adversum eum pinxit, non
127 traversum, et abunde intellegitur amplitudo.   dein, cum 10
omnes quae volunt eminentia videri candicanti faciant colore, quae condunt nigro, hic totum bovem atri coloris fecit
umbraeque corpus ex ipsa dedit magna prorsus arte in aequo
extantia ostendente et in confracto solida omnia.   Sicyone
et hic vitam egit, diuque illa fuit patria picturae.   tabulas 15
A.U.C. 698. inde e publico omnis propter aes alienum civitatis addictas
128 Scauri aedilitas Romam transtulit.   post eum eminuit longe
ante omnis Euphranor Isthmius olympiade CIIII, idem qui
inter fictores dictus est nobis.   fecit et colossos et marmorea
et typos scalpsit, docilis ac laboriosus ante omnis et in quo- 20
cumque genere excellens ac sibi aequalis.   hic primus vide-

---

4. **apographon**: there were at the
time many artists who were solely
occupied in the business of copying;
at Athens Lucian, *Zeux.* 3, sees a
copy of the ' Kentaurs ' of Zeuxis; cf.
also Dionysios περὶ Δινάρχου vii,
p. 644; Quinct. x, 2, 6 ; x, 2, 2 ;
above, § 91 (Helbig, *Untersuchungen,*
p. 63). From the exorbitant price
paid, however, it is possible that the
apographon was a replica by the
artist himself.

5. **Athenis**: Lucullus   visited
Athens in B.C. 88-87 as Sulla's
Quaestor; cf. below, on § 156.

§ 126. 7. **boum immolationem**:
for the subject cf. § 93 (note on *pompam*).

§ 127. 11. **eminentia**: §§ 92 (*digiti eminere videntur*); 131.

13. **umbrae corpus ex ipsa
dedit**: the effect was simply pro-

duced by modelling, without the help
of any extraneous colour, precisely as
the Kentaurs of the white marble
slab at Naples (Helbig, *Wandgem.*
1241) appear in strong relief through
the skilful though slight modelling,
Wickhoff, *Wiener Genesis*, p. 47.

in aequo omnia: in modern
parlance Pausias excelled at giving
the 'impression of artistic reality with
only two dimensions' (cf. Berenson,
*The Florentine painters of the Renais-
sance*, p. 4), i.e. at representing depth,
the third 'dimension, on a flat surface.

15. **patria picturae**: cf. xxxvi, 9.

16. **propter aes alienum**: since
Sulla's Mithridatic war the Sikyonians
had fallen into debt and distress
(see especially Cic. *ad Att.* i, 19, 9;
ib. 20, 4; *Tusc. Disp.* iii, 22,
§ 53) and were consequently forced
to sell their art treasures.

with a wreath, one of the famous pictures of the world, called the στεφανηπλόκος [wreath-binder], or by others the στεφανόπωλις [wreath-seller], because Glykera had supported herself by selling wreaths. A copy of the picture, an ἀπόγραφον as it is called, was bought by Lucius Lucullus for two talents [£420 circ.] at the festival of Dionysos at Athens. Pausias, however, also painted **126** large pictures, as for example the famous sacrifice of oxen in the Gallery of Pompeius. He devised an innovation which has often *He devises* been imitated but never equalled. The most striking instance is *a new application* that wishing to display an ox's length of body, he painted a front *of light* and not a side view of the animal, and yet contrived to show *and shade.* its size. Again, while all others put in the high lights in white **127** and paint the less salient parts in dark colour, he painted the whole ox black, and gave substance to the shadow out of the shadow itself, showing great art in giving all his figures full relief upon the flat surface, and in indicating their form when fore-shortened. He spent his life at Sikyon, for many years the home of painting. Later on, in the aedileship of Scaurus, all the **56 B.C.** pictures of Sikyon were sold to liquidate the public debt, and were brought to Rome.

After Pausias in the hundred and fourth Olympiad [364–361 **128** B.C.], *Euphranor* of the Isthmos, whom I have already mentioned *Euphra-* among the statuaries, far excelled all rivals. He furthermore *nor.* produced colossal statues, works in marble and reliefs. Receptive and of indefatigable industry, he attained in every branch a high level, below which he never fell. He first, it is believed, gave to

17. **Scauri aedilitas**: viii, 64, and often.

§ 128. **post eum**: of time (Furtwängler, *Plinius*, p. 15); but a date posterior to Pausias is irrecon-cilable with Ol. 104 below and xxxiv, 50. The mistake arises, as Robert, *Arch. Märchen*, p. 89, points out, from Pliny's confusion between the Elder Aristeides (§ 75) and Aristeides of Thebes. In his original scheme he doubtless intended to keep E. in his right chronology immediately after Euxeinidas and his pupil Aris-teides; but as in that case the ac-count of the supposed pupil would have preceded that of the supposed master (§§ 98, 111), Pliny was misled into the present anachronism.

18. **qui inter fictores**: xxxiv, 77, *et colossos* ib. § 78, Euphranor's marble works are only mentioned here.

20. **typos**: in which he would be able to bring out his double skill as painter and artist; the Greek relief, as we know it from the Sidonian Sar-kophagi, being in reality a sort of raised picture (Wickhoff, *Wiener Genesis*, p. 46 ff.; cf. Winter, *Arch. Anzeiger*, 1894, p. 8 ff.); a γραπτὸς τύπος, *Anth. Pal.* vii, 730.

in quocumque genere excel-lens: Quinct. xii, 10, 12 *Euphra-norem circa plurium artium species praestantem.*

21. **hic primus**: introduces his

tur expressisse dignitatis heroum et usurpasse symmetrian,
sed fuit in universitate corporum exilior et capitibus articu-
129 lisque grandior. volumina quoque composuit de symmetria
et coloribus. opera eius sunt equestre proelium, XII dei,
Theseus, in quo dixit eundem apud Parrhasium rosa pastum 5
esse, suum vero carne. nobilis eius tabula Ephesi est, Ulixes
simulata insania Iovem cum equo iungens et palliati cogi-
130 tantes, dux gladium. ..undens. eodem tempore fuere Cydias
et . . . , cuius tabulam Argonautas HS. CXXXXIIII Hortensius orator mercatus est eique aedem fecit in Tuscu- 10
lano suo, Euphranoris autem discipulus Antidotus. huius
est clipeo dimicans Athenis et luctator tubicenque inter
pauca laudatus. ipse diligentior quam numerosior et in
coloribus severus maxime inclaruit discipulo Nicia Atheni-
131 ense qui diligentissime mulieres pinxit. lumen et umbras 15
custodiit atque ut eminerent e tabulis picturae maxime

8. cydi et cydias *codd.* ; Cydias *Detlefsen.*

special contribution to his art, cf.
Introd. p. xxvii f.

1. **dignitatis heroum**: so Varro,
Vita Pop. Rom., *ap.* Char. p. 126,
praises E. for his *altitudo* or loftiness.

symmetrian: note on xxxiv, 65.

2. **exilior**: see Addenda.

capitibus articulisque: the
judgement is identical with that passed
on Zeuxis in § 64, where see note.

§ 129. 3. **volumina** . . . composuit: like Apelles, § 79, Pamphilos (note on § 76), Melanthios, &c.
Introd. p. xl f.

4. **equestre proelium**: in the Stoa
of Zeus Eleutherios at Athens, Paus.
i, 3, 4 ; the picture represented the
cavalry engagement which preceded
the battle of Mantineia (B. C. 362, cf.
Plut. *Glor. Ath.* ii, p. 346); according
to Paus. viii, 9, 8, a copy of it was to
be seen in the gymnasion at Mantineia.

XII dei: in the same Stoa,
Paus. i, 3, 3 ; for the Zeus in this
picture see Val. Max. viii, ext. 5 ; for
the Hera, Luc. εἰκόνες 7.

5. **Theseus**: likewise in the Stoa
Eleutherios ; the hero was represented

with Demokratia and Demos, Paus.
loc. cit. Both Theseus and Demos
were subjects that had been treated
by Parrhasios (above § 69). Demos
was also painted by Aristolaos, § 137.
For the distribution of Euphranor's
pictures in the Stoa Eleutherios see
Hitzig and Blümner, *Pausanias,* p. 141.

in quo dixit eundem: Plut.
Glor. Athen. ii, p. 346 Εὐφράνωρ
τὸν Θησέα τὸν ἑαυτοῦ τῷ Παρρασίου
παρέβαλε λέγων, τὸν μὲν ἐκείνου ῥόδα
βεβρωκέναι, τὸν δὲ ἑαυτοῦ κρέα βόεια.
Münzer (*op. cit.* p. 527) aptly compares
the Aristophanic verse (Fr. 180) upon
Euripides, recorded by Antigonos of
Karystos, *ap.* Diogenes iv, 3, 18 παρη-
τημένος (sc. Πολέμων) ἅ φησιν Ἀριστο-
φάνης περὶ Εὐριπίδου " ὀξωτὰ καὶ σιλ-
φιωτά," ἅπερ, ὡς ὁ αὐτός φησι, " κατα-
πυγοσύνη ταῦτ' ἐστὶ πρὸς κρέας μέγα."
Introd. p. lxiii f.

7. **simulata insania**: ὅτε συστρα-
τεύει τοῖς Ἀτρείδαις μὴ θέλων, Lucian,
περὶ οἴκου 30, where the whole picture is
described in detail. The same subject
was painted by Parrhasios (Plut. *aud.
poet.* 3), we are not told for what city.

heroes their full dignity, and mastered the theory of symmetry; he made the body, however, too slim and the head and limbs too large. He also wrote on symmetry and colour. His works are : 129 a cavalry engagement, the Twelve Gods and a Theseus, of which *He compares his* he said that the Theseus of Parrhasios had fed on roses, but his *'Theseus'* on flesh. At Ephesos is his famous picture of Odysseus feigning *to that of* madness and yoking an ox with a horse, with cloaked figures *Parrhasios.* in meditation, and their leader sheathing his sword. *Kydias* 130 and . . . lived at the same time; his picture of the Argonauts was purchased for 144,000 sesterces [£1250 circ.] by the orator Hortensius, who built a shrine for it on his estate at Tusculum. †*Antidotos* was a pupil of Euphranor. He painted a warrior *Antidotos.* fighting with a shield, to be seen at Athens, a wrestler and a trumpeter, a picture praised as are but few. He was a laborious rather than a prolific artist, and severe in his scheme of colouring ; his chief claim to renown is that he was the master of *Nikias* of *Nikias of* Athens, who painted women with minute care. Nikias was pains- *Athens.* taking in his treatment of light and shade, and took special care 131

palliati cogitantes: these must be identical with the πρέσβεις in Lucian's description.

8. gladium condens: Παλαμήδης . . . πρόκωπον ἔχων τὸ ξίφος, i. e. the sword was half out of the sheath, and it was uncertain whether Palamedes was drawing or replacing it. So too in § 59, Pliny says of a picture by Polygnotos that it was uncertain whether the man represented was 'ascending' or 'descending.'

§ 130. fuere Cydias et . . . .: the *fuere* combined with the evidence of the MSS. compels one to assume the loss of an artist's name. Whether Cydias should appear in the first place or the second is uncertain. Overbeck's explanation *Schriftquell.* 1969ᵃ (which I presume is also Detlefsen's), that *fuere* refers to both Cydias and Antidotus, is quite unwarranted.

9. Hortensius orator : xxxiv, 48.

12. luctator tubicenque : votive pictures ; for the latter, probably of a winner in a herald's competition, see note on xxxiv, 88.

13. numerosior: see on xxxiv, 58. in coloribus severus : for similar judgements ; § 98 *durior paulo in coloribus ;* § 134 *austerior colore Athenion ;* § 137 *e severissimis pictoribus (Aristolaus)* ; ib. *durus in coloribus (Nikophanes).*

14. discipulo Nicia : Euphranor and Praxiteles being contemporaries (xxxiv, 50), a chronological difficulty arises from the statement that Nikias, who assisted Praxiteles to paint his statues, was the pupil of a pupil of Euphranor. Pliny himself felt the difficulty ; in § 133 he hints at the solution in the words *non satis discernitur . . .* ; there were evidently two artists named Nikias ; to the Elder, the assistant of Praxiteles (fl. ab. B. C. 370-330), and probably the painter of Alexander (r. B. C. 336-323), belongs the date Ol. CXII, while the Younger, who was the pupil of Antidotos, flourished about the time of Athenion (on whom see note).

§ 131. 15. lumen et umbras : §§ 29, 127. Cf. Introd. p. xxxiv.

16. ut eminerent : §§ 92, 127.

A.U.C. 679. curavit. opera eius: Nemea advecta ex Asia Romam a
Silano quàm in curia diximus positam, item Liber pater in
A.U.C. 724. aede Concordiae, Hyacinthus, quem Caesar Augustus delectatus eo secum deportavit Alexandrea capta—et ob id
Tiberius Caesar in templo eius dicavit hanc tabulam et 5
132 Danaen—, Eph˙si vero est megabyzi sacerdotis Ephesiae
Dianae sepulchrum, Athenis necyomantea Homeri. hanc
vendere Attalo regi noluit talentis LX, potiusque patriae
suae donavit abundans opibus. fecit et grandes picturas,
in quibus sunt Calypso et Io et Andromeda, Alexander 10
quoque in Pompei porticibus praecellens et Calypso sedens.
133 huic eidem adscribuntur quadripedes, prosperrime canes
expressit. hic est Nicias de quo dicebat Praxiteles interrogatus quae maxime opera sua probaret in marmoribus:
quibus Nicias manum admovisset, tantum circumlitioni eius 15

5. tabulam et Danaen] *Bamb.*; tabulam—et Danae *Detlefsen.*

2. **Silano**: ii, 100; governor of
Bithynia, B.C. 76–75. The picture
had possibly belonged to Pergamon.

diximus: § 27, where see note.

3. **Hyacinthus**: from Paus. iii,
19, 4, it appears he was represented
in the bloom of youth, in special
allusion to Apollo's love for him.

4. **Alexandria capta**: on the
works of art brought by Augustus
from Alexandria, and dedicated by
him at Rome, see Wunderer's mono-
graph, *Manibiae Alexandrinae*, Würzburg, 1894.

5. **in templo eius**: i.e. in the
temple built to the memory of
Augustus by Livia and Tiberius in
14 A.D., Dio Cassius lvi, 46; cf.
Plin. xii, 94. To it belonged both
a porticus and a library (xxxiv, 43).

et Danaen: the Danae is awkwardly coordinated with the *Hyacinthus*. That it did not come from
Egypt, as Urlichs (*Chrest.* p. 372)
supposes, is shown by the fact that
Pliny would in that case have made
the relative sentence refer to both
pictures (Wunderer, *op. cit.* p. 9).

§ 132. 6. **megabyzi**: note on
§ 93.

7. **sepulchrum**: for another grave
picture, by Nikias, at Triteia in
Achaia, see Paus. vii, 22, 6; cf. the
expirantium imagines of Apelles, in
§ 90; the *anapauomene* of Aristeides,
in § 99.

necyom. Homeri: *Odyssey* xi.
The picture, described *Anth. Pal.*
ix, 792, was the artist's most celebrated work. While he was engaged
upon it, according to an entertaining
tale told by Plutarch, *An sen. sit ger.
rep.* v, 4, Nikias used to ask those of
his household whether he had washed
or breakfasted.

8. **Attalo regi**: familiarity with
the high prices paid by Attalos (vii,
126; xxxv, 24) induced Pliny into
error. The date of Attalos is irreconcilable with that of Nikias, so
that Plutarch is probably right in
telling the story of Ptolemaios
(Soter, B.C. 306–284), Πτολεμαίου
δὲ τοῦ βασιλέως ἑξήκοντα τάλαντα τῆς
γραφῆς συντελεσθείσης πέμψαντος αὐτῷ
μὴ λαβεῖν μηδ᾽ ἀποδόσθαι τὸ ἔργον.

that his figures should be relieved against the background.   His *His treat-*
works are : the picture of Nemea brought to Rome from Asia by *ment of*
Silanus, and placed, as I have said, in the Council Chamber ; *light and shade.*
a Dionysos in the temple of Concord ; the Hyakinthos carried 75 B.C.
away on the fall of Alexandria by Caesar Augustus, who took such 30 B.C.
great delight in the picture that as a consequence Tiberius Caesar
dedicated it in the temple of Augustus together with the Danae ;
at Ephesos a painting for the grave of a μεγάβυζος or priest of 132
Artemis of Ephesos, and at Athens the νεκυομαντεία [questioning
of the dead] of Homer.   This picture the artist refused to sell to
King Attalos for sixty talents [£12,600 circ.] but preferred, as he
was a rich man, to present it to his own country.   He also painted
large pictures, amongst them Kalypso, Io, Andromeda, the excellent portrait of Alexander which is in the Gallery of Pompeius, and
a Kalypso seated.   Pictures of animals are also ascribed to him, 133
and he was very successful in painting dogs.   It is of this Nikias *He colours*
that Praxiteles, when asked which of his marble statues pleased *the statues of Praxi-*
him most, said, 'Those which the hand of Nikias has touched,' *teles.*
such was his tribute to this artist's colouring of the accessories.
It is not clear whether this or another Nikias is the one placed

Non posse suav. vivere sec. Ep. xi, 2.
The court of Alexandria had been
more fortunate in purchasing the
Hyakinthos (§ 131).

patriae suae donavit : cf. in
§ 62 the similar statement concerning
Zeuxis.

9. grandes picturas : in opposition to the smaller pictures painted in
encaustic.

10. Calypso : a standing figure
from the fact that the second Kalypso
is expressly described as *sedens*.

Io : Helbig (*Untersuchungen*, pp.
113, 140), inclines to see in the Io
of the House of Livia on the Palatine,
a copy of the Io of Nikias, a composition which seems to have inspired
Prop. i, 3, 20.

Andromeda : the composition
seems preserved in the well-known
relief of the Capitol, Helbig, *Class.
Ant.*461 = Schreiber,*Hell. Reliefs*, xii;
cf. the Pompeian paintings, Helbig,
Wandgemälde, 1186–1189. Add.

11. Pompei porticibus : note on
§ 59.

§ 133. 12. prosperrime canes :
κεῖται δὲ ἐνταῦθα ... Νικίας τε ὁ Νικο-
μήδους (cf. Köhler, *Ath. Mitth.* 1885,
p. 234, 2), ζῷα ἄριστα γράψαι τῶν ἐφ'
αὑτοῦ, Paus. i, 29, 15. The description appears to be from the inscription
on the grave.

15. circumlitioni : the process
must be kept distinct from the γάνωσις
or toning down of the whole statue
(Vitr. vii, 9, 4) ; *circuml.* was
admirably explained by Welcker (in
Müller, *Handbuch*, p. 431), to consist
in a painting of hair and accessories,
intended to give *relief* to the statue—
to be in a word identical with *circumlitio* as understood in painting,Quinct.
viii, 5, 26 *nec pictura, in qua nihil
circumlitum est eminet* (cf. *id.* xii,
9, 8). Since then, the discovery of the
Sidonian sarkophagoi has revealed
precisely such a use of colour for hair,
dress, &c., as was divined by Welcker,

tribuebat. non satis discernitur alium eodem nomine an
134 hunc eundem quidam faciant olympiade CXII.   Niciae
conparatur et aliquando praefertur Athenion Maronites
Glaucionis Corinthii discipulus, austerior colore et in auste-
ritate iucundior, ut in ipsa pictura eruditio eluceat.   pinxit 5
in templo Eleusine Phylarchum et Athenis frequentiam
quam vocavere syngenicon, item Achillem virginis habitu
occultatum Ulixe deprendente, et in una tabula VI signa,
quaque maxime inclaruit agasonem cum equo.   quod nisi
135 in iuventa obiisset, nemo compararetur.   est nomen et 10
A.U.C. 586. Heraclidi Macedoni.   initio naves pinxit, captoque Perseo
rege Athenas commigravit, ubi eodem tempore erat Metrodorus pictor idemque philosophus, in utraque scientia magnae
auctoritatis.   itaque cum L. Paulus devicto Perseo petiisset
ab Atheniensibus uti sibi quam probatissimum philosophum 15
mitterent ad erudiendos liberos, item pictorem ad triumphum
excolendum, Athenienses Metrodorum elegerunt professi
eundem in utroque desiderio praestantissimum, quod ita

while flesh parts are seen to have been
left in the tone of the marble ; cf. the
Artemis of Vienna, *Jahrb. d. Oesterr.
Kunstsamml.* v, 1887, pl. i, ii, and
R. v. Schneider's remarks, *ib.* p. 22, on
the former colouring of the Hermes
of Praxiteles. See also Wickhoff, in
Wiener Genesis, p. 48.

1. **non satis discernitur**: above,
note on *discipulo Nicia*.

§ 134. 4. **austerior** : i.e. *Nicia,
cui comparabatur ;* cf. above, note on
severus in § 130.

5. **eruditio** : cf. § 76 *omnibus
litteris eruditus* of Pamphilos.

pinxit ... syngenicon : the two
pictures mentioned here belonging
to the class of votive offerings, and the
locality of each being specially noted,
B. Keil (*Hermes*, xxx, 1895, p. 229 ;
cf. Münzer, *ib.* p. 540) considers the
whole sentence to be an addition
to the main account from the work
of Heliodoros περὶ ἀναθημάτων, see
Introd. p. lxxiv f.

6. **Phylarchum** : Pausanias (i,

26, 3) mentions a cavalry captain
Olympiodoros (presumably identical
with the archon of Ol. 121, 3 = B.C.
294) in the time of Kassander (d. Ol.
121 = B.C. 296), who distinguished
himself in an engagement at Eleusis
against the Makedonians, and was
accordingly honoured with a portrait
there. He may quite well, therefore,
be identical with the Olympiodoros
painted by Athenion, a contemporary of the younger Nikias. For
lit. see Hitzig-Blümner, *Pausanias,*
p. 283.

7. **syngenicon** : the Greek word
introduced because P. is not quite
assured of his Latin equivalent ; for
the subject see note on *cognatio,* in
§ 76.

Achillem ... deprendente : the
subject had been treated by Polygnotos in the Pinakotheke of the
Propylaia (Paus. i, 22, 6) and often.
We know it from a series of Pompeian
wall paintings, Helbig, *Wandgemälde,*
1296-1303 (the most famous, 1297, is

by some authorities in the hundred and twelfth Olympiad [332-329 B. C.]. †*Athenion* of Maroneia, the pupil of Glaukion of 134 Corinth, is compared with Nikias, and preferred to him by some. *Athenion, pupil of Glaukion.* He used a severer scheme of colouring than Nikias, and produced a more pleasing effect withal, thus manifesting in his execution his grasp of the abstract principles of his art. He painted in the temple of Eleusis a captain of cavalry; at Athens an assembly called a συγγενικόν; also Achilles, in the guise of a maiden, at the moment of detection by Odysseus; a picture containing six figures, and the groom with a horse on which his fame chiefly rests. Had he not died young, no artist would be comparable to him.

†*Herakleides* of Makedon, who began life as a ship painter, also 135 enjoys a great reputation. After King Perseus was taken prisoner, *Herakleides.* he repaired to Athens, where was then living *Metrodoros*, who was 168 B.C. at once painter and philosopher, and had won high distinction *Metrodoros.* in either capacity. Accordingly, when Lucius Paulus after his victories over Perseus asked the Athenians to send him their best philosopher to teach his children, and a painter to commemorate his triumph, they chose Metrodoros, declaring that he could best fulfil both requirements, as indeed Paulus found to be the case.

given in Roscher, i, p. 27), none of which however can be traced back with any certainty to Athenion; cf. Helbig, *Untersuch.* p. 158. Addenda.

§ 135. 11. **Heraclidi**: below, § 146.

captoque Perseo rege: Ol. 153, 1, Robert, *Arch. Märch.* p. 135, note, points out that the last date for a painter having been Ol. 121 (§ 134), there was precisely the same gap in the chronology of the painters as in that of the bronze sculptors (xxxiv, 52 *cessavit deinde ars* (Ol. 121) *ac rursus Ol.* 116 *revixit*). It is evident that the Greek sources ended for painting as for sculpture with approximately the same period, and that the additions concerning Herakleides and Metrodoros, both of whom are connected with Roman exploits, like the additions made in xxxiv, 52 to the Greek lists of the sculptors, are extraneous to the original history of art

forming the basis of the Plinian account, Introd. p. lxxx f.

12. **Metrodorus**: he is most likely identical with the Metrodoros in the Index to this book. Further he is possibly the same as the Metrodoros of Stratonikaia, mentioned by Diogenes Laertios x, 9, and Cic. *De Orat.* i, 11, 45, as being a pupil of Karneades (cf. Brunn, *K. G.* ii, p. 293; Urlichs, *Malerei*, p. 16; Helbig, *Untersuch.* p. 5).

16. **ad erudiendos liberos**: the two younger sons who died at the time of the triumph; cf. the charming passage in Plutarch, *Aem. Paul.* vi Οὐ γὰρ μόνον γραμματικοὶ καὶ σοφισταὶ καὶ ῥήτορες, ἀλλὰ καὶ πλάσται καὶ ζωγράφοι καὶ πώλων καὶ σκυλάκων ἐπιστάται καὶ διδάσκαλοι θήρας Ἕλληνες ἦσαν περὶ τοὺς νεανίσκους (i. e. the elder sons, the younger Scipio and Fabius Maximus, after their father's triumph over the Ligurians, B.C. 181).

136 Paulus quoque iudicavit. Timomachus Byzantius Caesaris dictatoris aetate Aiacem et Mediam pinxit ab eo in Veneris Genetricis aede positas, LXXX talentis venundatas. talentum Atticum X̶ V̅I̅ taxat M. Varro. Timomachi aeque laudantur Orestes, Iphigenia in Tauris et Lecythion agili- 5 tatis exercitator, cognatio nobilium, palliati quos dicturos pinxit, alterum stantem, alterum sedentem. praecipue 137 tamen ars ei favisse in Gorgone visa est. Pausiae filius et discipulus Aristolaus e severissimis pictoribus fuit, cuius sunt Epaminondas, Pericles, Media, Virtus, Theseus, imago 10 Atticae plebis, boum immolatio. sunt quibus et Nicophanes eiusdem Pausiae discipulus placeat diligentia quam

§ 136. 1. Timomachus Byz. Caesaris ... aetate: from what we know of the famous Aias and Medeia (see following note), Pliny seems guilty of an anachronism in placing Timomachos in this period (so Brunn, Dilthey, Helbig, Urlichs and Furtwängler; see Brandstätter, *Der Maler Timomachos*, where all the evidence concerning the artist's date is collected); he presumably found no date in his author, and tried to obtain one out of the purchase by Caesar (Furtwängler, *Plinius*, p. 14), [*Caesaris dictatoris aetate* in imitation of *Magni Pompei aetate* xx, 144; xxii, 128; xxvi, 12; xxxiii, 130, 156.— H. L. U.]

2. Veneris G. aede: above, § 26 where see note.

Aiacem et Mediam: apparently identical with the Aias and Medeia mentioned by Cicero, *Verr.* II, iv, 60, 135, where he enumerates thirteen works of art, each of which was the pride of the city that owned it: *quid arbitramini merere velle Cyzicenos, ut Aiacem aut Mediam amittant?* Now the Verrine orations date from B. C. 70, and since the pictures had then attained a worldwide celebrity, similar to that enjoyed by the Eros of Praxiteles, the heifer of Myron, &c., we must suppose they

had been some time in existence; thus the latest date which could well he assigned to the pictures would be about 100–90 B. C., but this cannot he called the 'age of Caesar.' Indeed since all the artists (i. e. Pythagoras, Myron, the two Praxiteles, Protogenes and Apelles) mentioned by Cicero are of the fifth and fourth centuries, it seems reasonable to suppose that Timomachos also lived not later than the fourth century. From the subjects of his pictures he was probably a contemporary of Apelles (Brandstätter, *op. cit.*). The two pictures were composed as pendants, at least so we gather from the juxtaposition of the subjects in Ovid, *Trist.* ii, 525:
Utque sedet vultu fassus Telamonius iram
Inque oculis facinus barbara mater habet.
The composition has survived on a number of gems (Berlin, Cat. 673, 674, 1357, 4319, 4327, 6491; Br. Mus. Cat. 1426, 1427). Copies of the Medeia have survived in two wall-paintings (1) from Pompei, Helbig, *Wandgemälde*, 1262, (2) from Herculaneum, Helbig, 1264 (single figure of Medeia, but taken apparently from a large composition similar to the former): Medeia meditating the murder, while the children

Timomachos of Byzantion in the time of the dictator Caesar **138**
painted the Aias and the Medeia, placed by Caesar in the temple *Timoma-chos.*
of Venus the Mother, which cost eighty talents [£16,800 circ.].
(Marcus Varro values the Attic talent at 6000 denarii.) Other
pictures by Timomachos meet with a like praise ; his Orestes and
Iphigeneia among the Tauroi ; his portrait of Lekythion, a master
of gymnastics ; an assembly of notable persons, and two men in
cloaks just ready to speak, one standing, the other sitting. Art,
however, is thought to have granted to him his greatest success in
the Gorgon which he painted.

†*Aristolaos,* the son and pupil of Pausias, was an artist of the **137**
severest school ; he painted pictures of Epameinondas, Perikles, *Aristolaos, son and pupil of Pausias.*
Medeia, Valour, Theseus, a personification of the populace of
Athens, and a sacrifice of oxen.

†*Nikophanes,* another pupil of Pausias, is admired by a small *Niko-phanes.*

quietly play in charge of the *paidagogos*—a scheme which corresponds to Lucian's description περὶ οἴκου, 31. The picture was very probably inspired by the Medeia of Euripides. From § 145 we learn that it was left unfinished. The Medeia gave occasion for a number of epigrams (see Overbeck's *Schriftquellen* 2126-2139). *Anth. Plan.* iv, 137, shows that it was painted in encaustic—ἐν κήρῳ. (Against the view advanced here that Timomachos is a painter of the fourth century, see Robert, in *Arch. Märchen,* p. 132, who defends Pliny's *Caesaris aetate,* and lately Wickhoff, in *Wiener Genesis,* p. 72). Addenda.

5. Orestes, Iphigenia in Tauris : one picture, the two parts of which are given asyndetically, see J. Müller, *Stil,* p. 39 f. For the subject cf. the Pompeian wall-painting, *A. Z.* 1875, pl. xiii : on the right, above, Iphigenia with her maidens emerging from the temple, on the left, below, Orestes and Pylades brought prisoners to the temple ; as Robert points out (*ib.* p. 133 f.), there are no grounds for identifying the Pompeian picture as a copy of the original by Timomachos. See also the composition on the

sarkophagos, Robert, *Sarkoph. Reliefs* pl. lvii. Addenda.

agilitatis exercitator : he would be a less exalted personage than an ἐπιστάτης ἀθλητῶν (xxxiv, 82), but more on a level with the *praestigiator* Theodoros, and the *saltator* Alkisthenes in § 147. The picture was presumably a votive portrait.

6. cognatio nobilium : above, note on § 76.

palliati : i. e. wrapped in the *pallium = ἱμάτιον,* whence they were presumably portraits ; cf. on the *duo palliata* in xxxiv, 54.

quos dicturos : [cf. the Elder Philostratos εἰκόνες ii, 31 ὅρα καὶ τὸν Θεμιστοκλέα τὴν μὲν τοῦ προσώπου στάσιν παραπλήσιον τοῖς λέγουσιν. — H. L. U.] ; also Sittl, *Gebärde,* p. 7, note 5.

8. in Gorgone : i.e. a Gorgoneion or mask of Medusa ; we may compare in sculpture the ' Medusa Rondanini ' (Munich, Glypt. 128).

§ 137. Pausiae : above, § 123. The account of Aristolaus has been torn asunder from its original context.

9. e severissimis : note on § 130.

11. boum immolatio : note on § 93 ; cf. § 127.

Nicophanes : above, § 111.

intellegant soli artifices, alias durus in coloribus et sile
multus ; nam Socrates iure omnibus placet ; tales sunt
eius cum Aesculapio filiae Hygia, Aegle, Panacea, Iaso et
piger qui appellatur Ocnos, spartum torquens quod asellus
138 adrodit.   hactenus indicatis proceribus in utroque genere 5
non silebuntur et primis proximi : Aristoclides qui pinxit
aedem Apollinis Delphis.   Antiphilus puero ignem conflante
laudatur ac pulchra alias domo splendescente ipsiusque pueri
ore, item lanificio in quo properant omnium mulierum
pensa, Ptolemaeo venante, sed nobilissimo Satyro cum pelle 10
pantherina, quem aposcopeuonta appellant.   Aristophon
Ancaeo vulnerato ab apro cum socia doloris Astypale
numerosaque tabula in qua sunt Priamus, Helena, Credulitas,
139 Ulixes, Deiphobus, Dolus.   Androbius pinxit Scyllum
ancoras praecidentem Persicae classis, Artemon Danaen 15

12. Ancaium (Angaium *e corr.*) vineratumo *Bamb.* ; Ancaeum vulneratum
Detlefsen.   Astypalaea *coni. Brunn K. G.* ii, p. 53, *Detlefsen.*

1. soli artifices : Münzer, *op. cit.*
p. 519, points out that this reference
to the opinion of artists recalls the
passage on Telephanes, xxxiv, 68.

durus in coloribus : § 130 *in
coloribus severus*, where see note.

2. nam : [elliptical, i. e. the case
of the painter Sokrates is different,
for *he* pleases everybody (*omnibus*),
whereas Nikophanes is only for the
few (*sunt quibus*) ; cf. the use of
nam in xxxiv, 7 ; x, 210 ; xvii, 58,
151.—H. L. U.]

Sokrates : he appears in such
close connexion with Aristolaos and
Nikophanes, that he is presumably also
a pupil of Pausias. In xxxvi, 32, Pliny
mentions a sculptor Sokrates, whom
he distinguishes from the painter,
though according to some authorities
they were identical.   Introd. p. l. f.

3. Aesculapio : i. e. a votive
picture for a recovery ; for the subject
cf. the reliefs, Friederichs-Wolters,
1148, 1150.

4. Ocnos : for the subject, which
had already been represented by
Polygnotos in the Delphian Lesche

(Paus. x, 29, 2), cf. the *puteal* in the
Vatican (Helbig, 373).

§ 138. 5. utroque genere : i. e.
both large and small pictures.

7. aedem Ap. Delphis : nothing
further is known of these paintings.

Antiphilus : above, §§ 89, 114.

puero ign. confl.: for the same subject in statuary cf. the splanchnoptes
of Styppax, xxxiv, 81.

8. domo splendescente : for effects
of reflected light cf. above, note on
§ 78, and Wickhoff, *Wiener Genesis*,
p. 79.

9. lanificio : cf. the subjects of
Peiraïkos in § 112, of Philiskos in
§ 143.

10. Ptolemaeo : above, § 89.

11. aposcopeuonta : i. e. raising
his hand to shade his eyes in the
satyric dance called σκώπευμα (Athen.
xiv, p. 629 f.).   Variations of the
motive have been recovered in a number of statues and statuettes, which
can all be traced back to one original
type of which the finest instance is a
bronze at Berlin ; Furtwängler, *Satyr
aus Pergamon*, p. 14 ff.

circle for an industry which painters alone can really appreciate ; apart from this merit he was too harsh in colouring, and too lavish in his use of yellow ochre.   The merit of †*Sokrates* on the other *Sokrates.* hand is, as it should be, patent to everybody, thanks to his pictures of Asklepios with his daughters Hygieia, Aigle, Panakeia and Iaso, and of a sluggard, called Ὄκνος [sloth], twisting a rope which an ass is gnawing.

So far I have spoken only of the leading artists in both styles, but I do not purpose to omit those of the second rank.

†*Aristokleides* painted the temple of Apollo at Delphoi.   *Anti-* *philos* is praised for his picture of a boy blowing a fire, and for the reflection cast by the fire on the room, which is in itself beautiful, and on the boy's face ; for his picture of wool-weaving, where all the women busily ply their tasks ; for his Ptolemaios hunting, and, most famous of all, for his Satyr with a panther's skin, called the ἀποσκοπεύων, or Gazer.

Aristophon is celebrated for his Ankaios wounded by the boar, *Aristo-* grouped with Astypale, the partner of his woe, and a crowded *phon.* picture containing Priam, Helen, Credulity, Odysseus, Deiphobos and Guile.   †*Androbios* painted Skyllos cutting the cables of the Persian fleet ; †*Artemon* a Danae and the pirates marvelling at her ;

[right margin notes:] 138 *Painters of second rank arranged alphabeti- cally. Aristo- kleides. Antiphilos.* 139

Aristophon: brother of Poly- gnotos, above, note on § 60.

12. Ancaeo: not the Arkadian Ankaios, but the Argonaut with his mother Astypale. Benndorf, *Gjölbas-* *chi*, p. 114 f., inclines to believe the wounded hero was supported by his mother, a Polygnotan scheme, echoes of which seem to have survived on both the Phigaleian and Gjölbaschi friezes. The hero being a Samian, the picture was probably at Samos.

Astypale: [shortened for *Asty-* *palaia,* so Zeuxis commonly for Zeux- ippos ; cf. A. Fick, *Die Griechischen* *Personennamen,* 2nd. ed., p. 35. In Hyginus, *Fab.* 167 (ed. Bunte, 122, 1, 6), *Astyphile* is unnecessarily restored by Bunte to Astyphalaea.— H. L. U.] The reading *Astypale* is also kept by Benndorf (*op. cit.*).

13. numerosa : Brunn, *K. G.* ii, p. 53, explains this adjective applied to a picture which contained only six

figures, from Quinct. v, 10, 10 *vulgo-* *que (inter opifices) paullo numero-* *sius opus dicitur argumentosum.*

Priamus . . Dolus: from the presence of Helen and of Deiphobos it appears that the picture represented a scene from the siege of Troy subse- quent to the death of Paris; on the whole composition cf. Jahn,*A.Z.* 1847, p. 127.   For the personifications of *Dolus* and *Credulitas* cf. the διαβολή in Apelles' picture (above, note on § 89).

§ 139. 14. Scyllum : he dived and cut the cables of the Persian fleet, Paus. x, 19, 1 ; cf. Herod. viii, 8.

15. D. mirantibus eam prae- donibus : according to the legend, it was Dictys. a fisherman, who rescued Danae.   There may have been a variant tradition or the *praedones* may come from misinterpretation of the picture. Helbig, *Untersuchungen,* p. 145, brings *Wandgemälde* 119 into connexion with the ' Danae.'

mirantibus eam praedonibus, reginam Stratonicen, Herculem
et Deianiram, nobilissimas autem, quae sunt in Octaviae
operibus, Herculem ab Oeta monte Doridos exusta mortali-
tate consensu deorum in caelum euntem, Laomedontis circa
Herculem et Neptunum historiam.   Alcimachus Dioxip- 5
pum, qui pancratio Olympiae citra pulveris iactum, quod
140 vocant ἀκονιτί, vicit, Coenus stemmata.   Ctesilochus Apellis
discipulus petulanti pictura innotuit, Iove Liberum parturi-
ente depicto mitrato et muliebriter ingemescente inter
opstetricia dearum, Cleon Cadmo, Ctesidemus Oechaliae 10
expugnatione, Laodamia, Ctesicles reginae Stratonices
iniuria.   nullo enim honore exceptus ab ea pinxit volutan-
tem cum piscatore quem reginam amare sermo erat, eamque
tabulam in portu Ephesi proposuit ipse velis raptus. regina
tolli vetuit utriusque similitudine mire expressa.   Cratinus 15
141 comoedos Athenis in Pompeio pinxit, Eutychides bigam,
regit Victoria.   Eudorus scaena spectatur—idem et ex

1. **reginam Stratonicen**: there
were several queens of this name;
the most celebrated, who may be the
one intended here, was daughter of
Demetrios Poliorketes (Plut. *Dem.*
liii), married first to Seleukos Nikator,
then to his son Antiochos (Val. Max.
v, 7, *Ext.* 1); Introd. p. lx.

    Herculem et Deianiram : this
and the following picture seem part
of a cycle representing the Labours of
Herakles.   Addenda.

3. **Herculem . . . in caelum
euntem** : for the Apotheosis of
Herakles in later art see Furtwängler,
ap. Roscher, i, 2250.

5. **historiam** : probably in a series
of pictures.   One scene, the freeing of
Hesione by Herakles, was also the
subject of a picture by Antiphilos
(above, § 114).

    Dioxippum : he was in the army
of Alexander the Great, and in B.C.
328, during the Median campaign,
he overcame in an athletic contest
the Makedonian Koragos who had
challenged him.   By this feat, however, he drew upon himsef the dis-

pleasure of Alexander, and being
slandered to the king he finally took
his own life.   Diod. xvii, 100–101 ;
Ailian, Ποικ. Ἱστ. x, 22 (see G. H.
Förster, *Sieger in den Olympischen
Spielen*, i, p. 27, 381), Ol. 113, 3 =
326 B. C.

6. **Olympiae** : instead of the usual
construction, *Olympia vincere*, imitated from the Greek.

7. ἀκονιτί = χωρὶς κόνεως : usually
because the appointed antagonist
failed to appear; according to Paus.
vi, 11, 4, Dromeus of Mantineia was
the first to gain a victory ἀκονιτί; cf.
id. vi, 7, 4 ; *I. G. B.* 29.   See for
all possible conditions of such a
victory K. E. Heinrichs, *Ueber das
Pentathlon der Griechen* (Würzburg,
1892), p. 74.   For the expression
sine pulvere, which was proverbial,
Otto, *Sprichwörter*, p. 290.

    stemmata: portraits fitted into
some kind of genealogical tree (xxxv,
§ 6); cf. note on *cognatio*, in § 76.

    § 140.   **Ctesilochus** : if iden-
tical, as is generally supposed with
the Κτησίοχος of Souidas (*s. v.*

a portrait of queen Stratonike; a Herakles and Deianeira, and the celebrated pictures in the galleries of Octavia : the one represents Herakles on Mount Oite in Doris, putting off his mortality in the flames, and going up to heaven by consent of all the gods ; *Alkima-* the other shows the story of Laomedon, Herakles and Poseidon. *chos paints a portrait* †*Alkimachos* painted a picture of Dioxippos, who won in the pan- *of the Pan-* kration at Olympia a victory without dust, ἀκονιτί, as it is called. *kratiast Dioxippos.* †*Koinos* painted family trees. *Ktesilochos*, a pupil of Apelles, 140 became famous by a burlesque painting of Zeus giving birth to *Ktesilo- chos paints* Dionysos ; the god wears a head-dress and, moaning like a woman, *a grotesque* is receiving the good offices of the goddesses. †*Kleon* owes *picture of the birth of* his reputation to a picture of Kadmos, †*Ktesidemos* to a siege of *Dionysos.* Oichalia and a Laodameia, while †*Ktesikles* is best known by the *Ktesikles :* affront he offered to queen Stratonike, who had received him *his venge- ance upon* without any mark of honour. He in consequence painted her *Queen* lying in the arms of a fisherman, her reputed lover, and had the *Stratonike.* picture exhibited in the port of Ephesos, after he himself had sped away with all sails set. The queen, however, would not allow the picture to be removed, as both portraits were excellent likenesses. †*Kratinos* painted comic actors in the Pompeion at Athens, *Eutychides*, a two-horsed chariot driven by Nike. †*Eudoros*, who 141

Apelles), he was the brother of Apelles.

8. petulanti pictura : the picture was probably intended as a parody. Heydemann, *Hall. Winckelmannspr.* x (1885), p. 5 ff.

Iove ... mitrato : an absurdity because, among Greeks at any rate, the μίτρα was only a feminine adornment ; above, § 58 *capita earum* (sc. *mulierum*) *mitris versicoloribus operuit ;* but vi, 162 *Arabes mitrati.*

9. inter opstet. dearum : i. e. the *Eileithyiai.*

10. Ctesidemus : the master of Antiphilos, above, § 114.

Oechaliae expugn. : by Herakles, Strabo, ix, p. 438.

11. Laodamia : the subject is of frequent occurrence (gem Br. Mus. Cat. p. 67, no. 327 ; numerous sarkophagi, cp. especially Baumeister, *Denkm.*, p. 1422, fig. 1574), but there is no ascertained copy of Ktesidemos's picture.

Stratonices iniuria : cf. on § 139.

15. Cratinus comoedus : I see no need for doubting his identity with the writer of comedies (fl. middle of fifth cent.). This first mention of Kratinos was detached from its context with Eirene, daughter of Kratinos (§ 147), in order to be introduced into the alphabetical list (see Münzer, *op. cit.* p. 535 ; Introd. p. lxv.).

16. in Pompeio : at the entrance to the Kerameikos, Paus. 1, 2, 4.

§ 141. Eutychides : in xxxiv, 78, he is mentioned as a sculptor in bronze.

bigam, regit Victoria : for the subject cf. Helbig, *Wandgemälde*, 938, 939.

17. scaena : i. e. a scenic decoration intended to be fastened to the *scaenae frons ;* cf. § 23.

et ex aere signa fecit : he is however not mentioned in xxxiv.

aere signa fecit—Hippys Neptuno et Victoria. Habron
amicam et Concordiam pinxit et deorum simulacra, Leon-
tiscus Aratum victorem cum tropaeo, psaltriam, Leon
Sappho, Nearchus Venerem inter Gratias et Cupidines,
142 Herculem tristem insaniae poenitentia, Nealces Venerem— 5
ingeniosus et sollers iste, siquidem, cum proelium navale
Persarum et Aegyptiorum pinxisset, quod in Nilo, cuius est
aqua maris similis, factum volebat intellegi, argumento
declaravit quod arte non poterat; asellum enim bibentem
143 in litore pinxit et crocodilum insidiantem ei—Oenias 10
syngenicon, Philiscus officinam pictoris ignem conflante
puero, Phalerion Scyllam, Simonides Agatharchum et
Mnemosynen, Simus iuvenem requiescentem, officinam
fullonis quinquatrus celebrantem, idemque Nemesim egreg-
144 iam, Theorus se inunguentem, idem ab Oreste matrem 15

15. se inunguentem] *Sillig*; emungentem *Bamb.*; et inungentem *Ricc.*;
erumpentem *Detlefsen* (*coni. Benndorf*).

1. **Hippys**: the name has been
conjecturally restored from Polemon,
ap. Athen. xi, p. 474 d; cf. above,
note on *anus* in § 78.

2. **amicam**: simply the portrait
of a *hetaira* (cf. Furtwängler,
Dornauszieher, p. 94, n. 53). Some
commentators, however, assume a
misunderstanding on Pliny's part of
the Greek φιλία, and suggest the
reading *Amicitiam*, by analogy with
Concordia = ὁμόνοια.

3 **Aratum ... tropaeo**: according to Hardouin (*ad loc.*), to commemorate the victory over Aristippos,
Plut. *Aratus*, xxix; the identification
with the Sikyonian Aratos (frees
Sikyon B.C. 251), however, seems
doubtful, since none of the known
painters in the list belong to so late a
period; below, note on *Nealces;* cf.
Brunn, *K. G.* ii, p. 292.

psaltriam: cf. xxxiv, 63 and note.

§ 142. 5. **Herculem tristem**: i.e.
after the murder of his children; cf.
in sculpture the kindred subject of
Athamas, xxxiv, 140. A gem, which
Stephani (*Ausruh. Her.* p. 145)

thought he could trace back to the
picture of Nearchos, has been shown
by Furtwängler (*ap.* Roscher, i, 2175)
to be merely an adaptation by an
artist of the Renascence of a type
created for Aias (above, note on § 136).

Nealces: Münzer, *op. cit.* p. 532,
note 2, rightly disputes his identity
with the painter Nealkes, the friend
of Aratos (Plut. *loc. cit.* xiii), since
in that case Pasias, the pupil of Nealkes's own pupil Erigonos (§ 145),
would belong to the late second
century, outside the lower limit of the
lists; to this consideration may be
added that the story recounted of
Erigonos (*loc. cit.*) is closely connected
with a number of other stories, which
cannot have arisen later than the
commencement of the third century.
Münzer's discovery, however, with
regard to the picture by Nealkes
(note on *proelium*) at once settles the
question in favour of an earlier painter
of the name.

6. **ingeniosus**: cf. the praise
bestowed upon Timanthes in § 73.

proelium ... asellum. Münzer

also made statues in bronze, is known by a scene painted for a theatre, *Hippys* by a Poseidon and a Nike, †*Habron* by a portrait of his mistress, a picture of Concord and figures of the Gods. †*Leontiskos* painted Aratos as victor with a trophy, and a woman playing on the cithara, †*Leon* a Sappho, †*Nearchos* an Aphrodite attended by the Graces and Loves, and a Herakles in grief repenting of his madness, †*Nealkes*, an Aphrodite. This Nealkes was a man of ingenious devices; he had painted a naval battle between the Egyptians and Persians, and wishing to show that it was fought on the Nile (the waters of which are like those of the sea) he indicated by a symbol that which art alone could not express, painting an ass drinking on the river's brim and a crocodile lying in wait for it. †*Oinias* painted a family gathering; †*Philiskos* an artist's studio with a boy blowing the fire; †*Phalerion* a Skylla; †*Simonides* an Agatharchos and Mnemosyne; *Simos* a youth resting, the workshop of a fuller who is keeping the festival of Minerva, and a Nemesis of great beauty. †*Theoros* painted an athlete anointing himself, an Orestes slaying

142 *Nealkes.*

143

144 *Theoros: his picture*

(*loc. cit.*) has had the signal merit of fixing the occasion for the picture and thereby the date of the artist. It must have referred to one of the battles by which Artaxerxes III Ochos, (B. C. 358–337), successively reduced Egypt in B. C. 350. 'Popular conceptions of the wicked enemy, of the ass-shaped Seth Typhon, had won for the hated king the nickname of the " Ass" among the Egyptians, while among the Greeks who fought in thousands on either side, the pun ὦχος—ὄνος had quickly spread (cf. Deinon, *ap.* Plut. *de Iside*, 31 διὸ καὶ τῶν Περσικῶν βασιλέων ἐχθραίνοντες μάλιστα τὸν Ὦχον ὡς ἐναγῆ καὶ μιαρόν, ὄνον ἐπωνόμασαν : Ailian, Ποικ. Ἰστ. iv, 8). The allusion which Nealkes introduced into his picture was clear to his contemporaries and to the point; later its meaning was forgotten, and people had recourse to the silly explanation recorded by Pliny.'

§ 143. 11. **syngenicon** : above, § 136; cf. note on § 76.

ignem conflante puero. The studio must have been that of a

painter in encaustic; cf. the picture by Antiphilos, in § 138. Introd. p. lxxi.

12. **Scyllam**: uncertain whether the sea monster or the daughter of Nisos; cf. Brunn, *K. G.* 300; a Scylla by Nikomachos in § 109.

13. **Mnemosynen**: cf. the relief of Archelaos of Priene in Br. Mus.

Simus: possibly identical with the sculptor Simos of Salamis (in Kypros), known from two inscriptions (*I. G. B.* 163, 164), which from the character of the epigraphy may be dated about the third century B. C., Brunn, *K. G.* i, p. 467; H. v. Gaertringen, *Jahrb.* ix, 1894, p. 39.

iuvenem requiescentem: [perhaps a grave picture, in which the dead youth was represented lying down, i. e. an ἀναπαυόμενος (§ 99 and note), an *expirantis imago* (§ 90).—H. L. U.]

14. **quinquatrus** : the feast, which was of two kinds, the Greater and the Lesser, was kept by all those whose trades were under the special protection of Minerva. Addenda.

§ 144. 15. **Theorus** : the name belongs to the class of those given,

et Aegisthum interfici, bellumque Iliacum pluribus tabulis,
quod est Romae in Philippi porticibus, et Cassandram, quae
est in Concordiae delubro, Leontium Epicuri cogitantem,
Demetrium regem, Theon Orestis insaniam, Thamyram
citharoedum, Tauriscus discobolum, Clytaemestram, Pani- 5
145 scon, Polynicen regnum repetentem et Capanea. non omit-
tetur inter hos insigne exemplum. namque Erigonus tritor
colorum Nealcae pictoris in tantum ipse profecit ut celebrem
etiam discipulum reliquerit Pasian, fratrem Aeginetae
pictoris. illud vero perquam rarum ac memoria dignum 10
est suprema opera artificum inperfectasque tabulas, sicut
Irim Aristidis, Tyndaridas Nicomachi, Mediam Timomachi
et quam diximus Venerem Apellis, in maiore admiratione
esse quam perfecta, quippe in is liniamenta reliqua ipsaeque
cogitationes artificum spectantur, atque in lenocinio com- 15
mendationis dolor est manus, cum id ageret, exstinctae.
146 sunt etiamnum non ignobiles quidem, in transcursu tamen

according to Fick (*Gr.Personcnnamen*, p. 360), in allusion to the bearer's profession (see, however, H.L. Urlichs' note on *Euchira*, in § 152). That there is not the slightest evidence for following Brunn (*K. G.* ii, p. 255), in charging Pliny with the fabrication of *Theorus* out of a misunderstanding of *Theon*, has been shown by Urlichs in *Hölz. Pferd*, p. 18, n. 17.

se inungentem : votive portrait of an athlete, represented in the act of anointing himself, a subject familiar in statuary, Furtwängler, *Masterpieces*, p. 257 ff. ; against the Beundorf-Detlefsen reading *erumpentem* see H. L. Urlichs, in *Woch. f. Klass. Phil.* 1895, p. 548.

ab Oreste matrem et Aegisthum interfici : cf. the construction in xxxiv, 59 (*fecit*) *Apollinem serpentemque eius sagittis configi*. For the subject cf. the Pompeian picture, *A. Z.* xli, 1883, pl. ix, 1 (Robert, *ib.* p. 259), and the Sarkophagos in St Petersburg, Robert, *Sark. Rel.* pl. liv, p. 165 f. Wickhoff, *Wiener Genesis,* p. 85.

1. bellumque Iliacum pluribus tabulis : probably one of the oldest instances of a serial representation of scenes from the Trojan war, such as became so fashionable in imperial days (cf. the *Troiae halosis*, Petron. 87, also the pictures of the Fall of Troy, seen by Aineias in the Palace of Dido, Virg. *Aen.* i, 456–493). From Pompeii we have a series of pictures, which, even if not close imitations of the pictures by Theoros (see Helbig, *Untersuch.* p. 142), serve to illustrate how these cycles were conceived ; see Brüning, *Jahrb.* ix, 1894, p. 164 (*Ueber die vildlichen Vorlagen der Ilischen Tafeln*).

2. Philippi porticibus : note on § 66.

Cassandram : it may have been part of the Trojan series (above), and have become separated from it ; more probably it was a picture by itself.

3. Leontium : note on § 99.

4. Demetrium : i.e. Poliorketes ; cf. note on xxxiv, 42.

Theon : of Samos ; mentioned by Quinct. xii, 10, 6, among the seven

his mother and Aigisthos, a cycle of pictures of the Trojan war, *of ' Orestes* now in Rome in the Gallery of Philip, a Kassandra, now in the *slaying his Mother.'* temple of Concord, Leontion, the pupil of Epikouros, in medita- tion, and king Demetrios.   *Theon* painted the madness of Orestes, *Theon : his* and a portrait of Thamyras, a player on the cithara ; *Tauriskos* *picture of the 'Mad-* painted the portrait of a quoit - thrower, a Klytaimnestra, a *ness of* Παυίσκοs or young Pan, a Polyneikes claiming the throne, and *Orestes.'* a Kapaneus.

Nor must I forget to mention here the noteworthy case of 145 †*Erigonos*, who ground the colours of Nealkes, and eventually *Erigonos : his rise* became so good a painter that he could even train a great artist in *from ob-* his pupil †*Pasias*, the brother of the painter †*Aiginetas*.   Another *scurity to fame.* most curious fact and worthy of record is, that the latest works of *Singular* artists and the pictures left unfinished at their death are valued *value and* more than any of their finished paintings, for example the Iris by *charm of unfinished* Aristeides, the children of Tyndaros by Nikomachos, the Medeia *works.* by Timomachos and the Aphrodite by Apelles, mentioned above. The reason is that in these we see traces of the design and the original conception of the artists, while sorrow for the hand that perished at its work beguiles us into the bestowal of praise.

There still remain certain painters whom, though artists of 146 repute, I can do no more than name in passing, †*Aristokydes*, *Second al- phabetical list.*

most important painters of the age of Alexander, as *praestantissimus* ... *concipiendis visionibus, quas φαντασίαs vocant ;* cf. also Ailian, Ποικ. Ἱστ. ii. 44, where the warrior charging out of a panel is described.

   Orestis insaniam : τὴν 'Ορέστου μητροκτονίαν, Plut. *de aud. Poet.* 3.

   Thamyram citharoedum : cf. the *Gorgosthenes tragoedus*, by Apelles, in § 93, the *tibicina* of Lysippos, xxxiv, 63, the *psaltria* by Leontiskos, in § 141, &c.

   5. **Tauriscus** : his identity with one of the sculptors of the ' Farnese Bull ' can neither be proved nor dis- proved.   He is perhaps the same as the silver-chaser of xxxiii, 156, whom in xxxvi, 33, Pliny is careful to dis- tinguish from the sculptor.

   discobolum : votive picture for an athletic contest.

§ 145. 7. **tritor colorum** : cf. above, § 85 *qui colores tererent ;* for the story of Erigonos's rise from poverty to fame, cf. Lysippos, xxxiv, 61, Protogenes, above, § 101, Introd. p. xlix.

   8. **Nealcae** : above, §§ 104, 142. **ut discipulum rel.** : so likewise Seilanion, xxxiv, 51, though himself a self-taught artist, leaves a celebrated pupil in Zeuxiades, Introd. *loc. cit.*

   9. **Aeginetae** : for the ethnic as proper name cf. Fick, *Gr. Personen- namen*, p. 333.

   12. **Aristidis** : above, §§ 75, 98, 108 ; for Nikomachos, § 108.

   Mediam Timomachi : §§ 26, 136.

   13. **quam diximus** : above, §§ 87, 91.

   14. **quippe** ... **extinctae** : rheto- rical ; for *liniamenta reliqua* cf. note on § 68.

dicendi Aristocydes, Anaxander, Aristobulus Surus,
Arcesilas Tisicratis filius, Coroebus Nicomachi discipulus,
Charmantides Euphranoris, Dionysodorus Colophonius,
Dicaeogenes qui cum Demetrio rege vixit, Euthymides,
Heraclides Macedo, Milon Soleus Pyromachi statuari 5
discipuli, Mnasitheus Sicyonius, Mnasitimus Aristonidae
filius et discipulus, Nessus Habronis filius, Polemon
Alexandrinus, Theodorus Samius et Stadios Nicosthenis
147 discipuli, Xenon Neoclis discipulus Sicyonius. pinxere
et mulieres : Timarete Miconis filia Dianam quae in tabula 10
Ephesi est antiquissimae picturae, Irene Cratini pictoris filia
et discipula puellam quae est Eleusine, Calypso senem et
praestigiatorem Theodorum, Alcisthenen saltatorem, Aristarete Nearchi filia et discipula Aesculapium. Iaia Cyzicena
perpetua virgo M. Varronis iuventa Romae et penicillo 15
pinxit et cestro in ebore imagines mulierum maxime et
Neapoli anum in grandi tabula, suam quoque imaginem ad
148 speculum. nec ullius velocior in pictura manus fuit, artis
vero tantum ut multum manipretiis antecederet celeberrimos
eadem aetate imaginum pictores Sopolim et Dionysium, 20
quorum tabulae pinacothecas inplent. pinxit et quaedam
Olympias, de qua hoc solum memoratur, discipulum eius
fuisse Autobulum.

§ 146. 2. **Arcesilae** : from his
date he may be identical with the
Arkesilaos, Paus. i, 1, 3, whose picture
of Leosthenes and his sons (a συγγενικόν) was in the sanctuary of Athena
and Zeus in the Peiraieus. The exploits of Leosthenes, mentioned by
Pausanias, took place B.C. 323.
  Tisicratis : pupil of Euthykrates
of Sikyon, xxxiv, 83.
  Nicomachi : §§ 108, 145.
  3. **Euphranoris** : § 128.
  5. **Heraclides** : above, § 135.
  Pyromachi : note on xxxiv, § 84.
  6. **Mnasitheus** : the identification
with the Mnasitheos of Plut. *Arat.*
vii, suggested by Brunn, *K. G.* ii,
p. 292, is more than doubtful.
  Mnasitimos : son of Aristonidas,
I. G. B. 197, above xxxiv, 140.

  7. **Habronis** : above, §§ 93, 141.
  8. **Theodorus Samius** : on the
different painters of this name see
Brunn, *K. G.* ii, p. 285 ; if the identity
of his fellow-pupil *Stadios* with the
sculptor Stadieus of Paus. vi, 4, 5,
the master of Polykles (note on xxxvi,
35), were certain, his date would be
towards Ol. 150 = B.C. 180.
  § 147. 10. **Timarete** : the account
of the women painters bears strong
traces of Duris ; cf. Münzer, *op. cit.*
p. 525 ; Introd. p. lxv. The names
are given in inverted alphabetical
order. In connexion with the lady
painters it is interesting to note the
charming Pompeian wall paintings,
Helbig, *Wandgemälde,* 1443, 1444 =
Blümner, *Techn.* iii, p. 226, iv, p. 460,
the first of a woman painting a statue,

†*Anaxander*, †*Aristoboulos* of Syria, *Arkesilas* the son of Teisi-krates, †*Koroibos* the pupil of Nikomachos, †*Charmantides* the pupil of Euphranor, †*Dionysodorus* of Kolophon, †*Dikaiogenes* who lived at the court of king Demetrios, †*Euthymides*, †*Hera-kleides* of Makedon and †*Milon* of Soloi, both pupils of Pyro-machos the statuary, †*Mnasitheus* of Sikyon, *Mnasitimos* the son and pupil of Aristonidas, †*Nessos* the son of Habron, †*Polemon* of Alexandria, *Theodoros* of Samos and *Stadios*, pupils of †Niko-sthenes, and †*Xenon* of Sikyon, the pupil of Nealkes.

Women too have been painters : †*Timarete* the daughter of 147 Mikon, painted an Artemis at Ephesos in a picture of very archaic style. *Eirene*, the daughter and pupil of the painter Kratinos, painted a maiden at Eleusis, †*Kalypso* painted portraits of an old man, of the juggler Theodoros, and of the dancer Alkisthenes ; †*Aristarete*, the daughter and pupil of Nearchos, painted an Askle-pios. †*Iaia* of Kyzikos, who remained single all her life, worked at Rome in the youth of Marcus Varro, both with the brush and with the cestrum on ivory. She painted chiefly portraits of women, and also a large picture of an old woman at Naples, and a portrait of herself, executed with the help of a mirror. No artist worked 148 more rapidly than she did, and her pictures had such merit that they sold for higher prices than those of †Sopolis and Dionysios, well-known contemporary painters, whose works fill our galleries. †*Olympias* also was a painter ; of her we only know that †*Auto-boulos* was her pupil.

Women painters.
Timarete.
Eirene.
Kalypso.

Aristarete.

Iaia of Kyzikos.

Olympias.

the second of a woman seated at her easel.

Miconis filia : § 59 ; Eirene and Aristarete likewise figure both as daugh-ters and pupils ; cf. Münzer, *loc. cit.*

11. antiquiss. picturae : the exact meaning is difficult to comprehend ; Brunn suggests that she affected an archaicising style.

Irene : Εἰρήνην τὴν Κρατίνου θυγα-τέρα, Clemens Alex. (quoting from Didymos) *Strom.* iv, 124, p.620, Pott; cf. § 140.

12. puellam : translation of the Greek κόρα, so first Raoul Rochette, *Peint. Inédites*, p. 222 ; cf. Brunn, *K. G.* ii, p. 299.

13. praestigiatorem . . . saltato-rem : chiastic order.

14. Nearchi : above, § 141.

Iaia Cyzicena : the alphabetical order is broken to insert a passage taken from Varro, Introd. p. lxxxiii.

16. cestro in ebore : i.e. in encan-stic on ivory (below, § 149), as opposed to *penicillo* in the ordinary method of tempera.

17. in grandi tabula : on a wood panel of course, and presumably with the brush ; cf. Blümner, *Technol.* iv, p. 445, note 1.

§ 148. 20. Sopolim : the name is still known only from Pliny, for in Cic. *ad. Att.* iv, 18, 4, it seems certain that *solidis pectoribus* is the reading, and not *e Sopolidis pictoribus* (see Baiter & Kayzer's critical apparatus).

Dionysium : § 113.

21. inplent : rhetorical, cf. xxxiv, 36, *replevit urbem.*

149   encausto pingendi duo fuere antiquitus genera, cera et in
ebore cestro, id est vericulo, donec classes pingi coepere.
hoc tertium accessit resolutis igni ceris penicillo utendi,
quae pictura navibus nec sole nec sale ventisque cor-
rumpitur.   5

§ 149. 1. Encausto pingendi:
§ 122. Owing to Pliny's obscure
wording of the following passage the
whole subject of ancient encaustic is
beset with the gravest difficulties. For
the literature up to 1887 see Blümner,
Technol. iv, pp. 442 ff.; a good *ré-
sumé*, with new suggestions, by Cecil
Smith, art. *Pictura*, in Smith's *Dict.
of Ant.* ii, pp. 392 ff.; cf. also A. S.
Murray, *Handbook*, pp. 394 ff.; a highly
important contribution has lately been
made by the painter Berger, *Beiträge zur Entwickelungsgeschichte der
Malertechnik*, i, ii (1893 and 1895),
who has succeeded in proving painting
in encaustic to be a totally different
process from the καῦσις of walls
painted with an admixture of olive-oil
and Punic wax (Plin. xxi, 83), described by Vitruvius (vii, 9). This
discovery has freed the subject from
some of its worst difficulties.

duo genera: (1) *cera et cestro* on
the usual materials, i.e. wood. (2)
cera et cestro, on ivory, a less common
material, so that Pliny mentions it
specially. Of the first method, the
portraits from the Fayoum now afford
numerous examples (see Berger, ii,
pp. 50 ff.; Cecil Smith, *loc. cit.*, &c.).
The second method remains obscure,
but cf. the painted ivory fragments
mentioned by Berger, i, p. 41 (in *Pal.
Conserv.* at Rome) and the ivory panel
in the British Museum with figure of
a nymph, Murray, *Handbook*, p. 396,
fig. 117. It is noteworthy that the
lady painter Iaia (§ 147) is the only
artist known to have employed this
technique.

From the earliest times two methods of painting in encaustic 149 existed—one with wax, the other further on ivory—by means of *Painting in wax.* a cestrum or sharp point. When it became the fashion to paint ships of war, a third method was introduced, of melting the wax by fire and using a brush. Paint applied to ships in this way cannot be destroyed either by the action of the sun or of the brine or wind.

2. cestro . . . vericulo : it is Berger's merit (*Beiträge*, i, p. 35 ff.) to have identified the *cestrum* among the instruments found in the grave of St. Médard (*ib.* figs. 2, 3; Blümner, *Technol.* iv, figs. 66, 67), and among the Naples bronzes (*Beitr.* i, p. 43 ff.). The one end is shaped like a spoon: with it the colours are held to melt over the *cauterium* or fire-pan (the misnamed *boîte à couleurs* of the St. Médard grave), and then poured over the panel; the long handle thickens at the upper end, which is used to level the colours.

donec classes pingi coepere : Berger, i, p. 38, explains the introduction of the brush for ship painting to have been necessitated by the impossibility of pouring fluid colour from the *cestrum* on to the *vertical* sides of a ship. This explanation seems correct, in so far at least as the meaning of the writer of the Plinian passage is concerned. It would be in the manner of certain ancient art-writers to imagine a conventional development of technique from cestrum to brush, and then to prove the point by appeal to practice.

3. resolutis ceris : i.e. in a separate, preliminary process, whereas in the first two methods the colours were both heated and applied by means of the cestrum.

II. PLASTICE.

151 DE pictura satis superque. contexuisse his et plasticen conveniat. eiusdem opere terrae fingere ex argilla simili-tudines Butades Sicyonius figulus primus invenit Corinthi filiae opera quae capta amore iuvenis, abeunte illo peregre, umbram ex facie eius ad lucernam in pariete lineis circum- 5 scripsit, quibus pater eius inpressa argilla typum fecit et cum ceteris fictilibus induratum igni proposuit, eumque
A.U.C. 608. servatum in Nymphaeo, donec Mummius Corinthum ever-
152 terit, tradunt. sunt qui in Samo primos omnium plasticen invenisse Rhoecum et Theodorum tradant multo ante 10
A.U.C. 97. Bacchiadas Corintho pulsos, Damaratum vero ex eadem urbe profugum, qui in Etruria Tarquinium regem populi Romani genuit, comitatos fictores Euchira, Diopum, Eugram-mum, ab iis Italiae traditam plasticen. Butadis inventum

§ 151. 2. eiusdem opere terrae: with these words Pliny harks back to his main theme in § 1 (*Restant terrae ipsius genera lapidumque*) of which the History of the Painters has been but an episode ; so again in § 166 he begins *Verum et ipsius terrae ;* see Fröhner, in *Rhein. Mus.* 47, 1892, p. 294.

2. similitudines primus inve-nit: Boutades 'invents' (1) faces in relief, (2) faces applied as tile-ends, (3) how to take the cast of the model for a statue, whereas Lysistratos (4) shows, finally, how to take the cast from a living model. The whole de-velopment has a strong Xenokratic tinge ; see Introd. p. xxxiv. f.

3. Butades Sicyonius: the fol-lowing anecdote is told with slight variations by Athenagoras, Πρεσβεία,

17 ed. Schwartz, p. 18 (see App. xi).

Corinthi: cf. § 16; Corinth and Sikyon now appear as the cradles of the art of modelling. As Cecil Smith points out (*Pictura*, p. 401), the legend that the Sikyonian Bou-tades worked at Corinth, suggests an attempt to compromise the rival claims of both cities to artistic priority.

4. abeunte illo peregre: accord-ing to Athenagoras, the youth was not going away, but asleep.

8. donec Mummius Corinthum: the sack of Corinth in B.C. 146 had evidently become a conventional date with which to connect the disappear-ance or destruction of works of art in Greece.

9. sunt qui: introduces paren-thetically a variant version of the origin of πλαστική ; from the mention

II. MODELLING.

OF painting I have said enough and more than enough, but it may be well to add some account of clay modelling. It was by the service of the selfsame earth that †*Boutades*, a potter of Sikyon, discovered, with the help of his daughter, how to model portraits in clay. She was in love with a youth, and when he was leaving the country she traced the outline of the shadow which his face cast on the wall by lamplight. Her father filled in the outline with clay and made a model; this he dried and baked with the rest of his pottery, and we hear that it was preserved in the temple of the Nymphs, until Mummius overthrew Corinth. According to some authorities clay modelling was first introduced in Samos by *Rhoikos* and *Theodoros*, long before the expulsion of the Bacchiadai from Corinth, and when Damaratos fled from that city to Etruria, where his son Tarquinius, afterwards king of Rome, was born, he was accompanied by three potters, *Eucheir*, †*Diopos*, and †*Eugrammos*, who introduced the art of modelling into Italy. Boutades first added red ochre or modelled in red clay, and

151
Boutades of Sikyon discovers modelling in clay.

146 B.C.
152
Rhoikos and Theodoros of Samos.
657 B.C. (Grote)
Greek potters follow Damaratos to Etruria.

of the followers of Damaratos this alternative account seems taken from Cornelius Nepos (above, § 17, Introd. p. lxxxv). The subject of Boutades is resumed below at *Boutadis inventum*, and again at *idem et de signis*.

10. **Rhoecum et Theodorum**: xxxiv, 83.

11. **Damaratum**; above. § 16.

13. **fictores**: πλάσται, *fingere* like πλάσσω being used of the artist who works in soft substances such as earth or wax, also who fashions by the hand (cf. the *fingitque premendo* of Vergil, *Aen.* vi, 80); see on xxxiv, 7, and below, on § 153.

Euchira . . . Eugrammum: respectively the skilled handicraftsman (εὔχειρ), and the skilled draughtsman (εὔγραμμος), while Diopus = δίοπος is connected with διόπτης or διόπτρα, an instrument for taking levels, the invention of which (vii, 198) is attributed by Pliny to Theodoros, Urlichs, *Chrestom.* p. 373. [A. Fick, *Die Griechischen Personennamen*, 2nd ed. p. 254, believes these names to be given with regard to the bearer's trade or occupation, and in many cases to have supplanted the real name (cf. note on *Theorus*, in § 144). They seem to me more likely to have been favourite names in artist families, and to have been given at birth.— H. L. U.] For Eucheiros see Comm. on p. 220.

est rubricam addere aut ex rubra creta fingere. primusque
personas tegularum extremis imbricibus inposuit, quae inter
initia prostypa vocavit, postea idem ectypa fecit.   hinc et
fastigia templorum orta.   propter hunc plastae appellati.

153   Hominis autem imaginem gypso e facie ipsa primus 5
omnium expressit ceraque in eam formam gypsi infusa
emendare instituit Lysistratus Sicyonius, frater Lysippi de
quo diximus.   hic et similitudines reddere instituit, ante
eum quam pulcherrimas facere studebatur.   idem et de
signis effigies exprimere invenit, crevitque res in tantum ut 10
nulla signa statuaeve sine argilla fierent.   quo apparet antiquiorem hanc fuisse scientiam quam fundendi aeris.

154   Plastae laudatissimi fuere Damophilus et Gorgasus, idem
pictores, qui Cereris aedem Romae ad circum maximum

2. personas tegularum: numbers
of these tile-faces from Etruria are to
be seen in almost every Museum ; cf.
also the terra-cotta fragments from
the treasuries at Olympia (*Olympia* ii,
Baudenkmäler, taf. cxx).

4. fastigia : in Pliny used as a rule
of the figures of the akroteria, and
not of the actual pedimental figures,
cf. xxxvi, 13 ; xxviii, 16 ; xxxvii, 14 ;
xxxvi, 6, &c., below § 157 ; this meaning is borne out (1) by Vitruv. iii, 3,
5 *ornanique signis fictilibus aut
aereis inauratis earum fastigia Tusca-
nico more, uti est ad Circum maximum
Cereris, et Herculis Pompeiani, item
Capitolii*, (2) by Cicero, *de Divin.* i,
10, 16 *cum Summanus in fastigio
Iovis opt. max., qui tum erat fictilis,
e caelo ictus esset, etc.*, (3) by Festus,
s. v. *Ratumena*.   Further, in Plut.
Caesar lxiii, ἀκρωτήριον corresponds to
the *fastigium* of Suet. *Jul.* 81 ; see
Furtwängler, *A. Z.* 1882, p. 346;
Fowler in *Amer. Journ. of Archaeol.*
viii, 1893, p. 385.

orta : because the figured akroteria
arose out of the earlier tile-faces.

§ 153. 5. Hominis . . . studebatur : the proper place for the ' invention ' of Lysistratos is after the third
invention of Boutades, below (B. dis-

covered how to make models of
statues ; Lysistratos, however (*autem*),
found out how to take casts of living
people, see note on § 151).   The displacement arose, doubtless, from confusion of notes ; it may be due to Pliny
himself, or to his nephew when he prepared the last books of the *Hist. Nat.*
for publication ; cf. Brunn, *K. G.* i,
p. 403, Furtwängler, *Plinius*, p. 59 f.,
Münzer, *op. cit.* p. 510.

e facie ipsa: i.e. from the living
model ; the invention attributed to
Lysistratos has nothing whatever to
do with the custom of taking masks
from the face of the dead.

8. ante eum q. pulcherrimas :
the observation is correct ; by the time
of Lysippos realistic portraiture had,
if not superseded ideal or typical representation, yet asserted its right to
co-existence. It was, in a word, the age
when an athlete could be idealized as
the '*Apoxyomenos*,' or portrayed with
the brutal realism of the bronze boxer
from Olympia (*Olympia* iv, *Bronzen*,
taf. ii), cf. the note on xxxiv, 16.

9. idem et : refers back to Boutades.

11. sine argilla : Pliny means that
to make a bronze statue without a clay
model is impossible, though he—or

placed masks as tile-fronts on the eaves of buildings, originally called πρόστυπα, or low reliefs; later on he made ἔκτυπα, or high reliefs, and these led to the ornamentation of the gables of temples. Since the time of Boutades artists who worked in clay have been called modellers. (*Lysistratos* of Sikyon, brother of the Lysippos whom I have mentioned in an earlier book, was however the first who obtained portraits by making a plaster mould on the actual features, and introduced the practice of taking from the plaster a wax cast on which he made the final corrections. He also first rendered likenesses with exactitude, for previous artists had only tried to make them as beautiful as possible.) The said Boutades discovered how to take casts from statues, a practice which was extended to such a degree that no figure or statue was made without a clay model. Hence it is clear that the art of clay modelling is older than that of bronze casting.

Most highly praised among modellers were †*Damophilos* and †*Gorgasos*; they were also painters, and united both arts in the decorations of the temple of Ceres at Rome near the Great

153
Lysistratos of Sikyon takes casts from the living face.

Boutades makes clay models for statues.

154
Damophilos and Gorgasos decorate the Temple of Ceres.

his author—have used an ambiguous expression, which might imply that there had been previous bronze statues, but made without a clay model, cf. Furtwängler, *Plinius*, p. 60. The use of clay models for marble statues seems to have been of altogether later date, cf. § 155.

antiquiorem: so in xxxiv, 35, *prior* (sc. *plastice*) *quam statuaria fuit.*

§ 154. 13. Damophilus: [although Damophilos is the Doric form of Demophilos, and both represent the same name, it is yet impossible to deduce from this fact the identity of the Damophilus mentioned here with the *Demophilus Himeraeus* who appears in § 61, the master of Zeuxis. Himera was an Ionic city, and it is out of the question that one of its citizens should ever have called himself by a Doric form of his name. Yet we cannot on the other hand doubt the form *Damophilus* given here by Pliny; for he evidently had it from an authority who was familiar with the actual in-

scription (*versibus inscriptis Graece*) Thus if we get rid of the false assumption that this Damophilus could be identical with the master of Zeuxis, we get rid of all the far-fetched combinations necessary to reconcile the date of D. of Himera (whose pupil Zeuxis fl. about B.C. 404) with the date of the temple of Ceres, B.C. 493. —H. L. U.]. The difficulty of reconciling *Demophilus* and *Damophilus* has been perceived by Freeman, *Hist. of Sicily*, ii, p. 411: 'It is a little startling to hear that the master of Zeuxis, with his colleague Gorgasos, painted the Roman temple which was vowed by Aulus Postumius, victor at Regillus.' Freeman, however, inclines to a conciliation: 'Chronology may be appeased by the easy conjecture that the painting of the temple, and the Greek letters which recorded the names of the artists, came a generation or two later than the temple itself.'

14. Cereris aedem: note on xxxiv, 15, and the passage from Vitruvius quoted above under *fastigia*.

utroque genere artis suae excoluerant versibus inscriptis
Graece quibus significarent ab dextra opera Damophili esse,
ab laeva Gorgasi. ante hanc aedem Tuscanica omnia in
aedibus fuisse auctor est Varro, et ex hac, cum reficeretur,
crustas parietum excisas tabulis marginatis inclusas esse, 5
155 item signa ex fastigiis dispersa.   fecit et Chalcosthenes
cruda opera Athenis, qui locus ab officina eius Ceramicos
appellatur. M. Varro tradit sibi cognitum Romae Possim
nomine, a quo facta poma et uvas alitem nescisse aspectu
discernere a veris.   idem magnificat Arcesilaum, L. Luculli 10
familiarem, cuius proplasmata pluris venire solita artificibus
156 ipsis quam aliorum opera ; ab hoc factam Venerem Genetricem in foro Caesaris et prius quam absolveretur festina-
tione dedicandi positam, eidem a Lucullo HS. |X̄| signum
Felicitatis locatum, cui mors utriusque inviderit ; Octavio 15

9. alitem nescisse] *Traube*; item piscis (pisces, *Bamb.*) *codd.*; item pisces
non possis *Jan, Detlefsen.*

1. **utroque genere artis** : i.e. the
decorations consisted of painted terra-
cottas ; fine examples (from T. of
Jupiter Capitolinus?) exist at Rome
in Pal. Conserv., Helbig, i, p. 447 f.

2. **ab dextra . . . ab laeva**: cf. the
similar inscription, *Anth. Pal.* ix, 758 :
Κίμων ἔγραψε τὴν θύραν τὴν δεξιάν,
τὴν δ' ἐξιόντων δεξιὰν Διονύσιος.

4. **cum reficeretur**: after the fire
of B.C. 31 ; restored by Augustus, B.C.
27, re-dedicated B.C. 17 (Tac. *Ann.*
ii, 49).

5. **crustas** : for reliefs cf. xxxiii,
157, *crustarius.*

excisas : cf. Vitruv. ii, 8, 9, a
typical instance of the care taken in
the first century B.C. to preserve
archaic works.

tabulis marginatis : below, §
173.

6. **ex fastigiis**: above, note on
§ 152.

*§ **155. Chalcosthenes** : more
correctly *Kaïkosthenes ;* see on xxxiv,
87. From a basis (Δελτίον, 1891,
p. 25 f. and p. 84) found in the actual
Kerameikos, we learn that K. was

of the deme Thria. Lolling (*loc.
cit.*) dates the inscr. towards the close
of the third century B.C.

7. **cruda opera** : these have been
identified by Milchböfer (*Arch. Studien,
H. Brunn dargebr.* 1893, p. 50 ff.)
with the ἀγάλματα ἐκ πηλοῦ, representing Dionysos feasting in the house of
Amphiktyon, which adorned a chapel
—οἴκημα—of the god's τέμενος, in the
Kerameikos (Paus. i, 2, 5) ; the monument was presumably the votive offering of a guild of Dionysiac artists.
The Italian work of the Della Robbias
may help us to a notion of what the
group or relief looked like.

8. **appellatur** : the etymological
attempt suggests Varronian authorship ; cf. note on xxxiv, 11, on xxxvi,
14 (*lychniten*).

9. **poma et uvas** : cf. the excellent
carvings of fruit, leaves and flowers on
a relief of the Museo d. Terme, Wickhoff,
Wiener Genesis, p. 22, figs. 7, 8, 9,
10, and the beautiful garlands of fruit
and flowers that adorned the *Ara
Pacis* of Augustus.

alitem nescisse : cf., in con-

Circus, placing on it a metrical inscription in Greek to say that on the right hand were the works of Damophilos, on the left the works of Gorgasos. Varro tells us that in all earlier temples decorations in the Etruscan style only were to be found, and that when this temple was restored the ornamentation of the walls was cut out and framed, and the statues that crowned the roof were dispersed.

Chalkosthenes also modelled in unbaked clay in the Potter's Quarter at Athens, so called after his workshop. Marcus Varro says that at Rome a man named †*Possis* was known to him who made clay apples and grapes which the very birds could not distinguish from nature. He also praises †*Arkesilaos*, the friend of Lucius Lucullus, for whose clay models artists would pay more than was given for the finished works of others ; he made the statue of Venus the Mother in the forum of Caesar, which was set up before it was really finished, so eager were his patrons to dedicate it. He also accepted a commission from Lucullus to make a statue of Good Fortune for 1,000,000 sesterces [£8750 circ.]. Death, however, cut them both off before the statue was completed. Arkesilaos also made a plaster model for a talent [£210 circ.] for a Roman knight named Octavius, who proposed

(marginal notes:) 155 *Chalko-sthenes. Possis. Arkesilaos. Value of his clay models.* 156

firmation of Traube's reading, above, §§ 23, 65, 66.

10. idem magnificat : cf. in xxxvi, 41 *Arcesilaum quoque magnificat Varro*, hence the identity of authorship for both passages.

Arcesilaum : for his marble works see xxxvi, 33, 41 ; his *Venus Genitrix* and his *Felicitas* are mentioned here because they apparently remained at the stage of clay models.

L. Luculli familiarem : Urlichs (*Arkesilaos*, p. 4) suggests that Lucullus brought back Arkesilaos with him from Athens when he visited that city in B.C. 88-7, cf. above, § 125.

11. proplasmata : see the excellent remarks of Wickhoff, *Wiener Genesis*, p. 25 f. and p. 41, on the extensive use of the clay model in the first century B.C., and its influence on the technique of marble ; cf. above, on § 153.

§ 156. 12. Venerem Genetricem : from the Roman coins which most

probably reproduce the statue, it appears that the *Genetrix* of Arkesilaos was adapted from a Greek statuary type which recent criticism has traced back to the 'Aphrodite in the gardens' of Alkamenes (note on xxxvi, 16) ; cf. Furtwängler, *ap.* Roscher i, p. 413.

14. signum Felicitatis : the temple of *Felicitas* had been built by C. Licinius Lucullus, xxxiv, 69 ; xxxvi, 39.

15. mors utriusque : Marcus Lucullus died B.C. 58, and his brother only survived him a short time (Plut. *Luc.* xliii) ; hence since Arkesilaos was still at work for Caesar in B.C. 46 (below), we must either imagine that he left an order of his patron unattended to for fifteen years, or follow Urlichs (*op. cit.* p. 5), in supposing that it is the young Lucullus (*clarissimus adulescens*, Cic. *Phil. x*, 48), whose death (at Philippi in B.C. 42) is alluded to here. From

equiti Romano cratera facere volenti exemplar e gypso
factum talento.   laudat et Pasitelen qui plasticen matrem
caelaturae et statuariae scalpturaeque dixit et, cum esset in
omnibus his summus, nihil umquam fecit antequam finxit.
157 praeterea elaboratam hanc artem Italiae et maxime Etru- 5
riae, Vulcam Veis accitum cui locaret Tarquinius Priscus
Iovis effigiem Capitolio dicandam, fictilem eum fuisse et
ideo miniari solitum, fictiles in fastigio templi eius quadrigas,
de quibus saepe diximus, ab hoc eodem factum Herculem
qui hodieque materiae nomen in urbe retinet.   hae enim 10
tum effigies deorum erant lautissimae, nec poenitet nos
illorum qui tales deos coluere, aurum enim et argentum ne
158 diis quidem conficiebant.   durant etiamnum plerisque in
locis talia simulacra.   fastigia quidem templorum etiam
in urbe crebra et municipiis, mira caelatura et arte suique 15
firmitate, sanctiora auro, certe innocentiora.

xxxiv, 93 (where see note) we learn
that he rededicated a statue of
Herakles originally set up by his
father; it is therefore not surprising
to find him commissioning Arkesilaos,
an old friend of his family, with
a statue for the temple built by his
grandfather.

Octavio equiti : according to Urlichs, *Arkesilaos*, p. 17, perhaps identical with the upstart (*terrae filius*) who
pestered Cicero with invitations to
dinner, Cic. *Fam.* vii, 9, 16.

2. Pasitelen : xxxiii, 156; xxxvi,
40.

3. scalpturae : here = *sculptura*
[so also Plin. the Y. *Ep.* i, 10, has
scalptor for *sculptor.*—H. L. U.]; the
term is generally used of the graver's
art, as an equivalent of the Greek
γλυπτική.

§ 157. 5. maxime Etruriae : the
remark is fully confirmed by the
splendid remains of large terra-cotta
figures, discovered in Italy; cf.
especially the pedimental figures from

the temple at Luni, Milani, *Mus. d.
Ant. Classica*, i, 1884, pp. 89-112;
where see further literature.

7. Iovis effigiem . . fictilem:
cf. Juv. xi, 115 *fictilis et nullo vio-
latus Iupiter auro*. From Servius'
(on *Eclog.* x, 27) description of the
Roman *triumphatores*, who were
adorned *Iovis optimi maximi ornatu*
we learn that the god was represented
standing with the thunderbolt in his
right (cf. Ovid *Fast.* i, 201 *inque
Iovis dextra fictile fulmen erat*) and
the sceptre in his left. This ancient
image was destroyed B.C. 83, in the
fire which laid the temple in ashes.
It was replaced by a gold-ivory
Jupiter—the work of an Apollonios
—after the model of the Olympian
Zeus of Pheidias (cf. Chalcidius on
Plato's *Timaios*, 338 C, p. 361, ed.
Wrobel, and Loewy on *I. G. B.* 343,
p. 242).

Capitolio : note on xxxiv, 38.

8. miniari solitum : *enumerat
auctores Verrius quibus credere ne-*

to have a goblet cast from it. Varro further praises *Pasiteles*, who said that modelling was the mother of chasing, statuary and sculpture, and who, though he excelled in all these arts, never executed any work without first making a clay model. The art of modelling, again, according to Varro, was developed in Italy, and more especially in Etruria, and Tarquin the Ancient summoned an artist called †Vulca from Veii to make a statue of Jupiter for the Capitol. This statue was of clay and was therefore painted red ; the four-horse chariots on the gables of the temple, which I have mentioned so often, were also of clay. Vulca further made the Hercules still known at Rome as 'the clay Hercules.' These were the most magnificent statues known in those days, and we have no reason to be ashamed of the men who worshipped deities of clay, and would not, even for their gods, change gold and silver into images. Effigies of clay still exist in different places, while gable ornaments in clay are still to be seen even at Rome as well as in provincial towns. The admirable execution of these figures, their artistic merits and their durability make them more worthy of honour than gold, and they are at any rate more innocent.

Pasiteles. He pronounces upon the value of the clay model.

158

Beauty and simplicity of the ancient clay images.

cesse .sit Iovis ipsius simulacri faciem diebus festis minio inlini solitam . . . Plin. xxxiii, 111 ; see also Servius on *Ecl.* vi, 62 ; x, 27 ; cf. in Greece the painting with white, at her festival, of the image of Athena Skirrophoria.

fictiles . . . quadrigas : also the work of Veientine artists, Plut. *Poplic.* xiii ἅρμα κατὰ κορυφὴν (sc. νεὼ τοῦ Καπ. Δι.) ἐπιστῆσαι κεραμεοῦν ἐξέδωκε (sc. ὁ Ταρκουίνιος) Τυρρηνοῖς τισιν ἐξ Οὐηΐων δημιουργοῖς. These are the chariots whose miraculous swelling in the potter's furnace was interpreted as an omen of the future greatness of Rome (Plin. xxviii, 16 *cum in fastigium eiusdem delubri* (Jup. Cap.) *praeparatae quadrigae fictiles in fornace crevissent*). These chariots were replaced in B.C. 296 by a *Iovem in culmine cum quadrigis*, apparently of bronze (Liv. x, 23, 12). The roof of the temple of the Tarquins

was richly adorned with painted decorations ; cf. Cic. *de Div.* i, 10, 16 ; Liv. *per.* 14; and see note on § 154 for possible remains of these decorations.

9. **saepe diximus**: viii, 161; xxviii, 16.

Herculem : often identified (but on the very slightest grounds) with the *Hercules fictilis* of Martial xiv, 178.

10. **hae enim tum effigies**: this rhetorical tribute to the simplicity of the ancient Roman images was as old as —Cato, or as Cato reported by Livy (xxxiv, 4, 4) *infesta, mihi credite, signa ab Syracusis illata sunt huic urbi. iam nimis multos audio Corinthi et Athenarum ornamenta laudantis mirantisque et antefixa fictilia deorum Romanorum ridentis. ego hos malo propitios deos et ita spero futuros, si in suis manere sedibus patiemur.*

C. PLINII SECUNDI

NATURALIS HISTORIAE

LIBER XXXVI, §§ 9-44

(*SCULPTURA*)

SCULPTURA.

9 MARMORE scalpendo primi omnium inclaruerunt Dipoenus
et Scyllis geniti in Creta insula etiamnum Medis imperantibus priusque quam Cyrus in Persis regnare inciperet, hoc
est olympiade circiter quinquagensima. hi Sicyonem se
contulere, quae diu fuit officinarum omnium talium patria. 5
deorum simulacra publice locaverant iis Sicyoni, quae prius
quam absolverentur artifices iniuriam questi abiere in
10 Aetolos. protinus Sicyonem fames invasit ac sterilitas
maerorque dirus. remedium petentibus Apollo Pythius
respondit: si Dipoenus et Scyllis deorum simulacra per- 10
fecissent, quod magnis mercedibus obsequiisque impetratum

5. talium] metallum *omnes praeter Bamb.*

§ 9. 1. Marmore scalpendo: with
the exception of the ἄγαλμα of the
Lindian Athena ἐκ λίθου σμαράγδου,
mentioned on the doubtful authority
of George Kedrenos (Overbeck,
Schriftqu. 327; cf. Brunn, *K. G.* i,
p. 44), Dip. and Skyllis seem only to
have made wooden images, Paus. ii, 15,
1 ; 22, 5; Clement of Alex. προτρεπτ.
λόγ. iv, p. 42; the gilt bronze images
mentioned by Moses of Chorene
(*Schriftqu.* 326) were more probably
of gilt wood. It is evident that in the
original Greek authority (Xenokrates
from the character of the passage
and the stress laid on Sikyon; see
Introd. p. xxv) these artists had been
discussed in connexion with the
beginnings of bronze statuary;
Münzer, Hermes, xxx, 1895, p. 523;
cf. Robert, *Arch. März.* p. 22.

2. geniti in Creta: contains a
trace of the legend preserved in Paus.
ii, 15, 1, that they were the sons of
the Athenian Daidalos and a woman
of Gortyn. By representing artists
born in Crete as active in Sikyon,
a similar compromise between the
rival claims of ancient art centres is
effected to that noted in the case of
Boutades, xxxv, 151; cf. Münzer, *loc.
cit.*

Medis imperantibus; the Ar-
menian historian Moses of Chorene
recounts that Ardashir (= Kyros) took
away from Kroisos three statues of
Artemis, Herakles and Apollo by
Dipoinos and Skyllis. The date
assigned to the artists seems calcu-
lated with reference to this event as
follows: Kyros could take away
works by D. and S. at the time of his

SCULPTURE IN MARBLE.

As sculptors in marble, the first to win fame were *Dipoinos* 9
and *Skyllis*, born before the fall of the Median empire, and *First be-*
before Cyrus began to reign in Persia, that is about the fiftieth *sculpture.*
Olympiad [580-577 B.C.], in the island of Crete. They migrated
to Sikyon, which was long the home of all such crafts. The
state of Sikyon gave them a commission for certain images of the
gods, but before these were completed the artists, aggrieved at
the treatment they met with, departed into Aitolia. Sikyon soon 10
afterwards was visited by famine, failure of the crops and dire
affliction. The inhabitants sought relief from the Pythian Apollo,
and received the answer that the evil would cease when Dipoinos
and Skyllis should complete their statues of the gods, a concession
which was hardly won from them by money and by personal defer-

conquest of Kroisos (B. C. 546), therefore the artists must have been of
repute even before the accession of
Kyros (B.C. 556), Robert, *op. cit.*
p. 18 f.

4. **circiter**: cf. xxxiv, 49: *circiter CCC urbis nostrae annum.*

Sicyonem ... patria: cf. xxxv,
127 *diuque* (Sikyon) *illa fuit patria
picturae.*

6. **prius quam absolv.**: the
following anecdote, whose artificial
character is obvious, has been shown
by Petersen, *de Cerere Phigalensi,*
p. 13 ff., to be a mere adaptation
of the local myth recorded Paus. ii,
7, 7.

7. **iniuriam questi**: γενομένου
δὲ σφισι (Apollo and Artemis)
δείματος ... οἱ μὲν ἐς Κρήτην ... ἀπε-
τράποντο, Paus. *loc. cit.*

in **Aetolos**: named by the
legend as the artists' place of refuge
because there existed in that region
works by D. and S., i. e. at Ambrakia (§ 14), which, though not in
Aitolia, was towards the close of the
third century the most prominent city
of the Aitolian league. A Greek
writer of that date (Antigonos? cf. Introd. p. xxxvii) might say indifferently
εἰς ᾿Αμβρακίαν or εἰς Αἰτωλούς; Münzer, *op. cit.* p. 524.

§ 10. 8. **protinus ... dirus**: τοὺς
δὲ ἀνθρώπους ... νόσος ἐπέλαβεν, Paus.
loc. cit.

9. **remedium ... impetratum
est**: καὶ σφᾶς ἐκέλευον οἱ μάντεις
᾿Απόλλωνα ἱλάσασθαι καὶ ῎Αρτεμιν ...
ὑπὸ τούτων δὲ πεισθέντας τοὺς θεούς
φασιν ἐς τὴν ἀκρόπολιν ἐλθεῖν.

est. fuere autem simulacra ea Apollinis, Dianae, Herculis, Minervae quod e caelo postea tactum est.

11 Cum hi essent, iam fuerat in Chio insula Melas scalptor, dein filius eius Micciades, ac deinde nepos Archermus, cuius filii Bupalus et Athenis vel clarissimi in ea scientia fuere 5 Hipponactis poetae aetate, quem certum est LX olympiade fuisse. quodsi quis horum familiam ad proavom usque retro agat, inveniat artis eius originem cum olympiadum 12 initio coepisse. Hipponacti notabilis foeditas voltus erat, quamobrem imaginem eius lascivia iocorum hi proposuere 10 ridentium circulis, quod Hipponax indignatus destrinxit amaritudinem carminum in tantum ut credatur aliquis ad laqueum eos conpulisse. quod falsum est, conplura enim in finitimis insulis simulacra postea fecere, sicut in Delo, quibus subiecerunt carmen non vitibus tantum censeri 15 Chion sed et operibus Archermi filiorum. ostendunt et 13 Iasii Dianam manibus eorum factam. in ipsa Chio narrata est operis eorum Dianae facies in sublimi posita, cuius voltum intrantes tristem, abeuntes exhilaratum putant. Romae eorum signa sunt in Palatina aede Apollinis in 20

17. Iasii] *Riccard.*; Lasii *Bamb., Detlefsen*; lasi *Voss.*

1. **Apollinis ... Minervae** : the list is alphabetical ; the statues therefore were no part of a group but single works, H. L. Urlichs in *Görlitz. Verhandl.* p. 330, note 2.

Dianae : possibly identical with the ξόανον of Artemis Munychia mentioned by Clement, προτρεπτ. λόγος, iv, p. 42 : cf. Urlichs *loc. cit.*; Robert, *Arch. Märch.* p. 22.

§ 11. 3. **Cum hi essent** : to the account of D. and S. is now opposed (from another source) that of the Chian school. Introd. p. xxvi.

Melas ... Micciades ... Archermus : the three names appear on the famous inscription from Delos (*J. G. B.* 1 ; best restored by Lolling, Ἐφ. ἀρχ. 1888, p. 71 ff.; cf. E. A. Gardner in *Class. Rev.* 1893, p. 140), where Ἀρχερμος (2nd line) appears as son of Μικκιάδης (1st line). The

Melas (Μέ[λ]α[ν]ος πατρώϊον ἄσ[τυ νέμοντες]) of the third line is presumably not the father of Mikkiades, but, as Schöll and Robert pointed out (*Arch. Märch.* p. 116 f.), a local hero cf Chios, son of Oinopion; Ion *ap.* Paus. vii, 4, 8. The account in Pliny rests upon this or a similar inscription; the blunder with regard to Melas may have been committed early by a Greek writer; cf. note on Demarate in xxxiv, 88.

scalptor = *sculptor ;* cf. note on xxxv, 156.

4. **Archermus** : besides the Delos inscription, the name occurs on a later inscr., in the Ionic alphabet, from the Athenian Akropolis, C. I. A. iv, 373, 95.

5. **Bupalus et Ath.** : the fact that they were sons of Archermos was doubtless also taken from an inscription; Münzer, *op. cit.* p. 524.

ence. The statues in question were of Apollo, Artemis, Herakles, and Athene: this last was afterwards struck by lightning.

Before their day, however, the sculptor *Melas* had already lived **11** in the island of Chios, succeeded by his son *Mikkiades* and his *The school of Chios.* grandson *Archermos*, whose sons, *Boupalos* and *Athenis*, were masters of great renown in their craft in the time of the poet Hipponax, who certainly lived in the sixtieth Olympiad [540–537 B.C.]. Thus counting four generations backwards to their great grandfather, the birth of sculpture is found to coincide with the first Olympiad [776–773 B.C.]. Hipponax was conspicuous for **12** his ill-favoured countenance, which incited the sculptors in wanton jest to display his portrait to the ridicule of their assembled friends. Incensed at this Hipponax lampooned them so bitterly that, as some believe, they were driven to hang themselves. This, however, cannot be true, for they afterwards made in the neighbouring islands, as for example, in Delos, a number of images of the gods, under which they carved verses saying that Chios was not honoured for her vines alone but for the works of the sons of Archermos. Iasos too can show an Artemis made by their hands, **13** while in Chios itself we hear of a mask of Artemis by them, which is placed at a height in the temple, and presents a gloomy countenance to those who enter the temple, a cheerful one to those who are leaving. At Rome statues by them are to be seen on the summit of the temple of Apollo on the Palatine, and

6. **LX olympiade**: the Parian Chronicle gives his date as Ol. 59, 3 = B. C. 542.

8. **olymp. initio**: the calculation is based on the false assumption that a generation = the average full life of sixty years; cf. Furtwängler, *Plinius*, p. 17.

§ **12.** 9. **notabilis foeditas**: cf. Metrodoros of Skepsis, *ap.* Athen. xii, 552 c. The only ascertained factor in the whole anecdote is the poet's attacks (*acer hostis Bupalo*) upon the two artists (Bergk, *Lyr. Gr.* ed. 4, fr. 10–14; Collignon, *Hist. Sculpt.* i, p. 141); it is probable that when the real cause for these attacks had been forgotten, a new one was elaborated out of the statues of Boupalos and Athenis, the archaic character of which struck later generations as simply grotesque; cf. Robert, *Arch.*

Märch. p. 115 f.

12. **ad laqueum**: this portion of the story is the *doublette* of the story of Lycambes and Archilochos. The *credatur aliquis* introduces it as apocryphal, while in the following sentence it is proved an invention.

14. **in Delo**: like their father Archermos.

17. **Iasii**: in the neighbourhood of Chios. The words *ostendunt . . . putant* betray mere periegetic curiosity (Furtwängler, *Plinius*, p. 61); they are from a different source to the earlier part of the account, which is based upon a study of inscriptions. Since Mucianus visited Iasos (ix, 33) it is reasonable to attribute this information to him; Introd. p. lxxxix.

§ **13.** 20. **in Palatina aede**: xxxiv, 14.

fastigio et omnibus fere quae fecit divus Augustus.   patris
quoque eorum et Deli fuere opera et in Lesbo insula.
14 Dipoeni quidem Ambracia, Argos, Cleonae operibus refertae fuere.   omnes autem candido tantum marmore usi
sunt e Paro insula, quem lapidem coepere lychniten appel- 5
lare, quoniam ad lucernas in cuniculis caederetur, ut auctor
est Varro, multis postea candidioribus repertis, nuper vero
etiam in Lunensium lapidicinis.   sed in Pariorum mirabile
proditur glaeba lapidis unius cuneis dividentium soluta
15 imaginem Sileni intus extitisse.   non omittendum hanc 10
artem tanto vetustiorem fuisse quam picturam aut statuariam, quarum utraque cum Phidia coepit octogensima tertia
olympiade, post annos circiter CCCXXXII.   et ipsum Phidian tradunt scalpsisse marmora, Veneremque eius esse
16 Romae in Octaviae operibus eximiae pulchritudinis.   Al- 15
camenen Atheniensem, quod certum est, docuit in primis
nobilem, cuius sunt opera Athenis complura in aedibus
sacris praeclarumque Veneris extra muros quae appellatur
Aphrodite ἐν κήποις.   huic summam manum ipse Phidias

in fastigio : i. e. the *signa* were
akroterial figures (see note on xxxv,
152), the pedimental and other decorations also consisting of archaic sculpture ; cf. the archaic Amazon published
by Petersen, *Röm. Mitth.* iv, 1889,
p. 36 f.

1. et omnibus fere : rhetorical
exaggeration : cf. the *ex omnibus
clarissima quaeque* in xxxiv, 84, H. L.
Urlichs, *Rhein. Mus.* 1889, p. 487.

§ 14. 3. Dipoeni : harks back
to § 10.

Ambracia : see note on *Aetolos*
in § 9 ; the foundation of Ambrakia by Gorgos son of Kypselos
(Strab. x, 452) affords us an upper
limit for the activity of D. and S. in
that city.   The Ambrakiot works
of art were taken away to Rome by
Fulvius Nobilior, B.C. 189.

Argos : for which D. and S.
made of ebony wood a group of the
Dioskouroi and their families; Paus.
ii, 22, 5.

Cleonae : for which they made
the image of Athena ; Paus. ii,
15, 1.

refertae : rhetorical : cf. in xxxv,
148 *quorum   tabulae pinacothecas
implent.*

4. omnes autem : i. e. the Chian
sculptors as well.

5. lychniten : the etymology is
thoroughly Varronian, cf. notes on
xxxiv, 11 ; xxxv, 155 ; according to
Lepsius, *Griechische Marmorstudien*,
p. 45, it rests on fact : the marble
came from the underground quarries
about five miles N.E. of the ancient
city of Paros ; Lepsius noticed here
a number of holes cut obliquely into
the walls of the rock, the purpose of
which he believes was to suspend the
workmen's lamps by their hooked
handles.

10. imaginem Sileni : cf. the similar story, Cic. *Div.* i, 13, 23 : *fingebat
Carneades   in   Chiorum   lapicidinis
saxo diffiso caput exstitisse Panisci.*

indeed in almost all the temples built by the god Augustus. Works by their father Archermos existed at Delos and in the island of Lesbos. Ambrakia, Argos, and Kleonai were filled full 14 of the works of Dipoinos. All these artists used none but white Parian marble, called lychnites [λυχνίτης], as Varro says, because *Marble of* it was quarried by lamplight in underground passages. Since *Paros.* then many marbles of a purer white have been discovered, and again quite recently in the quarries of Luna. A marvellous story tells how in the quarries of Paros a block which was being split with wedges, opened and disclosed a figure of Seilenos.

Nor must I forget to say that the art of sculpture is much 15 older than that of painting or of bronze statuary, both of which *Sculpture older than* began with Pheidias in the eighty-third olympiad [448-445 B. C.], *painting* some 332 years later. It is said that *Pheidias* also worked in *and bronze statuary.* marble, and that an Aphrodite by him of surpassing beauty is at Rome in the gallery of Octavia. It is certain at all events that he taught *Alkamenes* of Athens, a sculptor of the first rank, 16. many of whose works are in the temples of Athens, while out- *Alka-* side the city is his famous statue, known as ' Aphrodite ἐν κήποις,' *menes.* or ' in the gardens.' Pheidias himself, according to tradition,

§ 15. hanc artem : sc. *sculp-turam* by implication, although the kind of art has not been previously mentioned ; cf. notes on xxxiv, 56 (*hanc scientiam*); xxxv, 153 (*hanc scientiam*).

12. quarum utraque : xxxiv, 49 ; xxxv, 54; as regards painting Pliny forgets that he had himself argued that its beginnings were still earlier than Pheidias. Introd. p. xxx.

14. tradunt : [tradition as opposed to real fact, i. e. whether he was a sculptor in marble or not, it is certain (*quod certum est*) that he taught Alkamenes. So in xxxv, 54, *tradatur* is opposed to *in confesso sit ;* in xvii, 49, *sunt qui . . . adspergant. quod certum est . . . sol confert*, H. L. U.]

scalpsisse marmora : Pliny's Greek authors had laid chief stress on the bronze works of Pheidias, xxxiv, 54; that he must have been equally celebrated for his works in marble is evident from the sculptures of the

Parthenon and the whole tendencies of his school, and from the express testimony of Aristotle, *Eth. Nicom.* vi, 7 : τὴν δὲ σοφίαν ἔν τε ταῖς τέχναις τοῖς ἀκριβεστάτοις τὰς τέχνας ἀποδίδο-μεν, οἷον Φειδίαν λιθουργὸν σοφὸν καὶ Πολύκλειτον ἀνδριαντοποιόν, ἐνταῦθα μὲν οὖν οὐδὲν ἄλλο σημαίνοντες τὴν σοφίαν, ἢ ὅτι ἀρετὴ τέχνης ἐστίν.

15. Octaviae operibus: cf. § 35, where another Aphrodite (*aliam Venerem*) by Philiskos is mentioned as being in the same gallery.

§ 16. Alcamenen: xxxiv, 49 and 72. The only dateable work by Alka-menes is his group of Athena and Hera-kles, dedicated in the Herakleion at Thebes after the downfall of the Thirty Tyrants in 403 B. C. (Paus. ix, 11, 6). Pliny's account of Alkamenes and Agorakritos seems borrowed from Antigonos, Introd. p. xlii.

17. Athenis : see note on xxxiv, 49, *Olymp.* lxxxiii.

19. ἐν κήποις: on the Ilissos, Paus.

17 inposuisse dicitur. eiusdem discipulus fuit Agoracritus
Parius et aetate gratus, itaque e suis operibus pleraque
nomini eius donasse fertur. certavere autem inter se ambo
discipuli Venere facienda, vicitque Alcamenes non opere
sed civitatis suffragiis contra peregrinum suo faventis. 5
quare Agoracritus ea lege signum suum vendidisse traditur,
ne Athenis esset, et appellasse Nemesin. id positum est
Rhamnunte pago Atticae, quod M. Varro omnibus signis
praetulit. est et in Matris magnae delubro eadem civitate
18 Agoracriti opus. Phidian clarissimum esse per omnes gentes 10
quae Iovis Olympii famam intellegunt nemo dubitat, sed ut
laudari merito sciant etiam qui opera eius non videre, pro-
feremus argumenta parva et ingeni tantum. neque ad hoc
Iovis Olympii pulchritudine utemur, non Minervae Athenis
factae amplitudine, cum sit ea cubitorum XXVI,—ebore haec 15
et auro constat—sed in scuto eius Amazonum proelium
caelavit intumescente ambitu, in parmae eiusdem concava
parte deorum et Gigantum dimicationes, in soleis vero
Lapitharum et Centaurorum, adeo momenta omnia capacia

i. 19, 2. According to a generally
accepted theory of Furtwängler, the
Alkamenian statue is reproduced in the
statues of the ‘Venus Genitrix’ type
(Louvre, Giraudon, 1175; Florence
Alinari, 1331).

huic summam manum: the
words almost imply that the same
reproach attached to Alkamenes as
to Agorakritos, namely, that Pheidias
allowed his own work to pass off as
his pupil’s, cf. Pallat in *Jahrb.* ix,
1894, p. 14.

§ 17. 1. Agoracritus: Overbeck,
Schriftquellen, 829–843.

3. nomini . . . donasse: the
scandal recorded here without special
allusion to any one work was used
by Polemon (*ap.* Zenobios v, 82)
as an argument wherewith to vin-
dicate for Pheidias the authorship of
the Agorakritan Nemesis. Introd.
p. xxxix.

certavere: cf. the story of the
competition between Pheidias and

Alkamenes recorded by John Tzetzes,
χιλιάδες, 931.

7. Nemesin: Wilamowitz (*Antigonos v. Karystos*, p. 11) points out
that the story of the Nemesis having
been intended for an Aphrodite
originated in the fact that the
Rhamnusian Nemesis differed from
the type usual at a later date. Cf.
Paus. i, 33, 7: Πτερὰ δ’ ἔχον οὔτε
τοῦτο τὸ ἄγαλμα Νεμέσεως οὔτε ἄλλο
πεποίηται τῶν ἀρχαίων . . . οἱ δὲ ὕστερον,
ἐπιφαίνεσθαι γὰρ τὴν θεὸν μάλιστα ἐπὶ
τῷ ἐρᾶν ἐθέλουσιν, ἐπὶ τούτῳ Νεμέσει
πτερὰ ὥσπερ Ἔρωτι ποιοῦσι; cf. Am-
mianus Marcellinus, xiv, 11, 25–26
(ed. Gardthausen, p. 42), and Kalkmann, *Pausanias der Perieget*, p. 206.

8. Rhamnunte: a fragment of
the colossal head of the Nemesis was
discovered here, and is now in the
Brit. Mus. (*Cat. Sculpt.* i, 460).
Numerous fragments of the basis (Leda
bringing Helen to Nemesis, Paus. *loc.
cit.*) were recovered in 1890, and are

put the last touches to this work. He also taught *Agorakritos* of ¹⁷
Paros, whom he so loved for his youthful grace, that he allowed *Agora-*
several of his own works to pass under his name. The two *kritos.*
pupils made statues of Aphrodite for a competition, and Alkamenes received the prize, not from the merit of his work, but
because the Athenians voted for their fellow-citizen against
a foreigner. The story runs that Agorakritos thereupon sold his
statue, imposing the condition that it should not be set up at
Athens, and called it Nemesis. It now stands in Rhamnous,
a deme of Attica, and Marcus Varro esteems it above all other
statues. There is another statue by Agorakritos in the same city,
in the shrine of the Great Mother.

The renown of Pheidias among all peoples who realize the ¹⁸
glory of his Olympian Zeus cannot be brought in doubt ; yet so *Pheidias.*
that even those who have not seen his works may know that his *ventive*
praises are well deserved, I shall cite those minute details in which *genius in*
it was only left to him to display the resources of his inventive *details.*
faculty. For this purpose I shall not appeal to the beauty of his
Olympian Zeus, nor to the size of his Athena at Athens, though
she is 26 cubits [37 ft. 10 in.] in height, made all of gold and
ivory ; but I shall instance her shield, on the convex face of which
he represented the battle of the Amazons, and on the concave
surface the conflict between the gods and giants, while on the side
of her sandals were the Lapithai and the Kentaurs. So true was
it that in his eyes every tiny space afforded a field for art. The

published, *Jahrb.* ix, 1894, pl. 1-7, pp. 1-22 (Pallat). Pausanias, who is never curious in the matter of ascriptions, simply attributes the work to Pheidias, as he likewise did the 'Mother of the Gods' by Agorakritos, and the Athena by Kolotes (see note on xxxv, 54).

9. **Matris magnae del.** : Μητρὸς θεῶν ἱερόν, Paus. i, 3, 5, where the statue is erroneously ascribed to Pheidias himself. For the type of the goddess see the fine relief of undoubted Pheidian style, *A. Z.* 38, 1880, pl. i ; Roscher, ii, p. 1663, fig. 5. Addenda.

§ 18. 11. **Iovis Olympii** : xxxiv, 49 ; 54 ; full description of the statue in Paus. v, 10, 2 : beneath the feet of Zeus was the artist's inscription, Φειδίας Χαρμίδου υἱὸς Ἀθηναῖος μ' ἐποίησε : the

numerous references in other authors coll. by Overb. *Schriftquell.* 692-754.

14. **Minervae** : xxxiv, 54 ; Paus. i, 24, 5 ; Overbeck, 645-696 ; a rough Roman copy in the statuette from the Varvakeion (Athens, Central Mus. ; cast in Br. Mus., *Cat. Sculpt.* i, 300 ; cf. 301).

16. **scuto** : a small late copy is preserved in the 'Strangford' shield, Brit. Mus. *Cat. Sculpt.* i, 302 ; for the latest discussion of the style of the reliefs and of the supposed portraits of Pheidias and Perikles, see Furt-wängler, *Masterpieces*, p. 48.

18. **soleis** : cf. in the Mus. Conserv. at Rome the colossal foot wearing a sandal adorned along the edge with a train of Tritons (Helbig, *Class. Ant.* 596).

19 artis illi fuere. in basi autem quod caelatum est Pandoras
genesin appellant : dii adsunt nascenti XX numero. Victoria
praecipue mirabili periti mirantur et serpentem ac sub ipsa
cuspide aeream sphingem. haec sint obiter dicta de artifice
numquam satis laudato, simul ut noscatur illam magnifi- 5
20 centiam aequalem fuisse et in parvis. Praxitelis aetatem
inter statuarios diximus, qui marmoris gloria superavit
etiam semet. opera eius sunt Athenis in Ceramico, sed
ante omnia est non solum Praxitelis verum in toto orbe
terrarum Venus quam ut viderent multi navigaverunt 10
Cnidum. duas fecerat simulque vendebat, alteram velata
specie, quam ob id praetulerunt quorum condicio erat Coi,
cum eodem pretio detulisset, severum id ac pudicum arbi-
trantes. reiectam Cnidi emerunt inmensa differentia famae.
21 voluit eam a Cnidiis postea mercari rex Nicomedes, totum 15
aes alienum quod erat ingens civitatis dissoluturum se pro-
mittens. omnia perpeti maluere, nec inmerito, illo enim
signo Praxiteles nobilitavit Cnidum. aedicula eius tota
aperitur ut conspici possit undique effigies dea favente ipsa,

1. caelatum est — Pandoras genesin appellant — dii *Gerhard, Detlefsen*.
2. adsunt nascenti] *Urlichs in Chrest.*; sunt nascentis *Riccard.*; sunt nascentes
reliqui; sunt adstantes *Detlefsen*.   3. ac] *post verbum* aeream *pos. Panofka,
Detlefsen*.   4. aeream] *Bamb., reliqui*; aureum *Urlichs, Detlefsen*.

§ 19. 1. Pandoras genesin : Paus.
i, 24, 7 : from the hesitating manner
in which the statement is introduced
by *appellant*, it appears that either
Pliny or his Latin author had not
thoroughly grasped the meaning of
the Greek; cf. Jahn, *Kunsturtheile*,
p. 127.
   2. dii adsunt : the composition
is preserved on the basis of the Pergamene copy of the Athena Parthenos,
Jahrb. v, 1890, p. 114, fig. 9.
   Victoria : καὶ Νίκην ὅσον τε
τεσσάρων πηχῶν . . . ἔχει. Paus. *loc.
cit.*
   3. ac sub ipsa . . : sphingem :
the reading adopted by Detlefsen
brings Pliny into agreement with
Pausanias (καὶ πλησίον τοῦ δόρατος
δράκων ἐστίν), but does intolerable
violence to the MSS. (cf. Gurlitt,

Pausanias, p. 98). We have there
fore retained the MSS. reading, which
can be construed though the sense is
not absolutely clear. The confusion,
however, is more likely due to Pliny's
hurrying over details, than to the
copyists. *Sub ipsa* I take to mean
' about on a level with '; *aeream* is
evidently correct, for had the sphinx—
according to Pliny—been of gold, like
the rest of the statue, there would
have been no need to mention its
material.
   § 20. 7. diximus : xxxiv, 69-70.
   8. in Ceramico : refers to grave
statues by Praxiteles in the Athenian
cemetery. Pausanias (i, 2, 3) mentions
a grave ἐπίθημα ἔχων στρατιώτην
ἵππῳ παρεστηκότα· ὄντινα μὲν οὐκ οἶδα,
Πραξιτέλης δὲ καὶ τὸν ἵππον καὶ τὸν
στρατιώτην ἐποίησεν (notes on xxxiv,

relief on the base is known as the γένεσις of Pandora; the 19
gods present at the birth are twenty in number. The Victory is
most wondrous, but connoisseurs admire also the serpent and
further the bronze sphinx beneath the spear of the goddess. Let
these passing remarks on a sculptor whose praises can never end,
serve at the same time to show that even in the smallest details
the opulence of his genius never fell short.

Praxiteles, whose date I gave among the bronze workers, outdid 20
even himself by the fame of his works in marble. Statues by his *Praxiteles.*
hand exist at Athens in the Kerameikos, while famous not only
among the works of Praxiteles, but throughout the whole world,
is the Aphrodite which multitudes have sailed to Knidos to look *Aphrodite*
upon. He had offered two statues of Aphrodite for sale at the *of Knidos.*
same time, the second being a draped figure, which for that
reason was preferred by the people of Kos with whom lay the
first choice; the price of the two figures was the same, but they
flattered themselves they were giving proof of a severe modesty.
The rejected statue, which was bought by the people of Knidos,
enjoys an immeasurably greater reputation. King Nikomedes 21
subsequently wished to buy it from them, offering to discharge
the whole of their public debt, which was enormous. They, however, preferred to suffer the worst that could befall, and they
showed their wisdom, for by this statue Praxiteles made Knidos
illustrious. It stands in a small shrine, open all round so that

70, 71, and on the *expir. imagines* of
Apelles in xxxv, 90). For the Plinian
phrase, cf. Cicero, *de Leg.* ii, 26, 64:
*amplitudines sepulcrorum, quas in
Ceramico videmus;* Wolters, *Athen.
Mitth.* xviii, 1893, p. 5 f. and note 1.

10. Venus . . . Cnidum: the
statue is represented on coins of
Knidos, Gardner, *Types*, xv, 21; for
a revised list of the marble copies, see
Furtwängler, *Masterpieces*, p. 322,
note 3; the best known is in the
Vatican, Helbig 316 (good cast without drapery in South Kensington
Museum). The notices in ancient
writers coll. by Overbeck, *Schriftquell.*
1227-1248. The information as to
the Knidian Aphrodite is from Mucianus. Introd. p. lxxxvii.

11. velata specie: this second
Aphrodite is still to seek; for a possible echo of the work, see Furtwängler, *op. cit.* p. 322 f.

§ 21. 15. voluit . . . mercari: at
the close of the first Mithridatic war,
B. C. 84, when Nikomedes III (King of
Bithynia B.C. 90-74), who had been
expelled from his kingdom by Mithridates, was reinstated by the Romans.

16. aes alienum: for the heavy
contributions exacted by Sulla from
the Greek states of Asia Minor, cf.
Appian, Μιθριδ. 63.

18. aedicula: for a detailed description of the statue and its shrine,
cf. Lucian, Ἔρωτες, 13.

19. dea favente ipsa: in allusion
to the legend that the goddess herself

ut creditur, facta. nec minor ex quacumque parte admiratio est. ferunt amore captum quendam, cum delituisset noctu, simulacro cohaesisse, eiusque cupiditatis esse indicem
22 maculam. sunt in Cnido et alia signa marmorea inlustrium artificum, Liber pater Bryaxidis et alter Scopae et Minerva, 5 nec maius aliud Veneris Praxiteliae specimen quam quod inter haec sola memoratur. eiusdem est et Cupido obiectus a Cicerone Verri, ille propter quem Thespiae visebantur, nunc in Octaviae scholis positus, eiusdem et alter nudus in Pario colonia Propontidis, par Veneri Cnidiae nobilitate et 10 iniuria, adamavit enim Alcetas Rhodius atque in eo quoque
23 simile amoris vestigium reliquit. Romae Praxitelis opera sunt Flora, Triptolemus, Ceres in hortis Servilianis, Boni Eventus et Bonae Fortunae simulacra in Capitolio, item Maenades et quas Thyiadas vocant et Caryatidas, et Sileni 15 in Pollionis Asini monumentis, et Apollo et Neptunus.
24 Praxitelis filius Cephisodotus et artis heres fuit. cuius laudatum est Pergami symplegma nobile digitis corpori

served the artist as model. Clement of Alexandria, προτρεπτ. λόγος 53, names the courtesan Kratina as model.

2. amore captum: cf. below, § 22, § 39. Similar stories were told also of a Hebe by Ktesikles, Adaios, *ap.* Athen. xiii, p. 606 a, of an Ἀγαθὴ τύχη near th Prytaneion in Athens, Ailian, ποικ. ἱστ. ix, 39.

§ 22. 5. Bryaxidis: below, § 30; xxxiv, 42, 73.

Scopae: below, §§ 25, 28, 30, 31 ; xxxiv, 49.

7. Cupido: given as a present to Phryne, Paus. i, 20, 1 ; cf. Athen. xiii, p. 591 b. The Eros was brought from Thespiai to Rome by Gaius Caligula, restored to Thespiai by Claudius, and finally brought back to Rome by Nero ; it was destroyed in a fire, in the reign of Titus (Paus. ix, 27, 3). Furtwängler (*Masterp.* p. 314 ff.) follows Visconti in recognizing copies of the statue in the 'Eros of Centocelle' (Helbig, 185) and its numerous replicas.

obiectus : Verres had robbed Heius of Messana of another Eros by Praxiteles ; Cicero's allusion to the Thespian statue was to impress upon the judges *mirum quendam dolorem accipere eos, ex quorum urbibus haec auferantur.*

8. propter . . . visebantur: Cic. *Verr.* II, iv, 2, 4 : *Cupidinem fecit (Praxiteles) illum qui est Thespiis, propter quem Thespiae visuntur; nam alia visendi causa nulla est;* cf. *ib.* 60, 135.

9. Octaviae scholis : part of the complex of buildings known as the *Opera Octaviae ;* these were probably rooms opening on to the gallery or *porticus* itself.

alter nudus: the type was first identified by Furtwängler on coins of Parion (*ap.* Roscher, i, 1358); later Benndorf (*Bull. della Comm. Arch.* 1886, p. 74) recognized a marble copy in the 'Genius Borghese' of the Louvre (phot. Girandon, 1201).

the statue, which was made, as is believed, under the direct inspiration of the goddess, can be seen from every side, nor is there any point of view from which it is less admirable than from another.

There are in Knidos other marble statues by great sculptors, **22** a Dionysos by *Bryaxis*, another Dionysos, and also an Athena by *Skopas*, and there is no more forcible panegyric of the Aphrodite of Praxiteles than the fact that among all these it alone is remembered. Praxiteles also made the Eros with which Cicero *Eros of* taunted Verres, that Eros for whose sake men travelled to *Thespiai* Thespiai. It is now in the 'schools' of Octavia. He made a second nude Eros in the colony of Parion, on the Propontis, a figure as celebrated as the Aphrodite of Knidos.

At Rome the works of Praxiteles are : Flora, Triptolemos and **23** Demeter in the gardens of Servilius, the images of Good Luck and Good Fortune in the Capitol, further the Mainads, the figures known as Thyiades and Karyatides, the Seilenoi in the gallery of Asinius Pollio, and an Apollo and Poseidon.

Kephisodotos, the son of Praxiteles, was also the heir to his **24** genius. Greatly admired is his celebrated group at Pergamon of *Kephiso-dotos.*

in Pario colonia : v, 141 ; xxxiv, 78 ; it was the seat of a very ancient cult of Eros, Paus. ix, 27, 1 (Furt-wängler, *ap.* Roscher, i, 1342).

§ 23. 12. Romae : at this point begins a description of works of art in Rome, which is continued with only a few interruptions to the close of the history of the marble sculptors in § 43.

13. Flora, Tript., Ceres : pre-sumably in a group ; *Flora* must be the Greek Κόρα, and owes her Latin name to the wreath she was holding as on the relief. Overbeck, *Kunst. Myth.* pl. xiv, 3, 4 ; 'Εφημ. ἀρχ. 1893, p. 35.

hortis Servilianis : from Suet. *Nero*, 47, this must have been on the *Via Ostiensis ;* cf. Tacitus, *Ann.* xv, 55 ; *Hist.* iii, 38 ; *C. I. L.* vi, 8673, 8674.

Boni Ev. et Bonae Fort.= 'Αγαθὸς δαίμων and 'Αγαθὴ τύχη ; for the received Attic type of these divi-nities see the votive relief in the Brit. Mus. (*Mus. Marbles*, xi, pl. 47).

15. Maenades : for Attic fourth-century types of the maenads see Rapp *ap.* Roscher, ii. 2270.

Thyiadas : γυναῖκες μέν εἰσιν 'Αττικαί, φοιτῶσαι δὲ ἐς τὸν Παρνασὸν παρὰ ἔτος . . . ἄγουσιν ὄργια Διονύσῳ, Paus. x, 4, 3. Καρυατίδες, maidens of Karyai, who danced at the festival of Artemis, Paus. iv, 16, 9.

16. Pollionis Asini mon. : in the Museum connected with the famous library, Plin. vii, 115 ; both apparently adjoined the *Atrium Libertatis*, which was restored by Asinius Pollio, cf. Suet. *Aug.* 29 ; Ovid, *Tristia*, iii, 1, 72 ; Gilbert, *Rom*, iii, p. 338, note 2.

§ 24. 17. Cephisodotus : xxxiv, 51, 87.

18. Pergami : the information is from Mucianus, Introd. p. lxxxix. [From Tac. *Ann.* xvi, 23, it appears that a number of works of art were still at Pergamon in the reign of Nero.— H.L.U.]

symplegma : [probably here of

verius quam marmori inpressis. Romae eius opera sunt
Latona in Palati delubro, Venus in Pollionis Asini monumentis et intra Octaviae porticus in Iunonis aede Aescula-
25 pius ac Diana. Scopae laus cum his certat. is fecit
Venerem et Pothon, qui Samothrace sanctissimis caerimonis 5
coluntur, item Apollinem Palatinum, Vestam sedentem
laudatam in Servilianis hortis duosque campteras circa eam,
quorum pares in Asini monimentis sunt, ubi et canephoros
26 eiusdem. sed in maxima dignatione delubro Cn. Domitii
in circo Flaminio Neptunus ipse et Thetis atque Achilles, 10
Nereides supra delphinos et cete aut hippocampos sedentes,
item Tritones chorusque Phorci et pistrices ac multa alia
marina, omnia eiusdem manu, praeclarum opus, etiam si
totius vitae fuisset. nunc vero praeter supra dicta quaeque
nescimus Mars etiamnum est sedens colossiaeus eiusdem 15
manu in templo Bruti Callaeci apud circum eundem, prae-

7. campteras] *Bamb.*; camiteras *reliqui*; lampteras *Jan, Detlefsen.*

an erotic couple, cf. Martial, xii,
43; Arnobius, vii, 33 (ed. Reifferscheid, p. 267), and for this use of
σύμπλεγμα, Soph. Fr. 556, Plato,
Symp. 191, Aeta.—H. L. U.] That
this *symplegma* had an erotic significance is proved by the comparison
with the group of Pan and Olympos
(§ 35) *quod est alterum in terris symplegma nobile.*
    digitis ... inpressis : cf. Herondas,
iv, 59 f. (ed. Crusius) :
    τὸν παῖδα δὴ ⟨τὸν⟩ γυμνὸν ἦν κνίσω
        τοῦτον
    οὐχ ἕλκος ἕξει, Κύννα;
    2. Latona: Crusius (German transl.
of *Herondas*, p. xiv, note) suggests
possible identity with the Leto which
had stood in Kos, Herondas, ii, 98.
    Palati delubro: below, § 32.
    3. Iunonis aede: below, § 35;
§ 42.
    Aesculapius: according to Cru-
sius (*loc. cit.*), possibly identical
with the Asklepios by 'the sons of
Praxiteles' (οἱ Πρηξιτέλεω παῖδες) in
the temple of Kos; Herond. iv, 20 ff.

§ 25. 4. Scopae laus : § 22 ; § 30.
    5. Venerem et Pothon : the Samo-
thrakian cult seems to have developed
out of that of Demeter and Hermes
Kadmos ; cf. Crusius, *Fleckeisen's
Jahrb.* 128, p. 298; *Beiträge z.
Griech. Myth.* p. 15. For the temple
of Aphrodite at Megara. Skopas had
made statues of Eros, Himeros, and
Pothos ; Paus. i, 43, 6.
    Samothrace : Mucianus, who had
visited Samothrake, is again Pliny's
authority here, Introd. p. xc.
    6. Apoll. Palatinum : for the
temple, cf. xxxiv, 14; above, § 24;
below, § 32. Propertius, ii, 31, 15,
describes the statue as follows:—
    deinde inter matrem deus ipse in-
        terque sororem
    Pythius in longa carmina neste
        sonat.
(The Apollo referred to in l. 5 f. of
the same elegy has been shown by
Hülsen, *Röm. Mitth.* ix, 1894, p.
240 f., to refer to a quite distinct statue
which stood in the courtyard of the
temple.) The Skopasian Apollo, the

figures interlaced [σύμπλεγμα], in which the fingers seem to press on flesh rather than on marble. At Rome his works are: the Leto in the temple on the Palatine, an Aphrodite in the gallery of Asinius Pollio, and the Asklepios and Artemis in the temple of Juno within the portico of Octavia.

The praise of *Skopas* vies with theirs. He made the Aphrodite 25 and Πόθος, or Desire, which are worshipped in Samothrake with *Skopas.* the holiest ritual, also the Apollo on the Palatine and, in the gardens of Servilius, a seated Hestia which is praised, and beside her two pillars whose pendants are in the galleries of Asinius, where also is his κανηφόρος [basket-bearer]. But most highly 26 esteemed of all his works is the group in the temple built by Gnaeus Domitius in the Circus of Flaminius: it comprises Poseidon himself with Thetis and Achilles, Nereids riding on dolphins and sea monsters or on sea horses, and Tritons and the train of Phorkos, with sea beasts and a tumult of creatures of the deep, the whole by the same hand, a wondrous work, even were it that of a life-time. Yet in addition to the works I have named and those which are unknown to us, we have by the same artist an Ares, a colossal seated figure, now in the temple built by Brutus Callaecus close to the Circus of Flaminius, besides a nude

Kitharoidos, is represented on coins of Nero (Overb. *Apoll. Münztaf.* v, 47, 48, 50, 51).

7. **campteras**: i. e. goals or columns marking in the *stadium* the turning-point for runners or chariots (κάμπτειν); cf. the *metae* on the sarkophagos, Helbig, *Class. Ant.* 339; these columns might be profusely adorned with sculpture.

§ 26. 9. **delubro**: i. e. of Neptune. It is uncertain which of the Domitii built it; Urlichs (*Griechische Statuen im Rep. Rom*, p. 19) inclines to attribute the original building to the consul of B. C. 121, who celebrated with great splendour his triumph over the Arverni, and its restoration to his great-grandson, the consul of B. C. 32; this later Domitius now placed in the temple the great Skopasian group, presumbly brought from Bithynia, of which he was governor B. C. 40–35, and where was a famous temple of

Poseidon at Astakos-Olbia (Urlichs, *Skopas*, p. 130).

10. **circo Flaminio**: cf. Gilbert, *Rom*, iii, p. 89.

ipse: i.e. the temple-statue; Becker, *Top.* p. 619, note 13; cf. *simulacrum ipsum* in xxxiv, 66.

Thetis . . . marina: the group represented the passing of Achilles to the Isles of the Blest; Urlichs, *Skopas*, p. 133 ff.; cf. Fleischer *ap.* Roscher, i, p. 53. Pliny's description is tinged by reminiscences of Virgil, *Aen.* v, 240.

15. **Mars . . . sedens**: the Ares Ludovisi (Helbig, 883)—a statue distinctly Skopasian in style—is probably a reduced copy of this work; see Furtwängler, *Masterpieces*, p. 304.

16. **Bruti Callaeci**: (D. Junius) cos. B. C. 138; celebrated his triumph over the *Callaici* B. C. 132; the architect of the temple was Hermodoros of Salamis, Nepos *ap.* Priscian, *Fragm.*

terea Venus in eodem loco nuda Praxiteliam illam ante-
27 cedens et quemcumque alium locum nobilitatura. Romae
quidem multitudo operum, etiam obliteratio ac magis offi-
ciorum negotiorumque acervi omnis a contemplatione tamen
abducunt, quoniam otiosorum et in magno loci silentio talis 5
admiratio est.   qua de causa ignoratur artifex eius quoque
Veneris quam Vespasianus imperator in operibus Pacis suae
28 dicavit antiquorum dignam fama.   par haesitatio est in
templo Apollinis Sosiani, Niobae liberos morientes Scopas
an Praxiteles fecerit, item Ianus pater in suo templo dicatus 10
ab Augusto ex Aegypto advectus utrius manu sit, iam
quidem et auro occultatus.   similiter in curia Octaviae
quaeritur de Cupidine fulmen tenente.   id demum adfirma-
29 tur, Alcibiaden esse principem forma in ea aetate.   multa
in eadem schola sine auctoribus placent : Satyri quattuor, 15
ex quibus unus Liberum patrem palla velatum umeris
praefert, alter Liberam similiter, tertius ploratum infantis

Hist. Rom. 13, p. 227; cf. Gilbert,
Rom, iii, p. 88.
    § 27. 2. **Romae quidem**: for the
sentiment of the whole passage, cf.
Hor. *Ep.* i, 10. [It became a commonplace of silver Latinity to contrast the
noise of the city with the quiet of the
villas, see also Pliny's Introd. to Bk.
xiv; Pliny, *Ep.* iii, 18, 4 *nunquam porro
aut valde vacat Romae, aut com-
modum est audire recitantem ; Ep.*
iii, 5, 13 *haec inter medios labores
urbisque fremitum ;* and *Ep.* i, 9;
cf. C. F. Herrmann *über d. Kunstsinn
der Römer*, p. 46.—H. L. U.]
    7. **operibus Pacis**: connected
with the Temple and Forum of Peace,
xxxiv, 84.
    § 28. 9. Apollinis Sosiani: xiii, 53,
the surname from C. Sosius (the legate
of Antony), who brought the sacred
cedar-wood image of the god from
Seleukia, and restored the temple ;
note on xxxv, 99.
    Niobae : if the group was identical
with the original of the Florence
statues, the style—especially of the
heads—can leave no doubt that it

was by Skopas (cf. Amelung, *Basis
des Praxiteles*, p. 67).   The ancient
critics evidently confused Skopas
and Praxiteles, precisely as do the
moderns.
    10. **Ianus pater**: a bearded double
terminal bust, rechristened at Rome as
Janus. [What divinity it originally
represented is impossible to tell, for
the Romans were absolutely without scruple in renaming statues; cf.
Pseud. Dio Chrys. xxxvii, 42 Κορινθ.
for a Poseidon rededicated as Jupiter.
—H. L. U.]   According to Wernicke,
Jahrb. v, 1890, p. 148, this 'Janus'
may be identical with the Skopasian
herm (*not* Hermes), *Anth. Plan.* 192.
    in suo templo : the shrine in the
Forum (xxxiv, 33) can scarcely have
been spacious enough to hold a second
statue : it is still doubtful which
temple is meant ; Roscher, (*Lex.* ii,
26 f.) suggests a temple of Janus
belonging to the Forum Augustum,
while Jordan (*Hermes*, iv, p. 239)
thought of the temple in the Forum
Holitorium ; cf. Peter, Ovid's *Fasti*,
ii, p. 11.

Aphrodite now in the same place, which surpasses even the
Praxitelean goddess, and would suffice to make famous any other
spot.   At Rome indeed the works of art are legion ; besides, one 27
effaces another from the memory, and above all, beautiful as they *Multitude
of works in*
are, people are distracted by the overpowering claims of duty and *Rome ob-*
business, for to admire art we need leisure and profound stillness. *scures their
fame.*
For this same reason we are ignorant of the sculptor of the
Aphrodite dedicated by the emperor Vespasian in the galleries of
his temple of Peace, a work worthy of the old masters.   It is likewise 28
uncertain whether Skopas or Praxiteles made the dying children
of Niobe in the temple of the Apollo of Sosius, and again which
of them made the Father Janus brought by Augustus from Egypt
and dedicated in his own temple ; the Janus, moreover, is now
disguised by gilding.   The same difficulty arises in the case of
the Eros holding a thunderbolt, in the Council Chamber of
Octavia ; this only is certain, that it is the portrait of Alkibiades,
the handsomest man of his day.   Many groups by unknown 29
artists attract us in this gallery ; such as the four Satyrs, one of
whom is carrying on his shoulders a cloaked Dionysos, the second
carries Ariadne in the same way, the third is soothing a crying

11. ex Aegypto : cf. xxxv, 131,
28, and notes.

   iam quidem : in exculpation.

   12. auro occultatus : the gilding is
specially mentioned, as unusual in the
case of a marble statue; cf. Wunderer,
Manibiae, p. 10 ; note on xxxiv, 63.

   similiter . . . quaeritur : from
works as to which it was doubtful
whether they were by Skopas or
Praxiteles Pliny passes on to general
doubts, and thence to statues by
unknown masters (*sine auctoribus*) ;
Wernicke, *op. cit.* p. 150.

   in curia : certain rooms of the
opera Octaviae served occasionally for
meetings of the Senate ; Dio Cassius,
lv, 8 ; Josephus, *Bell. Jud.* vii, 5, 4 ;
Gilbert, *Rom,* iii, p. 249, note 1.

   13. fulmen tenente : Ἔρως κεραυνο-
φόρος.

   id . . . adfirmatur : Wernicke (*loc.
cit.*) explains Pliny's meaning to be as
follows : the individuality of the features leads people to suppose this is a

portrait—and a portrait of Alkibiades ;
I take no responsibility in the matter,
but thus far is certain, that Alkibiades
was the most beautiful man in the
period to which the statue belongs.

   14. Alcibiaden : the statue had
most probably nothing to do with
Alkibiades, but the connexion in the
popular mind arose from the well-
known ἐπίσημον on his shield (Plut.
Alkib. 16).

   § 29. 15. eadem schola : Gilbert,
loc. cit.

   16. Liberum . . . palla velatum :
the description of the fully draped figure
suggests the Dionysos supported (not
carried) by a Satyr in the ' Ikarios'
relief (Schreiber, *Hell. Reliefs,* xxxvii).
palla = πέπλος, usually understood of
the cloak worn by women, though
practically identical with the ἱμάτιον.

   17. Liberam similiter : a Maenad
carried by a Satyr, misunderstood as
an Ariadne ; cf. Furtwängler, *Plinius,*
p. 10.

cohibet, quartus cratere alterius sitim sedat, duaeque Aurae
velificantes sua veste. nec minor quaestio est in saeptis
Olympum et Pana, Chironem cum Achille qui fecerint,
praesertim cum capitali satisdatione fama iudicet dignos.
30 Scopas habuit aemulos eadem aetate Bryaxim et Timo- 5
theum et Leocharen, de quibus simul dicendum est, quoniam
pariter caelavere Mausoleum. sepulchrum hoc est ab uxore
Artemisia factum Mausolo Cariae regulo, qui obiit olympiadis CVII anno secundo. opus id ut esset inter septem
miracula hi maxime fecere artifices. patet ab austro et 10
septentrione centenos sexagenos ternos pedes, brevius a

11. centenos] *Urlichs in Chrest., Detlefsen* ; *om. Bamb., reliqui.*

ploratum infantis cohibet : recalls the well-known group in the
Louvre (phot. Giraudon, 1182) and
its numerous replicas (Rome, Helbig,
11 ; phot. Alinari, 6673) of Seilenos
nursing the babe Dionysos.

1. duaeque Aurae : cf. the so-
called ' Nereids ' of the Xanthian tomb
(Brit. Mus.), which have been shown by
Six, *J. H. S.* xiii, p. 131, to represent
the Αὖραι : Pindar, *Ol.* ii, 70, μακάρων
νᾶσος ὠκεανίδες περιπνέοισιν ; see also
Max. Mayer *ap.* Roscher, ii, 2147 ff.

2. nec minor quaestio : above,
note in § 28 on *similiter . . . quaeritur.*

in saeptis : i. e. in the galleries
which surrounded the voting-place
of the Comitia, after the luxurious
alterations planned by Caesar (Cic.
Att. iv, 16, 14) and completed by
Augustus ; cf. Dio Cassius, liii, 23.

3. Olympum et Pana : the group
in Naples of the bearded Pan teaching
a young boy the syrinx (Friederichs,
Bausteine, 654 ; Helbig, *Untersuch.*
p. 156) is commonly thought to
reproduce this work.

Chironem cum Achille : the
subject is preserved in wall-paintings
(Helbig, *Wandgem.* 1291–1295), of
which the best preserved and most
famous is Helbig 1291. A head
from a marble copy is in the Pal.
Conservat. ; Helbig, *Class. Ant.* 572.

4. capitali satisdatione : xxxiv,
38.

§ 30. 5. Scopas : the dates for
his activity are comprised between
his work for the temple of Athena
Alea at Tegea (after the fire B.C.
394, Paus. viii, 45, 4) and his work
for the Mausoleion (about B. C. 353)
and for the Artemision of Ephesos
(after the fire of B. C. 356, below § 95).

aemulos : cf. xxxiv, 49, *aemuli ;*
xxxv, 64.

Bryaxim : xxxiv, 73 ; for his signature Βρύαξις ἐπόησεν on the basis
adorned with reliefs of horsemen see
Δελτίον, 1891, p. 35 ; *Bull. Corr. Hell.,*
xv, 1891, p. 369, plate vii ; 'Εφημ. ἀρχ.
1893, plates 6, 7. The inscription is
of about the date of the Mausoleion
(cf. plates 4, 5, for a torso of Nike
found not far from the basis, and
which Kavvadias, *ib.* p. 46, supposes
to have crowned the monument).

Timotheum : xxxiv, 91 ; he
may have been already advanced in
years when he worked upon the
Mausoleion ; the inscription (Kavvadias, *Fouilles d'Epidaure,* no. 241,
l. 36 f.) recording his contract for fur-
nishing models and sculptures for the
Temple of Asklepios at Epidauros,
Paus. ii, 32, 4, is dated by Kavvadias
(p. 85) at the commencement of the
fourth century, while Foucart, *Bull.*

child, and the fourth quenches the thirst of another child out of a goblet; further, the two wind goddesses spreading their robes as sails. It is equally uncertain who made the groups in the voting enclosures of Olympos and Pan, and of Achilles and Cheiron, and yet such is their renown that the custodians are obliged to pledge their lives for their safety.

Bryaxis, Timotheos, and *Leochares* were rivals and contempor- 30 aries of Skopas, and must be mentioned with him, as they *TheMauso- leion.* worked together on the Mausoleion. This is the tomb erected by Artemisia in honour of her husband Mausolos, prince of Karia, who died in the second year of the hundred and seventh Olympiad [351 B.C.], and its place among the seven wonders of the world is largely due to these great sculptors. The length of the south and north sides is 163 feet; the two façades are

---

Corr. Hell. xiv, 1890, p. 589 ff., places it at about B. C. 375.

6. Leocharen : for his date see on xxxiv, 50.

7. Mausoleum : a history of its discovery, a discussion of the restora-tions proposed, and the chief literature up to 1891 are given by Newton in Smith's *Dict. Ant.* ii, p. 155 ff. Students will read with interest the latest restoration, attempted by E. Oldfield, *Archaeologia,* 1895, pp. 273–362. But it is as useless and unsatisfactory as others so far as the Plinian text is concerned. Mr. Oldfield starts by rejecting *in toto* the variant readings of *cod. Bamb.,* and does this without adequate knowledge of the character of this MS. Especially unsatisfactory is his rejection of *circumitum,* for the besetting sin of the *Bamb.* is not the introduction of words or syllables, but their omission (cf. H. L. Urlichs' note on xxxiv, 69 *Liberum patrem*). Fur-ther, the facts that Mr. Oldfield writes in ignorance of anything more recent than Sillig's second edition, that he is unacquainted either with Detlefsen's edition, or with his article on the PlinianMSS. in the *Philologus* (t. xxviii), or with the *Chrestom.* of Urlichs, and that he confuses *Otto Jahn* (p. 284 and p. 290) with *Ludwig von Jan,* show how

little trust can be placed in his criticism of the text.—On architectural grounds alone, Mr. Oldfield's reconstruction may have merits of which the present writer feels incompetent to judge. We have translated faithfully from *cod. Bamb.,* and in the notes I attempt no harmonizing of the Plinian description with monumental evidence, nor can I point out discrepancies, for the simple reason that any impartial student must admit that the real shape of the Mausoleion and distribution of its parts remain as much a riddle now as before.—The whole description of the Mausoleion is taken from Muci-anus, Introd. p. lxxxviii.

8. Mausolo . . . regulo: he was, as a fact, only a satrap under the king of Persia ; Diodoros, xvi, 36, gives B. C. 353 as the date of his death.

9. inter septem miracula : it figures in the oldest canonical lists. The various lists of the 'Seven Won-ders' are conveniently printed together by Orelli in the Appendix to his edition of Philo Byzantius, pp. 141–150. *Ib.* pp. 192–194 will be found all the ancient descriptions of the Mausoleion.

11. centenos: this addition is unavoidable if we are to accept the total 440 feet as correct.

frontibus, toto circumitu pedes CCCCXXXX, attollitur in
altitudinem XXV cubitis, cingitur columnis XXXVI. pteron
31 vocavere circumitum.   ab oriente caelavit Scopas, a septentrione Bryaxis, a meridie Timotheus, ab occasu Leochares,
priusque quam peragerent regina obit.   non tamen recesse- 5
runt nisi absoluto iam, id gloriae ipsorum artisque monimentum iudicantes, hodieque certant manus.   accessit et
quintus artifex.   namque supra pteron pyramis altitudine
inferiorem aequat, viginti quattuor gradibus in metae
cacumen se contrahens.   in summo est quadriga marmorea 10
quam fecit Pythis.   haec adiecta CXXXX pedum altitudine
32 totum opus includit.   Timothei manu Diana Romae est in
Palatio Apollinis delubro, cui signo caput reposuit Avianius
Evander.   in magna admiratione est Hercules Menestrati
et Hecate Ephesi in templo Dianae post aedem in cuius 15

---

1. CCCCXXXX] *Bamb.*; quadringentos undecim *reliqui*.   2. XXXV
Detlefsen.   11. altitudine] *Bamb.*, *Riccard.*, *Lips.*; altitudinem, *Detlefsen.*

2. pteron vocavere : cf. in § 19,
Πανδώρας γένεσιν *appellant.*
§ 31. 3. ab oriente . . . Scopas
. . . Leochares: the endeavours to
identify the styles of each sculptor
in the extant slabs have up to now
been unsatisfactory. The dominant
thought and design seem Skopasian.
Vitruvius (vii, *praef.* 12), in his account
of the Mausoleion, names Praxiteles
as one of the sculptors (on this point
see Amelung, *Die Basis des Praxiteles
aus Mantinea*, p. 55 f.).
9. inferiorem: Newton, *loc. cit.*,
rightly points out that, according to
ordinary rules, the word to be supplied
would be *pyramidem*, which, however,
he considered iuadmissible, as he
found no evidence for a pyramidal
substructure.   On the other hand,
Detlefsen's *altitudine*[*m*] does unwarranted violence to the text.
10. quadriga marmorea: a restoration of the extant fragments may now
be seen in the Mausoleion room of
the Brit. Mus.   That the so-called
'Artemisia' and 'Mausolos' can,
however, never have been placed in

the chariot has been made clear by
P. Gardner, *J. H. S.* xiii, p. 188 ff.
11. Pythis: Vitruvius, *loc. cit.*, gives
the name Phyteus (MSS.), but the
identity is not certain.
§ 32. 12. Timothei manu : the style
of this artist can now be satisfactorily
studied in the sculptured decorations
of the Asklepieion at Epidauros ; from
the inscription (above, note on § 30, 5)
we learn that he contracted (ἕλετο) to
construct (ἐργάσασθαι) and provide
(παρέχεν) models (τύπος)—presumably
for the pedimental sculptures—and for
the akroteria or angle figures of one of
the gables (ἅτερον αἰετόν).   From the
relation of the akroterial figures of
the west front (Centr. Mus. Catal.
155–157) to one another and to the
figures of the Amazon battle from the
corresponding west pediment, there
is every ground for regarding them as
the work of one artist, i. e. of
Timotheos; Amelung, *Basis des Praxiteles*, p. 69 f., where the kinship of
the group of Leda and the Swan (best-
known replica in the Capitol; Helbig,
459) to the Epidaurian sculptures is

shorter, and the whole perimeter is 440 feet; its height is 25 cubits [37½ feet], and it has thirty-six columns. This colonnade is called a πτερόν. The sculptures of the eastern front are 31 carved by Skopas, those on the north by Bryaxis, on the south by Timotheos, and on the west by Leochares. The queen died before the work was finished, but the artists carried it through to the end, deeming that it would be an abiding monument of their own glory and of the glory of art, and to this day they compete for the prize. A fifth sculptor also worked on the monument. Above the colonnade is a pyramid, of the same height as the lower structure, consisting of twenty-four retreating steps rising into a cone. On the apex stands a chariot and four horses in marble made by *Pythis*. Including this the height is 140 feet.

In the temple of Apollo on the Palatine at Rome stands an 32 Artemis by Timotheos, the head of which has been restored by Avianius Evander. Greatly admired is a Herakles by †*Menestratos*, and a Hekate at Ephesos in the temple of Artemis, behind the

pointed out (the likeness noted simultaneously by Winter, *Ath. Mitth.* xix, 1894, p. 157 ff.). Add.

13. **Avianius Evander** : cf. Hor. *Sat.* i, 3, 90 :—
    Comminxit lectum potus mensave
        catillum
    Evandri manibus tritum deiecit ;
where the scholiast Porphyrio remarks that Evander was both chaser and sculptor (*plastes statuarum*), that Alexander brought him from Athens to Alexandria, whence he was taken to Rome *inter captivos*, doubtless on the capture of the city by Augustus in 25 B.C. ; cf. further Cic. *Fam.* xiii, 2 ; 21 ; 27, and vii, 23, where Avianius figures rather as art-dealer than as artist ; cf. Brunn, *K. G.* i, p. 547.

14. in **magna admiratione** : these words introduce the fifth parenthetical mention of works elsewhere than in Rome. [The construction of the passage down to *incluta* is curious ; we get (i) admirable works (in *magna adm.*) ; (ii) works equally admirable (*non postferuntur*) ; (iii) a work of which nothing need be said,

for all the world understands the greatness of the drunken old woman by Myron—this last work being abruptly introduced by a *nam*, which implies an ellipse of the preceding sentence, according to a usage noted in xxxiv, 7, xxxv, 137. H. L. U.]

Menestrati : possibly identical with the sculptor of a statue of the unknown poetess Learchis ; Tatian, πρὸς Ἑλλ. p. 34, ed. Schwartz.

15. **Hecate Ephesi** : the information, like that on the Mausoleion, appears derived from Mucianus (*Introd.* p. lxxxviii).

post aedem : interpreted by Sillig (*Dict. of Artists*, s. v. Menestratos) as 'the back part of the temple,' i. e. the ὀπισθόδομος. But it is doubtful whether *post* can be susceptible of such a meaning. It therefore seems more reasonable to suppose that the Hekate of M. was contained in a separate shrine, within the precinct (*in templo*), but behind the great temple (*post aedem*). That the Hekate was in a closed locality, and not merely outside the temple in the open air, as

contemplatione admonent aeditui parcere oculis, tanta
marmoris radiatio est. non postferuntur et Charites in
propylo Atheniensium quas Socrates fecit alius ille quam
pictor, idem ut aliqui putant. nam Myronis illius qui in
aere laudatur anus ebria est Zmyrnae in primis incluta. 5
33 Pollio Asinius, ut fuit acris vehementiae, sic quoque spectari
monumenta sua voluit. in his sunt Centauri Nymphas
gerentes Arcesilae, Thespiades Cleomenis, Oceanus et Iuppiter Heniochi, Appiades Stephani, Hermerotes Taurisci,
34 non caelatoris illius sed Tralliani, Iuppiter hospitalis Papyli 10
Praxitelis discipuli, Zethus et Amphion ac Dirce et taurus

9. Heniochi] *Jan* ; eniochi *Bamb.* ; enthochi *Riccard., Voss.* ; Antiochi
Urlichs *in Chrest, Detlefsen.*

some authorities suppose, is evident
from the story of the *marmoris
radiatio ;* the mysterious gleam of the
marble can only be understood if the
statue was seen in the half-light of a
shrine, and becomes nonsense if the
Hekate was out of doors.

1. aeditui : the fact that the
statue was shown by temple attendants
is another argument in favour of its
being in a closed locality.

2. marmoris radiatio : the face
of the statue, like the hands and feet,
would be left in the original colour
of the marble, or just toned by wax
(see in xxxv, 133 note on *circumlitioni*) ; the white face would be seen
gleaming through the dusk of the
shrine—the imagination being doubtless stimulated by a sense of the
mysterious personality of Hekate.—
M. S. Reinach kindly points out to
me that we seem to detect in the
legend traces of the old belief that
mortals might not look in the face of
the gods without being struck blind ;
cf. Teiresias and the mysterious
Epizelos of Herodotos.

Charites : the type is known from
two reliefs in Rome (most famous
in the Vatican, Helbig, 83) and three
in Athens, two of which were found on
the Akropolis (*Ath. Mitth.* iii, 1878,

p. 181 ff., Furtwängler). They are all
after an original of the period ab. B. C.
470 ; cf. Furtwängler, *Masterpieces,*
p. 23, note 1, Introd. p. 1, note 2.

in propylo Athen.. Paus. i, 22,
8 : κατὰ δὲ τὴν ἔσοδον αὐτὴν ἤδη
τὴν ἐς ἀκρόπολιν Ἑρμῆν, ὃν Προπύλαιον
ὀνομάζουσι καὶ Χάριτας Σωκράτην
ποιῆσαι τὸν Σωφρονίσκου λέγουσι ; cf.
note on xxxv, 101 for the unusual form
propylon, and Introd. p. 1.

3. Socrates fecit : it is curious
to note that Pliny knows nothing of the
popular identification of the sculptor
Sokrates with the philosopher,
accepted by Pausanias, *loc. cit.,* and
a number of other authorities (Overb.
S. Q. 907–914), Introd. *loc. cit.*

alius . . . idem : contains the
trace of a similar controversy to that
noted in the case of Pythagoras,
xxxiv, 60 ; Introd. p. 1.

4. Myronis illius : xxxiv, 49 ;
57–59.

5. anus ebria : the identification
of the work with the well-known
statue of an old woman nursing an ivy-
crowned wine-jar (Helbig, *Class. Ant.*
431, p. 318, where see list of replicas
and literature) is nothing less than
certain. Nor do the grounds for
attributing the work, on account of
the subject, to a later Myron seem

shrine, in looking at which the temple guardians advise visitors to be cautious, so dazzling is the lustre of the marble. Not inferior are the Charites in the gateway at Athens ; the *Sokrates* who made them is to be distinguished from the painter, though some believe in their identity. As to *Myron,* the celebrated *Myron.* bronze caster, his statue at Smyrna of an intoxicated old woman ranks among the most famous works.

Asinius Pollio with his characteristic enterprise was eager that his 33 galleries should attract attention. They contain Kentaurs with *Gallery of Asinius* nymphs on their backs by †*Arkesilas,* Thespiades by *Kleomenes, Pollio.* figures of Okeanos and Zeus by †*Heniochos,* nymphs of the Appia by *Stephanos,* terminal busts of Eros by *Tauriskos* (not the famous chaser, but Tauriskos of Tralles), a Zeus of strangers by †*Papylos* 34 the pupil of Praxiteles, and Zethos and Amphion, with Dirke, the

reasonable. The figures from the angle of the west pediment of the temple at Olympia show that the presentation of aged women was not alien to the art of the early fifth century. The epithet *ebria,* like the *temulenta* applied to the flute-player of Lysippos in xxxiv, 63, rests perhaps on some slight misapprehension of the motive, or mistranslation from the Greek.

§ 33. 7. monumenta : above, note on § 23.

Centauri Nymph. gerentes : for the subject cf. the wall-painting, Helbig, *Wandgem.* 499; cf. also the Kentaurs (bearing Erotes) of Aristeas and Papias (Capitol, Helbig, 512, 513).

8. Arcesilae: xxxv, 155; below, § 41.

Thespiades : same subject by Teisikrates, xxxiv, 66 ; by Praxiteles, below, § 39.

Cleomenis: his identity with—or relationship to—the sculptor of the so-called 'Germanicus' in the Louvre (*I. G. B.* 344), or of the altar with sacrifice of Iphigeneia in Florence (*I. G. B.* 380), is quite uncertain. (*I. G. B.* 513, from Medicean Venus, is a modern forgery.)

9. Heniochi: [von Jan's reading may be considered certain, the names *Arcesilae . . . Taurisci* being in alphabetical order.—H. L. U.].

Appiades: so called doubtless from their resemblance to the statues of the nymphs of the Appian aqueduct which adorned a fountain of the Forum Julium ; cf. Ovid, *Ars Amat.* i, 79; iii, 451 ; cf. *Rem. Amor.* 660 ; Gilbert, *Rom,* iii, p. 226, note 1.

Stephani : probably identical with the pupil of Pasiteles, whose inscription is read on the statue of an athlete in the Villa Albani, *I. G. B.* 574; cf. *ib.* 375, where he is named as the master of Menelaos, the artist of the famous group in the Museo Boncompagni (Helbig, 887).

Hermerotes : terminal busts of Eros ; for extant instances in statuary see Furtwängler, *Masterpieces,* p. 69 (Eros), p. 60 (Athena), p. 234 ff. (Herakles). The old interpretation that the several divinities were combined with Hermes in a double terminal bust is without support from the monuments, though it is favoured by Cicero, *Att.* i, iv. 3 : *quod ad me de Hermathena scribis, per mihi gratum est: est ornamentum Academiae proprium meae, quod et Hermes commune omnium et Minerva singulare est eius gymnasii.* Add.

10. caelatoris : xxxiii, 156.

§ 34. hospitalis = ξένιος.

11. Zethus . . . taurus : a group

vinculumque ex eodem lapide, a Rhodo advecta opera
Apolloni et Taurisci.   parentum hi certamen de se fecere,
Menecraten videri professi, sed esse naturalem Artemidorum.
eodem loco Liber pater Eutychidis laudatur, ad Octaviae
vero porticum Apollo Philisci Rhodi in delubro suo, item 5
Latona et Diana et Musae novem et alter Apollo nudus.
35 eum qui citharam in eodem templo tenet Timarchides fecit,
intra Octaviae vero porticus aedem Iunonis ipsam deam
Dionysius et Polycles, aliam Venerem eodem loco Philiscus,
cetera signa Pasiteles.   idem Polycles et Dionysius Timar- 10

9. Polycles aliam, Venerem *Detlefsen.*

('Toro Farnese,' Naples, Friederichs-
Wolters, 1402), which is generally
accepted as the identical one mentioned by Pliny, was discovered in
1546 in the Thermae of Caracalla.

1. ex eodem lapide: cf. below,
§ 36; § 37; § 41; the 'Bull' and
the 'Laokoon' are however constructed
of several pieces, and the same was
most likely the case with the 'Lioness'
of Arkesilaos, and the chariot-group of
Lysias. With regard to the 'Laokoon'
and the 'Lioness' Robert, *Arch.
März.* p. 143, note, had suggested
that *ex uno lapide* meant a group
disposed on one basis, in opposition
to groups composed of statues set
each upon a separate basis. But the
grammatical propriety of this interpretation   is   doubtful, cf.   Urlichs,
Arkesilaos, p. 16, note 2.   Förster
(*Görlitz. Verhandl.* p. 298) believes
that Pliny in saying that the Bull and
the Laokoon were *ex uno lapide* had
been deceived by the appearance of
the groups. As a fact, the expression
seems, in all four cases, to imply little
beyond the desire to heighten the
impression of technical difficulty, by
adding one of those details which
readily appeal to popular imagination; cf. *Anth.* ix, 759 (εἰς ἄρμα
λίθινον) :—

Εἰς λίθος, ἄρμ᾽, ἐλατήρ, ἵπποι, ζυγόν,
    ἡνία, μάστιξ.

Ib. 760 :—

Εἰς δίφρος, ἄρμ᾽, ἐλατήρ, ἵπποι, ζυγός,
    ἡνία, νίκη.

Rhodo: much light has recently
been thrown on the dates of the
Rhodian school by two papers of
Maurice Holleaux (*Rev. de Phil.*
xvii, 1893, pp. 171–185), and H. von
Gaertringen (*Jahrb.* ix, 1894, pp. 23–
43). According to the latter, the
inscriptions fall into two periods: (i)
from close of third century to B. C.
163 (Pydna); (ii) from B. C. 88, at
the close of the Mithridatic war, to
the total reduction of the Rhodian
state by Cassius Longinus and Cassius
of Parma in B.C. 43 (Appian, Ἐμφ.
iv, 60–74; v, 2). It was then that
many a Rhodian work of art was taken
to Rome.

2. Apolloni et Taurisci: a
basis found in the theatre of Magnesia
on the Maiander bears the inscription
Ἀπολλώνιος Ταυρίσκου [Τραλλιανὸς]
ἐποίει : it is published by H. v. Gaertringen (*Athen. Mitth.* xix, 1894,
p. 37 ff.), who dates it from early
Imperial times, so that the Ταυρίσκος
of the inscription (though of course not
the Ἀπολλώνιος) may be one of the
sculptors of the Bull, which would be
executed previous to B.C. 43 (see previous note). The names were probably
recurrent in a family of artists.

parentum hi certamen :   the

bull and the cord, all carved out of one block. It is the joint work of *Apollonios* and *Tauriskos*, and was brought from Rhodes. These two sculptors occasioned a controversy as to their parentage, by declaring that Menekrates was their nominal, Artemidoros their real father. In the same collection is a fine Dionysos by Eutychides. Near the gallery of Octavia in the *Other Roman galleries* temple of Apollo stands a statue of the god by *Philiskos* of Rhodes, together with Leto, Artemis, and the nine Muses and another nude Apollo. *Timarchides* made the Apollo with the cithara in the same temple, and *Dionysios* and *Polykles* the statue 35 of Juno within her temple in the portico of Octavia. A second Aphrodite in the same place is by *Philiskos*, and the other statues by *Pasiteles*. The same Polykles and Dionysios, the sons of

words are rhetorical, or rest on a Roman misunderstanding of the Greek inscription. According to a custom of which the Rhodian inscriptions afford numerous instances (cf. *inter alia*, *I. G. B.* 174. 181), the artists had added to their signature not only the name of their real father, but that of their father by adoption. H. v. G. suggests the following restoration :
Ἀπολλώνιος καὶ Ταυρίσκος Ἀρτεμιδώρου, καθ' ὑοθεσίαν δὲ Μενεκράτεος, Τραλλιανοὶ ἐποίησαν.

4. **Eutychidis** : probably not the pupil of Lysippos (xxxiv, 78), who was a bronze statuary ; the name was common ; see Loewy in *I. G. B.* 143.

5. **in delubro suo** : i. e. the temple of Apollo Sosianus ; notes on xxxv, 99, above, § 28.

6. **Musae novem** : Amelung (*Basis des Praxiteles*, p. 44 f. and Append.) shows that this is probably the group which inspired the artists of the Muses on the basis from Halikarnassos (Trendelenburg, *Der Musen Chor*, Winckelmannspr. xxxvi, 1876) and of the Muses on the relief of the Apotheosis of Homer (Brunn-Bruckmann, plate 50), both in the Brit. Mus. It is significant that both works are from Southern Asia-Minor, i. e. from the neighbourhood of Rhodes.

§ 35. 7. **Timarchides**: son of Polykles of Athens, xxxiv, 52, and brother of Timokles, *ib.*; his two sons, Polykles II and Dionysios, are mentioned below; together with his brother (οἱ Πολυκλέους παῖδες) he made for Olympia the statue of the pugilist Agesarchos of Triteia, and for Elateia statues of Asklepios and of Athena (Paus. vi. 12, 9 ; x, 34, 6 ; 8).

8. **aedem Iunonis** : erected together with the adjacent temple (*proxima aedes*) of Jupiter by Q. Caecilius Metellus after his triumph of B. C. 149 ; Vell. Paterc. 1, 11.

ipsam deam : the temple statue; cf. *Neptunus ipse*, above, § 26 ; *simulacrum ipsum Trophonii*, xxxiv, 66.

9. **Dionysius et Polycles** : identical with the *Polycles et Dionysius Timarchidis filii*, below.

aliam Venerem : Urlichs (*Quellenreg.* p. 8) has shown that these words refer back to § 15, where an Aphrodite by Pheidias, in the *porticus Oct.*, had already been mentioned.

10. **Pasiteles** : note on § 39.

Dionysius : together with his nephew Timarchides II, he made the statue of C. Ofellius, found in Delos ; it bears the inscription Διονύσιος Τιμαρχίδου καὶ Τιμαρχίδης Πολυκλέους Ἀθηναῖοι, *I. G. B.* 242.

chidis fili Iovem qui est in proxima aede fecerunt, Pana et
Olympum luctantes eodem loco Heliodorus, quod est
alterum in terris symplegma nobile, Venerem lavantem se
36 *sedaedalsas* stantem Polycharmus. ex honore apparet
in magna auctoritate habitum Lysiae opus, quod in Palatio 5
super arcum divus Augustus honori Octavi patris sui dicavit
in aedicula columnis adornata, id est quadriga currusque et
Apollo ac Diana ex uno lapide. in hortis Servilianis reperio
laudatos Calamidis Apollinem illius caelatoris, Dercylidis
pyctas, Amphistrati Callisthenen historiarum scriptorem. 10
37 nec deinde multo plurium fama est, quorundam claritati in
operibus eximiis obstante numero artificum, quoniam nec
unus occupat gloriam nec plures pariter nuncupari possunt,
sicut in Laocoonte, qui est in Titi imperatoris domo, opus
omnibus et picturae et statuariae artis praeferendum. ex 15
uno lapide eum ac liberos draconumque mirabiles nexus de
consili sententia fecere summi artifices Hagesander et Poly-

4. Sesedaedalsas stantem *Bamb.*; sesededalsa stantem *Ricc.*, *Voss.*; se sed et
aliam stantem *Sillig*; sese Daedalus, aliam stantem *Detlefsen.*

1. Iovem : above, note on *aedem
Iunonis.*

Pana et Olympum : the names
are significant as showing that these
συμπλέγματα were mostly erotic
groups, composed perhaps in the
scheme familiar from the groups in
Dresden.

Heliodorus : xxxiv, 91; the signature of his son (Πλούταρχος
'Ηλιοδώρου 'Ρόδιος ἐποίησε) closes the
great inscription, discovered in Rhodes
by Hiller v. Gaertringen, which since
it contains the names of L. Murena
and L. Lucullus has been dated by
Mommsen at B.C. 82-74 (*Jahrb.* ix,
1894, p. 25 ff.; cf. also Maurice
Holleaux, *Rev. de Philol.* xvii, 1893,
p. 173; and *I. G. B.* 194-196).

3. alterum: harks back to the similar group by Kephisodotos in § 24.

'Venerem lavantem se: the
'Vénus Accroupie' in the Louvre
(Friederichs-Wolters 1467) is looked
upon as a copy of this work, but
see Add.

§ 36. 6. super arcum: the arch was
part of the *Propylaea* which formed
the entrance to the *area* of Apollo,
Gardthausen *Augustus I*, p. 962; *ib.
II*, p. 575.

Octavii patris : Suet. *Aug. 3.*
8. ex uno lapide : note on § 34.
hortis Servilianis : above, § 23.
9. illius caelatoris : xxxiii, 155;
xxxiv, 47 ; he is presumably identical
with the bronze statuary, xxxiv, 71.

10. Amphistrati : known also
from Tatian (πρὸς 'Ελλην. p. 34, ed.
Schwartz) as sculptor of the portrait
of an unknown poetess Kleito.

Callisthenem : of Olynthos, pupil
and nephew of Aristotle ; according
to Diodoros, xiv, 117, his 'Helleuika'
were a history of the years B.C.
387-357 (Peace of Antalkidas to the
Phokaian war).

§ 37. 14. in Laocoonte : the original group was found on Jan. 14, 1506,
near the Baths of Titus, whither it may
have been moved from his Palace at
a date posterior to Pliny (on the cir-

A. THE FAMILY OF POLYKLES.

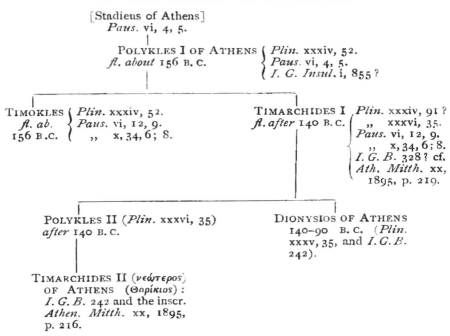

[Stadieus of Athens]
Paus. vi, 4, 5.

POLYKLES I OF ATHENS ⎰ *Plin.* xxxiv, 52.
fl. about 156 B. C. ⎱ *Paus.* vi, 4, 5.
⎱ *I. G. Insul.* i, 855 ?

TIMOKLES ⎰ *Plin.* xxxiv, 52.
fl. ab. ⎱ *Paus.* vi, 12, 9.
156 B .C. ⎱ ,, x, 34, 6; 8.

TIMARCHIDES I *Plin.* xxxiv, 91 ?
fl. after 140 B. C. ⎰ ,, xxxvi, 35.
Paus. vi, 12, 9.
⎱ ,, x, 34, 6; 8.
I. G. B. 328 ? cf.
Ath. Mitth. xx,
1895, p. 219.

POLYKLES II (*Plin.* xxxvi, 35)
after 140 B. C.

DIONYSIOS OF ATHENS
140–90 B. C. (*Plin.*
xxxv, 35, and *I. G. B.*
242).

TIMARCHIDES II (νεώτερος)
OF ATHENS (Θορίκιος) :
I. G. B. 242 and the inscr.
Athen. Mitth. xx, 1895,
p. 216.

B. THE FAMILY OF ATHANODOROS.

ATHANODOROS I Paton inscr.

HAGESANDROS I Paton inscr. Lindian decree, &c.

HAGESANDROS II*

POLYDOROS*

ATHANODOROS II*
(adopted by Dionysios,
Lindian inscr.)

* The sculptors of the Laokoon.

[*To face* p. 208.]

Timarchides, made the Zeus in the adjoining temple, where are also the Pan and Olympos interlaced by *Heliodoros*, ·second in renown among such groups in all the world, an Aphrodite bathing . . . . standing by †*Polycharmos*. The 36 distinction conferred on the work of *Lysias* shows how highly it was esteemed, inasmuch as the god Augustus dedicated it in honour of his father Octavius; it was placed within a small building adorned with columns upon the arch on the Palatine. It consisted of a team of four horses, a chariot, Apollo and Artemis, all carved out of one block of marble. I find that in the gardens of Servilius are an Apollo by *Kalamis*, the well-known silver chaser, boxers by †*Derkylidas*, and a portrait of Kallisthenes the historian by *Amphistratos*, all of which are mentioned with praise.

Not many celebrated artists remain to be named; in the case 37 of certain masterpieces the very number of the collaborators is an *Collabo-ration of* obstacle to their individual fame, since neither can one man take *different* to himself the whole glory, nor have a number so great a claim *sculptors.* to honour. This is the case with the Laokoon in the palace of the Emperor Titus, a work superior to all the pictures and bronzes of the world. Out of one block of marble did the illustrious artists *Hagesander*, *Polydoros*, and *Athanodoros* of Rhodes, after taking counsel together, carve Laokoon, his children, and the

cumstances of the find see Michaelis, *Jahrb.* v, 1890, p. 16); it is now in the Vatican (Helbig, 153). The full literature from 1755 to 1879 is given by Blümner, Comm. to Lessing's *Laokoon*, 2nd ed. p. 722; cf. also Friederichs-Wolters, 1422, and the three papers by Förster, (1) in *Gör-litz. Verhandlungen*, pp. 75–94, and 293 to 307; (2) *Jahrb.* vi, 1891, p. 177 ff. ; (3) *Jahrb.* ix, 1894, p. 43 ff.

in Titi imp. domo ; xxxiv, 55.

15. statuariae : note on xxxiv, 54 (*toreuticen*).

ex uno lapide : note above on § 34: Michelangelo Buonarotti and Giovanni Cristofano, 'che sono i primi scultori di Roma, negano ch'ella sia d'un sol marmo, e mostrano circa a quattro commettiture'; Trivulzio, quoted by Michaelis, *loc. cit.* note 49.

16. de consili sententia: that these words mean neither ' by decree of the Emperor's Privy Council' (Lach-mann, *A. Z.* 1848, p. 236 = *Kleine Schriften*, p. 273), nor ' by decree of the Council of Rhodes,' nor yet ' after consultation of the artists with their friends' (Mommsen, *Hermes*, xx, 1885, p. 268), but are to be under-stood in the simple sense given to them above, has been brilliantly proved by Förster in *Görlitz. Ver-handl.* pp. 75 ff. ; for the usage, cf. Cicero *Verres*, II, iii, 18 ; v, 12, 53, 54, 114 ; *pro Balbo*, 11, 19, 38, and often ; Caesar, *B. G.* iii, 16 ; Livy, xlv, 26 and 29 ; Plin. *Ep.* v, 1, 6 ; 3, 8 ; vi. 31, 12.

17. Hag. et Pol. et Ath. Rhodi : the name of Athanodoros occurs on seven inscriptions published in fac-simile by Förster, *Jahrb.* vi, 1891, pp.

38 dorus et Athenodorus Rhodi. similiter Palatinas domos
Caesarum replevere probatissimis signis Craterus cum Py-
thodoro, Polydeuces cum Hermolao, Pythodorus alius cum
Artemone, et singularis Aphrodisius Trallianus. Agrippae
Pantheum decoravit Diogenes Atheniensis, in columnis 5
templi eius Caryatides probantur inter pauca operum, sicut
in fastigio posita signa sed propter altitudinem loci minus
39 celebrata. inhonorus est nec in templo ullo Hercules ad
quem Poeni omnibus annis humana sacrificaverant victima,
humi stans ante aditum porticus ad nationes. sitae fuere 10
et Thespiades ad aedem Felicitatis, quarum unam amavit
eques Romanus Iunius Pisciculus, ut tradit Varro ; admirator

12. admirator] *Bamb.* ; admiratur *reliqui, Detlefsen.*

191-195. Of these, the Lindian decree
in honour of Athanodoros, son of
Hagesander, has been lately fully
published by H. v. Gaertringen
(*Jahrb.* ix, 1894, p. 34), and shown to
be not earlier, but possibly somewhat
later, than the Ploutarchos-Helio-
doros inscription (B.C. 82–74) mentioned above. With the help of lines
16, 17 of the inscription published
by Paton, *B. C. H.* xiv, p. 278,
['Aγησ]ανδρος 'Aγησάνδρου [τοῦ]
'Aθανοδ[ώ]ρο[υ], H. von Gaertringen
(*op. cit.*) reconstructs the annexed
table. The Hagesander who worked
on the Laokoon would more probably
be the elder brother than the father of
the other two sculptors. The present
writer can see nothing in the technique
or style of the Laokoon to prevent our
accepting for it the date suggested by
the inscriptions. Helbig however
has again quite lately (*Class. Ant., loc.
cit.*) maintained that the Laokoon
belongs to the period previous to the
Pergamene altar, and that the Athanodoros inscriptions belonged to copies
of his works.

§ 38. 2. replevere: rhetorical, cf.
refertae in § 14 ; *implent,* xxxv, 148,
&c.

Craterus ... Aphrodisius : Pliny's

contention is quaintly confirmed,
since not a single one of these artists
is known outside his text (see however
I. G. B. 427).

4. Agrippae Pantheum : xxxiv,
13.

5. Diogenes: identity with the
Diogenes of the inscription found at
Nineveh (Brit. Mus., *I. G. B.* 361 ;
A. S. Murray in *J. H. S.* iii, p. 240 ff.)
is possible, but doubtful.

in columnis ... Caryatides: the
late discoveries in connexion with
the Pantheon have, unfortunately,
thrown no light on the architectural
function performed by these Caryatides. Stark, *Arch. Zeit.* xviii, 1866,
p. 249 f., supposes *in col.* to mean
down among the columns as opposed
to the statues *in fastigio ;* in this case
the Kar. would be not architectonic,
but dancing figures like the Karyatides
of Praxiteles ; above, § 23. Addenda.

§ 39. 8. inhonorus est: rhetorical indignation ; cf. in xxxiv, 89,
the passage on the Bull of Phalaris.

Hercules : a Phoenician or Tyrian
Melkart, presumably brought from
Carthage by the younger Scipio B. C.
146 (cf. Peter, *ap.* Roscher, i, 246 ;
Urlichs, *Griech. Statuen im Rep.
Rom,* p. 13).

wondrous coils of the snakes. So, too, on the Palatine, †*Krateros* 38
and his colleague †*Pythodoros*, †*Polydeukes* and †*Hermolaos*, a
second †*Pythodoros* and †*Artemon*, and †*Aphrodisios* of Tralles,
who worked alone, have filled the mansions of the Caesars with
excellent statues. The sculptures of the Pantheum of Agrippa are *Pantheon.*
by †*Diogenes* of Athens; the Karyatides of the temple columns
are in the very first rank, and so are the statues of the pediment,
though less well known because of the great height at which they
stand. Dishonoured and without a shrine is the Hercules to 39
whom the Carthaginians offered annual human sacrifice; it
stands on the ground in front of the entrance to the Gallery
of the Nations. By the temple of Felicity stood also the
Thespiades, of one of which, according to Varro, a Roman knight,
Junius Pisciculus, was enamoured. Varro likewise admires

10. **humi stans**: i.e. the statue
was without pedestal or basis.

port. **ad nationes**: Serv. on
Aen. 8, 721: *porticum Augustus
fecerat in qua simulacra omnium
gentium collocaverat, quae porticus
adpellabatur ad nationes;* it must not
be confused with Pompeius' *porticus*
of the fourteen nations, below, § 41.

11. **Thespiades**: Cic. *Verr.* II, iv,
4: *atque ille L. Mummius, cum Thespiadas, quae ad aedem Felicitatis sunt,
ceteraque profana ex illo oppido [Thes-
piis] signa tolleret, hunc ... Cupidinem*
(above, § 22) ... *non attigit.* The
statues must have been among those
which L. Lucullus borrowed from
Mummius, to adorn the temple up to
the day of his election, and cleverly
managed not to return (Strabo, viii,
p. 381; cf. Dio Cassius, fr. 75). From
Varro (*Ling. Lat.* vi, 2) we learn that
the *Thespiades* = *Musae.* It is usually
assumed that the *Thespiades* are identical with the *signa quae ante aedem
Fel. fuere*, by Praxiteles, cf. xxxiv, 69,
where see note; but the fact that the
latter were of bronze sufficiently disposes of the identification. The pro-
venance, however, of the *Thespiades*,
their celebrity, the subject and the
story of Pisciculus, show them to have
been Praxitelean works. The famous

group of the Muses found at Tivoli,
now in the Vatican (Helbig, 268–274),
may be looked upon as copies; their
Praxitelean character has been search-
ingly analysed by Amelung, *Basis
des Prax. aus Mantinea*, 1895, pp.
25–49.

aedem **Felicitatis**: xxxiv, 69;
built by L. Lucullus to commemorate
his Spanish campaigns of B.C. 150–
151 (Urlichs, *Arkesilaos*, p. 7), ded.
142 B.C., Dio Cass. fr. 75. On the
temple-statue, see xxxv, 156.

12. **ut tradit Varro**: V. is evidently the authority for the whole
passage from *sitae fuere ... auctor est*
in § 41. His name is brought in at
this point because Pliny looks upon
the story of Pisciculus as of doubtful
authenticity, and therefore lays all
responsibility upon his author.

admirator **et Pasitelis**: the
reading is proved by the context
Arcesilaum quoque magn. Varro in
§ 41, where the *quoque* has no sense
unless Varro's admiration of some
other artist had been previously recorded; Furtwängler, *Plinius*, p. 41;
cf. the citations from Varro in xxxv,
155–157: *Varro tradit sibi cognitum
Possim ... idem magn. Arcesil ...
laudat et Pasitelen.* On Pasiteles, see
Introd. p. lxxvii.

et Pasitelis, qui et quinque volumina scripsit nobilium
40 operum in toto orbe.   natus hic in Graeca Italiae ora et
civitate Romana donatus cum his oppidis Iovem fecit ebo-
reum in Metelli aede qua campus petitur.   accidit ei, cum
in navalibus ubi ferae Africanae erant per caveam intuens 5
leonem caelaret, ut ex alia cavea panthera erumperet non
levi periculo diligentissimi artificis.   fecisse opera complura
41 dicitur, quae fecerit nominatim non refertur.   Arcesilaum
quoque magnificat Varro, cuius se marmoream habuisse
leaenam aligerosque ludentis cum ea Cupidines, quorum 10
alii religatam tenerent, alii cornu cogerent bibere, alii calci-
arent soccis, omnes ex uno lapide.   idem et a Coponio
quattuordecim nationes quae sunt circa Pompeium factas
auctor est.   invenio et Canachum laudatum inter statuarios
42 fecisse marmorea.   nec Sauram atque Batrachum obliterari 15
convenit qui fecere templa Octaviae porticibus inclusa natione ipsi Lacones.   quidam et opibus praepotentes fuisse
eos putant ac sua inpensa construxisse inscriptionem sperantes, qua negata hoc tamen alio modo usurpasse.   sunt

1. fraxiteles *Bamb.*; passitelis *reliqui*; Pasiteles *Detlefsen.*

1. nobilium operum : the Greek
title would be περὶ ἐνδόξων ἔργων.
§ 40. 3. civitate . . . oppidis :
during the social war of B.C. 90–89,
when by the *Leges Iulia* and *Plautia
Papiria* the right of citizenship was
extended to all the cities of Italy.
4. in Metelli aede : i.e. the temple of Jupiter mentioned above, § 35.
qua campus : sc. *Martius*, therefore the temple was on the north side
of the *porticus Octaviae*.
5. navalibus : the naval docks
of the Campus Martius, on the Tiber,
over against the *prata Quinctia*; cf.
Liv. iii, 26, 8, and xlv, 42, *sub fin.*;
Gilbert, *Rom*, pp. 146–150. The event
referred to may have happened in B.C.
55, when wild beasts were brought
from Africa for the games of Pompeius; Plin. viii, 53, 64.
8. non refertur : i.e. by Varro.
§ 41. Arcesilaum : xxxv, 155,
where see notes.

9. se . . . habuisse : xxxiii, 154,
where Varro is likewise cited as owner
and authority. His works of art were
scattered in the proscriptions of B. C.
43. Introd. p. lxxxiv.
marmoream . . . leaenam : the
subject recalls the beautiful relief in
Vienna of a lioness (Schreiber, *Hell.
Rel.*, pl. i), which, with its companion (sheep suckling a lamb), can
help us to recover the style of sculptures of animals executed by Arkesilaos
and Pasiteles, Wickhoff, *Wiener
Genesis*, p. 26.
13. quattuordecim nationes : to
correspond to the number of nations
subjugated by Pompeius (Plut. *Pomp.*
xlv; cf. Vell. ii, 40; Plin. vii, 98
mentions only thirteen nations; the
fourteenth statue was apparently added
to commemorate the triumph over the
pirates, a mention of which closes
the Act. Triumph. for the year 693;
Gilbert, *Rom*, p. 326, note 2). These

Pasiteles, the author of five books on the celebrated works of art *Pasiteles*. in all the world. This artist was born on the Greek coast of **40** Italy, and received the Roman citizenship when it was given to the cities of that district. He made the ivory statue of Jupiter in the temple of Metellus on the way to the Field of Mars. It happened that once at the docks where were the wild beasts from Africa, as he was looking into a den to make a study of a lion on a relief, a panther broke out of another cage, to the great peril of the conscientious artist. His works are said to be numerous, but they are nowhere mentioned by name. †*Arkesilaos* also is highly **41** esteemed by Varro, who possessed a marble group by his hand *Arkesilaos.* of a lioness with winged Loves sporting about her; some are holding her by a cord, others are forcing her to drink out of a horn, and others are putting shoes upon her; the whole is carved out of one block. Varro is again my authority for saying that †*Coponius* made the fourteen statues of the nations which stand round the theatre of Pompeius. I find too that *Kanachos*, famous for his bronzes, worked also in marble, nor must I overlook †*Sauras* and †*Batrachos*, Lakonians by birth, who built the temples **42** enclosed by the galleries of Octavia. Some say that they were *Sauras and Batrachos.* rich men who built the temples at their own cost, hoping that their names would be inscribed upon them. Foiled in this, they yet achieved their object in another way, so it is said, and it is

statues are the earliest instances of those personifications of conquered peoples so conspicuous in Roman art. It is noteworthy that the artist was a Roman (Brunn, *K. G.* i, p. 602). These may be the statues concerning the placing of which Atticus advised Pompeius, Cic. *Att.* iv, 9.

circa Pompeium: Suet. *Nero*, 46.

14. Canachum: xxxiv, 50, 75.

§ 42. 15. Sauram atque Batrachum: names of animals were familiar in Greece as proper names (cf. Ταῦρος, Σκύμνος, Τέττιξ, Μῦς, and the long lists in Fick, *Gr. Personennamen*, p. 314 ff.). Moreover, it was a usual Roman custom to introduce—on grave-reliefs—some allusive emblem to the name of the deceased: a boar for Titus Statilius Aper (*C. I. L.* vi, 1975; Helbig, *Class. Ant.* 423); a calf

for C. Tullius Vitulus (Fabretti, *Inscr.* p. 187). By an extension of this custom, the architects S. and B. might carve a frog and a lizard in lieu of signature among the ornaments of a column. The serious objection to the story is that Vitruvius (iii, 2, 5) names Hermodoros of Salamis as the architect of the temples. We must therefore conclude either that the story is aitiological—the ornaments of the columns giving rise to a story to which the custom of allusive emblems noted above lent plausibility— or that S. and B. were architects-adjoint, or perhaps merely donors of the said columns, whom at a later date legend turned into architects of the temples.

18. inscriptionem sperantes: this portion of the anecdote is, in any case, apocryphal.

certe etiamnum in columnarum spiris inscalptae nominum
43 eorum argumento lacerta atque rana.   in Iovis aede ex iis
pictura cultusque reliquus omnis femineis argumentis constat, erat enim facta Iunoni, sed, cum inferrentur signa,
permutasse geruli traduntur, et id religione custoditum 5
velut ipsis diis sedem ita partitis.   ergo et in Iunonis aede
cultus est qui Iovis esse debuit.   sunt et in parvolis marmoreis famam consecuti Myrmecides, cuius quadrigam cum
agitatore operuit alis musca, et Callicrates, cuius formicarum
pedes atque alia membra pervidere non est.   10
44   Haec sint dicta de marmoris scalptoribus summaque
claritate artificum.

2. **lacerta atque rana**: cf. the lizard and frog carved on the capital of one of the columns of San Lorenzo fuori le mura, transferred from some ancient building.

§ **43. in Iovis aede**: above, §§ 35, 40; according to Vell. Paterc. i, 11, who states that the temple of Jupiter was the first in Rome to be built of marble; the temples being *sine inscriptione*, legend naturally soon became active on the subject.

7. **parvolis marmoreis**: a confusion of Pliny's, who in vii, 85, mentions Myrm. and Kall. as workers in ivory.

8. **Myrmecides**: of Athens, according to Choiroboskos (quoted by Schol. to Dionysios Thrax = Overb.

Schriftquell. 2194), or of Miletos (Ailian, ποικ. ἱστ. i, 17).   He is generally represented as making the chariot conjointly with K.   Another marvel of their μικροτεχνία was a grain of sesame engraved with an elegiac distich (according to Plutarch, *adv. Stoicos*, xiv, 5, two lines of Homer).   There is no clue to the date of either artist.

quadrigam: in vii, 85 it is mentioned as of ivory, while Choiroboskos (above) says iron; and the grammarian Theodosios (*S. Q.* 2201), bronze; it looks suspiciously as if the *quadriga* were apocryphal.   Yet the execution of a microscopic chariot was quite within the power of the ancient goldsmith, cf. the tiny chariot led by

undeniably true that a lizard and a frog, typifying their names, are still to be seen carved on the bases of the columns. Of these 43 two temples the one dedicated to Jupiter contains only paintings and decorations relating to women, for as a matter of fact it was built for Juno; but the porters made a mistake, it is said, when they brought in the statues, and superstition consecrated the error, as though this division of their shrines were due to the gods themselves. In the same way the temple of Juno has the ornaments appropriate to Jupiter.

Miniature works in marble likewise secured renown for *Myrme-* *Miniature* *kides*, whose four-horse chariot and charioteer could be covered *works.* by the wings of a fly, and for *Kallikrates*, whose ants have feet and limbs too small to be distinguished by the human eye.

This closes what I have to say of workers in marble and of the 44 most famous sculptors.

a Nike, with Erotes at each side, belonging to the ear-pendant, *Ant. du Bosphore Cimmérien*, ed. Reinach, pl. xii, 5, 5ᵃ. Reinach (p. 4) justly sees in it a confirmation of the praises bestowed by the ancients on the μικρο-τεχνία of Theodoros, Myrmekides, and Kallikrates. Perhaps, therefore, we should look upon all these artists as practising the art of goldsmiths by the side of the greater art of statuary in bronze or marble (see note on xxxiv, 83).

9. **Callicrates**: of Lakedaimon (Ailian and Choiroboskos).

formicarum: the fashioning of ants and bees is attributed by Cicero (*Acad. prior.* ii, 38, 120) to Myrmekides—rightly, to judge from the man's name, which is doubtless a nickname won for him by his skill.

10. **pervidere non est**: cf. Varro (*Ling. Lat.* vii, i), who says of the works of Myrmekides that they could only be properly seen when placed on black silk. ,

APPENDIX.

I.

125   IDEM hic imperator edixit ne quis ipsum alius quam
Apelles pingeret, quam Pyrgoteles scalperet, quam Lysippus ex aere duceret, quae artes pluribus inclaruere exemplis.

126 Aristidis Thebani pictoris unam tabulam centum talentis
rex Attalus licitus est, octoginta emit duas Caesar dictator, 5
Mediam et Aiacem Timomachi, in templo Veneris Genetricis dicaturus.   Candaules rex Bularchi picturam Magnetum exiti, haud mediocris spati, pari rependit auro.   Rhodum
non incendit rex Demetrius expugnator cognominatus, ne
tabulam Protogenis cremaret a parte ea muri locatam. 10

127 Praxiteles marmore nobilitatus est Gnidiaque Venere praecipue vesano amore cuiusdam iuvenis insigni, sed et Nico-
medis aestimatione regis grandi Gnidiorum aere alieno
permutare eam conati.   Phidiae Iuppiter Olympius cotidie
testimonium perhibet, Mentori Capitolinus et Diana Ephesia, 15
quibus fuere consecrata artis eius vasa.

II.

198   Normam autem et libellam et tornum et clavem Theodorus Samius (*sc.* invenit).

VII, 125. 2. **Apelles**: xxxv, 8₅;
cf. Hor. *Ep.* II, 1, 239; *Edicto vetuit,*
ne quis se praeter Apellen | Pingeret,
aut alius Lysippo duceret aera | Fortis
Alexandri vultum simulantia . . .

    Pyrgoteles: xxxvii, 8.

    Lysippus: see note on xxxiv,
63.

    § **126.** 4. **Aristidis Thebani**:
xxxv, 98.

    centum talentis: after the sack

of Corinth this sum was offered by
Attalos, or rather by Philopoimen
on his behalf, for the 'Dionysos and
Ariadne' of Aristeides; upon which
Mummius, staggered at the value set
upon the picture, retained it (xxxv, 24
and note).

    6. **Mediam et Aiacem Timom.**:
xxxv, 26; 136.

    7. **Bularchi picturam**: xxxv, 55
and note.

I.

BOOK VII

THE emperor Alexander also issued an edict that none but 125
Apelles might paint his portrait, none but Pyrgoteles engrave it,
and none but Lysippos cast his statue in bronze. Several famous
likenesses of him exist of these three kinds.

King Attalos bought a single picture by Aristeides of Thebes 126
for a hundred talents [£21,000 circ.], and the dictator Caesar
gave eighty [£16,800 circ.] for two by Timomachos, a Medeia
and an Aias, which he intended to dedicate in the temple of
Venus the Mother. King Kandaules paid its weight in gold for
a picture of no small dimensions by Boularchos, representing the
destruction of the Magnetes. King Demetrios, surnamed the
Destroyer of Cities, refrained from setting fire to Rhodes, for fear
he should burn a painting by Protogenes which was near the
part of the city wall threatened. Praxiteles owes his fame to his 127
marble sculptures and to his Aphrodite at Knidos, which is best
known by the story of the youth who fell madly in love with it,
and also by the value King Nikomedes set on it when he offered
to take it in acquittal of the heavy state debt of the Knidians. Zeus
of Olympia daily bears testimony in honour of Pheidias, as for
Mentor do Jupiter of the Capitol and Artemis of Ephesos, to
whom the cups made by his hand have been consecrated.

I.

The rule and line, the lathe and lever, were invented by 198
Theodoros of Samos.

8. Rhodum non incendit:
xxxv, 104.

§ 127. 11. marmore nobilitatus:
xxxvi, 20; cf. xxxiv, 69 *Prax.*
quoque marmore felicior.

14. Iuppiter Olympius: xxxiv,
49, 54; xxxvi, 18.

15. Capitolinus . . . Ephesia:
xxxiii, 154 and note.

§ 198. 17. Theodorus Samius:
xxxiv, 83 and note.

III.

205   Picturam Aegypti et in Graecia Euchir Daedali cognatus
ut Aristoteli placet, ut Theophrasto Polygnotus Atheniensis
(*sc.* condere instituerunt).

IV.

LIB. XVI.

213   Maxime aeternam putant hebenum et cupressum cedrum-
que, claro de omnibus materiis iudicio in templo Ephesiae 5
Dianae, utpote cum tota Asia exstruente CXX annis per-
actum sit. convenit tectum eius esse e cedrinis trabibus.
de simulacro ipso deae ambigitur. ceteri ex hebeno esse
tradunt, Mucianus ter cos. ex his qui proxime viso scripsere vitigineum et numquam mutatum septies restituto 10

214   templo, hanc materiam elegisse Endoeon, etiam nomen
artificis nuncupans, quod equidem miror, cum antiquiorem
Minerva quoque, non modo Libero patre, vetustatem ei
tribuat.

V.

LIB. XXI.

4.   Arborum enim ramis coronari in sacris certaminibus 15
mos erat primum. postea variare coeptum mixtura versi-
colori florum, quae invicem odores coloresque accenderet,
Sicyone ingenio Pausiae pictoris atque Glycerae coronariae
dilectae admodum illi, cum opera eius pictura imitaretur,
illa provocans variaret, essetque certamen artis ac naturae, 20
quales etiam nunc exstant artificis illius tabellae atque in
primis appellata stephaneplocos qua pinxit ipsam.

11. Endoeon] *Sillig*; eandem con *codices.*

§ 205. 1. Aegypti: xxxv, 15.

Euchir: in xxxv, 152 he figures as
one of the Corinthian modellers who
accompanied Damaratos to Italy; in
Paus. vi, 4, 4 as the master of Klearchos
of Rhegion, the master of Pythagoras.
At least it seems probable that it is
one and the same personage to whom
different parts are assigned in various
apocryphal traditions concerning the
beginnings of the several arts, cf.
Robert *Arch. März.* p. 131, note 2.
For an artist of the name in late
historic times see xxxiv, 91.

2. Theophrasto: on the misunderstanding involved here see
Introd. p. xxx.

XVI, 213. 5. templo Ephesiae:
below, xxxvi, 95.

9. Mucianus: Introd. p. lxxxv ff.

11. Endoeon: the name was restored by Sillig from Athenag. Πρεσβ.
17 (below, App. xi) for the corrupt
eandem con of the MSS.   Besides
Ephesos, Endoios also worked in
Asia Minor at Ernthrai (Paus. vii,
5, 9); further, in one of his two inscriptions (*I. G. B.* 8, stele of

III.

Painting was first invented by the Egyptians, and introduced 205 into Greece, according to Aristotle, by *Eucheir,* a kinsman of Daidalos, but according to Theophrastos by *Polygnotos* of Athens.

IV.

Book XVI

Ebony, cypress, and cedar wood are thought to be the most 213 durable, every wood having been signally tested in the temple of Artemis at Ephesos, which all Asia joined to build, and which was completed in a hundred and twenty years. While all agree that the roof is made of cedar beams, we have varying accounts of the image of the goddess. All other writers say that it is of ebony, but among those who have written after close inspection, Mucianus, who was thrice consul, declares that it is of vine-wood, and has remained unchanged though the temple has been restored seven times. The material, he says, was the choice of *Endoios,* the 214 maker, whose name he gives somewhat to my surprise, since he holds the image to be not only earlier than the Dionysos, but also than the Athene.

V.

Book XXI

Branches of trees were originally used for crowns in the sacred 4 games. Later on the fashion of intertwining flowers of different hues, to strengthen each other's scent and colour, was invented and introduced at Sikyon by the painter Pausias and Glykera, a wreath-seller whom he loved. He imitated her wares in painting, and she varied them to challenge him, thus making art and nature vie together. Pictures by Pausias in this style are still extant, the most noteworthy being the στεφανηπλόκος, or wreath-binder, a portrait of Glykera herself.

Lampito) he uses the Ionic dialect, while in the other ('Αρχ. Δελτ., 1888, p. 208) he uses the Ionic alphabet. It is probable, therefore, that he was an Ionian, whom the later art-historians turned into an Athenian, as they did Alkamenes and others (see *Add. to Introd.* p. 232). From their epigraphy the inscriptions must be dated between B.C. 532 and 508; for the

latest discussion of Endoios and his date see Lechat in *Rev. des Études Grecques,* v, 1892, p. 385 ff. The most famous work of Endoios was the seated Athena (below, App. xi; Paus. i, 26, 4) dedicated on the Athenian Akropolis by one Kallias.

XXI. 4. 18. Pausiae ... Glycerae: xxxv, 125 and note.

VI.

90   Lemnius (*sc.* labyrinthus) similis illi columnis tantum
CL memorabilior fuit, quarum in officina turbines ita librati
pependerunt ut puero circumagente tornarentur. architecti
fecere Zmilis et Rhoecus et Theodorus indigenae.

VII.

95   Graecae magnificentiae vera admiratio exstat templum 5
Ephesiae Dianae CXX annis factum a tota Asia. in solo
id palustri fecere, ne terrae motus sentiret aut hiatus timeret,
rursus ne in lubrico atque instabili fundamenta tantae molis
locarentur, calcatis ea substravere carbonibus, dein velleribus
lanae. universo templo longitudo est CCCCXXV pedum, 10
latitudo CCXXV, columnae CXXVII a singulis regibus
factae LX pedum altitudine, ex is XXXVI caelatae, una
a Scopa. operi praefuit Chersiphron architectus.

VIII.

177   Elide aedis est Minervae in qua frater Phidiae Panaenus
tectorium induxit lacte et croco subactum, ut ferunt, ideo, 15
si teratur hodie in eo saliva pollice, odorem croci sapo-
remque reddit.

IX.

184   Pavimenta originem apud Graecos habent elaborata ante
picturae ratione donec lithostrota expulere eam. celeberri-

12. una a] *Bamb.*; una *Ricc., Voss.*

XXXVI, 90. 1. **Lemnius** (lab.):
by error for the Samian labyrinth,
see note on xxxiv, 83.

§ **95. 5. templum Ephesiae Dianae**: the description seems borrowed
from Mucianus, Introd. p. lxxxviii;
cf. xvi, 213, but the account is very
confused, referring partly to the first
temple (begun close of seventh century
B.Č. and burnt 356 B.C. by Herostratos,
Strabo, xiv, p. 640) and partially to
the second, upon which Skopas would
be employed. The reconstruction of
the Ephesian Artemision is beset with

almost as grave difficulties as that of
the Mausoleion, but see the interesting
attempt lately made by A. S. Murray,
*Journal of the R. Inst. of Brit.
Archit.*, 1895, p. 41 ff. The ancient
literature is fully given and discussed
by Brunn, *K. G.* ii, p. 345 ff.

8. **ne in lubrico . . . lanae**: this
was done by the advice of Theodoros,
Diogenes Laertios, ii, 8, 103.

10. **universo templo**: i.e. measuring the length along the lowermost
step of the platform, see A. S. Murray,
op. cit. p. 44.

VI.

The labyrinth of Lemnos is like that of Krete, but is distinguished by its columns, a hundred and fifty in number. Their drums were raised from the ground in the stone-yard and balanced on a pivot, so that a boy could set them spinning round and smooth their surface. The architects who built it were *Smilis*, *Rhoikos*, and *Theodoros*, natives of the island.

VII.

Our genuine admiration for the magnificence of the Greek genius 95 is roused by the temple of Artemis at Ephesos, which was built in a hundred and twenty years by the exertions of all Asia. The temple was placed on a marshy site, that it might not suffer from earthquakes, or be in danger from the cracking of the ground, while on the other hand, to prevent any insecurity or shifting in the foundation on which the massive weight of the temple was to rest, a substratum was laid of pounded charcoal covered with fleeces. The full length of the temple is 425 feet, and its breadth 225; there are 127 columns 60 feet high, each made by a different king. Of these 36 are carved, one of them by *Skopas*. The chief architect was *Chersiphron*.

VIII.

There is at Elis a temple of Athena in which we are told that 177 Panainos, the brother of Pheidias, mixed the plaster on the walls with saffron and milk; hence to this very day if the finger is wetted in the mouth and rubbed on the wall, it smells and tastes of saffron.

IX.

The Greeks were the first to introduce paved floors, which they 184 decorated with painting until mosaic took its place. The most

12. **una a Scopa** : this is the reading of Cod. Bamb.; it was kindly verified for this edition by Mr. Fischer. Chronologically it is quite possible that Skopas worked for the second Ephesian temple, see note on xxxvi, 30.

13. **Chersiphron** : the first architect of the first temple, vii, 125.

§ 177. 14. **Elide** : xxxv, 54, both Panainos and Kolotes had been employed on the statue of Athena, and it is evident from the present passage that Panainos must have decorated the temple with wall-paintings.

§ 184. 19. **lithostrota** : the earliest instance of a mosaic floor in Greece

mus fuit in hoc genere Sosus qui Pergami stravit quem
vocant asaroton oecon, quoniam purgamenta cenae in pavi-
mentis quaeque everri solent velut relicta fecerat parvis
e tessellis tinctisque in varios colores. mirabilis ibi columba
bibens et aquam umbra capitis infuscans. apricantur aliae 5
scabentes sese in canthari labro.

LIB.
XXXVII.
8

X.

Polycratis gemma quae demonstratur intacta inlibataque
est. Ismeniae aetate multos post annos apparet scalpi
etiam smaragdos solitos. confirmat hanc eandem opinionem
edictum Alexandri magni quo vetuit in hac gemma ab alio 10
se scalpi quam ab Pyrgotele non dubie clarissimo artis eius.
Post eum Apollonides et Cronius in gloria fuere quique
divi Augusti imaginem simillime expressit, qua postea
principes signant, Dioscurides.

XI.

Athena-
goras,
Πρεσβεία

Αἱ δ' εἰκόνες μέχρι μήπω πλαστικὴ καὶ γραφικὴ καὶ ἀνδριαν- 15
τοποιητικὴ ἦσαν, οὐδὲ ἐνομίζοντο· Σαυρίου δὲ τοῦ Σαμίου καὶ

is that of the *Pronaos* of the temple of Zeus at Olympia, *Olympia, Baudenkm.* ii, pl. cv (cf. *ib.* i, pl. ix). Mosaic came into general use in the time of the Diadochoi; cf. Athen. xii, 542 d, *ib.* v, 206 d.

.2. asaroton oecon: cf. the mosaic in the Lateran (Helbig, *Class. Ant.* 694) strewn with fragments of food, and the mosaic (Brit. Mus.) representing strewn leaves.—Statius *Silv.* i, 3, 56.

4. columba bibens: a similar subject in the famous mosaic of the Capitol, found in the villa of Hadrian; Helbig, *Class. Ant.* 450; cf. the mosaics in Naples, *Mo.* 9992 and 11428r. From the words *mirabilis ibi* it appears that the dove drinking was part of the larger composition representing the unswept floor. Doves on the edge of a vase are a subject of frequent occurrence on

coins, cf. Drexler, *Zeitschrift f. Numismatik*, vol. xix.

XXXVII, 8. 7. Polycratis gemma: according to Pliny in § 4 of this book it was a sardonyx, and was preserved at Rome, in the Temple of Concord, set in a horn, the offering of Augusta (sc. Livia).

intacta inlibataque: on the other hand, Strabo, xiv, p. 638, speaks of its being splendidly graved, and Herodotos (iii, 41) of its being a seal of emerald (i. e. emerald-prase, see Brunn, *K. G.* ii, p. 468; Furtwängler, *Jahrb.* iii, 1888, p. 194) mounted in a gold ring σφρηγὶς χρυσόδετος; it was reputed the work of Theodoros, cf. Paus. viii, 14, ι, and see note above on xxxiv, 83.

8. Ismeniae: Plut. *Per.* i; Apuleius, *de Deo Socr.* 21; Boethius, *Inst. Mus.* I, 1 (ed. Friedlein, p. 185,

celebrated worker in mosaic is †*Sosos*, who laid the floors of a house at Pergamon, known as the ἀσάρωτος οἶκος, or Unswept House, because he represented in small bits of many-coloured mosaic the scraps from the table and everything that is usually swept away, as if they had been left lying on the floor. Among these mosaics is a marvellous dove drinking and casting the shadow of its head on the water. Other doves are pluming their feathers in the sun on the lip of a goblet.

X.

The gem shown as that of Polykrates is uncut and untouched. 8 We find that at a much later date, in the days of Ismenias, even emeralds were engraved. An edict of Alexander the Great confirms this: he forbade any one but *Pyrgoteles*, who was beyond doubt the greatest master of the art, to engrave his likeness on these gems. After Pyrgoteles, †*Apollonides* and †*Kronios* won fame, and *Dioskourides* who engraved that perfect likeness of the god Augustus which later emperors have used as their seal. 9

XI.

Images of the gods were not had in honour at all before the arts of modelling, of painting and of statuary were introduced,

20). Dionysodoros is known only from Pliny.

9. smaragdos : emerald, however, does not appear to have come into use till Hellenistic times, and then only unimportant gems were cut in this stone.

11. ab Pyrgotele : vii, 125 (App. I) ; cf. Apuleius, *Florida*, i, p. 7 (ed. Krueger, 1865) ; he is unknown outside literature.

13. Augusti imaginem : a full list (needing revision however) of portraits of Augustus on gems is given by Bernoulli, *Röm. Iconographie*, ii. p. 46. None can be traced back to Dioskourides.

14. Dioscurides : of the numerous extant gems bearing the signature of D. six only are recognized as genuine by Furtwängler, *Jahrb*. iii, 1888, pp. 218-224 ; *ib*. pl. iii, 1 ; pl. viii, 22, 23, 24, 25, 26. To these signed instances should be added, according to R. von Schneider (*Album der Wiener Sammlungen*, p. 16, text to plate 41), the great Vienna cameo representing the family of Augustus. —Three sons of Dioskourides,— Hierophilos, Hyllos, and Eutyches, —are known from their signatures on gems to have been gem-engravers ; see Furtwängler, *op. cit.* p. 304 ff.

15. Αἱ δ' εἰκόνες . . . : the rhetoric of Athenagoras seems evolved out of the same curious notion appearing in Plin. xxxiv, 9, 16, that art progressed from lesser objects to statues of the gods.

16. Σαυρίου . . . Σαμίου : we again

περὶ Χρισ-
τιανῶν, 17
(ed.
Schwartz,
p. 18).

Κράτωνος τοῦ Σικυωνίου καὶ Κλεάνθους τοῦ Κορινθίου καὶ κόρης
Κορινθίας γενομένων καὶ σκιαγραφίας μὲν εὑρεθείσης ὑπὸ Σαυρίου
ἵππου ἐν ἡλίῳ περιγράψαντος, γραφικῆς δὲ ὑπὸ Κράτωνος ἐν πίνακι
λελευκωμένῳ σκιὰς ἀνδρὸς καὶ γυναικὸς ἐναλείψαντος, ἀπὸ δὲ τῆς
κόρης κοροπλαθικῆς [εὑρέθη] (ἐρωτικῶς γάρ τινος ἔχουσα περι- 5
έγραψεν αὐτοῦ κοιμωμένου ἐν τοίχῳ τὴν σκιάν, εἶθ᾽ ὁ πατὴρ ἡσθεὶς
ἀπαραλλάκτῳ οὔσῃ τῇ ὁμοιότητι (κέραμον δὲ εἰργάζετο) ἀναγλύψας
τὴν περιγραφὴν πηλῷ προσανεπλήρωσεν· ὁ τύπος ἔτι καὶ νῦν ἐν
Κορίνθῳ σῴζεται), τούτοις δὲ ἐπιγενόμενοι Δαίδαλος Θεόδωρος
Σμῖλις ἀνδριαντοποιητικὴν καὶ πλαστικὴν προσεξεῦρον. ὁ μὲν δὴ 10
χρόνος ὀλίγος τοσοῦτος ταῖς εἰκόσι καὶ τῇ περὶ τὰ εἴδωλα πραγ-
ματείᾳ, ὡς ἔχειν εἰπεῖν τὸν ἑκάστου τεχνίτην θεοῦ. τὸ μὲν γὰρ
ἐν Ἐφέσῳ τῆς Ἀρτέμιδος καὶ τὸ τῆς Ἀθηνᾶς (μᾶλλον δὲ Ἀθηλᾶς·
ἀθήλη γὰρ ὡς οἱ μυστικώτερον οὕτω γὰρ) τὸ ἀπὸ τῆς ἐλαίας τὸ
παλαιὸν καὶ τὴν Καθημένην Ἔνδοιος εἰργάσατο μαθητὴς Δαιδάλου, 15
ὁ δὲ Πύθιος ἔργον Θεοδώρου καὶ Τηλεκλέους καὶ ὁ Δήλιος καὶ
ἡ Ἄρτεμις Τεκταίου καὶ Ἀγγελίωνος τέχνη, ἡ δὲ ἐν Σάμῳ Ἥρα
καὶ ἐν Ἄργει Σμίλιδος χεῖρες καὶ Φειδίου τὰ λοιπὰ εἴδωλα ἡ
Ἀφροδίτη ⟨ἡ⟩ ἐν Κνίδῳ ἑτέρα Πραξιτέλους τέχνη, ὁ ἐν Ἐπιδαύρῳ
Ἀσκληπιὸς ἔργον Φειδίου. συνελόντα φάναι, οὐδὲν αὐτῶν δια- 20
πέφευγεν τὸ μὴ ὑπ᾽ ἀνθρώπου γεγονέναι. εἰ τοίνυν θεοί, τί οὐκ
ἦσαν ἐξ ἀρχῆς; τί δέ εἰσιν νεώτεροι τῶν πεποιηκότων; τί δὲ
ἔδει αὐτοῖς πρὸς τὸ γενέσθαι ἀνθρώπων καὶ τέχνης; γῆ ταῦτα καὶ
λίθοι καὶ ὕλη καὶ περίεργος τέχνη.

catch here the echo of some art-writer who had contrasted the claims of island and mainland schools ; cf. Introd. pp. xxiii, xxvi.

1. **Κλεάνθους** : Plin. xxxv, 15.

κόρης Κορινθίας : Plin. xxxv, 151.

6. **αὐτοῦ κοιμωμένου** : while in Pliny the lover is represented as going away.

8. **ἔτι καὶ νῦν ἐν Κορίνθῳ** : *donec Mummius Corinthum everterit*, Plin. xxxv, 151; hence it appears that

Athenagoras is quoting—though not necessarily at first hand—from an author older than B.C. 146.

14. **τὸ ἀπὸ τῆς ἐλαίας** : Paus. i, 26, 6. Athenagoras is the only writer who attributes the statue to Endoios.

15. **Ἔνδοιος** : above note on xvi, 214 = App. IV.

μαθητὴς Δαιδάλου : Paus. i, 26, 4.

16. **ὁ δὲ Πύθιος** : Diodoros, i, 98.

ὁ Δήλιος : Paus. ii, 32, 5; cf. Plut. *de Mus.* 14 (= Bernardakis, vi,

but are later than the days of †*Saurias* of Samos, †*Kraton* of Sikyon, *Kleanthes* of Corinth, and a maiden, also of Corinth. Linear drawing was discovered by Saurias, who traced the outline of the shadow cast by a horse in the sun, and painting by Kraton, who painted on a whitened tablet the shadows of a man and woman. The maiden invented the art of modelling figures in relief. She was in love with a youth, and while he lay asleep she sketched the outline of his shadow on the wall. Delighted with the perfection of the likeness, her father, who was a potter, cut out the shape and filled in the outline with clay ; the figure is still preserved at Corinth. After these came *Daidalos, Theodoros,* and *Smilis,* who introduced the arts of statuary and modelling. In fact so short a time has passed since statues and the making of images were introduced, that we can name the maker of each several god. *Endoios,* the pupil of Daidalos, made the statue of Artemis at Ephesos, the old olive-wood image of Athena (or rather of Athela [the unsuckled], for so those better acquainted with her mysteries call her), and the seated image ; the Pythian Apollo is the work of *Theodoros* and *Telekles ;* the Apollo and Artemis at Delos are by *Tektaios* and *Angelion ;* the statues of Hera in Samos and in Argos are by the hand of Smilis, and the other statues are by *Pheidias ; Praxiteles* made the second Aphrodite at Knidos, and Pheidias the Asklepios at Epidauros. In a word, there is not one of them but is the work of man's hands. If, then, these are gods, why were they not from the beginning, and why are they younger than those who made them ? What need had they of men and human art to bring them into being ? They are but earth and stones and wood and cunning art.

p. 500) ; for the type see P. Gardner and Imhoof-Blumer, *Num. Comm.* CC xi–xiv.

17. ἡ Ἄρτεμις : known only from Athenagoras.

ἡ δὲ ἐν Σ. Ἥρα : Paus. vii, 4, 4 ; for the type cf. P. Gardner, *Samos and Samian Coins,* pp. 19, 75 ff, pl. v, 1–9. Smilis was himself a Samian,

above notes on App. VI. and on xxxiv, 83.

18. ἐν Ἄργει : this Argive Hera by Smilis is known only from Athenagoras ; but see Brunn, *K. G.* i, p. 27.

19. Ἀφροδ. ἐν Κνίδῳ : Plin. xxxvi, 20.

20. Ἀσκληπιός : see Introd. p. liv, note 1.

ADDENDA

I. INTRODUCTION

Page xliii, note 2. F. Münzer provides me with a final proof of the indebtedness of Antigonos to Duris for the story of the Nemesis; he points out (in a private letter) the striking similarity between the story told in Pliny, of the vengeance taken by Agorakritos, and the following fragment from Duris in Plutarch (*Lysander* 18 = Fr. 65, Müller): Ἀντιμάχου δὲ τοῦ Κολοφωνίου καὶ Νικηράτου τινὸς Ἡρακλεώτου ποιήμασι Λυσάνδρεια διαγωνισαμένων ἐπ᾽ αὐτοῦ (sc. Lysander) τὸν Νικήρατον ἐστεφάνωσεν, ὁ δὲ Ἀντίμαχος ἀχθεσθεὶς ἠφάνισε τὸ ποίημα. Πλάτων δὲ νέος ὢν τότε καὶ θαυμάζων τὸν Ἀντίμαχον ἐπὶ τῇ ποιητικῇ, βαρέως φέροντα τὴν ἧτταν ἀνελάμβανε καὶ παρεμυθεῖτο, τοῖς ἀγνοοῦσι. . . . 'There were two other poets, Antimachus Colophonian, and Niceratus born at Heraclea, which did both wryte verses to honour him (Lysander), striving whether of them should do best. Lysander *judged the crown and victory unto Niceratus: wherewith Antimachus was so angry that he rased out all that he had written of him.* But Plato, who at that time was young, and loved Antimachus because he was an excellent poet, did comforte him, and tolde him that ignoraunce . . .' (North, ed. Wyndham, vol. iii, p. 247).

P. li. Still another story of a self-taught artist, preserved this time not in Pliny but in Pausanias, has been pointed out to me by F. Münzer, whose communication on the subject I translate verbally: 'The account of Pausanias (v, 20, 2) concerning Kolotes may be classed with the stories from Duris noted *Hermes*, xxx, p. 532 f.: εἶναι δέ φασιν ἐξ Ἡρακλείας τὸν Κολώτην. οἱ δὲ πολυπραγμονήσαντες σπουδῇ τὰ ἐς τοὺς πλάστας Πάριον ἀποφαίνουσιν ὄντα αὐτόν, μαθητὴν Πασιτέλους, Πασιτέλην δὲ αὐτοδιδαχθῆναι (Buttmann's reading for the αὐτὸν διδαχθῆναι of the MSS., which it is impossible to retain except by assuming a lacuna). Thus the same is recounted here of Pasiteles as of the several men noted *loc. cit.* Like the Seilanion, Protogenes, Erigonos, and Lysippos of Duris, Pasiteles is represented as having had no teacher; like Seilanion, Erigonos and Pythagoras of Rhegion, he had one pupil. Pasiteles is as completely unknown as these three pupils, and as the master of the philosopher Demokritos invented by Duris (fr. 56). I accordingly believe that the view combated by Pausanias must be traced back to Duris. It is uncertain whether Antigonos had already combated it, or whether he combined it with the current tradition, inasmuch as he transferred Kolotes from the Parian to the Athenian school. To alter the birthplace of Kolotes from Herakleia to Paros, whereby he was made into the countryman of his fellow-pupil Agorakritos, was a slight matter in the eyes of Duris, for he had turned Kleoboulos of Lindos into a Karian, and proclaimed the foreign origin of other of the seven sages (Müller, *F. H. G.* ii, p. 482, fr. 53–55); probably also he had transferred the scene of an anecdote from Kroton to Agrigentum (Plin. xxxiv, 64, cf. *Hermes*, xxx, p. 537, n. 1).' In the light of the preceding note of Münzer's, it has become plain to me that Duris must be held responsible for the tradition that represented Alkamenes as a native of Lemnos (Λήμνιος; Souidas, *s. v.* ᾽Αλκαμένης ; νησιώτης, Tzetzes, *Chil.* viii, 340), whereas Antigonos turned him into an Athenian (Plin. xxxvi, 16). It is natural to find Duris— a Samian—repeatedly championing the claims of the Greeks of Asia Minor and the islands to artistic pre-eminence. Nor must we forget that, careless of accuracy though he was, he doubtless had at his command detailed information which was no longer within reach of the later art-historians, who were content to group artists about the chief art-centres. Thus Endoios, who was probably really an Ionian (note on Appendix XI), is represented in Pausanias simply as ᾽Αθηναῖος. One great error of modern archaeologists is to attempt to harmonize the variant traditions instead of tracing them to their different sources, which will generally be discovered in periods wide apart.

P. li, note 6 : *The masters of Pheidias.* I am pleased to find what I wrote six months back concerning the masters of Pheidias confirmed by the comments of Michaelis (*Deutsche Litteraturzeitung*, 1896, no. 25, p. 788 ; rev. of E. Gardner's *Handbook of Greek Sculpture*) on the untrustworthiness of the Hagelaïdas tradition : the same scholion on Aristoph. *Frogs,* 504, which names Hagelaïdas as the master of Pheidias, also contains a mistake concerning the Herakles Alexikakos of Hagelaïdas ; this same untrustworthy scholion is the source for the information of Tzetzes and Souidas (above, p. li, note 3). Michaelis accordingly disputes the strange contention of E. Gardner (*Handbook*, p. 194 ; cf. pp. 248, 265) that ' the relation of Pheidias to Ageladas is the best established by literary evidence,' ' *vielmehr ist Phidias' Schülerverhältniss zu dem Attiker Hegias einmal, aber gut, das zu Hageladas viermal, aber schlecht bezeugt.*' To the unsatisfactory character of E. Gardner's proposed emendation of Dio Chrys. Or. lv. 1 (*Class. Rev.* viii, 1894, p. 70) I have drawn attention elsewhere (*ib.* p. 171, note 1).

P. lxi. The story of the angry artist and the sponge is told by Dio Chrysostom (Or. lxiii, 4 = *Schriftqu.* 1889) of Apelles and his picture of a war horse. I find that Mr. A. S. Murray (*Handbook*, p. 384) has already pointed out, in connexion with Apelles, that the story seemed the anecdotic illustration of the line of Agathon.

P. lxii. From a remark in note 1 on p. 537 of his article in the *Hermes*, it would seem that Münzer also inclines to attribute the story of Zeuxis and the five maidens to Duris. But Münzer makes Duris responsible for the transference of the scene of the story from Kroton to Agrigentum (cf. above, Add. to p. li). Possibly, therefore, we may some day be able to drive the story home to a source whence Duris himself quoted—or misquoted.

P. lxxxv. *Fabius Vestalis* : it is worth noting that, since in each of the three notices his name appears last on the Plinian lists, he was probably only a supplementary author (comm. by Dr. Münzer).

BOOK XXXIII

P. 6, 2. *crustarius* : there are superb examples of ἐμβλήματα among the cups of both the treasures of Hildescheim (Berlin) and of Bosco Reade (Louvre); cf. Winter, *Arch. Anz.* 1896, p. 93. For the most part the *emblema* appears in the shape of a bust in full relief, soldered to a silver plate.

BOOK XXXIV

P. 6, 18. *proscriptum ab Antonio* : cf. Gardthausen, *Augustus*, i, p. 136.

P. 8, 19. *tricliniorum pedibus fulcrisque* : that the *fulcrum* was 'the frame-work on which the pillows of a couch or the cushions of a chair were placed' has been maintained and fully proved by W. C. F. Anderson, *Class. Rev.* iii, 1889, p. 322 ff.

P. 14, 7. *ubi omnium . . . iconicas vocant* : the latest discussion of this passage is by Dittenberger and Purgold, *Olympische Inschriften*, col. 236, 295 f, where it is pointed out that in the inscr. recording the Olympic victory of Xenombrotos of Kos (*ib.* no. 170 ; Paus. vi, 14, 12) the τοῖος ὁποῖον ὁρᾷς of the fifth line proves that the statue was iconic; yet the epigram and the silence of Pausanias both show that X. was no τρισολυμπιονίκης.

P. 16, 13. *elephanti* : on triumphal chariots drawn by elephants see, however, Gardthausen, *Augustus*, ii, p. 257.

P. 23, 13. *Statues of Demetrios of Phaleron* : the lines from Varro run—

  Hic Demetrius aeneas tot aptust
  Quot luces habet annus absolutus

(for the first line, as emended by Scaliger, Bormann, *Arch. Ep. Mitth.* xvii, 1894, p. 233 f., proposes *hic Demetrius est [tot aera nac]tus*). Wachsmuth (*loc. cit.*) is probably right in tracing back the legend of the number of statues put up to Demetrios to an epigram—'as many statues as there are days in the year'—a playful turn which was afterwards accepted as serious fact, giving rise not only to the statements in Varro and Pliny, but to the improved version in Diogenes that all these statues were erected to Demetrios in a period less than a year: εἰκόνων ἠξιώθη χαλκῶν ἑξήκοντα πρὸς ταῖς τριακοσίαις, ὧν αἱ πλείους ἐφ' ἵππων ἦσαν καὶ ἁρμάτων καὶ συνωρίδων, συντελεσθεῖσαι ἐν οὐδὲ τριακοσίαις ἡμέραις.—Cornelius Nepos, *Miltiades*, vi, and Plutarch, *Praec. reip. gerend.* 27 E (Bernardakis, v, p. 116), mention 300 as the number of the statues, a round sum, more or less representing the truth. The 1,500 statues mentioned by Dio Chrysostom (xxxvii, 41) are mere foolish rhetoric. The distich from Varro was presumably inscribed, in his *Imagines* (cf. Plin. xxxv, 11 ; A. Gellius, *Noct. Att.* iii, 10, 1 ; 11, 7), beneath a portrait of Demetrios ; see Bormann, *loc. cit.*

P. 28, 18. *Rhodi etiamnum* : the passage from Jerome is referred by Mommsen (*Ueber den Chronographen, &c.*, p. 692) to a Roman history 'of the period of Caesar and Augustus,' by Reifferscheid (p. 360, n. 224) to Suetonius ; cf· Gardthausen, *Augustus*, i, p. 67.

P. 32, 25. *Arvernis* : the temple is presumably the one described by Gregory of Tours (i, 30), of which the foundations were discovered in 1874, see Mowat, *Rev. Arch.* 1875, p. 31 ff., where the five inscriptions *Mercurio Arverno* are discussed. As to the type of Zenodoros' Mercury, Mowat, *Bull. Monum.* 1875, p. 557 ff., conjectures that we possess an echo of it in the seated Mercury on an altar from Horn in Holland (inscr. Bramhach, *C. I. R.* 2029, p. xxvii) ; cf. S. Reinach, *Bronzes Figurés*, p. 80, no. 68.

P. 34, 5. *in officina* : perhaps it is scarcely correct to refer this to the workshop or studio of Zenodoros. From the size of the colossus it is probable that a special workshop was erected for the artist.

P. 34, 21. *sphingem* : Münzer points out to me that Quinct. vi, 3, 98, accords with Pliny in giving bronze as the material of the sphinx. Now 'in this

chapter of Quinctilian several *bons mots* of the personages of the Ciceronian age
and of Cicero himself have been shown by Wissowa (*Hermes*, xvi, p. 499 ff.)
to be borrowed from the book of Domitius Marsus, *de urbanitate*, which
Quinctilian frequently quotes in this chapter.' Therefore we may assume the
same D. Marsus, who appears in the Index to Bk. xxxiv, to have been Pliny's
authority for the story of Hortensius and the sphinx. (This observation of
Münzer's will shortly be published in his *Beiträge zur Quellenkritik der
Naturgeschichte des Plinius*.)

P. 36, 11. *Hagelades*: E. Gardner, *Handbook of Greek Sculpture*, p. 192,
proposes to read the 'Αγελαίδα of *I. G. B.* 30 (bathron of Praxiteles) as
ὁ 'Αγελαίδα, and, accordingly, takes the name of the Argive master to have
been Agelaïdas. The form Hagelaidas (Greek Hagelaïdas), which we print
in the translation, is also retained by Dittenberger and Purgold, *Inschr. von
Olympia* 631, where see literature.

P. 38, 1. *Argium*: owing to its position a proper name, and not, as often
surmised, the ethnic of Asopodoros, in which case it would have been placed
after the name it qualified, cf. *Gorgias Lacon* (§ 49), *Demean Clitorium*; Dittenberger and Purgold in *Inschriften von Olympia*, col. 647, where see literature.

P. 38, 1. *Asopodorum*: for the inscription on the bathron of Praxiteles, see
now *Inschr. von Olympia*, 630, 631, where Dittenberger and Purgold rightly
reject Röhl's proposed identification of the Plinian *Asopodorus* and *Athenodorus*
with the artists of the bathron.

P. 38, 2. *Clitorium*: Paus. x, 9, 7, οὗτοι (sc. 'Αθην. καὶ 'Δαμέας) δὲ 'Αρκάδες
εἰσὶν ἐκ Κλείτορος.

P. 38, 5. *Leochares*: I refer the passage concerning the statue of Isokrates by
Leochares in *Vit. X Orat.* 27 to Heliodoros on the authority of Keil, *Hermes*,
xxx, 1895, p. 202.

P 40, 1. *Date of Seilanion*: Furtwängler, *Statuenkopien im Alterthum*,
p. 562, shows, however, that the connexion attempted by Delamarre between
C. I. G. S. 414, and *C. I. G. S.* 4253, 4254, is unfounded: D.'s conjecture that
the latter refers to the revival of the games in 329-8 B.C. is unproven; 4253
refers not to the games but generally to the *Hieron* of Amphiaraos and the
Penteteris, while 4254 is a decree in honour of the officials in charge of the games.
There is nothing in either inscription implying a revival. Thus the only evidence
we are left with for the date of 414 is derived from the epigraphy ; according to
Dittenberger the upper limit is 366 B.C. Now if we accept the extant portraits of Plato as copies after an original by Seilanion (Helbig, *Class. Ant.*
265, p. 183 f.), and adopt Furtwängler's identification of the Theseus at Ince-
Blundell Hall (*Statuenkopien*, pl. ii, iii, *ib.* p. 559 ff.) as a copy of the Theseus
of Seilanion (Plut. *Thes.* iv), there would be artistic grounds for placing the
artist as far back in the fourth century as the epigraphy of *C. I. G. S.* 414
allows.—No great weight can be attached to the date assigned to Seilanion in
Pliny's chronology, the mention of Seilanion having been loosely tacked on by
a later hand to the old Xenokratic chronology, Introd. p. xlix, note 2.

P. 40, 2. *Zeuxiaden*: the identity of the portraitist of Hypereides with the
pupil of Seilanion is, however, doubtful, cf. Introd. p. liii.

P. 42, 4. *formae cognomen* = lit. 'the surname of beauty'; for *forma* = beauty,
cf. below § 78, *cliduchon eximia forma* ; xxxv, 86, *ob admirat. formae* ; O. Jahn,
Arch. Zeit. 1847, p. 63 (cf. Brunn, *K. G.* p. 182), believe the Greek epithet
of the goddess to have been Μορφώ, which occurs as an epithet of Aphrodite at
Sparta (Paus. iii, 15, 8). Other conjectures are καλλίμορφος and καλλίστη.

P. 42, 5. *cliduchum* : it is Pliny's rule to mention the names of gods, while he almost invariably omits to name mortals ; their statues are referred to by their motive, e.g. *diadumenus, discobolus, apoxyomenus, mala ferens nudus, &c.* Hence it is that the *cliduchus* cannot be regarded as the Athena Promachos (so Urlichs in *Chrestom.*), nor the *astragalizontes* of Polykleitos as the Dioscuri (so Furtwängler in *Masterpieces*, p. 292, note 1), nor the *mala ferens nudus* as a statue of Herakles.

P. 42, 10. *diadumenum* : another fairly complete copy of this statue, recently found in Delos (*B. C. H.* 1895, pl. viii), is—to judge from the publication—of poor workmanship, inferior to the Madrid copy; cf. Furtwängler, *Statuenkopien im Alterthum*, p. 548.

P. 44, 1. *telo incessentem* : I ought to have stated more fully that Furtwängler (*loc. cit.*) shows the impossibility—on grammatical and other grounds—of the reading *talo*, which is supported by Benndorf. The latter supposes the statue referred to, to have stood on an astragal basis—a forerunner to the Kairos of Lysippos (*Schriftqu.* 1463-1467), further, to have been described by some Greek writer as γυμνὸς ἀστραγάλῳ ἐπικείμενος where Pliny then translated the ἐπικείμενος in its alternative sense of 'advancing' or 'pursuing.' But in that case *talo incessens* could only mean *advancing towards* or *pursuing a knucklebone*, which is nonsense. *Talo* can only be the instrument, the weapon *with which* the man is attacking, so that everything combines to commend Benndorf's own earlier conjecture *telo*.

P. 44, 3. *in Titi imperatoris atrio* : the reading of *Cod. Bamb.* seems to be: in titi imperis atrio duo (see our facsimile); incliti in patrio duo *Bamb. e corr.*

P. 44, 6. *Portrait of Artemon* : in *Class. Rev.* 1894, p. 219, I pointed out that the erection of the portrait should probably be connected with the Samian expedition of 439 B.C., at which date Furtwängler (*Masterpieces*, p. 119) conjectures the Perikles by Kresilas to have been put up. Meanwhile grave doubts have arisen in my mind as to the authenticity of the Polykleitan Artemon. The confusion already noted by Plutarch with the Artemon of Anakreon is suspicious. The notice in Pliny is clearly derived from an anecdotic source other than that from which his main narrative is borrowed. Possibly, as Münzer hints, *Hermes*, xxx, p. 537, we have here further traces of Duris.

P. 46, 1. *pristas* : the MSS. are unanimous ; hence, since H. L. Urlichs (*loc. cit.*) has satisfactorily shown that a group of sawyers—put up doubtless by some successful master-builder—is absolutely in harmony with fifth-century traditions, I had not thought it necessary to refer to Loeschcke's proposed emendation of *pristas* to *pyctas*—an emendation, however, which threatens to come into favour again.

P. 46, 14. *puerum . . . tabellam* : for the motive Reisch (*l. c.*) compares the vase in Munich (Cat. 51), Benndorf, *Griechische u. Sicilische Vasenbilder*, i, pl. ix.

P. 48, 16. *The Apoxyomenos of Lysippos* : the copy in the Braccio Nuovo of the Vatican (Helbig, 31) seemed to me too well known to need mention. For the writer from whom Pliny got the story of Tiberius's passion for the statue, see Introd. p. xcii, n. 4.

P. 50, 6 : for portraits of Alexander, see also Helbig, *Sopra un Busto Colossale d'Alessandro Magno* in Mon. Antichi (R. Acad. Lincei), vol. vi, 1895.

P. 60, 1. *Portrait of Perikles* : Blümner and Hitzig (*Pausanias*, p. 307) remark that the word ἀνδριάς, used by Pausanias (i, 25, 1), does not apply to a terminal bust. Cf. further Bernoulli in *Jahrb.* xi, 1896, p. 107 f.

P. 60, 3. *Minervam mirabilem . . . et aram*: while still proposing to see
a copy of this Athena in the 'Pallas de Velletri' whose original he refers to
Kresilas (see Introd. p. lxxv, n. 2), Furtwängler recognizes a copy of the
Zeus in a fine statue at Ince-Blundell Hall, *Statuenkopien im Alterthum*,
plates i and iii, *1*, *ib*. p. 551 ff., the original of which he attributes on stylistic
grounds neither to Kresilas nor to the unknown Kephisodoros, but to the
elder Kephisodotos.   The reasons adduced, however, are scarcely strong
enough to warrant the alteration in the Plinian text of the MS. reading
Cephisodorus to *Cephisodotus.*

P. 60, 10. *celetizontas*: for the motive cf. further a statue in the Palazzo
Orlandi at Florence, Arndt-Bruckmann, *Einzelverk.* 242.

P. 66, 7. *Hermaphrodite of Polykles*: the Berlin statue (193) is now published by Furtwängler, *Statuenkopien*, pl. xii, who sees in it a copy of the work
of Polykles (*ib*. p. 582 ff.).

P. 68, 3. *nec hominem ex aere fecit, sed iracundiam*: while admitting—
what is indeed incontrovertible—that this phraseology is common to Silver
Latinity, I now believe that an epigram is after all concealed behind it (Introd.
p. lxx), all the Plinian criticism and analysis of Greek works of art being Greek
in their origin ; cf. note on xxxv, 61.

P. 68, 8. *Theodorus*: cf. also vii, 198 ; xxxv, 152.   Identity with the artist
of *C. I. A.* 373, 90 (from Akropolis, middle of sixth century) is probable but
not certain.

P. 70, 4. *infans . . . anserem strangulat*: in his translation of Herondas
(1893), p. xiv, Crusius alludes to the group in Herondas as being wholly
marble.   The attempt to establish identity with the Plinian group seems futile,
seeing how common the subject was in antiquity; cf. E. Gardner in *J. H. S.* vi,
1885, pp. 7 ff.

P. 72, 2. *Apellas*: cf. also *I. G. B.* 100 (=*Inschriften von Olympia*, 634),
from the basis supporting the horses of Kyniska in the Pronaos of the Temple
of Zeus, Paus. v, 12, 5 (*I. G. B.* 99 =*Inschr. von Ol.* 160).

P. 72, 8. *Hermes nursing the infant Dionysos by Kephisodotos*: the identity
of this group with the famous group at Olympia seems to me probable.   The
latter is attributed to Praxiteles on the authority of Pausanias (v, 17, 1) only.
I believe that in this case, as often in that of works attributed to Pheidias (xxxv,
54, Athena by Kolotes; xxxvi, 17, Nemesis and Mother of the Gods by Agorakritos), all of which are put down to Pheidias by Paus. (Introd. p. xl, cf. p. liii,
note 1), Pliny represents the more detailed—and perchance the more trustworthy—tradition, while Pausanias gives only the popular attributions.   If the
Hermes of Olympia was really by Praxiteles, but could pass in the eyes of
certain critics as the work of his father or elder brother, it follows that the
statue belonged, as Brunn has maintained, to the artist's earlier period and not
to his later as recently argued by Furtwängler (*Masterpieces*, p. 307 f).   It may
be questioned whether we are not too completely under the spell of Pausanias,
whose untrustworthiness in the matter of attributions is notorious, and who,
writing some 600 years after the artists of the great period, was as liable to
blunder concerning their works as the compiler of a modern guide-book
concerning the artists of the Renascence and their works.   However, I am at
present neither prepared nor equipped to challenge the Praxitelean authorship
of the Hermes on morphological or aesthetic grounds.   A long and complete
reinvestigation of all the extant material would first be necessary, but I think
it worth while to point out distinctly that there were probably two ancient

traditions concerning the authorship of the statue, and that the comparative trustworthiness of each should be investigated. I may add that the resemblance of the Kephisodotian Eirene holding the child Ploutos to the Hermes nursing the child Dionysos is so strong as only to be satisfactorily accounted for by referring them to the same artist: both figures are posed in the same manner, while the children are, as has often been noted, practically identical (cf. Furtwängler, *op. cit.* p. 296).

P. 72, 12. *Cenchramis*: cf. for Kenchramos, Purgold on *Inschriften von Ol.* 638.

P. 74, 2. *tubicine*: cf. Urlichs, *Pergamenische Inschriften*, p. 24. The commentary is not quite clear at this point; the explanation of Winckelmann (*Geschichte*, ed. 1776, p. 660 ff. = tr. Lodge, vol. ii, p. 204 ff.) applies to the 'dying Gaul' of the Capitol, and not to the Plinian *tubicen*.

P. 74, 2. *matri interfectae*: that this was a Gaulish woman seems to have been *first* suggested by Urlichs, *loc. cit.*; on the whole subject of these works by Epigonos see G. Habich, *Die Amazonengruppe des Attalischen Weihgeschenks* (Eine Studie zur Pergamenischen Kunstgeschichte), Berlin, 1896, p. 14 ff.

P. 76, 8. *Scopas uterque*: G. Habich, *Die Amazonengruppe*, p. 66, note 2, is of opinion that *scopas* refers to the works of art made by each of two artists (*uterque*), and explains these works to have been dancing satyrs. Habich supports his theory by appeal to the Munich vase. I must abide, however, by the opinion which I arrived at about a year ago after careful study of the vase in question, and which I have expressed in the Commentary.

P. 78, 1. *Callimachus*: for his date consult Winckelmann, *Geschichte* (ed. 1776), p. 460 (= tr. Lodge, vol. ii, p. 123), Furtwängler, *Masterpieces*, p. 437.

BOOK XXXV.

P. 92, 13. *M. Agrippa*: for Agrippa's interest in art, see now Gardthausen, *Augustus*, i. p. 749 ff.

P. 102, § 57, § 59. For the pictures in the *Poikile Stoa*, see now Hitzig and Blümner, *Pausanias*, p. 201 f.

P. 106, 2. *Zeuxis of Herakleia*: I have not sufficiently emphasized the difficulties at the commencement of Pliny's account of Zeuxis. It seems to me probable that the two conflicting dates of his birth given by Pliny represent the conflicting opinions of Greek art-historians (Antigonos and Duris? cf. Introd. p. xxxiii, on the beginnings of encaustic; Introd. p. xxvi, on the origin of sculpture). The epigram against Zeuxis attributed to Apollodoros should have been alluded to among the epigrams discussed, Introd. p. lvii.

P. 108, 7. *Herakles strangling the snakes in presence of Alkmena and Amphitryon*. The vase-painting in the Brit. Mus. (F. 479) is now published, *Cat. of Vases in Brit. Mus.* vol. iv, pl. xiii. The clumsiness of the figures, the coarseness of the picture as a whole, and the absence of Amphitryo must make us wary of accepting it as more than a distant echo of the picture by Zeuxis.

P. 134. *The Pompeian Mosaic*: now at last well photographed by Alinari, Naples 12050.

P. 136. *The 'Thesmothetai' of Protogenes*: the view of Curtius seems to me probable. For dissentient opinions and the full literature of the subject, see Hitzig-Blümner, *Pausanias*, p. 145.

P. 140. *The Resting Satyr*: the subject occurs likewise in painting; a well preserved instance in the *Casa Nuova* at Pompei, phot. Brogi, Naples 11216. But, at present, no safe connexion can be established between these paintings and the work of Protogenes.

P. 142, 17. *shortened methods of technique*: recent study in the Museum of Naples has convinced me that the clue to these words is afforded by a singular group of 'Campanian' pictures—the most striking of which is Helbig 1111 (= phot. Alinari, Naples 12035), known since the days of Böttiger as 'Evening prayer in front of the Temple of Isis.' The picture is not a work of the first rank, but it proves that the ancients possessed to as great a degree as any moderns all the secrets of impressionism : the broad flight of steps is indicated by a few bold dashes of white; the heads of the crowd on either side are roughly modelled within two bands of dark shadow ; white is applied with extraordinary intelligence and variety, now for an effect of light, now for the white garments that contrast with the dark skin of the Egyptian priests. Closely connected with this picture is the similar subject, Helbig 1112, and the two pictures of the 'Trojan horse' ((1) phot. Sommer, Pompei 9218, (2) Helbig 1326). Egyptian origin is attested from their subjects for the Isis pictures, while for those of the Trojan horse it has been proved both from the treatment and motives by L. von Urlichs (*das Hölzerne Pferd*). There seems little doubt that these pictures are an example of that *compendiaria*, that shortened method hated by Petronius, as in modern times by Ruskin, which was successfully cultivated and perhaps first brought into fashion by Antiphilos, and imitated in Greece by Nikomachos.

P. 154, 2. *exilior*: Robert, *Hall. Winckelmannsprogramm*, xix, 1895, p. 25, maintains that the adjective in its usual sense of *slender*, *slim* or *thin*, cannot be properly applied to the figures of an artist who expressed the *dignitates* of heroes, or who boasted that 'his Theseus had been fed on meat.' Robert, accordingly, proposed to see in *exilior* the (mis)translation of some such word as βραχύτερος = *short, thick-set* or *stumpy*. Robert's arguments have been vigorously controverted by Furtwängler (*Statuenkopien im Alterthum*, p. 568 f.), who defends the received interpretation of the passage. It seems to me that the contradictions in the criticisms passed upon Parrhasios, which vex Robert, and which Furtwängler attempts to reconcile, are the effect of the present juxta-position in Pliny of two or more appreciations of Euphranor, derived from totally different sources : the sentence *videtur expressisse dignitatis heroum . . . articulis-que grandior* is plainly Xenokratic in its origin (Introd. p. xxvii) ; here there can be no real contradiction between the *dignitates* which Euphranor expressed and the fact that he was *in universitate corporum exilior*, for the first refers to the artist's ethical conception of his heroes, the latter to their physical present-ment. As regards the saying attributed to Euphranor concerning his Theseus, I have pointed out both in the note on the passage and in the Introduction (p. lxiii f.) that its source is anecdotic, and can be traced back—perhaps through Antigonos—to Duris of Samos.

P. 155. *Andromeda*: for the finest and best preserved of the Pompeian pictures see phot. Alinari, Naples 12034.

P. 156. *Achilles detected by Ulysses* : phot. Alinari, Naples 12001, *id.* 12000 ; a different scheme seems preserved in the recently discovered picture in the *Casa Nuova* at Pompei, phot. Brogi 11226.

P. 159. *Medeia of Timomachos* : the picture Helbig 1262 (= phot. Alinari, Naples 12024) seems to me on close inspection to be really a copy after a good original, presumably, then, after the Medeia by Timomachos. The single figure of Medeia, on the other hand, appears to me extremely inferior in conception and execution ; pose and accessories are different, and I can see not the slightest reason for referring it to the same original as the former picture.

P. 159. *Orestes and Iphigeneia* : phot. Alinari, Naples 12020.

P. 162. *Herakles and Deianeira* : for the subject, treated with considerable mastery, and evidently after a good original, see the Pompeian picture, phot. Alinari, Naples 12026 (cf. Helbig, *Wandgemälde*, 1146).

P. 166, 14. *quinquatrus celebrantem* : Simos' picture apparently lent itself to a Roman interpretation, which by Pliny's time had superseded the true Greek explanation of the subject.

BOOK XXXVI.

P. 190, 9. *Statue of Mother of Gods by Agorakritos* : Furtwängler, *Statuenkopien*, p. 577 ff., claims to have discovered a copy of this work in a statue of the Villa Pamfili in Rome.

P. 202, 12. *Timotheos* : I have lately examined the 'Leda and the Swan' in the Capitol ; the connexion established between it and the Epidaurian sculptures by both Amelung and Winter seems to me to stand the test of minute criticism ; it is, however, disputed by Arndt (Arndt-Bruckmann, *Phot. Einzelverk.* ii, p. 30).

P. 205, 9. *Hermerotes* : the point made by Cicero (*loc. cit.*) was probably suggested by the word *Hermathena*, rather than by the actual monument. Cf. also *Att.* i, 1, 5 ; *ib.* 10, 3 (*Hermeracles*). A terminal figure at Newby Hall (Michaelis, *Anc. Marbles in Great Britain*, p. 531) affords a doubtful instance of an *Hermeros*. Michaelis brings it into connexion with the work of Tauriskos.

P. 208, l. 4. *Venerem lavantem se ... Polycharmus* : concerning this difficult passage I can only arrive at negative results. (1) The reading *sese Daedalus* must, I think, be rejected, the best codices offering no evidence for it whatsoever ; the corrupt *sedaedalsas* of *Cod. Bamb.* conceals either further descriptive words or the name of the locality where the statue was. (2) The current attribution of the *Venus lavans se* to one Daidalos of Bithynia, known only on the authority of Eustathios (*Schriftqu.* 2045), which seemed to receive support from the recurrence of a crouching or bathing Aphrodite on Bithynian coins (see Bernoulli, *Aphrodite*, p. 317), must also be renounced ; the type on the coins occurs elsewhere, and belongs to a series whose origin can be traced back to high antiquity (cf. Friederichs-Wolters, p. 571). (3) The notion that two statues are mentioned in the passage, and that the first was *crouching*, in opposition to the *Venus stans* of Polycharmos, is entirely without support ; *stantem* may be used here, not necessarily of an upright *versus* a stooping figure, but in the sense of 'placed,' 'situated.' Brunn, *K. G.* ii, p. 528, Müller, *Handbuch*, 377, note 5, take the whole sentence to be descriptive of *one* statue by Polycharmos.

P. 210. *Caryatids of the Pantheon*: see also Helbig, *Class. Ant.* i, and Gardthausen, *Augustus*, ii, p. 429 f.

P. 212. *Lioness by Arkesilaos*: Mr. Cecil Smith kindly reminds me, in this connexion, of a ' fine mosaic in the Brit. Mus., from Pompei (an early one), representing a lion and three Cupids : one has bound the lion with a cord, one seems to hold a drinking-vessel, and the third holds an object which seems to be a large dart. It is a good illustration of the Arkesilaos subject, and is evidently a copy from a Hellenistic relief.'

N.B.—The student will find all references concerning Roman topography admirably put together by Hülsen in the *Nomenclator Topographicus* to Kiepert and Hülsen's *Formae Urbis Romae Antiquae*, Berlin, 1896.

INDEXES

INDEX I

NAMES OF ARTISTS

INDEX II

MUSEOGRAPHIC

THE END

ImTheStory.com

'SIA information can be obtained at www.ICGtesting.com
ed in the USA
'01s1050220114

'6LV00005B/773/P

9 781313 818353